CW01081179

The Music of Frederick Delius

The Music of Frederick Delius

Style, Form and Ethos

Jeremy Dibble

THE BOYDELL PRESS

First published 2021
The Boydell Press, Woodbridge

ISBN 978-1-78327-577-9

The Boydell Press is an imprint of Boydell & Brewer Ltd
PO Box 9, Woodbridge, Suffolk IP12 3DF, UK
and of Boydell & Brewer Inc.
668 Mt Hope Avenue, Rochester, NY 14620-2731, USA
website: www.boydellandbrewer.com

A catalogue record of this publication is available
from the British Library

This publication is printed on acid-free paper

Printed and bound by TJ Books Limited

In the eyes of Delius the primary necessity for an artist was to develop his personality at all costs, to follow the dictates of one's nature in spite of all opposition and all possible consequences, to realize one's own peculiar angle of vision – what Cézanne called his *petite sensation* – however greatly it conflicts with that of the rest of the world.

– Cecil Gray, *Predicaments.*

Contents

List of Illustrations

Illustrations can be found between pages 250 and 251.

FACSIMILES

List of Tables

List of Music Examples

Preface and Acknowledgements

My introduction to the music of Delius took place while I was a schoolboy of about fourteen years of age. A copy of Eric Fenby's *Delius* in the Faber series of 'The Great Composers' lay among the books on music in my grammar school library at Buckhurst Hill, though I suspect its presence was due to my most enlightened and gifted music master, John Rippin. Such teachers make a lifetime of difference. After communicating an interest in this unfamiliar composer, I was plied with scores and records of numerous Delius works. I particularly remember being given a ten-inch LP recording of Anthony Collins's interpretation of *The Walk to the Paradise Garden* and *On Hearing the First Cuckoo in Spring,* recordings which I still hold dear. Before I was sixteen, however, I had come to know the *Songs of Sunset* (with John Shirley Quirk and the immortal Janet Baker), the *Requiem, Paris* (a work I have always loved for all its unevenness), the *Dance Rhapsodies, A Village Romeo and Juliet, In a Summer Garden* and *The Song of the High Hills.* Through Rippin's careful tutelage, I read Eric Fenby's *Delius As I Knew Him* by which I became acquainted with *A Song of Summer, Cynara,* the Violin Sonata No. 3 and the *Songs of Farewell.* With John I made the pilgrimage to the grave at Limpsfield and I also had the chance to meet Fenby, just before he was about to fly out to Jacksonville in 1978 to receive an honorary degree and also at the Bracknell Festival where he appeared in the capacity of conductor. My last meeting with Fenby was just before I was about to begin my PhD in 1980. As a sales assistant in the Toys Department of John Lewis in Oxford Street, I encountered him one afternoon when he appeared with a grandson, looking for a small bicycle with stabilisers. After the transaction was completed, I think he was most bemused to confront an unassuming sales assistant interested in Delius, but who also recognised him as the composer's amanuensis! I shall never forget this kind man, and how he expressed such an interest in my own research (at that time, on Parry) on which I was about to embark.

My fascination and passion for Delius's music has always been aroused by those aspects of lyricism and poetry in sound that the composer so abundantly possessed. But more latterly I have been equally intrigued by the question of form and style in his music. To those who, early on, loved his music – Max Chop, Fritz Cassirer, Hans Haym and Herman Suter, Henry Wood, Thomas

Beecham, Percy Grainger, Balfour Gardiner, Philip Heseltine, Patrick Hadley and Eric Fenby – the question of form was never in doubt, and the verdict of the critic of *The Times* (probably H. C. Colles) in 1929 fairly summarised Delius's unique properties: 'The strength and weakness of Delius is his solitariness. He belongs to no school, follows no tradition, and is like no other composer in the forms, content, or style of his music'.[1] But other judgements, past and present, of Delius's music have invariably focused more negatively on a lack of structural thinking and handling of tonality, and Delius's own disparagement of analytical thought (and I have no doubt he would have found this book intolerable), of theory, and 'academics', has not helped his cause. Writing in *The Sackbut* in 1929, Edwin Evans encapsulated that sense of doubt:

> When Delius is deliberately formal, as, for instance, in the piano concerto, he usually overdoes it, which does not argue a good natural conception of form. Otherwise his style is too fluid to produce points of sufficient salience to give comfort to a listener who needs to hang his attention upon them. He rears edifices which have no corner stones, or at best inconspicuous ones. The effect is to invite greater passivity from the listener. The stream down which he drifts has the most alluring banks, but few landmarks, and these unobtrusive. But it is a winding stream whose graceful curves are not planned without a sense of direction, if such is necessary to your happiness. Often it is quite sufficient to feel that you are definitely getting somewhere. But I confess that sometimes curiosity as to the stages of the journey remains unsatisfied, and then my personal reaction is that the music is formless, for a form so elusive is scarcely form at all. Even in the sense in which a painter employs his quantities Delius's form is too often unsatisfying to me, and no amount of recurrence in his *motifs* is capable of furnishing a remedy. This factor affects the reactions of all but the most enthusiastic listeners to Delius's music, but its influence upon their final judgment differs, as I have explained, with the importance which each one of them individually attaches to it.[2]

Yet, Evans's supposition of formlessness in works such as *Paris*, *Lebenstanz* and *In a Summer Garden*, or the robust opening chorus of *A Mass of Life*, with their eccentric but nevertheless demonstrable applications of sonata, *Appalachia* and *Brigg Fair* with their imaginative use of variation form, the adroit rondo

---

[1] *The Times*, 2 November 1929.

[2] Evans, E., 'Delius: A Personal Reaction in the Form of a Letter', *The Sackbut* (December 1929), 121.

structure of *Sea Drift* or the controlled one-movement forms of the later concertos and sonatas, seems at best strangely unaccommodating or at worst demonstrably untrue. Of late, however, there has been a tendency to gainsay the popular notion of Delius the 'improvisor' and the 'anti-academic' in favour of a more balanced view of a composer who knew his classics (however much he might have scorned them as an older man), benefited from his Leipzig training (even though he might have profited from it, had he stayed on longer), learned his lessons from the study of scores (notably Wagner and Strauss) and the immediacy of live performances. Allusions to Delius's cosmopolitan style are evident in Christopher Palmer's *Delius: Portrait of a Cosmopolitan*, and there is much to be gained from Anthony Payne's thoughtful article 'Delius's Stylistic Development' and Deryck Cooke's more pleading 'Delius and Form: A Vindication'. More recently, however, this question has become a more pressing one in Andrew Boyle's *Delius and Norway*, and especially in Daniel Grimley's *Delius and the Sound of Place*. I have also largely avoided an extensive assessment of Delius's reception history, since this is abundantly provided by Martin Lee-Browne and Paul Guinery's *Delius and His Music*.

This study therefore seeks principally to investigate the vexed question of form and style in Delius's music *ab initio*, and the individual ethos which these two critical phenomena combine to create. To a large extent, the study is an analytical one in which I argue that we can only do true justice to Delius's music by understanding *how* his music coheres, and that the question of form in his music is just as vital as those more established ones of lyricism, poetry and orchestration.[3] However, I have also attempted to reinforce my scrutiny of Delius's scores through access to the Delius archives in the British Library, the Grainger Museum in Melbourne and the Jacksonville University Library, as well as the detailed catalogues of the manuscripts provided by Rachel Lowe and Robert Threlfall. Moreover, I have made much use of Eric Fenby's *Delius As I Knew Him* as one of several rich biographical sources now available on the composer in order to give what I hope is a helpful context. In particular, I should like to pay tribute to Lionel Carley's two scholarly volumes of *Delius: A Life in Letters* (*1862–1908* and *1909–1934*); and also his *Grieg and Delius*; these have been my bible and a regular source of contextual reference throughout this book. My thanks also go to Lionel for his eagle eye in his correction of factual errors. I should also offer homage to the work of Stephen Lloyd, Philip Jones, Barry Smith, Jérome Rossi, Christopher Redwood, Roger and Lesley Buckley, Stephen Banfield, Lyndon Jenkins and

---

[3] It should be noted that this study does not set out to examine every single one of Delius's compositions.

Robert Montgomery, to whose scholarship I have freely referred. I should like to acknowledge the financial assistance of Durham University and the Delius Trust, who made it possible for me to make regular archival visits to London.

There are, of course, many other people I would like to thank. I have mentioned Lionel Carley already, but his unwavering friendship, expertise and encouragement has also been invaluable to me, not least in animating me to begin this study. I must extend my gratitude to Dick and Kate Packer, for I shall never forget their willingness to escort me and my wife to Jacksonville to see the manuscript holdings in the university library there; nor will I forget a memorable visit we made to the restored Delius dwelling in the grounds of the university, the excursion we made to the location of Solana Grove along the St Johns River in Florida (where Delius had his plantation of citrus fruits) and our visit to Melbourne University to see the Delius holdings in the Grainger Collection. I should also mention my old school friend, Anthony Purkiss, who patiently drove me to the Delius house at Grez one warm summer afternoon after a 'wine crawl' in Alsace. I should like to acknowledge the assistance of Nicolas Bell for access to the Delius Archive in the British Library, before it was officially catalogued. My thanks also go to the staff at Melbourne University who treated me as family. I should like to thank my mother for her support, and especially my brother, Christopher, to whom this book is dedicated. There have been numerous times in my early academic life when he selflessly stepped in to support my work; this study acknowledges the debt I owe him. As to my friends and colleagues, I extend my thanks to Jonathan and Rachel Clinch, Lucia Gri (my much-loved Italian tutor, who has often been the victim of conversations about Delius's unusual life), Vigdis Mykland (my long-suffering and most amiable Norwegian tutor who opened up a new world of Norwegian and Scandinavian culture to me; without her, my task would have been much more difficult), Christine and Tony Borthwick (for the therapeutic visits to Beg Meil in Brittany), Rumon Gamba, Christopher Mark, Anthony Boden, Martin Lee-Browne, Paul Guinery, Stephen Lloyd, Bo Holten (for encouraging me to learn Norwegian), Anthony Payne, the late Peter Evans, Julian Horton, Tuomas Eerola, Daniel Grimley and Geraint Lewis. Above all, however, I must thank my dearest wife, Alison, for her devotion, interest, sacrifice and support. Without her, my work on Delius would not have been possible.

Jeremy Dibble
Coxhoe,
Durham, 2020

List of Abbreviations

ARCHIVES AND OTHER COLLECTIONS

AU-Mgm	Grainger Museum, Melbourne University.
DTA	Archive of the Delius Trust.
GB-DRu	Durham University, Special Collections.
GB-Lbl	British Library.
GB-Mr	John Rylands University Library, Deansgate Branch, Manchester.
US-Jul	Jacksonville University Library, Florida.
US-Stu	Memorial Library of Music, Stanford University.

LITERATURE

MC	Beecham, T., *A Mingled Chime* (London: Hutchinson & Co., 1944).
TB	Beecham, T., *Frederick Delius* (London: Hutchinson, 1959).
DN	Boyle, A., *Delius and Norway* (Woodbridge: The Boydell Press, 2017).
DPY	Carley, L., *Delius: The Paris Years* (London: Triad Press, 1975).
DLL1	Carley, L., *Delius: A Life in Letters, Vol. 1: 1862–1908* (Aldershot: Scolar Press, 1983).
DLL2	Carley, L., *Delius: A Life in Letters, Vol. 2: 1909–1934* (Aldershot: Scolar Press, 1988).
GD	Carley, L., *Grieg and Delius: A Chronicle of their Friendship in Letters* (London and New York: Marion Boyars Ltd, 1993).
FDML	Carley, L. (ed.), *Frederick Delius: Music, Art and Literature* (Aldershot: Ashgate, 1998).
MCh	Chop, M., 'Frederick Delius: Eine biographische Studie mit Bildbeilage', *Musikalisches Wochenblatt*, Nos. 35–37 (1907).
CD	Delius, C., *Frederick Delius: Memories of My Brother* (London: Ivor Nicholson & Watson Ltd, 1935).
DSJ	*Delius Society Journal.*

EF   Fenby, E., *Delius As I Knew Him* (London: G. Bell & Sons Ltd, 1981 [1936]).

DG   Grimley, D. M., *Delius and the Sound of Place* (Cambridge: Cambridge University Press, 2018).

PH   Heseltine, P., *Frederick Delius* (London: The Bodley Head, 1923).

AH   Hutchings, A., *Delius* (London: Macmillan, 1949).

AJ   Jefferson, A., *Delius* (London: J. M. Dent & Sons Ltd, 1972).

MLPG   Lee-Browne, M. and Guinery, P., *Delius and his Music* (Woodbridge: The Boydell Press, 2014).

RL   Lowe, R., *Frederick Delius 1862–1934: A Catalogue of the Music Archive of the Delius Trust, London* (London: Delius Trust, 1974).

MT   Montgomery, R. and Threlfall, R., *Music and Copyright: The Case of Delius and his Publishers* (Aldershot: Ashgate, 2007).

DC   Redwood, C. (ed.), *A Delius Companion* (London: John Calder, 1976).

FDPW   Smith, B., *Frederick Delius and Peter Warlock: A Friendship Revealed* (Oxford: Oxford University Press, 2000).

RT1   Threlfall, R., *A Catalogue of the Compositions of Frederick Delius: Sources and References* (London: Delius Trust, 1977).

RT2   Threlfall, R., *Frederick Delius: A Supplementary Catalogue* (London: Delius Trust, 1986).

DMA   Threlfall, R., *Delius' Musical Apprenticeship* (London: Delius Trust, 1994).

PART I

THE SEEDS OF COSMOPOLITANISM

CHAPTER 1

An Unconventional Apprenticeship:
Bradford, Florida and Leipzig (1862–1888)

BRADFORD, LONDON AND A EUROPEAN EDUCATION

Granted the freedom of the city of Bradford in 1932, Frederick Delius was reported to have remarked: 'I love Bradford … and it would have been the greatest pleasure in my life to have been able to visit the city to have the freedom bestowed on me there'.[1] Rather less complimentary, and probably nearer to the truth, was his uncompromising disparagement of the Yorkshire conurbation as a 'filthy place, full of factories' imparted to Eric Fenby in his last years;[2] and his memories of childhood in Bradford, for all the fondness he retained for the outlying moors, were tainted by the strictness of life at home. A propensity to exaggerate may have been a symptom of his illness, or, as Arthur Hutchings has suggested, 'the [inheritance] of his father's hardness'.[3] There is a widespread acceptance that Delius's father Julius warranted the description 'Prussian martinet'. At home he exercised a 'reign of fear' at the family home at Claremont. An obsession with his sense of formality, to the point of militarism, may have been suffocating for his twelve children, but it belies the fact that Julius and his wife emanated from a well-established tradition of German *Kultur* where music was considered a valuable part of a broader education.[4] Elise Delius (née Krönig) had come from a music-loving family in Bielefeld, and Julius himself was undeniably fond of music. Even Delius, according to Heseltine, admitted this: 'My father loved music and used to tinker on the piano when he knew he was alone'.[5] What is more, Bradford, a significant, prosperous and expanding Yorkshire conurbation when Julius

---

[1] *Yorkshire Observer*, 25 July 1932.

[2] In Ken Russell's film *A Song of Summer*, BBC Monitor Films, 1968.

[3] *AH*, 8.

[4] *CD*, 52. This is also evident from Delius's own memories of his father in *FDPW*, 3 and in *DLL1*, 381. Ibid., 51.

[5] *PH*, 3.

Delius arrived there in 1850, was the beneficiary of various musical initiatives characteristic of expanding provincial music in northern Victorian England. In addition to the mill and pit bands, choral music thrived, and after the St George's Hall was opened in August 1853, the citizens of Bradford were able to enjoy large-scale concerts of orchestral and choral works, particularly after the Hallé Orchestra started to visit the city in 1858. Among the sponsors was no other than Julius Delius.[6] In 1865 the Bradford Subscription Concerts began; Julius Delius was a committee member. The presence of many German industrialists in Bradford – and the area, 'Little Germany', where they worked – also generated musical interest in a *Liedertafel* in which Julius also took part, and the substantial house Claremont was also a relatively frequent venue for chamber music, bringing quartet parties from Manchester and Leeds. Chamber concerts were also sponsored by the pianist, writer and Leipzig-educated Samuel Midgley, who knew the Delius family and who became a well-known figure in Bradford's music-making.[7] Heseltine maintained that this 'surfeit of good things became a little wearisome and developed in him a distaste for chamber music which lasted many years', a view Hutchings largely rejected.[8] It is also indisputable that Julius, with his Teutonic love of chamber music, encouraged Fritz (as he was known then). Recognising his son's natural talent, which he demonstrated somewhat autodidactically on the family piano, he placed a violin in Fritz's hands no doubt with the thought that domestic music-making and its social advantages would be beneficial; and certainly among the many German immigrants the ability to play met with approval. This was certainly the case when Joseph Joachim and his Italian colleague, the cellist Alfredo Piatti, came to play at Claremont and, owing to the absence of a third performer, Fritz was able to acquit himself in performance with these two European giants as well as before the assembled audience.[9] Fritz's ability as a violinist, what is more, had been supported by Julius and his connections with the German fraternity of musicians and the Hallé Orchestra through the employment of William Bauerkeller, a violinist in the orchestra, who came all the way from Manchester to teach him in 1868. A second teacher, George Haddock, a noted violinist in Leeds and Bradford and leader of the Bradford

---

[6] Kennedy, M., *The Hallé Tradition: A Century of Music* (Manchester: Manchester University Press, 1960), 67.

[7] Russell, D., *Popular Music in England, 1840–1914: A Social History*, 2nd edn (Manchester: Manchester University Press, 1997), 232.

[8] *AH*, 11.

[9] *CD*, 47.

Amateur Orchestra, took over his lessons in 1869. Haddock was a pupil of Vieuxtemps and Molique, owned an array of Stradivari and Guaneri violins and became the director of the Bradford School of Music. Sometime around 1875 Fritz began more formal lessons on the piano, an instrument which clearly opened up wider horizons to him beyond purely the matter of learning pieces. 'From then on', Clare Delius claimed, 'if he were not doing lessons or reading a book, he was reading music at the piano'.[10]

As is well documented, however, there was a world of difference in the perception of Julius and Elise Delius between pursuing music as a social pastime and embracing it as a career. It was a familiar trope. In this Julius was immovable, and to exacerbate the *impasse* between father and son, Fritz's love of music only grew as he approached manhood. As Clare Delius recollected, 'throughout all his schooldays, his greatest joy was going to concerts. No matter how classical they were, or how bored a great part of the audience might be, Fred was always lost in a trance of bliss'.[11] At the age of ten he was touched by the piano music of Chopin, and the music of Wagner made an early impression through hearing the Hallé play the 'Walkürenritt' and a performance of *Lohengrin* (albeit in Italian) on 8 May 1875 at Covent Garden. As Hutchings has commented, save for the occasional concert given by the Hallé, or the Bradford Subscription Concerts, the centre of Fritz's musical world until he left Bradford Grammar School was home.[12] His removal to the International College, Spring Grove, Isleworth, in 1877 promised certain opportunities. An institution with a liberal educational policy, the College aimed to bring young men together from cosmopolitan backgrounds. Lessons were conducted on business, accounting and, with an emphasis on the acquisition and practice of modern languages, Fritz would have felt some sympathy, given his fluency in German (which was spoken at home in Bradford),[13] French (presumably from school) and English (which he spoke with a Yorkshire accent). He continued piano and violin lessons, the latter with the accomplished German violinist Carl Deichmann who made regular appearances in London and the provinces,[14]

---

[10] Ibid., 51.

[11] Ibid., 48.

[12] *AH*, 11.

[13] Although Delius was essentially bilingual, Jelka Rosen always maintained to Philip Heseltine that '[his] idiom is English, his language is English'. See letter from Heseltine to Jelka Delius, [May 1929], *FDPW*, 466.

[14] *PH*, 7. See also Goldbach, K. T., 'Remarks on Delius's Violin Teacher, Carl Deichmann', *DSJ* No. 154 (Autumn 2013), 74–88.

and the regime at Isleworth was liberal enough to allow him to attend musical events in London and join an amateur orchestra.[15] We have no record of these exactly but the years 1875 to 1879 in Britain's capital cannot pass without some remark. British orchestras and conductors at the Crystal Palace and at the Philharmonic Society were rapidly discovering Wagner, particularly in the form of the orchestral extracts from *The Ring* and, in 1877, the presence of Wagner in London for the 'Wagnerfest' at the Royal Albert Hall, must have been a major attraction. After its first hearing in Cambridge under Joachim, Brahms's First Symphony was introduced to London audiences in 1877 as was Verdi's *Requiem*. Standards of orchestral playing, already sound under the baton of a figure such as August Manns, underwent a further transformation with the commencement of Hans Richter's 'Orchestral Festival Concerts' at St James's Hall and of German opera at Drury Lane in 1879. To the adolescent Fritz these happenings would have been too mouth-watering to ignore, and, for the price of short train journey, much would have been easily accessible.

After the liberal atmosphere of Isleworth, Fritz's return to Bradford must have seemed like a prospective life sentence. The desire to pursue music as a career, though a remote prospect at that time, combined with his total reluctance to enter the family firm, inevitably instilled in him a mutinous mentality in which Julius would be constantly tormented by his son's incorrigibility. Somehow Julius hoped that, with travel and experience, Fritz would come round to the realities of commerce and the benefits of a comfortable, secure career. For Fritz, conversely, trade missions at home or abroad were but opportunities to seek further musical edification and instruction on top of what he had managed to secure during his formal education. Conscious of his own innate musical abilities, one senses that probably the greatest frustration for him was the need for systematic tuition. As Clare Delius remarked, he was 'almost wholly self-taught',[16] and this was certainly the case when it came to piano lessons, for he largely rejected the imperative of learning scales or the benefits of finger exercises. What technique he acquired was a means to learning *about* music, however rudimentary it was, by the time he reached the age of eighteen. Certainly, by the time he was ensconced at the Bradford warehouse in early 1880, the piano at Claremont was his only source of refuge.[17] Here the appetite to improvise and invent was initially ignited. In addition, as he was sent away by his father to gain orders

---

[15] *PH*, 7.

[16] *CD*, 50.

[17] Ibid., 58–9.

for the firm, the motivation was always to use the situation to his advantage. Moreover, the need to extricate himself from the stultifying environment of Bradford and the suffocating presence of his father encouraged a powerful sense of *Wanderlust* in him. Stroud, an attractive Cotswold town in pleasing surroundings, was an important national centre for the textile industry in the south west of England, and he was sent there for a period as agent for his father's firm. It was also near enough to London to attend concerts.

Soon enough, however, the opportunity to visit Germany presented itself.[18] Chemnitz in Saxony, one of Germany's major textile hubs, was conveniently located between Dresden to the north east, Leipzig to the north west and Zwickau to the south west. Known as 'Das Sächsische Manchester' ('The Saxon Manchester'), Chemnitz was a growing industrial town with smokestacks comparable with the skyline of Bradford. Culturally, however, it was much more congenial. It boasted a modest theatre for opera and there was a healthy concert life with a resident orchestra expected to perform a wide range of duties from church services to balls, entertainments at local music clubs and taverns, opera, outdoor events and formal concerts.[19] Although the Chemnitz orchestra was used to a staple repertoire of Mozart, Haydn, Beethoven and the Leipzig circle of Mendelssohn, Schumann and Gade, it was also acquainted with the music of Wagner, and Liszt's symphonic poems had made their way from Weimar. With the arrival of the Czech-born Hans Sitt in 1873, the music of Smetana had been added to the programme while Brahms's First and Second Symphonies were performed under the composer's direction in 1877 and 1880 respectively.[20] How much interaction there was between Sitt and the young Delius is not known exactly, but we do know that Delius arrived in Chemnitz at a time when Sitt was experiencing difficulties with the Chemnitz authorities and that he resigned from his post in September 1880. Given that Delius arrived in Chemnitz on 24 April 1880, this left only the best part of four months for them to become acquainted and for Delius to arrange lessons.[21] The concert season was over, leaving the summer months

---

[18] As a youngster, Delius, 'der kleine Engländer' as he was known among his German relatives, had been to Bielefeld to see his mother's family, and later, around 1880, he spent a summer along the Rhine which also included visits to Frankfurt, Stuttgart and Nürnberg. See letter from Jelka to Philip Heseltine, 3 September 1929, *DLL2*, 354.

[19] Jones, P., 'A Reluctant Apprentice: Delius and Chemnitz', *DSJ* No. 118 (Winter/ Spring 1996), 23.

[20] Ibid.

[21] Ibid., 27.

for light music which lasted until September. At this point Sitt gave his farewell concert on 8 September which included Liszt's *Les Préludes*, the overture to Wagner's *Tannhäuser*, Mendelssohn's Violin Concerto (with Sitt as soloist) and *Meeresstille und Glückliche Fahrt* and a movement from his own Symphony in C minor.[22] For the rest of Delius's time in Chemnitz, which lasted until April 1881, concerts were initially overseen by the orchestra's leader Fritz Hartung until the appointment of Sitt's replacement, Fritz Scheel, whose programmes also included music by Liszt and Wagner as well as Nicolai, Goldmark and the emerging Norwegian, Svendsen.[23] There was also a good deal of opera at the Städtisches Schauspielhaus whose repertoire included *Der Fliegende Holländer*, *Lohengrin*, *Il Trovatore*, *Martha*, *Don Giovanni*, *Fra Diavolo*, *Zampa*, *Les Huguenots*, *Undine* and *Der Freischütz*, all of which was typical of a provincial German opera house of the time. To this Delius added a hearing of Goldmark's celebrated *Königin von Saba* (which remained in the operatic repertoire in Vienna until the late 1930s) at the newly restored Semperoper in Dresden and, more auspiciously, *Die Meistersinger* at the Staatsoper in Berlin, an experience which must have been deeply formative.

A year in Germany undoubtedly kindled Delius's *Wanderlust* which gave some purpose to the ensuing visit he made to Norrköping, Sweden's centre of the textile industry. The capital, Stockholm, had its appeal, especially during the summer months. But his susceptibility to the grand landscape of neighbouring Norway's fjords and mountainous country and to Scandinavia's unique phenomenon of summer outdoor culture, engendered by the long warm nights and the midnight sun, was immeasurable. This, for Delius, and the respite of Norway's more informal social customs, in stark contrast to those of Bradford, was life-affirming.[24] Norway also brought the additional enchantment of being a culture 'outside' the European musical mainstream; 'it really does one's heart good to meet such honest, unaffected & unspoiled people', he affirmed in his diary of 1887.[25] As a country it was being 'discovered' during the nineteenth century by holidaymakers, walkers and travel writers, while the Norwegians themselves, uneasy in their union with

---

[22]　Ibid., 26.

[23]　Ibid., 28.

[24]　An impeccable source of information on Delius's Norwegian diaries is now available. Roger Buckley's doctoral thesis is titled *Delius's Red Notebook: Transcription and Critical Analysis, Volume 1 – The Red Notebook: Facsimile, Transcription and Annotation*, Anglia Ruskin University, 2017.

[25]　From Delius's summer diary of 1887 (the 'Red Notebook', now in the Grainger Museum and reproduced in *DLL1*, 383–93); see *DLL1*, 384.

Sweden, found the vehicle of music, painting and literature an ideal means of expressing the desire for political and cultural separation. The music of Svendsen and Grieg, attracted as they were by their country's traditional song and dance music, embodied a sense of novelty and 'otherness' which clearly captured Delius's imagination. Quite when he was first introduced to the music of Grieg is uncertain, but he claimed that it was as a boy that he first heard the *Humoresques* Op. 6.[26] We also know that he was familiar with at least one of Grieg's Violin Sonatas, the one in G major, as a seventeen-year-old violinist,[27] and it is quite probable that he drew additional enthusiasm from Sitt who orchestrated Grieg's *Norwegian Dances* Op. 35.

A sense of rebellion awakened by Chemnitz and Norway and visits to the tedious industrial environment of St-Étienne in France, a large industrial city southwest of Lyon, only served to heighten Delius's need to escape the constraints of his present circumstances. With little prospect of music in a place not renowned for its cultural riches, his escape to the more amenable Riviera offered not only earnings from gambling but also the opportunity of local concerts. After returning to Bradford, once again as the prodigal son, he visited Paris to see his father's brother, Theodor, which must have placed artistic temptations in his way, not least because in Theodor, more unconventional in temperament, Delius quite likely perceived the possibility of sympathy and patronage.[28] Music, nevertheless, must have seemed a distant dream with all the complications of how he might support himself. Moreover, at this stage of his life, when most prospective music students had begun their formal studies, he must have also been rudely aware that he was largely untrained; and it was by no means clear how a career in music might be achievable. What he had learned so far was a practical proficiency on the violin and a pianistic adequacy to allow him to become acquainted with piano music or other scores. This in itself would not be enough to forge a career in music other than as a jobbing instrumental teacher, a fact Julius, who had entertained numerous professionals in his home, may well have recognised; and he would naturally have wished to avoid the kind of tragedy later portrayed in Somerset Maugham's 1931 short story *The Alien Corn* where George Bland, the son of a well-to-do family, rejects the family tradition of a place in the regiment

---

[26] Letter from Delius to Philip Heseltine, 24 September 1918, *GB-Lbl* Add MS 52547–52549.

[27] Carley, L. and Threlfall, R., *Delius: A Life in Pictures* (Oxford: Oxford University Press, 1977), 6.

[28] *DLL1*, 3.

and a parliamentary seat in favour of a career as a pianist, only to kill himself
after two years' study in Germany when he learns he will never be more than
a 'competent amateur'. Yet Fritz would not be deflected from his goal. If he
was to secure a proper, systematic musical education, he would, as Clare
Delius suggested, need to find a suitable occupation which could fulfil several
vital functions.[29] Enough physical distance between him and his father could
afford him sufficient personal independence to conduct his own affairs; and,
if this were possible, while paying lip-service to commerce, he could pursue
his musical goals without hindrance.[30] It was a strategy that would demand
patience, tenacity and the playing of the long game, but for Delius it must have
seemed like the only realistic option.

FLORIDA AND THE MUSIC OF THE AMERICAN SOUTH

A second visit to Sweden in 1882, one to Manchester, and another visit to
Paris in 1883 did nothing to alter Delius's resolve, but as Carley has alluded,
the departure of his brother Ernst to New Zealand to take up sheep farming
intimated at least that something other than the wool trade was negotiable
without the more dreadful prospect of being cut off financially altogether
by his father.[31] The notion of cultivating oranges and grapefruit in Florida, a
commercial venture to which Julius was well disposed, must therefore have
given Delius cause for hope. The remote Spanish plantation, at Solana Grove,
between Picolata and Tocoi, some forty-five miles upriver to the south of
Jacksonville along the St Johns River, and located on the edge of virgin forest,
placed a tolerable distance between him and Julius. 'I used to get up early and
be spellbound watching the silent break of dawn over the river', he recollected
to Fenby. 'Nature awakening – it was wonderful! At night the sunsets were
aglow – spectacular'.[32] Citrus fruit grew naturally in Florida's tropical climate
and much of the harvesting could be achieved with the help of negro workers.
If management of the plantation required little time, then there would be
more for music. Charles Douglas, Delius's business partner, may or may not
have been privy to this scheme, but after arriving at Solana Grove, he did not
stay long, and it is quite clear from the surviving reminiscences that Delius

---

[29] *CD*, 68.

[30] Ibid., 68–9.

[31] *DLL1*, 4.

[32] Lloyd, S. (ed.) *Fenby on Delius* (London: Thames Publishing, 1996), 127.

devoted as much time as he could to music and practising his violin. This was all that mattered.[33] The serendipity of meeting Thomas Ward in Jacksonville, the organist of the Jesuit church of St Peter and St Paul, Brooklyn, New York, whether under the differing circumstances relayed by Heseltine or Beecham, was undoubtedly significant.[34] It was Ward who helped acquire a piano for Solana Grove, and, with Douglas gone, there was room at Solana Grove for him to stay, and there would be unrestricted time to learn the rudiments and theory of music without the prying eye of Delius's father.

And this is what transpired. Delius threw himself into work. After all, at twenty-two he had much time to make up. Correspondence with Bradford evaporated as he laboured from sun-up to sun-down, sometimes even working during the small hours of the night.[35] Finally Julius received a letter from his son explaining that he had 'taken up the serious study of music with a friend – that he had made so much progress and was so confident of the future that he now regarded orange planting as a mere background to his existence'.[36] This was confirmed by Julius's emissary Mr Tattersfield, who visited the plantation,[37] and by the reminiscences of Julia Sanks, the sister-in-law of Delius's foreman Albert Anderson.[38] As we know from the writings of Heseltine, Clare Delius, Beecham, Grainger and Fenby, Delius was full of praise for what he learned from Ward during the months he spent at Solana Grove from the summer until early autumn 1884 and that it was, so he claimed, the only teaching of value he received.[39] What we actually know of Ward's musical abilities is very sparse in spite of what Don Gillespie's *In Search of Thomas Ward* tells us about the man. We do know that Ward (1856–1912) grew up as an orphan in Brooklyn, graduated at St John's College in 1873 and studied composition there with the organist John Loretz. Afflicted with tuberculosis, he had moved to Florida for his health in 1884, his arrival in Jacksonville coinciding exactly with that of Delius.[40] After leaving Florida, and an abortive attempt to become a priest in

---

[33] Ibid., 5.

[34] *PH*, 17; *TB*, 27–8.

[35] *CD*, 74–5.

[36] *CD*, 75.

[37] *DMA*, 76.

[38] *DLL1*, 5.

[39] How long Delius and Ward spent together at Solana Grove is not clear, but six months is likely to be an overestimate.

[40] Looser, D., 'Frederick Delius' Houston Connection', http://agohouston2016.com/blog/2016/02/22/frederick-delius'-houston-connection, 31 March 2018.

a Benedictine monastery in central Florida, Ward eventually moved further south to Texas where he taught the piano, organ and composition in Houston. Nevertheless, as Threlfall has commented, 'details of Delius's actual work with Ward ... are still confined to his pupil's own later reminiscences',[41] so that we ultimately lack a completely objective account of Ward's musicianly capacities. Fenby recounted that '[Ward] showed a wonderful insight in helping [Delius] to find out just how much in the way of traditional technique would be useful to [him]'.[42] Beecham echoed this view of the two working together, 'the younger man benefiting incalculably from the instruction of the elder ... in the mechanics of counterpoint and fugue'.[43] In this instance Beecham may have been influenced by Fenby's attribution of a notebook which he gave to Jacksonville University in 1962 inscribed 'Delius MSS Note-book 1884 / containing his earliest exercises in counterpoint / with numerous alterations, which he worked on / with Thomas Ward at Solano [sic] Grove'. Robert Threlfall subsequently identified this notebook as belonging to Delius's period in Leipzig.[44] In 1923, with Delius's *imprimatur*, the value and role of Ward's instruction was amplified even further in Heseltine's biography:

> Ward was an excellent musician, some nine years older than Delius, and it is not too much to say that the whole of Delius's technical equipment is derived from the instruction he received from Ward in the course of his six months' sojourn on the plantation. The young composer developed very rapidly. He worked with a demoniacal energy and in a short time he had as good a knowledge of musical technique as the average student at the institutions acquires in the course of two or three years. In his teaching, Ward wisely confined himself to counterpoint, seeing that his pupil's natural instincts had already provided him with a finer sense of harmony than could ever be gained from text-books and treatises.[45]

Ward may have introduced his pupil to the creative value of counterpoint, but it nevertheless seems equally plausible that Delius must have undergone

---

[41] *DMA*, 17.

[42] *EF*, 168–9.

[43] *TB*, 28.

[44] Threlfall, R., 'Delius's Student Exercises: A Fresh Look at the Chronology', *DSJ* No. 104 (Spring/Summer 1990), 3–5. This misattribution was acknowledged by Fenby in *DSJ* No. 105 (Autumn 1990), 23. See also *DMA*, 28.

[45] *PH*, 18.

some training in the way of functional harmony and all the technical armoury necessary for natural fluency and a comprehension of tonal syntax. After all, in order to develop a proficiency in *tonal* counterpoint (where the vertical concept of harmony and the linear one of counterpoint are essentially interdependent) it is vital to have already gained a facility in harmony. It is most likely that Ward opened up the discipline of this world to Delius who, hitherto, had had no formal instruction and, in doing so, must have instilled in him a sense of elation and gratitude as he shifted from a condition of intuition to a state of technical control and theoretical comprehension.

With the help of Ward, Delius made the acquaintance of a number of professional and amateur musicians in Jacksonville which was, contrary to the suggestion of Beecham and Clare Delius,[46] by no means a backwater with its several music shops, an array of private teachers and a thriving local itinerary of concerts. There was also the propinquity of Mrs Jutta Bell, the Kristiana-born wife of Lieutenant Charles Bell, who lived on the neighbouring estate. Besides being the alleged object of Delius's passion,[47] as an acquaintance of Grieg she shared the Yorkshireman's enthusiasm for the Norwegian composer. It is interesting to note that Delius set himself up in Jacksonville as a violin teacher in July and August of 1884 and appeared in at least one concert in St James House in the city; all the while Ward was organist at the Church of the Immaculate Conception and taught the piano and singing privately.[48] Some of the musicians with whom Delius interacted were trained in Leipzig. Indeed, this was a period in American musical history when many a budding native composer, no doubt persuaded by the many immigrant German musicians who not only lived and worked in the United States but populated the emerging orchestra and places of learning, looked to Europe for musical tuition. This can be observed in the numerous 'Boston' school of composers such as John Knowles Paine (Berlin), George Whitefield Chadwick (Leipzig), Horatio Parker (Munich), Arthur Whiting (Munich), Henry Holden Huss (Munich) and Edward MacDowell (Paris and Frankfurt) who considered it *de rigueur* to study in European musical institutions before returning to America. Among those in Jacksonville was

---

[46] *TB*, 25–6; *CD*, 71.

[47] *DN*, 19.

[48] Randel, W., 'More on that Long-lost Mistress', *DSJ* No. 96 (Spring 1988), 10–11; see also Randel, W., 'Delius in America', in Redwood, C. (ed.), *A Delius Companion*, revised reprint (London: John Calder, 1980 [1976]), 153–4. As Randel has insinuated, the presence of Delius teaching in Jacksonville suggests that his time at the plantation was limited.

the Leipzig-educated William Jahn. Delius certainly knew him and, according to local opinion, took lessons from him.[49] Jahn, together with Ward, were probably the principal influences in persuading Delius to consider a future musical education in Leipzig, though his German background and the prevalence of Leipzig-trained musicians in Jacksonville (and in America in general) at this time may have been equally persuasive.[50]

Delius's first published piece was a polka for piano 'Zum Carneval' with a dedication to Jahn who held the copyright and, even though it bears a copyright date of 1892 (when the US copyright law came into effect), was most probably composed sometime in 1884 or 1885.[51] Written in a very simple repetitive form, 'Zum Carneval' was clearly intended as a popular dance for the mass market. In terms of its musical content, it shows a limited and rather crude handling of harmonic resources in its fluctuation between C major and its relative minor (in which it concludes), and some quirky uses of the odd chromatic progression, not to mention a solecistic augmented sixth (b. 56) and some unabashed consecutive fifths. The rhythmically banal 'Pensées mélodieuses' (No. 2), dated 10 June 1885, shows a wider harmonic vocabulary in its tonal scheme. The emphasis on harmonic colour rather than on melody is perhaps indicative of a prevailing interest on the part of the composer, though it falls short of the sophistication and fluency that Heseltine claimed Delius possessed even at this early juncture. The two songs of 1885 offer rather more clues to Delius's creative future. First, they show his earliest propensity for setting Scandinavian poetry. 'Over the mountains high' used selected verses from an English translation of Bjørnstjerne Bjørnson's 'Over de høje Fjaelle' from (from Chapter 14 of Bjørnson's peasant romance *Arne*) which had been published in Boston in 1869.[52] Though simple in terms of its strophic form and harmonic resources, it nevertheless reveals a more discriminating method and, perhaps, the earliest evidence of Grieg's influence.

---

[49] *DMA*, 19.

[50] The influence of his American colleagues, together with Delius's own German background, is significant since it appears at no time did Delius ever consider study in his native country, either at the Royal Academy of Music in London or the newly founded Royal College of Music which had opened its doors in 1883. By the 1880s the reputation of the Leipzig Conservatorium, now rivalled by centres in Berlin, Munich and Frankfurt, relied largely on its past glories.

[51] *RT1*, 183.

[52] For the four verses (1, 5, 6 and 7), see Plesner, A. and Rugeley-Powers (eds), *Arne: A Sketch of Norwegian Country Life* (Cambridge and Boston, MA: Sever, Francis & Co., 1869), 125–6.

The larger tonal scheme of each verse (C major – E major – C major) recalls numerous instances of the same tonic–mediant relationship in Grieg's songs and piano miniatures. The opening progression of the flattened submediant to the tonic is a definite Grieg thumbprint as is the horn call in bb. 4–5; moreover, this partiality for the tonic–submediant fluctuation (another Grieg hallmark) is further accentuated in the second part of each verse, and the submediant is also neatly incorporated into the cadence into E major (see b. 17). A second setting of Scandinavian words, 'Zwei Bräune Augen', this time of Hans Christian Anderson's 'To brune Øjne' in a German translation by W. Henzen probably came Delius's way through Grieg's setting of the poem in his song collection *Hjertets Melodier* [*Melodies of the Heart*] Op. 5. Although the technical resources of this song are still somewhat modest, they reveal a partiality for chromatic voice-leading within the inner voices of the accompaniment. A lesson has clearly been learned here from Grieg in the tonal shift from G major to the major submediant E by way of the relative minor (Example 1.1) which projects the reflective sensibility of Andersen's words ('nein nie und nimmer vergess' ich dein') together with Delius's marking 'nachdenkend'. The return to G major is subtly accomplished through the contrapuntal movement of the A sharp and B (forming a sensual dominant thirteenth over the tonic pedal) of the vocal line, while the final gesture of the voice ('nimmer'), with its unresolved A falling to D, is thoroughly characteristic.[53]

These piano pieces and songs provide categorical evidence that Delius gleaned a good deal from Ward and that he had learned a degree of technical competence in harmony as well as counterpoint. More significantly, however, the two songs of 1885 suggest that, with this greater proficiency, he had learned a degree of self-criticism. While this would prove important as a spur to his aspiration for a more systematic training at Leipzig, the isolated environment in which he lived for much of the time at Solana Grove with its tropical heat, vivid dawns and sunsets, Spanish moss and vegetation, did much to whet Delius's highly impressionable appetite. There was always time for work, and the reading of orchestration treatises by Cherubini and Berlioz. But, away from the concert halls and opera house, the heavily forested ambience of Florida's landscape was often the only environment in which he heard music (beyond that of his own making), and this largely in the form sung or played by the negro workers employed on the plantation. Inheritors of

---

[53] Bo Holten's sympathetic orchestration of this song serves only to enhance the stylistic character of this early miniature.

Example 1.1. 'Zwei braune Augen', bb. 16–34.

the generations that had experienced slavery and the horrors of the American Civil War, these men and women sang their old slave songs or played them on the banjo. As Clare Delius recounted: '[Delius] spent most of his time on the river in his boat, accompanied by his old nigger servant, whose duty it was to play to him on the banjo some of the old slave songs. Every evening, too, the same old nigger was summoned to the veranda, where he would sing to Fred old plantation melodies'.[54] Jelka Rosen, Delius's wife, recalled that he would play negro melodies on his violin: 'Fred had his violin and played negro melodies on it for us. He played it rather like the Norwegian peasants play the Hardanges-Fele (fiddle) as much as possible with the harmonies'.[55] Later Fenby famously related one of his earliest memories of Delius calling for a recording of 'The Revellers', a male vocal quartet with piano accompaniment, who recorded 'Ol' Man River' in the late 1920s.[56] This undoubtedly helped to prompt memories of Delius's days in Florida, but more than that, the spontaneous close harmony reminded him of the collective singing of his negro workers. 'They showed a truly wonderful sense of musicianship and harmonic resource in the instinctive way in which they treated melody ... and, hearing their singing in such romantic surroundings, it was then and there that I first felt the urge to express myself in music'.[57] Integral to this testimony were several germane factors. Although Delius had begun to bring some technical discipline to his composition (which was vital if he was to bring a sense of order to his musical thoughts), he always cleaved to the notion that composition involved an *instinctive* impulse, impossible to articulate in words. It was entirely consistent with other convictions he articulated (according to Fenby), that 'contemplation, like composition, cannot be taught',[58] or his somewhat vague *dictum* 'a sense of flow is the main thing, and it doesn't matter how you do it so long as you master it'.[59] Again, to Fenby, he divulged: 'It is fatal with most of the critics if a composer has found it necessary to reject German forms and refuse to mould his thought into standardised patterns. One can't define form in so many words, but if I was asked I should say that it was nothing more than imparting spiritual unity to one's thought'.[60] Yet, as Hutchings remarked, neither is it plausible to believe, as Delius reputedly did in later life, that rejecting the 'immortals' and 'going out into the fields'

---

[54] *CD*, 76. Please note that the racially outdated terms quoted in this volume reflect the language used by Delius and his contemporaries at the time, and illustrate the ways in which the composer was shaped by his experiences in the American south.

[55] Delius, J., 'Memories of Frederick Delius', in *DLL1*, 411.

[56] This recording must have been recently acquired by Delius, since the first appearance of the piece, a 'synthetic' slave song by Jerome Kern and Oscar Hammerstein, had only recently appeared in the 1927 musical *Show Boat*, and Fenby arrived at Grez-sur-Loing in 1928.

[57] *EF*, 25.

[58] Ibid., 164.

[59] Ibid., 169.

[60] Ibid., 200.

could lead rationally to creative coherence.[61] He was never well disposed to the business of rationalising composition; for him, the singing of the negroes in Florida not only embodied an instinctive, *anti*-intellectual position, but the simplicity of this music also reinforced his particular partiality for the two distinct components of melody (essentially diatonic) and harmony, particularly the notion of a colourful supporting harmony and how this could be conceptually exploited. Given Ward's mutual interest in black music,[62] it is more than likely that the elaborate harmonisation of negro tunes was encouraged and practised. At this juncture of his life he had yet to assimilate the necessary apparatus to explore this *topos* fully, but there can be little doubt that the confluence of his surroundings and the experience of hearing this choral sound in the open air ignited the compulsion to pursue composition (rather than any practical aspirations he may have had for the violin). Cecil Gray, in his book *Musical Chairs*, even postulated that it was precisely this rapt encounter with negro music of the American south, albeit in a very general sense, which fuelled Delius's creative impulse:

> That which is known to the mystics as "the state of illumination" is a kind of ecstatic revelation which may only last for a split second of time, but which he who has known it spends the rest of his life trying to recapture … those who have experienced it can always recognize the presence of the peculiar quality of that which appertains to it. The music of Delius is an example, and I was immediately aware of it in the first work of his I heard … I knew, too, the exact moment at which that experience must have occurred in Delius's life, and when I asked him if it were so and if I were right, he was surprised and admitted that I was. The occasion was one summer night, when he was sitting out on the verandah of his house in his orange grove in Florida, and the sound came to him from the near distance of the voices of the negroes in the plantation, singing in chorus. It is the rapture of this moment that Delius is perpetually seeking to communicate in all his characteristic work.[63]

Singing in parts, therefore, became an irresistible and powerful metaphor for Delius, particularly in how it naturally appealed to his harmonic imagination;

[61] *AH*, 21.

[62] *DLL1*, 5.

[63] Gray, C., *Musical Chairs or Between Two Stools* (London: Home & Van Thal, 1948), 191, quoted in Palmer, C., *Delius: Portrait of a Cosmopolitan* (London: Duckworth, 1976), 3.

it also became a vital element in shaping those genres in which he chose to work, whether in opera, works for chorus and orchestra or partsong.

After leaving Solana Grove with a sense of purpose (and in the most welcome charge of his brother Ernest), Delius had but one thing on his mind, and that was to earn sufficient money beyond his day-to-day expenses to cover his passage back to England, albeit with the challenge of persuading his father to allow him to study in Leipzig. Danville, Virginia, where he made a reasonable living as a teacher, brought him into contact with further Leipzig-educated musicians, notably his employer, Frederick Rueckert (who advertised pianos and organs) and Robert Phifer, a music professor at Roanoke Female College, company which affirmed his intention to pursue his studies in Germany.[64] As a town of the 'New South', Danville was a centre for the tobacco industry and many hundreds of negro workers worked in the stemmeries where they would sing in large groups.[65] Delius would often listen to their singing and would have become familiar with the practice of 'basing' (where a refrain from the chorus would follow the lead of a soloist). In this way, likewise, he would have retained a repertory of songs, several of which emerged in the *Neger Lieder*, the *American Rhapsody* and, above all, *Appalachia*.

Delius may have continued to compose in Danville and after he left for New York and Rhode Island. He certainly owned manuscript paper bought from Carl Fischer of New York (which he took to Leipzig).[66] But there is little surviving evidence of anything written in 1886, except perhaps the song 'Der Fichtenbaum'. This may have been written in America, but corrections in blue pencil suggest that Delius submitted it for scrutiny in Leipzig where it may have been conceived along with numerous other settings of Heine's poems.[67] After sailing from New York to Liverpool in June 1886, Delius made for Bradford before arranging his travel to Leipzig. Fortunately, he was spared any unpleasant confrontation with his father, for, by this time, Julius had acceded to his son's wishes. Initially Delius's proposal to study in Germany had been rebuffed, in spite of a supportive letter received from Phifer in Danville.[68] Nevertheless, when nothing of Delius was heard of for several months, Julius had begun to fear for his son's well-being and replied to Phifer,

---

[64] Randel, W., 'Delius in America', 157.

[65] Ibid., 160.

[66] See *DMA*, 46.

[67] Ibid., 18.

[68] *CD*, 78.

not about musical study, to which he was still implacably opposed, but about his son's whereabouts. Having subsequently learned that Delius was happily supporting himself as a music teacher, Julius relented, perhaps sensing that his continued antagonism might drive Fritz away for good. Moreover, as Beecham has intimated (in a bid to scotch the assertion that Julius dismissed music as an unsuitable profession for a gentleman), if his son could make a living in provincial Danville, how might he fare in one of America's larger cities where a decent living could be made?[69] Seeing the logic of Fritz's aspiration, he finally granted his son the chance to study in Leipzig.

LEIPZIG

Delius arrived in Leipzig in August 1886. He followed in the footsteps of numerous English musicians such as Sullivan, Dannreuther, Carl Rosa and Stanford who had chosen to study there, while among the contemporary student body were his countrymen Percy Pitt and Ernest Hutcheson. Even if the Conservatoire no longer boasted the likes of Mendelssohn, Schumann, Gade or Hiller on the staff, its present range of teachers was still regarded as distinguished and the list of student applicants was still healthy. Fritz's certificate of admission acknowledged his studies on the violin with Deichmann in London, with Bauerkeller in Bradford and with Sitt in Chemnitz. His abilities as pianist were noted as being self-taught as was his knowledge of musical theory. More importantly, it was recorded that he had aspirations to compose.[70] His teachers were Carl Reinecke, the Director and Principal Conductor of the Gewandhaus Orchestra, who oversaw 'Ensemble Work' and also taught him the piano; Salomon Jadassohn taught the theory of music (essentially harmony and counterpoint), Oscar Paul 'Aesthetics and History' and Heinrich Klesse 'Singing'. To this was added violin lessons with Sitt who numbered among several string teachers including Adolf Brodsky (who was famous for his Quartet) and the cellist Julius Klengel. There was also a forum for frank criticism at student concerts on Friday evenings (essentially for performers), and, as Pitt recalled, the chance for composers to hear their works played through at Bonorand's restaurant before a proper audience,

---

[69] *TB*, 32. Beecham's comments were almost certainly aimed at Clare Delius (see *CD*, 91).

[70] Jones, P., 'Delius's Leipzig Connections 1886–1888', *DSJ* No. 102 (Autumn 1989), 3.

though this demanded 'a hundred marks for the bandmaster's tip and the musicians' beer', which, for less pecunious students, was a deterrent.[71]

A student at Leipzig would have found the musical life of the city irresistible and Delius was no exception in this regard. He arrived at a time when the Leipzig Opera, one of the best in the country, was led by Artur Nikisch with Gustav Mahler as his assistant. The city boasted the substantial Stadttheater where many of Wagner's later operas had been heard for the first time outside Bayreuth (thanks largely to the efforts of Angelo Neumann who set a challenging precedent for future theatre managers). The Leipzig Opera company accommodated a chorus of sixty-three singers, twelve female and fourteen male soloists, an orchestra of seventy-seven instrumentalists (furnished by the Gewandhaus Orchestra) and a team of three directors led by Max Staegemann.[72] The repertoire was well rehearsed and performed, besides the operas of Mozart and Weber, works by Bellini (*Norma*) and Meyerbeer (*La prophète, Les Huguenots, Dinorah* and *Robert le diable*), Beethoven's *Fidelio*, Rossini's *The Barber of Seville*, Bizet's *Carmen*, Goetz's *Der Widerspenstigen Zähmung*, Marschner's *Der Templer und die Jüdin*, Kretschmer's *Heinrich der Löwe*, Halévy's *La Juive* and Wagner's early operas (*Rienzi, Der fliegende Holländer, Tannhäuser* and *Lohengrin*). There was much to learn from this rich diet, but more auspiciously, Delius was in Leipzig when it was announced in November 1886 that Nikisch would conduct a complete *Ring* cycle and there would be later productions of *Tristan und Isolde* and *Die Meistersinger*.[73] With the new theories of Wagner's music dramas attracting increasing attention in Germany and elsewhere, this was an opportunity not to be missed. For Delius, hearing Wagner on a regular basis would be deeply formative. In addition, the Gewandhaus, which accommodated the best orchestra in Europe, was a magnet for many of the continent's finest composers. Berlioz, Rubinstein, Liszt, Bruch, Brahms, Grieg and Wagner had all conducted their music there, and, in 1887, Delius was able to hear Tchaikovsky direct several of his own works including the Fifth Symphony, the First Orchestral Suite, the overture *Romeo and Juliet*, the Suite *Mozartiana* and the Serenade for Strings. Brahms was also in Leipzig to conduct his Double Concerto (with Joachim and Hausmann) as was Busoni to hear his

---

[71] Chamier, J. D., *Percy Pitt of Covent Garden and the BBC* (London: Edward Arnold, 1938), 33, quoted in *DLL1*, 7.

[72] Riedel, S., 'Mahler in Leipzig: His First Season', in Böhm, C. (ed.), *Mahler in Leipzig* (Leipzig: Kamprad, 2011), 53.

[73] Ibid., 61–2. As it transpired, Nikisch was ill and Mahler conducted *Das Rheingold*, *Die Walküre* and *Siegfried* to considerable acclaim.

string quartets in the Kammermusiksaal. There were concerts every Saturday in the Kammermusiksaal, and every Thursday evening (save the summer break) in the large new hall of the Gewandhaus (which had opened in 1885); students could attend Wednesday rehearsals. For church music the choirs of St Nicholas and St Thomas were famous. As for obtaining scores, Leipzig was the music-publishing capital of the world.

All of this was meat and drink for the avaricious Delius, hungry to absorb and assimilate after his two years in America, and his experiences in the opera house and concert hall acted like a dynamic catalyst to aid his rapid development as a composer. 'Leipzig is a very nice town with a fine Opera house & concerts almost every night', he wrote to Gertrude Rueckert in Danville; 'All the greatest Artist[s] come here so we have fine opportunities to hear good music'.[74] And there were many opportunities to play music: 'I have a quartet at my lodgings every sunday morning. A fine violinist, cellist & viola, I play the piano. It is indeed very enjoyable. We play Schumann, Beethoven, Mozart, Haydn etc.', he told Rueckert.[75] Nevertheless, what he must have hoped for in Leipzig was to acquire enough technique to realise his compositional aspirations, and at the heart of this were the lessons he took with Jadassohn. Delius (so Heseltine maintained) was scornful of Jadassohn who was 'neither a beautiful player nor a cultured musician',[76] a harsh appraisal of an accomplished pianist and an experienced teacher, even if his own music failed to make its mark. As Threlfall has carefully identified, Delius worked diligently through selected parts of Jadassohn's *Musikalische Kompositionslehre* which consisted of five components.[77] Of these, the *Lehrbuch der Harmonie* (published in 1883) and the *Lehrbuch des Contrapunkts* figured centrally in his course of exercises, a fact corroborated by the consecutive numbering of them in Delius's surviving notebooks.[78] Delius also owned a copy of Jadassohn's *Die Formen in den Werken der Tonkunst*, published only a year before he arrived in Leipzig, a treatise which contained many wise and interesting concepts including the notion that form was intrinsically connected with the character

---

[74] Letter from Delius to Gertrude Rueckert, 11 December 1886, *DLL1*, 9.

[75] Ibid.

[76] *PH*, 25.

[77] *DMA*, 25–7.

[78] Three of Delius's Leipzig notebooks have survived. One is located in the Carl S. Swisher Library, Jacksonville University, one in the Grainger Museum, Melbourne University (*AU-Mgm* C2/DELI-23-1), and one in the Delius Trust Archive (now *GB-Lbl* MS Mus 1745/2/11/1).

and content of its thematic ideas. From Jadassohn's writings on harmony and counterpoint we can see that Delius undertook selected exercises on harmony, notably on the handling of the dominant-seventh and secondary-seventh harmonies, pedal points, modulation and enharmonic change; there is also evidence of harmonisation of German chorales such as 'Nun dankt alle Gott',[79] sometimes with figured bass, and four-part exercises in open score with C clefs. Much of the time, however, was spent on a strict course of species counterpoint from the *Lehrbuch des Contrapunkts*. Delius no doubt found this process trying and mechanical. The short exercises were dry and unappealing, such was the nature of learning species counterpoint. But the object of such a course was to develop contrapuntal *fluency* and we can see from the notebook dated from 29 March 1887 that Delius was completing his exercises on a regular basis, and that these exercises were sketched first (evident from other notebooks) and copied neatly into this one.[80] This was achieved in an incremental fashion and we can observe Delius learning, step by step (with corrective markings from his tutor), to manage first species (one against one) and second species (two against one, as well as four against one), and, within a three-part texture, first species with second together. Further exercises also involve four-part contrapuntal textures using a *cantus firmus* and the introduction of fifth species (full rhythmical freedom). In addition, the process of species counterpoint also introduced the vital concept of invertibility, and we can observe Delius's comprehension of both invertibility in two parts and three, and triple invertibility with a free fourth voice, and, in some instances quadruple invertibility. Jadassohn also insisted on the rigour of canon at various intervals, and with invertibility in three parts (two canonic voices and a free voice) and four (three canonic voices and a free voice). All of this was *de rigueur* for students of harmony and counterpoint at Leipzig (and differed little from the similar demands made by the B.Mus. degree of British ancient universities for its written papers in harmony and species counterpoint). By October and November of 1887, Delius had learned enough contrapuntal technique to undertake three-voice fugues which showed a reasonable, if not especially inventive, degree of fluency.[81]

There was also time for free composition under Jadassohn's tutelage. The notebooks show numerous sketches and fair copies of a variety of short pieces ranging from miniature piano works (including *Tarantelle, Tempo di Valse,*

---

[79] *DMA*, 46.

[80] Ibid., 80–90.

[81] These fugues are transcribed in Ibid., 92–101.

March, Tema con variazione) to partsongs with German texts.[82] Such tasks were intended to be the first steps towards an appreciation of simple forms and tonal schemes. There is also a sketch of fifteen bars of a first movement of a Piano Sonata in D minor, heavily influenced by Grieg's Piano Sonata Op. 7 (which had been published in revision in Leipzig in 1887).[83]

It is perhaps no accident that Delius spent much of this time focusing on the partsong. The sound of unaccompanied voices had appealed to him in Florida, which, conflated with the familiar tradition of the German *Männerchor* and *Chorgesänge*, provided an ideal opportunity to hone his harmonic skills within an essentially Romantic genre and allowed a flexibility of homophonic and contrapuntal texture. While none of these pieces is particularly characterful, the handling of voices, the sense of harmonic coherence and a facility for modulation suggest that Delius had learned his lessons thoroughly. Three songs ('Durch den Wald', 'Sonnenscheinlied' and 'Frühlingsanbruch'), reveal the composer's partiality for a dance-like compound duple metre (which Delius was to adopt with frequent alacrity in his livelier essays), and the more pensive setting of 'Abendfeier in Venedig' ('Ave Maria') from Emanuel von Geibel's *Jugendgedichte*, dated March 1887, gives the odd glimpse of chromatic colour in response to the text. Moreover, his continued fascination with Scandinavia drew him once again to Bjørnson's poetry in Lobedanz's translation (which had been published in Leipzig in 1881) for 'Sonnenscheinlied' and 'Frühlingsanbruch'. Delius probably acquired a volume of Heine's *Lyrisches Intermezzo* and *Die Heimkehr* in Leipzig, perhaps in the knowledge that this poetry had provided prime material for Schubert, Schumann, Robert Franz and Brahms. His interest in Heine clearly encouraged him to sketch two partsongs 'Die Lotosblume anstigt' and 'Der Mond is aufgegangen'; and two others, 'Lorelei' and 'Aus deinem Augen fliessen meine Lieder', may possibly have his authorship.[84] And there are at least two sketches of songs 'Warum sind den die Rosen so blass' and 'Ein Fichtenbaum', the latter a later and quite different version of a completed setting made in 1886 and showing a major advance harmonically in its unabashed pirating of the harmonic progression (i–vi–i) from the 'Tarnhelm' leitmotiv, first introduced by Alberich in *Das Rheingold* (suggesting that Delius may have composed this in 1887 after hearing *The Ring* cycle in Leipzig).[85]

---

[82] See particularly *AU-Mgm* MG C2/DELI-23-1.

[83] *DMA*, 78–9.

[84] Ibid., 109–14.

[85] Ibid., 102–4.

Delius's social intercourse with the Norwegian fraternity in Leipzig has been well documented in various sources, notably in Andrew Boyle's *Delius and Norway*. The former experiences of the Norwegian landscape as a young man, his friendship with Jutta Bell in Florida and his admiration for Grieg's music had already sealed his fascination for the country's fresh and emerging cultural accent; now the chance presented itself at first hand to interact with Norway's exciting new generation of musicians who were either studying at the conservatoire or visiting the city. His circle included the instrumentalists Borghild Holmsen, Olaf Paulus Olsen and Camilla Jacobsen (all pianists), Arve Arvesen, Halfdan Jebe, Hjalmar Børgstrøm and Johan Halvorsen (all violinists, though Halvorsen would later distinguish himself as a capable composer), the conductor Iver Holter, and the composers Georg Washington Magnus and Christian Sinding. From 1882 Sinding began to develop a reputation as a published composer, principally with songs, piano works and chamber works such as the Piano Quintet Op. 5 and the String Quartet *Alte Weisen*. A private bursary enabled Sinding to return to Leipzig for further study in 1886 at which time he met the twenty-four-year-old Delius, fresh from his American travels. The two became immediate friends and a correspondence between them continued until at least 1905.

During a walking tour of Norway during July and August of 1887, when he travelled up from Stavanger to Odda (a favourite route for English tourists),[86] and then through the fjords to Sandeid, Skånevik and Fjæra, Delius sketched in another notebook a series of Norwegian tunes.[87] Joining with those Norwegians, including Grieg, who were eagerly collecting folk tunes in many parts of the country, he no doubt thought that this, together with the live experience of Norwegian folk dances, would act as a useful catalyst in the formation of his own musical language.[88] One also suspects that his motivation to take down these melodies was also driven by his desire to emulate Grieg's *Lyriske småstykker* Op. 12, the *25 norske folkeviser og dandse* Op. 17 (after L. M. Lindemann's *Aeldre og nyere norske fjeldmelodier* and Kjerulf's *Norske Folkviser* published in 1875) and the *Folkelivsbilleder* Op. 19. 'Norske Wiser', taken down on 18 July 1887, presents sixteen bars of a distinctly Griegian tune in E minor, fully harmonised and replete with a characteristic V–VI–i cadence. Others, 'Sæters Sang', 'Til Fjeldet', 'Til Sætern' and 'Fiskaren på Sejegrunden'

---

[86] *DN*, 24.

[87] See *GB-Lbl* MS Mus 1745/1/38 and *DMA*, 120–24.

[88] It is evident from Delius's 'Red Notebook' that he witnessed a good deal of spontaneous Norwegian folk song and dance.

were also sketched but only as melodies. Another Norwegian-like melody was begun as a canon, several Griegian piano miniatures were attempted (which clearly refer to various of Grieg's *Lyrics Pieces*);[89] one of them, an 'Allegro risoluto' in C major, complete, and a sketch setting in German translation of Ibsen's 'Wiegenlied' (a text which eventually found its way into the *Seven Songs from the Norwegian* published in 1892) were made on his way back to Leipzig on 5 August.[90]

Back in Leipzig Delius resumed his studies with Jadassohn and it was through his close friendship with Sinding, with whom he dined regularly at Leipzig's Panorama restaurant, that he was introduced to Grieg. It was an encounter of such import that Delius later dictated his memories, 'Delius: Recollections of Grieg', to Percy Grainger.[91] Sinding, Halvorsen and the Griegs had formed a circle after Grieg's arrival in Leipzig in September 1887, but after the meeting with Delius, the fraternity increased to five. Moreover, Grieg introduced Delius to the twenty-year-old Ferruccio Busoni who had just arrived in Leipzig to study with Wilhelm Mayer and Reinecke.[92] 'He was Anti Wagnerian, whilst we others were Wagner-Enthusiasts', Delius later remembered; 'A few years later he became quite a Wagnerian – always a little too late. In the years following he tried to be modern and encouraged everything modern, but at heart he remained the Classic'.[93]

With the bonding of this new Anglo-Norwegian 'clique', Grieg's music became a central focus. Delius had much enjoyed hearing the first public performance of Grieg's new Violin Sonata in C minor Op. 45, performed by Brodsky, a few days before his meeting with the composer, but thereafter, the young man from Bradford basked in the company of his idol and the younger generation of adoring Norwegians. Grieg was clearly flattered by this 'English-American', as he first perceived Delius, and was absorbed by his knowledge of Norwegian geography, particularly of the Jotunheim area. Perhaps even more significantly, Grieg was deeply enamoured by Delius's belief in the older man's cultural mission, a sentiment he would later appreciate from the young Percy Grainger.[94] Moreover, in appreciating Delius's lionisation of him, Grieg repaid the compliment by recognising and supporting Delius's aspirations

---

[89] See *DMA*, 125–8 for Threlfall's transcriptions of these sketches.

[90] Ibid., 129–31.

[91] See Appendix IV, *DLL1*, 394–6.

[92] Dent, E., *Ferruccio Busoni* (London: Eulenberg, 1974), 67.

[93] Letter from Delius to Ernest Newman, 9 March 1933, *DLL2*, 417.

[94] *DN*, 33.

as a composer. In the few months left to the 'circle' (who were enshrined by the famous studio photograph made in the spring of 1888), they attended performances of *The Ring*, *Die Meistersinger* and *Tristan*, and Grieg's String Quartet Op. 27 was played by the Brodsky Quartet in Leipzig on 18 February 1888. After this performance Delius declared his unbridled devotion to Grieg in a letter: 'It will be of little importance to you if I tell you how much I love you & esteem you, but it is true & comes from my heart & so I thank you for all the pleasure that I feel in your works'.[95] Of a more intimate, domestic nature was the celebrated (and traditionally Norwegian) Christmas Eve party at which Delius was presented with a signed copy of Grieg's Piano Concerto as a gift. Nina Grieg sang her husband's *Tolv Melodier* Op. 33, and Grieg's Violin Sonata No. 2 in G major was played by Halvorsen. There were also songs by Sinding and his *Suite in alten Stil* Op. 10 for violin, and Delius's contribution to the evening was a piano piece, *Norwegische Schlittenfahrt*, now only known in its orchestration of 1890 (when, renamed and probably revised, as *Winter Night*, it became the second of his *Three Small Tone Poems*). The piece, fashioned in very much the same way as one Grieg's own piano miniatures, was in every way a tribute to the Norwegian in its veiled references to the *Humoresques* Op. 6 and to the more boisterous dance movements from the *Lyric Pieces*. Some effective details, such as the relationship between the 3/4 'Andante molto tranquillo' and the 4/4 'a tempo' of the 'trio', already reveal Delius's flair for thematic invention, and the 'unprepared' juxtaposition of D major and F sharp major (a Griegian thumbprint) corroborates his inclination to use third-related tonalities in such a context. One also senses Delius's sensual enjoyment of the dominant thirteenth of F sharp at the goal of the 'accel. Poco agitato' (b. 78).

While Delius resumed his counterpoint studies with Jadassohn in the autumn of 1887,[96] he was also eager to complete his first significant orchestral work, *Florida*, a four-movement suite intended to be a coherent cycle of pieces, or as Delius subtitled the work, 'Tropische Szenen für Orchester', spanning a typical day on a Floridian plantation (presumably his own at Solana Grove). Delius probably finished work on it in early 1888 since he was able to hear a play-through for two hours of his work at Bonorand's restaurant (made possible by the statutory payment of a barrel of beer), conducted by his violin teacher Hans Sitt, in the company of Sinding and the Griegs. In the summer of 1889 Delius returned to the score, mainly to review the

---

[95] *GD*, 37.

[96] Heseltine states that work on *Florida* began in 1886; see *PH*, 158–9.

instrumentation which, he admitted, contained some 'orchestral brutalities'.[97]
Two movements were revised though only one, numbered 'II' survives with
the French title 'Au coucher du Soleil – Pastorale' which, supplemented by
a cor anglais and bass clarinet for additional colour, is still retained as the
third movement in the published score.[98] For someone who had been at
the Conservatoire for barely fifteen months, *Florida* was a considerable
achievement in terms of its technical assurance, its indications of imaginative
scoring (in spite of Delius's later misgivings), its youthful élan and, moreover,
by dint of its portrayal of America's deep south, its entirely original subject
material. To its private audience in Leipzig, the American ethos of this music,
especially the quasi-negro dance melody (the 'Allegretto' in F major) with its
pentatonic scale, 5–6–8 melodic opening and 'banjo' scoring for pizzicato
strings and harp, was not lost on those present. As Delius remembered to
Grainger: 'In the Suite was a very noisy nigger dance where I had used the
trombones very noisily, and *ff*, and Grieg after the performance said to me
that he found it "scheusslich interessant"'.[99] What effect it might have had on
an English audience is tantalising. Certainly nothing would have been heard
of its type at the Crystal Palace, for it was under its conductor, August Manns,
that Delius hoped to secure a public performance. Both score and parts were
sent to Manns in the latter part of 1888, but finding no time to accommodate
the work, he returned Delius's score in March 1889.[100]

The simplicity of the structural invention in *Florida*, with its propensity for
simple formal designs (especially those of a ternary species), reveals that Delius
had gleaned much from the example of Grieg's *Peer Gynt* with its propensity of
atmospheric orchestral 'pictures', song movements and dances. This is clearly
evident in the 'Tanz der Majorbauer' (the main body of the first movement),
the song movement 'Am Fluss' (which is more of an Intermezzo) and the
slow movement 'Sonnenuntergang – Au Coucher du Soleil' where the central
section bears many similarities to Grieg's lively 'Troll' dances. By contrast,
the last movement, 'Nachts', is an arch form (ABCBA). The ternary forms,

[97] Letter from Grieg to Delius, [undated, but early June 1889], *DLL1*, 42.

[98] In the surviving manuscript of *Florida* at the University Melbourne (*AU-Mgm* MG
      C2/DELI-23-1), the original title of the third movement was 'Sonnenuntergang
      – Bei der Plantage'. The manuscript of the revised third movement (*AU-Mgm*
      MG C2/DELI-12-2) shows that the central section was marked 'Auprès de la
      Plantation / Dance des Nègres'.

[99] *DLL1*, 395.

[100] Letter from Manns to Delius, 14 March 1889, *DLL1*, 38.

however, with their strongly contrasting 'trio' sections, give the impression of separate movements, which collectively give the suite's four movements a sense of greater variety. Indeed, Delius may have intended the four-movement design of his work outwardly to resemble a symphony, even though the treatment of his extended thematic material is largely unsymphonic in spirit. Nevertheless, Delius undoubtedly conceived his suite as a cyclic entity which is apparent by the truncated recapitulation of the introduction from the first movement at the beginning of the last, a reference to the 'trio' material of 'Am Fluss', and by the augmented 'memory' of the 'Tanz der Majorbauer' in the closing bars of the work. These are deftly placed, effective moments. But *Florida*, for all its inchoate and over-repetitive elements, divulges clues to the future Delius. In spite of the 'orchestral brutalities', the handling of woodwind (especially in affecting solo passages such as the oboe which opens 'Tagesanbruch'), the nocturnal horn writing in the last movement (where, one suspects, Delius had learned his lesson from Mendelssohn's 'nocturne' from the incidental music to *A Midsummer Night's Dream*) and the 'banjo' music exhibit an instinctive sensibility for the orchestra as an agency of poetry. Harmonically, too, there are moments of genuine resourcefulness embodied most persuasively in Delius's ability, following the example of Grieg, to modulate effortlessly (without transitional progressions) to third-related tonalities: the 'negro dance' of the third movement is one such example where a shift from A major to F is fluently enacted. Moreover, Delius's harmonic vocabulary already demonstrates a natural predisposition for those enhanced dominant chords of the ninth, eleventh and thirteenth (such as one finds in the principal theme of the last movement – see Example 1.2a), so prevalent in Grieg's rich diatonic palette. But perhaps most remarkable are the opening bars of the introduction where the falling semitonal sequential phrases of the oboe are mirrored by a series of colourful progressions facilitated by the use of the augmented sixth in last inversion (Example 1.2b). This *topos* of a falling chromatic bass is also reflected in the harmonic model of the 'Tanz der Majorbauer' together with other falling chromatic steps in the upper voices (Example 1.2c).[101] While this chromatic model may be rudimentary, it nevertheless provides a glimpse of Delius's fertile harmonic mindset of the future.

---

[101] It is evident from the manuscript that the F natural in violins 1 and 2 (thirteen bars after b. 6), the E flat in violins 1 and 2 (fifteen after b. 6) and the A flat (sixteen after b. 6) in the viola, and later the E sharp and E natural in violins 1 and 2 (twenty-seven and twenty-nine after b. 6) were added later in pencil, which may have been a revision by Delius or Jadassohn.

Example 1.2a. *Florida*, 'At Night', main theme.

While *Florida* took its cue from the nineteenth-century tradition of the orchestral suite, *Hiawatha*, dated 'January 1888',[102] was a student attempt at a programmatic American 'Tongedicht für Orchester / nach Longfellows Gedicht' (tone poem for orchestra after Longfellow's poem), as the title page of the manuscript shows.[103] Again Delius showed some characteristic independence of mind in basing his orchestral essay on the 'exotic' subject of native Americans. What is more, he must have been conscious also that Longfellow's epic (influenced strongly by the Finnish *Kalevala*) explored a historical idea which allowed the poet to break with traditional European models, a factor which enhanced the exotic nature of his musical canvas. It is also an important instance of a European work influenced by the Hiawatha story. It is unlikely that Delius knew earlier American orchestral compositions by Robert Stoepel or Ellsworth Phelps; it also predates Dvořák's interest around the time of his Ninth Symphony 'From the New World' of 1893 and Coleridge-Taylor's cantata-triptych by a decade.

---

[102] Beecham suggests that *Hiawatha* was begun in late 1887; see *TB*, 36.

[103] See *GB-Lbl* MS Mus 1745/1/1.

Example 1.2b. *Florida*, 'Daybreak', bb. 10–20.

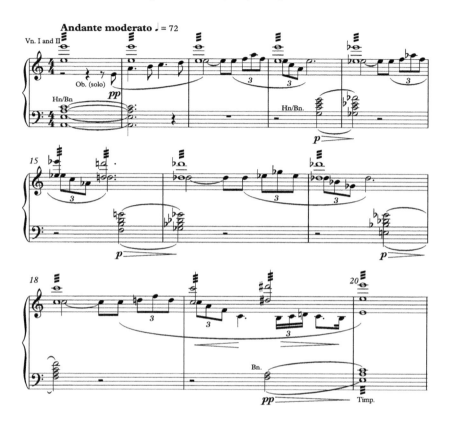

Example 1.2c. *Florida*, harmonic model of the opening
of 'Tanz der Majorbauer' [La Calinda]

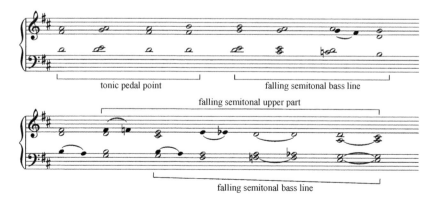

Example 1.3a. *Hiawatha*, first subject.

The incomplete autograph score of *Hiawatha* (completed by Threlfall) is prefaced by ten lines from the introduction to Longfellow's poem in twenty-two parts (beginning 'Ye who love the haunts of Nature / Love the sunshine of the meadow') and it is evident from erased quotations in three places in the score (ff. 1, 11 and 25) and two that were left intact towards the conclusion (f. 33), which are taken from Part XXII 'Hiawatha's Departure', that Delius imagined his work as a series of more symphonic episodes depicting principal events in the poem and Hiawatha's life. Why Delius erased three of these quotations is not certain, but he may have entertained second thoughts about their role, perhaps in the interests of musical coherence. The fact that the manuscript is also incomplete might also suggest that the composer was dissatisfied with the larger structure and that he was not quite ready for the symphonic challenge he had set himself. Nevertheless, for all the unsatisfactory elements of the work, and the most glaring of these is the laboured banality of the 'working-out' process, the more ambitious nature of the individual musical paragraphs with their more far-reaching tonal schemes reveals that Delius was attempting to develop his thematic material at greater length. There is also a clear sense of tonal dialectic between the first subject in A major ('Hiawatha') and the second in C major ('Minnehaha'), though one which Delius fails to work out in the later pages of the score. A more tonally fluid animated, dance-like section in B minor, which lies at the heart of the work, suggests the rhetoric of a development. This culminates in a delicious scherzo-like 'pastoral' in A flat and

Example 1.3b. *Hiawatha*, second subject.

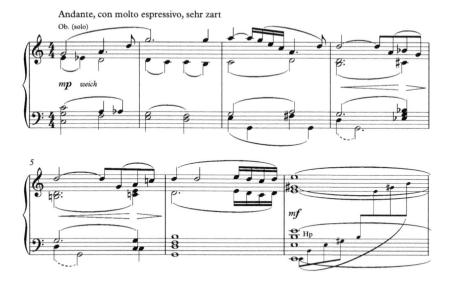

the tragedy of Minnehaha's death while the final section (as we know from the surviving quotations) depicts Hiawatha's resolve to depart. Although Grieg's influence is detectable in the dance character of the developmental phase and the general inclination of the work to form individual 'pictures' more redolent of a suite (and here the affinity with *Florida* is still strong), *Hiawatha* is as much about Delius's enthusiasm for Wagner, *Siegfried* and the *Siegfried Idyll*. The representation of nature in the introduction and closing section of the work are indebted to the 'Waldweben' (forest murmurs) in Act II of *Siegfried*, while the first subject bears a strong kinship with the opening thematic material of the *Siegfried Idyll* (Example 1.3a), works we know Delius would have keenly studied. Indeed, Delius's use of E major (the key of the 'Waldweben' and the *Siefried Idyll*) at the end of the tone poem further reinforces the connection. Of greater interest, however, is the second subject which, as Fenby suggested, looked forward in its melodic behaviour and harmonic support (replete with chromatic inner-voice work) to the lyrical viola theme in *Paris* over a decade later (Example 1.3b).[104] This process of self-reference or even direct self-borrowing would be a practice Delius chose to exercise freely for most of his creative career.

---

[104] *EF*, 68.

CHAPTER 2

Creative Self-Communion: *Paa Vidderne, Lieder aus dem Norwegischen, Légendes, Drei Symphonische Dichtungen*, Songs (1888–1891)

WITHDRAWAL FROM LEIPZIG AND ARRIVAL IN PARIS

By the spring of 1888 Delius was impatient to move on; moreover, the *coterie* of Norwegians was about to fragment. 'Our wonderful time in Leipzig has now melted away into the past', he later wrote to Grieg from Bradford; 'I have never lived through such a congenial time. It has been a cornerstone in my life'.[1] Halvorsen was the first to depart and Delius followed a fortnight later and had no intention of returning.[2] The Griegs left in April, leaving only Sinding to languish in solitude. Delius's withdrawal from Leipzig, as Philip Jones has argued, was entirely voluntary (which somewhat contradicts the assertion that his father had only granted him a limited period of eighteen months of study). His letter to Gertrude Rueckert of December 1886 makes it clear that he expected to be in Leipzig for three years like other fellow students,[3] but given that he attended few of the classes for which he was registered (with the exception of those with Reinecke, Jadassohn and Sitt), it is not surprising that he saw little point in continuing.[4] The wonder is that Leipzig granted him

---

[1] Letter from Delius to Grieg, 25 April 1888, *GD*, 45.

[2] *GD*, 41.

[3] Letter from Delius to Gertrude Rueckert, 11 December 1886, *DLL1*, 9; see also Jones, P., 'Delius's Leipzig Connections 1886–1888', *DSJ* No. 102 (Autumn 1989), 4.

[4] Apart from theory lessons with Reinecke and Jadassohn where he was 'very hard working', and violin lessons with Sitt, he attended very few of Oscar Paul's history lectures, did little for Reinecke's ensemble class, and failed to attend any classes for singing. His piano teachers did not regard him as a serious student (see Jones 1989, 4–5).

a diploma at all.[5] Delius's later disparagement of Leipzig, the 'Double Fugue Institution' as Sinding sarcastically described it,[6] is well known.[7] At a time when he made these comments, autodidacticism was deeply fashionable; likewise, popular 'anti-intellectualism' in composition and criticism deemed the word 'academic' (especially in the hands of Bernard Shaw) a pejorative term. Yet, Delius's experiences there, whether in the classroom, at the opera or in the concert hall, inculcated a sense of professionalism in his work and, more significantly, his later methods, with an incisive degree of self-criticism. However, possessed with youthful arrogance and (more importantly) belief in his own abilities, like many of his peers, he undoubtedly felt that he could make more progress on his own without Jadassohn's watchful eye. In January 1889, in a letter to Delius, Sinding ruefully commented: 'it is queer how Jadassohn impresses the stamp of his own personality on his pupils, if they cannot emancipate themselves from it'.[8] Emancipating himself clearly was Delius's desire. As he declared to the much younger Heseltine: 'Harmony is only a means of expression which is gradually developing. I don't believe in learning harmony and counterpoint'.[9] And, recalling his days with Jadassohn to the young Charles Wilfrid Orr, he counselled: 'Go by all means to the Guildhall school of music for a while and see how you profit by it – But do not get hold of a professor who teaches you little 4 or 8 bar counterpoint exercises and little harmony exercises – Trust your own ears and try to express your emotions in any way you can'.[10]

Delius must have imparted his disenchantment with Leipzig to his father on his return to England, and, quite understandably, Julius must have chaffed at the funds he had futilely disbursed, a fact hinted at, but not fully explicated, by Heseltine.[11] Nevertheless, the myth has persisted, probably through Clare Delius's biography of her brother, that his time in Leipzig had been circumscribed by his father.[12] Added to which, and contrary to those

---

[5]   That Delius received his diploma is largely owing to the efforts of Sinding; see letters from Sinding to Delius, 6 October 1888 and 26 January 1889, *DTA*.

[6]   Letter from Sinding to Delius, 16 January 1889, *DTA*.

[7]   *EF*, 168.

[8]   Letter from Sinding to Delius, 13 January 1889, *DTA*.

[9]   Letter from Delius to Heseltine, 4 December 1911 in *FDPW*, 10.

[10]   Letter from Delius to C. W. Orr, 10 April 1917, *DLL2*, 178–9.

[11]   *PH*, 28.

[12]   *CD*, 95. This myth continued to be reiterated in *TB*, 39, *AH*, 21, and *AJ*, 22. Clare Delius's account of Delius '[rushing] back to Grieg [to] unbosom himself to his friend' also makes no sense in light of the chronological evidence.

who asserted that Delius learned nothing at the Conservatorium,[13] had Delius decided to stay on at Leipzig, he might well have learned a good deal more to supplement his technique which, if no longer rudimentary, still required considerable refinement and amplification. This he must have realised, but while he placed no further trust in Leipzig, he must have fretted about where his future in music lay. Having returned to Bradford he made it plain to Grieg that 'I do not think that I shall stick it out for very long here',[14] and he was adamant not to enter his father's firm. Julius was not, however, incapable of showing some sympathy. He gave Fritz the score of *Tristan und Isolde*,[15] and plans were evidently made for a recreational journey to Paris and to Spain. But before this took place, Delius had conspired with Grieg while he was still in Leipzig to construct a formal letter addressed to him in German from the Norwegian master which could be read by his father:

> I was pleasantly surprised, indeed stimulated, by your manuscripts [most likely *Florida* and *Hiawatha*] and I detect in them signs of a most distinguished compositional talent in the grand style, which aspires to the highest goal. Whether you will reach this goal only depends upon what turn your affairs take. If you will permit me, in the interests of your future, to offer you a piece of advice, (it is as an older artist that I take the liberty of doing this) it would be this, that you devote yourself now, while you are still young, fully to the pursuit of your art, rather than accept a formal position, and that you follow both your own true nature and the inner voice of your ideals and your inclinations. However, in order to achieve this it is essential that you choose the national and artistic environment as dictated to you by your genius.

> It is my most fervent wish that you will one day find in your own country the recognition which you deserve, as well as the material means towards the achievement of your splendid goal and I do not doubt for a moment that you will succeed.[16]

---

[13] See Heseltine, P., 'Frederick Delius', in Eaglefield-Hull, A. (ed.), *A Dictionary of Modern Music and Musicians* (London: J. M. Dent, 1924), 116–17.

[14] Letter from Delius to Grieg, 12 April 1888, *GD*, 42.

[15] Letter from Delius to Grieg, 25 April 1888, *GD*, 46.

[16] Letter from Grieg to Delius, 28 February 1888, *DLL1*, 13.

Having proclaimed Delius's great potential, the letter contained all those things which Delius desired to pursue (a proper, unfettered environment for work abroad with immediate effect) and avoid (the possibility that he might have to return to a teaching post, perhaps in America where he was known and had formerly found some success). The letter, moreover, was part of a careful strategy. Julius Delius and Grieg were destined to be in London at the same time. Julius was on business, Grieg was on a tour of England, so the two could meet. The intention of the letter, from the great 'Herr Grieg', was to impress, and to dispel any doubts Julius retained about his son's musical talent, but it was also intended to appeal to his paternal benevolence, since such a course of action would require money. The meeting between Grieg, Julius and Fritz Delius took place at the Hotel Metropole in London on 4 May 1888 and produced the desired results. Julius yielded, though in truth, his mind was set on his son returning to America to make a living.[17] With an agreed allowance from his father, Fritz would go to Paris and stay, for the time being, with his father's brother, Theodor Delius, who had, hitherto, shown some sympathy for his nephew's artistic aptitude. Delius, delighted that his strategy had worked, left the following day for the French capital.[18]

The choice of Paris to begin his period of creative self-communion may well have been logistically determined by the presence of Delius's uncle there, but he may also have sensed that the city, in the wake of the catastrophe of the Franco-Prussian war, had become the most vibrant musical centre in Europe. Indeed, while musical histories tend to be preoccupied with the Austro-German modernism of Strauss, Reger, Mahler and Schoenberg at the end of the nineteenth century, Paris boasted an extraordinary and unequalled array of musical creativity far beyond anything the Austro-German axis could offer. Paradoxically, just as the Prussian army was occupying the streets of the city, the founders of the Société Nationale de Musique were proclaiming the motto of 'Ars Gallica' to promote new French music and a new, vibrant era of musical creativity. By 1889 the Société, enlivened by its sense of nationalism and its bid to counteract the enormous popularity and influence of Wagner, attracted such a large membership that it received funding from the Ministère des Beaux Arts. The concert hall prospered by way of Lamoureux's Société des Nouveaux Concerts, the concerts of Édouard Colonne as well those at the Conservatoire, the Salle Pleyel and Salle Érard (who hosted the Société Nationale de Musique). Opera also flourished through the work of the Opéra-Comique

---

[17] See letter from Eloise Delius to Delius, 13 January 1900, *DLL1*, 166.

[18] Carley, L., *Edvard Grieg in England* (Woodbridge: The Boydell Press, 2006), 91–2.

(which had originally been scandalised by the premiere of *Carmen* in 1875) and the Opéra Garnier. Besides the older generation of Massenet, Messager, César Franck (though actually Belgian), Gounod, Saint-Saëns, Widor, Chausson, Lalo, Pierné, Guilmant, Duparc and Fauré who were enjoying their heyday (and Bizet who had died tragically young), musical modernism in the 1890s was represented by a glittering and unrivalled assortment of new talents in the likes of d'Indy, de Séverac, Bruneau, Charpentier, Schmitt, Debussy, Ravel, Chabrier, Hahn, de Bréville, Vierne, Lekeu and Dukas. 'Realism' and 'Naturalism' preoccupied literary circles together with the objectivity of the Parnassians, and Impressionism dominated the world of French painting, though it would soon be eclipsed by Post-Impressionism. And the agency which helped to lubricate the links between these artistic movements was Paris's pulsating salon culture and regular *soirées* into which the young Delius would ingratiate himself. As Arthur Symons remarked:

> The atmosphere of London is not the atmosphere of movements or of societies. In Paris it is the most natural thing in the world to meet and discuss literature, ideas, one's own and one another's work; and it can be done without pretentiousness or constraint, because, the Latin mind, art, ideas, one's work and the work of one's friends, are definite and important things, which it would never occur to anyone to take anything but seriously.[19]

After settling in his uncle's apartment at 45 rue Cambon, in the vicinity of the Jardins des Tuileries, the Place de la Concorde and the Champs-Élysées (and a short walk to the Opéra Garnier), Delius took no time in acquainting himself with the musical life of the city. As he explained to Grieg, it was intoxicating: 'I have now settled down a bit & must confess that I feel very happy here. There is something in the atmosphere that is quite different from Germany or England. The hustle & bustle here is extraordinary'.[20] There was also the lure of Wagner and contemporary French repertoire:

> The concerts are over. I heard the last Lamoureux Concert & must confess that as far as ensemble & finesse are concerned the orchestra is far superior to Leipzig. I heard Parsifal Prelude, Tannhäuser Overture, Lohengrin

---

[19] Dowson, E. C. and Symons, A., *The Poems and Prose of Ernest Dowson, with a Memoir by Arthur Symons* (London: J. Lane, 1905), 6.

[20] Letter from Delius to Grieg, [mid-May 1888], *GD*, 48.

Prelude to 1st Act, Women's March & Prelude to 3rd Act, Dance Macabre Saint Saens, L'Arlesienne Bizet and something from Bizet's opera The Pearl Fishers, quite excellent. I am meeting a lot of artists, musicians & writers. But I can't do much work … I will soon have to have some peace & quiet. I heard a new opera [Le Roi d'Ys] by Lalo at the Opera Comique, but found it utterly trivial. Also Aida at the big Opera, quite excellent.[21]

Sinding, with whom Delius had begun to correspond, was bemused by the French penchant for German music:

I am glad to hear that you are well, and I can quite understand your sympathy for the French men and women, you old Joseph. I dare say you were in your element. With regard to music, however, it may actually be better here? It was, after all, mostly German music in this murderous programme which you sent me, and the other concerts are perhaps similar? What I mean is that German music sounds better in Germany than in France.[22]

But by June Delius had launched himself into a furious bout of work which continued until the winter. His appetite for composition was unquenchable as was his ambition. 'I have been working the whole time', he told Grieg, '& have written a lot, several songs, and Ibsen's *Paa Vidderne*, for tenor voice, & an orchestral piece'.[23] He was also writing a Suite for Violin and Orchestra and was looking for a libretto for an opera. As Sinding inquired: 'What are you doing? Have you got a text for an opera? Will you be able to have your suite performed this season?'[24] During the summer months he gave up the idea of a holiday to Spain in favour of St Malo in Brittany where he continued to work feverishly on a wide variety of genres including *Three Pieces for String Orchestra*, the *Rhapsodische Variationen für grosses Orchester* and a string quartet. He had discussed the idea with Grieg of making Bulwer Lytton's novel *Zanoni* into an opera but later abandoned the idea: 'I have dramatized *Zanoni*, the novel by Bulwer Lytton (I talked to you about it once)', he informed Grieg, '& am writing incidental music for it, as an opera doesn't go

[21] Ibid., 48–9.

[22] Letter from Sinding to Delius, 22 May 1888, *DTA*.

[23] Letter from Delius to Grieg, 20 June 1888, *GD*, 49.

[24] Letter from Sinding to Delius, 1 June 1888, *DTA*.

well'.[25] Such a list of works was ambitious, even overambitious, but typical of an uninhibited young composer with grand ideas. His regular correspondence with Grieg and Sinding further accentuated his Norwegian purview which would serve to shape his compositional parameters for years to come.

The *Three Pieces for String Orchestra* was one of several works in 1888 to come to nothing. One may freely speculate that Delius had in mind Grieg's string arrangement of his *Holberg Suite* (made in 1885) or perhaps the *Two Elegiac Melodies* Op. 34 of 1880 (arrangements of two songs from his Op. 33 Vinje songs) which reveal some imaginative and varied scoring across the uncomplicated strophic forms. The String Quartet in four movements (in C minor?) probably arose from his enthusiasm for Grieg's Quartet Op. 27 in Leipzig with the Brodsky Quartet. Sinding saw this work towards the end of 1888: 'You are indeed a real devil for work. In addition to all you've already done this year – another quartet for strings. How did you hit upon this idea? I shall be very glad to see it if you send it here, and I shall do everything to get Brodsky to accept it'.[26] Sinding found the work interesting but returned it in April 1889; Brodsky was too busy to play it. The quartet evinced a penchant for Griegian lyricism. It was not, however, a work that Delius forgot, for, almost thirty years later, he was to re-employ material from the second movement in his String Quartet of 1916. The manuscript of the *Rhapsodische Variationen*, dated 'St Malo / September 1888' consists of six completed variations and an incomplete seventh.[27] The theme, presented in the horns, trumpets and trombones without harmony combines the character of a Norwegian folk tune with the same pentatonic preoccupations of Delius's 'banjo' tune in *Florida* (notably the $\hat{5}$–$\hat{6}$–$\hat{8}$ opening gambit). The work was evidently conceived for a large orchestra. Besides the additional piccolo and third bassoon, the instrumental specification at the head of the score shows two cornets as well as two trumpets, though these do not figure in the surviving variations. Nevertheless, Delius may have anticipated deploying them in later variations, possibly for a climactic brass effect, given the 'fanfare-like' potential of the theme. One suspects that he had in mind a form which, as the larger sum of its individual variations, amounted to a symphonic rhapsody, not unlike the model of Grieg's *Ballade in Form von Variationen über eine norwegische Melodie* Op. 24 for piano of 1875 (or of his *Gammelnorsk romanse med variasjoner* [*Old Norwegian Melody with Variations*] Op. 51 for two pianos, which post-dates

[25]   Letter from Delius to Grieg, [mid-August 1888], *DLL1*, 22.

[26]   Letter from Sinding to Delius, 27 November 1888, *DTA*.

[27]   See *GB-Lbl* MS Mus 1745/1/3, ff. 52–68.

Delius's work by only two years) and Sinding's *Variations for Two Pianos* Op. 2 of 1882–1884. Grieg's technique of variations in the *Ballade* demonstrates a predilection for phraseological contraction and extension in which harmonic alteration (engendered by the highly chromatic detail of his theme) contributes to a succession of contrasting character pieces strongly underpinned by the one key (Grieg only deviates from G for a total of nine bars). Such an approach runs counter to the classical paradigm of processual organic reconstitution (including significant tonal divergence) that one finds in Beethoven or Brahms. Unsurprisingly Delius's surviving variations couched in E major are suggestive of a similar Griegian approach. The theme, with its irregular three-bar periodicity, is of interest, and this is subject to some resourceful manipulation from the second variation onwards. Likewise, the differentiated character element of each variation gives hints of original thought. The lively third variation, a *moto perpetuo*, is marked 'Alla Negra, vivace ma non troppo', the fourth, marked 'Eleganza', is a graceful waltz replete with effective countermelody, the fifth is a 'troll dance' (with a neat sidestep to G sharp major at its centre), while the sixth, a slow movement, suggests a palpable spiritual affinity with the theme of Grieg's *Ballade* by dint of its triple metre, falling bass line and chromatic inner voices. The abortive seventh variation, by contrast, is the first to be cast in a new key, the relative (C sharp minor). Of less merit than its forbears, it may have been the reason why Delius abandoned the work, though it may well be that his experience in handling variation form in the hybrid manner he envisaged still had some time to mature.

A PASSION FOR IBSEN

In his search for a suitable operatic libretto, Delius originally alighted on Bulwer Lyttons's Rosicrucian novel *Zanoni*, but deemed it ultimately unsuitable for operatic treatment. The choice of Lyttons's supernatural novel, centred on love and the occult, was significant since it was at a time when his work was enormously popular with the Victorian public. The story of Zanoni, a Rosicrucian brother, juxtaposes his immortality with the love of a mortal woman, Viola Pisani, an opera singer. In marrying her, he loses his immortal powers and dies at the guillotine during the French Revolution. The surviving sketches suggest that, in the absence of a libretto (which would have had to have been concocted), Delius had in mind a play or spoken drama similar to the manner of *Peer Gynt* (which had its revival in Copenhagen in 1886, shortly before Grieg came to Leipzig) in which there were plentiful opportunities for an overture, preludes, and interludes. Surviving sketches in short score of music to Acts I, II and III,[28] suggest that Delius had made progress with his drafts in the late summer of 1888 in St Malo, and in October Sinding was eager to know: 'And what and by whom is "Zanoni"?' – but it seems likely that, by early 1889, he had abandoned it, perhaps in favour of incidental music to Ibsen's *Kejser og Galilæer* [*Emperor and Galilean*], an even more forbidding play in two parts, each of five acts. This was folly, as Delius admitted to Grieg: 'Perhaps I am crazy, but I am writing incidental music for Emperor & Galilean'.[29] Nothing of this music survives, but it nevertheless confirms a strong affinity Delius felt at this time for Ibsen's anti-Christian sentiment. Having read Ibsen's *Brand*, he remarked to Grieg in early January 1889 that the Norwegian playwright 'was the *only one* who handles the Christian religion without kid gloves & says what he really feels without beating about the bush & without regard for anything at all'.[30] For this he worked hard on his Norwegian language (albeit with the help of dictionary). Later, probably in 1889 or 1890, he would sketch material for a lyric drama based on Emma Klingenfeld's German translation of Ibsen's *Das Fest auf Solhaug* though this too was given up when Delius discovered that the rights had been assigned to Hugo Wolf.[31]

Delius's love affair with Ibsen's writings, together with his infatuation for the Norwegian mountain landscape and the peace he craved away from the commotion of Parisian life, manifested itself in *Paa Vidderne* [*On the Mountains*] which he began to compose soon after arriving at his uncle's apartment. 'An original idea to make "Paa Vidderne" into a recitation. How did you hit on that?' wrote Sinding from Leipzig.[32] An initial conception of the work had been some kind of solo 'scena' or cantata for tenor and orchestra, but this soon transformed into a melodrama. This was a bold choice. Melodrama as a genre had been explored earlier in the century in well-known operatic contexts such as Weber's *Der Freischütz*, Marschner's *Hans Heiling*, Offenbach's *Orphée aux enfers* and the symphonic context of Berlioz's *Lélio* (though there are also examples in Mendelssohn, Schumann and Wagner). However, for melodrama

---

[28] See *GB-Lbl* MS Mus 1745/1/39, ff. 3–13; see also *RL*, 134–5.

[29] Letter from Delius to Grieg, [February 1889], *GD*, 76.

[30] Letter from Delius to Grieg, [early January 1889], *GD*, 73.

[31] See *DN*, 111. Evidence of Delius's work on Ibsen's *Das Fest auf Solhaug* can be observed in a partsong in the original Norwegian ('Herude, herude skal gildet stå' – see *GB-Lbl* MS Mus 1745/1/36, ff. 10–11), but there are also surviving sketches in *GB-Lbl* MS Mus 1745/1/10, ff. 24–7, in the notebook *GB-Lbl* MS Mus 1745/1/38, ff. 31–6 and in a short draft of full score in *GB-Lbl* MS Mus 1745/2/10, ff. 24–5; see also *DMA*, 146–51.

[32] Letter from Sinding to Delius, 6 October 1888, *DTA*.

as a discrete genre, Delius claimed that he had not seen any in the genre before (although he must have been aware of Grieg's setting of Bjørnson's *Bergliot* Op. 42 of 1871 which had been orchestrated by the composer in 1885 and published in Leipzig in 1887).[33] The dedication of the work, when it was completed, was to Grieg, though the correspondence between Delius and his idol shows that not only was Grieg critical of the instrumentation and its potential to overwhelm the reciter,[34] but that he himself had aspired to set the poem, possibly in the same idiom.[35] This criticism may have caused Delius to shelve the work permanently. Nevertheless, an examination of this unique work in his output tells us much about the composer's rapid development.

There is no doubt that Delius identified closely with Ibsen's radical questioning of traditional morality and social behaviour, and in *Paa Vidderne*, a tragedy in ballad form published in 1859, he recognised something of his own personality. In ascending to the heights, the principal character forsakes his love for a higher existence in Nature, without the traditional Christian tenets of sin or remorse. Yet, he encounters a mysterious lone hunter who endorses the choice of his 'vagabond' life rather than the 'path of the church' trodden by his mother and his beloved. Tempted to return to the comforts of home, he is subsequently 'tested' as he watches his mother's house below in the valley is consumed by fire and, in true Heine-esque fashion, he witnesses the marriage of his lover to another. All this so that, having outlived his lowland life, he may, with a new independence and self-reliance, 'obey the call to wander on the heights'. Ibsen's poem was, in part, inspired by notions of national identity, and the ballad style of the poem was strongly linked with Norse tradition. Furthermore, the notion of the 'test' was also derived from Viking history (a subject Ibsen explored in many of his earlier writings, such as *Hærmændene paa Helgeland*, *Kongs-Emnerne* and *Gildet paa Solhoug*). While Delius was undoubtedly aware of the growing swell of Norwegian nationalism in the late 1880s, his understanding of Ibsen had different goals. Ibsen (and others such as Bjørnson) articulated a pastoral vision of self-discovery and a new moral freedom in which Norway was idealised as an unspoiled source of new creative fecundity. He had, of course, only experienced the country's mountainous landscape, the 'Hardangervidda', in the memorable summer months when the sunlight and the longer days (the 'lyse nætter' as Drachmann

---

[33] Letter from Delius to Grieg, [December 1888], *DLL1*, 30–31.

[34] Letter from Grieg to Delius, 9 December 1888, *DLL1*, 28. Interestingly, Grieg endorsed Delius's original concept of a solo singing voice.

[35] Letter from Grieg to Delius, 9 August 1888, *DLL1*, 20.

described them) had a special iridescence. Grieg was the first to disabuse him of spending longer periods in a country where its population had to endure long, dark winters.[36] Nevertheless, with the memory of his 1887 walk, and the longing for further holidays in the Jotunheim with like-minded friends, Delius would always imagine Norway as a transcendental refuge.

Delius elected to set all nine parts of Ibsen's poem using Louis Passarge's liberal German translation. Each section forms a tableau, usually (but not exclusively) cast in one key in which the adopted form (like those of *Florida*) is frequently tripartite. This is not always the case, however. The second tableau is suggestive of a sonata structure, though Delius retains the subdominant key (C major) in the recapitulation of his second subject in order to provide a smooth transition to the third section in F major. The opening tableau, in which the high peaks are depicted, was clearly intended as a through-composed, open-ended exposition in which the important musical seed on the cor anglais is presented (at letter B). Variations on this one idea, in which Delius's lifelong rhythmic preoccupation with the downbeat triplet and subsequent minim, abound; the cell also metamorphoses into a glossary of thematic ideas and ubiquitous horn calls as the work unfolds, tableau by tableau until the 'quodlibet' of the final tableau. Besides the familial rhythmical connections of the many thematic strands (Examples 2.1a, 2.1b, 2.1c and 2.1d), a fixation on the melodic degrees $\hat{3}$–$\hat{5}$–$\hat{6}$–$\hat{5}$ is also shared across the entire canvas. The idea of mountain and metaphor together with the significance of the horn and herding calls in *Paa Vidderne* has been identified and expounded by Boyle.[37] These horn calls, of which there are numerous variants, provide the first auspicious instances in Delius's output of the Scandinavian landscape and would be of considerable symbolic meaning in shaping the subject matter and form of his later music.

The most significant factor of *Paa Vidderne* as a melodrama is, without, doubt, Delius's first attempt at an extended dramatic form. Whether he was wise to set the entire text, rather than a truncated form, is debatable – the work seems overlong and the tonal organisation insufficiently tight to underpin moments of *anagnorisis* [revelation] and *peripeteia* [reversal]. Nevertheless, the cumulative process of thematic development is well sustained, particularly in the final tableau where all the horn calls combine in the 'quodlibet' of the closing bars. The self-evident dominance of the orchestra as the vehicle of dramatic momentum also provides glimpses of Delius's attempt to emulate

---

[36]   Letter from Grieg to Delius, 6 November 1888, *GD*, 61.

[37]   *DN*, 44–8.

Example 2.1a. *Paa Vidderne*, tableau I, 'horn call', b. 14.

Example 2.1b. *Paa Vidderne*, tableau I, 'horn call', b. 37 and main theme.

Example 2.1c. *Paa Vidderne*, tableau I, 'horn call', b. 76.

Example 2.1d. *Paa Vidderne*, tableau I, 'horn call', b. 80.

Wagner's fluid method of musical prose and variegated periodicity, and though the division of nine tableaux militates against this on a large scale, some of the tableaux (such as the seventh and ninth tableaux) individually exhibit clear signs of internal symphonic development. Delius's enthusiasm for Wagner is also conspicuous in other ways. Ibsen's poem afforded opportunities for colourful orchestration, not only in the deployment of the traditional glossary of Romantic imagery, but also those of a more Wagnerian kind, such as the opening of the ninth tableau in which *Tristan* is unmistakable from the chromatic cello line, the accompanying 'Tristan' chord and the instrumentation (Example 2.1e). One senses, too, that the storm music of the seventh tableau drew its inspiration from *Der fliegende Holländer*. Grieg's influence, as one might expect, is also prominent. The fifth tableau, exclusively for muted strings, is an 'Elegiac melody' (could this have been one of the 'lost' pieces for string orchestra?), the chromatic harmony of the second tableau (at letter H) owes much to the distinctive progressions of movements such as 'Melancholie' Op. 47 No. 5, while the triumphant chorale at the end of the ninth tableau recalls 'Vektersang' ['Watchman's Song'] and 'Fedrelandssang' ['Fatherland's Song'] Op. 12 Nos. 3 and 8 of the *Lyric Pieces*.

During the composition of *Paa Vidderne*, Delius also devoted time to songs which were eminently more marketable as commodities. Dated 1888, 'Hochgebirgsleben (a setting of Ibsen's 'Høifjeldsliv' ['Life on the High Mountains'] from the *Digte* of 1859 in Passarge's German translation) might easily have been a study for the melodrama in its earlier form for voice and orchestra, sharing, as it does, a similar preoccupation with horn calls. An unusual through-composed structure, it begins in D flat (its opening gesture and key distinctly prophetic of the finale of *A Village Romeo and Juliet*) before shifting upwards to F major in bar eight at the end of the second vocal phrase. The framing tonality of the song, F major, yields unconventionally to the dominant by way of a series of Griegian parallel ninth chords in third inversion; but even more striking is the elliptical return to F ('so glänzend nieder schaut') at the song's conclusion in which Delius makes striking use of the enharmonic triads of A major, D flat major (a subtle memory of the song's opening) and F major. A setting of 'O schneller mein Ross' (which may date from his time at Leipzig, given his use of Geibel's poetry in the partsongs) emulates Grieg's use of accompanimental melodic doubling in the outer voices and the oblique nature of the progression ii^7–V–I (heard at the opening) shows some artistic variegation, particularly at the climax. The song suffers, however, from being too overblown, and Delius's attempt to outdo Schumann and Grieg (cf. 'Hvor er du nu' Op. 4 No. 6) in the extended

Example 2.1e. *Paa Vidderne*, tableau IX,
influence of *Tristan und Isolde*, bb. 608–10.

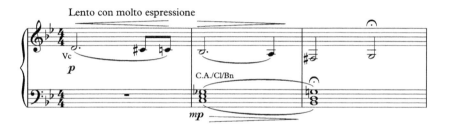

postlude seems tautologous. In the guise 'Plus vite mon cheval' (as part of
5 Chansons ... Musique de Fritz Delius), it was a rare instance of a French
publication in Paris in 1896.

Although Grieg's verdict on Paa Vidderne was muted, his evaluation of
songs which Delius sent him (with a dedication to Nina) were extremely
positive. 'There are so many beautiful and deeply felt things in them', he
wrote, quoting from the closing progressions of 'Sehnsucht'.[38] Apart from this
song, the dating of the twelve Norwegian songs is only open to conjecture,
though most of them probably date from 1888 and early 1889.[39] Augener,
who published them in 1890 (as Fünf Lieder aus dem Norwegischen) and
1892 (Sieben Lieder aus dem Norwegischen), in translation by W. Grist in
English and Lobedanz in German, no doubt thought that they had greater
commercial prospects in these languages.[40] Eight of the poems had already
been used in songs by Grieg, a fact which he acknowledged.[41] It is of course
possible that Delius chose these independently, but it is more than likely that,
since his acquaintance with Grieg at Leipzig (and Nina Grieg who sang many
of her husband's songs), he had developed a close working knowledge of this
especially fertile part of his colleague's output.

On entering the commercial 'song market' for the first time, Delius
may well have decided to restrict his Fünf Lieder aus dem Norwegischen to a
simple formula in that all of them followed a strophic design. This simplicity,
however, did not detract from some attractive invention in their harmonic
resource. This is demonstrated in Bjørnson's 'Der Schlaf' ['Slumber Song'] in
which Delius's handling of enhanced seventh, ninth, eleventh and thirteenth
chords is combined with a heightened awareness of chromatic voice-leading
in the transition from G major (the tonic) to G flat. We subsequently learn
the purpose of this tonal shift at the close of each verse where the gentle
benediction ('Ja so selig') gains intensity from the effortless semitonal shift
from the dominant of G flat to the dominant of the home key, G major.
'The Nightingale', using a poem by Welhaven, deploys a striking sequence of
seventh harmonies in last inversion (in a similar manner to the parallel ninths
of 'Hochgebirgsleben') culminating in a stabbing 'Tristan' chord to illustrate

---

[38] See letter from Grieg to Delius, 23 September 1888, GD, 57.

[39] See RT1, 92–3 for an account of the dating of the two sets of Norwegian songs.

[40] Delius claimed later to Ernest Newman that his Norwegian songs had first been
set in the original language, although the evidence suggests that, as Arthur Holland
alludes – see Holland, A. K., The Songs of Delius (Oxford: Oxford University Press,
1951), 14 – he used the German translations (see also RT1, 93).

[41] See letter from Grieg to Delius, 23 September 1888, GD, 57.

the sense of anguish. Delius's fascination for Wagnerian chromaticism is clear from the central progressions and postlude of 'Am schönsten Sommerabend war's' ['Summer Eve'], couched within a rich F sharp major. 'Sehnsucht' ['Longing'] makes repeated play on the 'Tristan' chord, particularly in the prelude and at the conclusion where it is a prominent feature. Delius also makes skilful use of the fluctuation between the tonic, D major, and B minor, particularly in the recovery from the central 'Lento' in D flat. The *Sieben Lieder (aus dem Norwegischen)* are, by comparison, more structurally complex. The simplest of them are the strophic 'Klein Venevil' ['Young Venevil'], a coquettish scherzo, which deftly fluctuates between C major and a more impish A minor and the much more Wagnerian 'Heimkehr' ['The Homeward Journey']. Other examples of Delius's Wagnerian experimentations were his settings of Bjørnson's 'Abendstimmung' ['Twilight Fancies'], where, besides the characteristic horn call of the 'herd-boy' (an effective feature of Delius's 1908 orchestration), the 'Tristan' chord is notably conspicuous as part of a more dense milieu of chromatic progressions (e.g. 'Schweig stille, O Kleiner, du fesselt mir, ach!'), and 'Verborg'ne Liebe ['Concealed Love'], whose more dramatic temperament is projected by sections of contrasting tempi. Three Ibsen settings affirm that, while their texts had already been used by Grieg, Delius was also beginning to assert his own individualism in markedly different interpretations. Grieg's 'Margretes Vuggesang' from *Romancer* Op. 15 No. 1 in A flat major reveals an uncomplicated ternary structure of Ibsen's three verses. There is innocence too in the simple phrasing, but Grieg's harmonic progressions are characteristically arresting. After concluding the first verse in A flat, the second verse, with its parallel octaves (a sound Delius often embraced) moves to F major before the third verse restores the opening material. Delius's conception as 'Wiegenlied' ['Cradle Song'] is somewhat larger and more elaborate. The pastoral sounds of the opening D flat harmony are rapidly surrendered through an unconventional move to F major, mimicking the little Haakon's dreams of the starry heavens; yet this move is a blind, for Delius then sets his second verse in the dominant, A flat, allowing a smooth return to D flat for the third verse which itself contains some beguiling chromatic progressions at its conclusion, conveying perhaps a glimpse of the mother's anxiety as she watches over her child. For the disturbing text of 'Spielmann' (*Sex Digte af Henrik Ibsen* Op. 25 No. 1) both Grieg and Delius share a through-composed approach, but while Delius opted for an agitated lyricism, Grieg chose an unusual blend of restrained melody and recitation verging on melodrama. 'Eine Vogelweise' [The Bird's Story'] in Grieg's hands (*Sex Digte af Henrik Ibsen* Op. 25 No. 6) is a remarkable mix of melody and declamation in which humour and irony are depicted. Key to Grieg's scheme is a series of arresting modulations. The first verse, in A flat, ends quizzically with a half-close and a paused progression to enable the second verse to begin in C flat major. This heightened animation is intensified by a move to E flat, the dominant key, but with a shift towards F minor, the mood changes as the lovers, having vowed never to part, say their farewells forever. The last verse then seeks to encapsulate the humour and irony of the previous verse. Beginning in A flat, Grieg gives us a series of stepwise modulations through B flat major, C major and D flat major before reaching a climax with the return of the tonic. Delius's interpretation of Ibsen's text, which he later orchestrated,[42] is a similar quirky fantasy. The first verse passes through three keys a major third apart, F major–A–C sharp minor and back to F, emerging with the warbling blackbird. The second verse is couched in A minor, though Delius's pace of modulatory change is rapid to imitate the quixotic behaviour of the lovers. The third verse, rather than returning immediately to the home key (as Grieg does), starts forebodingly in D minor recalling the stormy second part of verse one before the opening melody returns, not in F but in A, for Delius deftly reserves the restatement of the home key for the exultant coda. A further song, set only in Norwegian, of Bjørnson's 'Skogen gir susende langsom besked', is dated 1890 and may well have been intended for the *Sieben Lieder aus dem Norwegischen*, but was left unpublished. A further fragment is dated 'Aulestad, le 11 Juillet 91' and was probably left as an autograph when Delius was staying with Bjørnson during his Norwegian excursion, perhaps in acknowledgement of Bjørnson's daughter Bergliot who had presented Delius with the text to set.[43] Rather more economical in its thematic material, this twenty-eight-bar through-composed aphorism is a notable example of Delius's affinity for modal harmony. The middle section, in the submediant D major, is significant for its use of a Neapolitan seventh (its D flat linking subtly with the C sharp of the dominant thirteenth in the next bar), its unconventional use of augmented-sixth harmony (in b. 17) and the VI–I cadence (at this point almost a cliché).

It is perhaps not surprising that, after the exceptional industry of 1888, Delius's productivity began to moderate in 1889. Although life in Paris was exciting, and it was infinitely preferable to Germany, he craved quietness and isolation for work. Writing from St Malo, where he had spent a long, productive summer, he announced to Grieg: 'I can't do anything sensible

---

[42] 'Twilight Fancies' (then known in Grist's translation as 'Evening Voices') and 'The Bird's Story' were orchestrated for Henry Wood's wife, Olga Michailoff, who sang them in Liverpool on 21 March 1908. 'Cradle Song' and 'Young Venevil' were later orchestrated by Thomas Beecham for the 1946 Delius Festival.

[43] *RT1*, 100.

in Paris, the environment is just not suitable'.[44] He was also not entirely sympathetic with the French artistic sensibility: 'The French are very artistic, but it is always merely art, the great vitality of Nature is missing, at least in music'.[45] For this reason, he left his uncle's apartment in November, moving to the western suburb of Ville d'Avray, about seven-and-a-half miles from the centre of Paris. It was far enough away for the seclusion he needed, but near enough for concerts and the opera. 1889 also established something of a pattern in Delius's existence.

In the spring and summer his irresistible *Wanderlust* took him to foreign parts. Norway would be a regular haunt. 'Your kind note made me feel happy', he wrote to Grieg, 'but you can't be happier than I am. For months now our meeting in Glorious Norway has been my be all and end all'.[46] Grieg's home in Bergen was of course, a magnet, but he had other friends, such as the violinist Arve Arvesen, Sinding, Bjørnson and others, who would accommodate him. In August of 1889, Delius, Grieg and Sinding walked in the Jotunheim. It was Delius's first visit and left a powerful impression which is evident from his detailed diary.[47] On his return to France he moved into a new apartment at 8, Boulevard de la Mairie, Croissy-sur-Seine (a small affluent town on the western periphery of Paris which was more amenable than the cold and damp of his accommodation at Ville d'Avray) and work began again in earnest.

With the composition of *Florida* still relatively fresh in his mind, Delius's American memories surfaced again in the two *Neger Lieder im Volkston* or *Negro Songs* for solo, chorus and orchestra which, it has been suggested, date from 1889–1890.[48] In this largely undocumented work Delius presents a format of a leading singer (the 'base') who begins the text of each verse and the chorus who provide the refrain, in much the same manner as many slave songs were sung. The properties of both negro melodies 'I will meet you when the sun goes down' and 'Let me dance tonight' betray strong pentatonic properties and a characteristic syllabic nature of repetitive pitches, while the choruses are homophonically simple, with a strong penchant for plagal major–minor

---

[44] Letter from Delius to Grieg, 19 October 1888, *GD*, 59.

[45] Letter from Delius to Grieg, 20 June 1888, *GD*, 49.

[46] Letter from Delius to Grieg, [early June 1889], *DLL1*, 41.

[47] See *DN*, 56–65.

[48] Threlfall, R., 'An Early Manuscript Reappears', *DSJ* No. 130 (Autumn 2001), 20. As Threlfall noted, the fertile material of the *Neger Lieder* had the power to provoke thoughts and sketches of other works, including the suggestion of a 'Negro Rhapsody' and sketches of music for Act II of *Koanga*.

cadences, revealing the composer's incipient love of chromatic voice-leading. Perhaps not surprisingly both songs have potent affinities with *Florida*, the first in its handling of Griegian diatonic harmony to support the solo melody and the almost crude juxtaposition of F major and A major for the keys of adjacent verses, and the second in its obvious connection with the 'Plantation Dance' from the third movement of the Suite. More significantly, however, in these partsongs we find a paradigm of delivery of a soloist leading a responsive choir which Allen, Ware and Garrison recognised in their publication of *Slave Songs of the United States* in 1867:

> There is no singing in *parts*, as we understand it, and yet no two appear to be singing the same thing – the leading singer starts the words of each verse, often improvising, and the others who "base" him, as it is called, strike in with the refrain, or even join in the solo, when the words are familiar. When the "base" begins, the leader often stops, leaving the rest of his words to be guessed at, or it may be they are taken up by one of the other singers. And the "basers" themselves seem to follow their own whims, beginning when they please and leaving off when they please, striking an octave above or below (in case they have pitched the tune too low or too high), or hitting some other note that chords, so as to produce the effect of a marvellous complication and variety, and yet with the most perfect time, and rarely with any discord.[49]

Delius's experiences of this manner of singing had been experienced at first hand in both Florida and Virginia and their 'realisation' in these two choral and orchestral songs would prove vital in the gestation of *Koanga* and *Appalachia* at a later date. A footnote, a quotation from Fanny Kemble's *Journal of a Residence on a Georgian Plantation in 1838–1839*, provided by Allen, Ware and Garrison to their comments on the performance practice of the negro songs, also seemed uncannily prophetic of Delius's later familiarity with this music and of his vision for its operatic potential:

> The high voices, all in unison, and the admirable time and true accent with which their responses are made, always make me wish that some great musical composer could hear these semi-savage performances. With a very little skilful adaptation and instrumentation, I think one or

---

[49] Allen, W. F., Ware, C. P. and Garrison, L. M. (eds), *Slave Songs of the United States* (New York: A. Simpson & Co., 1867), v.

two barbaric chants and choruses might be evoked from them that would make the fortune of an opera.[50]

While the genre of solo song, and the fecund example of Grieg's work in the genre, was undoubtedly still uppermost in his mind, it is evident from another Scandinavian work, *Sakuntala*, that Delius continued to ponder the question of Wagnerian musical prose as exemplified by the symphonic art of the *Musikdrama*. That Delius was fascinated and hungry to imbibe Wagner's symphonic practices using both instrumental and vocal forces is evident from a series of undated copied passages from *Die Meistersinger* and *Parsifal* which he made. Two passages from *Die Meistersinger* include four bars from Act II Scene 3 – the passage where Hans Sachs sings 'Es klang so alt' – which must have left an enduring impression.[51] Another more extensive section, from Act III of *Parsifal* ('Von dort her kam das Stöhnen' to 'Oh Gnade! Höchstes Heil! Oh!') runs to twenty pages of score (equivalent to pp. 9–60 of the full score). The desire to understand and assimilate the methods of these two particular works, moreover, is corroborated by a desire to obtain the pocket scores at the end of a notebook of c. 1895.[52] Add to these monuments of Wagner's operatic legacy Delius's obsession with *Tristan* (the score of which we know he possessed), it is not difficult to appreciate how absorbed he was in his formative years with the entire Wagnerian paradigm of opera, philosophy and German progressivist art.

The need to digest Wagner's symphonic processes was unquestionably provoked by Delius's aspiration to pursue opera, but before he was ready to take on this challenge, he set himself the less onerous task of setting Holger Drachmann's most famous poem *Sakuntala*. This first appeared in his novel *En Overkomplet* of 1876 but was reissued as a poem in 1879 in the collection *Ranker og Roser: en samling sange*.[53] The German translation became available in 1881, one which Delius must have seen while he was Leipzig, not least because Sinding had set the poem in his song collection of Drachmann poems *Ranker og Roser* Op. 4 in 1886, only three years prior to Delius's own. Drachmann had, by the end of the 1890s, become a major figure in new European literary thinking. Though he has not achieved the international

---

[50] Kemble, F., *Journal of a Residence on a Georgian Plantation in 1838–1839* (London, 1863), 218.

[51] See *GB-Lbl* MS Mus 1745/2/13/5, f. 25.

[52] See *GB-Lbl* MS Mus 1745/2/11/3, f. 110.

[53] *RT1*, 74.

renown achieved by Hans Christian Andersen and Ibsen, Drachmann and his compatriot, Jens Peter Jacobsen, were highly esteemed, and their reputations spread rapidly after German translations of their work began to appear in the 1870s. Again, it was through this channel, by means of Edmund Lobedanz's anthology of Bjørnson and other poets, that Delius came to Drachmann and indeed later to Jacobsen.[54] Both these authors were influenced initially by the radical work and publications of the Danish critic and scholar Georg Brandes. Brandes had published works on modern French aesthetics, notably on Realism and Naturalism, and he was clearly interested in the rights of women, having published a translation of John Stuart Mills's *The Subjection of Women*. More significant, however, was his *Hovedstrømninger i det 19de Aarhundredes Litteratur* [*Principal Currents in Nineteenth-Century Literature*] based on his lectures at the University of Copenhagen. These later appeared in four volumes between 1872 and 1875 and this in turn led to the even more significant publication in 1883 of *Det moderne Gjennembruds Mænd* [*The Men of the Modern Breakthrough*] which specifically included not only Jacobsen and Drachmann but also Ibsen and Bjørnson. As Bergsagel has noted, Drachmann and Jacobsen shifted their focus from Brandes's concentration on naturalism to another French fascination, that of symbolism, but both were also interested in the promotion of a new Danish cultural romantic nationalism.[55]

Drachmann's text of *Sakuntala* offered Delius the opportunity to create a 'scena', a larger, more developmental vocal genre which found its roots in Wagner's *Wesendonck Lieder*. The presence of the orchestra as the accompanimental medium (rather than the piano) had numerous possibilities: the immense palette of instrumental timbres had the potential to characterise a musical gesture, to intensify realistic effect, to clarify structure and to heighten that inherent sense of polyphony between voice and accompaniment so quintessential to the late nineteenth-century organic ideology of Austro-German music. Indeed, the orchestra, as supreme agent of contrapuntal thinking, did much to accentuate the symphonic dimension of Lieder composition, and, in the case of Mahler and Strauss (who were already authoring works of this kind), connected the concept of song directly with the techniques essayed in Wagner's music dramas. More significantly, Drachmann's interpretation of the Kalidasa drama had all the ingredients and artistic characteristics of Tristanesque longing, a sentiment Delius had

[54] See Lobedanz, E., *Ausgewählte Gedichte von B. Björnson und anderen neueren nordischen Dichtern* (Leipzig: Wilhelm Friedrich Verlag, 1881).

[55] Bergsagel, J., 'Delius and Danish Literature', in *FDML*, 293–4.

already encountered in his 'Længsel' ['Longing'] from his *Five Norwegian Songs*. Sakuntala, a Brahmin girl, made pregnant by King Dushyant, is his only wife to bear him a child, but deceived by his other wives, she is abandoned by him. Yet, before giving birth she returns to the court. Crucially, however, she lacks the ring which would identify her to the king because it has been lost in the river. The king therefore does not recognise her and she is rejected. Fortunately for her, a fisherman finds the ring in the river where she had once bathed, brings it to the court, enabling Dusyant and Sakuntala to be reunited once more. Drachmann witnessed Kalidasa's Sanskrit play in Munich. He was drawn to the actress who played the role of Sakuntala, but there were also resonances of his one-time failed marriage to Vilhelmine Erichsen, the love of his early life. His years of courting her had been turbulent; neither of the families approved. Drachmann left for England in the summer 1871 during which time he wrote his book *English Socialists*. It was a difficult period of emotional strain, but on returning to Denmark he married Vilhelmine in November. The restless marriage only lasted four years, but afterwards Drachmann pined for Vilhelmine, especially after she married again and destroyed all the love letters and poems Drachmann had written for her.[56]

Hence *Sakuntala* expressed both a mythical and human longing, articulated at the very beginning of the poem, and the 'cris de coeur' as refrains to each verse reinforce this sense of yearning, just as Dowson's poem 'Cynara' was to do decades later. In addition to the lovesickness, the canvas of *Sakuntala* embodies many of those Wagnerian elements of *Tristan*. The expressive appoggiaturas of the opening, accompanied by the restive finger tremolandi in the strings, embody that restive mood of Act II. Even the extended pedal point refers to the slow-moving harmonic pace of Wagner's music drama. Certainly, that Griegian love of unexpected modulation is brought to bear here in numerous ways. Having established G major at the outset, Delius appears to take us to E, but that is not the goal. Instead we shift to E flat enharmonically, and with yearning dominant ninths 'med sød Musik' ['with sweet music'] the sensuous eroticism is intensified not least through the colourful nature of Delius's wind instrumentation (which owes much to the orchestral originality of *Florida*). The second verse moves enharmonically again, to G sharp minor and to a bleaker, more Norwegian modal tone redolent of Grieg once more. But Wagnerian gestures are never far away, as is evident from the progressions which accompany the question 'Where do my

---

[56] Anderson, H., 'Vilhelmine: The Muse of Sakuntala', *DSJ* No. 127 (Spring 2000), 12–13.

footsteps roam?' Of course, one of the most striking elements of *Sakuntala* is the declamatory nature of the text, even more one might argue than the proto-Wagnerian manner of 'Verborg'ne Liebe' of the Norwegian songs. With the original concept of the orchestral accompaniment, and the experience of the melodrama of *Paa Vidderne* behind him, Delius clearly responded to the new syntax and relationship of voice and orchestra. Not only could he provide nuance, timbre and sensual texture to comment on the text, but he could also explore that essential sense of polyphony central to Wagner's instrumental concept of opera. From G sharp minor at the end of verse two, the yearning motive helps to enunciate a modulation to B major (that most Tristanesque of keys) at which point Delius introduces a thoroughly Wagnerian 'love motive' (which later became the second subject of the finale of the Suite for violin and orchestra) typified by its chromatic inner voice and cadential dominant thirteenth appropriately accompanying a sense of ecstasy at the recognition of Sakuntala. The Wagnerian manner is not only evident from the way in which the orchestra initiates the melodic development but it is also further accentuated by the sequential nature of the thematic treatment as Delius takes us back to E flat major and then more passionately to the dominant of G. Here Drachmann's personal interpretation comes to the fore as the sense of physical distance is emphasised, and this sense of self-dejection and despair, despite the memory of the 'love motive', haunts much of the last stanza.

SOME COSMOPOLITAN ORCHESTRAL INITIATIVES

As he spent more and more time in and around Paris, Delius began to cultivate an increasing number of acquaintances and friends through the lively artistic salon culture abundantly offered by the French capital. His friendship with Arvesen was one of several Scandinavian associations he developed, including Johan Selmer, Edvard Munch, Gudmund Stenersen, and the Franco-Norwegian composer William Molard who was known for his artistic circle of Scandinavians at his studio in rue Vercingétorix.[57] With Grieg and Sinding he continued to correspond, but there was also an opportunity for Delius to see Grieg since his mentor was due in Paris to give a concert at the Salle Pleyel on 4 January 1890.[58] More crucially, Grieg came armed with a letter of introduction to d'Indy who, with Chausson, was joint secretary to the Société Nationale

---

[57] *DLL1*, 45 *passim*.
[58] Carley, L., *Edvard Grieg in England*, 195.

de Musique and who might provide useful access to French concert circles.[59] With Sinding, in particular, Delius mentioned the possibility of travelling once more to Florida. 'Go to Florida? Yes, by God, I should like to, but it will hardly be feasible', Sinding responded.[60] Sinding had, however, been badgering his friend to come to Leipzig and in late May 1890 Delius relented. This was partly in order to see his old friend and Selmer, but also to avail himself of the chance to try over some of the music he had composed in the last two years with a Leipzig rehearsal orchestra (a practical experience he had so far not enjoyed since the hearing of *Florida* at Bonorand's).[61] Leipzig also afforded him the opportunity to hear the latest cycle of Wagner operas which was undoubtedly important in the gestation of his operatic ambitions. In the summer of 1890, he returned to his favourite French haunts in Normandy and Brittany where he worked happily in solitude. The following year, while spending no less than four months in Norway, he was also able to visit Bjørnson at his home at Aulestad (by dint of the latter's daughter studying singing in Paris with Mathilde Marchesi at her vocal school in the rue Jouffroy-d'Abbans), and there were opportunities for walking tours with Grieg, Sinding and Iver Holter, and the summer nights with Munch at Åsgårdstrand.

1889 and 1890 had witnessed the revision of *Florida* and two orchestrations – one of his *Norwegische Schlittenfahrt* and the other, dated '2 December 1889', of Grieg's piano piece 'Norwegischer Brautzug im Vorüberziehen' from the collection *Aus dem Volksleben: Humoresken* Op. 19 (which Halvorsen had also orchestrated for Grieg's *Peer Gynt* as Op. 23 No. 2).[62] In fact the short orchestral piece as a genre preoccupied Delius for much of the year. Having been disappointed by Manns' inability to include *Florida* at the Crystal Palace concerts, it seems that he must have given some thought to Paris's orchestral concert scene since a series of short pieces with French titles was produced in the hope, perhaps, that they might be accepted by Lamoureux or Colonne and even by French publishers. This is surely suggested by the revised third movement of *Florida* with their French designations, 'Le coucher de soleil' and its central section 'Auprès de la Plantation / Dance des Nègres'. The *Idylle de Printemps* for small orchestra, described in French as a 'morceau symphonique' may also have been intended for the same venues, although

59 *DLL1*, 45.

60 Letter from Sinding to Delius, 20 March 1889, *DTA*.

61 *DLL1*, 50.

62 See *GB-Lbl* MS Mus 1745/1/3, ff. 69–78. This has remained unpublished (but has been performed).

there is no record of any performance. A strangely unbalanced piece formally, it provides an early example of Delius's unconventional handling of sonata structure. Two contrasting thematic ideas are presented in G major and in B major respectively which, in shortened form, are presented in reverse order in the reprise. However, it is in the unusual developmental phase that the movement, with its unmistakable reference to the *Liebestod* of *Tristan* (notably the C sharp appoggiatura on the subdominant of B), reaches its lyrical climax. Delius, indeed, may have sensed the work's disproportion and caused him to withhold the piece. Another work, the *Petite Suite d'Orchestre*, with its five 'French' movements – 'Marche', 'Berceuse', 'Scherzo', 'Duo' and 'Tema et Variazione [*sic*]' – might also have been intended for performance in Paris. The fashion for orchestral suites in France was at its height. Massenet's *Scènes Dramatiques*, *Scènes Hongroises*, *Pittoresques*, *Scènes de Féeries* and *Scènes Alsaciennes*, not to mention Saint-Saëns' Suite Op. 49, d'Indy's *Suite dans le style ancien* Op. 24, Bizet's *Petite Suite d'Orchestre Jeux d'Enfants* and the two *Suites l'Arlésiennes*, Debussy's *Petite Suite* and Chabrier's *Suite Pastorale* typified the French concert taste for music which exhibited a flair for brilliant orchestration. Indeed, one wonders whether Bizet's *Jeux d'Enfants* could have been the model for Delius's first conception in that it shares three movements ('Marche', 'Berceuse' and 'Duo') with the same title and genre.

The 'Marche', in a revised form as 'Marche Caprice', was retained for a new French suite of three pieces, the *Suite de 3 Morceaux Caractéristiques pour orchestre* which was completed in 1890.[63] One may conjecture that 'La Quadroone (une Rhapsodie Floridienne)' could have been intended for a revised version of *Florida*; certainly it recalled Delius's time in Florida and quite possibly his familiarity with, in this case, a woman of mixed race; or it may have been instigated by the many characters described in nineteenth-century American literature such as Lydia Maria Child's *The Quadroons* (1842), Longfellow's poem *The Quadroon Girl* (1842) or the more recently published writings of George Washington Cable which described many of the Creole peoples of America's deep south in *Old Creole Days* (1879), *The Grandissimes* (1880), and *Madame Delphine* (1881). Such was Delius's interest in this culture and history that he would later look to Cable's *The Grandissimes* for an operatic subject. 'La Quadroone' recalls something of the colour and exoticism of *Florida* implicit in its partiality for *flamenco*-like I–flat VII progressions relating to the old Spanish presence in Florida. Rather more

---

[63] Delius also sketched a 'Marche française' and a 'Marche des Marionettes' (see *RT2*, 128) which may have been destined for this suite but were subsequently rejected in favour of the 'Marche Caprice'.

sophisticated in design and instrumentation than 'La Quadroone' (which also suggests that it may be earlier) are the 'Scherzo' in E major and the 'Marche Caprice'. The 'Scherzo' is a movement of much felicity and owes much in terms of its gossamer scoring to Mendelssohn's music for *A Midsummer Night's Dream* and Berlioz's 'Queen Mab' Scherzo. Not until *La Ronde se déroule* and *Lebenstanz* do we see Delius engaging again with this same manner of delicate orchestration and pulsating velocity. There are also indications of more subtle structural procedures such as the tangential introduction of no less than thirty-three bars which begins on the subdominant. By degrees we arrive at the tonic E major, though not before a characteristically halting chromatic interpolation (marked 'poco rit.') just before resumption of the Scherzo proper. With the advent of the dominant, and the continued use of the same material, there is a strong suggestion that a monothematic sonata movement is in operation. This phase is, however, transitional to the presentation of a second thematic idea in A flat whose falling chromatic semitonal harmony gives us a taste of the composer's later language. These two thematic strands subsequently combine both in bringing the tonality back to E but also as a proper recapitulation in which they are grounded in the tonic key. The 'Marche Caprice', in its revised orchestration, exhibits a professionalism worthy of Bizet and his 'Marche (Trompette et Tambour)' from *Jeux d'enfants* (especially the recurrent trumpet fanfares and the added percussion). By means of a beautifully managed arch form (ABCBA), Delius contrasts his march theme (A) in C major (Example 2.2a) with a more modal idea (B) which moves from D minor to A minor (Example 2.2b). The 'trio' (C), in A major, then consists of a variant of (B). With true legerdemain, the 'trio' capitulates to (B) which is used as a modulatory agency to return to the march theme (A) in the last nine bars. Executed with a slickness worthy of Bizet's polish and elegance, Delius's miniature essay gives us more than a glimpse of his mature characteristics. The chromatic consequent phrases by the wind (embodying a sequence of ii^7–V progressions) and the modal properties of the second thematic idea (replete with their own chromatic harmonisations) are decidedly prophetic, as is the transitional harmonic progression immediately before the return of C major (eight bars after E).

A variety of character movements for the French style of orchestral suite appears to have preoccupied Delius for much of 1889 and 1890. There are many sketches of unfinished movements – namely 'Valse lente', 'Serenade', 'Ouverture', 'Élégie', 'Idylle de nuit', 'Plainte d'amour' with French titles,[64]

---

[64]   See *GB-Lbl* MS Mus 1745/2/10, ff. 65–78 and 87–94.

Example 2.2a. *Marche Caprice*, opening, bb. 1–5.

Example 2.2b. *Marche Caprice*, secondary theme, bb. 16–19.

and portion of a movement with an Italian title 'A l'Amore'.[65] These may have been intended for the *Petite Suite d'Orchestre* of 1889 mentioned above, or for another work by the same title of three movements dated 1890. Beecham referred to this latter work as 'short suite in two movements',[66] referring to the 'Allegro ma non troppo' and 'Con moto' which are both cast in G minor, but a third movement, 'Allegretto', in E major clearly belongs to the set by dint of its foliation.[67] Beecham's description of 'short' does, however, appositely refer to the diminutive character of each movement which is much slighter than the earlier *Petite Suite*. The folk-like nature of the material, especially evident in the first movement with its Breton tune and highly unusual sequences of parallel root-position chords, suggests that Delius may have been attempting to emulate the nationalist tendency of various French composers who were, at that time, incorporating French folk tunes into their works (three such

[65] See *GB-Lbl* MS Mus 1745/1/39, ff. 19–23 and 1745/2/10, ff. 56–70.

[66] *TB*, 60.

[67] See *GB-Lbl* MS Mus 1745/1/48a, ff. 1–13r.

examples of this era being Saint-Saëns' *Rhapsodie d'Auvergne* Op. 73 and d'Indy's *Symphonie sur un chant montagnard français* Op. 25 and *Fantaisie sur des thèmes populaires français* Op 31). Again one can only conjecture, but his protracted visits to Brittany in 1888 and 1890 (not to mention 1892) may have stimulated an interest in the vibrant Breton Renaissance Movement led by such contemporary musical figures as Émile Durand, Louis-Albert Bourgault-Ducoudray and (later) Guy Ropartz.

A further suite, one for violin and orchestra, Delius's first completed work for solo instrument with orchestral accompaniment, may well have materialised through the influence of Grieg's and Sinding's interaction with the eighteenth-century genre. Grieg had recently completed his *Holberg Suite* in 1885 which was published in Leipzig the year before Delius arrived there. Sinding's partiality for dance suites (which recurred with some regularity throughout his life) gave rise to his five-movement Suite for Piano Op. 3 in 1888 and Delius was able to hear two performances of the 'Suite im alten Stil' Op. 10 by Halvorsen at the 1887 Christmas Eve party when the work had just been published by Peters. The work may also have been a product of his friendship with Arvesen who was studying with Martin Pierre Marsick at the Paris Conservatoire.[68] Heseltine dated this work as 1888 and this is supported by an early notebook sketch of the first movement,[69] but the French instrumental nomenclature and two of the titles of the four movements ('Pastorale' and Élégie') in the manuscript score (undated by the composer) may date it to 1890 or even 1891 and may point to an intended French performance and publication.[70] Although not played in the composer's lifetime, Delius evidently thought highly enough of his work to recommend it to Beecham and the young English violinist Marie Hall, in 1907.[71] The first movement, 'Pastorale', is another of Delius's unusual interpretations of sonata form. Abridged, the exposition begins with a sarabande 'im alten Stil' in E minor before launching into a more extrovert secondary idea in E major (using the tell-tale triplet rhythm on the first beat and longer note value on the second). By way of G sharp major, a second subject of flowing triplets establishes itself in C sharp major and a fourth idea in the orchestra (with accompanying trills from the soloists) brings the exposition to a close. The recapitulation, which begins

---

[68] *RL*, 24. Marsick's later pupils included Carl Flesch, Jacques Thibaud and George Enescu.

[69] See *GB-Lbl* MS Mus 1745/1/38, f. 23v and *DMA*, 144.

[70] *RT2*, 92.

[71] Letter from Delius to Thomas Beecham, 1 December 1907, *DLL1*, 318.

immediately, presents the sarabande idea in G sharp minor before the tonality is 'rectified' to E major with the restatement of the remaining thematic material. The bucolic-styled ternary 'Intermezzo', replete with drones, has the character of a Scherzo, its dance-like chromatic accompaniment (especially from b. 21) looking forward to the 'fa la la' mannerisms of the later works such (as *A Village Romeo and Juliet* and *A Mass of Life*). The 'Élégie' provides what must be the first example in Delius's music of an extended, self-developing melody for the soloist, one which is furnished with countermelody by horns and trumpet in the reprise. The finale, also an abridged sonata, looks back to Mendelssohn's Violin Concerto (a work Delius knew and performed) for its opening theme, material which sits uncomfortably with the more personal lyrical second subject in the submediant, an idea which gives us a first taste of Delius's flair for wind sonorities.

Having completed the Suite for Violin and Orchestra, Delius's attention also became temporarily fixed on a work for piano and orchestra. As his masters at Leipzig recognised, Delius had a limited facility for the piano which (like Tchaikovsky) meant that virtuoso writing for the instrument had to be learned. Delius was, of course, thoroughly conversant with Grieg's Piano Concerto. He not only owned the score but had heard it in Paris with the pianist René Chansarel.[72] Furthermore he was very much aware that Sinding had enjoyed some success with his own Piano Concerto in D flat Op. 6 in Christiania in February 1889. A good deal of surviving sketch material of works for piano and orchestra suggests that Delius was unsure of what form to adopt. A three-movement work in C sharp minor was tried but rejected,[73] and other sketches reveal that he also worked briefly on a *Fantaisie pour Piano & Orchestre* in G minor.[74] Another, more extended draft, albeit unfinished, was the *Légendes* (or *Sagen*) *pour Piano & Orchestre* in which Delius evidently wished to retain a one-movement form but this time as a series of variations based on a theme in F sharp major. The concept of the *Légendes* was ambitious, perhaps still too ambitious for the level of technique Delius had achieved. For one thing, Delius's chosen theme of twenty-six bars was a good deal more extensive than what had been attempted in the *Rhapsodische Variationen*, a decision which gave rise to a series of six variations of much greater substance as individual

---

[72] *DLL1*, 27. Chansarel was the dedicatee of Debussy's *Fantaisie* for Piano and Orchestra of 1889–1890. Its premiere was cancelled in 1890 and the work was not performed until after Debussy's death.

[73] See *GB-Lbl* MS Mus 1745/2/10, ff. 1–19.

[74] See *GB-Lbl* MS Mus 1745/2/10, ff. 20–23.

'fairy tales'. Moreover, the length of each variation was important in allowing space for more creative interaction between orchestra and soloist as one might more traditionally find in the rhetoric of a concerto. Indeed, each variation of Delius's unfinished structure has the status of a self-contained movement in which the composer's developmental technique is given genuine space to evolve. This is especially conspicuous in the second variation ('Misterioso, allegretto') in which the familiar Delian *topos* of the falling semitonal bass makes a bold appearance for the first time (Example 2.3a) and, in the fourth and fifth variations ('Allegro con moto'), Delius also demonstrates a much more fruitful understanding of the voice-leading properties and functions of consecutive augmented sixth harmonies (Example 2.3b). Quite what kind of structural scheme Delius hoped to embrace in the *Légendes* we shall never know. After the last of the extant variations, a chorale in E flat major, a return to F sharp major is indicated. Was a large-scale finale, a sonata movement, contemplated at this point, in the same mould as César Franck's cyclic *Variations Symphoniques* (which shares the same tonic), a work premiered at the annual orchestral concert of the Société Nationale de Musique on 1 May 1886 and since then a highly regarded and established classic of the repertoire? Delius may not have known himself how to resolve the question, and it may well have been the reason for the work's unfinished state. Nevertheless, the *Légendes* provides a useful insight into the composition of Delius's Piano Concerto seven years later.

Delius may have hoped to break into the French concert scene with his orchestral suites, the Suite for Violin, and even the abandoned *Légendes*, but if he did, his attempts were patently unsuccessful. It is significant therefore that in 1890 his *3 Symphonische Dichtungen* should have been aimed at a German audience where, perhaps, new opportunities might be found. The *Schlittenfahrt*, which Delius orchestrated from his original piano score, became the second of the triptych, while the other two pieces, *Sommerabend* (*Summer Evening*) and *Frühlingsmorgen* (*Spring Morning*), in the model of Griegian *Lyric Pieces*, were similar in length if different in structure. *Sommerabend*, the first of the three, is by the far the most substantial and best worked. Ternary in structure, like many of the movements of Delius's 'French' suites, its thematic material bears numerous hallmarks of the composer's mindset – an opening triplet figuration and a contiguous cadential dominant thirteenth. To this Delius also interpolates an arresting diversion from the dominant of D to an entirely unexpected 6/4 of the flat submediant, B flat, and superbly manages the recovery to the tonic through the subsequent II^{11}–V cadential progression. This progression is then expertly incorporated into the sequential melodic extension of the melody after letter B. The 'trio', which consists of two melodic

Example 2.3a. *Légendes*, Variation 2, bb. 98–109.

fragments, begins in G, but the rest of the section provides a glimpse of the increasing ease with which Delius was able to handle more complex tonal apparatus. The love of Griegian unconventional modulation is there, but now handled with greater fluidity as a repetition of the thematic idea (and its countermelody) moves from F sharp major to D flat and then to the dominant of A flat. However, instead of fulfilling the standard cycle of fifths, Delius skilfully reinterprets this dominant as an augmented sixth, taking us to a 6/4 on D and a cadence into G. This process, using the augmented sixth, is subtly repeated first to the dominant of B and subsequently to the dominant of B

Example 2.3b. *Légendes*, Variation 4, bb. 173–80.

flat, using the opening material, and with the arrival in B flat, Delius is able to use the flat submediant of D as a means of replicating his original cadence to the tonic. Perhaps even more impressive, however, is the climax at letter J where the original interpolation of B flat undergoes further extension to the dominant of E, a thoroughly fitting and well-judged variation in both thematic and harmonic terms and one also outstandingly orchestrated. Although *Frühlingsmorgen* provides an apposite counterpart to *Sommerabend*, and the climactic part of the piece (from b. 64) re-echoes the Wagnerian pinnacle of *Idylle de Printemps*, its tonal organisation is more laboured.

SONGS

A prolific production of songs in the years of 1890 and 1891 suggests that, having enjoyed a modicum of success with the publication of his first set of *Lieder aus dem Norwegischen* with Augener, Delius pondered on the lucrative gain from the composition of new songs. Earlier sketchbooks show a particular attraction to the lyrical poetry of Heine,[75] and the fact that he looked to the poet's *Neue Gedichte* and *Buch der Lieder* (the source for 'Der Fichtenbaum' and 'Warum sind den die Rosen so blass') strongly indicates that Delius was

---

[75] See *DMA*, 18 *passim*.

still drawn to the German lieder tradition. What is more, by dint of Heine's short lyrical verse, the three short songs are similarly concise and through-composed. An examination of the late nineteenth-century chromatic vocabulary Delius deploys also intimates that it was to German influences of Wagner and the literature of German song that Delius looked to emulate, rather than those Griegian characteristics and components of the Norwegian songs. The chromatic voice-leading of 'Mit deinen blauen Augen', a love song, is overtly more Teutonic in method, and the fluid modulations which, within the space of ten bars, carry us from the tonic (F major) to the dominants of the mediant (A) and the Neapolitan (F) sharp), reveal Delius's eagerness to absorb contemporary German harmonic processes.[76] In 'Ein schöner Stern geht auf in meiner Nacht' the entire edifice of the song is supported by a robust tonal scheme and by the contrary motion of the voice-leading in the outer lines. Cast in B major, moreover, the song's yearning climax and hushed coda have a strong Tristanesque aura, and the raised Lydian fourth on the tonic (b. 20) is a recognisably Delian characteristic. One senses too in this song, and in 'Hör' ich das Liedchen klingen', that Delius was also learning to handle his apparatus with a new sense of prose, engendered largely by the elasticity and fluctuation of tempi.

It seems the Heine songs were never offered for publication, but the *Three English Songs (poems by Shelley)* were accepted by Augener in 1892 and, being 'more suitable' than the Norwegian songs,[77] were intended for the rapidly expanding market of vernacular solo song in England during the 1890s.[78] Admired by Beecham, Delius's three Shelley lyrics exceeded the sales of the Norwegian songs and became some of his most popular works in the genre.[79] Though more substantial in length, they continued to build on the expanding technique of the Heine settings with even greater attention to structural

---

[76] An interesting question surrounds a fourth song, 'Aus deinen Augen fliessen mein Lieder' which appears with the Heine songs in *GB-Lbl* MS Mus 1745/1/36, ff. 35–6 in a copyist's hand. Thought originally to be by Delius (see *TB*, 60), it is in fact the first of Franz Ries's *Drei Lieder* Op. 21 (c. 1875). How it came to be part of the Heine set is unclear, but it may be that Ries's example of chromatic harmony and elasticity of tempi may have been a useful paradigm.

[77] See letter from Delius to Augener, 16 January 1892 in *MC*, 41.

[78] These songs were set exclusively in English before a French translation was provided in 1896 for 'Indian Love Song', and before the English words were paralleled with German translations in 1910 by Jelka Rosen (Nos. 1 and 2) and G. Tischer (No. 3) for Tischer & Jagenberg.

[79] *FDPW*, 466.

invention and vocal adventure. 'Indian Love Song' (best known by its first line, 'I arise from dreams of thee') begins as a lullaby, and much of the first verse and the opening of the second is occupied by a protracted tonic pedal. But, rather like the second of the Heine songs, after reaching a tonal fulcrum, in this instance to the dominant (B flat major) through the agency of a stepwise bass descent, the more fluid resourcefulness of Delius's harmonic vocabulary gives rise to a more operatic style of passion ('Oh lift me from the grass!'). And, as a counterbalance to the long pedal of the opening, Delius furnishes two further extended pedal points on V (from b. 57) and its secondary dominant (b. 47) as preparation for the singer's climactic top B flat before the reprise of the lullaby. 'Love's Philosophy', rivalled only by Quilter's later setting, is notorious for its demanding and virtually unrelenting left-hand figurations. Although the 'neighbour' harmonies of the opening two bars recall similar configurations in the first movement of *Florida*, Delius's carefully paced progressions reveal a much more calculated structure. The first verse of Shelley's poem outlines a tonal shift from G major to B, while the second verse, mirroring the more turbulent imagery of the words, is more fluid. Deft touches are the move from E major to the subdominant C ('And the moonbeams kiss the sea') and the use of minor ii^7 at the critical arrival of the line 'If thou *kiss* not me' at the head of the understated coda. Notwithstanding its ungratefully dense and somewhat overblown accompaniment (which would have been better scored for orchestra), 'To the Queen of my Heart' has a Wagnerian *Schwung* in its athletic vocal line, its harmonic formula recalling the climax of Act I of *Tristan*. Reserving the climax for the end of the central paragraph is also an adroit touch since this makes room for a wistful conclusion to the song in which Delius makes early use of his tell-tale 6 and 9 appoggiaturas in the final bars.

It may have been the eminently musical nature of Tennyson's *Maud* Part I which attracted Delius, or the emotional complexity of the poet's once controversial poem, but it is not clear what moved him to set five of the sections with accompaniment for small orchestra in 1891. Was there some possibility of a performance? Or, like *Sakuntala*, did the exercise offer him further experience in the interaction of voice and orchestra, pertinent in this instance since he was at work on his first opera, *Irmelin*? The separate manuscript gatherings of the five songs also give no confirmation of a title, the sequence of songs, or that they were even intended as a cycle. Beecham, who proposed the order in which they are now published, saw merit in the songs,[80]

---

[80] *TB*, 59. Beecham's reason for the order was largely determined by the order of the five poems within Tennyson's scheme, but he evidently felt that that 'Birds in the

and hoped to perform them in the 1929 Delius Festival, only to be rebuffed by Delius, who, perhaps recoiling from their Victorian sensibility almost forty years later, could not be persuaded to exhume them.[81] As Beecham remarked, the first item, 'Birds in the high-hall garden' runs to some 102 bars,[82] while the last, 'Come into the garden, Maud', to 214. Reinforced by their colourful orchestral garbs, both give the impression of operatic 'scenas' rather than the much shorter edifices of the other three, less distinguished, songs which do not exceed fifty bars. A hint of this theatrical ambience is perhaps evident in the opening of the first song, which is almost a quote from the Prelude to *Irmelin*, and the vocal delivery (as one sees in the climactic material, just before the reprise – see bb. 70–78) sits tantalisingly between the lyricism of his songs and the declamatory manner he was striving to achieve in his first opera, by then close to completion. The last song, well known through Balfe's thoroughly operatic setting of 1857, suffers from over-inflation, a fault Beecham identified.[83] Nonetheless, the operatic temperament of the first song finds an even more theatrical home here, with enriched scoring for strings. Delius, moreover, uses a sonata structure to embrace all ten of Tennyson's verses with four distinct thematic ideas. The first two are well delineated in G major and D, but a third, in F sharp minor articulates a dance phase of the song, using syncopations familiar from the 'Tanz der Majorbauer' in *Florida* which continues with a more exotic fourth idea in C major. The last three verses are used for the reprise of the first, second and fourth ideas, all grounded in the tonic, though the restatement of the fourth idea, in its initial E flat, is strategically used (together with the introduction of the heavy brass) to enhance the mood of anticipation ('She is late!').

One further song that dates from 1891 is a setting of Drachmann's poem 'Lyse Nætter' (Example 2.4). A highly significant text for Delius, the poem captures a spellbound stillness of a summer evening. The term in Norwegian relates specifically to the period of the midnight sun (known as the astronomical twilight) where the evening dusk melds with the morning dawn without any intervening night. It was a marvel of nature Delius adored as he told Percy Grainger many years later: 'In the summer I have always a great longing to go to Norway & live among the Mountains. I love the light nights

---

high Hall-garden' and 'Come into the garden, Maud', substantially longer than the other three, should begin and end the set thereby slightly altering the order.

81   *FDPW*, 467.

82   *TB*, 59.

83   *TB*, 59.

Example 2.4. 'Lyse Nætter', version 1.

so'.[84] Fascinated by this natural phenomenon, Delius was moved at least three times to set Drachmann's verse. After a first, rejected sketch in Danish only,[85] a second version was made with Danish and English words, the translation provided by Delius himself.[86] The result was an enchanting lullaby in 6/8 which is based, save for an interlude of four bars on a dominant pedal seven bars before the end, entirely on a tonic pedal over which Delius placed his lullaby 'charm'. What is also apparent from this mesmerising song of thirty-three bars – the most original vocal miniature he had composed to date – is that its chord progressions (in particular the prevalence of the added-sixth harmony and the tender ninth and thirteenth appoggiaturas) are a product

---

[84] Letter from Delius to Percy Grainger, 10 June 1907, *DLL1*, 293.

[85] See *GB-Lbl* MS Mus 1745/1/36, f. 14.

[86] See *GB-Lbl* MS Mus 1745/1/36, ff. 42–3 draft in Danish only dated 1891; ff. 44–5 with Delius's English translation.

of a profound study of the love duet from Act II of *Tristan und Isolde* ('O sink hernieder') or Wagner's study for that opera, 'Träume – Studie zu *Tristan und Isolde*' from the *Fünf Gedichte für Frauenstimme*. As has been observed, the Heine and Shelley songs furnished compelling evidence of Delius's desire to incorporate Wagnerian techniques of harmony and declamation into his style. 'I want to tread in Wagner's footsteps and even give something more in the right direction', he related to Jutta Bell in 1894.[87] This song, above all, confirms the extent and momentum of that appetite.

---

[87] Letter from Delius to Jutta Bell, 29 May 1894, *DLL1*, 86.

CHAPTER 3

A Wagnerian Odyssey: *Irmelin* and
The Magic Fountain (1891–1895)

FORMAL EXPANSION

The publication of the *Shelley Songs* by Augener was undoubtedly a welcome development for Delius, but there seemed little prospect of hearing anything of his orchestral labours. Even though he attended the Lamoureux concerts and acquainted himself with performers at the Paris Conservatoire, the French concert scene seemed closed to him. It may indeed have been this particular circumstance – the need to be 'in the thick of things' – that persuaded him to move from Croissy to a rented apartment at 33 rue Ducouëdec in the Montrouge quarter, now in the southern suburbs of Paris. This would be his home for several years. From there the centre of Paris was only two-and-a-half miles, and even closer was Montparnasse where, in regularly frequenting Madame Charlotte's *crémerie* for a cheap meal, he would socialise with his artist friends Gauguin, Mucha, Monfreid, Slewinski, the Molards, Charles Boutet de Monvel and Munch.

Although songs and the less complex, smaller movements of his suites and the more diminutive symphonic poems had been useful *loci* for stylistic experimentation, Delius was clearly aware that, after the less developed exercise of the melodrama *Paa Vidderne*, he had yet to attempt a larger, more testing symphonic canvas for orchestra. Conscious, perhaps, that the melodrama had its flaws, Delius returned to Ibsen's poem but now with the intention of composing an entirely new concert overture with the same title. The first draft of the overture was completed sometime before the end of 1890, since a letter from Grieg states: 'I should love to hear your overture 'På Vidderne'.'[1] It seems that the score was in the possession of Iver Holter, conductor of the Christiania Musikforening at the end of 1890, but was received too late to be included before Christmas. Holter then asked if he could retain the score and parts with a view to performing the work in the autumn of 1891.[2] Holter

---

[1] Letter from Grieg to Delius, 22 December 1890, *GD*, 106.
[2] See Letter from Holter to Delius, 19 March 1891, *DLL1*, 56.

carried out his promise and performed it on 10 October 1891.[3] Delius, who extended his stay in Norway to hear it, was there with Grieg and Sinding. This 'Concert ouverture for stort Orkester' was later revised as a symphonic poem (in accordance with the date on the manuscript) but was not performed again until 25 February 1894 when, thanks to the assistance of Isidore de Lara,[4] whom Delius befriended in 1892, it was played under the direction of Arthur Steck and the Orchestre Philharmonique de Monte-Carlo in a revised form as a 'symphonic poem' *Sur les Cimes*. The work was not heard again until November 1946 when, as *On the Mountains*, Beecham conducted it with the Royal Philharmonic Orchestra at the Albert Hall.

Although conceived as a sonata design, the thematic behaviour of Delius's movement is far from conventional. An opening paragraph in E minor, outlining a dialogue between the lower strings, horns and wind, soon leaves that key for the dominant of B (a key central to the recapitulation), and then, by way of a sequence of bold Griegian modulations, the section alights on the dominant of G. Delius's next step, however, is a second, more introspective subject in B minor which, given its relative brevity, functions as a transition to a more substantial secondary theme in B flat. At this point, he attempts to fashion a more tonally fluid developmental phase by use of a Straussian figure in the bass which drives upward, the consequence of which is a set of climactic, if over-laboured fanfares. By contrast, the tranquil later part of the development is more sensual, giving us a taste of those poetical encounters of oboe, horn and strings (Example 3.1) in which Delius excelled, though this is somewhat undermined by the forced transition to the recapitulation. The return to E minor and the restatement of the first subject and transition is disappointingly unchanged. Yet, with the reprise of the second subject, Delius chose to couch this entire paragraph in B major, as if to create a passionate Tristanesque apotheosis to the movement before fanfares bring it to a rather abrupt, premature close.

Delius's preoccupation with B major found further expression in a Violin Sonata which was dedicated initially to a teacher at the Conservatoire, Charlotte Vormèse, though this dedication was later erased. The Sonata was tried over privately in 1893 by the English-born pianist Harold Bauer, who was in Paris for a year studying with Paderewski, and the American-born violinist, Achille Rivarde, who had been, until recently, principal violinist

---

[3] Lowe, R., 'Delius's First Performance', *The Musical Times*, Vol. 106 No. 1465 (March 1965), 190.

[4] De Lara, I., *Many Tales of Many Cities* (London: Hutchinson & Co., 1928), 99.

Example 3.1. *Paa Vidderne*, development, bb. 168–83.

of the Lamoureux orchestra. Such performers were well chosen because Delius made considerable demands of both players. As in *Paa Vidderne*, all three movements show an inclination for self-developing, organic themes of some rhythmical intricacy, especially for the violinist, while the support in the piano is harmonically complex. This type of elastic thematic mindset suits the simpler ternary structure of the slow movement more readily, particularly its Griegian central section. In the structurally unorthodox finale, however, it seems almost relentless. It is also evident that Delius, within this newer chromatic context, had learned to understand the strategic value of the Straussian 6/4 as a means of modulation (e.g. in the first movement, the first major modulation to the Neapolitan, C, in b. 25, the climax of the second subject in b. 121, and the commencement of the development in b. 124), a technique he had already put to effective use in *Summer Evening* some two years earlier and in the pages of Act III of *Irmelin* (see below).

Delius sent the Sonata to Max Abraham, the owner of Peters Edition, in Leipzig, but it was returned. Grieg, a close friend of Abraham, had pronounced

the work 'full of talent' and that the 'Adagio [was] wonderful', but had warned
that the orthography, with its excess of double sharps, would be testing for the
most professional of musicians.[5] This was one disadvantage; but there were
others, as Abraham explained:

> I regret that I cannot publish the Sonata, because the form is too free, the
> key is changed too frequently & the first & last movements are so difficult
> to play that reasonably large sales for the work are unthinkable. I would not
> write to every composer in this way, but I have the honour of knowing you,
> & I know also that you want frankness on my part.[6]

The Sonata was perhaps wisely shelved, but Delius was much more successful
and judicious in another work for violin, the *Légende*, where the support of
the orchestra liberated him from the unsympathetic properties of the piano.
Far less 'active' than the Sonata, the violin is allowed to breathe as part of a
much more interactive exchange between soloist and orchestra. Moreover,
the arch structure of the *Légende*, with its unusual tonal dialectic of E flat, its
major Neapolitan, E major, and differentiation of tempi between primary and
secondary material, is more fluent and lacks the self-conscious sonata thinking
of the Violin Sonata's outer movements. The autograph full score of the
Légende is dated 'Paris 1895' which is when Delius probably orchestrated the
work.[7] Though bearing no dedication, it may have been connected with the
Dutch violinist, Johannes Wolff, who had come to Paris in the early 1890s to
study with the very elderly Joseph Massart at the Conservatoire. It was Wolff,
with whom Delius kept in contact after he moved to London, who gave the
first performance of the *Légende* in London in January 1897, though Delius,
owing to his travels abroad, could not attend.[8]

---

[5] Letter from Abraham to Delius, 28 February 1893, *DLL1*, 73.

[6] Ibid.

[7] See *GB-Lbl* MS Mus 1745/1/8, f. 1. The date of the version for violin and piano is
     uncertain. After Delius's Violin Sonata No. 1 (see Chapter 15) was first performed
     in Manchester on 24 February 1915 by the violinist Arthur Catterall and pianist
     R. J. Forbes (with Delius in the audience), a second performance in London on 29
     April included a performance of the *Légende*. Catterall's role as leader of the Hallé
     Orchestra and Forbes's position on the staff of the Royal Manchester College
     were no doubt instrumental in seeing both the Sonata and *Légende* published by
     the Manchester firm, Forsyths.

[8] Letter from Delius to Jutta Bell, [23 December 1896], *DLL1*, 110.

A FIRST OPERATIC VENTURE: *IRMELIN*

Delius's love of opera had been affirmed both in Leipzig and in his first years in Paris, so it comes as no surprise that, after three years of secluded work, his compulsion for composition, combined with his ethic for hard work, should have included the challenge of opera. Even as far back as June 1888, Sinding was asking: 'Have you got a text for an opera?'[9] Much of the work on *Irmelin*, a 'Lyric Drama' as he termed it,[10] was done, according to Heseltine, between 1890 and 1892,[11] though as Carley has suggested, the greater part of it was composed in 1892.[12] At least two notebooks reveal sketches for *Irmelin* from around 1890,[13] but it seems most likely, given the considerable advance of Delius's technique, and in particular his grasp of Wagnerian methods, that material for the opera coalesced in 1892. After the opera was finished, a vocal score was made up principally by Florent Schmitt whom Delius had met through the Molards.[14] This was during the years 1893–1894 to aid his efforts to 'sell' the opera to prospective impresarios. Jelka Rosen, however, recalled that, even in January 1896, Delius was still working on the opera.[15]

In spite of the opposition in some quarters, Wagner's music gripped the imagination of many in Paris during the last two decades of the nineteenth century. But it was also an auspicious time for French opera, whether through the popularity of Bizet, especially *Carmen*, the elegant operas of Delibes (above all *Lakmé*) and Massenet (notably *Manon* and *Werther*), the late flowering of Verdi's art in *Aïda*, *Don Carlos* and *Othello* (not to mention the even later *Falstaff*) or the advent of *verismo* in Giordano's *Andrea Chénier*, Mascagni's *Cavalleria rusticana* and Leoncavallo's *Pagliacci*. Mascagni's and Leoncavallo's music, which we know Delius admired, would have provided a range of paradigms for his own work. Various subjects, as we know, had tempted him by Bulwer-Lytton and Ibsen. *Sakuntala*, the melodrama *Paa Vidderne*, and the array of songs written in 1890 and 1891 had provided

---

[9] Letter from Sinding to Delius, 1 June 1888, *DTA*.

[10] See letter from Delius to Jutta Bell, 12 August 1894, *DLL1*, 90.

[11] *PH*, 162. One of Delius's earliest champions, the critic J. F. Runciman, stated in his article in the *Musical Courier* (18 March 1903) on the composer that *Irmelin* was completed in 1891 (see Runciman, J. F., 'Fritz Delius, Composer', in *DC*, 14).

[12] *DPY*, 27.

[13] See *GB-Lbl* MS Mus 1745/2/11/2 and 1745/1/38.

[14] Schmitt drew up the vocal score in 1893 and 1894 (see *GB-Lbl* MS Mus 1745/3/1).

[15] Delius, J., 'Memories of Frederick Delius', in *DLL1*, 410.

important opportunities to develop areas of vocal delivery, formal design as well as thematic and harmonic continuity, and a series of orchestral works, culminating in the symphonic poem *Paa Vidderne*, had nurtured an advance in his instrumental technique. Add to this an obsession with *Tristan*, and Delius was hungry to try his hand at his first operatic canvas.

In opting to create a fairy-tale plot from the conflation of several literary sources, Delius consulted various writers, including the historian and novelist Charles Francis Keary, who acknowledged the collaboration, albeit short-lived, many years later.[16] In the end, however, it proved to be easier logistically for Delius to create his own libretto for *Irmelin*. Although Beecham maintained that the Irmelin legend was 'Northern and early medieval',[17] there is no source in the *Norske Folkeeventyr* collected by Asbjørnsen and Moe, nor in other Norwegian folk tales. More likely Delius gleaned enough from Jacobsen's poem 'Irmelin Rose' (published in his *Digte* of 1869), a text he eventually set as one of the *Seven Danish Songs* in 1897. This connection seems even more plausible when one observes Delius's use of Irmelin's leitmotiv from the opera in the song's refrain (Example 3.2a). The poem, sure enough, details the princess's rejection of all her suitors, much to the chagrin of her father, the king. As John White has suggested, 'King Thrush-Beard' from the Brothers Grimm tells of a haughty princess who mocks her suitors and of a king who insists that his daughter marry the next man who arrives at the gate. This turns out to be a minstrel (King Thrush-Beard in disguise), who after singing before the king, is ordered to marry her.[18] This seems closer to Delius's libretto than Beecham's other putative source, Andersen's 'The Swineherd', for, although Nils's role as swineherd to the chieftain Rolf and his band of robbers has its obvious parallels, Andersen's moral tale ends unhappily for the princess. At the end of Delius's opera, by contrast, the hero of Delius's opera, Nils, is recognised as a prince in disguise. With this epiphany, Irmelin and Nils quickly fall in love and the fairy tale concludes joyfully.

Beecham, in his 1959 biography of Delius, was full of praise for the composer's first operatic venture: 'Taking the work as a whole I have little hesitation in claiming for it the distinction of being the best first opera written by any composer known to me'.[19] A few years earlier, in 1953, when

---

[16] Keary, C. F., *The Brothers: A Masque* (London: Longmans, Green & Co., 1902), i.

[17] *TB*, 56.

[18] White, J., 'Words without Music: The Literary Sources of the Delius Operas', *DSJ* No. 135 (Spring 2004), 7–8.

[19] *TB*, 58.

Example 3.2a. *Irmelin*, Irmelin's motive.

Beecham was on the point of giving the world premiere of *Irmelin* at Oxford, he wrote equally warmly of Delius's achievement: 'As for the music, the writing for voices is smoothly singable, and that for the orchestra reveals an easy plasticity and wealth of colour, demonstrating that Delius had nothing here to learn from any other composer living at the time'.[20] This was, perhaps, an exaggeration. There was much still to refine in terms of declamatory processes and, though there is some evidence of the organic function of representative themes, his study of the contrapuntal and transformational behaviour of Wagner's leitmotivic processes had some way to go in terms of their organic malleability; nevertheless, many of Delius's leitmotivs, in particular Irmelin's theme (its diatonic melody, its supporting dominant pedal and inner chromatic voices outlining the progression of V^7 of V followed by V^7) and the 'Silver Stream' material (with its added-sixth colour), already exude that unmistakable perfume of Delius's parlance. It is also possible to hear the advance in Delius's sense of self-assurance as the opera progresses: the material of Act III, for example, is demonstrably more sophisticated and inventive than Act I. Added to which, there are many aspects of the opera which are not only intrinsically interesting from a purely musical point of view but which also point to those directions in which Delius wanted to take opera over the course of the next twenty years.

Some criticism has been levelled at Delius's libretto. Its stilted, 'Wardour Street' language and simple rhyme is undistinguished, but that is true of the character and content of many libretti, including those of Wagner. The weaknesses of the opera lie mainly in those areas of realistic depiction. The king's declaration to Irmelin of his wish to have her betrothed, and the presentation of the knights in Act I, are perfunctory, the 'Männerchor'

20 Beecham, T., 'An Unknown Opera of Delius's Youth', *Daily Telegraph* and *Morning Post*, 21 March 1953, quoted in Beecham, T., 'Beecham on Delius', in *DC*, 73.

drinking song lacks melodic and rhythmic invention, and the 'welcome' music of Act III Scene 1 (in spite of its novel I–V ostinato) is largely pedestrian in its regular phraseology. Delius had yet to master the litheness of Wagner's conflation of unperiodic recitative and declamation in these contexts. However, in the more set-piece instances of soliloquy, duet, and solo with chorus, which, even if they necessitated longer passages of introspection and inaction, demanded a more lyrical approach to self-developing melody and the symphonic role of the orchestra, he was much more successful. The first evidence of this is in Act I Scene 6 where Irmelin laments her parlous state of being forced to marry against her wishes. In true fairy-tale fashion, buoyed up by the sound of 'free' distant horns, Irmelin reassures herself that her prince will come. In this mood of greater optimism, the pastoral scene is enhanced by a distant chorus ('Away, far away to the woods let us stray') whose eight-part texture and 'tra la la la' refrain provide the first example of Delius's affinity for partsong. Indeed, the chorus's distant context surely invokes those Floridian experiences of the far away negro voices here romanticised in the clothing of a 12/8 dance. Furthermore, Delius's choral dance, with its transformational modulation to D flat, fuels Irmelin's belief in her destiny ('Ah! But he will come and then we'll wander in the groves and woods') and, besides furnishing an interlude to the larger musical scheme, functions as a transition to the last and even more impassioned part of Irmelin's soliloquy which concludes with strains from the opening orchestral prelude.

As a counterbalance to Irmelin's music in Act I, Act II is dominated by two extended soliloquies for Nils, and Rolf's ballad. The pictorial prelude in E major presents the 'Silver Stream' material (Example 3.2b) which provides the basis of the first part of Scene 1. Nils's first soliloquy is, however, devoted principally to narrative as he relates the circumstances of how, after seeking the Silver Stream, he was lured away by the 'fatal flowers'. Here Delius introduces a new, more 'angst-ridden' leitmotiv (Example 3.2c) in a more animated section, closely related to a fourth, which tells of his enslavement by Rolf's seductive women (Example 3.2d). This is also supplemented by a further figure symbolising 'yearning for the beloved' (Example 3.2e), a figure he would use with some frequency in later scores, and the introduction of a Griegian leitmotiv associated with Nils's *peripeteia* (bb. 219–221) consisting of contiguous cadences, the first in the Neapolitan, the second in the tonic.[21] This is consistently connected with Nils's changes of fortune, particularly in

---

[21]   This type of double cadence is anticipated in the first movement of Grieg's Piano Concerto, b. 56.

Example 3.2b. *Irmelin*, 'Silver Stream' motive.

Example 3.2c. *Irmelin*, 'Nils's regret' motive.

Example 3.2d. *Irmelin*, 'seduction' motive.

Example 3.2e. *Irmelin*, 'yearning for the beloved' motive.

Act III (see bb. 190–192 and 240–243) where this and the reintroduction of Irmelin's motive (b. 775) occur with even greater dramatic purpose. As a centrepiece of Act II, Rolf's ballad in Scene 2 (comparable in terms of genre with Senta's from *Der fliegende Holländer*), has a fluency and robustness, enhanced by the tonal colour Delius brings to the narrative. If anything, this section suffers from being dramatically underdeveloped. Nils's sense of regret, the struggle he faces in Scene 3 to free himself of the carnal attractions placed in his way by the women's ballet-chorus ('Ah! What bliss to love and kiss'), and the motivation to seek his princess, have distinct parallels with *Tannhäuser* (although Beecham considered the ballet episode to be more reminiscent of the Flower Girls in *Parsifal*).[22] Having successfully escaped the clutches of Rolf, Nils's discovery of the Stream in Scene 5 is depicted in an impressive tripartite structure in D major. Framed by a quasi-folksong idea (Example 3.2f) derived from music sketched for *Zanoni* (which seems uncannily redolent of Mahler, though Delius could not have encountered any of Mahler's music at the time),[23] Nils is revealed searching his way through the rocky terrain, his music being appropriately of a more turbulent and tonally unstable nature.

Although the wedding ceremony in the first part of Act III is, save for the joyful orchestral opening (again based on Irmelin's material), less characterful, the remaining part (from the arrival of Nils as a minstrel) is of a high order and confirms just how far Delius had progressed in terms of his command of contemporary musical mechanisms. The *peripeteia* motive and a prominent 'pipe tune' from the oboe appropriately punctuate the 'minstrel' scene (itself reminiscent of *Tannhäuser*) as Nils, somewhat inadvisedly, prefers to sing

Example 3.2f. *Irmelin*, quasi-folksong idea.

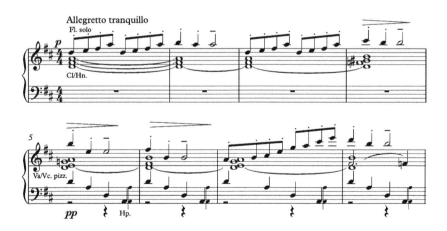

---

[22] *TB*, 57.

[23] See *RT1*, 22.

of his past as a swineherd rather than entertain the party with a song. This, not surprisingly, elicits a quizzical response from the chorus underpinned by the *peripeteia* motive ('What a strange song he sings') though the recurrence of Irmelin's motive signals her enamourment for Nils. All this, however, is a preparation for the two main pillars of Act III which exclusively involve Irmelin and Nils. At this juncture the parallels with *Tristan* are palpable. As the banquet comes to an end, and Nils has left, the men embark on a hunt while Irmelin is free to meet Nils in secret. The hunt acts as a frame for a tender scene which has the function of recapitulation as Irmelin's motive returns along with those of 'yearning', the music of the Silver Stream, as well as the addition of new 'love' music (Example 3.2g). As the hunt returns, Delius's libretto makes an unabashed reference to *Tristan* in Nils's words, 'O blissful dream, Let me not awake', and, in fear of being discovered, Nils departs with the promise that the two lovers will meet later that night in the garden. With the aid of an orchestral prelude (which also facilitates a scene change), sufficient anticipatory time

Example 3.2g. *Irmelin*, 'love' music.

is given for their second clandestine meeting in Scene 2, where, as Delius marks in the score, 'both lose themselves in the ecstasy of the moment'. The bond of Irmelin and Nils is sealed in poetic music of high quality material that is preludial to a love duet whose own transcendental fervour is not only modelled on that of Act II Scene 2 of *Tristan* (even to the point of allusions to 'so starben wir' – see bb. 909–13), but which also provides a telling apotheosis to the opera in its incorporation of the opening prelude (and here one becomes more aware of its *Tristanesque* melodic and harmonic affinities – see bb. 925–38).

As Beecham posited, much of the material in Act III of *Irmelin* represented a culmination of Delius's efforts since he arrived in Paris in 1888.[24] The opera provides overwhelming corroboration of his preoccupation with *Tristan und Isolde* and his desire to emulate the ideals of Wagnerian music drama. As he later declared to Jutta Bell in May 1894, 'I want to tread in Wagner's footsteps and even give something more in the right direction'.[25] Tantalisingly, Delius never elucidated what he meant by the idea of the 'right direction', but an examination of the larger structure and concept of *Irmelin* reveals that, while he was fixated on Wagnerian instrumental processes of symphonic continuity and with the larger themes of redemption and transcendence, he was little interested in issues of realism or of character development. As Hutchings observed:

> What, in simple terms, is the kind of libretto for composers like Wagner and Delius? First a legendary one, since such a story is already charged with romantic atmosphere, and these are romantic composers; the mystery of distance makes the legendary figures into symbols and prototypes of all heroes, all lovers, who express the struggles and yearnings of all generations. Secondly, a tale which provides scope for the voluptuous and ecstatic, and contains between its lines more than the lines themselves can communicate without musical expression.[26]

Beyond these character archetypes, Delius also seems to have been attracted by the simplification of operatic plot, devoid of complex dialogue, ensemble work and Aristotelian finales where, in keeping with the trend of many shorter dramatic works of the 1890s (e.g. Verdi's *Otello*, Humperdinck's *Hänsel und*

---

[24] *TB*, 58.

[25] Letter from Delius to Jutta Bell, 29 May 1894, *DLL1*, 86.

[26] *AH*, 123.

Gretel and Puccini's *La Bohème*), the opera's length was notably reduced. The three acts of *Irmelin*, lasting barely two hours, are uncomplicated; Acts I and II are heavily dependent on soliloquy from the principal characters, while Act III, made up of two scenes, is notable for its conspicuous love duet. Similarly, Delius's attraction to partsong led him often (though not exclusively) to use the chorus for set pieces such as interludes, ballet music, or even as accompaniment for the soloists. Already increasing in terms of its artistic and dramatic significance for Delius was, however, the operatic contribution and potential of the orchestra. Apart from the conceptually *instrumental* nature of Wagner's operatic works, which Delius clearly understood, he must also have been aware of those parts of *Tristan*, *Die Meistersinger*, *Der Ring des Nibelungen* and *Parsifal* where, either in the form of set pieces (such as *Siegfried's Funeral March*), preludes (such as *Tristan* and *Parsifal*) or extended interludes (such as *Siegfried's Journey Down the Rhine* or the entrance into the Hall of the Grail in *Parsifal*), the orchestra becomes uniquely articulate. Indeed, one of the striking features of *Irmelin*, particularly in Acts II and III, is the amount of music for the orchestra *alone* and which, like that of Wagner, moves beyond the conventional functions of traditional opera in order to express those things outside the scope of words. This is executed most effectively in the closing passage of Act III Scene 1 and the sixty bars of the Prelude to Scene 2 in which the lovers' 'ecstasy' is encapsulated in the climactic 6/4 on V of F sharp major (the tonality most closely associated with Irmelin, *viz.* the Prelude to Act I) and the equally ecstatic 6/4 on V of E major (Nils's key from Act II). One senses, too, that in this operatic context, Delius enjoyed the opportunity to expand his orchestral palette as an agency of pictorial and emotional intensity. Besides the spacious sound of mountain horns, the menacing connotations of the hunting horns, the delicate filigree of individual woodwind timbres and the nostalgic presence of the solo violin (all hallmarks of the composer's orchestral language), there is also evidence of increasing detail, especially in the texture and sonority of the strings in Act III where they are more frequently divided into at least eight parts, a lesson he had drawn from the last two songs of *Maud*. Such orchestral detail and simplicity of operatic plot would inform his next operatic endeavour, *The Magic Fountain*, but it would also symbolise poetically what opera as a genre meant to Delius. Having gorged himself at Bayreuth in 1894, where he heard *Tannhäuser* and multiple performances of *Parsifal*, *Die Meistersinger*, *Tristan* and *Der Ring*, he remarked that 'dramatic art [was] almost taking the place of religion'.[27] *Parsifal* had deeply impressed him at Bayreuth.

---

[27] Letter from Delius to Jutta Bell, 29 May 1894, *DLL1*, 86.

'Parsifal is magnificent', he wrote to Bell, 'the finest work of Wagner'.[28] But it was not so much the religious aura of Wagner's last opera that Delius responded to; rather it was how opera moved on, to become a new internalised experience where action onstage was of secondary importance to a higher level of human existence and spirituality, and where traditional operatic form merged ever more closely with the wordless ideals of the symphonic poem.

THE MAGIC FOUNTAIN

With the completion of *Irmelin*, Delius had it copied by his new-found friend, the Conservatoire music student Florent Schmitt, for the practical purposes of attracting impresarios and conductors across Europe. As another friend Léon Moreau informed him, 'Schmitt is very busy doing your reduction for you'.[29] But it is also evident that Delius and Schmitt were working closely *together* to get the vocal score ready. 'I am working with a friend all day at a reduction of my opera for piano and voice', he informed Jutta Bell.[30] Encouraged by the fact that Grieg and Messager admired what they saw in the opera,[31] and with the hope of attracting a German performance, sometime between July and September 1894, he travelled to Bayreuth in order to show the well-known Wagner conductor Hermann Levi the score.[32] Levi, who was unable to accommodate the opera at Munich, recommended a meeting with Richard Strauss, then Kapellmeister in the Bavarian capital, but no further progress was made.[33]

During the latter stages of the completion of *Irmelin*, Delius was evidently considering a new opera, since, in February 1892, he visited London to discuss the plot and libretto of the legend of Endymion.[34] Various versions of the legend had Wagnerian possibilities: Endymion's eternal sleep had parallels with Brünnhilde in *Die Walküre* as a punishment for his sexual relationship with Zeus's wife, Hera; another had Endymion put to sleep

---

[28] Letter from Delius to Jutta Bell, 12 August 1894, *DLL1*, 90.

[29] Letter from Léon Moreau, [22 May 1894], *DLL1*, 80.

[30] Letter from Delius to Jutta Bell, 29 May 1894, *DLL1*, 86.

[31] *PH*, 101.

[32] See letter from Delius to Jutta Bell, 12 August 1894, *DLL1*, 90.

[33] This runs contrary to Heseltine's assertion that a performance of *Irmelin* 'was never seriously contemplated by the composer'. See *PH*, 101.

[34] *DLL1*, 61.

by his lover Selene, the moon goddess, so that she could enjoy his beauty alone. Some musical ideas for the opera were sketched,[35] but soon the idea of Endymion was abandoned, much to Delius's frustration and which no doubt caused Sinding to sympathise in a letter of October 1892: 'God these opera texts! What a rotten business! It's a damned nuisance to be so dependent on others in this sort of thing. To do the text oneself would of course be easiest; I would do it too if I were able to discern the slightest talent in myself'.[36] By July 1894, Delius had in fact re-established contact with his former neighbour from Florida, Jutta Bell, with whom he was communicating on the libretto of a new opera, *The Magic Fountain*, which he described as a 'Lyric Drama in 3 Acts'. It was a fertile correspondence, for Bell now lived in Paris where she was studying singing with Mathilde Marchesi and was close at hand to discuss the opera's progress. Letters between them show that Bell participated substantially in the formation of the libretto even though she was not credited in the autograph manuscript. 'Only a woman could have conceived Watawa like you have done', he declared to Bell, 'therefore all your thoughts will be of great value'.[37]

In the same manner as *Irmelin*, Delius imagined a libretto that was simple in structure and message. 'I want to make the poem very *concise*', he told Bell, 'not a word too much philosophical or psychological – as the drama – as I have conceived it – requires'.[38] He had read widely round the subject matter of native Americans – Longfellow's *Hiawatha*, Fennimore Cooper's popular *The Last of the Mohicans* as well as Chateaubriand's highly influential romantic novels *Les Natchez* and *Atala* – but was seeking a plot in which there would be strong Wagnerian resonances. The setting for *The Magic Fountain* was sixteenth-century Florida when it was ruled by the Spanish. Delius, however, was keen that the Spanish element (though important as an underlying hostility between the native tribes of Florida and the Spaniards) should not be a significant focus for the opera. 'I want the Indian Characters to be the most important', he announced to Bell. 'The first Character is Watawa then comes Tamanünd the magician and Solana who in the end almost becomes an Indian himself and quite disappears – or loses his individuality in the last

---

[35] See *GB-Lbl* MS Mus 1745/2/10, f. 31.

[36] Letter from Sinding to Delius, 29 October 1892, *DLL1*, 68.

[37] Letter from Delius to Jutta Bell, 12 August 1894, *DLL1*, 90. That Delius was still working on the libretto for *The Magic Fountain* in August 1894 suggests that, while he may have sketched a good deal of the music, composition of the score probably took place in the latter part of that year.

[38] Letter from Delius to Jutta Bell, 12 August 1894, *DLL1*, 90.

act … He is no more Solana but the love of Watawa, who has not changed one iota since the beginning'.[39] An essential part of Delius's plot was based on the ancient idea of the 'Fountain of Youth' according to Gonzalo Fernández de Oviedo's *Historia general y natural de las Indias* of 1535 and Francisco López de Gómara's *Historia general de las Indias* of 1551, which Spanish explorer Juan Ponce de León was in search of when he landed in Florida in 1513. In lieu of the historical figure of de León, Delius's Solano is similarly fixated with his quest for the fountain, and, like Nils, his search for the Silver Stream and his belief in the fountain's prospect of salvation is all-consuming. It is this element of the plot, a monologue punctuated by the male chorus, which constitutes Act I Scene 1. On board ship (a parallel with Act I of *Tristan*), Solano's obsession, cursed by his exasperated crew, is frustrated by weeks of becalmed sea. Unafraid, and by the power of his will, he invokes a storm. This, in turn, raises the morale of his crew who sing joyously of the possibility of seeing land (their chorus in high spirits again has a strong parallel in the closing stages of Act I of *Tristan*). The violent tempest, as a substantial instrumental entr'acte, facilitates a scene change to a sandy beach on the coast of Florida after Solano's ship has been wrecked. Scene 2, markedly shorter and consisting of little more than 100 bars, functions essentially as a coda to Act I. After the wreck of his ship, Solano is discovered by a young native American princess, Watawa, last of the Jessamines massacred by the Spanish, who has sought refuge with the Seminoles of Florida.[40] The sight of Solano awakens in her sentiments of racial vengeance and of her reluctance to aid him (a further connection with Isolde's desire to wreak revenge on Tristan for a past wrong). While she retires into the grove, the task of rescuing Solano is left to the chief of the Seminole tribe, Wapanacki, and his tribesmen. The conciseness of Act I, which lasts no more than approximately thirty-five minutes, sets a precedent for Acts II and III, resulting in a work of little more than one hour and forty minutes in total.

Act II, marginally the longest of the three, is divided into two scenes framed by a prelude and postlude and divided by a choral ballet and interlude. A campfire provides the setting for Scene 1. Observed by Watawa, Solano declares to Wapanacki his wish to find the Fountain of Eternal Youth and that

---

[39] Letter from Delius to Jutta Bell, 29 July 1894, *DLL1*, 88–9. Self-evidently the name 'Solana' (which was eventually altered to 'Solano') was derived from Delius's former Floridian plantation, itself named after its first developers.

[40] Robert Threlfall has pointed out in his article 'A Note on Watawa – Last of Her Race', *DSJ* No. 118 (Winter/Spring 1996), 34–5, that the Seminoles were settlers to Florida in the early part of the eighteenth century and would not have been present at the time of Delius's *mise-en-scène*.

he is willing to pay gold for the knowledge. Wapanacki, aware of Unktahé's concealed sacred spring, advises him to seek counsel from Talum Hadjo, a Seer (rather than Delius's initial notion of Tamanünd the magician), who lives in the Everglades and promises to find him a guide. Leaving Solano to ponder, Wapanacki returns to his tent and enters a dialogue with Watawa. That Wapanacki might be tempted by the prospect of the white man's gold only serves to fortify Watawa's desire for retribution, so she offers to act as Solano's guide. Wapanacki, uneasy about Solano's defenceless predicament, and of the white man's growing prevalence in America, urges Watawa to reflect before she exacts revenge, counselling that she might consider asking for ransom. All these exchanges are punctuated by a choral ritornello for the tribesmen whose next role is in a choral ballet, a war dance. This, and a passage of orchestral music, provides sufficient opportunity for a scene change to the Everglades (what Delius termed a 'transformation scene') where Solano, enamoured with Watawa's beauty, rejoices in his quest. The scene transforms again to Talum Hadjo's abode where Watawa, affirming her desire to kill Solano, seeks advice from the seer alone. Like Wapanacki, Hadjo is disturbed by the depth and bitterness of Watawa's hate, but urges her to put away her poisoned knife since the waters of the fountain will kill Solano as he tastes them.[41] This is enough reassurance for Watawa as the scene changes once more to pastoral woodland. Here, as in Act I, this final section functions as a coda in which we are made aware, in the brief exchange between Solano and Watawa, that the emotional chemistry between them is transforming.

Act III, the shortest of the three (at just over half an hour), consists of only one scene and, in terms of its plot, was clearly conceived by Delius as a greater intensification of the trope of *Tristan*. The Prelude of Act III captures the conflicted emotions of Watawa: the opening passage provides us with a vision of the Magic Fountain (in a transparent Tristanesque B major), while the turbulent music which follows depicts Watawa's agitated frame of mind. She has fallen in love with fair Solano; she also cannot bring herself to slay him, yet she knows that it violates her solemn promise to her people not to do so. This struggle lies at the heart of her opening monologue. Tormented by Solano's amorous calls, she resolves to let the fountain decide his fate, but she cannot prevent herself from divulging her murderous intent to him. Undeterred by commands to leave her, Solano declares his undying love ('In thy will lies all my bliss') which initiates a love duet in another of Wagner's redemptive keys,

---

[41] Similar warnings can be found in *Zanoni*, although one wonders whether Delius had also become acquainted with the accursed blue flames of immortality in H. Rider Haggard's *She* of 1886–1887.

D flat major ('Every passion, that my soul entrances'), a tonality which frames the rest of the act. At the conclusion of the duet (where Solano and Watawa fall asleep in one another's arms), in returning to the music of the fountain, Delius very effectively incorporates a partsong for female ballet-chorus, a lullaby with orchestration of great delicacy ('Sleep and dream'), which provides a springboard for the lovers as they awaken to the sight of the fountain in a luminescent C major. While Solano is elated, Watawa is dismayed and reveals that, as Talum Hadjo warned, the waters are poison. Nevertheless, Solano beckons her follow him unto death, at which, shunning fear and in an act of selfless love, Watawa drinks and dies. Horrified by what has happened, Solano drinks and joins her in death.

The themes of revenge, forbidden love, and death as the highest expression of love, are all factors which link *The Magic Fountain* with *Tristan*, and the fact that Delius devotes his entire third act to the epiphany of mutual passion between Solano and Watawa also has a powerful Wagnerian resonance in their love duet, which has an unmistakable air of a proto-'Liebestod'. Delius's need to assimilate Wagner seems to have a greater urgency in his second opera, a fact confirmed in the more intensely chromatic language prevalent from b. 28 of the opening prelude (Example 3.3a). The new-found fluency with which Delius handles this apparatus gives greater élan to the monologues of Solano and Watawa in Acts I and III and to the splendid love music. This can be felt not only in the treatment of harmony and voice-leading but also in the flexibility of rhythm which, in moments of dramatic epiphany, particularly in Act III, has a new momentum. One senses too that, although Delius evidently shunned the notion of excessive 'psychologising', his principal characters have a greater complexity. This is especially the case with Watawa whose cankerous desire for revenge and of the struggle she feels to express her love for Solano (see bb. 83–162) reveals a conflicted character comparable with those of Brünnhilde, Isolde and Kundry. Moreover, in this fine soliloquy, it is evident that, concomitant with Delius's greater rhythmical freedom of his contrapuntal lines, the wider expressive vocal range of Watawa gives urgency to her emotional turmoil, one that is complemented by the irregular periodicity of her faltering phrase lengths.

Other features are also given a more coherent role within the operatic structure. Three closely related tonalities – E flat, A flat and D flat – function as the main pillars of the three acts: Act II is entirely framed by E flat, and the last part of Act III is dominated by D flat (the tonality underpinning the last parts of *Das Rheingold* and *Götterdämmerung*). The prevalence of these keys allows the luminescence of the fountain music in C major in Act III to stand out, and it is brilliantly summoned by the female partsong which Delius introduces to

Example 3.3a. *The Magic Fountain*, chromaticism of opening prelude.

accompany the ballet of water nymphs. Within the larger scale of tonal planning, Delius also exercised a much more integrated symphonic approach to each act. Except for the love duet in Act III, much of the opera is organised in a series of monologues. Solano's monologue, which dominates Act I, and Watawa's restive soliloquy in the first half of Act III abundantly illustrate Delius's ability to 'work out' his thematic ideas with a new organic thoroughness, one that has come about through the composer's greater confidence in handling chromatic voice-leading and the larger governing tonal framework of each scene and subordinate episodes. In particular, the love duet, with its own concentrated use of short thematic strands, demonstrates Delius's capacity to create a rich symphonic canvas from small kernels of material; indeed, the contraction and expansion of two prominent thematic strands (see Examples 3.3c and 3.3d) solely provide the basis of the love duet until the entry of the chorus (bb. 208–370). Solano's monologue also demonstrates how Delius had learned to use the chorus in the structural role of 'ritornello', a process which, while breaking up the monologue into a series of shorter sections, provides an adhesive to the larger cumulative scheme. This practice is repeated in Scene 1 of Act II where the wordless music of the native Americans (Example 3.3b) punctuates the exchange between Watawa, Solano and Wapanacki.

The chromatic language of *The Magic Fountain* and Delius's study of Wagner, even to the point of copying sections from Wagner's vocal scores to aid better acquaintance of process and harmonic syntax, has been mentioned above. However, it is evident from an examination of Delius's thematic ideas

Example 3.3b. *The Magic Fountain*, 'wordless music of the native Americans'.

in the opera that certain procedures were already becoming habitual. The tendency, in providing harmonic continuity, to deploy chromatically rising (Act I, b. 127–32) or falling (Act I, bb. 621–2) bass lines, is now much more conspicuous. Such falling bass lines are often manifested as a 'circle of fifths' sequence (Act I, bb. 289–90), and many functional perfect cadences are often substituted by augmented-sixth harmonies. In fact, it is not surprising that Delius identified this integral chromatic factor of his bass lines in borrowing the oboe melody and concomitant chromatic harmony unaltered from

'Daybreak' in *Florida*. Its inclusion in the opera is unforced and stylistically unobtrusive. The love of extended pedal points is exemplified in the 'magic fountain' leitmotiv (Example 3.3c), the opening music of Act I, the native-American music and much of the prelude and postlude of Act II. Delius had also clearly developed a liking for the colourful harmonic possibilities of parallel fourths which are used abundantly in the prelude to Act II, and with even greater deliberation to characterise the exotic nature of Talum Hadjo's leitmotiv in Act II (Example 3.3d). Hadjo's leitmotiv is but one of a rich matrix of thematic ideas in *The Magic Fountain* which sets it apart from the simpler content of *Irmelin*. Solano is characterised by several thematic elements in addition to the becalmed music and the 'phantom quest' of the opening of Act I. Besides the thematic borrowing from *Florida* which

Example 3.3c. *The Magic Fountain,* 'magic fountain' theme.

Example 3.3d. *The Magic Fountain,* 'Talum Hadjo' theme.

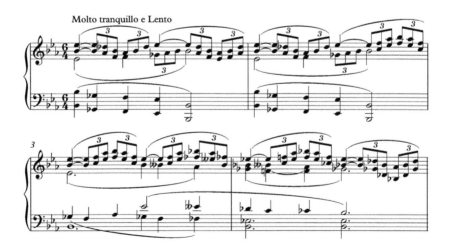

also locates him on the Florida coast (see Example 1.2b), Solano's dream of eternal pleasures (b. 152) and desire to search (b. 187) remain subordinate to the notion of 'Eternal Youth' (b. 133) which recurs climactically in Act II (b. 672) in association with his infatuation with Watawa (Example 3.3e). Watawa's own acknowledgement of her love for Solano occurs in the prelude to Act III (bb. 49–52), and from Solano's entry in Act III (from b. 287), when the couple admit their love for each other. Watawa also possesses a similar hierarchy of representative themes, most of which centre on her agitated monologue in Act III, but her principal idea, transparently diatonic, which occurs for the first time in Act I Scene 2, has all the typical hallmarks of Delius's style with its dominant pedal, pentatonic melody and the prevalence of the added sixth in the accompanying harmony (Example 3.3f). As Beecham mentioned, Delius later used this idea in the closing phase of *Sea Drift*.[42] The practice of borrowing material from earlier works was a practice Delius exercised without qualm throughout his life. There are numerous instances of borrowing thematic material from works which are virtually contiguous, but, as has been cited, it would take ten years before Watawa's theme would appear again. The music of Talum Hadjo's warning (Act II, bb. 615–19) bears a strong resemblance to the conclusion of the lyrical episode in *Légendes* (cf. bb. 114–88). *Florida* would also be an important source for several thematic ideas. In addition to recognising the opportunity to incorporate the 'Daybreak' theme in Act I, Delius must have seen, early on, the chance to recycle the 'very noisy nigger dance' (from 'Bei der Plantage') as a war dance

Example 3.3e. *The Magic Fountain*, 'eternal youth' theme.

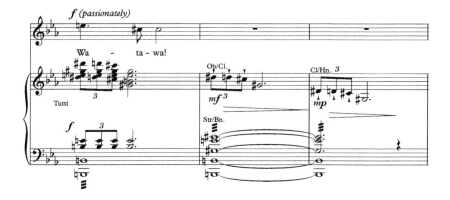

Example 3.3f. *The Magic Fountain*, Watawa's theme.

for the native Americans at the centre of Act II. More subtle, however, was the inclusion of the opening theme from 'Sonnenuntergang', which, with its extended pedal point, proved ideally suitable as tonicising material to close Act II (bb. 653–703).

For Delius *The Magic Fountain* was undoubtedly a major step forward from the impressive achievement of *Irmelin* in terms of its organisation, thematic involution and symphonic sophistication. The work exudes an increasing confidence which is palpable across the full technical array of operatic procedures, but is perhaps most greatly perceived in the handling of the orchestra where his sense of growing ambition can be measured by the scale of orchestral resources he brought to his score. Rather larger than the orchestra for *Irmelin* (which was itself larger than the standard romantic orchestra) and laid out with strangely old-fashioned origination, Delius's additional demands were for three trumpets, two harps, a generous contingent of percussion, triple woodwind and additional piccolo, cor anglais, bass clarinet and, more unusually for the first time, a contrabass sarrusophone, felt by some to be a more accommodating (and mellower) alternative to the contrabassoon across its whole range. Why Delius was persuaded to use this instrument may have been through his awareness of its use in contemporary French music of the time, notably in Saint-Saëns's *Les noces de Prométhée* (1867) and *Hymne à Victor Hugo* (1881) and, closer to the completion of Delius's opera, Massenet's *Esclarmonde* (1889) and symphonic poem *Visions* (1891). Such resources, symptomatic of the late nineteenth-century orchestra, also serve to accentuate the importance Delius attached to the orchestra in his operatic composition and of his desire to develop an orchestral technique, the highly nuanced palette of which such instrumental resources facilitated. As in *Irmelin*, significance of the orchestra cannot only be measured by its contrapuntal role, but also by the proportion of music assigned to the orchestra *without* voices. A fair amount of this is taken up with the preludial material to each act – the becalmed sea (Act I), the depiction of the Floridian wilderness (Act II) and the magic fountain (Act III). But Delius saw much opportunity in the entr'actes such as the eighty bars of storm music (effectively a melodrama) between Scenes 1 and 2 of Act I (bb. 524–65), and, at the beginning of Scene 2, another sixty bars depicting the Floridian coastline (bb. 514–74). The choral ballet occupies 100 bars of the entr'acte to Act II, and as Delius himself described in the score, for the 'transformation scene to the Everglades' at daybreak a quartet of horns (bb. 403–12) provides ten bars of 'nature' music evoking the dawn (an instrumentation he had already used in the last movement of *Florida*). While these sizeable passages contribute substantially to the colour of the opera, and leave us in no doubt of the *instrumental* dimension of Delius's operatic art, it is in the evocation of the more intangible element of the work – the suppressed feelings of love between Solano and Watawa – that Delius shows most subtlety. As mentioned above, Delius certainly aspired to this arena of wordless expression in *Irmelin*. Here, however, in Acts II and III of *The Magic Fountain*, the process is cumulative and perceptively increases by degrees. At the outset of Act II Scene 2, Delius has Solano and Watawa 'working their way through the thick undergrowth', but more suggestively Delius also remarks that 'Solano ever turns his face radiantly towards Watawa who notices him not'. Solano's enamourment is reflected in the passionate and opulently scored Strauss-like outburst for orchestra (bb. 413–26) immediately before Solano's entry ('And so towards eternal youth and love'), and his quest for love through discovery of the fountain is further emboldened by a second orchestral upsurge (bb. 453–71) before Talum Hadjo's appearance. This passage, which firmly tonicises E flat major, is also tonally linked with the postlude to Act II, where, replete with the borrowing from *Florida*, Delius quizzically reminds us of the couple's mutual attraction in his stage directions. With Watawa's entry in Act III, however, we are fully aware of her conflicted love for Solano, one made explicit in the *Tristanesque* climax of the prelude (bb. 42–54) and its reprise of the leitmotiv of 'Eternal Youth'.

Florent Schmitt made up a vocal score of the opera which is dated 1893,[43] but surviving correspondence with Jutta Bell confirms that it was not until

---

[43]   *GB*-Lbl MS Mus 1745/3/2.

at least July 1894 that Delius was satisfied with the libretto,[44] and even later 'the proper poetic form'.[45] The music and scoring was not finished, as Beecham suggested, until the summer of 1895,[46] a fact confirmed by a letter from Sinding: 'I was … most impressed that you have already produced a new opera'.[47] There were serious attempts to have it staged in Prague (which seemed initially promising) and, as he claimed to Jutta Bell, it was 'on the list at Weimar' under its conductor Bernhard Stavenhagen who was well known for directing new operatic works;[48] but it was withdrawn at the last minute by the composer who remained dissatisfied with the score.[49] The hope was also that, with the aid of a German translation and the title *Der Wunderborn*, it would be more readily accessible to German impresarios.[50] Delius was also advised to send the score to Mottl in Karlsruhe, and, on his way back from Norway in 1896, he visited the German conductor with the score and left it with him.[51] Mottl did not, however, take it up. In 1898 Delius returned to the score to make revisions and then showed the score to the young and receptive twenty-six-year-old German conductor Alfred Hertz, who conducted at Barmen-Elberfeld. 'I should like to pay you a *most genuine* compliment on your opera', Hertz wrote in August 1898. But Hertz felt unable to perform the opera because of the expense necessary for staging and changing of scenes. 'The Director hasn't a free enough hand to take so great a risk with the work of an author who is as yet unknown, & if it is *not* properly staged even a musically good performance can only do you harm'.[52] *The Magic Fountain* was, in the end, universally rejected for many reasons. Delius was unknown in Germany and, as Hertz related, impresarios saw his work as a potential

[44]   Letter from Delius to Jutta Bell, 29 July 1894, *DLL1*, 89.

[45]   Letter from Delius to Jutta Bell, 12 August 1894, *DLL1*, 90.

[46]   *TB*, 71.

[47]   Letter from Sinding to Delius, 25 June 1895, *DLL1*, 94.

[48]   Letter from Delius to Jutta Bell, 15 July 1896, *DLL1*, 108.

[49]   *CD*, 186–7.

[50]   Monochrome reproductions for the title page of the score were drafted for a German publisher as were the designs for costumes for *Der Wunderborn*, but publication did not materialise. The English words of Schmitt's vocal score are in Delius's hands. Besides the German translation, a French translation (*La source enchantée*), probably in Schmitt's hand, suggests that Delius may have contemplated offering it to a French opera company and even possibly a publisher.

[51]   Postcard from Delius to Jelka Rosen, 16 September 1896, *AU-Mgm*.

[52]   Letter from Alfred Hertz to Delius, 27 August 1898, *DLL1*, 129.

risk. One may also surmise that less than 100 minutes of music and a costly large orchestra failed to convince each of the opera companies of its economic viability, and the reality that Delius himself had no financial backing or potential sponsors – he had fallen out with his uncle Theodor who refused categorically to provide financial support for a performance of the opera – was a further obstacle.[53] In consequence, Delius shelved the work, and only by dint of including the preludial material of Act II in his next opera, did he ever get to hear any of the music of this considerable artistic achievement. But by then, his attentions were on the composition of his third operatic canvas, *Koanga*, which, in terms of dramatic challenges would eclipse those of his second opera. Though an attempt by Beecham to stage *The Magic Fountain* in 1953 came to nothing (and for which Fenby prepared a new vocal score), the opera was finally broadcast by the BBC and recorded under the direction of Norman del Mar in 1977, while there have been fully staged productions in Kiel (1997) and Glasgow (1999).

[53] *DLL1*, 92.

CHAPTER 4

A Stylistic Fulcrum: *Koanga, Danish Songs*, Piano Concerto, *Folkeraadet* (1895–1897)

The period of 1895 to 1897 saw Delius's musical style clearly undergoing some considerable change. It was also a time of some personal turbulence. Moving among the Parisian upper classes, and as part of the *Belle Époque*, he cut a dashing figure, was well dressed, charming and debonnaire. He was undoubtedly attractive to women and was something of a womaniser. Possessed of a strong sexual appetite, he was known to frequent Paris's notorious brothels, a habit in which he had possibly indulged since arriving in the French capital in 1888. The consequence of these pleasures was the infection of syphilis in 1895. In the knowledge that syphilis was incurable, and, until the advent of antibiotics, effective treatment was either extremely unpleasant or debilitating (the use of mercury was often worse than the disease itself), Delius must have been aware of the unpalatable prognosis, for sooner or later the tertiary phase of the disease would manifest itself. Yet, in the meantime, symptoms would disarmingly disappear while the disease lay dormant in the system and Delius, perhaps cynically, resolved to satisfy his carnal desires without care or hindrance.

Besides the ominous news about his health, the treatment which would have come at a price, Delius was short of money. There was even the possibility that he might have to sell his precious violin. Shunning the idea of obtaining a regular job, which might have brought some financial relief and stability, he preferred to rely on the allowance from his father. But news from Bradford was that Julius's business was in decline and that further income was by no means certain, nor from any other branches of the family such as his uncle or relatives in Germany. Similarly, the orange plantation Solana Grove brought no income, a situation Delius finally decided to resolve with a visit to Florida and Virginia in the first part of 1897. There were, however, sufficient funds for Delius to satisfy his continuing passion for Norway which he visited during the summer of 1896.

Frequenting Madame Charlotte's *crémerie* in Paris, he became better acquainted with Gauguin, the Swedish playwright Strindberg, whose enthusiasm for the writings of Nietzsche would prove highly influential on his imagination, and for a brief time in Norway, the novelist Knut Hamsun and the poet Vilhelm Krag. His association with the Molard 'salon' continued, he made new friendships with the Czech artist Mucha and the Norwegian playwright Gunnar Heiberg, and first met his wife-to-be, Jelka Rosen, in 1896. Even more so than Delius, Jelka came from a well-to-do German family. Well educated, she was the youngest child of Georg Rosen, an orientalist and diplomat, and was highly cultured through her musical mother, Serena Anna, the daughter of Ignaz Moscheles. Jelka's brother, a strong Anglophile, was also, for a short time in 1921, a senior member of the German government as foreign minister. All this would account for Jelka's remarkable powers as a linguist and translator, and her affinity for music, not least as an amateur singer. After her upbringing in Belgrade where her father was Consul General of the North German Confederation, she developed a skill for painting, which she decided to study in Paris under Gustave-Claude-Étienne Courtois at the Académie Colarossi, a private academy, in 1892, accompanied by her mother who had been recently widowed in 1891. Jelka enjoyed modest success as an artist, exhibiting at the Salon des Indépendants, one of the most influential locations for French modern art. She became acquainted with sculptors such as Auguste Rodin and Camille Claudel and painters such as Rousseau, Gauguin and Munch, and among her closest associates was Ida Gerhardi, a German Neo-Impressionist painter and a fellow student at the Académie. Jelka met Delius at the house of the Swedish sculptress Carolina Benedicks-Bruce in Paris on 16 January 1896; the friendship flourished through a mutual fondness for the songs of Grieg (which Jelka sang at Mme Bruce's 'salon'), the writings of Nietzsche and Jelka's delight in singing Delius's Norwegian songs.[1] Later that year Delius first became aware of the village of Grez-sur-Loing near Fontainebleau since it was where Jelka often painted, and it was here, thanks to Jelka's selfless devotion and support, that Delius eventually made this village along a tributary of the Seine his permanent dwelling. Through her Parisian home in Montparnasse, Jelka was also acquainted with various musical personalities in Paris, though it was not until she met Delius that she got to know the likes of Fauré, Ravel and Schmitt. But while he was cultivating his friendship with Jelka, he continued to womanise. He had a relationship with Marie Léonie Mortier de Trévise, Princesse de Cystria, wife of the Prince de Cystria Baron de Faucigny-Lucinge. An amateur singer, she organised salons in Paris which attracted Debussy, Ravel, and Déodat de

---

[1] Delius, J., 'Memories of Frederick Delius', in *DLL1*, 408–15 *passim*.

Sévérac, as well as Delius himself.[2] Another acquaintance of Delius was the bohemian American-born Winaretta Singer, Edmond Princesse de Polignac, who initiated her own musical salon in Paris in 1894. At their mansion in the Avenue Henri-Martin (today, Avenue Georges-Mandel), she encouraged not only the young Debussy and Ravel but also Chabrier, d'Indy and Fauré as well as English composers such as Ethel Smyth and Adela Madison. Delius was often to be seen there.

It was against this unsettling backdrop that Delius embarked on a new creative phase of composition which would prove crucial in the development of his harmonic language, the handling of form and of the genres in which he chose to work. All these brought fresh challenges and a range of solutions.

STUDIES IN A NEW MODERNISM

'I always have another work which I think of in the entr'acte of the present one'.[3] So it was with *Koanga* on which he began work barely before the ink was dry on *The Magic Fountain*. The latter was completed in June 1895; early drafts of *Koanga* were probably taking shape later that year, so that by February 1896 he was writing to Jutta Bell with the news that 'I am writing another opéra – *Please keep this quite to yourself* – I am taking the story of Bras-Coupé – in the Grandissimes. Read it and tell me what you think of it – I will send you shortly the libretto and no doubt you will be able to give me some help'.[4] Nevertheless, while his creative juices were flowing with a new stimulus, he would, with the help of friends and associates, keenly follow the progress of prospective performances of works already completed. This was, however, a slow and painful process. Even though Henrik Hennings, a Danish publisher and concert promoter, had initially shown some interest in *The Magic Fountain*, the rejection of the opera accentuated a period of considerable challenge to Delius. 'I am getting sick of all my futile efforts to get heard', he admitted to Jelka;[5] and in July he began to harbour doubts about having any of his works performed. 'I want to go & see Mottl in Karlsruhe', he told Jelka. 'Could you find out for me whether he will be in Karlsruhe at the end of August – or if not where he will

---

[2]   Guillot, P., *Déodat de Sévérac: la musique et les lettres* (Paris: L'Harmattan, 2000), 172.

[3]   Letter from Delius to Jutta Bell, 29 July 1894, *DLL1*, 88.

[4]   Letter from Delius to Jutta Bell, 9 February 1896, *DLL1*, 98.

[5]   Letter from Delius to Jelka Rosen, [end of June 1896], *AU-Mgm*.

be. I might go to him … I really did not smile when I said "all my efforts to be heard" For me they have been really efforts – at least what I consider efforts. But I know that I am not very gifted in such matters & that makes me doubt whether anything I may do in the "Effort" line will be successful'.[6]

The challenge to have opera, the most expensive of all musical commodities performed, was indeed a severe one and the properties of *The Magic Fountain*, with its brevity and large orchestral resources, only served to exacerbate Delius's predicament. But even with smaller items such as songs, where he had enjoyed some success hitherto, the response was mixed. A setting of Vilhelm Krag's 'Jeg havde en nyskaaren selrefløjte' ['I once had a newly cut willow pipe'] (from the author's play *Vester I blåfjeldet*), probably composed after he met the poet in Paris in 1893, remained unpublished, as did a setting of Jean Richepin's 'Nuages' (dated 1893). 'Jeg havde en nyskaaren selrefløjte' provides an interesting insight into the changing nature of Delius's approach to song. Krag's text tells of lost love combined with a stoicism in the final verse ('Sulio-sulio-lei!') which we have already met in the resigned responses of 'Heigh Ho!' in *Irmelin* and *The Magic Fountain*. Appositely Delius conveys these two contrasting demeanours in the persisting E flat minor which occupies much of the song's twenty-eight bars, yet, at the conclusion, it is G flat, which we heard fleetingly in the opening bars, which prevails. There is also a greater fluency in Delius's handling of the tonal structure. This is demonstrated by the detour to D major at the end of verse one and the eloquent recovery to E flat minor by way of the Neapolitan, E minor ('Jeg havde en fele med fine strænger'). And while one is aware of the Griegian lyricism, prevalent in the piano, the preponderant impression is one of Wagner, conveyed by the through-composed structure (now essentially normative in Delius songs), the declamatory, syllabic nature of the text, the constantly shifting chromatic harmony and the distinctly operatic outburst of the last line ('Men fanden er kanske saa venlig og ta den') with its orchestral gestures in the accompaniment. Indeed, this song appears to explore, in the form of a miniature study, those very stylistic and technical aspects Delius was learning to refine in *The Magic Fountain*, even to the point of the unresolved seventh harmonies (bb. 22–3) which played an important part in Act II of the opera (cf. the Prelude, bb. 91–6, and conclusion). Even more striking than 'Jeg havde en nyskaaren selrefløjte' is 'Nuages', unpublished during Delius's lifetime. A setting made in 1893 of a lyric by Richepin, Delius took the text from the author's gypsy novel *Miarka, la fille à l'ourse* of 1883, which he may have got to know through Alexandre

---

[6]   Letter from Delius to Jelka Rosen, 8 July 1896, *AU-Mgm*.

Georges' collection *Chansons de Miarka* (1888). Delius's setting, which only uses the first two verses of Richepin's verse, reflects the highly erotic sexual symbolism of the poetry. The declamatory vocal line, in which the repetitive sensual articulation of 'nuages' plays a central part, is illustrated throughout by a monorhythmic series of subtly shifting progressions. Delius's harmonic structure consists of a tetrachordal descending bass line from D flat (b. 1) to the 6/4 on A flat (b. 21) which is modulatory (though neither E nor F sharp achieve any form of cadence), and this is balanced from b. 21 by twenty bars of D flat tonicisation, coloured significantly by added-sixth harmony (see bb. 21, 23, 27, 29, 31, 36 and 38–40) in which Delius accomplishes final resolution by the falling of 6 to 5, a procedure he would use with increasing intensity in his later works.

A further two French songs drawing on the poetry of Paul Verlaine reveal an even greater degree of harmonic and structural experimentation. Although Heseltine gives the date of 1895 to both songs, it seems likely that Delius wrote them as a tribute to the poet who died in early January 1896. His setting of 'Il pleure dans mon coeur' was published as the fifth of *5 Chansons de F. Delius* by L. Grus Fils of Paris in 1896; the second setting, 'Le ciel est, par-dessus le toit', appeared in the short-lived literary journal *L'Aube* in July 1896 as 'Mélodie de F. Delius sur des vers de Paul Verlaine'. By 1895 Verlaine's reputation among his fellow poets and critics alike was at an all-time high, which may also have heightened Delius's awareness; and, according to Munch, he and Delius moved in circles which included Verlaine's close friends.[7] Through his acquaintance with Fauré, Delius would certainly have come across the settings of Verlaine in *Cinq melodies 'de Venise'* (1891), *La bonne chanson* (1894) and even 'Prison', completed in December 1894 though not published until 1896; his friend Schmitt had also set 'Il pleure dans mon coeur' as one of his *3 Mélodies* Op. 4 in 1895.

'Il pleure dans mon coeur', dedicated to André Messager, is an introspective lament which questions the nature of the poet's pain and longing. The essence of the song lies in the tonally ambivalent progressions of the first two bars, the first a 6/4 of D flat with an added sixth, the second a B flat minor triad with added seventh. This is complemented by an upper melodic fragment of B flat, A flat and F, though beginning with an appoggiatura of C. For the first six bars of the song, these two progressions act as an ostinato in which the tonality of the song is not permitted to settle (either in a putative D flat major or a putative B flat minor), and the climax of the verse, where we hear the melodic

7 *DN*, 119.

fragment again, anticipates a modulation to E flat, only for Delius to give us a sensuous 'sound moment' in the form of an unresolved dominant ninth of A flat. For the second verse, Delius deftly reverses the order of the two harmonies: B flat appears to establish itself in the first four bars but this yields to a 6/4 of D flat, subtly varied by the minor mode as if to accentuate the sad song of the rain ('Ô le chant de la pluie'). D flat minor persists throughout the third verse and the beginning of the fourth, as if to mirror Verlaine's 'la pire peine'. For the emotional crisis, however, the 'environment' of D flat and B flat is abandoned in favour of B minor and B major which, by dint of this entirely new tonality, throws the irony of Verlaine's text ('sans amour et sans haine') into relief. At the climactic 6/4 ('Pour-*quoi*') where Delius reaches the highest point of the vocal tessitura, the initial melodic fragment is heard again (bb. 29–30), typically up a semitone from its initial statement in bb. 1–2, but the inward, irrational pain so central to the poem is emphatically symbolised by the return of the ostinato material and by the quizzical, open-ended conclusion on the B flat minor triad.

Rueful of a wasted youth, Verlaine's four four-line verses in 'Le ciel est, par-dessus le toit' were treated by Delius as two eight-line units. At the outset of the song, B flat minor is strongly insinuated in the first four bars (as if, perhaps, to link it with the end of the first song). A chromatically descending bass line (bb. 5–6) sequentially takes us to a contrasting lyrical passage in 12/8 which underpins the end of Delius's first verse ('Un oiseau, sur l'arbre qu'on voit, Chante sa plainte'). Here Delius is tonally ambivalent. After arriving at E flat minor (b. 7), Delius settles on a 6/4 of G flat major for his last line of text. However, with more insistent repetition, the bass shifts down to a 6/4 of E flat major which becomes an extended pedal point (thoroughly Delian with its syncopation), straddling verses one and two. The last part of verse two differs markedly between the version Delius published in 1896 and the one which appeared as part of the *Deux Mélodies* published by Tischer & Jagenberg in 1910.[8] Delius's original conception was shorter and more lyrical in its vocal material. Moreover, the chromatically descending bass line, with a much brisker harmonic rhythm, reaches a climax as it arrives at the dominant of D flat major ('de ta jeunesse') and the song ends wistfully in that

---

[8] Delius's decision to revise 'Le ciel' can be observed in *GB-Lbl* MS Mus 1745/2/6 where the last two systems are crossed through in pencil and a bifolium of the revised ending in a copyist's hand pasted to the back of the second page. See also the *Stichvorlag* in *GB-Lbl* MS Mus 1745/4/1 and also 1745/1/36, f. 47r. Beecham's reference to 'Le ciel' is to the later version (*TB*, 83) as also is Holland's: *The Songs of Delius* (London: Oxford University Press, 1951), 38–9.

Example 4.1. 'Le ciel est, par-dessus le toit', conclusion of the original version.

key with a reference to the melodic fragment stated at the end of verse one (Example 4.1).

In the revised version, Delius's vocal delivery is much more declamatory and the harmonic rhythm merely one chord per bar. Moreover, as a parallel to bb. 5–6 of the first verse, the latter part of Delius's second verse is a more extended descending bass from F to C flat (bb. 18–24) with a characteristic series of slow-moving chromatic seventh harmonies (many of them variations on the augmented-sixth configuration). This leads, as before, to a recurrence of the 12/8 thematic idea ('De ta jeunesse?') in G flat, in which the song more cathartically concludes. Delius's structure (in both versions) reveals a fascinating two-part construction in which each of his eight-line verses, goal-directed towards its 12/8 thematic material, begins obliquely. The design is made that much more subtle by the lack of tonicisation Delius provides for the first verse where the unresolved dominant of G flat is deflected by the shift away to E flat, a move which subsequently provides the tangential beginning of the second verse. Although Delius apparently considered these two songs best with the piano accompaniment,[9] Heseltine clearly perceived that the piano parts more readily suggested an orchestral sensibility (a tendency prevalent in many of Delius's later songs) and orchestrated them for a performance at the Grafton Galleries under Beecham on 25 January 1915.

The experimental nature of the songs was also reflected in two orchestral works that occupied Delius's attention while he was composing *Koanga*. The first of these, the Fantasia or Fantasy-Overture *Over the Hills and Far Away* (or in its German version *Über die Berge in der Ferne*), was written sometime between 1893 and 1897.[10] After its completion, Delius hoped to have it played at the Lamoureux Concerts under Camille Chevillard,[11] but this did not materialise, the latter date probably corresponding to its first performance at Elberfeld under Hans Haym on 13 November 1897. Unpublished during Delius's lifetime (it was not published until 1950), it received at least two other performances, both in London, the first under Alfred Hertz in 1899, and later under Thomas Beecham in 1908. Beecham, who described the work as a 'tone poem', admired the work for its 'combination of serene content and lively impulse' which 'rarely contrive to come together' in his music.[12] Describing the work as a loosely shaped structure, Max Chop believed it reflected something of Delius's memory of Yorkshire as well as Norway.[13]

---

[9]   Letter from Jelka Delius to Philip Heseltine, 6 September 1929, *FDPW*, 494.

[10] Literary sources differ widely about the date of this work. *MCh* states that it was completed in 1893, *FDPW* in 1895, Fenby's copy of the manuscript, now in *US-Stu* is dated 1897, while in *TB* it was completed in 1897 (p. 93).

[11] See letter from Delius to Jelka Rosen, 25 January 1898, *DLL1*, 126.

[12] *TB*, 93.

[13] Chop, M., 'Frederick Delius', in Jones, P. (ed.), *The Collected Writings of the German Musicologist Max Chop on the Composer Frederick Delius* (Lewiston, NY, Queenston, ON and Lampeter: Edwin Mellen Press, 2002), 82–3. One wonders

The substitution of 'anti-symphonic' for 'loose' would be a more appropriate description of Delius's overture, not least since the artistic decision he had opted to take was in marked distinction to that of his friend Sinding who informed him of the performance of his Symphony in D minor in Berlin under Weingartner.[14] *Over the Hills and Far Away* relies more quintessentially on the contrast of thematic episodes in an arch form (ABCBA). Delius's first paragraph (A) is similarly constructed out of three divergent musical ideas underpinned by C major. Horn calls at the opening are supported by a pedal point on E. This forms a passing polarity in E minor (bb. 7–10) confirmed by the cadential melodic figure in the solo horn (Example 4.2a). With the repeat of the material from b. 11, the pull towards E minor is further accentuated through the augmented sixth (bb. 13–16). E minor, what is more, persists thereafter to act as a dominant to a secondary theme in A major. Here Delius falls back on one of his favourite Griegian models, a (drone) pedal point with contrapuntal detail above. In this instance, however, the behaviour of Delius's upper voices is conspicuous for its deliberate avoidance of resolution (until b. 39), particularly through use of the added-sixth and added-ninth dissonances which figure prominently (Example 4.2b) as well as the colouring of lower chromatic auxiliaries (E sharp and D sharp). This premonition of a truly Delian sound (which looks forward to *A Village Romeo and Juliet*) is followed by a march theme in A minor more redolent of an earlier style (such as the 'Marche Caprice'), though intimations of *Die Meistersinger*, heard as Delius restores C major in b. 59 (the key of Wagner's *Vorspiel* to Act I), remind us of the composer's continuing fixation with Wagner's music. A weaker contrasting section (B) sets out in D minor though C major is soon restored together with horn calls reminiscent of *Paa Vidderne*. The central paragraph (C) is differentiated by its variation structure, a (quasi-folk) theme in A major and two variations in E.[15] Aping Grieg's method of dense harmonic elaboration, Delius brings an increasingly chromatic resource to his harmonisation of the diatonic melody. Moreover, with each variation

---

whether, in choosing the title of his overture, Delius was making conspicuous reference to the seventeenth-century English folksong 'Over the hills and far away', a reference which would chime with Chop's comparison with Yorkshire. Boyle has also suggested that it may have been suggested by W. E. Henley's poem in *The Song of Swords and Other Verses* (*DN*, 128).

[14] Letter from Sinding to Delius, 1 September 1895, *DLL1*, 95.

[15] Philip Jones has a suggested the theme's similarity with the American Civil War song 'Marching through Georgia'; see Banfield, S. (ed.), *The Fourth Delius Festival*, 8–14 March 1982, University of Keele, 1982, 6.

the harmonisation changes, a technique common to the Norwegian's string arrangements of his songs such as 'Hjerteår' Op. 34 No. 1 or even more so in 'I folketonestil' Op. 63 No. 3, published in 1895 at much the same time as Delius's work was being composed). Something of this approach was latent in the early *Rhapsodische Variationen*, especially the variation in C sharp minor, but here Delius's stylistic intentions are much clearer and deliberate. The resumption of the arch structure has the effect of throwing the central variation structure into relief, and it is clear from the tonal behaviour of the B section that Delius intended to use it as a transition back to C major. Bars 183– 92 reveal that he wished to do this obliquely through A minor (accentuating the prevalence of both keys at the beginning of the work), though Beecham (rightly) considered this an awkward corner and cut the offending bars (*pace* his 1936 recording). As if to emphasise the 'anti-symphonic' nature of the overture, much of the recapitulation of section A is a (disappointing) verbatim repeat save for the reference to the variation theme in the coda. One feature, however, stands out, and that is Delius's serene reorchestration of the passage in A major (bb. 205–24), the numinous solo horn being truly prophetic of so many rapt moments in the composer's later orchestral scores.

A second orchestral work, dated 1896 by the composer and also left unpublished during his lifetime, was *Appalachia: American Rhapsody for Orchestra*. There is evidence among undated surviving sketches that Delius

Example 4.2a. *Over the Hills and Far Away*, opening theme.

Example 4.2b. *Over the Hills and Far Away*, secondary theme, bb. 27–39.

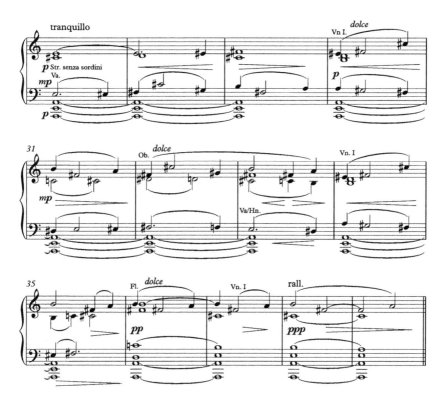

continued to be haunted by the memories of Florida and entertained notions of writing another work inspired by the American south.[16] It was not until the end of 1896, however, that he announced to Jutta Bell that he had completed an 'American Rhapsody' for orchestra. Its American subject may have been provoked by the national flavour of *Koanga* on which he was still working, but the more contemporary tone of the thematic material used in the work suggests that it reflected Delius's own impressions of a country still smarting from the tragedy of its bloody civil war. Delius hoped that the work might be performed in Bradford, perhaps by the Hallé Orchestra who were visitors to the city.[17]

---

16 Several of the sketches in *GB-Lbl* MS Mus 1745/2/10 reveal Delius's continued interest in this source of inspiration.

17 Letter from Delius to Jutta Bell, [23? December 1896], *DLL1*, 109.

Yet, renewing his pessimism about the fate of his works in the concert hall, he despondently recognised that 'the bigger & better orchestras of England are unreachable for me at present and I have neither wish nor energy enough to go kicking around the ante chambers of well known Conductors'.[18] It is perhaps not surprising that Delius held the work back from publication: its ternary form, consisting of an atmospheric prelude and postlude (which share the same material) and a central though truncated episode of variations, fails to cohere nor does it achieve a satisfactory climax. Nevertheless, it is evident that he was seeking new solutions to the problem of formal cohesion in the same manner as the experiment of *Over the Hills and Far Away*. Delius based his variations on a tune he had heard in Florida and later in Danville, sometimes used as a hymn in negro churches,[19] though the final result may well have been a synthetic creation.[20] Having established this theme in D flat (bb. 42–97), Delius sets out in his first variation (in F minor and a slower tempo) with the same process of dense chromatic harmonisation as one finds in *Over the Hills*, though here the multiple descending lines of Delius's chromatic counterpoint begin to assume a new rationale and syntax which, one suspects, may have owed something to Grieg's later experiments in the 1890s. It is notable that Grieg's *19 norske folkeviser* Op. 66 of 1896–1897 should have been composed and published at exactly the same time as Delius was composing the *American Rhapsody* and *Koanga*. These short pieces for piano reveal a new phase of Grieg's exploration of chromatic harmony, with particular emphasis on the understanding, function and extended potential of augmented-sixth progressions, as well as the use of seventh, ninth and thirteenth chords. In a sketch such as 'Siri Dale Visen' Op. 66 No. 4, which begins modally and conventionally enough, Grieg's gradual intensification of the harmony concludes with a fascinating structural bifurcation of the diatonic melody and the chromatic harmony beneath (Example 4.3). Carl Dahlhaus described this as 'the rift between melody and harmony' in which 'melodic pitches so straightforward as to have ineradicable

---

[18] Ibid., 109–10.

[19] Randel, W., 'Frederick Delius in America', *The Virginia Magazine of History and Biography*, Vol. 79 No. 3 (July 1971), 361, reprinted in Redwood, C. (ed.), *A Delius Companion* (London: John Calder, 1980 [1976]).

[20] Sketches featuring this theme, for 'A Southern Night', reveal that Delius intended it to be central to his earliest concepts of *Appalachia* (see *GB-Lbl* MS Mus 1745/2/13/5, ff. 1–2). Its key, D flat, also confirms its kinship with *Koanga*. There are also indications that he was sketching other 'southern' pieces such as a 'Nigger Rhapsody' (f. 3) which included the banjo, or banjo-like music and a Scherzo 'Negro Games' (f. 18).

tonal implications are forced into almost bizarre nonfunctional roles in the harmony'.[21] It is where tonal (or even modal melodies) collide with harmonic progressions that are increasingly chromatic but where cohesion is retained by the tonal relationship and structure of the *melody*. At the same time its tonal context is constantly forced into situations of 'non-functional' harmony, where the behaviour of the chords begins to assume a new structural rationale determined by the contrapuntal movement of the voices.[22] It is this incipient process we see essayed in the variations of the *American Rhapsody*, though, tantalisingly, Delius decided not to develop this technique any further in this work. Instead, a third variation is combined with 'Yankie doodle' and 'Dixie', tunes undeniably American in flavour but which render the former variation structure irrelevant (and no further reference to them or the negro theme is made in the work). One suspects that Delius realised that the *American Rhapsody* was flawed, and, wisely, sought to rework some of the material at a later date in *Appalachia* of 1902–1903, a much more cohesively constructed work based on variation form.

Example 4.3. Edvard Grieg, *19 norske folkeviser*
Op. 66 No. 4, 'Siri Dale Visen', conclusion.

---

[21] Dahlhaus, C., *Nineteenth-Century Music*, trans. Bradford Robinson, J. (Berkeley, CA: University of California Press, 1989), 310.

[22] Further examples can be seen in 'En Kong hersked i Österland' Op. 66 No. 3, 'Det var i min Ungdom' Op. 66 No. 5, the end of 'Ranveig' Op. 66 No. 12 and 'Bådnlåt' Op. 66 No. 15.

KOANGA: A SLAVE OPERA

It was to Jutta Bell that Delius made known in July 1894 his desire to write three operas: 'One on the Indians, one on the Gypsies and one on the Negroes & quadroons'.[23] His 'Indian' opera had been achieved with *The Magic Fountain*, and, in time, he would undertake an opera with a 'gypsy' element; but by February 1896 he had already sketched the first act of *Koanga* with a plot taken from an episode in George Washington Cable's lengthy novel *The Grandissimes: A Story of Creole Life*, published in America in 1880. It was a significant choice of literature. Cable was well known in American literary circles for his work on the multi-racial and multi-cultural aspects of New Orleans and wider Louisiana where he lived until 1885. At the very time when Delius was in Florida in the mid 1880s, Cable felt forced to leave the South owing to his advocacy of racial equality and opposition to the Jim Crow laws that promoted segregation. For many southerners he was the cause of much white resentment and the source of bitter controversy, though during his 1898 visit to England, where the abolition of slavery was some six decades old, Cable proved something of a celebrity.[24] On the matter of slavery, segregation and oppression of the negroes, however, Delius is frustratingly silent. On the politics of race, the civil war, of slavery, emancipation and the rights of the negro, he left no comment, and while he retained cordial relations with the negroes on his plantation, the difference in social class always remained a factor. As Grainger pointed out, 'his interest was purely that of an onlooker – a highly sympathetic onlooker, but merely an onlooker never the less'.[25]

In truth what Delius was seeking in *Koanga* was another novel source of colour and fantasy consistent with the unusual plots and subject matter of his two previous operas. 'I am working on a work which I believe will be *unique* in its way', he told Jutta Bell.[26] No-one hitherto had considered the possibility of staging a work about the plight of slaves in the American south, and it would be some ten years before the completion of Scott Joplin's *Treemonisha* (1911), which did not receive its first public hearing until 1972, and forty years before

---

[23]   Letter from Delius to Jutta Bell, 29 July 1894, *DLL1*, 88.

[24]   Randel, W., '*Koanga* and its Libretto', *Music & Letters*, Vol. 52 No. 2 (April 1971), 152.

[25]   See Hubert Foss's revision of Heseltine's *Frederick Delius* (London: The Bodley Head, 1952), 171. See also Grainger, P., 'About Delius', in Gillies, M. and Clunies Ross, B. (eds), *Grainger on Music* (Oxford: Oxford University Press, 1999), 361.

[26]   Letter from Delius to Jutta Bell, 15 July 1896, *DLL1*, 108.

George Gershwin would put *Porgy and Bess* (based on the play *Porgy* by Dorothy Heyward and DuBose Heyward) on the Boston stage in September 1935. *Koanga* also offered Delius the additional chance to reignite his passion for the negro music he had heard in the romantic tropical setting of Florida; furthermore, the chorus of the opera would consist entirely of slaves, for which there would be much opportunity for the quotation of negro melody, for the genre of partsong and the application of those stylistic principles of harmony and melody incipiently essayed in *Over the Hills and Far Away* and the *American Rhapsody*. Delius was, however, conscious that his opera should also fulfil his preoccupation with the Tristanesque paradigms of 'forbidden love' and 'love in death', the former of which had been realised in *Irmelin* and both in *The Magic Fountain*, so there would be the need of considerable adaptation of Cable's plot if anything was to come of his new operatic venture.

Delius identified possibilities for the enactment of these dramatic elements in chapters 29 and 30 of Cable's *Grandissimes* which focus specifically on the arrival of Mioko-Koanga (an African prince of the Jaloff race) on Don José Martinez's plantation along the Mississippi in Louisiana. In Cable's novel, Koanga, aware of his royal heritage, refuses to work on the plantation and attempts to escape. When he is brought before Martinez, no-one can understand his Jaloff tongue, so Palmyra, a quadroon and in love with Honoré, a creole member of the Grandissime family, is asked to interpret. Koanga at once falls in love with her and wants to marry her. Palmyra, while admiring Koanga, has no desire for marriage. She tries to reason with Koanga but fails. Later, at a wedding on the plantation, Koanga, blind drunk, fells Martinez to the ground, curses the lands of the Grandissimes, and flees into the swamps. The voodoo curse brings about crop failure and fever. Martinez, sick with the fever, implores Koanga to lift the curse, but the Jaloff prince refuses, in spite of Palmyra's entreaties, and leaves. Koanga is then apprehended, flogged, hamstrung, and has his ears cut off (a particularly gruesome punishment which strained the sympathy of Cable's publishers), but still he maintains the curse unmoved by Martinez's death. Only the sight of Martinez's baby son persuades him to relent, after which, seeing a vision of Africa, he dies.

Delius was fully aware of the need to alter Cable's story. In February 1896, having fully sketched Act I, he was uncertain about how the opera should conclude. 'I must change the real end', he told Jutta Bell; 'Make Bras Coupé kill himself & Palmyre or something of that sort'.[27] By 25 February he had sketched

---

[27] Letter from Delius to Jutta Bell, 9 February 1896, *DLL1*, 98.

the entire libretto. As he informed Bell, to whom he evidently owed the first phase of *Koanga*: 'I wrote the music and the words at the same time'.[28] To satisfy Delius's requirements, the main changes involved Don José's overseer, Simon Perez, who has designs on marrying Palmyra. Although Palmyra is not required to translate for Koanga (who has somehow acquired a knowledge of English), Martinez, who notices how enamoured Koanga is with Palmyra, suggests marriage as a way of bringing him round. In Act II this prospect alarms Perez and Martinez's wife, Clotilda, who object on the grounds that Palmyra, baptised a Christian, cannot marry a pagan; Perez, on the other hand, hopes that Honoré will save the day by returning from his travels. Koanga (who has now been described as being from Dahomey, where Voodoo was practised) reiterates his vows and devotion. Yet Palmyra, deeply impressed by Koanga's defiance and dignity, begins to identify with his plight and position (rather than act as an accomplice to his downfall). Martinez arrives with the priest for the wedding, but Clotilda objects that the priest is too drunk for the proceedings. By this time Palmyra has set her heart on Koanga and slips away. Koanga, in his attempt to find her, strikes down the whip-bearing Martinez and utters curse after curse over his body. He then escapes into the swamps calling on the protection of his Voodoo religion. Using this set of circumstances, Delius attempted to lay the ground for his scenario of forbidden love and the prospect of death by suicide in the final act.

If the dramatic components of Acts I and II were not problematic enough, then the denouement of Act III is the least satisfactory part of Delius's scheme in terms of dramatic cohesion and continuity. In the swamps, Koanga's invocation of the Voodoo gods (in the company of various slaves and a Voodoo priest) allows him to see the destruction caused by his curse on the Martinez plantation, but which also inadvertently includes the slaves and Palmyra. On hearing Palmyra's voice, he withdraws his curses. In Scene 2, Martinez, who appears unaffected by the famine and fever, chides his overseer for giving credence to Voodoo, and promises to hunt down Koanga. A sick Palmyra, wondering where her former lover Honoré is, rejects the advances of Perez who, trying to flee, is killed by Koanga Yet, Koanga is soon apprehended by Martinez's horsemen, flogged and left to die before Palmyra. This experience is so horrifying to her that she renounces her Christian faith (an act with which Delius would have had some sympathy), embraces Voodoo and takes her own life.

---

[28] Letter from Delius to Jutta Bell, 25 February 1896, *DLL1*, 99.

That Delius felt uncomfortable about his abilities to construct a satisfactory libretto is evident from his correspondence with Bell. He was also undecided about the larger structure of the opera and needed advice:

> I find I must really get some one to work with me – My literature is not on a level with my music – And I believe in Colaboration [*sic*] a greater effect may be attained – Please advise me – As you see I have not decided about the end Shall I make a 3rd Act or only the 2 – You see the 2nd Act is much shorter and might have 2 parts. I thought of an epilogue like the prologue ie. bringing the scene back to the old negro – his tale now finished – I want a finale – Have you an idea? a dramatic one? Do you think you have time to help me in this? I think the music is a success – It is more of an opera than the last one – with quartetts Trios, quintettes & chorus … I am employing the Banjo in my orchester. The effect will be strange.[29]

Instead of continuing with Bell, who was a distance away in London, Delius opted to consult Keary with whom he had briefly discussed *Irmelin*. Keary also lived at Bourron, not far from Grez-sur-Loing, which was logistically convenient in his growing friendship with Jelka.[30] Staying at a local hotel in Bourron, he wrote to Jelka: 'The weather here is delightful. Keary and myself go for long walks every day Yesterday we went to Barbizon. We passed by Grez the other day. Not a soul there. But we had a delightful walk across the fields – and also saw the first swallows'.[31] Yet how much Keary actually assisted with the production of the libretto is uncertain. As Jelka reminds us, '[Delius] was not enthusiastic about Keary's words either. They were 'ungeschickt' and 'mal habile' in the extreme, and in the more lyrical parts rather highflown, and the two kinds of words never fitting together. However Fred was not very critical as he was so eager to get to work. He destroyed the worst of the stilted words and got Keary who was a charming man and friend, to make some more'.[32] By July, when Delius was spending much time in Valdres in Norway, Keary had sent on Act II.[33] At that time he clearly valued Keary's insights, and by December 1896, when he was staying with his family in Bradford over

---

[29] Letter from Delius to Jutta Bell, 25 February 1896, *DLL1*, 99.

[30] See Delius, J., 'Memories of Frederick Delius', in *DLL1*, 410.

[31] Letter from Delius to Jelka Rosen, 11 April 1896, *AU-Mgm*.

[32] Delius, J., 'Memories of Frederick Delius', in *DLL1*, 410–11.

[33] Letter from Delius to Jelka Rosen, 8 July 1896, *DLL1*, 107.

Christmas, he was evidently satisfied with the outcome of their collaboration since he was already well advanced with the orchestration: 'It ought to be wonderfully effective & original and is full of color & contrast I think I told you that C. F. Keary wrote the libretto', he told Bell; 'we worked together & the result is all that I could wish'.[34]

Koanga was completed by early 1897 and Delius clearly entertained notions of having it given in London.[35] However, through his connections with the composer Adela Maddison, who lived in Paris, the opera, in this earliest version, was first played privately at the Maddison's Parisian residence in the presence of Fauré, 'the best young french musicians' and the Prince and Princess de Polignac in March 1899.[36] By this time Delius had been making detailed arrangements for his renowned London concert on 30 May 1899 at St James's Hall at which the finale to Act I, the whole of Act II and the Prelude to Act III were given. It was the first time he would hear any of his operatic music in live performance.

It is evident from his first dealings with Bell that Delius had a fair idea of the scope of *Koanga's* larger structure. His suggestions of a prologue and epilogue were adopted and his more ambitious allusion to ensemble work for the soloists, in which he allowed himself a richer and more numerous *dramatis personae*, eventually took form in a three-act design much like those of *Irmelin* and *The Magic Fountain*. While this was a more ambitious undertaking, he did not abandon the terseness of the earlier operas since *Koanga* is also an opera of less than two hours. The first two acts are little more than half an hour each, and but for the fact that Delius opted to insert an additional monologue for Palmyra in Act II for the performance at Elberfeld in 1904, Act II would have been appreciably shorter; Act III, in which Delius envisaged a climactic finale, is just over fifty minutes in length. Such brevity would undoubtedly have been a challenge to any opera impresario of the time. Nevertheless, Delius brought to *Koanga* a number of innovations which he had not explored in his other operatic essays. The unique role of Koanga is for a high baritone whose tessitura extends to a high A flat (perhaps more in the manner of the 'Verdi baritone'). Such unusual demands for the principal soloist inevitably created difficulties for its performance since singers in this range were not easy to come by. Ensemble and chorus also

---

[34] Letter from Delius to Jutta Bell, [23?] December 1896, *DLL1*, 109.

[35] Letter from Delius to Jutta Bell, 15 July 1896, *DLL1*, 108.

[36] Letter from Delius to Jelka Rosen, [March 1899], *DLL1*, 149.

play an extensive role. This can be observed in the Prologue whose tonally oblique opening provides an effective accompaniment to the action of the girls as they appear on the verandah of the plantation. Here, ephemerally, Delius provides us with a taste of G flat major, an important tonal reference to the character of Koanga in the opera, though it passes soon enough as the prologue settles into the first of many partsongs ('Look how the shadows of night are falling') which support the larger narrative of the work. The intense chromaticism of the Prologue, which shows Delius building on his enthusiastic assimilation of Wagner's symphonic development of leitmotiv in *The Magic Fountain*, sets a firm precedent for the much of the solo material in the rest of the opera. A major contrasting feature, however, is the use made of *diatonic* negro melodies which imbue *Koanga* with a unique American flavour, somewhat before the sounds of this music emerge incipiently in the music of George Whitefield-Chadwick (especially his *Symphonic Sketches* of 1895–1904) and Samuel Coleridge-Taylor, and, of course, well before such figures as Gershwin.

The Prologue, which carefully concludes in C major, a tonality signalled by Uncle Joe's mention of Koanga and Palmyra, provides a smooth dominant transition to the prelude of Act I in F. Here Delius introduces the first of his synthetic negro melodies. Like the one he introduced in the *American Rhapsody*, he probably retained it from his days in Danville. 'Come out, niggers, come out to cut the waving cane' (Example 4.4a), which he assigned to the tune, occupies the entire prelude in the form of a theme and variations (much in the same manner as the shorter model of the *American Rhapsody*). Imaginatively scored for divided cellos and muted upper strings, the melody begins in transparent diatonic apparel, but towards the final cadence of the melody, Delius by now almost instinctively brings a denser, more chromatic set of progressions into play. Much of this harmony remains functional, but in the first variation (like the variations we see in the *American Rhapsody*), the bifurcation between the diatonic melody and the chromatic bass line is clearly observable. A third variation is set in the subdominant (a practice copied in the *American Rhapsody*) which also has an elaborate set of cadential progressions, while the third variation, more truncated, shifts between the dominants of B flat minor and D flat major (a practice he probably drew from the opening of 'Il pleure dans mon coeur' which makes use of the same two tonalities in juxtaposition) which foreshadows the tonal dualism of Palmyra's opening monologue ('Ah, I cannot sleep'). Delius's use of the negro melody in the prelude to Act I was intended to establish an important facet of the opera's sound-world. 'I am getting all the Southern flavour of the music', he informed Bell, and in the same letter he added 'I am keeping the whole in the character of the negro melody'.[37] In making these two statements, Delius was undoubtedly mindful that the stylistic nature of *Koanga* would fluctuate between the largely diatonic world of the negro choruses which punctuates much of Acts I and II and the chromatic Wagnerian solo material. An examination of the first part of Act I, for example, reveals the scheme shown in Table 4.1.

Example 4.4a. *Koanga*, Prelude to Act I, negro melody 'Come out, niggers, come out to cut the waving cane'.

37   Letter from Delius to Jutta Bell, 9 February 1896, *DLL1*, 98.

Table 4.1. *Koanga*, first part of Act I, structural overview.

Section	Thematic/textual content	Key
Orchestral prelude	Negro melody (1) 'O Lawd, I'm goin' away'	F major/Bb major
Palmyra's aria	'Ah, I cannot sleep'	Bb minor/Db major
Perez	'Get out of bed you lazy lot'	Db major
Negro chorus (a6)	'It's dawn'	Bb minor
Negro chorus	Negro melody (1) 'O Lawd, I'm goin' away'	F major
Palmyra/Perez	'Ah, there's Palmyra'	Tonally fluid
Negro chorus (a6)	Negro melody (1) 'O Lawd, I'm goin' away'	Bb major
Palmyra/Perez	'Pale as moonlight your brow'	Tonally fluid
Perez and negro chorus (TTBB)	Negro melody (2) 'John say you got to reap where you sow'	C major
Martinez/Perez	'Well, what's the plan today'	Tonally fluid
Perez and negro chorus (TTBB)	Negro melody (2) 'John say you got to reap where you sow'	C major

It is at this strategic point, having set the scene, that Delius develops the drama by bringing Koanga forward in chains for his first monologue ('O Voodoo Manian'), replete with his own leitmotiv. This material becomes the focus of a much more extended declamatory section in which, more unusually, the four characters of Palmyra, Perez, Martinez and Koanga, initially in dialogue, form a quartet which occurs in conjunction with a third negro melody ('D'lilah was a woman fair' – Example 4.4b), the entire ensemble being enunciated by A flat major. With the addition of Clotilda (who enters the drama for the first time) this same structural model is then deployed in the final part of the act for further dialogue, a quintet in G flat major for Palmyra, Clotilda, Perez, Koanga and Martinez (where much of the material is freely derived from the triplet figures of the characteristically Delian introductory bars with their added-sixth harmony) and the recurrence of 'D'lilah was a fair woman'. Perhaps the most striking *coup de maitre*, however, is the way Delius marks his final statements of the third negro melody by modulating to E flat major where it appears first for unison chorus and latterly for orchestra. This might have been a convincing end itself, but the final bars are reserved for a nostalgic memory of the first negro melody, a highly effective reprise which, far from becalming the scene, seems full of an unsettling foreboding. That Delius chose to include the finale of Act I in his 1899 London concert suggests that he must have been proud of this impressive ensemble piece.

Act II of *Koanga* (which was performed in its entirety in London in 1899) reinforces many of the stylistic factors established in Act I. The opening, a

Example 4.4b. *Koanga*, Act I, negro melody 'D'lilah was a woman fair'.

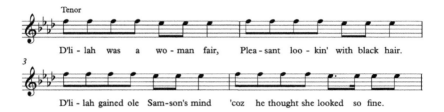

distant partsong for chorus ('Now once in a way, we are free for a day') and the orchestral introduction of another pentatonic negro melody, replete with two on-stage banjos, is as striking as the Prelude to Act I, while the negro melody itself is also subject to a process of free variation treatment. We are also given a taste of the dance music – the melody 'La Calinda' (an imported negro dance), borrowed from the first movement of *Florida* which occupies the core of the act in a much reworked form. The first part of Act II is also highly dependent on the structural role of the negro melodies. The first synthetic negro tune ('He will meet her when the sun goes down'), sung unaccompanied, bears an interesting generic connection both melodically and rhythmically with the melody of the *American Rhapsody*, but it is additionally interesting for its orchestral 'refrain' (replete with banjos), which functions as a transition to each new solo departure (Example 4.4c). The Wagnerian exchanges of Clotilda, Perez and Palmyra (whose lament from Act I reappears in a new variegated manner) also has an increased intensity, its chromatic fluidity thrown into relief by the anchor of A flat which provides an additional tonal link with Act I. The elaborate eight-part chorus also looks forward to numerous examples of Delius working within this sonorous idiom in his later choral works.

The central focus of Act II is, however, the dance sequence and the redeployment of the material from *Florida*. The sequence is at first no more than a rhythmical allusion which begins obliquely on the dominant of C in the guise of an off-stage chorus of negroes (although its significance is marked by the recurrence of the first negro melody from Act I). It is also deftly used to accompany the dialogue of Coltilda and Perez who, ironically, are eager to stop the wedding. With the exit of Clotilda and Perez, the original version of the opera would have continued with the dance material which also includes Martinez's brief invitation to Koanga (set apart in D flat) to greet his bride. However, at this point Delius chose to insert a love monologue for Palmyra for

Example 4.4c. *Koanga*, Act II, negro melody
'He will meet her when the sun goes down'.

the revised version of the opera performed at Elberfeld on 30 March 1904.[38] This is an impressive through-composed form in which Palmyra's 'love' motive for Koanga is introduced for the first time (see Examples 4.4d and 4.4e) and which appears at strategic points in the text, notably after Palmyra pledges her life to her beloved ('until I die'); it was material which also bore a strong kinship with the 'destiny' letmotif from Wagner's *Ring* cycle. Written at least seven years after the first version of the opera was completed, this music shows a great confidence in its shape and continuity; moreover, its climax foreshadows that outpouring of rapture which so characterises *The Walk to the Paradise Garden*, also composed some years after the original version of *A Village Romeo and Juliet* was finished. Another reason for the insertion of Palmyra's monologue was the need to counterbalance Koanga's substantial monologue and chorus ('Far, far away, Palmyra, my people mourn for me')

---

[38] This additional section, with German text only, can observed in the autograph manuscript in Jacksonville (*US-Jul*).

which not only recall leitmotivs from his lament in Act I, but also introduce new figures such as Koanga's love for Palmyra (Example 4.4e). At the conclusion of Koanga's monologue the transition from G major to D for the wedding feast is a smooth one. For this, Delius reworked the 'Tanz der Majorbauer' from *Florida* using the dance's original key structure and ternary design; and with a number of small inserted transitional passages (e.g. the choral 'Dansons la Calinda'), much of the primary material (including the coda) remained intact. Delius, however, decided to transform the movement into a choral ballet. For the outer sections he added vocal counterpoint, including a reference to the first negro melody ('He will win her when the sun goes down') for the reprise; the central section in A major became a purely orchestral 'Ballet of Creole Dancers'. Given that so much of Act II was devoted to integrated structures orientated around negro melodies, to the two monologues of Palmyra and Koanga and to the 'set piece' of the choral ballet, Delius was wise to reserve the most dramatic part of the act for a more open-ended sequence of action in which Koanga confronts Martinez, fells him to the ground and, before escaping, issues his deadly curse. This is effected with some dexterity, in particular, with Koanga's love motive which, from its F major origins (two bars before Fig. 19), undergoes considerable reworking within the province of F minor. Koanga's final pronouncement in E flat ('Voodoo Manian'), in spite of the somewhat pedestrian orchestral preparation, is well executed as is another of Delius's 'last-ditch' modulations to G flat at the conclusion. The reference to this tonality provides a tangible link to the quintet and chorus of Act I in that the intentions of Clotilda and Perez have successfully come to pass. Koanga may have found a degree of freedom from his slave-owner, but he has been deprived of his beloved Palmyra.

Act III of *Koanga* is more puzzling and it seems that Delius encountered problems in realising his ideals of opera satisfactorily. To open the act he originally conceived of a short prelude in E flat major of thirty bars which, after making reference to the first negro melody and Koanga's love motive, would pass into the first wordless chorus in A flat.[39] As Threlfall has demonstrated, the Prelude to Act II of *The Magic Fountain* was used instead; one suspects, too, that the unaltered employment of this material was a last-minute decision.[40] While

---

[39] This earlier version of the Prelude to Act III can also be seen in Florent Schmitt's copy of the vocal score (*DTA*).

[40] See Threlfall, R., 'The Early History of *Koanga*', *Tempo*, No. 110 (September 1974), 11. One senses that, in using such an extensive part of *The Magic Fountain*, Delius, reluctant to acknowledge this act of self-borrowing, effectively condemned his second opera to obscurity.

Example 4.4d. *Koanga*, Act II, Palmyra's love for Koanga.

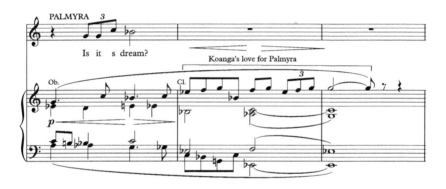

Example 4.4e. *Koanga*, Act II, Koanga's love for Palmyra.

Delius presumably hoped that this would provide a sufficient impression of the outlying swamps beyond the plantation, it also meant dispensing with those thematic allusions which linked the prelude with Acts I and II. Unfortunately, Delius's desire to create the exotic atmosphere of Voodoo magic also has the effect of undermining the opera's dramatic momentum at this point, which no amount of choral narrative, hymns of tribute, incantations, negro dances (which are surely also drawn from *Florida* and *The Magic Fountain*) can serve to mitigate. Indeed, the lack of action combined with the reflective chorus appears to have more generically in common with the paradigms of choral music than with the stage. Only with the entry of Martinez does the drama resume a real sense of forward motion ('Fools you are to weep and wail') as it is rescued by the dialogue of Palmyra and Perez (a passage which recalls Palmyra's lament at the beginning of Act I in the same key) and the horrifying, violent action which follows. Koanga's final monologue is, not surprisingly, dominated by the vengeful material from his first entry in Act I and increasingly by his love motive, an idea which actuates the coalescence of D flat major. This was familiar climactic tonal territory for Delius since it also formerly underpinned the dramatic culmination of *The Magic Fountain*. Here, the tonality also played an extended role, first in marking the death of Koanga (which coincides with a powerful occurrence of his love motive) but also in framing Palmyra's final monologue ('Koanga, dead!'), itself strongly anchored to B flat minor, the tonality of her first lament in Act I. The presence of B flat is nowhere more emphatic than in Palmyra's last pronunciation, 'Great Dahomey Prince', where Koanga's love motive is also powerfully prominent, but it also marks the moment where she takes her own life. After this point Delius embarked on what was in some ways the most remarkable passage of the opera, for having left Palmyra's monologue tonally unresolved, the last part of this scene, which reaffirms the composer's fixation with *Tristan*, is left to the affirmation of D flat and the depiction of Palmyra's self-sacrificial 'Liebestod' in no less than ninety-eight bars of pure orchestral music. Beecham referred to this extraordinary section as an 'intermezzo', perceiving the music as an extended transition to the Epilogue.[41] The scale and gesture of the music, however, implies something much more substantial, on par with the orchestral interludes of Wagner's *Ring* and the end of Act II of Humperdinck's *Hänsel und Gretel*. In this context, however, Delius's design represents the final denouement of the drama, a unique feature in late nineteenth-century romantic opera. Moreover, the formal dimension of this 'intermezzo' yields an interesting parallel with the Prelude to Act I in that Delius uses another loose variation structure. Suspended above one of his favoured tonic pedal points, the variations are based on a progression ($I^6–V^7–[I^6–V^7]–V^7$ of IV–V^7) enhanced by the inner chromatic voice-leading (Example 4.4f). A thematic idea for cellos constitutes a first variation, and a second variation is developed by the oboe. A third variation, replete with Tristanesque appoggiatura, underpins the ecstatic climax, and a fourth provides a transition to the Epilogue (in which the first negro melody is subject to one final, even more intense chromatic harmonisation), though Delius had cause to use the melody once more in the sweeping orchestral conclusion to the opera.

     Perhaps one of the most striking features of the history of Delius's *Koanga* is that, after the first hearing of the excerpts in London in 1899, the critical response from a range of national newspapers, journals and magazines was

---

[41]   *TB*, 100.

Example 4.4f. *Koanga*, Act III, harmonic progression for Palmyra's 'Liebestod'.

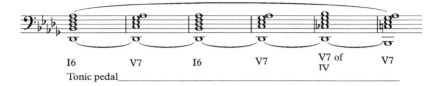

distinctly positive. 'Every bar of Mr Delius's music shows high musicianship, an astonishing mastery of notes, and a degree of vital energy quite as astonishing' was the unbridled verdict of the *Saturday Review* (10 June 1899), *The Morning Post* spoke of 'strong originality',[42] and the *Morning Leader* of 'vivid vitality of colour' in *Koanga*. There were similar judgements in *The Star*, *The Daily Telegraph*, the *Pall Mall Gazette* and the *Morning Advertiser* which commented on the effective use of the banjo, the imaginative scoring and Andrew Black's successful negotiation of the demanding role of Koanga. The only negative tone came from *The Times* (probably Fuller Maitland). Nevertheless, Delius remained unsatisfied with the work and, as mentioned above, made alterations for the three performances in Elberfeld in 1904 under Fritz Cassirer. The German press was also kind in deeming Delius a modernist who had learned his art from Wagner and a dramatic realism from Verdi. Fenby, who played a central role in Beecham's revival of the opera in 1935, contended that Delius maintained a special relationship with the opera in that 'it held some secret bond that tied him to his youth in Florida; and in old age it was the one work he regretted he was never likely to hear again (and so it proved)'.[43] True though this may be, and while the flawed libretto required revision (one which Douglas Craig and Andrew Page duly carried out in 1974), Delius surely recognised in *Koanga* a stylistic fulcrum in which his assimilation of Grieg and Wagner found a new personal consolidation, particularly in the interaction of melody and harmony. Furthermore, *Koanga* seemed to point the way in terms of those genres which were best adapted to his highly individual musical voice, notably partsong, the possibilities of variation technique as a form admirably suited to his instinct for harmony, and the potential of orchestral music as a vehicle for poetry. Indeed, with regard to the latter, *Koanga* indicated a major change in Delius's approach to

---

[42] *The Morning Post*, 31 May 1899.

[43] Fenby, E., sleeve note for EMI recording of *Koanga* (2003), 4.

opera where physical drama was subservient to musical substance. As Delius remarked, *teste* Heseltine: 'Every gesture of the actors in my work must be controlled and ordered by the conductor, for my music is conceived in that spirit. Only thus can *the whole* be made comprehensible to the public. An actor stage-manager will be no good whatever, *for he will make the singers act from the stage and not from the music*'.[44] Although Beecham described the work as being 'frankly and unashamedly "operatic"',[45] essentially due to the more gesticulative solo material and the presence of more elaborate ensemble music, the presence of the purely orchestral sections, especially that of the extended conclusion of Act III, suggests a new chemistry in which the expression of drama *without* words was an equally important part of Delius's rhetorical armoury.

DANISH POETRY, JACOBSEN AND *DANISH SONGS*

The midnight sun is a time of special recreation in Scandinavia during the warm days, the glow of the evenings and the vivid sunsets, occasions which are celebrated in nordic poetry and in music. Such poems were undoubtedly seized upon by Delius as an expression of his love of the northern climes and the experiences of those unusual physical phenomena, notably Paulsen's 'Jeg reiste en deilig Sommerkvæld' ('Summer Eve'), Andreas Munch's 'Solnedgang' ('Sunset') and Drachmann's 'Lyse Nætter' ('Dreamy Nights'). In June 1896 Delius wrote of his experiences to Jelka:

> I am living on a big farm in Valders, situated on the mountain side of a lovely valley – and working at my opera – the air is delicious & the living excellent, and before leaving I hope to have completed the 1st Act – The nights are *grand*; light all night & the color of the atmosphere, the hills & the woods and the water is most beautiful – The sun sets at about 8.30 behind the mountains and immense shadows begin to creep across the great valley – at 10.30, only the tops of the hills, covered with fur [*sic*] trees are lighted by the sun's rays – and stand out as if in gold. Then the whole disappears in a mystic – half light, a very dreamy & mysterious effect It is light enough to read & to distinguish every detail at the other end of the valley and on the mountain tops – Only one drawback. I cannot sleep – It

[44] *PH*, 58.
[45] *TB*, 99.

is quite day at 2.30 AM And my room has 4 windows looking out over the valley ... The result is that all thro' the night I have a most gorgeous and wonderful sunrise effect in my room – I wake up regularly at 2.45.[46]

It was this languorous sensibility which he brought to several of his *Danish Songs*. Five of them had been completed by the end of 1896 as he told Jutta Bell: I have written 5 songs to J. P. Jacobsen's poems[;] I think they are good'.[47] Written between 1896 and 1897 the songs in this collection, with the exception of a new version of Drachmann's 'Lyse Nætter', were all settings of Jens Peter Jacobsen, a poet for whom Delius would develop a special empathy.[48] As with the *Norwegian Songs* and *Sakuntala*, Delius probably came to the texts through the medium of German, though he claimed in a letter to Ernest Newman in 1929 (when some of the *Danish Songs* were being performed as part of the Delius Festival in London) that 'all my Danish Songs and also the Norwegian ones were first composed in their original language'.[49] As Robert Threlfall has suggested, Delius must have misremembered given what we know of the available German translations and his knowledge of Norwegian at the time.[50] One cannot dismiss the possibility that by 1897 his ability to read Norwegian and Danish had improved significantly, but it is likely that, like later Danish texts, he came to them more comfortably through German translation, even if they were set in the original language.

The autograph manuscript of the *Danish Songs* for voice and orchestra shows different orders of the songs and also different numbers. The first conception was of five songs,[51] the second of seven.[52] The songs were also made available in versions with piano accompaniment, though, for some of

---

[46] Letter from Delius to Jelka Rosen, 15 June [1896], *AU-Mgm*.

[47] Letter from Delius to Jutta Bell, [23? December 1896], *DLL1*, 110.

[48] A further setting of Jacobsen, the narrative 'Pagen højt paa Taarnet sad', was, as Threlfall has suggested (*RT1*, 111), probably intended for the *Danish Songs*, but was subsequently rejected.

[49] Letter from Delius to Ernest Newman,19 August 1929, *DLL2*, 353.

[50] *RT1*, 93.

[51] The order in *GB-Lbl* MS Mus 1745/1/12, ff. 1–13 is (i) 'Through long, long years' ('Red Roses'), (ii) 'Let springtime come', (iii) 'There was a king' ('Irmelin Rose'), (iv) 'No leaflet stirs upon the silent shore' ('Summer Nights') and (v) 'Lift on high and clink the glasses' ('Wine Roses'). The title, in Jelka Delius's handwriting, is *Danish Songs*.

[52] The manuscript of the seven songs (also in the hand of Jelka Delius) bears the title *Seven / Danish Songs / Frederick Delius*, dated 1897 (*GB-Lbl* MS Mus 1745/1/12, ff. 16–30) and shows the order (i) 'Silken Shoes', (ii) 'Irmelin Rose', (iii) 'Summer

them, this was conspicuously less idiomatic. As for the texts, Delius opted to publish the German and English translations (which detracted from Jacobsen's more subtle language), Jelka providing the majority of those in German, Delius providing all the English ones. The decision to ignore the original language was made purely for commercial reasons.

The first of the set of seven, 'Silkesko over gylden Læst' ('Silken Shoes'), demonstrates vividly just how far Delius had come in the five years since the publication of the *Seven Norwegian Songs* of 1892. The song is a mere twenty-two bars, yet the concentration of thought reveals a steadily growing confidence and facility. The rich dominant thirteenth (with eleventh, ninth and seventh) of the two opening bars supporting Delius's rhythmical thumbprint of a triplet on the strong beat followed by a minim, is a mark of the mature composer. The presence of added sixths to simple diatonic triads (which, as Peter Evans has suggested, was a means of enriching the otherwise 'bare' nature of the traditional triad as part of the broader matrix of Delius's denser harmonic language)[53] is another emerging sonority familiar from *Koanga*, and while much of the harmony could still be said to be 'functional', the process of key change is now much more rapid, a lesson he had learned from the Wagnerian musical 'prose' of *The Magic Fountain* and *Koanga*. Indeed, at the epicentre of the song, Delius reaches F sharp major before recovering with impressive competence the home key of F in the space of only eight bars, all without a hint of hurried or forced modulation. The vocal line, meanwhile, is no longer shackled to traditional lyric melody, but is now a freer, elastic declamatory form more akin to opera, and while Delius gives some care to vocal rhythm, the meaning of the text (here one of infatuation with young feminine beauty) is conveyed more by the general tenor or mood of the larger musical canvas, where particular words are given special nuance through their harmonies and 'sound moments', a feature especially enhanced by Delius's sparing orchestration.

'Irmelin' clearly looks back to Delius's eponymous first opera in its use of Griegian modality and its fairy-tale narrative. What is more, Delius recycles the cadential music ('Irmelin's theme') of the Vorspiel to Act I of the opera for the 'refrain' to each verse ('Irmelin Rose'), elongating it with great sensual effect at the end of the song. The third song, Delius's second setting of Drachmann's 'Lyse Nætter' ('Summer Nights'), is quite unique in

---

Nights', (iv) 'In the Seraglio Garden', (v) 'Wine Roses', (vi) 'Red Roses', (vii) 'Let springtime come'.

[53] Evans, P., 'Delius', Evans Papers, *GB-DRu*.

concept, a fact recognised by the London critic of *The Musical Times* in 1899 who described it (together with 'Through long, long years') as 'remarkable for poetical conception and perfect sympathy for the text.[54] When Delius set this text in 1891, he had already treated it as a study in Tristanesque chromaticism; in this new version, significantly, his treatment was governed by similar criteria. His evocation of the seascape and balmy, long midsummer evenings is a series of nuanced, slowly changing harmonies which move from E flat to the close in A flat, above which is a freely declaimed vocal line. The mood is one of transcendence where nature is imbued with a longing for childhood days engendered by the kaleidoscopic richness of sensuous post-Wagnerian progressions. Epitomised by the perfumous added-sixth sonorities which initiate and conclude the song, the impressionistic style of Delius's divided strings and pointillistic use of horns for the most affecting harmonies reinforce the pertinence of the orchestral idiom, one which makes it virtually impossible to realise at the piano.

The symbolism of roses forms a recurrent motive for several of the *Danish Songs*. 'In the Seraglio Garden', tinged with that sense of exoticism of *Sakuntala* in its evocation of minarets and Turkish towers, has at its heart the perfume of flowers, the rose as a symbol of feminine sexual prime, and the rarified enclosed space of the Ottoman concubines. The added-sixth sonority of 'Summer Nights' is equally prevalent in this song, notably in the 'dreamy' melodic figure which presages *A Mass of Life*, one to which Heseltine drew attention as a hallmark.[55] 'Wine Roses', like 'Summer Nights', continues the theme of longing – 'a faded day, a time gone by'. The influence of Grieg can be heard in the more strident C sharp minor of the opening and the return to reality at the conclusion, but the core of the song is centred around a lush A major in which the memories of summer nights are captured. Here again, Delius's languorous added sixths are present, but even more intensely in this instance with multiple appoggiaturas (note the contour of 'wine roses') and modal inflections, all intended to invoke that heady sense of wine and deeply scented roses. This, as with 'Summer Nights' is Delius in the first flush of his maturity. The penultimate song of the Danish set, 'Through long, long years', is an aphorism similar to that of 'Silken Shoes'. An elegiac miniature, the song begins with a Griegian gesture in B flat, but the true goal of the song is D flat. At the close, Jacobsen's potent symbol 'Red, red roses' embodies

---

[54] 'Mr Fritz Delius', *The Musical Times and Singing Class Circular*, Vol. 40 No. 677 (July 1899), 472.

[55] *PH*, 148.

the rueful remembrance of youthful pleasures set against the background of Delius's menagerie of shifting harmonic colours.

Jacobsen's words seem truly to have inspired Delius and throughout the *Danish Songs* the sensibility of longing, that quintessential feature of *Weltschmerz* which Delius's music conveys with such luminosity, seems to grow in intensity and consciousness, hand in hand with a boldness to explore new harmonies and the development of a chromatic language that was personal to the composer. The last song, 'Let springtime come', notwithstanding the last eight bars revised by Delius in 1929, seems almost to be the most advanced song of all. While there is still some retention of a discernible tonal plan, from A major to F sharp major and back, underpinned by an extended pedal, the journey of Delius's harmonic 'arc' is by no means traditionally functional, and the fluctuating rhythmical figures that permeate much of the song serve to heighten the modernity of its harmonic world. This sense of modernity should also include the strikingly flexible and declamatory role of the voice, which is no longer trammelled by traditional notions of lyricism and repetitive melody but instead dictated by practices of opera, a genre which had, of course, preoccupied Delius for much of the decade. In this sense one might argue that the *Danish Songs* are no longer 'songs' in the traditional sense but an evolving genre, in much the way that Wolf, Mahler and Strauss were transforming the song, especially with the help of the orchestra as a determining stylistic ingredient. It would be a genre, moreover, in which Delius would excel.

That the composer considered his *Danish Songs* to be an important demonstration of his work is surely indicated by the inclusion of some of them in two of his earliest concerts. 'Irmelin', 'Summer Nights', 'Wine Roses', 'Through long, long years' and 'Let springtime come' featured in his self-financed concert at St James's Hall in 1899 under the baton of Alfred Hertz, the reception of which was decidedly positive: 'there can be no doubt concerning the expressive character of several miscellaneous songs, which were rendered by Mlle Christianne Andray', so read the review in *The Musical Times*, 'for those entitled "Through long, long years" and "On the Sea Shore" ['Summer Nights'] are remarkable for poetical conception and perfect sympathy with the text'.[56] 'Silken Shoes' and 'In the Seraglio Garden' were given at the Société Nationale de Musique – a rare appearance of Delius's music in the French capital – in a translation by William Molard on 16 March 1901, sung once again by Christianne Andray and conducted by Vincent

---

[56] 'Mr Fritz Delius', *The Musical Times and Singing Class Circular*, Vol. 40 No. 677 (July 1899), 472.

d'Indy. Among the audience was no other than Claude Debussy. As John Palache has commented, it was characteristic of the French composer to offer a deliberately non-analytical, impressionistic, not to say obscure observation of the music:[57] 'ce sont des chansons très douces, très blanches, de la musique pour bercer les convalescentes dans les quartiers riches … C'était ineffable comme tout, cette musique!'[58] It is interesting that Delius was ultimately dismissive of his talents for song in later life, but in the particular sub-genre of *orchestral* song he had as much to offer as his contemporaries, Mahler, Wolf, Strauss and Ravel. That he may have retained a special regard for the *Danish Songs*, is perhaps indicated by their revival for the Delius Festival in 1929.

PIANO CONCERTO IN C MINOR:
A PROBLEM OF FORM AND GENRE

After abandoning a good deal of material for piano and orchestra, including a *Fantaisie* and the *Légendes*, in the early 1890s, it is evident that the aspiration remained to compose a work for the idiom. In the time since Leipzig, Delius's proficiency as a pianist had not undergone any noticeable technical improvement. Much to Beecham's astonishment he had admitted to performing Chopin's piano music during a tour of Norway with his violinist friend, Halfdan Jebe (and the writer Knut Hamsun) in the summer of 1896. Aware of Delius's somewhat approximate technique, Beecham 'remained for quite a while undecided as to which of two possible explanations of the mystery could satisfy [his] curiosity: his own unbounded assurance, or the undeveloped state of musical culture in Norwegian provincial audiences'.[59] This lack of prowess as a pianist was not enough, however, to deter Delius from embarking on a new work, possessed as he was by this time with greater confidence as a composer.

In returning to Florida during the first half of 1897, in order to settle his affairs there, Delius devoted a good deal of time to the composition of a work for piano and orchestra. A *Fantasy* for Piano and Orchestra in C minor,

---

[57] Palache, J., 'Debussy as Critic', *The Musical Quarterly*, Vol. 10 No. 3 (July 1924), 361.

[58] Debussy, C., *Monsieur Croche et autres écrits* (Paris: Gallimard, 1971), 26. 'They are very sweet songs, very white, music to cradle the convalescents in the rich neighbourhoods … It was ineffable like everything, this music!'

[59] *TB*, 84.

probably begun some time in 1896 though completed in 1897,[60] initially confirmed his preference for a one-movement Schumannesque- or Lisztian-type form in the same manner as the earlier *Fantaisie* and *Légendes*.[61] Cast in five sections, the work is essentially a sonata structure in which a thoroughly Griegian slow movement, in D flat major (the same key as the corresponding movement in Grieg's Concerto), is inserted between the development and recapitulation. Delius also included a cadenza towards the end of the recapitulation before a final statement of the opening theme. After completing the *Fantasy*, Delius had the piano part copied in Paris. Having had a chance to hear the work, albeit in a two-piano version, it is evident that Delius was unhappy with its form and decided to recast it using a more traditional three-movement model. Precisely when Delius decided to revise the *Fantasy* is uncertain, but it was thoroughly reworked, much of the 'Fantasy' element being absorbed into the first two movements, while the last was an entirely new conception. Delius had it played over by Henri Falke,[62] a Premier Prix du Conservatoire, privately in Paris,[63] and by his old friend Harold Bauer who was still living in the French capital. It is also known that Busoni and Delius went through the work together in 1898.[64] Busoni had a liking for the work, and Hans Haym was particularly taken with the score: 'I am absolutely full of your Piano Concerto', he wrote in 1903; 'It is really a marvellous, ravishing work! Why have you held it back from me for so long? For two pins I would play it myself. I really don't need to go into raptures to you about its many beauties, its splendid thematic work etc etc, but I have already written enthusiastically to Buths'.[65] Although attempts were made to persuade the pianist Egon Petri to take up the Concerto,[66] its first public executant was indeed Julius Buths

[60] See *GB-Lbl* MS Mus 1745/1/11, ff. 1–38.

[61] Such one-movement forms had also become a prevalent part of the instrumental repertoire of the Société Nationale de Musique, notably among composers such as d'Indy, Franck, Dukas, Saint-Saëns and Chausson which may have been equally or even more influential on Delius's decision to pursue the model.

[62] See *GB-Lbl* MS Mus 1745/1/11, ff. 20–37 and letter from Delius to Jelka Rosen, 25 January 1898, *DLL1*, 126. Delius referred to the work as his 'concerto Fantaisie'.

[63] Delius, J., 'Memories of Frederick Delius', in *DLL1*, 415.

[64] *TB*, 125. Busoni had also promised Delius that he would play the three-movement version in Berlin in 1901, but this never materialised, much to Delius's chagrin (see *DLL1*, 180 and *EF*, 58).

[65] Letter from Hans Haym to Delius, 19 June 1903, *DLL1*, 216.

[66] Letter from Haym to Delius, 10 July 1903, *DLL1*, 217.

(who also made a two-piano version)[67] at the Stadtshalle, Elberfeld, under Hans Haym on 24 October 1904. Buths was very taken with the work: 'We think this Concerto still shows a little of Grieg's influence upon you but only in occasional passages. The main thing is that the whole expresses an original mind'.[68] Precisely what moved Delius to refashion his original scheme is not known,[69] but it is likely that he found the musical ideas of the *Fantasy* too large for the smaller structure and felt that a more conventional concerto design would accommodate them. A comparison of the exposition of the first movement of the Concerto with the opening part of the *Fantasy* reveals the transplantation of the same musical ideas though with expanded and recomposed transitional material as well as a good deal of rescoring. The first movement of the Concerto is in fact quite traditional in its sonata outlines. Indeed, apart from the opening statement (a modal 'motto' idea which Delius uses throughout the work), the soloist and orchestra share the uncomplicated structure and the surprisingly classical tonal scheme. There are some subtle touches. The second subject in E flat is a gentle poetic utterance thoroughly reminiscent of Grieg. The closing section of the development in A flat is also subtly executed. Here Delius presents his second subject in a more expansive version before piano and orchestra take up the motto theme in the minor as a false restatement. The reprise of the motto in C minor is then left to the piano alone. The recapitulation of the second subject, in C major, is well done, but the closing part of the movement, again left largely to the pianist, is disappointing and it concludes too precipitately. The slow movement is simpler still in terms of form. Two presentations of Delius's languorous Griegian melody in D flat, one by the piano alone, the other by the orchestra with pianistic filigree, provide the backbone of the movement. Deft incorporation of the 'motto' theme is noteworthy. Only briefly does the music step outside the domain of D flat and that is for a somewhat belated 'con anima' passage. This soon finds its way back to a dominant pedal of D flat and the reprise of the principal theme which, after a variation in the orchestra (with Delius's favourite nostalgic horn solo), distils down to the initial presentation for the pianist. The harmonic idiom of the last movement – also a sonata scheme – suggests that it was probably written sometime

---

[67] Buths' two-piano version, dated 'Spring 1898' (see *GB-Lbl* MS Mus 1745/1/10, ff. 1–19), was made some time before the Elberfeld performance.

[68] Letter from Julius Buths to Delius, 10 July [1903], quoted in *TB*, 125.

[69] It is more than likely that Delius's revision of the Concerto took place sometime in 1902 or 1903. It is significant that Delius, through a sense of dissatisfaction with the work, chose not to consider it for his London concert in 1899.

after the completion of the *Fantasy* – perhaps not long before the Elberfeld performance in 1904. In terms of thematic invention, it is by far the most interesting movement of the three, especially the virile second subject in the relative major. The developmental phase is dominated by the wide-ranging first subject, treatment which could have undermined Delius's conventional recapitulation, except for the fact that the intervention of his second-subject material in E flat provides just enough suggestion of a new tonal direction, making the return to C minor unexpected. Less satisfactory, however, is the overlong cadenza (which seems to add nothing to the movement's coherence) and the coda which, in a more majestic C major, belatedly recalls the second subject of the first movement as a peroration to the entire work.

After hearing the three-movement design at Elberfeld, Delius remained dissatisfied with the Concerto's larger form. The final movement lacked the traditional dynamism of a traditional romantic finale, and, though the movement contained some pleasing material, it lacked cohesion. Consequently, when the prospect presented itself for a performance on 22 October 1907 under Henry Wood, with the Hungarian pianist Theodor Szántó, who conveniently lived in Paris, Delius decided to jettison the last movement completely and return to the one-movement form originally suggested by the much earlier *Fantasy*. It was also an opportunity for Delius to revise the score completely, and while much of the first- and second-movement thematic material remained intact, extensive details of the scoring and consignment of thematic ideas were recast, which also included some judicious structural compression. One major feature – the transition to the slow movement – had to be composed afresh. For this Delius initially gave the strong impression that, with his protracted dominant pedal of C, this part of the movement would end in the tonic, but, in the last thirty-two bars, the music (with strong reminiscences of the 'intermezzo' from *Brigg Fair*) diverged sharply towards the subdominant where it quietly concluded, allowing the enharmonic effect of D flat for the slow movement to take place. For the last part of the Concerto in this abbreviated form, Delius provided a revised form of the recapitulation of the first movement (as in the *Fantasy*), again comprehensively rescored and, for the newly composed coda (arguably the weakest part of the work), the second subject is once again brought into play with the briefest of cadenzas (which refers, epigrammatically, to the motto theme) rather than the ill-judged length of the first version.

Delius's Piano Concerto has remained a subject of contention in his output. Chop considered it an example of the composer at the height of his powers. 'Of course it is not a piano concerto in the usual sense', he wrote to Delius after hearing the work in Berlin under Schillings, 'in spite of the over-elaborated virtuoso style of parts of the work. It is a dialogue of symphonic proportions between piano and orchestra, sometimes suggestive of an improvisation, and then again like a sunset landscape veiled beneath a blue haze, or an heroically inspired will, which nonetheless requires tender impressions in order to fulfil itself'.[70] In his musicological writings on Delius, Chop maintained that 'structural integrity [was] never compromised' in the Concerto,[71] and Wood considered it a work of great beauty.[72] Hutchings, on the other hand, was, without exception, excoriating: 'rarely has a great composer written such drivel'.[73] Heseltine believed that 'the recapitulation of subject matter from the beginning of the work ... gives it but an artificial coherence which is by no means convincing'.[74] Jelka referred to it as 'juvenilia',[75] while even Delius himself declared, *pace* Fenby, that he thought little of the work, 'not so much in terms of its form as embarrassment by its content'.[76] Nevertheless, the exercise was instructive. The traditional form of the Concerto was one never likely to suit Delius's true aesthetic outlook. A form which had evolved to project the dialectic of a 'contest' between soloist and orchestra was hardly an apposite one for Delius's poetical instincts; moreover, the classical strictures it placed on his growing affinity for freer structural designs gave rise to a tension which he only felt resolvable in the shape of fantasy-like schemes. It is therefore no accident that all Delius's later concerto essays consistently opted for the one-movement design. In many ways his unsympathetic relationship with the piano was always likely to undermine his affinity for the virtuoso romantic idiom, and this is certainly true of the ungainly nature of the piano writing in both the *Fantasy* and first version. In spite of his love for Chopin, Delius failed to comprehend the complex yet entirely rational contrapuntal matrix of Chopin's piano virtuoso figurations, a fluency which successors such as Scharwenka, Rachmaninov and Medtner clearly understood. Observing that this was entirely missing in Delius's composition, Szántó attempted extensively to rewrite the piano part at the same time transforming the soloist's role into one of a genuine virtuoso, alterations of which Delius

---

[70] Letter from Chop to Delius, 3 November 1907, *DLL1*, 308.

[71] Chop, M., 'Frederick Delius', in Jones, P., *The Collected Writings of the German Musicologist Max Chop*, 83–4.

[72] Wood, H., *My Life of Music* (London: Victor Gollancz, 1938), 359.

[73] *AH*, 95–6.

[74] *PH*, 137.

[75] Letter from Jelka to Lilli Gerhardi, 24 January 1933, *DLL2*, 415.

[76] *EF*, 112; see also Fenby, E., *Delius* (London: Faber & Faber, 1971), 74.

approved. It was first performed in this version by Szántó under Henry Wood on 22 October 1907 at Queen's Hall and earned for Szántó, who performed the Concerto a number of times at the Proms in 1912, 1913 and 1921, the work's dedication. Delius approved Szántó's embellishments for the London performance, but when further changes were made for publication by Harmonie Verlag, he was distinctly unhappy on the grounds that his original conception of the work had changed into one that, he believed, conformed with the popular notion of the concerto as one of showmanship. Again, this highlighted the conflict between the modern, accepted concerto idiom and Delius's approach to it. It gave rise to an uncomfortable correspondence with both Harmonie and Szántó. 'I hereby inform you that all the alterations in my Piano Concerto have been made without my permission', he told Harmonie. 'My Concerto is no piano showpiece with orchestral accompaniment, where the orchestra plays a subordinate role, as Herr Szanto seems to have conceived it'.[77] But Harmonie took Szántó's part and defended the artistic attitude the pianist had taken, describing Delius's unaltered version as 'an otherwise impossible work for piano'.[78] Delius was furious and even threatened legal action (which he probably could not afford to take). To Szántó he was equally indignant:

> The piece is *not* to become a piano showpiece with a faint orchestral accompaniment as you seem to wish … I admit that I have only been able – as I wrote to you – to take a cursory look at your altered score & as I wrote to you it is all quite nicely & cleverly done but the whole character has gone & the whole thing has become superficial. Particularly e.g. in the big climax where the brass has been completely cut out, it has become awfully banal, loses character & accent completely … There are already enough superficial piano concertos around without my enriching the world with yet another – & as you know, I would not take *one* step out of my way in order to attain a popular success.[79]

Ironically, however, even though contemporary opinion of Delius's Concerto is at best equivocal, and in spite of the composer's own misgivings towards the work, it was for many years the piece which brought Delius's name to unknowing audiences. Even Delius seemed eventually to come round to

---

[77] Letter from Delius to Harmonie Verlag, 17 October 1908, *DLL1*, 373–4.

[78] Letter from Harmonie Verlag to Delius, 15 October 1908, *DLL1*, 372.

[79] Letter from Delius to Theodor Szántó, 17 October 1908, *DLL1*, 373.

Szántó's interpretation of the Concerto.[80] Szántó's advocacy was echoed by no other than Vaughan Williams who was present at the first performance of the revised version on 22 October 1907,[81] and by the critic Robin Legge, who waxed lyrically about the 'sheer loveliness of that Largo'.[82] Moreover, Percy Grainger both adored and championed it especially after he moved to the United States in 1914,[83] R. J. Forbes performed it in Manchester, Moiseiwitsch in London to considerable acclaim, and so did Evlyn Howard-Jones whose interpretation Delius admired most of all.[84]

FOLKERAADET: A TRIBUTE
TO DIE MEISTERSINGER

After returning to Paris from Florida and Virginia in May 1897, Delius moved into the property Jelka had purchased at Grez-sur-Loing; for him it held all measure of advantages, both financial (in that Jelka had a private income) and artistic (in that Grez was quiet, good for work, and yet no more than a modest journey by train to the French capital). No sooner had he taken roots at Grez when Gunnar Heiberg, the Norwegian critic and playwright, arrived to discuss the incidental music for his play *Folkeraadet* due for performance in Christiania during the autumn. Delius was no stranger to such a task, after his early experiences with *Zanoni* and the sketches for Ibsen's plays, nor was he unfamiliar with the composition of shorter movements given his production of music for orchestral suites.

The object of Heiberg's play was to poke fun at the pomposity of parliamentary politicians, all of whom voice their love of country while urging others to go and fight for it. However, when parliament learns of the invasion

---

[80] Letter from Delius to Philip Heseltine, 21 October 1912, *DLL2*, 94.

[81] Letter from Vaughan Williams to Delius, 24 October 1907, *DLL1*, 305.

[82] Letter from Robin Legge to Delius, 22 October 1907, *DLL1*, 304.

[83] For details of Grainger's performances of Delius's Piano Concerto in the USA, see Kirby, C. S., *"The Art-Twins of Our Time-Stretch": Percy Grainger, Frederick Delius and the 1914–1934 American "Delius Campaign"*, MA Thesis, Melbourne University 2015, 26 *passim*. Although Grainger had played the Concerto privately to Delius as early as 1907, his first English performance was at the Torquay Festival in April 1914. A planned performance in February 1915 with the London Symphony Orchestra never took place.

[84] *EF*, 80.

by a foreign power, a resolution is passed asking the politicians to lead the attack. This ironic position was fairly summarised by Clare Delius:

> In the play all the parliamentarians get jockeyed into a situation in which they have to pass a vote declaring that they must all go out and fight, instead of merely mouthing patriotic sentiments. Once, however, they have taken the field the incurable habit politicians suffer from of quarrelling among themselves comes uppermost. The bullets intended for the enemy are turned upon one another. When the war had been brought to an end by the adroit explosion of a charge of dynamite, for which a hotel waiter is solely responsible, a great public funeral is arranged for the parliamentarians whom everybody believes have died in defence of their country. The mistake is discovered in time, and instead of the patriotic funeral, a triumph is accorded to the hotel waiter.[85]

The detailed events of the plot have been well documented by Carley,[86] and the colourful, not to say controversial reception which took place during the performances has been thoroughly covered both by Carley and Boyle.[87] Delius, who was not a political animal, could not have known that the staging of Heiberg's satirical play about parliamentary democracy would have coincided with a significant general election in Norway when aspirations for national independence from Sweden were running high. Certainly his old friends Grieg and Holter thought he was badly advised,[88] and Holter, who exercised considerable political power in Norway's musical circles, predicted, not without a degree of personal *animus*, that Delius's music would not figure in Norwegian theatres or concert halls for many years.[89] Most of the controversy rested on Delius's quotations,[90] especially those in the minor mode, of the Norwegian national anthem 'Ja, vi elsker dette landet' (which superseded the older 'Sønner av Norge'). Use of the new anthem in this manner was construed by many as a national slight, not helped by the fact that the composer was a foreign interloper. But Holter, somewhat distracted by his

---

85 *CD*, 17–18.

86 Carley, L., '*Folkeraadet*: Performance and History', in *FDML*, 211 *passim*.

87 Ibid., 228 *passim* and *DN*, 146.

88 *DN*, 163.

89 Ibid., 164.

90 The quotations of the folk tune 'Kjærringa med Staven' and the first of Grieg's *Twenty-Five Folk Songs* Op. 17 appear to have gone unnoticed.

annoyance at Delius's participation in the play, was wrong in his assessment of the score as 'run-of-the-mill stuff'.[91] Delius evidently thought well enough of his *Folkeraadet* music to include it, newly named as the *Norwegian Suite*, in his London concert of 1899. The four principal movements (the Prelude and three Interludes) had sufficient thematic and tonal cohesion and Delius's choice to emulate the comedic style of *Die Meistersinger*, even to the point of couching the movements in C, the key of Wagner's famous Vorspiel to Act I, was a deft one. Further parallels with the Vorspiel of *Die Meistersinger* included the opening fugato of the Prelude to Act I and Delius's emphasis on diatonic counterpoint which dominated the outer sections of the ternary design. However, Delius's use of counterpoint in this context is surely to convey the sense of parliament's 'learnèd pomposity' and of the parliamentarians' obliviousness to the people. This 'busy' polyphonic music is juxtaposed in an endearing pastoral 'trio' in F major, which depicts the 'love' theme of the play between the 'Poet' and Ella (the play's only female character). Typically, the poet is an idealist, a romantic dreamer, but his love is rejected by Ella unless he show himself capable of some great endeavour.[92] By contrast, the Interlude between Acts I and II, with its rustic drone and its spirit of a Norwegian dance, refers to the people and to Norway's agrarian majority. Here, of course, Delius reveals his indebtedness to Grieg's orchestral dances (with a confidence in orchestration he had developed in the pages of *Koanga*) and also appropriately quotes (in his own adapted version) a second Norwegian tune ('Kjaerringa med Staven') in the central section in E major. But perhaps the most distinctive material, residing in the highly characteristic love music (between the Poet and Ella) in the Interlude between Acts II and III (and which also informed the melodrama in Act V), especially in its full orchestral apparel, revealed many of the similar constituent traits Delius had already essayed in *Over the Hills and Far Away* (see Example 4.2b), notably the preponderance of the added sixth, the extended pedal point and upward chromatic appoggiatura. It is an idea which anticipated the secondary material of *La Ronde se déroule* completed two years later. Much of the Interlude between Acts II and III depicts the empty political rhetoric of the parliamentarians and their military indecision. Here Delius's 'tongue-in-cheek' quotations of the national anthem undoubtedly touched a nerve, as would its minor version, juxtaposed with the funeral march in the Interlude

---

[91] *DN*, 163.

[92] This challenge to the Poet (in Act II) is articulated by the first of the two melodramas in Delius's score: 'But a poem is also a deed. A poem nobody has equalled. A great poem, Ella?'

between Acts IV and V. In this final movement of his incidental score, Delius was also equal to Heiberg's biting satire where the diffident and subtly truncated recapitulation of the 'parliament' music in C major serves to remind us that it was not the politicians who saved the 'fatherland' but an unassuming hotel waiter, a gesture inherent perhaps in Delius's short but telling quotation (by the oboist) from the first of Grieg's *Twenty-Five Norwegian Folk Songs and Dances* for piano Op. 17 (published in 1870) in the tranquil bars before the coda.[93]

---

[93] See Carley, L., '*Folkeraadet*: Performance and History', 227.

CHAPTER 5

A Nietzschean 'Dance' Epiphany: Nieztsche Songs, *Mitternachtslied Zarathustras, Paris, La Ronde se déroule, Lebenstanz* (1898–1901)

The period of 1898 to 1901 was a major new phase of Delius's career as a composer. In spending a good deal of time in Paris, he must have still harboured aspirations to break into the French concert world, yet, with the exception of the performances of two of his *Danish Songs* under d'Indy's direction in 1901, this never materialised for him. Perhaps disillusioned by his failure to make any inroads into the Parisian concert scene, his sights instead fell on London and he travelled there in 1898 to explore means and ways of having *Koanga* performed and to make contacts with potential sponsors. London, at this time, was an important emerging musical centre. The music of Parry, Stanford and Mackenzie had enjoyed its heyday during the 1880s and 1890s and was still very much an extant influence; Sullivan was a household name, in part through the popularity of his operettas, but he was also admired as the composer of *Ivanhoe* and the conductor of the Leeds Festival. The young Elgar was also a name with which to reckon, especially after the success of his cantata *Caractacus* at Leeds, and younger men such as Samuel Coleridge-Taylor had come to prominence, the latter with his *Hiawatha* trilogy whose literary source had been of significant interest to Delius at the end of the 1880s. But equally noteworthy, and a fact Delius must surely have appreciated, even if he was ensconced at Grez for much of the time, was London's burgeoning concert scene, which was, in many ways, a serious rival to Paris.[1] It boasted many fine German, Italian and French musicians as part of its cosmopolitan mix, and the likes of Hans Richter, the Austrian conductor, enjoyed an annual

---

[1] It is likely that Delius kept abreast of musical events in London through the continental editions of one or other of the British newspapers, copies of which he read regularly until his death.

season in London and Birmingham with his orchestral concerts at St James's Hall, choral programmes at the Birmingham Festival and opera performances at Drury Lane. Good orchestral players at the Philharmonic Society, Richter Concerts, the Crystal Palace and Henry Wood's Promenade Concerts were a more abundant commodity, and if properly harnessed, could act as the major catalyst Delius needed to have his music adequately performed since, ten years from the advent of *Florida*, he had heard precious little of his own work.

Delius travelled to London with high hopes armed with letters of introduction, including one from Fauré. His real problem, however, was that he was barely known in London's musical circles, and since his early days as a student in Isleworth, he had never truly experienced England's professional musical world. The year after the Royal College of Music opened its doors in 1883, Delius was in Florida and when the decision was made to study music, his German orientation naturally drew him to Leipzig as a pedagogical centre rather than to London. This, and the difficulties he found establishing his place in the British capital, and the misapprehension that people would, in some unrealistic manner, throw themselves at his feet (an experience Elgar was uncomfortably to discover in London in 1889) contributed to a frustration and cynicism. 'How can art flourish here?' he wrote gloomily to Jelka,[2] and he was unjustly scathing of the city's musical status: 'London is hell & the [most] inartistic city in the world – Whether I will have my opera performed here is very doubtful'.[3] 'I hate London artistically', he reiterated to Jelka, '& I understand that everything fine & free must wither here'.[4] A particular arrogance, even aloofness, was equally unhelpful: 'the people here are a weak-headed lot – at least in the things I care about – I have a certain feeling of power here amongst them – if I could only get my fingers on the strings I could make the marionettes dance'.[5] Such comments need to be treated with good deal of scepticism. Delius had in fact arrived in London at a potentially auspicious time in the city's chequered operatic history, for, in pursuing the staging of *Koanga*, his contact with the London agency of Concorde Concert Control (to whom he had probably been introduced by Jutta Bell) coincided with an initiative spearheaded by a committee of nineteen members (which included Parry, Stanford, Mackenzie and Richter) to establish a permanent municipal opera (sung in English) financially supported by the newly

---

[2] Letter from Delius to Jelka Rosen, 20 November 1898, *DLL1*, 135.

[3] Letter from Delius to Ida Gerhardi, [December 1898], *DLL1*, 138.

[4] Letter from Delius to Jelka Rosen, [5 January 1899], *DLL1*, 143.

[5] Letter from Delius to Jelka Rosen, 28 November 1898, *DLL1*, 137.

instituted London County Council.[6] In addition there was another scheme, publicised by the Concorde company, which looked to set up a permanent opera controlled entirely by musicians with a policy of 'introducing to the public unknown works of originality and genuine merit'.[7] *Koanga* seemed like an ideal candidate, but by February 1899, Delius's mind was more fixed on the prospect of a concert of his own music rather than the staging of his opera.[8] Such a concert would, however, feature substantial parts of the opera.

Even before Delius had started to focus on the performance of his works in his native country, other creative initiatives had also begun to take shape. Foremost in his mind appears to have been the need to find a creative outlet to express his admiration for Nietszche; but very much connected with this compulsion was discovery of the play *Dansen gaar* ('The Dance Goes On') by his old friend, the Danish critic and writer Helga Rode. As Boyle has noted, Rode was himself an admirer of Nietzsche's ideas,[9] and much of his language and ideation struck a powerful note in Delius's imagination. However, when Delius suggested he might write an overture and incidental music for the play, Rode was indifferent. Unpleasant recollections of *Folkeraadet* no doubt lingered and Rode thought that a young Danish composer might be more politically suited to the task. In the end, Rode suggested that a prelude to the play might be suitable, to which Delius responded with *La Ronde se déroule* in 1899. This work and *Mitternachtslied Zarathustras* (also known as *Das Nachtlied Zarathustras*) would figure prominently in his London concert initiative.

A NIETZSCHEAN AWAKENING: *MITTERNACHTSLIED ZARATHUSTRAS* AND THE NIETZSCHE SONGS

Delius came to know Nietzsche's literature and poetry as early as 1889 when he had been spending some of the summer residing at the home of his friend Arve Arvesen in Hamar, Norway. This was corroborated by Fenby.[10] At this time Delius's imagination had already been ignited by Ibsen's iconoclasm, and

---

[6] White, E. W., *A History of English Opera* (London: Faber & Faber, 1983), 330–31.

[7] *TB*, 100; see also White, E. W., *A History of English Opera*, 332.

[8] *TB*, 103.

[9] *DN*, 171.

[10] *EF*, 171.

given his antipathy, not to say antagonism towards Christianity, it fortified his loathing of the social straitjacket he associated with his Bradford upbringing and the family values against which he had rebelled. This was made strikingly clear in a letter to Jelka after the funeral of Julius Delius in October 1901:

> The only one who has (any) brains at all in the family is my sister Clare with whom I am staying now. We buried the old man on Monday and indeed he died just in time to save the whole family from ruin ... My brother is a soft headed mope & broke down at the grave altho I know he has been waiting 18 years for this event & really did not care a straw. I was also surprised to see him kneel & do a bit of praying when the Parson drawled out his prayers. What a crowd of white livered fools they all are here – and not even honest at that. I am longing for Grez & my work again – To Hell with them all – as I really could see these sort of people wiped out by thousands with the greatest equanimity.[11]

But Delius was no intellectual, nor was he especially interested in Nietzsche's deeper philosophising, the indebtedness to Schopenhauer or Nietzsche's views of Wagner. Hutchings wryly remarked that 'it was not thought which led him [Delius] to the *Weltanschauung* of Zarathustra: he was Nietzschean by constitution, not by conversion. Zarathustra flattered his particular make-up, and one may observe that it is especially easy to take the first step towards a 'Master morality' if one has a good bank balance, or if one has been brought up among affluent relatives who will at least not let one starve though one has flouted their wishes in becoming a practising artist'.[12] As Beecham rightly observed:

> Too much stress has been laid on his alleged subservience to the teachings of Friedrich Nietzsche. Let it be freely admitted that he admired more than in any other modern thinker the literary style, the persuasive method of argument and the more than occasional psychological illuminations of the great iconoclast; but he certainly did not owe to him the discovery that there were dangerous fallacies inherent in the bulk of democratic doctrine, and that most of the world's significant changes had proceeded, not from the collective inaction of the masses, but from the inventions and ideas of

---

[11] Letter from Delius to Jelka Rosen, 9 October 1901, *DLL1*, 195.

[12] Hutchings, A., 'Nietzsche, Wagner and Delius', *Music & Letters* Vol. 22 No. 3 (July 1941), 237.

extraordinary individuals. All this he had heard pronounced with telling force by the greatest dramatist of the century [i.e. Ibsen], sometime well before he had dipped into *Also Sprach Zarathustra*, and it fell like soothing balm upon the distractions and indecisions of his youth.[13]

The main body of Nietzsche's writings had been produced during the 1870s and 1880s, and, by the 1890s, Nietzschean thought had become part of the modernist literary, philosophical and artistic *Zeitgeist* in Europe. Mahler had already been attracted to *Zarathustra* for 'Das trunkene Lied', the fourth movement of his Third Symphony (1895–1896), and Richard Strauss's tone poem *Also Sprach Zarathustra* was given its premiere in Frankfurt in November 1896. Nietzsche's work was also the subject of discussion with Strindberg whom Delius encountered in Paris. But his susceptibility to Nietzsche's poetry and ideas was ultimately nurtured by his relationship with Jelka, for they shared a mutual interest in *Also Sprach Zarathustra*.[14] Writing to her from Norway in June 1896 he exclaimed: 'I am leading a life quite Adam like – Mon Dieu, que je suis simple!! Your Zarathustra I need not say, is invaluable for my present state. A thousand thanks for having lent it me'.[15] It was Jelka who also drew Delius to the *Dithyramben*, written under Nietzsche's *nom de plume* 'Dionyssos' in the appendix to *Ecce homo*,[16] and it was through her that the impetus to set Nietzsche's words, particularly from *Zarathustra*, occurred. Having renounced religion as a young man, Delius found that Nietzsche's almost evangelical atheism struck a powerful empathetic note of emancipation, and the notion of the 'Übermensch' as a self-sufficient, empowered individual driven by destiny and purpose, were all ideas he had already embraced through Ibsen and, later, Jacobsen. Nietzsche the hedonist, Nietzsche the dreamer, Nietzsche the visionary also deeply appealed to him, as did the assertion, learned from Wagner and originally essayed in *The Birth of Tragedy*, that music depended on the equilibrium of Apollonian order and Dionysiac abandon. As a disciple of Dionysius, Nietzsche accepted life as it was in terms of a 'yea-saying' ecstasy, declared in his *Die fröhliche Wissenschaft* [*The Gay Science*], and one he associated with physical movement and revelry: 'when the millions sink into dust you shall approach Dionysiasm in which, singing and dancing, man

---

[13] *TB*, 219–20.

[14] Delius, J., 'Memories of Frederick Delius', in *DLL1*, 408.

[15] Letter from Delius to Jelka Rosen, 15 June [1896], *AU-Mgm*.

[16] Letter from Jelka Rosen to Delius, 20 June 1896, *DLL1*, 105.

expresses himself as a member of a higher community'.[17] For Delius the idea
of singing and dancing chimed with how he understood music as a visceral,
almost instinctive impulse. As we have already seen, ballet and dance had been
important to him since *Florida* and it figured prominently in both *The Magic
Fountain* and especially *Koanga*. Dance, in particular, was also a manifestation
of Nietzschean rapture (the 'Tanzlieder') which Delius took to heart and it
was this Dionysiac spirit which increasingly imbued his later works. Last,
but certainly not least, Nietzsche's view of work and creativity as the key to
personal contentment chimed with Delius's larger *Weltanschauung*. As he told
Fenby, 'I myself do not subscribe to everything Nietzsche said, but I hail in
him a sublime poet and a beautiful nature ... There is only one happiness in
life, and that is the happiness of creating'.[18]

If 1897 proved to be a stylistic fulcrum for Delius, then 1898 was one
of epiphany, for it was through the medium of Nietzsche's poetry that he
began to discover a new, modernist musical syntax that might carry the
synthesis of his assimilation of Grieg and Wagner. Taking his text from 'Das
trunkene Lied' ('The Intoxicated Song') at the end of Part IV of *Zarathustra*
(coincidentally the same text that Mahler had selected), his song for voice and
piano, 'Noch ein Mal' ('Once more') was a setting of Zarathustra's 'roundelay',
the very essence of the author's 'eternal joy and eternal silence' which had
earlier occurred in 'The Second Dance Song' (Part III). Couching his song so
symbolically in B major, it was as if Delius identified Wagner's ecstasy in the
'Liebestod' of *Tristan* with Nietzsche's death song. Of particular significance
in 'Noch ein Mal' is the slow harmonic rhythm of Delius's through-composed
structure, the simplicity of its tonal scheme (which is essentially an extended
dominant pedal and its delayed resolution until the last three bars), its mono-
motivic content, based on the figure C sharp–B–F sharp (the 'bell' motive)
and the vocal orientation around the sixth degree, G sharp. This pitch not
only characterises the opening vocal fragment with its emphasis on 'Mensch'
('O Mensch, Gib Acht!') and other operative words such as 'Traum', 'Lust'
and 'tiefe Ewigkeit' but it haunts the final tonic harmonies where the sixth
is unresolved (a truly prophetic sound of Delius's later works). Equally
fascinating, too, is the manipulation of harmony, for, in spite of the bass's
V–I structure, Delius studiously avoids the platitude of a perfect cadence.
Indeed, the only functional harmonic moment in the song is the climactic

[17] Nietzsche, F., *The Birth of Tragedy: or, Hellenism and Pessimism*, 3rd edn, ed. Levy, H.
      (London: George Allen & Unwin, 1923), quoted in *AH*, 68.

[18] *EF*, 181.

progression in bb. 17–19 which concludes on a 6/4 of V but fails to resolve to the customary 5/3. Such functional moments would often be associated with climactic points in his later works.

It was the hearing of this song played through by Delius one evening at Grez in 1898 which Jelka identified as the moment she resolved to devote her life to support him.[19] Soon after, Delius recast 'Noch ein Mal' as *Mitternachtslied Zarathustras* for baritone, male chorus and orchestra.[20] The decision to expand the scope of the song (which possesses the solemnity of a chorale in its ponderous rhythm) was noteworthy. Save for the much earlier *Neger Lieder im Volkston*, this was the first time Delius had ventured seriously into the domain of music for voices (i.e. solo and chorus) and orchestra, an idiom which the composer must have thought best suited to the solemn, oratorical nature of Nietzsche's text where a solo voice (as 'evangelist') 'leads' a male chorus of attendant 'disciples' with their hymn-like response (it is marked 'sehr feierlich'). To 'Noch ein Mal' Delius added a sizeable 'scena' for baritone which begins on the dominant of B and the presentation of Zarathustra's motive (see Example 8.1e). This leads to Zarathustra's first entry, taken from the end of section two of 'The Intoxicated Song' ('Kommt! kommt! kommt! Lasst uns jetzo wandeln') as he beckons his disciples to walk with him into night's darkness. Further statements of Zarathustra's theme conjoin with the 'bell' motive (see Example 8.1d) in a more tonally fluid orchestral transition. This yields to a thoroughly Wagnerian symphonic monologue for Zarathustra in which the 'bell' motive is accompanimentally ubiquitous and where statements of Zarathustra's motive have a greater urgency. The midnight bell of 'Noch ein Mal' beckons him, and it is to B major that the monologue returns climactically before Zarathustra anticipates the opening of the chorus ('Die alte tiefe, tiefe Mitternacht!').

The fact that Delius was determined to include *Mitternachtslied Zarathustras* in his London concert of 1899 is sufficient confirmation that he felt a confidence in his first Nietzschean composition. Critical reception of it was mixed, partly because the orchestral parts were not entirely accurate (in spite of the rehearsals) but partly because this Nietzschean brand heralded a genus of composition entirely new to English ears. From surviving correspondence, we know that Delius endeavoured to have this performed elsewhere, particularly

---

[19] Delius, J., 'Memories of Frederick Delius', in *DLL1*, 414. Fenby also recognised *Mitternachtslied Zarathustras* as a pivotal point of self-discovery in his talk appended to the EMI recording of *A Village Romeo and Juliet* of 1973.

[20] See *GB-Lbl* MS Mus 1745/1/14.

in Germany,[21] though, as a short work demanding substantial performing resources, it was again a challenge for concert promoters. Furthermore, the subject matter was also something of a deterrent. Buths, to whom Delius had sent the score, was critical. He was positive about Delius's choice of key which embodied a 'darkly longing mood',[22] but he felt it required more polyphonic detail. He also questioned the added-sixth sonority at the very end: 'Why should the symbol of eternity not be just as well the reposeful triad?'[23] Nikisch was reticent,[24] and there was no joy with Siegfried Ochs in Berlin. Eventually it was taken on by Hans Haym, in Elberfeld in 1902 and, under the aegis of Max Schillings (an important figure in Germany's post-Wagnerian world) at the festival of the Allgemeine Deutsche Musikverein in Basel, Switzerland, on 12 June 1903 under Hermann Suter. And even though Delius endeavoured to have it published in this form,[25] it was undoubtedly a powerful incentive towards the production of a much larger choral work based on *Zarathustra*. As an apotheosis in Nietzsche's text (at the end of Book IV), Delius evidently understood the possibility of it functioning in a similar way in *A Mass of Life* which he began to compose the year after his success in Basel.

The choice of the seminal text for 'Noch ein Mal' and latterly *Mitternachtslied Zarathustras*, Zarathustra's 'roundelay', was symptomatic of Delius's broader objective to set other prominent, well-known poems of Nietzsche. That same year, 1898, he composed four settings which, like 'Noch ein Mal', were short, pithy interpretations; in some instances no more than aphorisms. 'Busoni was quite begeistert [excited] with my Nietzsche songs and will try to help me with a Verleger in Germany', he proclaimed to Jelka.[26] And Busoni had good reason to be impressed by the modernist nature of Delius's highly fluid post-Wagnerian chromaticism and the epigrammatic concept of the songs which not only continued the diminutive trend of Wolf's *Italienisches Liederbuch* but looked forward to the aphoristic songs of Webern's first mature phase of composition. Indeed, Delius must have wondered whether these songs were realistically marketable. In spite of helpful indications from Busoni,

---

[21] See *DLL1*.

[22] Letter from Buths to Delius, 31 May 1901, *DTA*.

[23] Ibid. As Lowe has pointed out, in the revision of *A Mass of Life* (*RL*, 67), the last sixty bars do indeed conclude with a B major triad, in response to the added-sixth sonority of the chorus's final chord.

[24] Letter from Ida Gerhardi to Delius, [6 February 1900], *DLL1*, 169.

[25] See letter from Delius to Grieg, [mid-June 1903], *DLL1*, 216.

[26] Letter from Delius to Jelka Rosen, January 1898, *DTA*.

the songs did not find a publisher until 1924 and only the German text was used. As he remarked to his publisher: 'the English text is quite unusable & may not appear under any circumstances. No one in England would sing translations like this of such famous Nietzsche texts. The songs must either appear only with German text, or be translated by a true English poet. It would otherwise merely become a disgrace & laughing-stock'.[27]

For his four through-composed *Lieder nach Gedichten von Friedrich Nietzsche*, Delius took the first three from *Die fröhliche Wissenschaft* of 1882, a collection Nietzsche considered most personal to him and which contained the greatest number of poems he was to publish. Recurrent themes of human empowerment, courage, eternal love, longing and loneliness haunt the poetry in the same manner as those which Delius had set of Jacobsen in the *Danish Songs*. The first, 'Nach neuen Meeren' is a passionate love song which begins with a familiar progression in Delius's vocabulary: a diminished substitute for V with an unprepared dissonance (the G sharp) moving to Ib in E major with its own suspension. This and the vocal melody ('Dorthin will ich; und ich traue') look forward twenty-five years to the same material in the Violin Sonata No. 2. This allusion to E major is fleeting, however. The same dissonance in b. 1 occurs again in b. 7 ('Offen liegt das Meer'), now as V of A, but there is no resolution, and, quite unexpectedly, Delius's goal is C sharp major, a tonality which frames the remaining thirteen bars. Here the lover's infinite gaze is allied with accompanimental imagery of the ebb and flow of the sea and the skilful incorporation of the opening vocal phrase ('Nur dein Auge') in bb. 16–17 as part of Delius's larger melodic arc. The nineteen bars of 'Der Wanderer' outline the challenge of Nietzsche's text. Where is the wanderer to go, now that the old path (of traditional religion) no longer exists? This is mirrored by the highly oblique opening whose climactic goal is the dominant of B flat ('Vom Pfade wich dein Wille! Nun, Wandrer, gilt's!'), and a stern diatonic ending in G minor ('glaubst du an Gefahr') in which the menacing risks and dangers of life have to be confronted. The third song, 'Der Einsame' encapsulates much about Nietzsche's own solitariness, the conflict of will and loneliness and the stark choice of retaining individuality and the need for 'following the crowd'. In order to point up the conflict of this text, Delius set the first six lines in a declamatory style within the orbit of D major, throwing into relief the final four lines of contemplative lyricism in D flat. The last song, 'Der Wandrer und sein Schatten', taken from the earlier *Menschliches, Allzumenschliches* of 1878, is perhaps the most abstract and

---

[27] *MC*, 199.

experimental in its attempt to capture the mysteries of life, death and man's
role in nature, above all in the majestic closing lines ('Fünf Fuss breit Erde,
Morgenrot und unter mir Welt, Mensch und Tod'). Entirely declamatory in
style, the vocal line plays a more interdependent contrapuntal role with the
piano which explores the more extreme registers of the keyboard. There is
also little sense of any settled tonality until the emergence of a dominant
pedal of C sharp in b. 14, and even then the tonicisation of C sharp minor
at the close is achieved through a series of oblique progressions (somewhat
redolent of Richard Strauss) in which the conventional dominant is far away.
The relationship between the voice and piano in the last song also accentuates
the fact that all four songs would be more satisfactory if they were scored for
orchestra since many features – extended pedal points, sustained chords, the
wide range of harmonies and unperformable dynamics – do not lie well on
the piano. Such attributes only serve to confirm that, like the *Danish Songs*,
Delius was most effective in the province of *orchestral* song where, through
his own particular individual prowess as an orchestrator, the additional
ingredients of instrumental timbre provided the necessary subtle nuances of
his textual interpretations.

DELIUS AND THE DANCE:
LA RONDE SE DÉROULE AND *LEBENSTANZ*

Delius's response to Rode's *Dansen gaar*, which is likely also have influenced
his friend Edvard Munch in his own eponymous painting of 1899, was
twofold. The tragic figure of the painter, Aage Volmer, and his lover, Klara,
enter an engagement, but one they both know to be an impossibility given
the intentions of Klara's wealthy industrialist father. Only one outcome seems
possible and that is a Schopenhauer-like death in erotic ecstasy, reminiscent,
of course, of the end of *Tristan*. Klara in fact recoils from such an ending,
but Volmer's desire and longing to seek death is articulated by his climactic
realisation: 'It is beautiful to die in a state of exalted happiness ... Now we
can embrace all of life's greatness'.[28] Such sentiments were already firmly in
Delius's bloodstream, but Rode's Zarathustrian affirmation of life, symbolised
by Volmer's references to 'Livets Dans' ['Life's Dance'], also appealed to
Delius's Nietzschean sensibilities such that it induced him to include a
seminal quotation in Danish from the play – part of Volmer's rapturous

---

[28] *DN*, 172.

outpouring about the painting he aspires to create. Much of Rode's prose has a Nietzschean inflection, but the vocabulary – the erotic mention of red roses – has the ring of Jacobsen and of Delius's *Danish Songs*:

> The dance of life. My picture shall be called the dance of life! There will be two people who are dancing in flowing clothes on a clear night through an avenue of black cypresses and red rose bushes. The earth's glorious blood will gleam and blaze in the roses. He holds her tightly against himself. He is deeply serious and happy. There will be something festal about it. He will hold her to him so firmly, that she is half sunk into him. She will be frightened – frightened – and something will awaken inside her. Strength is streaming into her from him. And in front of them is the abyss.[29]

Written between September 1898 and February 1899, *La Ronde se déroule*, a French translation of Rode's title (which Delius may have considered more mainstream), also reflected another important emerging influence in Delius's style; this was the music of Richard Strauss who was enjoying a major vogue as Europe's new *enfant terrible*. Delius almost certainly knew *Don Juan* and *Tod und Verklärung*, but Strauss's new wave of symphonic poems, *Till Eulenspiegel* (1895), *Also Sprach Zarathustra* (1896) and *Ein Heldenleben* (1898), which were reaching out to European capitals after their German premieres (and were invariably conducted by their creator), were also known to him. Strauss's particular brand of post-Wagnerian chromaticism, allied with an advanced palette of orchestral timbres and virtuoso technique, set a new standard of orchestral playing which was already detectable in Delius's *Folkeraadet*, and the urge to produce orchestral music of a similar bent in *La ronde se déroule* proved irresistible. Added to which, the strong pictorial and programmatic dimensions of Strauss's tone poems, in which classical forms such as rondo and sonata, radically reinterpreted, were potent symbols of modernity at the end of the nineteenth century, and Delius, for one, was happy and fascinated to be carried along by the impetus of this new groundswell of symphonic invention. This is evident in the size of Delius's orchestra for triple wind (to which are added piccolo, bass clarinet and contrabassoon), brass, harp, percussion and a large complement of strings, which are laid out in German, as are the expression markings, suggesting that, after Hans Haym's performance of *Over the Hills and Far Away* in Elberfeld, Delius had both a German concert hall and publisher in mind for his next major orchestral

---

[29] *RL*, translation by R. Woods, 1965, 69.

work. This uncompromising size of forces would hereafter establish itself as a norm in Delius's orchestral voice. For some conductors, this artistic choice was a disincentive. Writing to the Concorde Concert Control in June 1899, during the aftermath of Delius's London concert, August Manns, with whom Delius had corresponded many years earlier, commented 'I will examine the *Orchestral* works (no Choral Scores, please) of M. Delius, although I see but little chance of introducing any of those works just now. From what I read in the London Journals about M. Delius Compositions, I gather that they are prominently "radicalistic" and require a very large modern Orchestra for doing them justice'.[30] Such music did not appeal to the present generation of conductors in Britain, such as Manns, Mackenzie, Sullivan, Stanford, Cowen and Richter (who evidently loathed Delius's music).[31] In truth it would require the enthusiasm of a younger band of British conductors – Henry Wood, Thomas Beecham, Hamilton Harty and Albert Coates – to appreciate and promulgate Delius's music, but that time was yet to come.

Styled not as an overture for Rode's play but as a 'Symphonische Dichtung',[32] the score, with its amplified opulence, projects many of the ideas of Volmer's 'declaration'. As Delius made plain to Ida Gerhardi: 'Dansen Gaar is an Impressionistic mood and one ought to know the play to be quite clear about it: it is symbolic of the Dance of Life just as Helge Rode has depicted it in his play'.[33] The dance *topos* is immediately evident from the elaborate nature of the scherzo-like first idea in B flat minor, a heady dance depicting Rode's two lovers, in which Delius experiments for the first time with cascading, florid passagework for wind and strings (Example 5.1a), and muscular scoring (in true Straussian manner) for massed horns. This is music for a virtuoso orchestra in which colour and effect are intrinsic to this modern instrumental aesthetic. A second, passionate idea for the violas, marked 'Langsam & stimmungsvoll' – a representation of Volmer's love for Klara (Example 5.1b) – provides a major contrast in mood. As one finds in the third movement of *Folkeraadet* (the Interlude between Acts II and III), whose expressive second subject behaves in a similar fashion, Delius's contrasting material, cast in

---

[30] *DLL1*, 159 n.2.

[31] Fifield, C., *True Artist and True Friend: A Biography of Hans Richter* (Oxford: Oxford University Press, 1993), 424–5.

[32] At first, however, Delius referred to *La Ronde se déroule* as an overture. See letter from Delius to Jelka Rosen, [5 January 1899], *DLL1*, 143 and [January 1899], *AU-Mgm*: 'I must finish my Overture! Ciel!'

[33] Letter from Delius to Ida Gerhardi, 4 January 1900, *DLL1*, 166.

Example 5.1a. *La ronde se déroule* [*Dansen gaar*],
opening thematic statement.

the tonic major and suspended above an extended dominant pedal, inclines
initially to the relative G minor with a melodic accentuation on G (by now a
familiar added-sixth sonority within the context of B flat); though it should
also be observed that the consequent material, which looks forward to the

Example 5.1b. *La ronde se déroule* [*Dansen gaar*], second subject.

thematic material of *A Mass of Life*, recoils to B flat. It was this melodic
shape that Heseltine singled out, together with its harmonic properties as
another 'Delian' thumbprint.[34] A full repeat of this thematic material with
more luxuriant orchestral apparel reiterates its affinity with *Folkeraadet*. A

---

[34] *PH*, 148.

developmental phase follows in which the trochaic rhythms of the first subject are inverted, first to iambs, then to an augmented form of dotted crotchets. Both are permitted their own moments of thematic disjunction (caused by the brief interpolation of different thematic material at a markedly slower tempo) and climactic arcs before subsiding, and the paragraph is left expectantly on the dominant of B flat at its close, however, with the promise of a new episode in B flat. This is another dance idea (Example 5.1c), the embrace of Volmer and Klara in a waltz marked 'schneller und tanzartig' and, featuring a solo violin, tinged with biographical associations of the composer. The point of Delius's recapitulation, with the first subject in B flat minor, is unequivocal. However, the second subject, very much associated with the passionate bond between Volmer and Klara, is restated in B flat major with greater force, Delius marking its restatement 'wachsender Begeisterung' ['mounting emotion'] in accordance with Klara's awakening ardour and strength. This material in its Straussian apparel dominates the coda, though diminishing to a wistful comment in the oboe in the deeply nostalgic closing bars. Here Delius finally gives us a cadence forebodingly into D flat minor together with a memory of the more turbulent development (which rhythmically looks forward to the waltz music of *Paris*), gestures which are surely suggestive of the 'abyss' which Delius quoted from Rode's play in the preface.

La Ronde se déroule received but one performance, at the London concert on 30 May 1899, after which it was relegated to the rank of precursor for a more extended version whose German title, *Lebenstanz*, was derived from a more direct translation of Rode's play. What appears to have persuaded Delius to revise his score (and this was a frequent habit for many of his later works) was a need to expand the symphonic conception of the work and, at the same time, its Straussian element of orchestral complexity. Though he had

Example 5.1c. *La ronde se déroule* [*Dansen gaar*], waltz of Volmer and Klara.

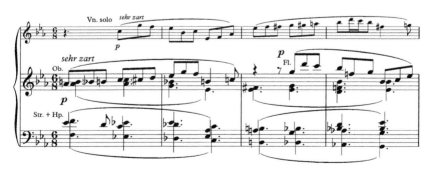

dubbed *La Ronde se déroule* a 'symphonic poem', its shorter form still retained the ambience of an overture, a feature which linked it strongly with its initial connection with incidental music. This particular aspect must have struck him after its hearing in London in May 1899, for by December 1900 it was being recast. 'I am working at "Dansen gaar"', he wrote to Jelka from Berlin, 'and it is becoming twice as good as before'.[35] In this enlarged form, completed in 1901,[36] it was first given under Julius Buths on 21 January 1904 at Düsseldorf and later that same year on 24 October under Haym (who also transcribed the work for two pianos in 1903). A final version of the score, however, with a new ending,[37] was not made until 1912 when it was published by Tischer & Jagenberg in Cologne and first performed by Oskar Fried and the Berlin Philharmonic Orchestra on 15 November that year.

The revision of *Lebenstanz* involved a yet more elaborate orchestra than its predecessor, admitting both a cor anglais, a double bassoon and the addition of a bass drum and glockenspiel (and the option of multiple harps if available), and Delius took the opportunity (as he often did with revisions of his orchestral works) to rescore it. More to the point, however, the formal expansion of the work was influenced by two further factors. First, the aplomb and *Schwung* of a second Straussian tone poem, *Paris*, written in the meantime, had bolstered his confidence in the new orchestral proficiency; and second, Delius clearly looked to develop the symphonic dimension of the work (he would often refer to his symphonic poems as 'symphonies') which *La Ronde se déroule* so palpably lacked, and in so doing, he conspicuously enhanced the Nietzschean 'dance' element while dispensing with his preface from Rode's play.

Delius's process of expansion in *Lebenstanz* can first be observed in the first subject which is more thematically and tonally ambitious than its precursor (especially notable is a new high point on V of A, four bars before Fig. 6). A new and longer transition, replete with cello solo, leads to the second subject which is more or less untouched in terms of its material and behaviour. With more voluptuous instrumentation, Delius recast this section in F major. By far the most substantial part of the symphonic poem to be revised was the developmental phase which amounted to no less than 133 bars of music. Though Delius retained the initial iambic figures from *La Ronde se déroule*, the rest of the original development was jettisoned in favour of a much more protracted 'dance' paragraph in which both first and second subjects played a

[35]   Letter from Delius to Jelka Rosen, 29 December 1900, *DLL1*, 278.

[36]   See *GB-Lbl* MS Mus 1745/1/16, ff. 1–28.

[37]   See *GB-Lbl* MS Mus 1754/1/17, ff. 1–42.

prominent role in a virtuoso display of orchestral scoring. While Delius may have dispensed with his literary preface, this part of his symphonic essay was strongly pictorial in his depiction of Rode's dancers. The spirit of the first subject, with its sense of abandon, also had an increased intensity, owing essentially to the enhanced rhythmical activity, but alive to the disjunctions and spasms of Strauss's *Till Eulenspiegel*, Delius introduced a number of vividly contrasting tempo changes – the sudden 'Lento molto' before Fig. 18 in which the second subject was deliberately isolated in a moment of B flat major, and the resumption, 'doppio movimento', immediately thereafter is one remarkable instant – and the reverie of the second subject in A flat (which occurs at the culmination of a strategic series of rising third-related tonalities) reveals the extent of Delius's careful planning. Furthermore, after a further passage in which the first idea is subject to additional reworking (betraying gestural similarities with comparable homophonic passages in *Paris*) and a brief glimmer of its augmented variant in *La Ronde se déroule*, the 'waltz' episode in B flat is truncated and relegated, more successfully, to the status of an interlude and transition to the recapitulation of the first subject. Although lavishly rescored, the recapitulation remained largely unchanged until the end of the second subject. At this point Delius opted to modify both the transition to the coda and the coda's conclusion (a change he made in 1912), one which retained the close in D flat, in the major, though one that also accentuated the final added-sixth sonority and (with its pungent A natural leading notes) its inherent ambiguous relationship with B flat minor.

DELIUS'S LONDON CONCERT, 30 MAY 1899

Much comment has been made of Delius's London concert at St James's Hall. Beecham has provided a detailed description of the event, and the forty-five letters of correspondence between Delius and his agent, R. Norman-Concorde, provide a wealth of minutiae about its planning, publicity, the procurement of soloists and orchestral players. Time spent in London towards the end of 1898 had acquainted him more with the capital's musical atmosphere. That he was prepared both to organise, and spend money on, a concert entirely of his own works says much about this particular juncture of Delius's life. The uncomfortable reality was that he had heard very little of his own music nor had much of it been published. During a decade of creative self-communion, moreover, in which his musical style had evolved into one that was now immensely personal, esoteric and of a modernist demeanour, comparable with his contemporaries, he had nevertheless been denied the satisfaction of hearing the material sound of his labours. In all those years, though he had been spared the arduous necessity of working for a living (the imperative of most musicians), he had by no means squandered his time; indeed, he had worked hard and, driven by a sense of purpose and self-belief in his own abilities, he had continued to compose a great deal of music without the stimulus of performances to test the viability of his stylistic vision. In part this was because, unlike many composers past and present, he had not enjoyed the practical exigencies of professional music-making (save for the modest insights he had gained in America). He was not a professional performer able to disseminate his own works, he had no conducting skills or experience, and though he appears to have known many musicians (as well as painters and writers), his desire for space and quietness necessary for composition militated against the regular intercourse with musicians which working in conservatoires, teaching or orchestral playing facilitated; nor did he have the practical experience in choral music that a church musician or organist might possess. Nevertheless, Delius was a driven man as he told Jelka from Paris in March 1899: 'The truth however is – that my artistic aspiration has drowned & smothered everything else in me – Am I going to the devil or not? I don't know, but I must go after my art & I know you understand it & want it so'.[38] The need, therefore, to break the mould was now urgent if Delius was ever to be known as a composer, a fact he understood only too well; added to which, he had little money and needed another source of income. As he told Jutta Bell: 'I must see that my works begin to bring me in a little money'.[39]

Delius's name in England, however, was entirely unfamiliar, save for the minimal impact of two of his songs 'Venevil' and 'Abendstimming' in a London recital by Minna Fischer on 14 March 1899,[40] so he relied a great deal on the advice from the Concorde Agency (a fact corroborated by the large surviving correspondence) and on his friendship with the Australian critic George Clutsam. Added to which, putting on a concert exclusively of his own music, and at his own expense, was a considerable personal gamble. As Heseltine observed, this phenomenon was, for the time, a rarity. With the support of Joachim, Stanford had come before the German public in a programme of his orchestral music in the Grosser Saal der Philharmonie in Berlin on 14 January 1889. Already well established as a composer and conductor, the ambitious Irishman nevertheless wanted to use the concert

---

[38] Letter from Delius to Jelka, [March 1899], *DLL1*, 149.

[39] Letter from Delius to Jutta Bell, [6 June 1899], *DLL1*, 156.

[40] *The Musical Times*, Vol. 40, No. 674 (April 1899), 248.

as a way of bringing himself firmly before the German critical press, and to some degree this worked.[41] Heseltine also reminds us that a youthful Granville Bantock superintended a concert at Queen's Hall on 15 December 1896 of his works and those of his fellow composers from the Royal Academy of Music to some acclaim.[42] The entrepreneurial Bantock also pursued a supportive regime of 'one-man' programmes of contemporary British composers during his time in New Brighton after 1897. Delius's concert, however, was especially singular and uncompromising in that it required the audience's attention for the best part of three-and-a-half hours until almost midnight. His chosen programme demanded a colossal orchestra, a chorus, eight soloists and a competent conductor (since Delius was in no position to direct himself), all of which, given the novelty of the music, necessitated hours of rehearsal. Although Hamish MacCunn, a young up-and-coming conductor, had been initially suggested,[43] he having recently conducted pioneering English-language productions of *Tristan und Isolde* and *Siegfried*, Delius favoured the enterprising Henry Wood (and the prospect of a concert at Queen's Hall), only to find that Wood was contracted to Robert Newman and was therefore unavailable.[44] Unwilling to heed the advice of his old student acquaintance, Percy Pitt, to wait until the autumn of 1899,[45] Delius decided to look further afield, and more providentially, to Germany and Elberfeld where some sympathy for his music had already been demonstrated. In securing Alfred Hertz, he not only acquired a conductor empathetic to his cause, but it almost certainly helped to turn his attention towards Germany in the aftermath of the London concert. Hertz, who had in fact recently moved to the Breslau opera, was an able and likeable practitioner, who, trained in Frankfurt, somewhat transcended the stereotypical German *Kapellmeister*. He was keen to spread his wings and the idea of bringing Delius's music before the English public presented an ideal opportunity. Heseltine even suggested that Hertz's direction of the Delius concert assisted the German's later appointment as conductor of

[41] Dibble, J., *Charles Villiers Stanford: Man and Musician* (Oxford: Oxford University Press, 2002), 203.

[42] The concert included music by William Wallace, who had already made his name with his symphonic poem *The Passing of Beatrice* (1892), Arthur Hinton, Reginald Steggall, Stanley Hawley and Erskine Allon. See 'Mr Bantock's Concert', *The Musical Times*, Vol. 38 No. 647 (January 1897), 24.

[43] *DLL1*, 142. MacCunn had established his credentials as an opera conductor with the Carl Rosa Opera Company.

[44] *TB*, 104.

[45] Ibid., 105.

the Metropolitan Opera, New York, in 1902.[46] Hertz's energy and enthusiasm proved infectious: 'Hertz is studying my scores very seriously & likes them more & more', he wrote to Jelka;[47] '[he] is all fire & flame & interest'.[48] Furthermore, Delius, who found himself untypically involved in the rehearsal process, gained some valuable insights into the preparation and performance of his own music, including the procurement of singers and chorus:

> The chorus is going a little better – have had 2 rehearsals – not enough men – but the women are intelligent & full of bonne volonté. Miss Dickens came & is very nice. I shall probably be obliged to fall back on Miss Palliser – Miss Strong a good soprano of covent garden asks 35 guineas! – I met the Duke of Manchester to day – quite a young man & very nice and interested – shall meet him again & have asked him to the orchestral rehearsals. Mrs Woodhouse also is full of interest & charming – Lady Lewis is getting up a musical party for me – so we may get a few people in the house – Hertz is a brick & working hard. I don't hope for any success whatever – it takes the English people too long to get accustomed to anything.[49]

After several choral rehearsals, at which 150 singers (some of them from the Covent Garden opera chorus) were mustered, orchestral rehearsals were fixed for 23, 25 and 29 April. The orchestra (of ninety-five players),[50] according to Delius, '[was] as good as can be had in London',[51] and trusting to old friendships, he relied on Halfdan Jebe to lead the orchestra. The soloists, on the other hand, required more careful handling. Some of them were expensive. 'Bispham asked 40 guineas to sing! – Ella Russell – whose price is 40 guineas – sings for 20 & Andrew Black also 40 guineas sings for 15 – the others offered to sing for nothing'.[52] He was also fortunate to enjoy the patronage of Lady (Elizabeth) Lewis, wife of the lawyer George Lewis, who was a leading hostess of the day and an advocate of composers such as Fauré, Messager and Hahn as well as painters such as Edward Burne-Jones (who painted her) and John Singer Sargent.

[46] *PH*, 41.

[47] Letter from Delius to Jelka Rosen, [27 April 1899], *AU-Mgm*.

[48] Letter from Delius to Jelka Rosen, [May 1899], *AU-Mgm*.

[49] Letter from Delius to Jelka Rosen, 7 May 1899, *AU-Mgm*.

[50] *The Times*, 30 May 1899.

[51] Letter from Delius to Jelka Rosen, [May 1899], *DLL1*, 154.

[52] Ibid.

It has already been intimated, in connexion with *Koanga*, that the reception of Delius's concert was generally more than favourable. It cannot be overemphasised that the programme Delius chose to put before his audience (and these works, for the most part, represented the cutting edge of his creativity) was strange, unprecedented and cosmopolitan. Apart from the *Légende* for violin and orchestra, the earliest piece and one which must have seemed rather more conventional to contemporary ears, the rest of the programme, with its range of Scandinavian, German and American influences, must have seemed uncannily exotic and modernist. Equally unfamiliar, too, were the literary sources and inspirations of Nietzsche (in *Mitternachtslied Zarathustras*), Heiberg (in the third and fourth movements of *Folkeraadet*), Jacobsen and Drachmann (in five of the *Danish Songs*), Rode (in *Dansen gaar*), and a historical libretto about sixteenth-century Floridian native Americans. Nor were the critics entirely ready to countenance an amalgam of Wagnerian chromaticism and Straussian élan together with an accretion of Griegian harmonic innovation. More to the point, the works Delius had programmed encapsulated many of those stylistic components which would form the *nuclei* of his mature voice. The sound was altogether perplexing or, in the words of the *Sunday Sun*, 'bizarre and cacophonous'.[53] Nevertheless, there was a consensus among commentators such as Vernon Blackburn (*Pall Mall Gazette*), E. A. Baughan (*Musical Standard*) and the volatile John Runciman (*Fortnightly Review*) that Delius's music exhibited a new, original talent. As Blackburn commented: 'The extreme originality of phrasing, the audacious harmonies, the moving of waters (as it may be described) within the depth of the music far below the surface, the obscurity of expression, the daring discords – these things began to unite now and then into such fine single effects that one felt them to be the signs, if not the proof, of something not unlike real greatness'.[54] And John Runciman, the self-appointed, irascible head of the 'new critics' and author of *Old Scores and New Readings* (1898), admitted that 'the truth was that we didn't know what the devil to make of this music, and most of us were frank enough to say so'.[55] As for Baughan, 'Delius's music sounded discordant to [his] ears, harsh, uninviting, and ugly', yet having undergone the same experience with Wagner, he predicted that he would come to admire Delius.[56]

---

[53] Quoted in *PH*, 44.

[54] Quoted in Ibid., 47–8.

[55] Heseltine, P. [Warlock, P.], *Frederick Delius, reprinted with additions, annotations and comments by Hubert Foss* (London: The Bodley Head, 1952), 61.

[56] Ibid., 61. Baughan would similarly confront the challenge of Schoenberg's *Five Orchestral Pieces* when they received their English premiere in 1912.

The lamentable outcome of Delius's concert was, however, that, having effectively achieved his goal – a decent audience and a positive critical reception – he failed to capitalise on his success. In part, he unreasonably felt indignant at the cost of the venture and blamed the Concorde Agency. Having expected a bill for somewhere in the region of £300, the one presented to him was £500, a result of the additional rehearsals and the abnormal size of the orchestra and a good deal of publicity (and in this Concorde did its work more than adequately). The financial pressure under which it placed him convinced him that if another similar venture were to take place in London, the cost ought to be defrayed by others. Such hopes were unfortunately predicated on the generosity of his German relatives in Bielefeld,[57] and when these were dashed, the idea of a second concert in 1900 evaporated. After the concert itself, Delius spent little time in London and retreated to France without any plans to take advantage of the publicity he and his music had received. Within twenty days of the concert, and in the same venue of the St James's Hall, Elgar's *Enigma* Variations were first performed to great acclaim under the direction of Hans Richter. The propinquity of these two events drew the attention of a critic of *The Gazette* in which an article on 'Two Promising Young Men: Elgar and Delius' focused on the Variations and *Koanga*. But while Elgar was in a position to press home his fame with other works, Delius's name, and the remarkable concert he arranged, slipped from memory, and for this only he himself can be blamed. However, the lack of consequences which the concert failed to generate should not, on the other hand, diminish the significance of this musical occurrence. It was, after all, the *first* substantial hearing of Delius's music and one that gave a first impression of the composer's range and vision. For that reason, and because the composer was on the cusp of his greatest fecundity, 30 May 1899 ought to be celebrated as one of the most noteworthy days in British musical history.

PARIS: A 'DANCE' POEM

Having spent ten years in the French capital – and his address was still (at least for the moment) 33 rue Ducouëdic – it is not surprising that Delius should have wanted to compose a tribute to a city where he had felt most culturally settled. Henri Murger's novel, *Scènes de la vie de bohème*, had been the inspiration behind Puccini's *La bohème* (premiered at the Teatro Regio in Turin in February 1896) which was first heard at Paris's Théâtre des Nations

[57] *TB*, 107–8.

with the Opéra-Comique on 13 June 1898. The city was the setting for Gustave Charpentier's enormously successful opera *Louise*, composed in 1899 (and premiered in Paris in February 1900), which tells the story of a young seamstress and her desire to find freedom with a young artist; and it was also a stimulus for Florent Schmitt's piano duet *Rhapsodie parisienne* (which Schmitt intended to orchestrate), completed in 1900.

Although much of the work on *Paris* appears to have been accomplished between October 1899 and February 1900,[58] Delius may have conceived the idea of a symphonic poem sometime earlier as is evident from numerous sketches.[59] Indeed, Delius was an inveterate and copious sketcher of his music. This is clear from surviving notebooks of earlier works; but it is also apparent from the many surviving fragments of harmonic outlines, pencil sketches and draft scores, that his music increasingly passed through many stages of careful honing before he was satisfied with the result; furthermore, we already know from *Lebenstanz* that he was also inclined to revise his music over a long period. The sketches for *Paris* emerged initially out of two earlier orchestral conceptions, *Scènes Parisiennes* and *Épisodes et Aventures*. At the beginning of 1935, when Fenby was going through Delius's manuscripts at Grez-sur-Loing, the autographs of these pieces were unearthed. As Fenby explained in a letter to Thomas Beecham:

> I have been perusing some almost undecipherable pencil sketches in full score, written on vast manuscript paper, of two unfinished works "Scenes Parisiennes" (l'heure de l'absinthe; heureuse rencontre; joyeuse nuit) and "Episodes et Aventures" in which may be found the nucleus of "Paris". These were unearthed today.

> "Scenes Parisiennes" opens with that low pedal D in the basses but the oboe tune at 1 […] is given first to the Eng. H.[orn] and then to the B.[ass] cl.[arinet]. The entry of the divided 'celli at bar 5 appears to have been an afterthought for there is a rough sketch of it in the margin. The viola figure at 3 bars after 2 is there as is the response in the 'celli two bars later, but the figure in the Fag., 5 bars before 3, is given to the oboe and echoed by the B. cl. The music now moves to the Vivace 6/8 at 8 and soon changes to 3/4 time, being a foretaste of the polyphony in the Allegretto grazioso

---

[58] A draft of the full score, *GB-Lbl* MS Mus 1745/2/13/1, ff. 106–37, is signed 'Frederick Delius Oct 1899 Feb 1900'.

[59] See *GB-Lbl* MS Mus 1745/2/11/3 ['Notebook 3'], ff. 117v and 120v, 1745/2/10, ff. 26–8 and 1745/2/9, ff. 5–9.

section in "Paris" (9 bars after 18) except that here the theme runs along in crotchets instead of quavers as in "Paris".

Looking towards the last part of the work, and particularly the recapitulation of the lyrical second subject:

> Then follows the skeleton of what was to be that moving passage between 27 and 28 except there is no violin solo. This all ends serenely as in "Paris" and then enters on a long 12/8 section in which there are many odd bars and decorative counterpoints the possibilities of which Delius obviously did not see at the time of composition, but which he was afterwards to develop so magically. So much for "Scenes Parisiennes".

> In "Episodes et Aventures" may be found the germs of all that vigorous treatment of the [F sharp–E–F sharp–E][60] figure in "Paris". In a Vivo section 3/4 in which the brass give out [A–G–A–G / F–E flat–F–G][61] etc to the accompaniment of all sorts of helter-skelterings in the strings and woodwind, but the chief interest in this work, and there are many, is that it provides that rollicking tune in "Paris" at 23. This is announced in Bb major by Eng. H., B. cl., Violins I and 'celli in octaves with a similar accompaniment of chords off the beat in the horns, but here with added inner strings.

> I hope I have not made myself a bore, but if I have stressed the obvious it is because I am rather excited for the moment by your exquisite music-making and what these rapidly pencilled sketches reveal.[62]

Fortunately the scores of *Scènes Parisiennes* and *Épisodes et Aventures* survive, so it is possible to observe something of the process of gestation of many of Delius's incipient ideas for *Paris* before they were assimilated.[63] Both works,

62   Letter from Eric Fenby to Thomas Beecham, 19 January 1935, *GB-Lbl* MS Mus 1745/1/40, ff. 1–3.

63   *Épisodes et Aventures* now forms part of *GB-Lbl* MS Mus 1745/1/40, ff. 18–31r. *Scènes Parisiennes* survives in two parts: the first section can seen in *GB-Lbl* MS Mus 1745/1/40, ff. 1–17v (pp. 1–27) and *GB-Lbl* MS Mus 1745/2/8 (pp. 28–53).

conceived in much the same spirit as *La Ronde se déroule*, were Straussian in ethos and scored for large orchestra: *Scènes Parisiennes* including six horns and two harps; *Épisodes et Aventures* has an even larger ensemble of triple woodwind, piccolo, cor anglais, bass clarinet and double bassoon, and three trumpets in F (with their broader tone). *Scènes Parisiennes* also makes allusion to a series of programmatic scenes. 'L'heure de l'absinthe' refers to the tradition of the 'l'heure verte' in Paris when many would visit the local cafés to drink absinthe (often known as 'la fée verte'); it was a favourite time for Parisian writers, artists and composers to fraternise at around four o'clock in the afternoon (though its addictive and potentially harmful effects led to its proscription in France and the rest of the Europe by 1915). 'Heureuse rencontre', refers perhaps to a chance encounter between two lovers. And much of the body of the orchestral work was taken up with 'joyeuse nuit', a time of gay abandon, amid the temptations of Paris's night life. Other references such as 'Caprice' and descriptions such as 'Côté mysterieuse & fantasque aux crepuscules étranges de joie et de tristesse' and 'ville de plaisirs' provide evidence of Delius's current fascination with programmatic material in emulation of Strauss. A further point of interest in both works is that one of their central features is the waltz, a characteristic which would prove highly formative in the creation of *Paris* as a 'dance poem'.

After *Scènes Parisiennes* and *Épisodes et Aventures* were rejected, Delius drafted a new symphonic poem, *Paris*, in which, as Fenby intimated, ideas from both works were assimilated into a new structure. Although the *Stichvorlag* (the autograph used by the publishers) of *Paris* is now lost, an earlier version contains an unspecified prose poem (perhaps by Delius or Jelka Rosen) which, by incorporating many of the descriptive and thematic elements of the earlier orchestral tone poems, and two subtitles – 'Impressions de Nuit' and 'Ein Nachtstück' – helped to define its nocturnal programme (written in English):

Mysterious city!
Asleep whilst the crowds hurry bye [*sic*]
to their many pursuits and pleasures:
Awakening as the twilight deepens.

City of pleasure,
of strange sensations
of brazen music and dancing
of painted and beautiful women.

Secret city,
unveiling but to those
who ever shunning day
return home in the pale blue light
of scarcely breaking dawn
and fall asleep to the song of awakening streets
and the rising dawn.[64]

Although Delius was adamant (in an appended note in German) that the poem should not be understood as a programme for the work, there are many elements of it – the onset of night, music, dancing, pleasure-seeking and the breaking of dawn – which define its broader depiction.[65] It is, however, significant that, when the score was published by Leuckart in 1909, Delius decided to dispense with the poem completely, and recast the name of work as *Paris: A Nocturne (The Song of a Great City)*. The poem, nevertheless, had not completely been disassociated with the symphonic poem for we know that Delius sent a shorter version of the poem to Heseltine in 1914.[66]

The orchestra for *Paris* – effectively a fusion of the considerable forces required for *Scènes Parisiennes* and *Épisodes et Aventures*, with a large contingent of percussion – was Delius's largest to date. The substantial number of strings was specified as twenty first violins, sixteen second violins, twelve violas, ten cellos and ten double basses (the same total number as that listed in the published score as 16.16.12.12.12 though differently distributed). Quite clearly the considerable size of the forces proved no deterrent to Delius's creative vision at this time.

---

[64] See the flyleaf of *GB-Lbl* MS Mus 1745/2/13. A German translation in Delius's hand was added later, to help promote performances in Germany (see *DLL1*, 174–5). This slightly earlier version contains abundant evidence of use for performance and was probably the score used for its premiere under Hans Haym at Elberfeld in 1901, for the numerous continental performances in Berlin, Düsseldorf and Brussels, as well as its English premieres by Beecham in Liverpool and London in 1908. This version also corresponds musically with the arrangement made by Haym for two pianos (c. 1903); see *GB-Lbl* MS Mus 1745/2/18.

[65] 'Dieses Gedicht soll nur die Stimmung angeben & soll durchaus nicht als Programme aufgefasst werden'. ['This poem is only intended to indicate the mood and should not be construed as a programme'.] Delius, in other words, preferred to perceive *Paris* as a '*Stimmungsbild*', a work which conveyed a mood rather than a sequence of events.

[66] *RT2*, 199.

It was Philip Heseltine who remarked that 'for Delius, Paris is not so much the capital city of France as a corner of his own soul, a chapter of his own memories. The superficialities of *la Vie Parisienne* have been dealt with by Offenbach, the trifler, and Charpentier, the vulgarian, with whom Delius would disdain competition'.[67] Together with *Lebenstanz*, *Paris* was the first major manifestation of his Dionysiac evangelism in purely orchestral terms. Here, it is the *dance* itself, the working out of youthful joy, energy, ambition, love and death, and two other genres, the 'song', a natural effusion of Delius's lyrical gifts, and the resolute march (prevalent in *Over the Hills*) that are recurrent metaphors; in fact, so much of Delius's music in 3/4 or 6/8 was allegorical of this philosophical fixation, one that embodied diverse elements of the lilting, pulsating dance metre, while the march, instead of being associated with the military or with empire, was internalised into an expression of desire, lack of inhibition and physical striving (having much in common with the dance). As Banfield rightly questioned, was Delius the first composer to write a symphonic waltz poem? Certainly the work seems to have prefigured Frank Bridge's *Dance Poem*, a large symphonic waltz of 1913, and by some two decades Ravel's homage to the waltz, *La Valse*.[68] It is perhaps significant that the critic of *The Musical Times* would remark that though 'Mr Delius's "Paris" is an original work, it cannot be said to conjure up any specifically Parisian atmosphere'.[69] In Delius's symphonic poem, the city of Paris itself becomes metaphorical of Nietzsche's Apollo-Dionysius dialectic, and, in consequence, the piece, replete with Delius's favoured slow-moving frame, becomes a symphonic working of the dance, the song and the march, three genres which would be become hallmarks of his later style. The extended introduction of *Paris* begins with a tranquil evocation, a pregnant pause before the revelling in which Delius introduces a series of melodic aphorisms which can be identified as some of the 'Cris de Paris', Parisian street cries of vendors, which, as Fenby, acknowledged, found their source in *Scènes Parisiennes*. It was strangely coincidental that the 'Cris de Paris' also formed a prominent role in the opening of the second act of Charpentier's *Louise*, evocative of dawn in Paris, though as Chop was keen to point out: 'The music of these two composers, Delius and Charpentier, is as different as it could possibly be; while Charpentier is superficial, Delius is profound.[70]

---

[67] *PH*, 131.

[68] Banfield, 'La ronde se déroule: Delius and the Round Dance', *British Music Society Journal*, Vol. 6 (1984), 29.

[69] 'New Symphony Orchestra', *The Musical Times*, Vol. 49 No. 782 (April 1908), 243.

[70] *MCh*, 24–5.

There are numerous fragments – a seemingly innocuous rising figure in the bass clarinet, and popular song in the oboe, horn calls, a more sinister interjection for the bassoons – all this is symptomatic of the composer's love of scene painting found in his earlier orchestral works. But this well-tried rhetoric yields to an orgiastic climax built essentially of one chord (an augmented sixth in last inversion, A flat–D–F–B flat) in which a reworked version of the bass clarinet idea combines in an almost improvised manner with the other fragments (a sound-world so far unfamiliar in Delius's music), while the rhythm of the dance (or, as Banfield has more precisely insinuated, the waltz)[71] is exaggerated by wind and tambourine. A return to the initial mood of tranquillity only serves to throw into relief the Allegro and the ebullient first dance (Dance No. 1 – Example 5.2a) heard in the brass. Headed by the sound of laughter (a figure which had already used in *Koanga* and would be used again in *A Village Romeo and Juliet*), this waltz makes use of the same iambic rhythmical figures as *Lebenstanz*. To this is appended (in oboes and clarinets) at Fig. 11 a subsidiary dance (Dance No. 2 – Example 5.2b) drawn from *Épisodes et Aventures*. After a buoyant transition, which departs from the tonic, D major, Delius takes us more than unconventionally to what rhetorically feels like a second subject, in C major. The tempo relaxes to Adagio, and we are carried into a more than familiar province of Delius's genius: a lyrical, nostalgic love song (surely the 'heureuse rencontre' of *Scènes Parisiennes*) reminiscent, as Fenby pointed out, of the second subject of *Hiawatha*, though in a much more reassured guise (Example 5.2c).[72] This overtly diatonic melody is then subject to a series of three variations (both in terms of harmony and instrumentation), recalling the bifurcated technique from the *American Rhapsody* and the

Example 5.2a. *Paris*, Dance No. 1.

---

[71] Banfield, 'La ronde se déroule', 28 *passim*.

[72] Fenby, E., *Delius* (London: Faber & Faber, 1971), 40.

Example 5.2b. *Paris*, Dance No. 2.

Example 5.2c. *Paris*, second subject, 'heureuse rencontre'.

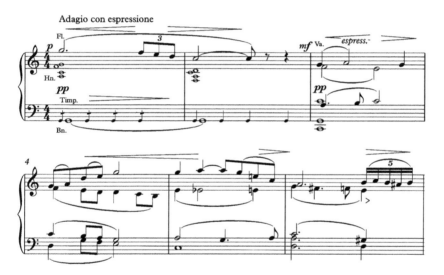

prelude to *Koanga*, though now far more complex polyphonically (see seven bars after Fig. 13 to Fig. 14). C major is quitted with a brief development of the 'song' theme in a guise which can almost be perceived as a paraphrase of *Ein Heldenleben*, but, Strauss-like in its sense of abrupt dramatic juxtapositions, Delius restores the dance (in D major) through the use of 'Dance No. 1', though it is clear this time that the tonal behaviour is increasingly unstable and highly fluid. Yet, just as we are ready to accept the conventional rhetoric of a sonata development, Delius diverts our attention. Dance No. 2, originally a thematic appendage, now takes on an important life of its own as it becomes a new, self-contained thematic episode (the 'molto Adagio' four bars before 17) in G major. In terms of the larger structural events this phase of the work, as its disjunct rhetoric would suggest, is an 'interlude' (prefiguring the rhetorical device Delius later used in *Brigg Fair*), and at its close we resume the tonally unstable development, this time with 'Dance No. 2' in a more suave, relaxed mood (marked 'Allegretto grazioso'). Soon, however, the Dionysiac intoxication returns and Delius creates his sense of climax through tonal catastrophe, where the sense of chromaticism is so intense that all sense of tonality is expunged (see before Fig. 21).

It is at this crucial point of tension that Delius introduces a *new* theme (March No. 1 – Example 5.2d), a strident, Lydian idea which coincides with a move to B flat, and at the rhetorical point of cadence (just before Fig. 23) a new fragment is heard, almost innocuously, in the flutes (March No. 2 – Example 5.2e). In one sense the triumphant nature of the material suggests that the work is about to take a new departure, yet at this very point, when the new tonality seems so strongly affirmed, Delius takes us unexpectedly to G flat major and the two new thematic ideas (now marked 'Tempo di marcia') combine as counterpoints and develop into full-blown melodies. This event marks a new phase in Delius's highly unconventional structure. In moving to G flat, the tenor of the symphonic poem 'relaxes', a tendency analogous to a sonata form as it moves flatwise in its closing phase. The reworking of these

Example 5.2d. *Paris*, March No. 1.

Example 5.2e. *Paris*, March No. 2.

ideas sets a trend for the reprise of other material in the work, which though familiar is not literally repeated.

'Dance No. 2' is recalled in G flat and provides a transition to what is surely the episode of greatest pathos, the recapitulation of the 'Song' in D flat major, replete with a new and inspired invertible countermelody (and an excellent example of Delius's genuine contrapuntal abilities) to give new fillip to his variation process. This sonorous tonal area is one that Delius reiterates for the reprise of the slow introduction (which we now understand to be an integral part of the larger structure), but in direct contrast to this seemingly stable area, the last part of the symphonic poem sets out from G major with 'Dance No. 1' (and ultimately ends in this key). This, in conjunction with the restatement of the 'Song', provides a recapitulation to 'balance' those thematic events at the beginning of the work, though this final stage of the 'dance', a *topos* which runs through the work as a continuum, is intensified by one further unexpected tonal event, the jubilant reiteration of both march themes in E major which, conflated as one extended melody, acts as a thematic apotheosis of the entire structure together with the tolling bell gesture. As Banfield has remarked, it is 'a definite death summons if we note its blatant debt to the passage announcing the hero's doom in Strauss's *Till Eulenspiegel*'.[73]

The complex structure of Delius's form (see Table 5.1) in *Paris* serves to show that, amid the abundance of thematic material, he was rapidly learning how to handle the apparatus of thematic development and transformation (contrary to Heseltine's assertion) while retaining his iconoclastic irreverence for conventional classical principles of key organisation. There is still some residual evidence of the sonata dialectic, notably between the first two dances and the slow lyrical love song, but Delius's form is also overtly more episodic which, with rather obvious and undigested transitions between major thematic statements, tends to undermine the sense of seamless organic coherence and 'continuing variation'. It is evident, however, that Delius's conversion to a more symphonic mindset with this work, and *Lebenstanz*, quickly emancipated him from an older Griegian formula which had more limited structural potential. But perhaps most significant for Delius at this juncture was that, musically and intellectually, he was thinking in a quite different way, akin to those practices of the modern German school which he was studying with considerable interest and curiosity. It is also clear that Delius was happy to 'play freely' with the traditional principles or pillars of classical tonal form. One governing key for an entire work no longer

---

[73] Banfield, 'La ronde se déroule', 31.

Table 5.1. *Paris*, structural overview.

Score ref.	Theme/genre	Key	Formal element
b. 1	'Cries'	D major	Slow introduction 'Twilight'
b. 82	Dance No. 1	D major	Exposition (first-subject group)
Fig. 11	Dance No. 2	D major	Exposition (first-subject group)
Fig. 13⁺³	'Song'	C major	Exposition (second subject)
Fig. 15	Dance No. 1	D major	Developmental
Fig. 16⁺⁵	Dance No. 2	G major	Developmental
Fig. 18⁺⁹	Dance No. 2	G major (fluid)	Developmental
Fig. 21⁺²	March No. 1	B♭ major	Developmental
Fig. 23⁻⁴	March No. 2	B♭ major	Developmental
Fig. 23	March No. 1, March No. 2	G♭ major	Developmental
Fig. 24⁺²	Dance No. 2	G♭ major	Reprise/transition
Fig. 27⁺⁴	'Song'	D♭ major	Reprise
Fig. 28	Dance No. 1	G major	Reprise
Fig. 31	March No. 1	E major	Reprise
Fig. 32⁻²	March No. 2	E major	Reprise
Fig. 35⁺²		D♭ major	Reprise of slow introduction as epilogue 'Dawn'
Fig. 36⁺⁴	'Cries'	G major	Coda 'Dawn'

applied, as Peter Evans has articulated: 'In Delius, neither the opening nor the closing bars are more significant tonally than the constant intermediate key fluctuations. Here again Delius was not setting out to *challenge* traditional usage but merely securing his effect by instinctive means; it happened that key as opposed to harmony had little to offer to him as a means of expression. He was intent on the immediate sensuous effect of this or that rich sound rather than the intellectually satisfying effect of large-scale tonal construction'.[74] This is certainly true of *Paris* and this period of orchestral 'liberation'.

Delius sent the score of *Paris* to Strauss who was initially reticent about performing it in Berlin. 'I am afraid I cannot decide to perform the work for the time being: the symphonic development seems to me to be too scant, and it seems moreover to be an imitation of Charpentier which has not quite succeeded – perhaps I cannot quite imagine the effect of the piece'.[75] To Ida

[74] Evans, P., 'Delius', Evans Papers, *GB-DRu*.

[75] Letter from Richard Strauss to Delius, 2 March 1902, *DLL1*, 199.

Gerhardi he also expressed some misgivings and thought it 'a little thin from a thematic viewpoint'.[76] Strauss seems, however, to have changed his mind, for Buths later reported that: 'Last Friday we played your two works "Paris" and "Lebenstanz" to Strauss in Cologne. The impression made on Strauss was definitely in your favour. Henceforth you will certainly have an advocate in him for the future Tonkünstlerversammlungen'.[77] As Delius also expressed in a letter to Grieg in September 1903, the orchestra, and the challenge of *symphonic* orchestral music, had become the chief focus of his attention:

> If you go to Germany next winter let me know for I have several performances ... & then I should so much like you to hear my music – You only know my very first efforts – Unfortunately I can't send you anything either as I still haven't found a publisher although I must say that I haven't tried very much either & am writing orchestral music exclusively. Every year I have 3 or 4 performances in Germany – Buths in Düsseldorf and Dr Haym in Elberfeld give my latest scores every year – Buths has arranged "Paris" The song of a great city – a symphonic work of mine for two pianos & Dr Haym has done the same for "Lebenstanz". I shall try to send you these arrangements if I get the chance. I don't need to tell you that *my* Mitternachtslied has absolutely no relationship with the Strauss Zarathustra, which I consider a complete failure. Yet I find that "Till Eulenspiegel" & Heldenleben especially are splendid works. Tod & Verklärung I find not so significant although there is much that is beautiful in it.[78]

After the completion of *Paris*, Delius's preoccupation with orchestral music came temporarily to a halt as he turned his attention to a new opera, *A Village Romeo and Juliet*, but even here the orchestra would play a pronounced role in the concept and form of the work.

He spent time in Norway and Denmark, mainly for pleasure, although work on the opera did continue during these weeks of recreation. Unable to repeat the concert in London, which had been his hope, he devoted much of the latter part of 1900 trying to interest German conductors to take up his music, anxious no doubt that performances of his works had once again stalled. It was a tortuous time, however. A rehearsal of *Paris* in Elberfeld went

---

[76] Quoted in *DLL1*, 199.

[77] Letter from Buths to Delius, 19 July 1903, *DLL1*, 219.

[78] Letter from Delius to Grieg, 28 September 1903, *GD*, 177.

badly,[79] and a visit to Hertz in Breslau resulted in letters of introduction to other conductors. There was, however, no joy in Berlin or Leipzig with Busoni, Weingartner, Nikisch, Maskowski and Ochs. It was a disconsoling time as he explained in a letter to Jelka:

> As far as I can see I have absolutely no chance here [Berlin] – Strauss plays his own things – Weingartner plays his own things & Nikisch plays nothing new – The last Concert was a Haydn Symphonie – Mendels[s]ohn Violin Concerto & a slow ungifted Dramatic Overture by Scharwenka "beaucoup de bruit pour rien" Strauss of course is always interesting – but as I am here I might as well stay a bit & hear as much new as I can … Here it is awful what mediocre talents hold the ropes in Music, painting & sculpture. A real genius would be hopelessly lost unless he had means – They only applaud the most awful rot – the "pfennig Gefühle" & the most sickly sentiment brings down the house – Well, it is so & cannot be altered just now.[80]

But, with some persistence and patience, *Paris* was finally taken up at Elberfeld on 14 December 1901 by Haym whose determination to perform Delius's music called forth the wrath of the town council who wanted music in a lighter vein.[81] As Delius informed Grieg in 1903, its success helped to carry his reputation forward, for it was also given in Berlin under Busoni in November 1902 (even though Delius maintained that the work was unrecognisable),[82] Buths in Düsseldorf in February 1903 and again in Elberfeld with Haym in October 1904. Henry Wood also rehearsed it in London in 1905,[83] but the work was not given there until February 1908 under Beecham. Such exposure finally went some way to giving Delius the springboard he needed to give his music a more international profile.

---

[79] Letter from Delius to Jelka Rosen, 18 November 1900, *DLL1*, 174.

[80] Letter from Delius to Jelka Rosen, 14 December 1900, *DLL1*, 176.

[81] *CD*, 148–9.

[82] *EF*, 58.

[83] Letter from Henry Wood to Delius, 6 November 1905, *DLL1*, 258.

PART II

THE VOICE OF INDIVIDUALITY

CHAPTER 6

Operatic Innovation:
A Village Romeo and Juliet and
Margot le Rouge (1898–1902)

GESTATION

Even before the opportunity to hear parts of *Koanga* in London in 1899, Delius had embarked on yet another work for the stage, as if he was anxious to move on from the aesthetic world of his third opera to pastures new. In fact, it appears that the ink of *Koanga* was barely dry before Delius approached Keary with a request for a libretto based on the Swiss author Gottfried Keller's short story 'Romeo und Julia auf dem Dorfe' from the collection *Die Leute von Seldwyla* written between 1856 and 1874. Keller was associated with the German-speaking literary movement of 'Bourgeois' or 'Poetic' Realism, one which promoted virtue in ordinary, local people, customs, events and morals. As Christopher Palmer has commented, it 'implied the statistical norm, the social generality; subject matter was drawn from the unexceptional rather than from the phenomenal, and settings tended to restrict themselves to the provincial and homespun'.[1] Keller, along with his contemporaries, Theodor Storm, Adalbert Stifter, Eduard Friedrich Mörike and Nikolaus Lenau, sought refuge in the settled order, observing value and honesty in rural, peasant life rather than in urban reality, and essentially represented a reaction to the insidious influences of materialism and industrialisation (just as Romanticism had earlier reacted to the starker truths of the Age of Reason) which threatened to overwhelm it. In one of his most famous stories, 'Romeo und Julia auf dem Dorfe', which was based on a newspaper report of a local tragedy, Keller tells of pauper lovers who commit suicide by drowning together. The progeny of two feuding farmers, Manz and Marti, who fall out over a coveted strip of land separating their fields, Sali and Vreli (Vreli) are forbidden to see each other (hence the reference to Shakespeare's famous

---

[1] Palmer, C., Delius: *Portrait of a Cosmopolitan* (London: Duckworth, 1974), 105.

drama). Riven with hate, the two fathers are impoverished by the cost of futile litigation – Manz becomes a humble publican, Marti sells all except his dilapidated cottage – and the families become homeless beggars; yet, with poetic irony, the ruinous process brings Sali and Vreli closer together and they grow up to fall in love. To exacerbate their predicament, a clandestine meeting at the cottage is discovered by Vreli's father, Marti, who, in attempting to remove his daughter, is felled violently to the ground by a more assertive adult Sali, but such was the force of his assault that Marti loses his reason and is confined to an asylum. Stigmatised by these events, the hapless couple dreams of marriage, only to realise that it is socially unacceptable for them to do so. Believing their predicament to be hopeless, they attend a local fair, are recognised, and, feeling oppressed by the staring crowd, seek refuge and solitude in an inn called 'The Paradise Garden'.[2]

Keller's tale is further punctuated by an inescapable curse: that of the illegitimate 'Dark Fiddler' (a character, which, at many turns, seems to embody Delius himself) whose dramaturgical behaviour is much like a *deus ex machina*.[3] Denied his rightful inheritance as the bastard son of the village 'trumpeter', he has become part of a group of vagabonds (a manifestation of Delius's aspiration to write an opera about gypsies), able to roam freely untrammelled by the conventions and social mores of everyday life. A more complex character, he seems at once a sinister presence: he is happy for the children to play on his land but announces his curse should the land be sold. At the heart of his warning lies the blight of avarice and jealousy under which Marti and Manz's friendship rapidly founders, yet, throughout the opera, the initial beneficence of the fiddler returns as he presents the despondent young couple with the choice of being their guide as well as joining him and his friends. 'Come and live with us and taste the cream of life!' Let others drink the sour milk of toil and strife!' he exclaims (a sentiment which was thoroughly in tune with Delius's own iconoclastic mentality), and offers to play for their wedding. Yet, such a course is beyond the scope of Sali, Vreli or Seldwyla's comfortable bourgeois culture and so, in more tragic vein, the fiddler appears once more on the verandah of the inn to accompany them in their death wish.

---

[2] This name appears in the original Keller story, but it has been commented that is may also have been derived from the nickname used by Delius's Norwegian friends to describe the garden at Grez-sur-Loing (see letter from Heiberg to Delius, 22 September 1897, *DLL1*, 120).

[3] Lyle, R., 'Delius and the Philosophy of Romanticism', *Music & Letters*, Vol. 29 No. 2 (April 1948), 163.

There were numerous elements of Keller's story which appealed to Delius. In much the same way as *Irmelin*, *The Magic Fountain* and *Koanga* had taken dramatic form, for *Romeo und Julia auf dem Dorfe* (as it was first published in c. 1906) or *A Village Romeo and Juliet* as it became in its anglicised version, it was still essential for Delius to acquire a libretto which embraced the idea of a Tristanesque 'death ecstasy'. This and the familiar underlying Shakespearean theme of doomed lovers in addition to the dark fiddler's curse (redolent of Alberich's curse in *The Ring*) made for a multi-layered narrative around which he could weave the additional themes of Nietzschean dance, the carefree vagabonds, and, as Boyle has suggested, the backdrop of a transplanted Norwegian landscape in which benign yet indifferent Nature could provide the inspiration for the larger symphonic canvas.[4] Following the example of *Koanga* there would be creative opportunities for ensemble, roles for several high baritones (a tessitura Delius increasingly seems to have favoured), and also more than adequate prospects for chorus in the marriage scene and the bustling market.[5] Yet, even more fundamental to Delius's design was a fairy-tale innocence removed from reality. 'These children', Heseltine remarked, 'unwitting in their wisdom, have come into the world with foreknowledge of evil, forewarned against the forces that accomplish the soul's corruption and disintegration. Death were a thousand times to be preferred to the tarnishing of the faith that is in them, to the slow fading of that dream which had been their best ideal, their great illusion'.[6] This fantastical aspect in particular would ultimately set Delius's opera apart from earlier efforts in its attempt to challenge the conventional tenets of opera as a genre.

Delius's first thoughts about adapting Keller's novella for operatic purposes were again to approach Keary; he was unsympathetic to the story. Writing to Delius in the summer of 1897, he remarked: 'For the moment I am stuck with R. & J. I don't see this 2nd (or rather 1st) act satisfactorily. If you have any suggestion to offer send it'.[7] *Teste* Ida Gerhardi, Keary found it a 'quite banal commonplace sentimental German love-story',[8] a reaction

---

[4] *DN*, 188–9.

[5] The high baritone tessitura of *Koanga* can not only be observed in the roles of Marti, Manz and the Dark Fiddler, but also in the bargemen in Scene 6. The lack of a prominent bass soloist in *A Village Romeo and Juliet* is conspicuous.

[6] *PH*, 84.

[7] Letter from Keary to Delius, [Summer 1897], *DLL1*, 115.

[8] *DLL1*, 117.

which led to the consideration of constructing a German libretto to be
made by Gerhardi's brother, Karl-August. However, by January 1899, Delius
began to think of taking on the task himself with Jelka's assistance.[9] Keary's
progress had been slow, but more detrimental to Delius's conception of the
work had been his Zola-like pursuit of realism. 'Everything must always be
true & realistic to an extreme', wrote Gerhardi to her brother, 'but that is
so dreadfully unmusical & reduces Delius constantly to despair'.[10] Once
the libretto had been drafted, much of the musical work of the opera was
undertaken between the end of 1899 and 1901. Act I was rapidly finished by
February 1900, but progress with Act II faltered. Holidays to his old haunts of
Normandy and Brittany, and to the Loire with Jelka, provided a diversion, but
attempts to revive his creative energy during an extended sojourn in Germany
in the winter of 1900 became a more fractious affair. Berlin, in particular, was
'so unsympathetic that my muse does not budge'.[11] After returning to Grez in
April 1901, the opera was completed, but we know from letters to Jelka that
he was still preoccupied with it in 1902, and Clare Delius also mentions that
revision of the work was still going on in 1905.[12]

In 1902 he once again asked his old friend Florent Schmitt, who was away
in Italy (having won the Prix de Rome with his cantata, *Sémiramis*, in 1900),
to undertake the preparation of the vocal score.[13] The score bears Delius's
original title of *Le Jardin du Paradis*, a reference to the inn at the end of the
opera, but also surely a further manifestation of Delius's 'Tristan' complex
in its allusion to idealist love. By c. 1906, however, when the vocal score was
published in German by the Parisian company Lévy-Lulx, Delius had opted for
the title of Keller's book, *Romeo und Julia auf dem Dorfe* (*nach Gottfried Kellers
gleichnamiger Erzählung*). These sources also reveal that Delius's original
adaptation had followed a similar model to that of *Koanga*, of a prologue and
three acts. This was the version that was first produced under Gregor (who

⁹ Letter from Delius to Jelka Rosen, [5 January 1899], *DLL1*, 143.

¹⁰ *DLL1*, 117.

¹¹ Letter from Delius to Jelka Rosen and Ida Gerhardi, 18 November 1900, *DLL1*,
    174.

¹² *CD*, 200.

¹³ The piano reduction of the manuscript vocal score, *GB-Lbl* MS Mus 1745/1/19, is
    in Schmitt's hand; the vocal parts are in Delius's. The German translation is in Jelka's
    hand and a French translation in red ink was provided by Robert d'Humières, friend
    of Proust and Oscar Wilde, translator of Kipling and the author of the silent drama
    Le Tragédie de Salomé (1907) for which Schmitt composed the score.

had directed *Koanga* at Elberfeld in 1904) at the Komische Oper in Berlin on 21 February 1907, though, by the time it was performed by Beecham at Covent Garden on 21 February 1910, its title and form had become *Romeo und Julia auf dem Dorfe: Lyrisches Drama in sechs Bildern nach Gottfried Keller* [*A Village Romeo and Juliet: Lyrical Drama in Six Scenes after Gottfried Keller*] in which the piano reduction, much altered from Schmitt's original version, was by Otto Lindemann. This scheme, published by Harmonie Verlag in 1910, subsumed the original conception (Table 6.1).

A PROBLEM OF GENRE

A comparison of these two schemes reveals that Delius revised his more traditional approach of three separate acts with an introductory prologue, similar to that of *Koanga*, into a continuous, homogenous symphonic drama of six scenes or tableaux, played without a break or interval. This is entirely consistent with several features. First, given the length of the opera at around one hour fifty minutes (in keeping with the conciseness of *Irmelin* and *The Magic Fountain*), the duration of each act would have seemed inordinately short, but as six scenes embodied a more substantial continuous structure. Second, Delius brought a greater homogeneity to his score which is conspicuous in the more mature and extensive symphonic development of his thematic material. And thirdly, this symphonic dimension was greatly enhanced by the exceptional role given to the *orchestra*. As Cecil Gray commented: Delius set himself the task of writing 'an opera in which the dramatic element of the representation only serves to interpret and elucidate the musical action; in which the stage action is only the realisation of the drama which is already embodied in the music, as the programme in the symphonic poem. In fact, the *Village Romeo* might be called a symphonic poem with the implicit programme made explicit upon the stage'.[14] Gray's conclusion, published in 1927, chimed with the passionate defence of *A Village Romeo and Juliet* expressed by Heseltine in his book on Delius of 1923. In fact, both men had contemplated the staging of the opera in a small theatre during the war where its intimacy might be better comprehended. Delius was not sanguine about the idea. 'I quite agree that The Village R ought to be given in a small theatre', he stated to Heseltine, 'but there must be an orchestra of at least 60. The piano Idea does

---

[14] Gray, C., *A Survey of Contemporary Music* (Oxford: Oxford University Press, 1927), 66.

Table 6.1. A *Village Romeo and Juliet*, comparison of the two dramatic schemes of 1907 and 1910.

1907 version		1910 version	Description
PROLOGUE	Vorspiel/prelude	Bild/Scene 1	–
	Scene 1		Fields of Marti and Manz – Marti ploughing his land.
	Scene 2		Enter Manz.
	Scene 3		Enter Sali and Vreli.
	Scene 4		Enter Dark Fiddler. Dispute between Marti and Manz.
ACT I	Vorspiel	Bild/Scene 2	–
	Scene 1		Outside Marti's house, Sali and Vreli swear their love.
	Interlude	Bild/Scene 3	–
	Scene 2		Sali and Vreli meet. Dark Fiddler. Sali and Vreli 'crown' each other.
	Scene 3		Marti discovers Sali and Vreli. Sali fells Marti to the ground.
ACT II	Vorspiel	Bild/Scene 4	–
	Scene 1		Interior of Marti's house. Vreli's lament. Enter Sali. Love duet.
	Scene 2		Sali and Vreli: Dream Scene [with chorus].
	Interlude		–
	Scene 3		Sali and Vreli awake. They resolve to go to Berghald for the fair.
ACT III	Vorspiel	Bild/Scene 5	[Dance]
	Scene 1		Fair and market [chorus].
	Scene 2		Sali and Vreli visit the fair. They are recognised and leave.
	Interlude		[Original replaced by *The Walk to the Paradise Garden*]
	Scene 3	Bild/Scene 6	'Dance along' [chorus]
	Scene 4		The Paradise Garden. Enter Dark Fiddler and vagabonds. They encounter Sali and Vreli.
	Scene 5		Sali and Vreli resolve to die together. Love duet.
	Orchestral postlude		–

not smile to me – My orchestra is too all important & almost the whole action on the stage is indicated in the Orchestra'.[15]

It was this very point which helped to focus Heseltine's argument on the issue of drama, or indeed on the accusations that Delius's opera was 'undramatic', a criticism which had emerged not only after the Berlin performances of 1907 but also after Beecham had undertaken the work at the Royal Opera House, Covent Garden on 22 and 25 February 1910. The Australian critic W. J. Turner echoed Heseltine's indignation in his own positive impression of the work:

> How ridiculous it is to complain that this story is not dramatic! One might as well complain of Burgundy for not sparkling. The fact is, our operatic public has got so used to fat tenors brandishing cardboard swords, and to daggers, poison, and revolvers, and to abductions, seductions, and desertions, that they do not know what to make of such a strange, inert flowerless passion as that of Sali and Vreli … The reticence and briefness of the love-passages between Sali and Vreli are extraordinarily refreshing, and in sensitiveness of outline and in harmonic colouring the music of modern Italian opera with its crude and blatant emotionalism will not bear comparison with it.[16]

Turner's remarks were profoundly insightful, but even more so in their prediction of the opera's fate: 'The Village Romeo and Juliet [sic] may not become a very popular work, but it is an opera that will wear better than three-fourths of the operas that are popular to-day, although it will always depend more than most on the way it is produced'.[17]

The polemic views of the opera began almost as soon as Fritz Cassirer, its first interpreter, began his acquaintance with the work in 1904. 'And I am very *grateful* to you for having done it! And for having dared to be so quiet, so simple, so sincere in an opera! And for having forgotten the "*Gallery*"! … All in all – this repressed ardour, this near-chaste anxiety of the modern soul, this deep, passionate stillness – you are the first who has dared on the operatic stage to speak so softly, to be so – "aristocratic"'.[18] Cassirer quickly

---

[15] Letter from Delius to Heseltine, 15 October 1916, *DLL2*, 172. Heseltine had in mind replacing the orchestra with two pianos (see letter from Heseltine to Delius, 11 October 1916, *FDPW*, 229).

[16] Turner, W. J., *Music and Life* (London: Methuen, 1921), 116–17.

[17] Ibid., 117.

[18] Letter from Fritz Cassirer to Delius, 13 May 1904, *DLL1*, 240–41.

understood that the opera challenged the traditional understanding of opera as a genre. It was Cassirer who introduced *A Village Romeo and Juliet* to the Berlin critic and musicologist Max Chop, who was 'utterly intoxicated' by it.[19] Chop was part of the 'committee' of judges present at Cassirer's soirée on 15 November 1906 (together with the producer Hans Gregor, his associate Otto Mertens, Maximilian Morris, the director, and Karl Walser, the illustrator and designer, and Cassirer's brother Bruno), to decide the fate of the work after reservations had been expressed about its suitability for the stage and the cost of production.[20] The decision to stage the opera was an agonised one, though Chop clearly played an important part in persuading Gregor to take it on.

The three performances at the Komische Oper were, according to Delius, something of a fiasco. Six years later, he recollected to Emil Hertzka of Universal edition that 'merely because of stage conditions, the entire hay-barge scene, and thus the entire ending, was left out. The orchestra was thoroughly 4th rate and in no state even to attempt to play the music'.[21] Yet this did not deter his greatest advocates such as Chop who supported Delius in the face of invective from the Berlin critics. In particular, Chop drew attention to the articles in the *Allgemeine Musik-Zeitung* and *Schlesische Zeitung,* both of which alluded to the immense forces of Delius's orchestra (which were even more extensive than *Paris* and *Lebenstanz* – and in this regard it is not difficult to appreciate Gregor's concerns about cost) and to the role of the orchestra in transforming the concept of opera as a genre:[22]

> His music, however, and in particular the orchestra with its brilliantly handled, colourful and gripping textures, reveals so much genuine and heartfelt emotion that one has to listen to this sound above all else. It is the orchestra which displays such astonishing powers of expression in the substantial symphonic interludes which connect the different scenes.[23]

---

[19] See letter from Cassirer to Delius, 6 December 1906, *DLL1,* 272–3.

[20] See letter from Cassirer to Delius, 26 November 1906, *DLL1,* 275.

[21] *MC,* 106.

[22] Besides the substantial material demands of his orchestra, Delius also asked for an on-stage violinist and six horns (although these could be provided by the orchestra), two cornets, two alto trombones, snare drum, tuned 'Stahlplatten', two 'Kirchenglocken' and an organ.

[23] Chop, M., 'Delius in Berlin', in Jones, P. (ed.), *The Collected Writings of the German Musicologist Max Chop on the Composer Frederick Delius* (Lewiston, NY, Queenston, ON and Lampeter: Edwin Mellen Press, 2002), 46.

The young Cambridge music lecturer Edward Dent, who was in Berlin to hear the opera, also remarked in his critique for *The Monthly Musical Record* that 'the main musical interest [was] in the orchestra, which [flowed] on, intangible and elusive, full of half-suggested phrases'.[24] But it was Heseltine who, if somewhat polemically (as was his wont), claimed that Delius's work broke new ground:

> To praise the music of this opera and cavil at the drama, as so many critics have done, is simply to expose the fact that the meaning of the music itself has not been grasped; for the drama is literally but the overflowing of the music from the region of the audible into that of the visible. If opera be defined as perfect co-relation between music and action, then *A Village Romeo and Juliet* is one of the most flawless masterpieces that have ever been given to the world. There is never any disparity between the music and the action; if the drama of the work is "undramatic" (according to the Italian-opera scale of values), then the music is too. What really matters is that the work is vitally expressive and that it illuminates things which matter in the lives of us all: and if this is not covered by the word *dramatic*, so much worse for the word.[25]

Writing in *The Musical Times* in 1920, after Delius had prohibited a performance of the opera at Covent Garden in November 1919 (on the grounds that insufficient rehearsal had taken place), he sought to clarify the opera's aesthetic significance:

> Opera, it should be remembered, is a *musical* form. It is not a play with music, though many such are termed operas or, more accurately, music-dramas. Opera is simply programme music with the programme enacted upon an external stage instead of in the imagination merely: and the scope of its programme may range from the crudest from of melodrama to the subtlest interplay of conflicting emotions.
>
> The old distinction between "operatic" and "symphonic" music has broken down as completely as the arbitrary differentiation of "programme" music from "abstract" or "absolute" music, which, in a word, is simply *music*.[26]

---

[24] Dent, E., 'English Opera in Berlin', in *DC*, 29.

[25] *PH*, 87–8.

[26] Heseltine, P., 'Delius's New Opera', *The Musical Times*, Vol. 61 No. 926 (April 1920), 237–8. The 1919 performance under Beecham was postponed until the following year.

Quintessentially what Heseltine identified in *A Village Romeo and Juliet* was that Delius, developing the prominent instrumental ethos of *Koanga* (especially at the end of Act III), makes unusually extensive use of the orchestra alone throughout the opera. Even Beecham was moved to remark: 'Delius has certainly a method of writing opera shared by no one else. So long as the singers are off the stage the orchestra plays delicately and enchantingly, but the moment they reappear it strikes up fiercely and complainingly as if it resented not being allowed to relate the whole story by itself'.[27] With the exception of Scenes 1 and 3 (which end abruptly), each scene begins and ends with a substantial passage of orchestral music, and in some instances such as Scenes 2 and 3, the concluding postlude of the former and the prelude of the latter elide to form an elongated interlude or miniature symphonic poem. Indeed, the preludial material of Scene 3 is a nature poem of no less than forty bars replete with mountain horn calls, built on the same rhetorical ideas from the opening of Scene 1. Scene 5 begins with a Nietzschean waltz and concludes with similar material, while the final scene ends with a substantial postlude. Scene 4, whose prelude anticipates Vreli's lament, is even more lavishly furnished with orchestral music in the 'Dream Scene'. Constructed in three sections totalling well over 100 bars, the first consists of a *Parsifal*-inspired ostinato of distant bells and a modal march (both preludial to a chorale sung by a distant choir), the second, a post-nuptial pealing of bells, and the third, an evocation of the dawn as an allegory of Sali and Vreli's conjugal love. But even this sizeable interlude is shorter than the conclusion of Scene 5. Originally this self-contained orchestral passage in E flat major, depicting the journey of the young couple to the 'Paradise Garden' (which was itself designed to link with the opening partsong of Scene 6 in the same key), was made up of forty-five bars (Example 6.1a). However, this was discarded in favour of the 132 bars which constituted its revision, now celebrated as a tone poem in its own right, *The Walk to the Paradise Garden*. Fenby maintained that Delius composed his new version on the suggestion of Beecham for the 1910 production in London.[28] This is, however, contradicted by Jelka Delius's letter to Heseltine of 28 September 1929 when she stated: 'The Entr'acte of the Village R. was composed or changed in 1906 for the Berlin performance ... The Entr'acte was composed at once after the Mass of Life and just before or in between Songs of Sunset'.[29] This is corroborated by

---

[27] MC, 88.

[28] Fenby, E., *Delius* (London: Faber & Faber, 1971), 49.

[29] RT2, 25.

a copy of the vocal score sent to Alfredo Mondello in Florence in 1907 which includes the revised entr'acte.[30] Having settled on this much longer interlude, it is clear that Delius considered its status entirely in keeping with the rest of the work. The notion of including protracted episodes of orchestral music within the larger symphonic framework of opera was, of course, not new. It is evident in much of *The Ring* and *Parsifal*, and Humperdinck, who attended one of the Berlin performances of Delius's opera,[31] used the device to great effect in the *Traumpantomime* at the end of Act II of *Hänsel und Gretel*. But Delius carried the concept of the orchestra as an articulate protagonist to a new extreme, asking his producer and director, actors and audience to imagine the drama beyond the physical presence of the stage towards romantic regions in which music *is* the drama. As Hutchings put it: 'music without words can suggest and express; words without music in such a place can hardly do more than describe, and in the precision and realism of description lies the danger of crudity and bathos'.[32] For Beecham, Delius's prescription seemed entirely natural, and for Heseltine, who believed the work to be a 'consummate masterpiece',[33] he was even ready to place the work above *Tristan*. 'Personally I must confess I am more and more bored by the first two acts of 'Tristan' every time I hear them', he wrote to Delius. 'For me the work is (historical considerations apart) only interesting as the fore-runner of the 'Village Romeo'.[34] The effect of *A Village Romeo and Juliet* on Heseltine's own music (as Peter Warlock) was such that he appropriated a similar conceptual paradigm in his most extended vocal and instrumental work, *The Curlew*. There, in a piece ostensibly dubbed a 'song cycle', the symphonic matrix provided by the chamber ensemble (which is as conspicuous a protagonist as the solo singer) emulates the process of Delius's opera in its extensive instrumental passages, thus exploring the possibilities of a much more complex, hybrid form.

As for Delius's view of his opera, we know that he believed fervently in what the work was trying to achieve. Yet, by 1913, he lamented the fact that it had not yet received a sympathetic staging. As he complained to Emil Hertzka at Universal Edition: 'Not a single one of my works has enjoyed an

---

[30] See letter from Delius to Alfredo Mondello [not Mondelli], 10 June 1907 (41D77) West Yorkshire Archive Service, Bradford. Mondello was a well-known theatre agent in Florence at that time. See also *RL*, 78 and *RT1*, 38.

[31] See letter from Engelbert Humperdinck to Delius, 12 March 1907, *DLL1*, 281.

[32] *AH*, 126.

[33] *PH*, 102.

[34] Letter from Heseltine to Delius, 11 November 1919, *FDPW*, 300.

immediate success. My music drama A Village Romeo & Juliet still awaits its true premiere; until now it has only been played under the most unfavourable circumstances and I still maintain that it will become a repertory piece'.[35] Indeed, he begged Hertzka to find a theatre which might at last give the opera the interpretation it needed: 'Is it not possible for you to place A Village Romeo and Juliet in a good theatre? The work is still awaiting its premiere. Only Vienna would be out of the question because of Gregor who has so mutilated it once already, by among other things omitting the whole of the ending, that he has done me great harm'.[36]

Example 6.1a. *A Village Romeo and Juliet*, original
orchestral interlude between Scenes 5 and 6.

35 *MC*, 106.
36 Ibid., 108.

Example 6.1a (continued).

SYMPHONIC FECUNDITY, SCENES 1–3

Besides the unique role of the orchestra in *A Village Romeo and Juliet,* one of the most striking elements is the advance Delius made in his understanding of thematic transformation and development, made possible not only by a greater sense of stylistic confidence (and by now he had finally experienced the 'viability' of his music in the concert hall) but also by a more sumptuous and varied thematic fecundity sustained by greater harmonic fluency. In this regard, Delius had moved on both technically and conceptually. Not only was the range, variety and character of his leitmotivs more evocative and complex, but the entire plastic nature of his leitmotivic world also assumed a richer generative life of its own. Having learned to handle a developmental process through the agencies of his symphonic poems, Delius now possessed the flexibility to transform his thematic ideas throughout the opera, a flexibility which also permitted a new interconnectivity between leitmotivs and one which more closely informed the dramatic events of the plot. This is evident from the outset in the prelude to Scene 1 where, in a variation structure more sophisticated than that of *Koanga*, Delius provides us with a rich 'seed bank' of material: the descending scale of the opening idea (borrowed from *Over the Hills and Far Away*), replete with a chorus of 'mountain' horns (a representation of nature and friendship) and a dominant pedal point, the familiar Delius thumbprint of the 'downbeat triplet' (3 bars after Fig. 1) used in a host of previous works, and the plagal cadential figure (3 bars after Fig. 2) are but three of the seminal ideas which are reworked at length (Examples 6.1b, 6.1c and 6.1d respectively). These ideas are seminal to the meta-structure of the opera, but Scene 1 also introduces other important ideas. The farmers at their ploughing recall an idea from *The Magic Fountain* (2 bars before Fig. 4) which provides much of the developmental fabric for the rest of the scene while the overtly contrapuntal sound of Delius's orchestra, written in the wake of *Lebenstanz* and *Paris*, has a Straussian opulence which

Example 6.1b. *A Village Romeo and Juliet*, Scene 1, opening idea.

Example 6.1c. *A Village Romeo and Juliet*, downbeat triplet idea.

Example 6.1d. *A Village Romeo and Juliet*, plagal cadential figure.

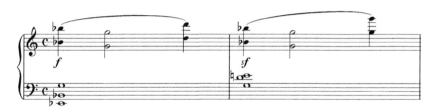

distinguishes it from the less elaborate pages of *Koanga*. The appearance of Sali and Vreli (3 bars after Fig. 12), with its Tristanesque appoggiaturas, already provides us with a sense of impending tragedy. Combining with a fragment which is derived from the opening 'nature' motive and the cadential material, this idea paves the way for the introduction of the 'Dark Fiddler' whose 'wind' music, based on a series of parallel ninths, shares a rhythmic similarity (Example 6.1e). The distinctiveness of these harmonic parallelisms has often been attributed to Debussy. Yet, Delius always maintained that the first Debussy he heard was the premiere in Paris of *Pelléas et Mélisande* in 1902 (a work he much admired). Dent, in his 1907 review, alluded to the influence of 'modern French tendencies'. If this was the case, it is more likely that Delius's awareness of this harmonic practice had been heightened by the modernisms of Fauré, Schmitt or Ravel whose 'fairy overture' *Shéhérazade* (recently been performed in Paris by the Société Nationale on 27 May 1899) was saturated with such devices. The 'Dark Fiddler' is not only inextricably associated with this material but also with his own melody (from Fig. 25). The bizarrely suave nature of the Fiddler's melody (introduced in the violin's lowest range) has an unsettling, even intimidating aura which is accentuated by this warning to the children and their fathers. This is set to music of considerable chromatic intensity (Figs 27–28) in which Delius's harmonic rhythm is notably profuse (a technique familiar from the variation structure of the second subject in *Paris*). A juxtaposition of all three ideas witnesses the Fiddler's departure in another substantial passage of orchestral music which hastens the dispute between Manz and Marti. In a rare display of realism, the violent enmity which transpires between the two, thematically imbued with the tragic appoggiaturas of the children and strains of the Fiddler, is enacted in no more than fifty-eight bars of music. Consistent with Delius's preference for conciseness, this concluding section is nevertheless an impressive and concentrated symphonic episode in which, besides the thematic allusions mentioned above, the entire

Example 6.1e. *A Village Romeo and Juliet*, 'Dark Fiddler' theme.

ill-omened paragraph is underpinned by a thorough working-out of the three-note chromatic figure (introduced imperceptibly in the cello and bass clarinet) which reaches a peak of ferocity after Fig. 35.

The prelude to Scene 2 introduces several new thematic ideas – one suggesting the menacing nature of Sali's visit to Marti's derelict property (Example 6.1f), the 'cry of despair' (Example 6.1g) and, more elusively, the underlying love of the cursed couple in bars 13–14, an idea brought to prominence thanks to Delius's skilled, strident instrumentation (Example 6.1h). The consummate fluidity of the orchestral counterpoint, well suited to Delius's endless fount of lyricism, also provides an increasingly fecund source for the extensive development of the opening figure in numerous guises (notably a chromatic Tristanesque version – Example 6.1i) from which much of Sali's declamatory material is derived. This, in combination with the rising triplet figure, strategically presented at Fig. 13, provides a telling reminiscence of their childhood 'normality' of Scene 1, one tellingly emphasised by the presence of C major which underpins not only the rest of the scene but much of the buoyant orchestral postlude. In the closing bars of the latter, Delius also took the opportunity, with a special ethereal serenity, to introduce an additional thematic fragment (Example 6.1j) representative of 'the bond of love' between

Example 6.1f. *A Village Romeo and Juliet*, 'Marti's derelict property'.

Example 6.1g. *A Village Romeo and Juliet*, 'cry of despair'.

Example 6.1h. *A Village Romeo and Juliet,*
'underlying love of the cursed couple'.

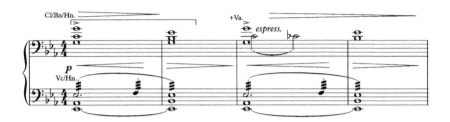

Example 6.1i. *A Village Romeo and Juliet,* chromatic
version of Scene 1, opening idea, 'doomed love'.

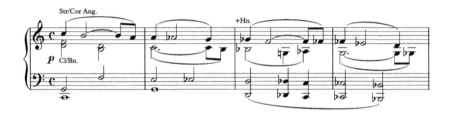

Example 6.1j. *A Village Romeo and Juliet,* 'the bond of love'.

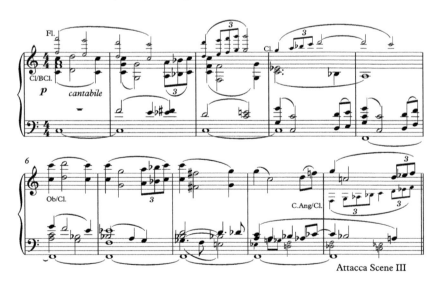

Attacca Scene III

Sali and Vreli, the effect of which was to anticipate, some dramatic distance
hence, the final scene where the couple decide to die together. The underlying
presence of the nature idea (see Example 6.1b) as a counterpoint to the
'bond' fragment surfaces again in another new form as a melodic 'suffix' to the
'mountain calls' of the prelude to Scene 3. Played by six on-stage horns, this
material undoubtedly referred to the rugged terrain of the distant mountains.
Certainly this was evocative of the Swiss landscape elucidated in Delius's stage
directions, but it was also a symbol of freedom and of the iconoclasm which he
had explored as far back as his Ibsenesque melodrama *Paa Vidderne*.[37] The slow
harmonic pace of the preludial material to Scene 3 is epitomised by the series
of pedal points which Delius favoured so much. It also provides a platform
for the ecstatic meeting of Sali and Vreli (recalling Act II of *Tristan*) and the
'nature' motive which again permeates their first section of dialogue (Figs 27
to 30), though this also combines with a further leitmotiv, one signifying 'ruin'
(Example 6.1k). Derived from material heard in the prelude to Scene 2 (see
Fig. 1), this idea curtails the first part of the scene. Central to Scene 3, however,
is the return of the Dark Fiddler whose ingress and exit are marked by the
distinctive parallel ninth progressions. In this context the troubling presence
of the Fiddler's melody is tempered by a degree of diatonic lyricism intended
to convey a sense of benevolence towards the young couple. 'I bear you no
ill will' the Fiddler exclaims, and issues his first proposition to them to join
his itinerant existence (see Fig. 34). The interaction of this material and the
Fiddler's melody is deftly executed for it provides a subtle enough chemistry
to support his ominous departing words 'We'll meet again no doubt, further
down the hill!' and Vreli's sense of fear, which is marked by a further recurrence
of the 'ruin' fragment (two bars after 40). The gentle, pastoral love duet which
ensues between Sali and Vreli introduces two further important thematic ideas,
the first a lullaby 'charm' (Example 6.1l) which embodies their 'incipient love'

Example 6.1k. *A Village Romeo and Juliet*, 'ruin'.

[37] *DN*, 190–91.

and the second, their 'kiss' (Example 6.1m) which concludes the duet. The innocence of this last leitmotiv, moreover, provides a sufficiently contrasting backdrop for Marti's discovery of Sali and Vreli which, as a fast-moving coda to Scene 3, provides a second phase of sinister realism to the drama. At this juncture Delius astutely took the opportunity to rework the same menacing bass figure from the end of Scene 1 in a transition whose passing Tristanesque appoggiaturas make plaintive reference to the couple's hapless involvement in their father's feuding. The coda itself is appropriately more violent in its portrayal of Sali's discovery of his adulthood as he fells Marti to the ground, though most impressive in these last bars of the scene are the references to the 'ruin' motive – Sali's anguished distillation, immediately followed by the 'cry of despair', and a second recurrence in the orchestra underpinned by C minor, a key which neatly closes off the first part of the opera.

OPERATIC TONE POEM, SCENES 4–6

It is already evident from an examination of the first three scenes of *A Village Romeo and Juliet* that, through the precedents of *Irmelin*, *The Magic Fountain* and *Koanga*, Delius's approach to opera was now assuming a particularly personal distinctiveness, not only in its terseness of form but also in the unusually extensive role played by the orchestra, a factor which functioned symbiotically with the profuseness of the thematic material and its overt symphonic behaviour. Much of the purely instrumental interaction took place in preludial and postludial contexts, but in the second part of the opera (Scenes 4–6), this contextual orbit widened considerably and with it a greater symphonic richness as the composer made fertile use of his already abundant thematic reservoir. One also senses that, in this later phase of the drama,

Example 6.1l. *A Village Romeo and Juliet*, 'incipient love' (with lullaby 'charm').

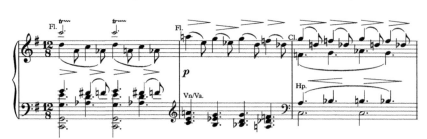

Example 6.1m. *A Village Romeo and Juliet*, 'kiss'.

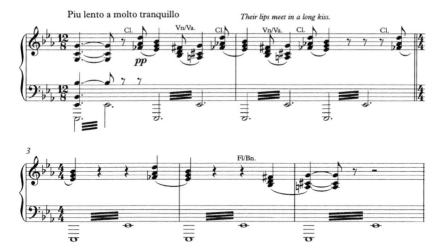

Delius became more attuned to the significance and dramatic functionality of key association. Much of Scene 4, for example, is centred around the keys of B flat and E flat, and only with the couple's new determination to enjoy life for the moment does the tonal orientation decisively change to E major (a key to which Delius also attached significance later in the opera). This strong sense of tonal cohesion also underpinned the essential simplicity of the scene's tripartite scheme in which the 'dream scene', a tableau for chorus and orchestra, was the central focus.

The richer symphonic ambiance of the opera is affirmed in the opening prelude of Scene 4. Framed by the 'kiss' motive, it features a further 'cry of despair' (Fig. 1) on one of Delius's favoured augmented-sixth harmonies (a characteristic 'sound moment' in his language) before making way seamlessly for 'doomed love' (see Example 6.1i). All this is preparatory for a new theme (Example 6.1n), a nocturnal lament (Fig. 3) which brings to mind the Grieg-inspired lyricism of *Irmelin*. This melancholy utterance is subject to a series of miniature variations within the orbit of B flat major, and later, when Vreli makes her vocal entry in a second series of variations around E flat. At the conclusion of her lament, a second, passionate reunion with Sali recalls *Tristan* once more, the sound of which is palpable in the gestures of despair and desire which Delius gives us (the presence of the 'Tristan' chord, three bars after Fig. 8, is evidence enough) in the preceding transition. That Wagnerian sense of symphonic continuity lies at the heart of the couple's first love duet ('O Sali, I should have died had you not come'). Here, in another series of variations, one phrase (Example 6.1o) is developed copiously on three transpositional levels before the presence of 'doomed love', fortified by the reprise of Vreli's lament, reasserts itself. Delius, however, subjects this leitmotiv to yet a further transformation (Fig. 21). In diatonic guise (and a nod in the direction of *Koanga*), it supports Sali's resolve to stand by his love ('What will you do?'), a noble determination strengthened by a rare instance of a perfect cadence into E flat ('Vreli, my love'); and the leitmotiv continues to be developed after E flat has been quitted for G major (Fig. 24) when it combines with a reprise of the triplet figure (see Example 6.1c), now a symbol of the lovers' new-found confidence ('to wander free and careless like gipsies on the great road'). This too concludes with a perfect cadence and a recurrence of the 'kiss' motive.

As a conduit to the 'dream scene', and in anticipation of its opening solemnity, Delius deftly provided a miniature strophic design in which Vreli's first verse ('Come sit beside me here') is answered by a Sali's second (as a variation). It is a moment of magical serenity, enhanced by the simplicity of the fluid modality (again suggestive of Grieg). The 'dream scene' itself is one of the most remarkable passages of Delius's opera and functions as an important dramatic and musical fulcrum to the work. Each section of the tripartite construction begins with the same opening melodic contour (derived loosely from the previous conduit – see Fig. 27) from which new music transpires (Example 6.1o – cf. Figs 31, 38 and 42). The distant bells, framing the first episode, suggest the influence of Act I of *Parsifal*. Adroitly, the two chimes, one defining B flat, the other D flat, reflects the tonal dualism of the austere procession (couched in B flat minor) and the chorale (in D flat), a gesture which recalls the opening of Act I of *Die Meistersinger*. From the earnestness of B flat minor, the second episode swiftly changes to the tonic major which also plays on a similar third relationship of B flat major and G minor. This relationship receives special accentuation in the elliptical cadence (vi–I)

Example 6.1n. *A Village Romeo and Juliet*, 'nocturnal lament'.

Example 6.1o. *A Village Romeo and Juliet*, first love duet.

immediately before the pealing of the church bells and it is further exploited in the subsequent purely orchestral 'carillon' which closes affirmatively in B flat. This concludes the wedding scene (and, in conventional dramatic contexts, might well have completed the scene), but Delius's *coup de maître* is yet to come, for a third episode, in G flat major, signals the dawn, both physically and in terms of the couple's realisation of their undying love. In what must be some of Delius's most passionate music, the composer introduces a new melodic figure (Example 6.1p) which, combined with 'incipient love' of Scene 3 and

Example 6.1p. *A Village Romeo and Juliet,* 'ardour'.

the triplet figure (see after Fig. 43), expresses a new sense of ardour, especially in the magnificent climactic progressions immediately before the cadence in to G flat. What is more, the sense of mutual discovery between Sali and Vreli is articulated entirely by *instrumental* means, an effect for which Delius had surely been seeking since his first foray into opera in the early 1890s. Indeed, the impression is of a mingling of opera and tone poem.

The juxtaposition of G flat and the D minor chord at Fig. 44 breaks the spell and the restoration of B flat major not only returns us to reality but also to the happy recognition that the lovers have shared the same dream. In the ensuing dialogue between Sali and Vreli, the fabric of the orchestral music is imbued with the revivified triplet figure and the 'dawn' motive, until, at the close of this lovely lyrical paragraph, Vreli utters the prophetic words, 'Oh how I long for one long day with you'. This invokes an even more intense series of references to the 'dawn' idea which so eloquently captures the couple's longing for happiness. But while Vreli is detained by melancholy, E major signals a joyful finale in which the chorus (of whom Delius demands abnormal vocal agility) join the soloists in a premonition of the 'dance' ethos of Scene 5, and the lovers forget their woes, a sentiment Delius highlights by recalling a transformed version of the 'ruin' motive.

Table 6.2. *A Village Romeo and Juliet*, Scene 5, structural overview.

Structure	Figure	Key
EXPOSITION		
First subject (orchestral introduction)		E♭ major
First subject (chorus and 'cries')	4	E♭ major
Second subject (trumpet theme and choral refrain)	7	F major
DEVELOPMENT		
Entrance of Sali and Vreli	13^{+5}	B♭ major – E major
'Cries' (first subject)	16	E major
Recognition of Sali and Vreli (second subject)	21	E major – A♭ major
Chorus of peasants (first subject)	25	F major
Vreli and Sali ('O Sali, it fits me quite') (second subject)	26	D major
Vreli ('Why do they stare at us?')	27^{+3}	
Chorus (second subject)	28^{+1}	F major
Orchestra (second subject)	29	A major
Sali and Vreli decide to leave	32	
RECAPITULATION		
Chorus, Sali and Vreli (second subject)	33	B♭ major
Orchestra (first subject)	35	E♭ major

Scene 5 is conspicuous in *A Village Romeo and Juliet* in that it is the one section of the opera which substantially features the chorus, and in this sense alone it provides some relief from the soloists as an interlude. The scene of the fair at Berghold is also a Nieztschean choral dance which not only recalls the waltz obsession of *Paris* but also its 'cries' among the fair's stallholders. But perhaps the most impressive feature of Scene 5 is its brilliant conception as a self-contained sonata movement (see Table 6.2).[38] Cast in E flat major, the fairground music (as a first subject) makes use of some of Delius's most advanced harmony (note the parallel sevenths of the tolling bells). The second subject, a composite idea, takes the form of a melody for solo trumpet (Fig. 7) with a choral refrain (Fig. 8) which cadences in F major. A developmental phase, in which these two contrasting thematic ideas interact,

[38] The self-contained form of Scene 5 made it an attractive and viable concert item which Beecham exploited as a partner to *The Walk to the Paradise Garden*. See *RT1*, 41.

marks the entry of Sali and Vreli. An initial episode in E major is succeeded by others in A flat and D major at which point the couple realise, to their discomfort, that they have become the subject of attention. At this juncture, the second subject returns (Fig. 28), first in F major with chorus, later more ebulliently in A major for orchestra and, after a brief interruption in which Sali and Vreli decide to leave for a place where they are less conspicuous, B flat major (Fig. 33). The scene then proceeds to conclude in E flat major with an orchestral form of the first subject, one which yields to *The Walk to the Paradise Garden*, Delius's extended entr'acte between Scenes 5 and 6.

After the set piece of Scene 5, which is the shortest of the opera, the more substantial Scene 6, situated at 'The Paradise Garden', juxtaposes a number of contrasting operatic style-forms in a bid to settle those parts of the drama which are still unresolved. As a prelude to the scene, Delius deploys a partsong ('Dance along') in E flat which, in linguistic terms, looks back to the partsongs of his student days at Leipzig, particularly those in 6/8 compound metre. Sung by the vagabonds, its distant horn-call gestures evoke that recurring theme throughout the opera of an untrammelled freedom, in nature, away from the conventions of human manners. It also anticipates the central role of the Dark Fiddler who plays a major part in the opera's denouement. Indeed, after a variation of the partsong for horns alone (at which the curtain is raised), it is the Dark Fiddler who moves forward to join his fellow vagabonds at the table and to whom, Wotan-like, he recounts the events of the drama in a ballad couched in F minor ('So, you want to know how that strife began?'). At the ballad's conclusion, as F minor gives way to a tender F major, Sali and Vreli make their entrance in the hope that they will not be recognised, only to meet the Dark Fiddler one more time. In promising to play at their wedding, he renews his offer of a life free of travail. This passage, based around E major, functions as a conduit to a second set piece, a partsong with a refrain 'Vagabonds are we'. The main body of this extended chorus is based in A flat, but enveloping it is the broader sweep of F major which underpins the conclusion. Sali and Vreli have been participants in this elaborate polyphonic choral paragraph – one of Delius's most intricate vocal ensembles – but after digesting the Dark Fiddler's proposal they decline, a reaction accompanied by a reprise of the 'ruin' motive. There follows at this juncture some of Delius's most heart-rending lyrical music headed by the recurrence of a final transformation of the upward triplet figure (Example 6.1q), this time as a wistful gesture of realisation at their hopeless predicament and of their 'tragic destiny'. The idea is presented in a manner now well associated with Delius's methods as a set of short variations and through a sequence of closely related tonalities.

One of several masterstrokes in this last phase of the opera is Delius's highly imaginative creation of the distant bargemen. Only a hint of this is given in Keller's novella:

[Vreli] "How beautiful it is around here! Listen! It seems to me there is somebody far away singing in a low voice".
[Sali]   "No, sweetheart, it is only the water softly flowing".
[Vreli] "And yet it seems there is some music – way out there, everywhere".
[Sali]   "I think it is our own blood coursing that is deceiving our ears".[39]

Example 6.1q. *A Village Romeo and Juliet*, 'tragic destiny'.

39 Keller, G., *Romeo und Julia auf dem Dorfe*, trans. Von Schierbrand, W. (Berliner Bilinguale Ausgabe, 2015), 64.

Delius's bargemen are symbols of a transformation as is clear from the stage direction: 'It seems as if something mysteriously beautiful had touched the garden by enchantment', a sentiment captured by Vreli's climactic phrase 'This is the garden of Paradise'. But, as wanderers along the river, the bargemen also embody a transience in their refrain 'travellers we a-passing by' and their music (also for high baritones) has a mellifluousness which links effortlessly with a second variation structure based on the 'bond of love' motive from the end of Scene 2 (see Example 6.1j). It is with the recollection of this poignant material and the more heartbreaking references to 'doomed love' and 'ruin', in which the couple resolves to die together, that Delius skilfully generates his 'prelude' to the forthcoming 'Liebestod'. Indeed, it is with the last repetition, in E major, a key much associated throughout the opera with the emotional states of joy and devotion, that their pledge is made ('and then to die, were not that eternal joy?') and a modulation to the 'Liebestod' in D flat major is smoothly effected.

That Delius's confidence and sophistication is abundantly evident in this opera should by now be self-evident. Scene 6, in particular, is used as an important opportunity for thematic recapitulation, nowhere more so than with the 'Liebestod' which presents a final reworking of the opening 'nature' motive ('See the moonbeam kiss the woods') taken from the original entr'acte between Scenes 5 and 6. Given its context, Delius presents the material as a barcarolle. The use of D flat not only recalls Wagner but also Delius's exploitation of the key at the close of *The Magic Fountain*. The Tristanesque setting is of course unabashed and much of Delius's polyphonic writing, imbued with its sequential semitonal progressions downward, has a palpable Wagnerian flavour (see Fig. 90), as does the powerful climax which restores E major and a memory of the cadential motive from the opening of Scene 1 (see Example 6.1d). But Delius reserves his most Wagnerian statement for the closing orchestral statement. This takes place after the Dark Fiddler's 'concerto', a virtuoso demonstration underpinned by a conflation of his theme, the whole-tone wind music and a valedictory gesture from the vagabonds. The harmonic rapidity and rising orchestral volume of this passage is very much commensurate with the dramatic action, as Sali lifts Vreli onto the boat, jumps on himself, casts off and withdraws the plug. Delius's *coup de maître* occurs with the final three parallel harmonies, 'sound moments', which in themselves are deeply evocative of that Schopenhauer-inspired expression of ecstasy as Sali throws the plug into the river and Vreli utters her lover's name for the last time. As the boat begins to sink, Delius reaches the dominant of C (a tonality so prominent in the first stages of the opera), and the expectation of resolution to C seems irresistible – except that Delius's elliptical cadence is to *B major* (yet a further reference to *Tristan*), a tonality which, over the final forty-four bars of the opera, chronicles the sinking of the boat. Although much of this passage is also purely orchestral (which re-emphasises the vital and extensive role of instrumental music within the work), it also affords the opportunity to re-invoke voices and music of the distant bargemen. Appended to this mystical gesture, what is more, is Delius's familiarly stoical 'Heigh-Ho!', a musical figure subtly linked to the 'kiss' motive (see Example 6.1m).

THE WALK TO THE PARADISE GARDEN

It has been mentioned above that the entr'acte, *The Walk to the Paradise Garden*, was probably composed as a longer replacement for the much shorter interlude Delius originally conceived for the first performances of the opera in Berlin in 1907. Whatever its actual date of composition may be, one thing, however, is abundantly clear: Delius continued to be profoundly inspired by the cornucopia of thematic material he had created and by the new operatic ethos of staged tone poem he had authored in *A Village Romeo and Juliet*. Such a mentality must have been in his mind when *The Walk to the Paradise Garden* came into being, since he obviously exercised no compunction in believing that an 'interlude' of 132 bars of music (in place of an entr'acte a third its size) would conform with the work's aesthetic aims. 'Interlude' was the term used by Heseltine,[40] and also by Beecham when the work was published as a separate entity, though later, in published form it was referred as 'Intermezzo'.[41] This is true insofar as the work is located between Scenes 5 and 6, but, given the work's final cadence in B major (as opposed to the original ending's seamless transition to Scene 6), it actually functions as a *conclusion* to Scene 5. The generous proportions of *The Walk to the Paradise Garden* also seem to owe something to the intervening years in which *Sea Drift* and *A Mass of Life* had been composed. These two works, perhaps more than any other precedents, exude that extraordinary sense of confidence and stylistic coherence which Delius had discovered between 1903 and 1905, and one senses that, in the pages of these works, especially the voluptuous passages in B major (notably from 'The Song of Life') which sensuously overflow in *A Mass of Life*, Delius's so-called 'interlude' derived much of its confidence and unmistakable harmonic syntax.

[40] *PH*, 85.

[41] The entr'acte first bore the title of *The Walk to the Paradise Garden* after publication by Universal in 1922.

Heseltine described the 'miraculously lovely orchestral interlude' as 'an epitome of the whole drama',[42] a perspicacious comment worthy of more elaboration. As intimated above, the original interlude focused entirely on the thematic figure which, as a transformation of the opening 'nature' music, later became the opening of the love duet (see Example 6.1a). In the revised version the first sixteen bars, defined by E flat, were retained. Thereafter the music took a different turn. Cast in G major (see Figs 41 to 45) the next paragraph is led by a development of the upward triplet figure (Example 6.1b) which combined with strains of the 'nature' motive and references to the 'cry of despair'. The climax, on the subdominant, is marked by statements of the transformed 'nature' idea in augmentation, before the raising of the curtain, revealing Sali and Vreli 'hand in hand on their way to the Paradise garden', and signals a new tonal departure. As a thematic consequence of his use of the triplet figure, and with great deftness, Delius appropriated the lyrical music of 'tragic destiny' from Scene 6 in a paragraph of unequalled beauty defined by E major. This is curtailed by a reprise of the 'kiss' motive above a dominant pedal of E (Example 6.1m) before a new phase of development sets out from E major with a statement of the original 'nature' motive (see Fig. 48), though central to this stage of the movement is the combination of 'tragic destiny' and the parallelisms of the Dark Fiddler's music (Fig. 49). The goal, however, of this reworking is the climax of the entire movement: a passionate statement of 'tragic destiny' in B major whose references to the plagal cadential motive of Scene 1 also haunt the final bars of the extended tranquil coda.

The Walk to the Paradise Garden is to all intents and purposes a tone poem in its own right and was first performed as a 'stand alone' work by the Birmingham Philharmonic Society on 14 February 1912 under Beecham; its first London performance took place at Queen's Hall under the aegis of the Philharmonic Society on 24 November 1914, again under Beecham's direction.[43] Championed by Beecham, as well as by others such as Wood, Harty and Anthony Collins, the work has often been the only means of hearing music from the opera. Heseltine's postulation that it encapsulates the essence of the drama has some truth: reference to those seminal leitmotivs from the opening of Scene 1 plays a central role, but it is their transformed counterparts of Scene 6 which play a dominant part in Delius's beautifully controlled through-composed structure. What is more, much of the tonal design – the opening in E flat (which refers back to Scene 5 as well as the beginning of Scene 6),

---

[42] *PH*, 85.

[43] *RT1*, 41.

the lyrical centrepiece in E major and the conclusion in B major, were clearly derived from those tonal areas employed in Scene 6. Thus, the tone poem not only provides a form of thematic anticipation, but also gives us a tonal foretaste of the opera's final scene.

A SCANDINAVIAN DIVERSION

Although Delius's attention was principally addressed towards opera between 1900 and 1902, the pull of Danish poetry, which had so absorbed him in 1896 and 1897 in the stylistically pivotal *Danish Songs*, remained a vital stimulus nourished by his continued fascination with Norway. The two settings of Ludvig Holstein, composed in 1900 (and originally published in both German and English in 1906), have a structural simplicity in their strophic designs, though the vocal lines resemble the more chromatic complexities of *A Village Romeo and Juliet*). A notable feature of the two verses of 'Viol' ('The Violet') is the oblique nature of the tonal organisation. It is only at the conclusion of each verse, with the mention of 'Viol', that G major is achieved (and here the setting of the Danish, which Delius also undertook, is more successful in its accentuation than either the German or English translations). The plaintive 'Efteraar' ('Autumn'), which sets the first, second and last verses of Holstein's poem, is distinctive for its dialogue between son and father and disconsolate refrain 'Ingen ved hvorhen' ('No-one knows whereto'). Verses one and two, which question the behaviour of nature in autumn, establish a strophic form in E flat major, though the final cadence of each refrain is to the minor. The last verse, even more earnest in tone, seeks an answer to human existence ('whither do we go?'), to which Delius aptly responded with more deliberate Wagnerian recitation and an even more unsettling elliptical cadence into G flat minor.

'Schwarze Rosen', from 1901 (though not published until 1915), is a setting of the eponymous verse by the Swedish poet and painter, Ernst Josephson. A deeply sorrowful poem (which looks forward to the sentiment of *Songs of Sunset*, not least with the refrain 'For sorrow has night-black roses'), the two verses (of Josephson's three) influence the two distinct parts of Delius's through-composed design, the first a tonally fluid preparation for the second, more animated section in B flat. The climax, on a 6/4 of B flat is carefully placed ('joy and peace'), though it is the return of the opening dissonant piano gesture in the final bars as the refrain and the longing, unresolved seventh of the final chord that conveys the song's unremitting melancholy. Two further songs, 'Jeg hører i natten' ('I hear in the night') and

'Sommer i Gurre' (Summer landscape'), looked to the more familiar poetry of Drachmann. The stormy 'Jeg hører i natten' conveys the fluttering fears of the text through the rapid rhythmic exchange of semiquavers between the hands, though it is the semitonal shifts of the harmony (and the motion between the hands), most notably through the motivic motion of the foreign G natural at the head of verse one (and which Delius repeats before verses two and four) that evokes the sense of inner turbulence. 'Sweet memories' and a deep sense of longing lie at the heart of the languorous 'Sommer i Gurre', dated April 1902. Even more than 'Schwarze Rosen', the concentrated harmonic language and nuance of this song suggests that it was a 'study' for those most sensual parts of *A Mass of Life* and *Songs of Sunset*. This can be felt in the opening drone (which anticipates 'Pale amber sunlight'), the thumbprint of the upward chromatic appoggiatura of the phrase 'Dagen vil sove' (which looks forward to 'Exceeding sorrow'), so effectively used for the reprise's climax ('og der fødes et Digt'), and the measured rhythm of the vocal delivery (such as in 'In dein Auge schaute ich jüngst' of *A Mass of Life*) with its deep sense of longing. After the delicacy of the central section ('Det sitter et Minde på hvert et Blad'), which seems prophetic of those poignant nature evocations in the *Requiem*, the truncated recapitulation, underpinned almost entirely by a dominant pedal, imparts a compelling feeling of resolution at the final cadence in B flat. Perhaps a further indication of Delius's aesthetic concept of this song can be heard in its more nuanced orchestrated version which the composer made in 1903; this may also be said of 'Viol' which was later scored for Olga Wood and performed in Liverpool on 21 March 1908.

MARGOT LA ROUGE: VERISMO OR NATURALISM?

Delius, we are told, was never especially attracted by the operatic phenomenon of *verismo* or realism expressed as continual physical action. In fact, according to Fenby, it was a form of drama he loathed.[44] For him, realism was an extension of the Wagnerian ideals of *Tristan*, where the action was psychological and internalised. Nevertheless, as has been demonstrated, he was an ardent advocate of reshaping opera into something terser and more succinct in design where such ideals were communicated with a new brevity. Such principles he reiterated with a characteristic lack of compromise to G. M. Stevenson-Reece in a rare interview for the *Evening News* in 1919:

[44] *EF*, 118.

The future of opera generally as an art-form? Length and cumbrousness, in my opinion, will be the first features to disappear, and that is the end towards which I am working – brevity and conciseness. Long dialogues and wearisome narrations must go, and will be replaced by short, strong emotional impressions given in a series of terse scenes. Ninety minutes to two hours is long enough for any opera, and by reducing intervals, as I have done in my own work, to three minutes instead of the usual half-hour necessitated by ponderous realistic decoration, this limit can easily be preserved.[45]

In *A Village Romeo and Juliet*, Delius had shown himself susceptible to 'poetic realism' in Keller's love of the parochial and the ordinary conditions of day-to-day life. What is more, extensive sections of *Koanga* and at least two brief passages of *Romeo and Juliet* revealed that he was far from incapable of presenting 'dramatic' action onstage when it was warranted.

Extraordinary though it may seem, even after the completion of *A Village Romeo and Juliet* and without the immediate prospect of any performances, Delius's appetite for opera had by no means diminished, and the prize for one-act operas initiated by the Italian publisher Edoardo Sonzogno offered a rare opportunity to produce a work which chimed with many of his dramatic aspirations, besides offering the prospect of a performance in Italy, international publicity and, as a bonus, a financial reward, always welcome in Delius's case. Although the Sonzogno award began in 1883, it was not until 1890, with the staging of Mascagni's *Cavalleria Rusticana* (which won the prize in 1889), that the one-act opera as an appropriate vehicle of *verismo* was born. What is more, Mascagni's masterpiece coincided with the beginning of a decade which marked the heyday of *verismo* in Europe with the popularity of Leoncavallo's *Pagliacci* (1892) and *Zazà* (1900), Puccini's *La Bohème* (1896) and *Tosca* (1900), Massenet's *La Navarraise* (1894) and *Sapho* (1897), Bruneau's *Messidor* (1897) and Cilea's *Adriana Lecouvreur* (1902), not to mention an entire series of works from the pen of Giordano, who, along with Mascagni, was one of the archetypal exponents of *verismo*. Although these operas could consist of up to four acts in length, the acts themselves were short, direct and uncomplicated in structure. It was the particular brevity of the one-act opera, such as one finds in Mascagni's *Zanetto* (1896) or in Puccini's later triptych *Il tabarro*, *Suor Angelica* and

---

[45] Quoted in *CD*, 199.

Gianni Schicchi (1918) which encouraged a return to the Aristotelian sense of unity in terms of time and place and which, in turn, lent the form a singular intensity in terms of emotional focus. Jérôme Rossi has also argued convincingly that Delius's choice of subject, a Parisian prostitute called Margot la Rouge, was almost certainly determined by his own experiences of Parisian night life, his frequentation of the café culture in the French capital, and the city's brothels.[46] What is more, the atmosphere was generated by the setting, a 'cabaret de banlieue', and the attendant characters – pimps, prostitutes, soldiers, criminals, impecunious artists, hardened drinkers – were those who typically inhabited the margins of society and appeared regularly in Zola's naturalist literature. What is more, Zola as novelist and playwright was very much to the fore in the late 1890s and the turn of the century. After the great success of *l'Assommoir*, the seventh of his cycle of twenty naturalist novels, known as *Les Rougon-Macquart*, Zola had become a leader in his profession. Universally admired, the admixture of realism and romanticism in his novels was highly influential in the theatre and the opera house, not least with Bruneau's *Messidor* and Charpentier's *Louise*.

During the 1890s Delius had become acquainted with a number of naturalist-leaning writers. Some, such as Jean Richepin, he knew through his association with the Molard circle. Other prominent naturalist authors such as Armand Abraham Blocq – known as Gaston-Danville – were from a more elevated class, but given Delius's own social mobility and standing, and his ability to interact with the culture-loving aristocratic houses of Paris, it was by no means impossible for him to gain such introductions either directly or through intermediaries.[47] Gaston-Danville's wife, Berthe, was also a writer under the *nom de plume* Karl Rosenval. More significantly she already possessed some experience in writing libretti for operettas such as *Leda* (1897) and *L'heure du Berger* (1900).[48] As Rossi has also suggested, she was enjoying a degree of exposure in Parisian theatrical circles just at the time when Delius was planning his Sonzogno opera.[49]

---

[46] Rossi, J., '*Margot La Rouge*, un verisme a la française', in Rossi, J. (ed.), *Frederick Delius et la France* (Paris: Delatour, 2014), 89. This dimension is given even greater emphasis in Chop's alternative title, *Eine Nacht in Paris: Musiktragödie in einem Aufzuge*, see Chop. M., *Frederick Delius* (Berlin: Harmonie Verlag, 1907), 20.

[47] Rossi, J., '*Margot La Rouge*', 97.

[48] Ibid., 94–5.

[49] Ibid., 95.

A ZOLA-ESQUE DRAMA

The manuscript of the full score of *Margot la Rouge* bears the date 'Spring 1901',[50] but we know from letters written to Jelka in June 1902 that it was not until this latter time that the opera was definitively completed (and in time for him to make another journey to Norway).[51] This is also confirmed by a pencil draft of the score, signed by the composer, 'commencé le 7 Avril – terminé le 6 Juin/1902'.[52] It had been the habit of Delius to ask his friend Schmitt to make up a vocal score, but Schmitt appears to have been unavailable, so, in October 1902, the task was given to Maurice Ravel, who must have been able to offer useful advice about the setting of the French language and in particular Gaston-Danville's libretto in its unusual form of versification, short, pithy lines, and somewhat characteristic of Zola, the use of onomatopoeia.[53] Schmitt, who had been in London, and was about to depart for Germany, certainly knew of Delius's work on *Margot*: 'Have you seen Ravel?' he asked Delius; 'If you get the chance give him my regards, and to Molard too. What are you working on at the moment. Have you sent off to the Sonzogno competition. I'd be very surprised if an Italian didn't get the prize!'[54] The work, replete with Italian translation, was not in fact entered for the Concorso Melodrammatico Internazionale until the final months of 1903 under Delius's *nom de plume* 'Paulò audacior'.[55] It was unsuccessful for the 1904 competition; the prize, as Schmitt anticipated, went to the young Italian composer, Lorenzo Filiasi, for his one-act opera *Manuel Menendez*, a work which enjoyed a procession of performances throughout Italy in 1904 and 1905 and also among the spate of *verismo* operas produced under the aegis of the Société Nationale in Paris in 1905.[56]

At the heart of Delius's naturalist plot, set in a suburban Parisian café, is the motive of jealousy and a chance encounter which leads to a double murder. Lili Béguin, one of several prostitutes to frequent the seedy establishment, loathes Margot la Rouge because of her liaison with the 'Artist'. Béguin has

---

[50] See *GB-Lbl* MS Mus 1745/2/13/6.

[51] See *DLL1*, 203.

[52] See *GB-Lbl* MS Mus 1745/2/13/3.

[53] *DLL1*, 207.

[54] *DLL1*, 208.

[55] *RL*, 81.

[56] Grayson, D., 'Finding a Stage for French Opera', in Fauser, A. and Everest, M. (eds), *Music, Theater and Cultural Transfer: Paris, 1830–1914* (Chicago: University of Chicago Press, 2009), 147n.

feelings for this unnamed character, but it is Margot the Artist has chosen. We learn of this underlying animus in the first two scenes, one analogous with the storm which straddles Scenes 2 and 3. Margot arrives in Scene 3 but prefers not to mingle with her gossiping fellow prostitutes. In Scene 4 the inclement weather drives in three soldiers, one of whom, Sergeant Thibault, is transfixed by Margot. A double *anagnorisis* takes place in Scene 5 and 6 as, little by little, both characters happily recognise each other. Thibault has plans to remove her from her present environment, but Margot is reluctant owing to her present loveless relationship with the Artist. The arrival of the Artist in Scene 7, mischievously summoned by Béguin, accelerates the action. A noxious, sinister individual, he is shunned by Margot, and Thibault is forced to intervene as the Artist attempts to stab her. Mortally wounded, Thibault dies in the struggle, and Margot, gripped by revenge, kills the Artist with Thibault's bayonet. Amid these 'crimes de passion', the police arrive to arrest Margot.

The realisation of this plot in musical terms is a cumulative structure of seven scenes in which the momentum of the drama is appropriately incremental. In a work of less than forty minutes of music, each scene not only has a terseness but also provides a vital role in the gradual hastening of the opera's dramatic pace towards the tragic and violent conclusion. In this sense Beecham was perhaps too precipitate in his criticism of the first part of Delius's score, which he deemed to be slow moving.[57] He also expressed disappointment in the fact that Delius cleaved so closely to the Italian *verismo* model of *Cavalleria Rusticana* where, with his characteristically lyrical gift, he might have produced an entirely different prototype. Yet it is hard to fathom how, in a work of such diminutive proportions, his 'tone poem' paradigm could have been made to work convincingly. Beyond the orchestral prelude and storm between Scenes 2 and 3 (a reminiscence of *The Magic Fountain*), how much room could have been afforded to the orchestra alone, and could such brevity of structure have supported a plot of any consequence or impact? In truth, *Margot la Rouge* is rich in lyrical material consistent with Delius's own subtitle of 'Drame lyrique' and this aspect is deftly handled in a fluent canvas shared contrapuntally between voices and orchestra in a manner learned from *A Village Romeo and Juliet*. And, like Delius's previous opera, it exhibits a profusion of distinctive thematic ideas, several of which are organically inter-related, which exude so many attributes of the composer's style. That Heseltine could dismiss it so summarily as bearing 'hardly a trace of the familiar Delius'

---

[57]   TB, 121. *Margot la Rouge* was one score Beecham never had occasion to hear so his impressions relied entirely on those furnished by the published vocal score.

was probably more a reflection of his aversion to melodrama. Furthermore, like the experiences of Beecham and an equally sceptical Hutchings,[58] his encounter of the work never went beyond the published vocal score.[59]

The translucent diatonic opening idea in A major (Example 6.2a) replete with tonic pedal, played by the cor anglais, beautifully depicts Parisian suburbia in late spring. Besides setting the scene and acting as a punctuative theme between scenes, it interacts effortlessly with Margot's leitmotiv, a cadential idea heavily coloured by the upward-leaning A sharp appoggiatura (Example 6.2b). A somewhat melancholy fragment, using a triplet figure borrowed from *Paris*, dominates Scenes 1, 2 and 3 (Example 6.2c) and this idea interacts with another cadential progression (II⁷b–V–VI) whose dotted rhythms (Example 6.2d) help to animate the underlying jealousy of Béguin (and the source of the scene's prevailing despondency in A minor and C minor). This idea continues to act as a conduit through much of the opera. A contrast occurs, however, with the expression of Béguin's passion for the artist in Scene 2 which is a fine lyrical theme in F major (Example 6.2e); a subtle chemistry of diatonicism and chromaticism (enhanced by Delius's luxuriant voice-leading in the orchestra), and the incorporation of the 'melancholy

Example 6.2a. *Margot la rouge*, Prelude, opening.

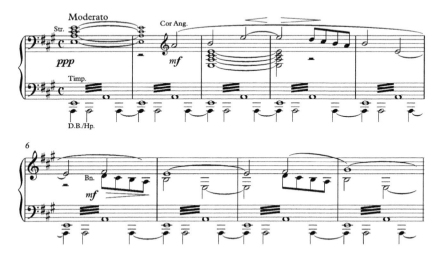

58 *AH*, 134.

59 *PH*, 101. Heseltine also offered no comment on Delius's recasting of *Margot*, since by the time the *Idyll* was produced in 1933, he was dead.

Example 6.2b. *Margot la rouge*, Margot's theme.

Example 6.2c. *Margot la rouge*, theme from *Paris*, 'melancholy'.

Example 6.2d. *Margot la rouge*, the jealousy of Béguin.

fragment' (see Example 6.2c) perfectly embodies her infatuation. After the gaiety of Scene 3, and the entrance of the soldiers in Scene 4, the triplet figure of Scene 1 assumes a form even closer to that of the dance material of *Paris*, and this music, strongly associated with Thibault (Example 6.2f),

Example 6.2e. *Margot la rouge*, Béguin's passion for the Artist.

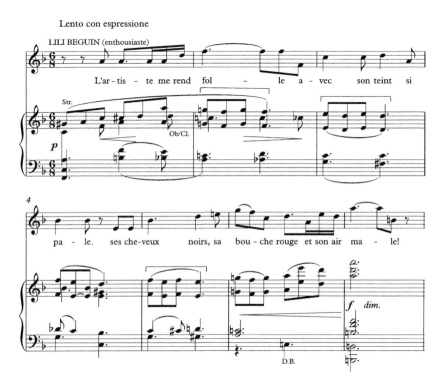

Example 6.2f. *Margot la rouge*, Thibault's theme.

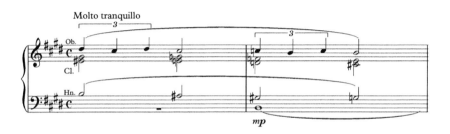

is appended to a second theme linked with Thibault's curiosity for Margot
(Example 6.2g). Enriching this already profuse matrix of thematic strands,
in which Delius exhibits admirable developmental facility, is another simple
two-bar fragment expressing Thibault's happiness at the chance encounter
(Example 6.2h). As Thibault's surmises are confirmed, his love music becomes
more fervent in Scene 5 in another idea thoroughly diatonic in nature and, as
if the memory of *A Village Romeo and Juliet* was still latent in Delius's system,
it combines with the upward triplet figure (Example 6.2i) which occupied
so potent a force in that work. In fact Scenes 5 and 6 provide particularly
fertile examples of Delius's handling of his thematic material for, as Thibault's
happiness intensifies, so does the reprise of earlier ideas in combination such
as one hears in Thibault's epiphany (Example 6.2j), derived from Béguin's
love music of Scene 2 (see Example 6.2e), and in the introspective moments
of Margot's shame (Example 6.2k). Scene 6, in particular, represents the high
point of Delius's invention which happily coincides with the one instance of
ensemble – the love duet of Margot and Thibault – in the opera. Here Delius

Example 6.2g. *Margot la rouge*, Thibault's curiosity for Margot.

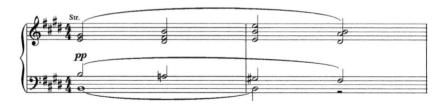

Example 6.2h. *Margot la rouge*, Thibault's happiness.

Example 6.2i. *Margot la rouge*, Thibault's love.

Example 6.2j. *Margot la rouge*, Thibault's epiphany.

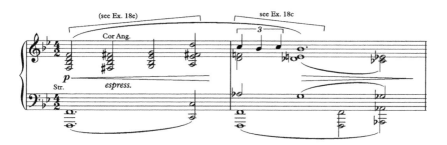

Example 6.2k. *Margot la rouge*, Margot's shame.

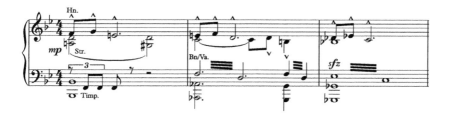

fell back on the technique used for the dramatic climax in Act III of *Koanga* (and one he had learned from Wagner) in his employment of strong tonally functional progressions, notably in modulation towards the subdominant. This is deployed with admirable effect at the high point of Scene 6 as Margot, in her moment of revelation, sings 'Mais je vais m'éveiller de nouveau dans la nuit'. At this point the tonality moves unequivocally to F major, a key Delius seems to have associated most with passionate ardour in this drama. The contrast of this lyrical effusion with Scene 7 is stark in almost every respect, since it is action and the declamation of the singers which become the focus, and the orchestra is somewhat relegated to the emission of melodramatic gesture. This was an idiom Delius had exploited with a modicum of success in *Koanga* and in the first two scenes of *A Village Romeo and Juliet*. In the context of *Margot*, it occurs with an even greater ferocity, though arguably sacrificing the leitmotivic cohesion of the previous scenes. Nevertheless, after the horrific murders and the summoning of the police, the tragic recollection of Thibault's love theme as he lies dying in Margot's arms is well executed as is Margot's theme in a transformation reflecting her defiance and stoical equanimity.

Regardless of the criticisms levelled at the opera by Heseltine, Hutchings and Beecham, *Margot* contains some of Delius's most characteristic thematic invention, and the coherent nature of its free-flowing, through-composed structure reveals an undeniable technical prowess. At no point does one sense that the opulent scheme of leitmotivs, skilfully integrated, are sacrificed to a tessellation of individual and disparate 'calling cards', while the use of key and modulation are carefully reserved for dramatic impact. There is no doubt, however, that the composition of *Margot* was a new experiment. Delius had seldom worked in the French language and it had been some time since the composition of his two Verlaine settings of 1895. In these two instances he had learned something of that typical syllabic delivery common to the style of French *mélodies* (and it is not without interest that, at the climax of *Margot*, Delius should have recalled a similar melodic figure to that of the opening of 'Il pleure dans mon coeur'). Nevertheless, for the purposes of *Margot* he had much to learn in order to provide a flexible and stylish realisation of Gaston-Danville's rapid declamation and dialogue; yet the results suggest that he was fully aware of the challenge and that Ravel, among others, was at hand to advise him. 'I am hard at work on "Margot la Rouge" & have already sketched 2 scenes', Delius told Jelka in the spring of 1902; 'I wonder what you will think of the libretto! I may make something good of it after all'.[60] As Carley has adroitly suggested, the year after *Margot*, Ravel produced his orchestral song cycle, *Shéhérazade*, in which a thorough acquaintance of French recitation is demonstrated (notably in the first song 'Asie'). Though only a conjecture, Ravel's involvement with Delius's opera may well have contributed to the conception of his song cycle. Another work which may also have assisted in his familiarisation with French vocal syllabisation was his enthusiastic encounter with Debussy's *Pelléas et Mélisande* which was premiered at the Opéra-Comique in Paris on 30 April 1902. 'Peleas [*sic*] and Melisande is *exquisite*' was the impression he related to Jelka; 'the best thing I have seen for years,

---

[60]   Letter from Delius to Jelka, [Spring 1902], *AU-Mgm*.

full of poetry and delicacy – Go and see it if possible'.[61] Debussy's masterpiece evidently made its mark, for he made the effort to hear it a second time in May.[62] *Margot*, as we know, was completed in June.

Although *Margot* did not make sufficient impression on the judges in Rome, it is quite clear from Delius's correspondence that he believed in the music. When writing to Mondello in Florence about the possible production of *A Village Romeo and Juliet* there, he was keen to offer *Margot* to the Italian theatre agent in the knowledge that *verismo* was still all the rage in Italian opera houses: 'Now I also have a small opera with French libretto and Italian translation: Margot le Rouge which will perhaps interest you. If you like it I could send you the libretto and the piano reduction. It's [on] a modern subject and very dramatic'.[63] Indeed, had Delius been so dismissive of his creation he would have foregone the expense and time of having the vocal score published in c. 1905 by Lévy-Lulx in Paris. Even though his attempt to interest Mondello was unfruitful, he continued to send copies of the vocal score to John Coates in 1907, hoping that it might be produced by the Moody-Manners Opera Company and that Coates himself might play the role of Thibault. 'It will be very effective when played', he assured Coates.[64] That Bantock in 1908 and Heseltine in 1913 also received copies indicates that he still believed in the score's merits. That its lack of performance lingered in his mind is, of course, evident from the fact that it became a subject of reworking to a different English text with Fenby and Delius in 1932. But, like the fate of *Irmelin* and *The Magic Fountain*, *Margot* was added to the list of operatic works he failed to hear during his lifetime; and the work was not actually given until June 1983 when it was staged by the Opera Theatre of St Louis in English under Fenby's direction. The Park Lane Opera Group gave its first hearing in French in March 1984 for the Camden Festival, over eighty years after its original conception.[65] As it transpired, however, the fate of *Margot* during Delius's lifetime would lie elsewhere.

[61] Letter from Delius to Jelka, [May 1902], *AU-Mgm*.

[62] See letter from Delius to Jelka, 14 May 1902, *AU-Mgm*.

[63] Letter from Delius to Alfredo Mondello, 10 June 1907 (41D77) West Yorkshire Archive Service, Bradford.

[64] Letter from Delius to John Coates, 16 December 1907, *DLL1*, 322.

[65] The only existing recording of *Margot le Rouge* uses the orchestral score that was commissioned by the Delius Trust from Fenby in 1979, since at this point the original score of the opera was not in possession of the Trust. This version, using Gaston-Danville's original French, and orchestration gleaned from the *Idyll*, was recorded for the BBC under Norman del Mar in December 1981. By the time the St Louis performance took place in 1983, the original score had come to light.

CHAPTER 7

American Apogee: *Appalachia* and *Sea Drift* (1902–1903)

A NEW 'AMERICAN SYMPHONY'[1]

English opera on a Swiss subject, Scandinavian songs and French Naturalism bear witness to Delius's European cosmopolitanism. Yet, even while he was preoccupied with *A Village Romeo and Juliet*, his propensity for revision had compelled him to revisit his old *American Rhapsody*. 'I am at my American Rhapsody again', he told Jelka from his Berlin apartment in March 1901. One suspects also that *Koanga* (some of which he had heard in London, and was also under revision) was still very much in his system as were the revived memories of Florida from his visit in 1897. *Appalachia*, 'Variationen über ein altes Sklavenlied mit Schlusschor für grosses Orchestra' ('Variations on an old slave song with final chorus for large orchestra'), was, according to Heseltine, completed in 1902.[2] Chop, on the other hand, dates it from 1903.[3] By this time we know from correspondence with Haym that he was asking for the score which was in fact in the possession of Buths in Düsseldorf. In a long, detailed letter to Delius, Buths was evidently coming to terms with the new work, having already performed *Paris* in February 1903 and with plans to do *Lebenstanz* in 1904:

> As the air surrounds a physical body so your sound surrounds your themes. In that sense I say you are endowed with a natural impressionism. "Paris" and "Lebenstanz" are elaborations of moods in accordance with the expressive import of each. In "Apalachia" [*sic*] there is in addition a new impetus, not so much in the psychic and sound element in the music as

---

[1] As Delius termed *Appalachia* in a letter from Haym to Delius, 10 July 1903, *DLL1*, 218.

[2] *PH*, 168.

[3] Chop, M., 'Tonsetzer der Gegenwart: Frederick Delius, Sein Leben und Schaffen', *Neue Musik-Zeitung*, Vol. 31 (1910), 313.

in the formal – and contrapuntal nature of it. I should like to call this the intellectual side of music, and it follows from this designation, as I have already said above, that I find the intensification of the mode of expression all the greater an advance. It also follows that the internal sense of what is legitimate should appear all the more clearly.[4]

Buths was delighted with *Appalachia* and admired Delius's intuitive flair. Nevertheless, sensing his friend's reliance on artistic intuition, he reminded him of the cerebral imperative: 'Instinct guides us, leads us, carries us away, inspires us, intellect must convince us'.[5] Like Haym, Buths was transfixed by the quality of Delius's ideas, yet he was bemused by the rejection of classical principles: 'In parts I find the piece quite outstanding, as outstanding as anything anywhere in music, but this absolute non-acknowledgement of rules and laws'.[6] Haym, who gave the first hearing of the work at Elberfeld on 15 October 1904, was less troubled. 'Appalachia has grown very dear to me', he assured Delius; 'I find the whole thing superb and as rich as an entire life. We shall yet live to see Buths agreeing with enthusiasm'.[7] Buths was duly persuaded, and gave a performance at the Lower Rhine Festival in Düsseldorf on 13 June 1905, though this was of particular disappointment to Max Schillings who had hoped to perform it in Graz. '[It] would have opened up completely *new* circles to you', Schillings claimed.[8] Nevertheless, word of Delius's highly unusual work had reached Oskar Fried in Berlin, who performed it with the Berlin Philharmonic on 5 February 1906, and his old friend Fritz Cassirer took the work to London where it received its English premiere on 22 November 1907 at Queen's Hall.[9] Enthusiastically reviewed, especially by Ernest Newman in the *Birmingham Post*,[10] *Appalachia* was the vehicle by which Delius's name came more permanently before the British public. It was at this performance that Beecham's devotion to Delius's music was sealed. 'Here at last', Beecham declared, 'was modern music of native

---

[4] Letter from Buths to Delius, 26 July 1903, *DLL1*, 221.

[5] Ibid.

[6] Ibid., 222.

[7] Letter from Haym to Delius, 25 July 1904, *DLL1*, 245.

[8] Letter from Max von Schillings to Delius, 28 February 1905, *DLL1*, 254.

[9] These performances of *Appalachia* did not come without some exacting costs. The work was still in manuscript, and the choral parts had to be lithographed. The full score was not published until 1906, and the vocal score not until 1907.

[10] *Birmingham Post*, 23 November 1907.

growth in which it was possible with uninhibited sincerity to take pride and delight. I formed the unshakeable resolution to play as much of it as I could lay my hands on whenever I had the opportunity'.[11] And to the young Percy Grainger, its experimental attributes were impressive and life-changing.

In returning to the material of his old *American Rhapsody*, Delius was keen to achieve several artistic goals. The first was to continue the trend of his Strauss-inspired symphonic poems which had achieved momentum with *Paris* and *Lebenstanz* using a large orchestra (which, in this case, continued the uncompromising predisposition of *Lebenstanz's* triple wind, cor anglais, bass clarinet, double bassoon and six horns with additional clarinet in E flat, two harps and an array of percussion). A second was to revisit those tropical pictorial recreations of *Florida*, the *American Rhapsody* and *Koanga* which continued to haunt Delius's imagination. Chop situated the setting of *Appalachia* to the 'American Mid-West, Louisiana, Alabama and Florida',[12] and even more exotically in an article after Fried's performance of the work in 1906, where, as a form of 'ethnographic' expression, he more succinctly summoned up:

> as a backdrop the region of Central America which contains the Allegheny mountains (the Appalachian System), Alabama, the central Atlantic States, Massachusetts and on up to the mouth of the St Lawrence River. Delius proves himself to be a mature artist of exceptional individuality. A wonderful array of sounds and contrasts of colour are present in abundance, whether he is depicting the rich tropical landscape of the Mississippi, the primeval forest, the midday heat or incorporating folk songs with their distinctive rhythms.[13]

Heseltine also remarked that appended to the full score (now lost) was a note from the composer (which Chop must have seen), which stated that the work 'mirrors the moods of tropical nature in the great swamps bordering on the Mississippi River which is so intimately associated with the life of the old slave population. Longing melancholy, an intense love for Nature, childlike

---

[11] *TB*, 149. Beecham also admitted in *A Mingled Chime* (pp. 74–5) that it was mainly through the counsel and conviction of Delius that, after a period of considerable indecision in his life, he resolved to become a professional conductor.

[12] Chop, M., 'Frederick Delius: A Biography', in Jones, P. (ed.), *The Collected Writings of the German Musicologist Max Chop on the Composer Frederick Delius* (Lewiston, NY, Queenston, ON and Lampeter: Edwin Mellen Press, 2002), 59.

[13] Ibid., 66–7.

humour and an innate delight in dancing and singing are still the most characteristic qualities of this race'.[14] It is highly unlikely that Delius ever saw this landscape so much further west from his locations in northern Florida and Virginia, but he would, nevertheless, have known the cotton-growing landscapes of typical southern plantations at Dan's Hill and Burleigh,[15] the high society of their owners and the long working hours of the negro workers for whom, even though the Civil War had been over for two decades, life was no less arduous in spite of emancipation. Indeed, given the nature of the mini-drama that occupies the finale of *Appalachia*, and the mixed emotions of parting and hope, it seems more likely that the character of the variations represents both sides of that disparate social world, one which Delius would have experienced at first hand and one which is surely epitomised in the title *Appalachia (Dixieland) (Eindrücke aus dem Süden)* used at the Düsseldorf performance in 1905. Directly linked to this was a third artistic goal, which was to re-employ the same negro melody which had occupied such an important role in the *American Rhapsody*, but in this instance (and perhaps instigated by Strauss's example in *Don Quixote*) to use it in a much more complex context of symphonic variations, a form, as we have observed, Delius found creatively amenable. What it is more, Delius's choice of variation form was stimulated not only by the negro melody and his love of the negroes' extemporised harmony, but by the coalescence of these factors into an eight-part choral song close to the work's conclusion. Moreover, it also provided a further opportunity for the composer to deploy his well-tested model of diatonic melody and chromatic accompaniment, incipiently essayed in the *American Rhapsody* and *Koanga* but more maturely assimilated and harnessed in *Paris* and *A Village Romeo and Juliet*.

One of the most fascinating features of *Appalachia* is its unusual variation structure. Though the underlying 'successional' concept of the form remains intact, the execution of the variations themselves is a complex one. What is more, before the variations get under way, the work commences with a substantial multifaceted introduction, tonally oblique in nature. An evocation of nature, in E flat major, encapsulates a dawn call 'a' (Example 7.1a), several fragments conveying the idea of awakening 'b' (Example 7.1b), particularly those triadic motions enriched by an added sixth or seventh. Typically contradicting the dominant C which concludes the first part, Delius shifts to

[14] *PH*, 124.

[15] Ridderbusch, M. R., 'The "Delius in Danville" Festival', *DSJ* No. 122 (Winter 1997), 36.

a dance passage in 12/8 on the dominant of B major with an operatic gesture which, suggesting the sound of banjos, might have come from *Koanga*. To this is added a third fragment 'c' (Example 7.1c) which will later have strong choral associations. Leaving the ecstatic but untonicised B major for C, Delius surreptitiously presents the opening notes of the negro melody (in the *minor* and in augmentation), and, before concluding the introduction, provides a tantalising cadential quote from *A Village Romeo and Juliet* (see letter G), material Delius was clearly unable to exorcise from his system.

Although the succession of variations in *Appalachia* has been suggested as consisting of fourteen 'events',[16] the nature of 'composite' variations, the suggestion of individual character movements, the interaction of other thematic ideas (including their later reprise) and the role of an 'intermezzo' or interlude make Delius's unconventional structure much more multi-

Example 7.1a. *Appalachia*, Dawn, 'evocation of nature', 'a'.

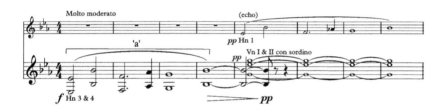

Example 7.1b. *Appalachia*, Awakening, 'b'.

16 *MLPG*, 139.

Example 7.1c. *Appalachia*, opening dance, 'c'.

dimensional, and one of the most intricate in what must have been the most fertile period of orchestral variation sets (See Table 7.1).[17]

Although the end of the introduction gives a foretaste of the negro melody in C minor, the eight-bar theme itself, heard on the cor anglais, is presented in C major (Example 7.1d). In this respect, Delius follows a traditional classical principle of simplicity – Hutchings even described it as 'jejune and banal'[18] – and a familiar periodicity of 2+2+4 in terms of the regular phraseology. The theme, however, exhibits attributes which Delius had explored in the *American Rhapsody, Koanga* (in particular the negro melody of the introduction and its subsequent recurrences) and the second subject of *Paris*, that is, a strong diatonic melody with a striking element of chromatic bifurcation in the accompanying harmony, particularly towards the final cadence; it was a formulation ideally suited to his stylistic aims. Fluctuation between major and minor modes for the theme, and reference to the descending chromatic bass line ('d'), would also remain important features of Delius's variations hereafter. After the presentation of the theme in C major, Delius immediately moves to F *minor* (Var. 1) in one of numerous variations in his set which exploits the minor mode. Haym particularly admired this aspect, though Buths was initially critical. 'His [Buths's] critical remarks derive for the most part straight from the schoolroom', Haym reassured Delius; 'e.g. re the repeated theme in Appalachia, first in C then in F, which I find particularly beautiful, it is just as if the tragic moment were already being foreshadowed in it, as if the theme wanted to say: I am not as harmless as may at first appear'.[19] Variation 2, in the major mode, retains the same

---

[17] See Dibble, J. C., 'Fantasy and Hybridisation in the British Variation Tradition', in Dibble, J. and Zon, B. (eds), *Nineteenth-Century British Music Studies*, Vol. 2 (Aldershot: Ashgate, 2002), 235–45.

[18] *AH*, 108.

[19] Letter from Haym to Delius, 25 July 1904, *DLL1*, 245.

Table 7.1. *Appalachia*, structural overview.

Score ref.	Structural role	Key	Comments		
b. 1	Introduction	E♭ major	'a' and 'b'		
B⁺¹²	'Banjo' music	B major	'c'		
F	Thematic anticipation	C minor	Augmentation of theme		
G⁺⁸	Theme	C major	Including 'd', falling chromatic bass line		
H	Variation 1	F minor			
H⁺⁸	Variation 2	F major	Harmonic rhythm doubled		
I	Variation 3	D minor / G minor / F major	Featuring 'd' and 'e', fanfare		
J	Variations 4–6, 'Old dance' (composite Var. 1)	F major	Var. 4	J–J⁺¹²	Introduction of 'f', begins obliquely in D minor
			Var. 5	K⁺²–K⁺⁵	F major
				K⁺⁹–K⁺¹²	G major
				K⁺¹³–L	G major
			Var. 6	L⁺⁴–M⁺¹²	D major, free fantasy
			Reprise of Var. 4	M⁺¹²–O	'e' used extensively as ritornellos, 'Lydian' ending

Table 7.1 (continued).

Score ref.	Structural role	Key	Comments		
O	Variations 7–8, 'Scherzo' (composite Var. 2)	C minor	Var. 7	O^{+15}–O^{+21}	F major, using 'e'
			Var. 8	P–Q^{+11}	F major and C major, 'popular song'
			Reprise of Var. 7	Q^{+11}–R	Coda – chorus
R	Variation 9, 'Interlude'	C major	'a' and 'b', coda – chorus, 'Lydian' ending (see Var. 4)		
U	Variation 10, 'Waltz'	F major	Based on 'f' and 'e', coda – chorus		
V	Variation 11, 'Elegy'	B minor – F major	Negro melody in augmentation, coda – chorus		
Y	Variation 12, 'March'	C major	Based on 'e' and 'f'		
Bb	Variation 13, 'Funeral march'	A minor	Chorale		
Cc	Variation 14, 'Partsong'	C major	Chorus *a cappella*		
Cc^{+16}	Variation 15, 'Lament'	A minor – Ab major			
Dd	Variation 16 [transition]	Ab minor			
Dd^{+9}	Finale [Variation 17]	F major	Combination 'c', 'e', final phrase of negro melody		

phraseological properties of its predecessor, though its harmonic rhythm is double the speed and 'd' (which falls over an interval of an octave and a half) is especially exaggerated. This sense of acceleration reaches a new point of departure with Variation 3. At the opening (at letter I) Delius derives a new fragment from the theme ('e'), but in diminution and in the character of a fanfare (Example 7.1e). This idea, and the chromatic bass figure 'd', dominate the variation, but the three strains of the negro melody are also present, in three different keys, D minor, G minor and, to conclude, F major. Variation 4 is the first of Delius's 'composite' variation structures which, in the larger sense, constitutes a single movement and a single variation, but in detail it is also made up of three separate variations. The first of these (Var. 4) begins obliquely in D minor before F major is established. Its character is one of an 'old dance', a baroque minuet with its distinctive Phrygian half close (J^{+5}), and an impression perhaps of a high-society gathering at a southern plantation house (as depicted at the beginning and end of *Koanga*). The variation may

Example 7.1d. *Appalachia*, negro melody and falling chromatic bass, 'd'.

Example 7.1e. *Appalachia*, Theme in diminution, fanfare, 'e'.

Example 7.1f. Appalachia, Theme as 'baroque minuet', 'f'.

begin with a reference to the eighteenth century, but the consequent material (onwards from the end of J^{+5}) is pure Delius in his favoured 6/8 metre (surely Peter Warlock found this music paradigmatical in the stylistic formation of his later *Capriol* Suite of 1926). Moreover, the melodic material ('f') adds a further fragment to the work's already rich thematic matrix (Example 7.1f). The dance is used as a reprise to round off the composite structure, but not before two further variations based around G major (Var. 5) and, to facilitate the recapitulation of the dance, D major (Var. 6), have provided a central paragraph.

The decorative orchestral filigree, which makes so much of the Straussian free fantasy of Variation 4 so engaging, is even more extensively developed in Variation 7's composite design. A Scherzo in ternary form, this movement also makes extensive use of 'e' in its opening section in C minor. Moving to F major and C major for the 'Trio', Delius gives us a 'popular song' version of the negro melody (initially scored for clarinet in E flat and high cellos) before elements of the original version combine with it (Q^{+1}–Q^{+11}). With the reprise of the Scherzo (from Q^{+11}) the original negro melody is presented triumphantly in the trombones amid a virtuoso display of three-part counterpoint for full orchestra. As Variation 7 winds down both in tempo and volume, the male chorus makes its first appearance with a simple, short 'la la' refrain or 'doxology' as Heseltine described it.[20] Sung at 'pp', it is barely audible, but this was undoubtedly Delius's intention. Here, manifestly, we have Delius's remembered impression of the negroes, singing in harmony on a distant plantation, exquisitely enhanced by the Lydian colours of the upper wind.

As Grimley has suggested, the next section functions as a form of tranquil interlude in C (Var. 9) in the which the negro theme appears among other fragments as memories of the previous 'exposition' of seven variations.[21] This is particularly telling in the section marked 'Misterioso'. At this juncture of repose, Delius recalls elements of the introduction – the 'dawn call' and 'awakening' – enveloped by an orchestral texture which recalls the Prelude to Act II of *The Magic Fountain* (and which also found its way into *Koanga*) before the 'dawn call' and negro melody intermingle, the latter sung as a parting refrain in augmentation by the almost imperceptibly hushed male chorus, replete with Lydian memories from the reprise of Variation 4.

Initiating a second series of variations, Variation 10, a waltz in F, is another sophisticated depiction of southern society. The eight-bar periodicity of the original theme is still perceptible, but the waltz theme is new as is the counterpoint for violin solo which recalls both *La Ronde se déroule* and *Lebenstanz*. In this context it is perhaps no surprise that the 'haughty' atmosphere of the 'old dance' of Variation 4 should appear as a consequent phrase as if to emphasise the kinship between this material and the 'fanfare'; Delius deftly introduces the latter to an already inventive polyphonic texture. Distant voices, more sympathetic with the livelier spirit of the dance, are once again heard at the conclusion. The elegy of Variation 11, using a contrapuntal figure derived from *Margot la Rouge*, stands out for the appearance of one strain of the negro melody in B minor in augmentation. This mood is quickly dispelled by a return to F and a full citation of the theme, but after the climax and cadence (at letter X), Delius used the rest of the movement to combine the elegiac material with the negro melody and the distant chorus and memories of the Interlude. For Variation 12, a march in C, the 'fanfare' motive comes into its own and dominates the variation, though Delius also makes subtle reference to 'f'. In stark rhythmical contrast, Variation 13, a funeral march in A minor, and its intense homophonic treatment of the negro melody suggests a solemn chorale. A shorter variation, it provides both the ideal prelude and conduit to the final variation (Variation 14) which is for chorus alone. After an entire series of instrumental variations, albeit some of them with choral 'refrains' at

---

[20] *PH*, 125.

[21] *DG*, 124.

their conclusions, the occurrence of this final *a cappella* variation is remarkable. In one sense, of course, we have come full circle in that the theme, in its initial form, returns in its original key (C major). As Peter Franklin has also remarked, the chorus is 'foregrounded' after its distanced locations in past variations.[22] But the purpose of this foregrounding is also to throw into relief several other factors: the very source which had inspired Delius's symphonic poem – the sound of the free-harmonising negroes and its romantic manifestation in the *partsong*;[23] the more intense chromatic harmonisation of the diatonic melody – and here Delius's technique is paradigmatical, for its attitudinising falling chromatic bass lines (as instances of 'd'), its dense harmonic rhythm, its sumptuous texture of up to eight vocal parts, and the climactic force of the phraseological extension of seven bars at the conclusion. Such choral writing, with its awkward intervals, chromatic density and challenging intonation, exacted special demands from its executants (and Delius made no practical allowances), and had not been heard by audiences in such a context before. The impact of this choral variation had a further self-evident impact in that its text articulated a somewhat melancholy setting – as Hutchings insinuated, 'a long twilight brooding'.[24] Using what were probably Delius's own words,[25] the chorus's evocation of nature, the tropical forest and the river ('the mighty stream') might have been Delius's own plantation at Solana Grove, Florida.[26]

The *a cappella* variation, as a transformed human embodiment of the original theme, has a further major consequence. Delius almost certainly must have realised that this choral variation would not be enough on its own to conclude his variation set, and that, in the tradition of nineteenth-century variation structures, some kind of large-scale final variation was required. Moreover, he also needed some form of counterbalance to the quasi-operatic introduction. As a unique response, therefore, Delius appended two more variations and choral finale in which the *a cappella* variation

[22] Franklin, P., *Reclaiming Late-Romantic Music: Singing Devils and Distant Sounds* (London and Berkeley, CA: University of California Press, 2014), 50.

[23] See Dibble, J. C., 'The Partsong as *Topos* in the Music of Frederick Delius', keynote lecture for the one-day conference on Delius at the British Library, 15 July 2016.

[24] *AH*, 108.

[25] An A5 pencil draft of the lyrics survives in *GB-Lbl* MS Mus 1745/2/39, f. 23. The succeeding folio shows a sketch for the last section labelled 'Negro chorus in finale'.

[26] Anyone who has had the good chance to visit the location of Delius's homestead at Solana Grove in Florida (now preserved in the grounds of Jacksonville University), along the huge expanse of the St Johns River, will testify to its powerful sense of place and tropical environment.

acted as *post hoc* narrative for all the 'impressions' already established by the orchestral symphonic poem, but also as a prelude for the darker narrative of the finale. Immediately after the *a cappella* variation, Delius plunges us into an oppressive, dirge-like lament in A minor with ostinato marked 'Misterioso lento' (Variation 15) in which augmented strains of the theme occur in augmentation. Haym was especially impressed by the scoring: 'The Mysterioso with the viola solo sounded wonderful. Altogether everything sounds good. Your sounds often require a soft pp. It makes many things intelligible & poetically effective'.[27] Indeed, at the end of Variation 15 one is left with the inescapable impression of tragedy, not least because of the strangely alien tonality of A flat major and a further gesture from the distant wordless chorus. This 'alienation' goes one step further in Variation 16 as the negro melody appears in A flat *minor* in another intensely chromatic harmonisation (replete with 'blue' notes). This variation is, however, transitional to the main (and most unexpected) event of the finale – a *scena* for solo baritone and chorus, taking a similar form to that of Delius's much earlier *Neger Lieder im Volkston* with its pentatonic 'base' intonation ('O Honey, I am going down the river in the morning') and response, first from the male voices and later from the whole chorus ('Heigh-ho, down the mighty river'). From the continuation of the soloist, and the chorus which follows, we learn from the text that the element of parting amounts to 'the separation of husband from wife and parent from child, when one might be sold for a slave to a distant plantation and the other left behind'.[28] Given the nature of Delius's text, and the closing mention of 'sweet Nellie Gray', one suspects that Delius was acquainted with Benjamin Hanby's pre-Civil-War popular song 'Darling Nellie Gray' (1856) which told of the sweetheart of a Kentucky slave forcibly taken away by slave owners to the distant, harsher conditions in Georgia (see Table 7.2).[29]

In placing the stylised 'Negro Volkslied' in A flat at this point in the structure, Delius gained even more dramatic effect by modulating to F major for his final choral statement (see Ee). And here, with text, motive 'c' (from the

---

[27] Letter from Haym to Delius, 25 July 1904, *DLL1*, 245.

[28] *PH*, 125.

[29] From a family of abolitionists, Hanby gave succour to the runaway slave, Joseph Selby, who hoped one day to be united with his lover, Nelly Gray. Exhausted and sick, Selby died at the Hanby home in Rushville, Ohio, but not before he had related his story to the family. 'Darling Nellie Gray' became enormously popular not only in the United States but also in Britain, so it is possible that Delius may have known the song even before he travelled out to Florida.

Table 7.2. *Appalachia*, structure of Finale.

Voice/chorus	Text	Key	Comments
Solo baritone	O Honey, I am going down the river in the morning.	A♭ major	'Base'
Male chorus	Heigh-ho, heigh-ho, down the mighty river.		Response
Full chorus	Aye! Honey, I'll be gone when next the whipper-will's a-calling.		
Solo baritone	And don't you be too lonesome love,		
	And don't you fret and cry;		
Full chorus	For the dawn will soon be breaking,	F major	'c', Var. 16
	The radiant morn is nigh,		
	And you'll find me ever a-waiting,		
	Heigh-ho, my own sweet Nelly Gray!		
	La la la,		'e'
	T'ords the morning lift a voice		
	Let the scented woods rejoice,		
	And echoes swell across the might stream.		Final phrase of negro melody
Postlude	[Wordless Chorus]	F major	'd', 'b', Lydian cadence

'banjo' music in the introduction) is recapitulated imitatively in all the voices in a climactic paragraph, expressing hope at the breaking of a new dawn ('For the dawn will soon be breaking'). But not only is it a moment of theatrical vision but also one of structural dexterity, for 'c' becomes part of a tripartite melodic structure (in broad imitation of the original theme) in that it combines with 'e' ('La la la') before concluding with the final phrase of the negro melody ('T'ords the morning lift a voice'), linking it with the final phrase and text of Variation 14. This deft quodlibet of motivic and melodic references, and the appearance of the theme (replete with high Cs for the sopranos) reminds us that the finale, for all its dramatic amplification, functions as the last variation (Variation 17), though the closing, long-suffering gesture ('Ah!') from the chorus (with its unusual modal inflection), its references to the chromatic falling bass ('d'), the 'awakening' motive ('b') and the Lydian cadence, leave us with a narrative without resolution.

The importance of *Appalachia* in Delius's output cannot be overestimated for several reasons. After the first complete performance of *Koanga* in March 1904 at Elberfeld, Haym's performance of the symphonic poem at Elberfeld later that year established a stronger bond with the German musical world. No longer was Delius's name an occasional appearance in a programme but one now associated with a fresh, alternative modernism, and, in the case of *Appalachia*, one of exoticism. Beecham also attributed the beginning of Delius's success to a reaction, in some parts of Germany, against the mania for Strauss's music which had taken most of Europe and America's capitals by storm.[30] The latest offering had been the *Symphonia Domestica* which Strauss conducted in the Carnegie Hall, New York, in April 1904. The reception was mixed. Certainly for Haym, *Appalachia* – a new 'American symphony' – was a much-needed antidote: 'How there can be any doubts about the choice between Appal. & Sinf. dom. I do not understand. What a watery concoction from Strauss this time! I have already had a rehearsal of it too & found the impression gained by my initial reading fully confirmed. Absolutely nothing new, no humour, no depth, really a terrible void. I had an argument with Buths over this too, of course he can't bring himself to drop Strauss so easily & is too much under the spell of the leges tabulaturae for this new "masterpiece" not to impress him highly'.[31] Haym, Buths, Cassirer, Suter and Schillings were to prove vital allies and catalysts in promulgating Delius's music, and with the momentum of other works – *Paris*, *Lebenstanz*,

---

[30] *TB*, 129.

[31] Letter from Haym to Delius, 25 July 1904, *DLL1*, 245.

Mitternachtslied Zarathustras and the Piano Concerto (and not least the Elberfeld concert on 24 October 1904 which contained three of his works) – his creative energy, encouraged by the culture of the German choral festivals, turned towards the concert hall.

SEA DRIFT: CONCERT DRAMA 'IN ONE ACT'

Buoyed by the interest of his German colleagues in his music, and by the environment of the German choral festivals (a culture by no means alien to him from his upbringing nor from his Leipzig education), Delius probably began work on his first large-scale choral work in 1903,[32] and the vocal score suggests that it was completed sometime during 1904,[33] a date confirmed by Chop.[34] The American transcendentalist literature of Walt Whitman was to be his source, one which he may have encountered in America (given the reprinting of the poem in 1881 shortly before he arrived there), though we also know that he was reading Whitman at the end of the 1890s at the same time as he was captivated with Nietzsche.[35]

Delius was by no means the first British composer to set Whitman: Stanford had done so in 1884 with his *Elegiac Ode*, a setting of 'When lilacs in the dooryard bloom'd', written by the poet in the aftermath of the assassination of President Lincoln in 1865 and in the form of a first-person monologue. This sense of narrative was a feature of Whitman which clearly greatly appealed to Delius. The poem *Out of the Cradle Endlessly Rocking* had a similar narrative element. Based on a reminiscence of an adult man, the poem relates the time when he was an adolescent boy, walking along the beach on Long Island. Absorbed by the busy sounds and scents of early summer, he recounted the bracing features of the Atlantic seaboard and two nesting mockingbirds (who mate for life), migrants from Alabama, in some seashore briers. The poem, however, had other irresistible features for the composer. The boy's observance of the devoted birds, as they pass back and forth tirelessly to the nest, aroused his admiration; but after the female (she-bird) fails to return to the nest, the male (he-bird) pines for her, ever hoping

---

[32] See *PH,* 168 and *CD,* 140.

[33] *RT1,* 60.

[34] Chop, M., 'Frederick Delius: His Life and Work', in Jones, P., *The Collected Writings of the German Musicologist Max Chop,* 109.

[35] *MLPG,* 169.

that she will return. With this heartrending event, the core of *Sea Drift* begins as the 'he-bird' grieves over the loss of his love, and the boy, deeply affected, discovers new adult emotions of sorrow through his compassion. Finally, in the realisation of the he-bird's permanent separation and lament, the boy, anthropomorphically, sings of lost love and happiness. As Gerald Abraham has suggested, those elements of human pain, in *Paa Vidderne*, *A Village Romeo and Juliet* and *Appalachia*, recur continually in Delius's work:

> It is generated by his view of life as something inexorably cruel to the individual, meltingly beautiful in its cruelty and with infinite power of renewal. He accepts it passively and underlines the beauty. Not for him the protest and struggle of Beethoven, the joyous all-embracing acceptance of Wagner, the renunciation of Brahms …; he takes life as Thomas Hardy took it. This brooding over beautiful cruelty would be repulsively morbid were it not for the ever-present faith in rebirth, the Nietzschean "ewige Wieder-kunft". Sali and Vreli, the lovers who find life together impossible, are mirrored in "Sea-Drift".[36]

The tragedy of parting, death and ecstasy almost certainly stirred once more Delius's *Tristanesque* sympathies as did so much of Whitman's Wagnerian propensity to internalise the drama of emotions; but most of all it is the sense of Nature's obliviousness and, as Hutchings has commented, 'the pathos of human bereavement, symbolised in the seagull's [*sic*] bereavement' which imparts such a powerful, deeply melancholy message.[37] The autograph manuscript of the work (*Stichvorlag*) is unfortunately lost, though, from facsimiles visible in Chop's monograph, it is possible to see that Delius composed his setting using Whitman's English text and that his wife, Jelka, provided the German translation underneath.[38] In fact, many years later, Delius claimed to Fenby that 'the shape of it was taken out of my hands, so to speak, as I worked, and was bred easily and effortlessly of the nature and sequence of my particular musical ideas, and the nature and sequence of the particular poetical ideas of Whitman that appealed to me'.[39] A somewhat irritable letter from Delius to Ernest Newman, of 19 August 1929, firmly contradicted Newman's

---

[36] Abraham, G. E. A., 'Delius and His Literary Sources', *Music & Letters*, Vol. 10 No. 2 (April 1929), 185.

[37] *AH*, 104.

[38] Chop, M., *Frederick Delius* (Berlin: Harmonie Verlag, 1907), 56.

[39] *EF*, 36.

assumptions that *Sea Drift* had been 'laboriously retranslated into English' from the German. 'I composed "Seadrift" in English and could not have done otherwise, as the lovely poem inspired my music. Owing to the entire lack of interest in my music in England at that time I was compelled to give it to a german Publisher and to have it performed a number of times in Germany before it was given in England. My wife therefore translated it into german (and a very arduous job it was, too, fitting the german words to my music)'.[40] Newman's view nevertheless prevailed for many years, owing to the larger and more prominent nature of the German text in the 1906 Harmonie edition.[41] In sensing the form of his choral work, Delius was also astute in his paring down of Whitman's text. It was by no means all usable. The first twenty-three lines were excised; a small central portion of seven lines, and the last fifty-three, which included much of the explication of the boy's vicarious relationship with the hopeless he-bird, were also dispensed with. The structure of Delius's 'concert drama' for solo baritone, chorus and orchestra was carefully measured. Its conception, too, was unique. The baritone (with a similar high tessitura as found in *Koanga* and *A Village Romeo and Juliet*) takes on the role of narrator, yet, in accordance with Whitman's poem, he becomes the central protagonist with a distinctly theatrical demeanour. The chorus, in addition, play a variety of roles, commenting here, accompanying there, besides punctuating Delius's beautifully balanced design with set pieces.

Though completed in 1904, it was not until 24 May 1906 that *Sea Drift* was first performed, under the aegis of the Allgemeine Deutsche Musikverein at the Tonkünstlerfest, Essen, with the baritone Josef Loritz under the baton of Georg Witte. Schillings, the work's dedicatee, thought about performing the work in Munich, but his programme for 1906 was too crowded already. A most important element which assisted the promulgation of *Sea Drift* was that Delius's music was now being published for the first time, by Harmonie, a new publishing house in Berlin set up by Alexander Jadassohn in 1897. That the vocal score was available to the chorus was a huge boon for the Essen performance and undoubtedly precipitated a second performance in Basel under Hermann Suter and its first English hearing at the Sheffield Festival under Wood in October 1908. Cassirer, another of Delius's devotees, also came to know *Sea Drift* through the published score: 'I had no idea that the things were already out', he wrote to Delius. 'I have now got to know Sea-Drift

---

[40] Letter from Delius to Ernest Newman, 19 August 1929, *DLL2*, 352–3.

[41] See Butcher, A. V., 'Walt Whitman and the English Composer', *Music & Letters*, Vol. 28 No. 2 (April 1947), 155.

today! What am I to write? I could have almost howled with delight. I will say no more. I am quite beside myself and wanted just to let you know briefly … You are now so glorious in your maturity'.[42]

Critical reception was mixed. Some drew parallels with French Impressionism and sensuality;[43] others, such as *Die Musik*, condemned it for its 'depressing cheerlessness'. A prevailing criticism, however, was of its perceived formlessness and lack of thematic material.[44] More importantly for Delius, he recruited a new disciple in the young, Danzig-born Carl Schuricht, who was quite evidently smitten by what he had heard at Essen:

> Now … I can at last *do* what I longed to: perform new works and good older ones; devote my energies to the service of the (terribly few) *real* composers. And so I am asking *you*, dear Maestro, who have so wonderfully revived my hopes for a new flowering of the purest, *most spiritual* and most perfect art, firstly: So long as I have no orchestra of my own, let me get *your* works better known privately.[45]

Schuricht was only 26, but, as a keen student of so many German and Austrian conductors – Mottl, Richter, Weingartner, Mahler (who conducted the premiere of his Sixth Symphony in the same Essen concert) and Nikisch – he would prove to be an influential ally in the progress of Delius's music in Germany. Schuricht honoured his promise and conducted *Sea Drift* in Frankfurt in November 1910 after he was appointed as director of the Rühlscher Oratorienverein. As the most fervent of Delius's German 'Liebhaber', Schuricht also remained devoted to *Sea Drift* which had been a Damascene experience for him: 'I wander around as if intoxicated, what a wonderful gift the piece was and is to me'.[46] But perhaps most significantly, Schuricht's energy and promotion of new music – he was hugely supportive of works by Mahler, Schoenberg, Reger and Strauss, especially at Wiesbaden after 1920 – gave Delius's music its much deserved European perspective.

---

[42] Letter from Fritz Cassirer to Delius, 6 October 1906, *DLL1*, 272.

[43] *The Musical Times*, Vol. 47 No. 761 (July 1906), 486.

[44] *Nazionale Zeitung*, 9 March 1907; see also *The Musical Times*, Vol. 49 No. 789 (November 1908), 727 and *Sheffield Daily Telegraph*, quoted in *MLPG*, 188.

[45] Letter from Carl Schuricht to Delius, 3 October 1906, *DLL1*, 271.

[46] Letter from Schuricht to Delius, 12 March 1908, *DLL1*, 340.

Contrary to the accusations of formlessness, or of possessing no determinable form,[47] *Sea Drift* reveals a surprisingly classical structure in which the element of key, not normally a significant part of the composer's cohesive process, plays a quintessential role. Throughout Whitman's poem the rhythm of the sea constantly offers a point of return and it is this which provides a metaphor for the opening rondo theme for orchestra in E major, a theme which recurs in various impressionistic transformations throughout the work as a symbol of nature's oblivion to the anthropomorphic drama (Example 7.2a). Besides this rotational dimension, there is also the suggestion of a larger ternary organisation in which an 'exposition', firmly couched in E major, is quitted for a more developmental and modulatory phase before all is resolved with a truncated climactic reprise of the opening material unequivocally in E.

A slow, sensuous, opening paragraph with chorus (which takes place in two sequential stages) sets a scene of gently rolling waves in E major ('Once Paumanok, when the lilac scent was in the air'), evoked by falling figures in the wind, the ever-sensuous presence of the composer's much favoured added-sixth harmony and a pulsating figure in the bass, E to F natural, which will prove important later in the work. One other feature, however, establishes itself with true vigour and ingenuity in *Sea Drift* and that is the composer's instinctive capacity for an individual orchestral sound and style. As Evans has remarked:

Example 7.2a. *Sea Drift*, rondo theme.

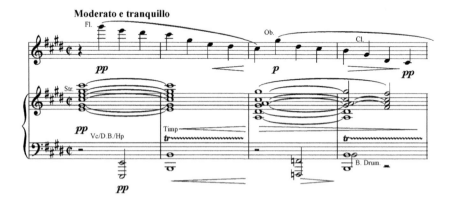

---

[47]   Gray, C., *A Survey of Contemporary Music* (Oxford: Oxford University Press, 1927), 70.

It may fairly be claimed, I think, that Delius is the most original and imaginative orchestrator England has yet produced. His methods are always much the same but have proved difficult to imitate convincingly: the Hollywood music purveyors whose abuse of his added-note chords we have already noted, seem unable to apply the Delian orchestral technique without a similar incursion of vulgarity. Genuine Delius scoring is occasionally miscalculated, we may think, but very rarely vulgar. His favourite disposition of the instruments is a thick string harmony (with much division, particularly in the middle parts) decorated by melodic snatches and arabesques passed among the woodwind group. Though he frequently uses triple w.w. [woodwind] he does so not for added weight but for the additional solo colours of cor anglais and bass clarinet or for the homogeneity of complete chords of one tone colour.[48]

The opening prelude of *Sea Drift* is the very epitome of this technique – divided strings, wind filigree, which culminates in a wind 'choir' (before Fig. 2). Such sensuality, such striving after beauty of sound, established itself as an aesthetic objective for Delius. Indeed, the lesson of *Sea Drift* seems to have taught him to temper his previous Straussian enthusiasms. Even though he retained his uncompromising need for large forces – the score requires triple woodwind, cor anglais, bass clarinet, double bassoon, six horns, three trumpets and two harps – the desire for *nuance* over volume guided Delius's orchestral imagination. As Evans also observed:

Fortissimo passages do tend to sound uncomfortable in Delius, his harmonies are usually more effective in quiet, lyrical passages, often with subtle distinctions in the dynamics of the essential and the "added" notes in the chords. Despite superficial resemblances in method, Delius' orchestral technique owes very little to the impressionist manner of Debussy. Not only is it much fuller (even its pianissimos) due to the greater complexity of its chords, but it is less patchy: the w.w. [woodwind] snatches are interwoven in a way quite unlike Debussy's successive solos, and indeed countermelodies or figures are an essential part of the "Delius" scoring. Debussy's and, still more, Ravel's felicities of orchestration stand out as such; in Delius they are so vital a part of the musical conception that their ingenuity is irrelevant.[49]

---

[48] Evans, P., 'Delius', Evans Papers, *GB-DRu*.

[49] Ibid.

The opening choral entry (which re-emphasises the link with F at Fig. 3) yields to the baritone's narrative ('And every day the he-bird to and fro'). Here again, E reasserts itself and, in spite of the direction of this first monologue to B major (which draws attention to the observing boy), it is to E which Delius accentuates with its F natural oscillation at the close of this passage. What is more, the first of the three partsongs ('Shine! Shine! Shine! Pour down your warmth, great sun!'), with its striking appoggiaturas, affirms the tonic in an explosion of diatonic harmony, radiating Whitman's expression of solar warmth. To this vocal texture, which is often intrinsically bound up with the orchestra, Delius invariably adds an upper counterpoint in the strings and wind, and it is this line that often provides the necessary rhythmical conduit between choral strains.

At the conclusion of what might aptly be described as a 'dance of joy', Delius provides a more operatic style of dramatic recognition (at Fig. 8). Moving to the Neapolitan minor ('Till of a sudden, may be killed'), a more detached style of recitation announces the demise of the she-bird. In response, as a measure of the sense of tragedy, Delius initially provides an orchestral gesture, heavily redolent of *Tristan* (before Fig. 9 – Example 7.2b) before returning to the unchanging E major seascape ('And thence forward all summer in the sound of the sea'). As the narrative begins to involve the boy's emotional reaction to the he-bird's anxiety, the initial E–F oscillations of the preludial material find a new meaning in the shift to F major (at Fig. 10) and the contemplative second dance-like partsong, 'Blow! Blow up winds along Paumanok's shores'. With considerable care, each of Delius's departures for the soloist become more extensive so that, with the conclusion of the second partsong, the narrative begins to become more animated in conjunction with greater tonal fluidity ('Yes, when the stars glisten'd'). This phase of more genuine symphonic development culminates in one of the most heartrending passages in all Delius – another *Tristanesque* transition, sequential in its series of 6/4 harmonies and replete with Delius's 'autobiographical' solo violin obbligato ('He called on his mate'). The agony of the boy is compellingly reflected in the baritone's high tessitura supported by the homogenous tone of the wind.

With yet another rondo statement of E major (Fig. 13), we are reminded of nature's inescapable insensibility while the boy's empathy for the he-bird ('my brother') intensifies. At this point the music takes a new, more animated symphonic turn as the sea itself becomes a character in the drama, a fact accentuated by the commentary of the chorus ('Soothe! Soothe!') and the colourful orchestral figuration. The upward direction of this exhilarating section, shaped by its own melodic fragment for the chorus, is towards a powerful solo and choral climax in C major as the voices of the he-bird and

Example 7.2b. *Sea Drift*, 'tragedy'.

Example 7.2c. *Sea Drift*, 'O rising stars'.

boy, now as one, sing relentlessly and frenziedly for *their* beloved ('You must know who I am, my love'). Emulating the Neapolitan motion of the E major – F major relationship, Delius repeats the same relationship here as C major gives way to C sharp minor (Fig. 18) for the third and final partsong ('O rising stars' – Example 7.2c). In this magnificent lament in the relative minor, in which Delius once more shows his affinity for *a cappella* eight-part choral sonority, the partsong idiom now becomes the sole support for the soloist. This emotional centrepiece, full of the most kaleidoscopic changes of harmonic nuance, also allows the first contemplation of death to surface ('death's carols!' as Whitman put it) in what is essentially a funeral song.

A further occurrence of the rondo (Fig. 20) in a much-distilled form ('O reckless despair') follows the lament (the E–F oscillations are still audible) and underpins one last desperate hope that the beloved might return. Yet, while the text may still convey this lingering hope, the shift to D flat major signals the beginning of a new threnody, founded on a paraphrase of 'so starben wir' from *Tristan* (Example 7.2d), and a secondary rising fragment, more alluring in rhythm and shape (Example 7.2e). Another of Delius's veiled tributes to his beloved Wagnerian opera, this wonderfully lyrical paragraph represents the expressive epicentre of the work in its acceptance of loss, a sentiment poignantly articulated by the understated cadence into D flat (seven bars after Fig. 22). With the return of D flat and the threnody material, Delius takes little time to reach the most forceful climax ('O darkness! O in vain!'), and the *Tristanesque* climax at 'fff', on an unresolved dominant minor thirteenth of E (additionally coloured by a minor ninth and eleventh), provides a substantial emotional fulcrum from a state of desolation to one of stoical acceptance; moreover, this epicentral sensation of hopelessness is powerfully

Example 7.2d. *Sea Drift*, 'O darkness, O in vain!'

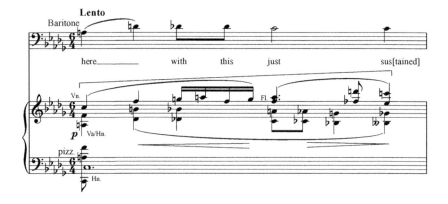

Example 7.2e. *Sea Drift*, 'threnody'.

apostrophised in the one naked moment of 'ad libitum' ('O I am very sick and sorrowful') that immediately follows. Delaying the return of E is, however, one of the most astutely judged moments of the work's deft formal construction, for in allowing further reworking of the threnody material, the larger dramatic function is not only one of tragic realisation ('O throat! O throbbing heart! And I singing uselessly all the night') but a passing from adolescence to adulthood for the distraught onlooker.

One of the most significant features of the reprise in E major is the conspicuous use of diatonicism. In this Delius had certainly learned lessons from both Wagner and Strauss who, at their most profound, invariably fell back on diatonic resources for their most profound climactic statements. Delius's climax (like that of *Koanga* in Act III) outlines a simple but sublime modulation to the subdominant ('Loved, loved'), an ecstatic moment aptly enunciated by the baritone's high F sharp. One senses that the borrowing of the descending diatonic figure from *The Magic Fountain* (Watawa's theme – see Example 3.3f), which pervades much of this valedictory paragraph (in combination with a memory of Example 7.2c), had much to do with its kinship with the work's preludial material.[50] Nevertheless, it provides a fitting and effective transformation of the opening idea before, as one last recurrence of the rondo's rolling waves, it is distilled in the last sixteen bars (see Table 7.3).

Sea Drift, as Heseltine commented, 'is essentially a dramatic work, but there is no such definite cast as even the most elastic form of opera would demand'.[51] It was a comment which adroitly summed up the hybrid nature of Delius's first major choral work. The extent of the soloist's role and its exacting range have much in common with opera, yet like all composers writing works for choral festivals, the imperative remains for a substantive participation by the chorus to whom a variety of creative roles is imaginatively assigned, more akin to that of cantata and oratorio (even though these traditional genres were anathema to the composer). Another strength of the form is its powerful narrative element – as Donald Mitchell commented, 'the only narrative poem Delius ever set'.[52] The secular nature and melancholy sentiment of *Sea Drift* must also have given the chorus at Essen in 1906 some pause for thought, since this was not the kind of repertoire with which they were familiar. In addition, Georg Witte, the conductor, must also have been aware that Delius

---

[50] Beecham noted this thematic correspondence (*TB*, 66–7), though did not offer any reason for Delius's act of self-plagiarism.

[51] *PH*, 103.

[52] Mitchell, D., 'Delius: The Choral Music', *Tempo*, No. 26 (Winter 1952–1953), 9.

Table 7.3. *Sea Drift*, structural overview as a rondo.

Main section	Subsection	Text	Key	Rondo structure
EXPOSITION	Orchestral prelude		E major	**Rondo theme**
	Chorus	'Once Paumanok when the lilac scent'	E major	Choral introduction
	Baritone soloist	'And every day the he-bird to and fro'	E major	Partsong 1
	Chorus	'Shine, shine, shine' [dance of joy 6/8]	E major	Transition
	Baritone soloist	Recit: 'Till of a sudden'	F minor	
	Baritone soloist	'And thence forward all summer in the sound of the sea'	E major	**Rondo theme**
	Chorus	'Blow! Blow up winds along Paumanok's shores'	F major	Partsong 2
	Baritone soloist	'Yes, when the stars glisten'd'	A major	
	Baritone soloist	'Yes, my brother'	E major	**Rondo theme** (modified)
DEVELOPMENT	Baritone and chorus	'Soothe! Soothe!'	D minor – C major	Symphonic development
	Baritone and chorus	'O rising stars'	C♯ minor	Partsong 3 'Lament'
	Baritone soloist	'O reckless despair'	E major	**Rondo theme** (distilled)
	Baritone soloist	'For somewhere I believe I heard my mate'	D♭ major	
	Baritone and chorus	'O darkness'	D♭ major	
	Baritone soloist	'And I singing uselessly'	E minor	Transition
REPRISE	Baritone soloist	'O past! O happy life!'	E major	Conclusion
	Orchestra and chorus	Postlude	E major	**Reprise of rondo material**

was not a composer who had emanated from a traditional choral background, whether from church or as a member of a choral society. As Fenby recorded, Witte made overtures to regularise Delius's choral writing in order to conform with more conventional techniques of voice-leading and texture in order to ease the problem of awkward intervals, challenging vocal ranges, and intonation. 'I should like to ask whether you will permit me to "touch up" the choral parts a little in the interests of more comfortable singing and of a better rendering of the German text'.[53] This elicited an indignant response from the composer who demanded that the original disposition of voices be restored.[54] But Delius's chromatic harmony and unconventional part writing inevitably compounded the already considerable demands of intonation, not least when passages such as the *a cappella* variation of *Appalachia* or 'O rising stars' from *Sea Drift* were expected (effortlessly) to retain pitch for the next entry of the orchestra. As John Rippin has rightly observed, 'Delius's music is risky territory for the amateur choir: few can cope with the intricacies of the parts and many professional singers have a job to keep the unaccompanied sections in tune … Only when the technical difficulties have been overcome can the singers find the time to add all those fine nuances necessary for a worthwhile performance'.[55] Cassirer entertained a range of views on the choral performance of *Appalachia* and *Sea Drift*: 'I have yet another idea. "Seadrift" requires a large choir, but "Appalachia" does not. What if I had the choral part performed by about twenty *professional* soloist singers. Perhaps young music students who are studying singing? Would this not be possible in London?'[56] But Heseltine took an even more extreme view and believed that Delius's intentions could not be properly realised until the choral forces were radically reduced: 'I am convinced that we shall never hear a perfect performance of "Appalachia", "Sea-Drift", or the "Songs of Sunset" until some one has the courage *to reduce the numbers of the choir to thirty-five, or at most fifty, while keeping the orchestra up to full strength*. It is absurd to use as large a chorus for "Sea-Drift" as for the "Te Deum" of Berlioz'.[57]

Even while German-speaking choirs were coming to terms with Delius's first choral essay, Henry Wood found the Sheffield committee obdurately set

---

[53] Letter from Georg Witte to Delius, 21 April 1906, *DTA*.

[54] *EF*, 203–4.

[55] Rippin, J. W., 'The Choral Music of Delius' (unpublished).

[56] Letter from Cassier to Delius, 9 October 1907, *DLL1*, 301.

[57] Heseltine, P., 'The Works of Delius', *The Musical Times*, Vol. 68 No. 1013 (July 1927), 643.

against the inclusion of it for the 1908 Festival, and neither its chorus nor its renowned chorus master, Henry Coward, showed any enthusiasm:

> I was rather hurt, to be candid, when they turned it down. I determined to produce it if possible, and wrote asking that I might meet the committee personally and play and sing the work to them. It was the subsequent enthusiasm of Walter Hall that brought about its inclusion in the programme. For all that, the chorus did not take kindly to it. They thought it an impossible work, and although Dr. Coward himself was not really in sympathy with it he managed to bring it off. I purposely asked for Frederic Austin to sing the solo part because I knew of no one else who could be trusted to sing it *con amore*.[58]

Although Delius, who attended the Sheffield performance, expressed reservations about Wood's choice of tempi, he was delighted with Coward's choir. 'The chorus was wonderful!', he told Jelka, 'but too loud'.[59] It was not, however, until Beecham took up the work up with the North Staffordshire Choral Society in December 1908, when it was given at Hanley and Manchester (again with Austin as soloist), that *Sea Drift* achieved some real traction, and this was largely due to that fact that its chorus master, James Whewall, had superbly schooled the singers (many of whom were more accustomed to Tonic Sol-fa) to produce a bright sound, with 'undeviating pitch and a sensibility that marked it apart from most other larger choral bodies of the day'.[60] Thereafter, Beecham championed *Sea Drift*, a fact confirmed by no less than the five recordings he made between 1928 and 1954.

GOOD FORTUNE

The promising omens of *Appalachia* and *Sea Drift* seemed to run parallel with Delius's changing fortune. All the time he had been in Paris and during the early days at Grez he had managed to eke out a living from the allowance he received from his father; and Jelka, after receiving a private income from her own family (which enabled her to pursue her career as a

---

[58] Wood, H., *My Life of Music* (London: Victor Gollancz, 1938), 279.

[59] Letter from Delius to Jelka, [8 October 1908], *DLL1*, 371.

[60] *TB*, 154.

painter),[61] inherited a small income from her mother. At his death, Delius's uncle Theodor left him a few thousands, and there were American shares which gave them a certain additional income.[62] After the death of his father in 1901, his allowance evaporated, and times were lean while he hoped to gain royalties from performances and publications of his music. Beecham, in vehemently gainsaying the claims of Clare Delius,[63] that Julius dealt with him fairly, came to the conclusion that, in pursuing his career as a musician, his father's unjust settlement towards him had been tainted by discrimination and recrimination.[64] His mother, too, loyally upheld Julius's unbending stance, and, apart from annual birthday presents, ignored her son's musical achievements (as her husband had done) well after she had left Bradford for the south of England.[65] Yet fortune smiled on Delius with an allowance from his German Aunt Albertine, and to take advantage of French tax laws, he and Jelka decided to marry in the summer of 1903. After returning from Florida in 1897, Delius had had the run of a wing in the house at Grez entirely for the purposes of his work which enabled him largely to discontinue the use of his Paris apartment. For Jelka, who was unstintingly devoted to Delius and his work, it marked the beginning of a new, more settled existence for them. For Delius, as Beecham has commented quite candidly, such devotion was not mutually returned (or at least not until much later); indeed, Jelka's attentiveness was a happy accommodation of his needs.[66] Such circumstances, nevertheless, left Delius in a favourable, not to say rare position in order to compose without disturbance at Grez-sur-Loing in relative comfort, and the fact that he never had to do a daily job of work, as was the lot of many musicians of his time, enabled him to realise his artistic goals with little distraction or obstruction. Had the position been otherwise, the blossoming of Delius's genius might never had happened. And now that he was on the very cusp of fulfilling his potential, the environment in which he found himself seemed almost providential. Writing retrospectively in 1907, Delius reflected on the realistic lot of an aspiring composer:

[61] *CD*, 143.

[62] Letter from Delius to Jelka, [Spring 1908], *AU-Mgm*, 155.

[63] See *CD*, 142–3.

[64] *TB*, 115–18.

[65] *CD*, 144.

[66] *TB*, 123.

No earnest musician should think of becoming what I may call a professional composer unless he has private means. A man who knows that his three meals a day are assured can devote himself to real individualistic composition and can wait for whatever good fortune may be in store for him.[67]

---

[67] *Musical Opinion*, December 1907.

Figure 1. Hans Sitt (Delius's violin
teacher in Chemnitz). Courtesy of
The Delius Trust and Lionel Carley.

Figure 2. Salomon Jadassohn
(Delius's composition teacher
at the Leipzig Conservatorium).
Ullstein Bild / ArenaPAL;
www.arenapal.com.

Figure 3. Studio photograph (Spring, 1888). *From left to right*: Nina Grieg, Edvard Grieg, Johan Holvorsen, Fritz Delius and Christian Sinding. KODE – Edvard Grieg Museum.

Figure 4. Edvard and Nina Grieg.
Courtesy of The Delius Trust
and Lionel Carley.

Figure 5. Christian Sinding.
Courtesy of The Delius Trust
and Lionel Carley.

Figure 6. Florent Schmitt (from a woodcut).
Courtesy of The Delius Trust
and Lionel Carley.

Figure 7. Maurice Ravel.
Courtesy of The Delius Trust
and Lionel Carley.

Figure 8. Hans Haym (champion
of Delius's music in Germany).
Courtesy of The Delius Trust
and Lionel Carley.

Figure 9. Julius Buths.
Courtesy of The Delius
Trust and Lionel Carley.

Figure 10. Jelka Delius, c. 1900. Courtesy of The Delius Trust and Lionel Carley.

Figure 11. Frederick Delius, London, May 1899. Courtesy of The Delius Trust and Lionel Carley.

Figure 12. Gunnar Heiberg (by Blix). Courtesy of The Delius Trust and Lionel Carley.

Figure 13. Alfred Hertz (conductor of Delius's London concert in 1899). Granger, NYC / TopFoto.

Figure 14. Henry and Olga Wood.
Courtesy of The Delius Trust and
Lionel Carley.

Figure 15. Percy Grainger.
Courtesy of The Delius Trust
and Lionel Carley.

Figure 16. Thomas Beecham (Delius's champion in England).
Royal College of Music / ArenaPAL; www.arenapal.com.

Figure 18. Philip Heseltine.
Courtesy of The Delius Trust
and Lionel Carley.

Figure 17. Balfour Gardiner.
Courtesy of The Delius Trust
and Lionel Carley.

Figure 19. Eric Fenby,
Delius's amanuensis
(by Gunn). Courtesy
of The Delius Trust
and Lionel Carley.

Figure 20. Beatrice Harrison (cellist)
and May Harrison (violinist).
Courtesy of The Delius Trust
and Lionel Carley.

Figure 21. *Front row from the left*: Amalie Gmür-Harloff (singer), Agathe Backer Grøndahl (pianist), Edvard Grieg (composer), Gerhard Schelderup (composer), Erika Lie Nissen (pianist) and Iver Holter (composer, conductor). *Back row from the left*: Ole Olsen (composer), Thorvald Lammers (singer), Christian Cappelen (composer, organist), Johan Halvorsen (composer, conductor), Nina Grieg (singer), Johan Svendsen (composer, conductor) and Christian Sinding (composer). Taken at the Music Festival in Bergen, 1898. KODE – Edvard Grieg Museum.

Facsimile 1. First page of 'Lyse nætter' (1891).
GB-Lbl MS Mus 1745/1/36, f. 45r.

Facsimile 2. Opening of first movement of *A Mass of Life*, Part I,
'O Du mein Wille!' *GB-Lbl* MS Mus 1745/2/13/7, f. 1v.

Facsimile 3. From third movement of *A Mass of Life*, Part I, opening
of fugue: 'Das ist ein Tanz'. *GB-Lbl* MS Mus 1745/2/13/7, f. 23r.

Facsimile 4. Orchestral opening of fourth movement of *A Mass of Life*, Part II,
'Heisser Mittag schläft auf den Fluren'. *GB-Lbl* MS Mus 1745/2/13/7, f. 37r.

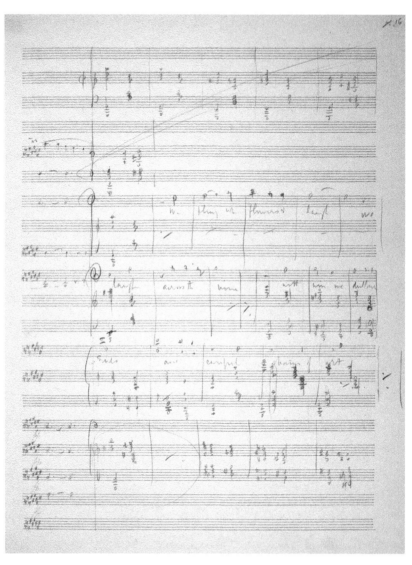

Facsimile 5. Pencil sketch of a discarded setting of
Ernest Dowson's 'Carthusians' ('We fling up flowers and
laugh'). *GB-Lbl* MS Mus 1745/2/13/4, f. 16r.

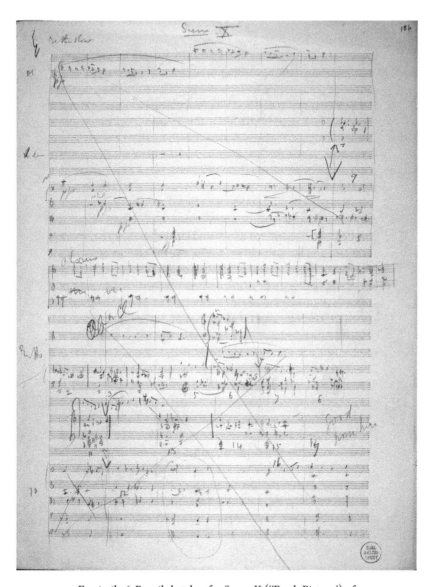

Facsimile 6. Pencil sketches for Scene X ('Tenth Picture') of
Fennimore and Gerda. *GB-Lbl* MS Mus 1745/2/13/4, f. 186r.

Facsimile 7. Opening of 'Midsummer Song' for unaccompanied chorus.
GB-Lbl MS Mus 1745/2/6, f. 178r.

Facsimile 8. Opening of first movement, 'Autumn: The wind soughs in the trees', from *North Country Sketches*. *GB-Lbl* MS Mus 1745/1/24, f. 2r.

Facsimile 9. From the slow movement of the Violin Concerto.
GB-Lbl MS Mus 1745/1/27, f. 10v.

CHAPTER 8

The Nietzschean
Obsession: *A Mass of Life*
(1904–1906)

A NIETZSCHEAN LIBRETTO

The notion of a large-scale work based on Nietzsche's *Also Sprach Zarathustra* had probably been gestating in Delius's mind since the end of the 1890s, after completion of *Mitternachtslied Zarathustras* and the four experimental Nietzsche songs. As we know, after the one flirtation with *Mitternachtslied Zarathustras* in 1898, his creative energies were still very much diverted by his attraction to the Tristan myth, whether in *Koanga* or in *A Village Romeo and Juliet*, and, as we have seen in *Sea Drift*, the need to sublimate his obsession with love, death and ecstasy.[1] Also the orchestral modernisms of Richard Strauss required some form of assimilation in *Paris*, *Lebenstanz* and *Appalachia* before a work such as *Sea Drift* was allowed to emerge with a new assurance. As mentioned previously, choral music was not an instinctive milieu for Delius. He had no practical experience of running a choir, nor participation in a choral society; indeed, Delius came more readily to the chorus through its role in opera. However, after the experience of *Sea Drift*, in which those facets of the opera house happily found a home in the concert room, it is not surprising that he soon came to the conclusion that choral music – on an epic scale – could, and should, be the most apposite symphonic vehicle for the expression of his concordance with Nietzsche's *Weltanschauung*.

Having *Mitternchtslied Zarathustras* already to hand may well have been the initial incentive to proceed with his grand Nietzschean choral project. Indeed, as Threlfall has pertinently commented, the revival of the work in

---

[1] See Lyle, R., 'Delius and the Philosophy of Romanticism', *Music & Letters*, Vol. 29 No. 2 (April 1948), 163.

Basel in 1903 under Suter (after its original hearing in London under Hertz in 1899) may well have provided the critical stimulus to begin work in earnest.[2] As we have seen repeatedly, Delius was never averse to the cannibalisation of his earlier music for new compositions, and the whole was taken over, save the final sixty bars, to be, as Fenby noted, the 'spiritual axis' of *A Mass of Life*.[3] Even the original dedication, to his cousin Arthur Krönig, was retained in the score (while the *Mass* in its entirety was dedicated to Fritz Cassirer). In addition, we know from a letter to Cassirer that the 'Tanzlied' (which probably became Part I No. 2 of the *Mass*) had been composed,[4] and from the many surviving sketches, skeletal strips of manuscript paper with series of progressions only comprehensible to their author, and various pencil drafts, many of the initial ideas may well have been committed to paper by mid-1904.[5] Having originally asked Cassirer, who was fresh from the performances of *Koanga* at Elberfeld, to write an opera libretto for him – this never materialised – Delius enlisted the German conductor's assistance in constructing a libretto for the work from *Also Sprach Zarathustra*, having already expressed some difficulty in selecting appropriate sections from Nietzsche's poem.[6] Cassirer was due to visit him at Grez in August,[7] and out of this meeting a cycling holiday transpired in Brittany, during which the two men put together a text. Hence, by September 1904, Delius found himself with an outline of his work which occupied him for the rest of the year and for much of 1905.[8]

Although we have relatively little evidence of the process of composition in *A Mass of Life* after the content of the work was decided, we can nevertheless extrapolate from the libretto and the supporting sketch material that it was conceived on a very large scale, larger indeed than Strauss's tones poems and *Eine Alpensinfonie*, and most of Mahler's symphonies. The

---

[2] Threlfall, R., 'Delius: A Fresh Glance at Two Famous Scores', *The Musical Times*, Vol. 125 No. 1696 (June 1984), 317.

[3] See Puffett, D., 'A Nietzschean Libretto: Delius and the Text for "A Mass of Life"', *Music & Letters* Vol. 79 No. 2 (May 1998), 246.

[4] Letter from Cassirer to Delius, 13 May 1904, *DLL1*, 240.

[5] Threlfall, R., 'Delius: A Fresh Glance', 317. The sheer number of scraps of paper, sketches, drafts in short score and drafts in full score (*GB-Lbl* MS Mus 1745/2/13/3) reveal that Delius was an inveterate sketcher and revisor of his work.

[6] *TB*, 132.

[7] Letter from Cassirer to Delius, 13 May 1904, *DLL1*, 241.

[8] At the foot of the MS autograph (*GB Lbl* Ms Mus 1745/2/13/7) it states 'Die Auswahl und Zusammenstellung des Textes hat Herr / Fritz Cassirer besorgt'.

orchestra was even larger than *Sea Drift* – besides the triple woodwind and additions of cor anglais, bass clarinet and double bassoon, Delius asked for a bass oboe, six horns, four trumpets, two harps and a battery of percussion including a large tamtam and bells. A good deal of the choral material is for double choir, and, as in many large-scale oratorios, there is a full complement of four soloists. The daunting dimensions of *A Mass of Life* compare more readily with Mahler's Symphony No. 8 (not heard until 1910 in Munich) and Schoenberg's *Gurre-Lieder* (not premiered until 1913 in Vienna), or in Britain the Wagner-inspired oratorical works of Elgar (such as *The Dream of Gerontius*, *The Apostles* or *The Kingdom*). None of these works could have had any tangible influence on Delius in the years 1904–1905, yet, it is clear that Delius was infected with the same *Zeitgeist* – the creation of an immense musical architecture – which permeated the imagination of composers in the decade before the First World War. Indeed, one might argue that Delius's conception was more analogous to his operatic designs in terms of sheer length, not to mention the theatrical and sensual nature of his musical gestures, yet the very mention of a 'mass' suggests that Delius and Cassirer between them aspired to produce a 'holy' work, an affirmation of life through the Dionysiac prism of *Zarathustra*, in much the same way that the mass – to those of a Catholic and Orthodox persuasion – is considered sacramentally epicentral to the Christian faith. As Derek Puffett has pointed out, the language and rhetoric of *Zarathustra* have a strongly biblical aroma. Exhortations, aspirations, oratory and a didactic higher morality (of an almost puritanical kind) all abound in the pages of Nietzsche's poem, and there are, from time to time, palpable references to the Christian liturgy, such as the litany in 'The Awakening' of Book IV. Elements such as 'The Last Supper' in Book IV undoubtedly have potent Christian parallels as does Zarathustra's abandonment by his own followers,[9] and much of the sensuous content seems to point to the opulent imagery of *The Song of Songs*. So, in one sense, Delius's *Mass* was by no means unconnected with the history of the mass or its large-scale concert genus which had emerged in the eighteenth and nineteenth centuries at the hands of Bach, Beethoven, Schubert, Bruckner and Dvořák. Threlfall has even speculated that sketches of a major orchestral introduction to the work, one that was later jettisoned, may even have been intended for a Requiem. Early sketches show that Delius certainly had a large orchestral

---

[9] Puffett, D., 'A Nietzschean Libretto', 249. The parallel of the Christian mass with Delius's work has also been conjectured by Robert Matthew-Walker in 'Aspects of Delius's *A Mass of Life*', *DSJ* No. 144 (Autumn 2008), 38–44.

prelude in mind and that one sketch, 'Prelude / Lebens Messe / Begin with / Marche Funebre' anticipates a draft of nine pages headed 'A Mass of Life / In Memoriam' beginning with the marking 'Lento con Solemnità'.[10] Whether this music was connected in any way with a mention of a Requiem in 1902, in letters to Jelka, we can only conjecture.[11]

The fact, however, that Delius seized on the title of A Mass of Life (Eine Messe des Lebens) intimates that he was attempting to capture a similar type of experience as one achieves from hearing a Concert Mass. Elements of drama combine with moments of awe, solemnity, joy, sadness and reverence as they relate to life and death – in other words the full gamut of the human experience – but without a narrative (in the case of the mass, the order of items is essentially determined by the liturgy). The Christian concert mass, with its familiar movements, outlines a cycle of different emotions intrinsically connected with faith. For Delius, A Mass of Life provided a major opportunity to select those texts he (and Cassirer) admired the most and into which he could pour all those 'items of faith': a devotion to elemental nature, the primacy of the human will (especially of work and the creative process), the physical abandon of the dance, the need for, and the role of, human love, the Nietzschean conviction of the 'Eternal Recurrence', and, above all, an affirmation of life itself. These fundamentals, together with Delius's love of Nietzsche's poetic language (the reason why the Mass was set in German), proved seminal to the construction of his libretto. As Abraham has commented, 'Delius, consciously or not, picked such passages as were remarkable for their poetry rather than their philosophy'.[12]

Besides a visit to Düsseldorf to hear Buths conduct Appalachia, Delius spent much of 1905 at Grez – hardly surprising given the amount of time he must have devoted to the completion of A Mass of Life. By November it was finished, and no-one was more delighted than Haym: 'I am enormously pleased to hear that the Mass of Life is finished. I am of course extremely curious & would like to do the piano reduction if it can wait till the New

---

[10]   Threlfall, R., 'Delius: A Fresh Glance', 317–18.

[11]   Delius mentions the possible composition of a Requiem (see letters from Delius to Jelka, [Spring] 1902) AU-Mgm, 111 and 10 June 1902) with which he was planning to collaborate with Robert d'Humières. The idea may well have been planted by his hearing of Verdi's Requiem in Berlin in February 1901 (see letter from Delius to Jelka, 14 February 1901, AU-Mgm, 120)

[12]   Abraham, G. E. A., 'Delius and His Literary Sources', Music & Letters, Vol. 10 No. 2 (April 1929), 187.

Year'.[13] Haym remained a devoted advocate of *A Mass of Life* which gave rise to a set of analytical notes published by Universal Edition in 1914,[14] but his hopes of performing the work had been undermined by the bad odour shown towards him by his Elberfeld employers. After the 'all-Delius' concert in 1904, he was attacked at a meeting of the town council for doing too much of Delius's music – an altercation which meant that any further production of Delius's works would have to be postponed. Although this did not suppress his efforts to promote Delius, Haym would not have the chance to conduct another Delius work for another five years.[15]

A study of Delius and Cassirer's libretto immediately reveals that Delius conceived the work in two parts. At first glance this was not dissimilar to the kind of oratorical model used at Birmingham where an interval provided some pause during the course of a whole evening's musical entertainment.[16] Yet, Delius's two parts are considerably disproportionate in size, Part I being almost half the length of Part II. It was almost as if the first part, of five movements (constituting well over half an hour's music), functioned as an extended prelude to the magisterial second of seven movements (lasting over one hour). A study of *Zarathustra* must have identified that Book I (of the poem's four books), with its unwieldy sermons, was unusable, so it was from Books II, III and IV that the content was chosen. What can be observed from a tabular representation of the grand architecture of the *Mass* is Delius's dependence principally on Books III and IV, with a special preponderance for individual sections of 'The Intoxicated Song' in Book IV which provides much of the text of Part II (see Table 8.1). It had, after all, been this part of the poem, full of Dionysiac imagery, that had drawn Delius to Nietzsche in 1898. But, besides these blocks of texts selected, Delius was also content to lift sentences from a combination of books (as in Part I No. 3 and Part II No. 1). Such amalgams also tended to accentuate the tendency of choosing those parts of the poem which ultimately chimed with Delius's own particular brand of atheism.

---

[13] Carley, L., 'Hans Haym: Delius's Prophet and Pioneer', *Music & Letters*, Vol. 54 No. 1 (January 1973), 10.

[14] An English version was printed by Universal Edition in 1925: Haym, H., 'Frederick Delius: *A Mass of Life* – Introduction to the Words and Music', trans. B. Gardiner (Vienna: Universal Edition, 1925).

[15] Carley, L., 'Hans Haym', 9.

[16] Typical examples of this paradigm can be seen in Mendelssohn's *Elijah*, Parry's *Judith* and Elgar's *The Dream of Gerontius*.

Table 8.1. *A Mass of Life*, libretto.

Section	Book	Subtitle*	Forces	First line
ERSTER TEIL [PART I]				
			[Orchestral prelude jettisoned]	
I/1	III	Invocation (from 'Of Old and New Law Tables')	Chorus	'O du mein Wille'
I/2	IV	The Song of Laughter (from 'Of the Higher Man')	Baritone [Zarathustra]	'Erhebt eure Herzen, meine Brüder'
I/3	III, IV	The Song of Life (from 'The Second Dance Song' and 'The Ass Festival')	Tenor and chorus	'In dein Auge schaute ich jüngst'
I/4	IV	The Riddle (from 'The Intoxicated Song')	Baritone and chorus	'Wehe mir! Wo ist die Zeit hin?'
I/5	II	The Night Song (from 'Das Nachtlied')	Baritone and chorus	'Nacht ist es: nun reden lauter'
ZWEITER TEIL [PART II]				
		On the Mountains	Orchestral prelude	
II/1	II, III, IV	[On the Mountains] (from 'The Sign', 'Of Old and New Law Tables' and 'The Rabble')	Soloists and chorus	'Herauf nun, herauf, du grosser Mittag'
II/2	IV	The Song of the Lyre (from 'The Intoxicated Song')	Baritone	'Süsse Leier'
II/3	II	The Dance Song (from 'The Dance Song')	Baritone and female chorus	'Lasst vom Tanze nicht ab'
II/4	IV	At Noon in the Meadows (from 'At Noontide')	Soloists and chorus	'Heisser Mittag schläft auf den Fluren'
II/5	IV	The Song of Rapture (from 'The Intoxicated Song')	Baritone and chorus	'Gottes Weh ist tiefer, du wunderlicher Welt'
II/6	IV	The Paean to Joy (from 'The Intoxicated Song')	Baritone	'Kommt, Kommt, Kommt! Lasst uns jetzo wandeln!'
II/7	IV	[Hymn] (from 'The Intoxicated Song')	Baritone and chorus	'Oh Mensch! Gib Acht!'
	IV	Coda	Soloists and chorus	'Lust will aller Dinge Ewigkeit'

* These subtitles are used by convention, but do *not* appear in Delius's score.

A MASS OF LIFE, PART I

Anthony Payne has persuasively suggested that the broad duration of *A Mass of Life* 'relates man's spiritual development to the passing of day, rising to the "glorious noontide" of maturity and then progressing to the midnight bell of death's call'.[17] This general narrative, and it is very general, appropriates the times of day (germane to Nietzsche's image of man's strength, independence and intellectual power) to Delius's scheme. These symbolic times of day also indicated something of Nietzsche's eclectic assimilation of Darwinist evolution and Comte's three phases of man's development leading to positivism – i.e. man emerging from his early animalistic state, at noontide midway into his course to becoming a Superman. Having reached this stage by evening, a new beginning is symbolised by the coming of morning. Delius no doubt realised, however, that the conclusion with midnight (with *Mitternachtslied Zarathustra*) would convey a negative sentiment, so it was entirely fitting to append additional text and sixty bars of music in order to affirm the quintessential Nietzschean ideal of 'Eternal Recurrence', allowing the work to emerge from the gloom 'into sunlit uplands'. This point is also reiterated in Puffett's study of the libretto.[18]

Very much confirming the biblical rhetoric and manner of *Zarathustra*, the first item of the *Mass* is sermon-like, delivered with a muscular evangelism. Delius took his text from the last section (section 30) of 'Of Old and New Law Tables' in Book III. Analogous to the New Testament's rejection of the 'old law' of Leviticus and Deuteronomy and the traditional values of Wisdom literature, Zarathustra's invocation to his followers is, by discovering one's true will ('O, Du mein Wille!'), to reject the trammels of Christianity. Delius's concept of this section must originally have been to depict man emerging from his 'primitive' phase in the initial pages of the orchestral introduction. This, as we know, was later rejected, though we know that Haym was discussing it in connection with the possibility of performing various numbers of the *Mass* individually.[19] The mood is forceful, self-confident, rhythmically dynamic (especially the opening statement), and clearly presented in a sonata scheme whose first and second subject components help to accentuate the composer's choice of text (Table 8.2).

---

[17] Payne, A., 'Delius, Frederick', in Sadie, S. (ed.), *The New Grove Dictionary of Music and Musicians*, 2nd edn (London: Macmillan, 2001), Vol. 5, 340.

[18] Puffett, D., 'A Nietzschean Libretto', 256–7.

[19] Carley, L., 'Hans Haym', 10.

Table 8.2. *A Mass of Life*, structural overview of I/1 [Invocation].

Section	Key	Text
First subject	F major	'O du mein Wille' (Animato)
Second subject (1)	D major	'Dass ich einst bereit und reif sei im grossen Mittage'
Second subject (2)	D major	'Bereit zu mir selber und zu meinem verborgensten Willen'
Transition		'O Wille, Wende aller Not'
First subject	F major	'O du mein Wille!'
Second subject (2)	F major	'O Wille, Wende aller Not'
Coda	F major	'Zu einem grossen Siege!'

The second movement (known as 'Song of Laughter'), taken from the twelfth section of Book IV ('Of the Higher Man') of Part I, might be described as 'Introduction and Dance' in which 'dance and laughter [figure] as symbols of a higher existence and freedom from bondage to earth'.[20] The opening recitative for baritone (who embodies the character of Zarathustra) begins with an exhortation ('Erhebt eure Herzen, meine Brüder' ['Lift up your hearts, my brothers'] – from section 17) reminiscent of the 'Sursum Corda' (the opening exhortation before the Preface to the Eucharistic Prayer in the Christian mass), in which the seeds of the forthcoming dance are planted. From B flat, Delius embarks on the first dance of the *Mass* ('Diese Krone des Lachenden' – section 18), another of his much-loved waltzes, in B major, where the rhythmical reminiscences of *Paris* are palpable. It was also a Neapolitan tonal relationship with which he had already experimented in the first of his *Danish Songs*. A short contrasting middle paragraph ('Dem Winde tut mir gleich' – section 20) moves from B back to B flat, a change of key which indicates the reprise of 'Diese Krone' and the restoration of the dance.

The second movement's buoyant dance, in an appropriate ternary form, provides an interlude before the main focus of Part I, 'The Song of Life'. Much more extended in form, the design of this centrepiece is more akin to those multi-sectional schemes of the larger mass movements such as the 'Gloria', 'Credo', and 'Offertorium' which often include set pieces such as fugue or sonata movements. The texts are taken (principally) from 'The Second Dance Song' in Book III and 'The Ass Festival' in Book IV. The meta-structure is framed by B major, a key area which we have already witnessed in the second movement. However, in this case Delius's use of the tonality is

---

[20] Haym, H., 'Frederick Delius: *A Mass of Life*', 8.

profoundly connected with the text of the last section 'O Mensch! Gib Acht!' in Part II. These words, and the key of B major, were inextricably linked with *Mitternachtslied Zarathustra* which, as we know, Delius placed at the end as a spiritual culmination of the entire work. One may surmise, therefore, that Delius recognised the significance of this text at the end of 'The Second Dance Song' and used both the text and key as a major anticipation and unifying force for the end of the entire work. The use of B major in this context is one of intense sensuality. It is a love affair with life ('In dein Auge schaute ich jüngst, O Leben'). Above the slow-moving opening pedal point (one of Delius's favoured drones) a wordless refrain (Example 8.1a) is numinously announced which Delius took from the last section of his Jacobsen setting 'I Seraillets Have' ('In the Seraglio Garden'), also from the *Danish Songs* of 1896. Functioning as a ritornello to the individual entries of the soloists (it was another of those favoured figures based round an added-sixth sonority),[21] it punctuates the whole of the first paragraph. The seductive nature of the soloists' material ('Gold sah ich in deinem Nachtauge blinken') which the tenor amply conveys with a melodic figure derived from *Lebenstanz* (Example 8.1b), yields to a second section centred around F major. Against the backdrop of the chorus's overtly simple diatonic tune, clearly intended to be innocuous and popular (using Delius's characteristically anonymous 'la la la' text), the lovers coyly pursue each other (Example 8.1c). As this behaviour grows in intensity, so does Delius's contrapuntal treatment. While the popular tune in octaves continues unabated (as a strangely archaic *cantus firmus*), the soloists furnish an increasingly rich texture of polyphony against which, with a perspicacity to match Wagner's contrapuntal *tour de force* in the Prelude to *Die Meistersinger*, the orchestra also provides at least two independent contrapuntal lines of its own. The confluence of this studious six-part polyphonic texture marks the return of F, now in the minor mode, and signals an inherent acceleration of tempo towards the centrepiece of the movement, a double fugue in C major.

It is almost a symptom of the oratorical nature of *A Mass of Life* that Delius should wish to produce on this rare occasion a fugue – a style-form which he had not written since his Leipzig days and which appears in no other work by him (save the *fugato* of *Folkeraadet*). Moreover, as if to accentuate its auspicious presence, it is a double fugue (i.e. both subjects *always* appear invertibly together, one a countersubject to the other), a contrapuntal *tour de force* (for which Delius needed to thank his Leipzig teachers). Of course,

---

[21] See *PH*, 148.

Example 8.1a. *A Mass of Life*, wordless refrain.

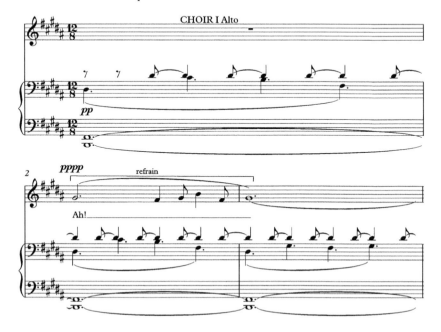

in another sense, it is, as Haym noted, a 'fugal dance' in accordance with the text ('Das ist ein Tanz über Stock und Stein') which itself symbolises the high point of the 'love-chase'.[22] Delius gives us a full exposition of four entries in accordance with traditional principles though this is more unconventionally interspersed with passages of homophonic laughter ('Ha ha ha') which constitute the lion's share of the episodic material, thereby providing a major contrast between the two components of the structure. All the while, the energy and momentum of the dance is provided by the orchestral *moto perpetuo* which has a rhythmical impetus akin to the scherzi of Mahler's later symphonies. A cadence into D major marks the end of the fugal exposition and the beginning of the first major episode. The eight-part contrapuntal texture is now exchanged for a homophonic, wordless one ('la la la') which acts as accompaniment to a three-part contrapuntal unit for the soprano, contralto and tenor soloists ('Ich tanze dir nach'). At the conclusion of the

[22]   Haym, H., 'Frederick Delius: *A Mass of Life*', 10.

Example 8.1b. *A Mass of Life*, 'Gold
sah ich in deinem Nachtauge blinken'.

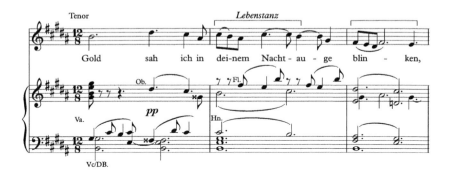

Example 8.1c. *A Mass of Life*, popular tune.

first episode, Delius arrives at F sharp major, a whole tritone away from the tonic. The fugal entry (which restores the original text 'Das is ein Tanz') in F sharp is announced by the soprano, its countersubject by the contralto. This remote key area and the introduction of 'false' entries (e.g. at Fig. 29 for the chorus) herald an increased sense of Dionysiac passion enhanced by the greater volume of laughter. A second entry in F sharp, given by the first choir, signals a stretto of entries which sequentially arrive in E (tenor), D (soprano) and C (bass). This facilitates a reprise of fugal entries in C and G for the full eight-part chorus including several 'false' ones. The fugue is, however, not completely over. Soloists and chorus join in an extended coda in which the laughter reaches a riotous climax 'over hill and dale'. Parallels with the central chorus of Act II of *Die Meistersinger* come to mind, although the 'dance' element vividly recalls the 'Fair' scene from *A Village Romeo and Juliet* (with its own wordless element).

After Delius's most unusual fugal essay has subsided, away from C major, Zarathustra's second exhortation ('O meine neuen Freunde'), taken from 'The Ass Festival' in Book IV, is framed by a third wordless popular tune for chorus. Although the laughter figurations of the fugue linger as memories, its more reflective tone relies on the elegiac suspensions from *Sea Drift* ('O darkness'). By closing this part in B major with the refrain (see Example 8.1a), Delius evidently considered this composite structure of four movements to be concluded. It was, however, for the last section to provide an apotheosis. This is supplied by the solo contralto who speaks of human love ('O Zarathustra! Jenseits von Gut und Böse'). Her extensive solo begins in E flat before moving once again to B major. At the arrival of this key, her opening melody is reannounced by the orchestra while the contralto's melancholy text invokes parallel images with Christ's atonement ('O Zarathustra, ich weiss es, dass du mich bald verlass willst!' ['O Zarathustra, I know that thou soon will have forsaken me!']). At this solemn conjunction, Zarathustra's 'Midnight Song' ('O Mensch, Gib Acht!') emerges chorale-like in the basses of the chorus forming a Neo-Baroque chorale prelude against the rich counterpoint of the contralto and soprano, the sumptuousness of which (with its tonal journey from E flat to B) looks forward to a similar tonal relationship in *The Walk to the Paradise Garden* (which, as we know, Delius composed after the *Mass*'s completion).

After the tranquil ending of the third movement, the fourth, 'The Riddle', is one of contrasting despondency as Zarathustra expresses misgivings about his aspirations ('Wehe mir! Wo ist die Zeit hin?'). It was the first of several textural references Delius made to 'The Intoxicated Song' of Book IV. More Wagnerian in its declamation, the vocal line is more gesticulatory and urgent as each question is uttered, and the chorus, functioning more like a *turba*, repeats each question with commensurate resolve. Motivically the movement is also important for its exposition of the rising fifths idea (Example 8.1d) which represents the midnight 'bell' (see 5 bars after 42). This idea recurs repeatedly throughout the movement, reaching a climax with the exclamation 'Wer soll der Erde Herr sein?', until it is stilled by the return of the 'Mitternachtslied' text 'O Mensch gib Acht', at which point the music settles in F major with a final question 'Was spricht die tiefe Mitternacht?'. As if to pacify Zarathustra's anxiety, conveyed by the through-composed transitional nature of the fourth movement, the fifth and final movement of Part I is a pastoral nocturne, taking up the tonality of F major established at the end of the fourth movement. As mentioned above, the song 'Summer Landscape', which also shares the same key, was very likely a 'study' for this striking essay. In 'The Night Song' (from 'Das Nachtlied' in Book II), an operatic scena in terms of its length and delivery, Zarathustra longs for love in his solitude. In the distance he hears the singing of love songs which are provided by the hushed tones of the chorus, whether in the form of extended melodic lines (such as the one provided by the basses at the beginning), brief wordless exclamations, choral comments more redolent of the partsongs in *Sea Drift*, or by appropriately pictorial

Example 8.1d. *A Mass of Life*, rising fifths, 'midnight bell'.

accompanimental figurations. The slow, languid pulse of Delius's 6/4 metre, almost suggestive of a lullaby, is hugely demanding for the baritone soloist in terms of range and length of line. Indeed, the comparison with the steady, self-developing lines of Tristan in Act II of *Tristan und Isolde* is a compelling one, not only for the sexually charged nature of the rich harmony – Delius's use of harmonic 'sound moments' is abundant here – but also for the powerful sense of voice-leading which inhabits the outer sections of the ternary design. This is nowhere more imposing than in the first climax ('die redet selber die Sprache der Liebe') and its counterpart in the reprise ('und auch meine Seele ist das Lied eines Lebenden') where, with the stepwise assent to the high G, Delius parades his love of the high baritone tessitura. What is more, for the reprise's climax, Delius once again relies on the simple but immensely effective modulation to the subdominant to create his highest point of ecstasy. The movement closes with the chorus. Straussian in its diatonic iridescence, the last eleven bars of B flat major communicate Delius's fondness for the sensuous added-sixth sonorities, now joined by an equal gratification in the added ninth, together with the gentle pulsation of timpani and the velvet tones of the horns (a timbre which dominates the luxuriant orchestration).

A MASS OF LIFE, PART II

It would have been quite reasonable for Delius to have quitted his Nietzschean rapture at this point, since Part I itself embraced a broad and coherent array of contrasting movements. Yet, judging from the poetical choices made in Part II, Delius and Cassirer felt that more of Zarathustra's emotional 'story' as a man needed to be told, so Part I effectively assumed the role of prologue.

The opening of Part II, 'Auf den Bergen' ['On the Mountains'], was the only time Delius actually provided a title for his individual movements. The landscape, a depiction of high peaks, fjords and answering horn calls, is surely Norwegian, though there is something of the Swiss Alps from Scene 3 of *A Village Romeo and Juliet* too. As Boyle has suggested, the horn calls, suspended above the extraordinary simplicity of protracted dominant and tonic pedals of F major (totalling some sixty-five bars, and here there is a parallel with the prolonged E flat major in the prelude to *Das Rheingold*), have an anonymity removed from the romanticism of animal herding or shepherd boys;[23] this is, instead, a landscape of enlightenment, contemplation and self-discovery, closer to Ibsen's *Paa Vidderne*. Indeed, it is the refuge of Zarathustra's meditations, as was Christ's desert wilderness. From this, Part II erupts with another massive choral statement for double choir in ternary form, this time in A major. In this instance, Delius's text was a free concoction of well-known closing lines of 'The Sign' (Book IV) and 'Of Old and New Law Tables' (Book III) for the outer paragraphs that contain two major thematic elements (see Table 8.3), while the great hope of 'summer's noontide' occurs in 'The Rabble' (Book II) towards D and later to F major.

Symbolising man in his prime, the first movement is a vigorous appeal to the artist to be hard-nosed in pursuit of his artistic goals ('Werdet hart!') to the exclusion of all else. It was an unpalatable philosophy Delius readily embraced, believing implicitly in the notion of creativity as man's foremost concern (and belying the notion that Delius's interest in Nietzsche was entirely poetical). It did not commend itself to Beecham,[24] Fenby was unimpressed,[25] and Jelka was only too often sacrificed for his egotism and his rejection of 'love' as a 'folly'.[26] In contrast to the whirlwind of the first movement, 'The Song of the Lyre' (another extraction for 'The Intoxicated Song'), Zarathustra seeks solace in his lyre and sings of the promised richness of the new world to come in a through-composed song ('Süsse Leier!'), couched in A flat major. Much denser harmonically, the flowing accompaniment provides a profuse matrix of different tinctures illuminating Nietzsche's highly nuanced vocabulary, particularly in those passages which contend with pain and anguish ('Jeder Schmerz riss dir in's Herz, Vaterschmerz, Urväterschmerz').

---

[23] *DN*, 201.

[24] *TB*, 219–20.

[25] *EF*, 171.

[26] This especially disagreeable image was recalled by Cecil Gray in his 'Memories of Delius', in *DC*, 142.

Table 8.3. *A Mass of Life*, structural overview of II/1 [On the Mountains].

Section	Subsection	Key	Text
A	First subject (chorus)	A major	'Herauf! Nun herauf du grosser Mittag!'
	Second subject	A major	'Dort hinaus, stürmischer als das Meer'
B	Third subject (soloists)	D major/ D minor	'Vorbei die zögernde Trübsal'
	Fourth subject (chorus)	F major	'Einem Stürme gleich'
A	First subject (chorus)	A major	'Herauf! Nun herauf du grosser Mittag!
	Second subject	A major	'Dort hinaus, stürmischer als das Meer'
	Coda	F major	'Zu einem grossen Siege!'

The text also formed an important part of the modified reprise: here the opening progressions are somewhat disguised by the continued descending quaver motion (from four bars after 70), as is the gradual crystallisation of A flat at the very end on its tonic pedal ('Die Welt ist tief und tiefer als der Tag gedacht'). One of the most remarkable facets of 'Süsse Leier' is not only its advanced chromatic harmony but the extended periods where there is little suggestion of key and no cadence. Only from time to time does Delius seem to relent with a defining 6/4 (often as part of an anchoring, tangible dominant pedal). As Evans has ventured to enunciate, apparent atonal tendencies gain direction by the vital structural role of the melody above:

> If, on the other hand, we can find no obvious tonal relationship between the chords Delius uses, we may feel that he is drifting into atonality. Sometimes the vagueness of this procedure helps him to secure just the nebulous effect which he is seeking – or rather which he intends, since the sounds in Delius seem not to be sought but [are] the inevitable medium for the ideas they convey [...]

Very often, however, an apparently atonal series of chords is given a clear tonality by the melodic line which is above it. This point is important and seems not be understood by those who glibly claim that the melody is unimportant in Delius or even that the harmony was the first inspiration and the melody a fabricated tag on which to hang it. I am convinced that this idea is altogether wrong. We are told by his biographers that the young Delius would spend hours at the piano decking out well-known tunes in ever more complex harmonies ... It is precisely because of this melodic starting-point that so many of Delius' chord series seem arbitrary or even

fantastic when isolated, yet spring naturally to the mind (or the *fingers*) as
a texture to fill the gap between the preconceived melody and the typical
chromatic descending bass.[27]

The third movement of Part II, 'The Dance Song', is perhaps the most overt
projection of Delius's Nietzschean obsession with the dance. Using excerpts
from the eponymous section in Book II, Delius drew on an episode in
Zarathustra's life where, in a nocturnal wandering through a forest, he comes
upon young girls dancing. Aware of Zarathustra's presence they disperse. He
begs them to continue and the dance is resumed; but as twilight deepens and
the dance becomes wilder, he is plunged into gloom and doubt. As Puffett has
pointed out, commentators such as C. W. Orr have suggested that the dance
constitutes the song itself,[28] but there is in fact no tangible song. A more
accurate description of this movement would be 'Solo and Choral Ballet', since
the wordless four-part female chorus embodies music which is clearly balletic
in style and momentum. Puffett has also suggested that the interruption of the
dancers makes reference to the Flower Maidens in *Parsifal*;[29] this is plausible,
though the precedent of the three-part balletic chorus in *The Magic Fountain*,
which shares a similar compound metre, seems more likely. The movements
take the form shown in Table 8.4.

Precisely what is depicted by the orchestral prelude to the third movement
is unclear. Some have suggested that it is the meadow, yet it is only after walking
through the forest (a typical romantic symbol of emotional turbulence) that the
meadow is reached along with the dancers. Is the scene not another of Delius's
nocturnal evocations, in which the dark forest symbolises Zarathustra's restless
state of mind? This is surely insinuated by the appearance of Zarathustra's
motive at the beginning of the 'Con moto moderato' (Example 8.1e). The
first episode of ballet music fluctuates between E minor and E major before
it yields to a counterstatement from Zarathustra ('Lasst vom Tanze nicht ab')
in F major (yet another instance of a Neapolitan relationship). The response
from the dancers is a more tonally fluid phase in which their thematic material
is developed and brought to a high state of headiness before all is becalmed
in a sunset underpinned by B major ('Die Sonne ist lange schon hinunter')
and in the recurrence of the 'refrain' idea, though it is the final melancholy
gesture in D major by the orchestra (replete with choral memory in the final

[27]   Evans, P., 'Delius', Evans Papers, *GB-DRu*.

[28]   Puffett, D., 'A Nietzschean Libretto', 251.

[29]   Ibid.

Table 8.4. *A Mass of Life*, structural overview of II/3 [The Dance Song].

Section	Key	Text
Orchestral prelude	[A minor]	
Chorus [ballet]	E minor/E major	'La la la'
Baritone solo	F major	'Lasst vom Tanze nicht ab'
Chorus [ballet]	Fluid	'La la la'
Baritone solo	B major	'Die Sonne ist lange schon hinunter'
Baritone solo [coda]	D major	'Abend ward es'

Example 8.1e. *A Mass of Life*, Zarathustra's motive.

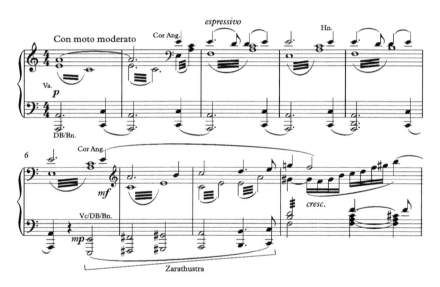

two bars) that Zarathustra's sadness is articulated in a reverie of exquisite lyricism. For the pervasiveness of the 'dance' spirit in this part of the *Mass*, Banfield has pointed to the idea, not of the waltz of *Paris* and *Lebenstanz*, but of the compound character of 'Sellinger's round', a model which he suggested would have been communicated to Delius through the 'tempus perfectum' of the apprentices' song at the end of Act I of *Die Meistersinger*, a work in which compound time is widely deployed.[30]

30 Banfield, S., 'La ronde se déroule: Delius and the Round Dance', *British Music Society Journal*, Vol. 6 (1984), 35–6.

For the rest of *A Mass of Life* Delius depended entirely on Book IV of *Zarathustra* and much of it on 'The Intoxicated Song'. For 'At Noon in the Meadows', he drew freely on lines from 'At Noontide'. In his solitude, Zarathustra, now come of age, has fallen asleep in the steamy heat of midday, rapt in blissful happiness. Even though this is the sacred time when no shepherd plays his pipe, a trialogue of pipes can be heard distantly. For this, Delius provides a timeless tableau of oboe, cor anglais and bass oboe in a series of three variations: first as a set of interacting contrapuntal entries (which looks forward to the opening of *Brigg Fair*), second as a harmonised version with descending chromatic bass, and third, having cadenced into the tonic, as a melody above the tonic pedal, replete with added sixth. As a pastoral scene, it is one of Delius's most characteristic (and least known) creations. The melody, distinctive for its Lydian inflection, haunts the first choral episode ('Heisser Mittag schläft auf den Fluren') where it also intermingles with the refrain from 'The Song of Life' in Part I. Zarathustra refuses, however, to be roused as he dwells upon his rapture. Appropriately Delius persists with further recollections of 'The Song of Life' refrain and the shepherd pipe tune; yet for all his blissful state, Zarathustra's restiveness erupts in the choral ejaculations ('Sein Glück lächt') and he is urged to stir himself in a mellifluous monologue ('Lasst mich doch! Still!'). A ternary structure, cast in C minor, the song is a tender lullaby whose repetitive 'charm' forms part of Delius's close-knit harmony (a paradigm which looks forward to the opening movement of *North Country Sketches*). The closing gestures for eight-part chorus ('O Glück!') are exquisitely handled as is the wonderfully poetic coda which closes euphoniously in E flat.

By dint of its brevity, the fifth movement, 'The Song of Rapture', functions both as an interlude between the fourth and final movements, and also as a transition to the *Mass*'s immense finale, to which it is conjoined without a break. Here we see Zarathustra in old age, at eventide, questioning his achievement as a rejected prophet ('Eine trunkene süsse Leier, eine Mitternachtsleier, eine Glockenunke, die Niemand versteht') in a short passage of declamation in which the 'bell' motive begins elusively to ring (four bars after 111). The tone is one of regret which is echoed by a commenting chorus in an extended, through-composed partsong ('Dahin! O Jugend! O Mittag! O Nachmittag!') whose homophony acts as one dramatic voice within the larger texture of the orchestral polyphony. The through-composed design also functions splendidly in expressing Zarathustra's cumulative elation and 'drunkenness', marked by the climax in which the chorus is joined by Zarathustra ('Lust is tiefer noch als Herzeleid'). Having reached a peak of almost dance-like fervour, chorus and soloist conclude without any resolution, yielding auspiciously to a solo kettle drum on F sharp, the dominant pedal of B.

At this point Delius inserted his *Mitternachstlied Zarathustras* virtually unchanged from the music composed in 1898 (except for the addition of the women's voices) in 'Noch ein Mal'. Remarkably, much of the music, especially 'Noch ein Mal', sits well in its later context, though the opening Wagnerian 'scena' does, to some degree, betray an earlier stage of development in which the composer was still perfecting his techniques of declamation. Nevertheless, its formal binary dialectic (not dissimilar to that of the 'Agnus Dei' and 'Lux Aeterna' of the Requiem Mass) is highly effective. The significance of Delius's finale and the key of B major have already been commented upon previously (see Chapter 5), in connection with redemption. However, Delius rightly understood that the music needed to emerge triumphantly from the solemnity of 'Noch ein Mal' to press home Nietzsche's fundamental principle of 'Eternal Recurrence', because the words also required a more triumphal consequence from their context in Part I, and because Delius needed to marshal all his forces, soloists, chorus and orchestra, in a grand peroration. This he managed in the final sixty bars in which the climactic crux materialises around the lines of section 11 of 'The Intoxicated Song' ('Lust will aller Dinger Ewigkeit') – 'Joy wants the eternity of all things' – and where the 'bell' motive re-echoes through the hushed tones of the chorus.

After *A Mass of Life* was completed in November 1905, Delius wasted no time, as we know, showing the score to Haym. It was almost certainly scrutinised by Cassirer, Suter and Schillings, though, not surprisingly, the scale and demands of the work, especially for chorus, caused them to have serious doubts. Writing from Switzerland, Suter felt he could not undertake it straightaway:

> The "Messe" is a very difficult proposition, particularly for soloists and choir … I have of course revived my own enthusiasm first and foremost for the deep poetry of the "Trunkene Lied"; I was particularly captivated by No III of the 1st part "In dein Antlitz sah ich jüngst"; in fact the wonderful poetry revealed by your music was a continual delight to me.[31]

And Schillings, somewhat daunted by the physical size of the score, remarked: 'Die Lebensmesse has arrived. At the moment I am still standing in awe before your gigantic score, whose secrets do not reveal themselves at the first

---

[31] Letter from Suter to Delius, 18 August 1906, *DLL1*, 269.

glance'.[32] Haym, as we know, had ideas of performing parts of the work (not least as a means of placating his hostile committee in Elberfeld). Chop, too, was delighted with the *Mass* and recognised that, as an 'evening-long' work, it made special demands on both performers and public.[33] Nevertheless, none of these men felt they were in a position to do the work justice. Cassirer's hopes for a performance in the winter season of 1906–1907 came to nought, but it finally fell to the singer and conductor Ludwig Hess to direct the whole of Part II (though with cuts in the third and fifth movements) into which the second movement of Part I would be interpolated, for the Tonkünstlerfest in Munich on 4 June 1908.[34] 'Your "Messe des Lebens" is one of those works where I have the feeling that there is such power and vitality in it', Hess wrote to Delius, 'that for the artist who renders it, putting all his power and love into it must make it an intensely rewarding experience'.[35]

The performance in Munich, attended by the composer, 'made an enormous impression',[36] but it fell to Beecham and his beloved North Staffordshire District Choral Society to give the first complete performance of the *Mass* in London's Queen's Hall on 7 June 1909. This was undoubtedly a red-letter day in London's musical calendar, for, in the wake of the London premiere of Elgar's First Symphony, Delius's work provided another major novelty to audiences now familiar with the modernisms of Reger, early Schoenberg, Debussy, Ravel, Vaughan Williams, Frank Bridge and Gustav Holst. Though people were familiar with *Sea Drift, Appalachia, In a Summer Garden* and *Brigg Fair*, few were prepared for the hybrid nature of Delius's work with its elements of oratorio, opera, ballet, partsong and solo (orchestral) song, often viewed through the prism of the 'dance', and for the significant role of the orchestra (as one finds in Part II Nos. 1, 3 and 4) with its own role as commentator (and here the pastoral evocation of Part II Nos. 1 and 4 are supreme examples of the composer's instrumentation). Nor were they ready for the immensely challenging choruses (many of them wordless and more instrumental in behaviour) and uncompromising vocal tessituras (especially for the sopranos), the particular nature of Delius's treatment of

---

[32] Letter from Schillings to Delius, 16 November 1906, *DLL1*, 274.

[33] Chop, M., 'Frederick Delius: His Life and Work', in Jones, P. (ed.), *The Collected Writings of the German Musicologist Max Chop on the Composer Frederick Delius* (Lewiston, NY, Queenston, ON and Lampeter: Edwin Mellen Press, 2002), 119.

[34] Carley, L., 'Hans Haym', 13.

[35] Letter from Hess to Delius, 16 April 1908, *DLL1*, 344.

[36] Letter from Delius to Bantock, 9 June 1908, *DLL1*, 351.

the chorus *with* orchestra, or the unfamiliar message the work was attempting
to convey. As Hutchings has suggested, the choruses are 'the counterparts of
the tableaux in medieval plays like *Everyman*, which depict the movement
of human life from the cradle to its "Destiny"'.[37] In this way the chorus is
deployed to affirm the condition of the human spirit, its changing moods, the
effect of age, the difference and complement of the sexes, and man's place in
nature. Much of the differentiation Delius achieves is through manipulation
of texture and colour. At one end of the spectrum, there is the imposing
muscularity of the opening eight-part choruses of Parts I and II; at the other,
the more chorale-like rhetoric of unison voices. At no point is counterpoint
considered a refuge of contrast. Even the 'dance-fugue', which occupies such
a singular place in his music, is not a conventional or cumulative structure,
not only in its bizarre tonal scheme across the tritone of C to F sharp and
back, but also in the concertante use of the soloists (other than Zarathustra)
as a contrast to the chorus itself. The soloists' role, as 'höhere Menschen', is
to provide an abstract dialogue against which Zarathustra is tested, as well
as a foil to the chorus. Only once do they appear with Zarathustra and this
moment is reserved for the work's major peroration in the closing bars.

For Zarathustra's material in *A Mass of Life*, a role which brings to mind
the demands of Wotan or Hans Sachs, Delius utilises a wide range of style-
forms – recitative, aria, arioso, lyric song and 'scena' – in a similarly wide
spectrum of rhetorical gestures from opera to song, and there is undoubtedly a
commodious chemistry between the lyricism of Nietzsche's prose and Delius's
poetical euphony. This is magisterial in the 'Nachtlied' at the end of Part I
where Delius was able to accomplish the same sense of reflective climax as
he did in the final section of *Sea Drift*, yet this same propensity for lyricism
conflicted, Haym contended, with the bombast of the last sixty bars: 'I don't
agree with the ending of the whole either. I feel that it is a great pity you do
not end on the wonderfully solemn mood of "O Mensch gib Acht", but instead
dissipate it in the *fortissimo* roar of the tutti. Is that necessary? Could you
possibly decide to scrap this ending and – as was the case with the fragment
I once performed here – send the audience away with the eternity-*pianissimo*
of a midnight sparkling with stars'. With particular discernment, Haym
understood where Delius's true gift resided: 'This *ff* ending is really not at all
like you, for the little *pp* tail which you have tacked on can't put it right again'.[38]

---

[37] *AH*, 72.

[38] Carley, L., 'Hans Haym', 15.

Delius, however, did not heed Haym's advice, preferring to end with what he clearly perceived as triumphant optimism.

To Haym's delight, however, the Elberfeld committee agreed to programme the *Mass* on 11 December 1909. After attending Beecham's performance, which he found unconvincing, he thoroughly rehearsed the work and made efforts to proselytise its merits among the committee members and the public. A second performance of the *Mass* took place in Elberfeld in 1911, the same year as a hearing in Vienna which brought the work to the attention of Béla Bartók (who, at that time, was engaged in the composition of his one-act expressionist opera *Bluebeard's Castle*). Bartók, and his young friend Zoltan Kodály, were greatly impressed, Bartók especially by the innovation of the wordless chorus. 'I think you are the first to have tried such an experiment', he wrote to Delius,[39] an interest which drove him to produce a review for the musical journal *Zeneközlöny*.[40] Although the *Mass* was very much championed by Beecham – it was one of the centrepieces of the Delius Festival in 1929 – it received further performances in Germany at Wiesbaden, Frankfurt and, after the war, in Hagen, Duisburg and Coblenz. One of its most fervent supporters, however, was Hamilton Harty, a great admirer of Delius, who conducted the work in Manchester with the Hallé Orchestra and Chorus with Roy Henderson in 1932 and 1933 to great acclaim. Indeed, it was said that Delius considered Harty's interpretation superior to that of Beecham's but never dared confess it for fear of offending his greatest advocate.[41]

A Mass of Life was undoubtedly Delius's most ambitious effort in terms of concert music. Years later, in 1916, he still claimed it to be his 'best work',[42] and in terms of its level of originality, design and content, it represents a high-water mark in Delius's mature output and a climax of that remarkably fecund period of creativity since the creation of *Paris* and *Lebenstanz* at the turn of the century. Moreover, as Mitchell has rightly intimated, 'there is many a post-Wagnerian echo in *A Mass of Life*, not because Delius was imitating Mahler or Strauss, but because he was their strict contemporary and – at least in the *Mass* – was engaged in similar pursuits'.[43] This was recognised in the words

---

[39] Letter from Bartók to Delius, [27 March 1911], *DLL2*, 70.

[40] See Bartók, B., 'A Delius Premiere in Vienna', in Suchoff, B. (ed.), *Béla Bartók Essays* (London: Faber & Faber, 1976), 449–50.

[41] Dibble, J., *Hamilton Harty: Musical Polymath* (Woodbridge: Boydell & Brewer, 2013), 213.

[42] See *DLL2*, 161.

[43] Mitchell, D., 'Delius: The Choral Music', *Tempo*, No. 26 (Winter 1952–1953), 10.

of the Swiss critic William Ritter, a champion of Mahler. Ritter corresponded with Delius and produced a lengthy review of Part II of *A Mass of Life* after its performance in Munich in June 1908 (Beecham attested that this was the crowning glory of his German career). In a comparison of Debussy and Delius, Ritter's critique for the journal *Lugdunum* (July 1908) surely stands as one of the most succinct accounts of style, form and ethos in Delius's music:

> Comme lui, il paraît vêtu d'arc-en-ciel dilué: une continuelle pâmoison de délicats frottements d'accords nous chatouille delicieusement et, cependant, quelque chose de fort et de salubre règne dans l'ensemble. L'architecture de l'oeuvre connaît une élévation à grandes lignes audacieuses et un plan large et aéré, mais ferme et défini. On sait d'où l'on part, où l'on va, et où l'on aboutit.[44]

> [Like him [Debussy], he [Delius] appears clothed in a diluted rainbow: a continual swarm of delicate chordal burnishing tickles us deliciously and yet, however, something strong and salubrious reigns over the whole. The architecture of the work has an elevation with bold outlines and a wide and airy plan, yet firm and defined. We know from where we are departing, where we are going, and whence we are destined.]

When heard sung in German, *A Mass of Life* seems to breathe more spontaneously the language of German modernism and in so doing, the work locates Delius very much within the mainstream of contemporary European music. Yet this very element, together with those other germane components such as didacticism and oration, make the *Mass* atypical, even uncharacteristic, in Delius's output (even though the sentiment comes closest to an artistic *apologia* for him). Indeed, there was still the need to look elsewhere for the most apposite agencies of his style to express that fragile admixture of lyricism, diatonicism and chromaticism which had become a natural utterance for him and which required forms more appropriate to the sense of eloquence he was rapidly discovering. Inspired by an English *fin-de-siècle* voice, that search ultimately began in *Songs of Sunset*.

[44] Quoted in *TB*, 150.

CHAPTER 9

'English' Interlude:
The Partsong as Innovative Genre
(1906–1908)

TOWARDS ENGLISH ROOTS

The success of Delius's works in Germany, with such advocates as Haym, Buths, Schuricht, Cassirer, Hess and others, and Chop's enthusiastic advocacy in print, might have persuaded Delius to ignore the lively environment of London and England altogether. Yet, for all his reported sarcasm about English music, he hankered after recognition in the country of his birth and the critical acclaim of *A Mass of Life* in London in 1909, together with the championship of his music by Beecham, must have been a source of some satisfaction to the transplanted Yorkshireman.[1] He was also known to his express his impatience with German society, especially the breed of tourist he met during his walking tours in Norway:

> When we returned for supper, a whole caravan of germans had arrived: there are more Germans traveling than any other nation &, I can assure you, they are most objectionable – They have, nearly all, very bad manners – eat like swine & talk very loud: – Then they take entire possession of the sitting room & begin to play the piano & sing in chorus german Folksongs & student songs. They are all fat & ugly: – Not one pretty girl or fine woman. When one comes into the room, he struts in proudly & snorts around a little & then retires banging the door after him – or he comes in, turns over all the books on the table – knocks a chair over &

---

[1] It is noteworthy that Delius largely dispensed with the Germanic version of his forename, 'Fritz', in 1903 in favour of the English 'Frederick', a fact visible from a scrutiny of his autograph manuscripts and letters.

then sits down at the piano. Both english & french have better manners, undoubtedly without exaggeration!²

Delius's process of 'anglicisation' began two years earlier. As Carley has noted, 'his music showed signs of being ready and sufficiently well-established to cross the Channel ... [and] friends there were tilling the ground on his behalf'.³ London, therefore, began to take on an aura of optimism. 'London is a wonderful place', he wrote to Jelka,⁴ and he was invigorated by the atmosphere of the capital: 'I lunch with Wood tomorrow & will write you the result. I have a wonderful appetite here & also sleep so well. The climate agrees wonderfully well with me. Mothers milk I suppose!'⁵ After meeting Wood he encountered Balfour Gardiner: 'I dined with Balfour Gardiner last night & they played Appalachia there (a few musicians were there) all were tremendously taken with it'.⁶ All this left the deep impression that London's musical world welcomed him. 'This is my real field & I ought to be here every year', he exclaimed to Jelka,⁷ and reiterated that 'everybody seems very keen on me here. Especially all the young lot. Cyril Scott I have also seen he is really very nice'.⁸ Indeed, with other admirers such as Grainger, Legge and Norman O'Neill, his position in London was already exalted:

My stay has been most successful & I should have no difficulty here to take the first place. Everyone wants me to come and live in London. I also met Percy Grainger, a most charming young man & more gifted than Scott & less affected. An Australien [sic] – you would like him immensely. We all met at his house on Thursday for music. My Concerto & Appalachia. I have become acquainted with the musical critic of the daily Telegraph – Robin Legge. He has a very charming wife & daughter & they have invited me already several times. He is all fire & flame. I left him the score of Appalachia & he & Percy Grainger are quite enthusiastic

---

² Letter from Delius to Jelka, 2 August 1908, *DLL1*, 365–6.

³ Carley, L., 'Hans Haym: Delius's Prophet and Pioneer', *Music & Letters*, Vol. 54 No. 1 (January 1973), 23.

⁴ Letter from Delius to Jelka, 9 April 1907, *AU-Mgm* 137.

⁵ Letter from Delius to Jelka, 11 April 1907, *AU-Mgm* 139.

⁶ Postcard from Delius to Jelka, [15 April 1907], *AU-Mgm* 142.

⁷ Postcard from Delius to Jelka, [17 April 1907], *AU-Mgm* 144.

⁸ Letter from Delius to Jalka, 18 April 1907, *AU-Mgm* 145.

about it. Enclosed a little note Grainger left at my house after he had seen & played the score. He is impulsive & nice. There is a splendid Baritone here a Mr Austin, *very musical* & I hope he will sing Sea-Drift at Sheffield & later the "Messe".[9]

Acquaintance with Bantock, known to be an active facilitator, also provided him with the courage to launch his initiative of a Musical League, an idea inspired by his experience of the Allgemeine Deutsche Musikverein (which had promoted his music in Germany) to support new English music, especially in the provinces,[10] and according to Grainger, a means of subverting the political dominion of Parry and Stanford.[11] Thus, performances of *Sea Drift* in Sheffield in 1908, and the *Mass* in London in 1909, served to reinforce his standing as a contemporary *English* musical figure with comparable eminence to Elgar (another mainstay of the Musical League). What is more, his rise to fame was reflected by his entry (authored by R. A. Streatfeild) into the supplement of the second edition of *Grove's Dictionary of Music and Musicians* and by at least one German critic who commented that Delius's gravitation towards England was worthy of acknowledgement by his Teutonic peers.[12] Interestingly, too, this shift of identity was also marked by the death of Grieg.

SONGS OF SUNSET: DOWSON AND THE *FIN DE SIÈCLE*

Perhaps most symbolic of Delius's 'anglicisation' was his composition of *Songs of Sunset* which he began sometime in 1906. The poetry of Ernest Dowson was very much a product of the 1890s, especially the two collections *Verses* (1894) and *Decorations* (1900). Richard Le Gallienne, whom Delius had known in the early 1890s during the composition of his first operas, had been an admirer of Dowson in the Rhymers' Club in London, and had, like Dowson, contributed to the well-known *Yellow Book*. Other admirers included Wilde, Symons and Browning. We are unsure whether it was Gardiner or

---

[9] Letter from Delius to Jelka, 21 April 1907, *DLL1*, 287.

[10] Lloyd, S., 'The Rumble of a Distant Drum [Granville Bantock]', *DSJ* No. 80 (October 1983), 21.

[11] Grainger, P., 'The Personality of Frederick Delius', in *DC*, 123.

[12] See *DLL1*, 329.

Jelka who introduced Dowson's works to Delius,[13] but what seems to have drawn him to the poet's beautifully shaped lyric poetry, so typical of the *fin de siècle*, were three distinct themes, very much influenced by Verlaine: the capturing of an ideal, rapt moment; desolation in its fleetingness and loss; and a dialectic of nature images, be they summer and winter, spring and autumn, 'bright' and 'faded' roses, 'full' and 'leafless' boughs, sunlight and the pale moon.[14] Such imagery became analogies for human love, ecstasy, parting and separation, aching memory, the oblivion of dreams and an overwhelming sense of longing. Some of this symbolism suggested parallels with Ibsen's and Nietzsche's natural images (not least Nietzsche's much-favoured metaphors of noon, eventide and the 'mystical, half-drunken ecstasy of midnight'),[15] but even closer were those of Jacobsen's 'wine roses' and Drachmann's 'summer nights' in Danish literature which he had already set to music. As Houston Baker has posited, in the poetry of Yeats, Eliot and Dowson 'the ideal moment is the bright, dream-like opponent of an undesirable reality'.[16] That Delius perceived these facets of Dowson is evident in the change he made from the original title of *Songs of Twilight and Sadness* to the evocative nature imagery of *Songs of Sunset*,[17] a choice probably determined by the opening setting of 'Moritura' ('A song of the setting sun!').

Characteristically Delius took some time to reach a final version of the *Songs of Sunset*. Some of the sketches show quite different musical ideas *ab initio* and different tonal behaviour. Even before reaching the more advanced stage of *Songs of Twilight and Sadness*, an earlier pencil draft shows that Delius considered a short setting ('We fling up flowers and laugh') of one stanza (the eighth of nine) from Dowson's 'Carthusians' (part of *Decorations*) between 'By the sad waters of separation' and 'I was not sorrowful'. This was jettisoned as was the inclusion of 'Cynara' (from *Verses*) for soloist and chorus before the last song 'They are not long the weeping and the laughter'.[18] The version of

---

[13] See Fenby, E., *Delius* (London: Faber & Faber, 1971), 58. The volume of Dowson's complete poetry, with accompanying essay by Arthur Symons, had been recently published in 1905: Dowson, E. C. and Symons, A., *The Poems and Prose of Ernest Dowson, with a Memoir by Arthur Symons* (London: J. Lane, 1905).

[14] Baker, H. A., 'A Decadent's Nature: The Poetry of Ernest Dowson', *Victorian Poetry*, Vol. 6 No. 1 (1968), 21.

[15] *PH*, 123.

[16] Baker, H. A., 'A Decadent's Nature', 28.

[17] See *GB-Lbl* MS Mus 1745/2/13/4, ff. 38–71.

[18] See *GB-Lbl* MS Mus 1745/2/13/4, ff. 25–33. Heseltine also informs us that 'Cynara' was to have formed the work's climax, but was omitted because Delius

Songs of Twilight and Sadness (which is the only autograph full score which survives; the *Stichvorlag* prepared for the publishers is lost) shows that Delius had settled on the eight songs and their running order, but, besides the title, he still had revisions to make on the scoring.[19]

As he declared to Bantock, Delius conceived *Songs of Sunset* as a 'cyclus of songs', in which aspects of Dowson's ideal world, removed from society's banality, are explored between the two lovers (the soprano and baritone) with comment and reflection from the chorus.[20] The genre of 'song' is, however, treated loosely, for Delius provides us with not only orchestral song, a genre in which he had already excelled, but also orchestral partsong, formerly essayed in *Sea Drift* and *A Mass of Life*. But these two generic concepts happily elide and expand to intimate other genres such as opera and oratorio in much the same way as in the *Mass* but, as Delius evidently intended, on a smaller scale and one that ultimately suited the special intimacy of his language.

Delius's first setting of Dowson in the cycle, 'A song of the setting sun!', uses three of the fours verses of 'Moritura' (from *Decorations*) to set the scene of a winter sunset, a chill wind, a 'cynic moon' and the image of fresh flowers, once worn 'in a lady's hair it stood', but now faded. Delius's musical imagery, evocative of the north wind with its highly chromatic inner parts and dense harmonic rhythm, dominates the choral texture of the first two verses. It is thanks, however, to the anchoring role of tonic and dominant pedal points that adventurous chromatic forays, into what appears to be close to atonality, are held in check. The tonal organisation of the partsong is subtly managed. Although C major controls the opening of the first verse, it is an arrival in E major that marks its end. The dominant of C also marks the beginning of the second verse ('A song of a winter day!'), but in accordance with the words, much of the verse's chromatic behaviour reflects the cold winter landscape.

---

believed it 'disturbed the proportions and interrupt[ed] the mood-sequence of the whole' (*PH*, 123).

[19] The original scoring of *Songs of Sunset* was to have been comparable with *A Mass of Life* except for the bass oboe. The published score shows, however, that, perhaps because of his desire for a smaller chorus (see letter from Delius to Bantock, 19 September 1907, *DLL1*, 300), three oboes were replaced by oboe, cor anglais and bass oboe, while the bass clarinet was omitted, a sarrusophone replaced the contrabassoon, and six horns were scaled down to four. An instruction on the title page – 'These songs must not all be played à la suite' – suggests that they did not have to be performed altogether, but if they were, they should follow the stipulated order. This instruction did not subsequently appear in the published edition.

[20] Letter from Delius to Bantock, 19 September 1907, *DLL1*, 300.

The return of C at the end of the verse provides a moment of stable respite before verse three ('A song of faded flower!') embarks in E major, and it is in this tonal region that Delius climactically expresses Dowson's 'ideal moment' ('fair and fresh for an hour') before a shift back to the dominant of C signals its passing ('Now, ah, now, faded it lies'), allied with the first appearance of a unifying melodic fragment (Example 9.1a), an *idée fixe* or 'motto',[21] which appears throughout the cycle and 'wanders through the score like a pale ghost'.[22]

For the second item, a duet for the two lovers, Delius used the second half of Dowson's 'Sapientia lunae' (from *Verses*), itself a paraphrase of Propertius ('Cease smiling Dear!'). Taking six of the eight verses (omitting the second and fourth), he created a fluent, through-composed symphonic structure in which the *idée fixe* fragment heard at the end of the first chorus is virtually ubiquitous. Longing for the moment to 'be perpetuate', the lovers lament the passing of 'divine, lost youth' and the incapacity to 'taste no more the wild and passionate love sorrows of today'. This anguish is expressed in a second familiar fragment, a typical rising triplet on the downbeat (Example 9.1b), though given special character here through Delius's choice of dissonance and orchestration. An elision of the first two verses forms a prelude to an even more passionate, sensual outpouring ('O red pomegranate of thy perfect mouth!') which owes much of its advanced harmony to the *Mass* (such as one finds in 'Süsse Leier' and 'Auf, du Schläfer'), although the upward trajectory of Delius's vocal parts (especially the soprano) is indebted to the careful voice-leading of *Tristan* and the strategic placing of 6/4 harmonies. The latter is deployed with particular poignancy at the sexually charged climax ('that we shall lie, red mouth to mouth, entwined') on a 6/4 of D flat from which the duet subsides towards A flat (as did the first section), a tonal event which is again marked by the recurrence of the lament figure. Moreover, the final cadence, enriched not only by the added sixth but by an added ninth, envelops the added-sixth properties of the *idée fixe*, hauntingly played by the cor anglais.

Omitting the fourth verse of 'Autumnal', ('Pale amber sunlight falls across the reddening October trees'), Delius's third item, another partsong, drew its pastoral disposition and its key structure from an earlier song, 'Summer landscape'. This picture of nature is, however, preludial to the main body of the song ('Let misty autumn be our part!') where the metre changes to 4/4 and Delius's pedal points are replaced by a functional diatonicism ('The twilight

---

[21] This figure was one to which Heseltine drew special attention (see *PH*, 148).

[22] *PH*, 122.

Example 9.1a. *Songs of Sunset, idée fixe* or 'motto' theme.

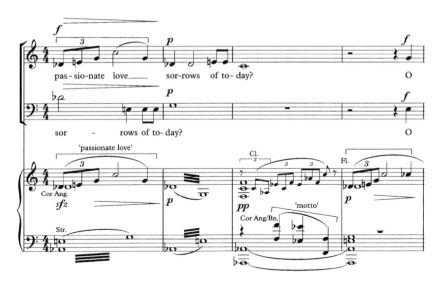

Example 9.1b. *Songs of Sunset*, 'passionate love'.

of the year is sweet') as the bass moves through a cycle of fifths. This diatony intensifies as the declaration of love is marked by a perfect cadence into the tonic (F major) and an effusive melodic sequence in the soprano, enhanced by some affecting countermelody in the overlapping woodwind phrases (this is surely the most archetypal Delius). But, in typical Dowson fashion, the last part of the song darkens ('A little while and night shall come'), and for this Delius called on material from *Margot la Rouge* (see from Fig. 18) and a solo

violin arabesque, somewhat reminiscent of the 'Dark Fiddler', to conclude the
song in the subdominant, B flat major.

For the through-composed soprano monologue 'Exceeding sorrow
consumeth my sad heart!', Delius made use of all four verses of 'O Mors!
Quam amara est memoria tua' (Verses), a quotation by Dowson from
Ecclesiasticus ('Oh Death, how bitter you are'), a text which Brahms
employed in his Vier Ernste Gesänge. To express the ardent longing of this
lyric, Delius relied on the constant variation of a four-bar phrase and the
exploitation of its expressive appoggiaturas and suspensions to support the
soprano melody (Example 9.1c). Delius's inventiveness can be measured
here not only by the extent to which this one idea is resourcefully reworked,
but also in the way the phrases of the soprano interact so as not to coincide
with the orchestra, thereby undermining any hint of regular periodicity.
The seamless sense of melody is also greatly enhanced by the absence of
cadence, which is achieved, elliptically, in the last two bars. Rarely again
did the composer attain such a tender expression of Weltschmerz. While the

Example 9.1c. *Songs of Sunset*, 'Exceeding sorrow consumeth my sad heart!'

Table 9.1. *Songs of Sunset*, structural overview of No. 5.

Verse	Text	Key	Theme
1 and 2	'By the sad waters of separation'	[C major]	'x'
3	'By the sad waters of separation'	C♯ minor	'y'
4	'If you be dead'	F minor	'z'
5 [first part]	'No man knoweth'	F minor	'z'
5 [second part]	'While the sad waters of separation' (reprise of verse 1)	F minor	'z'
Coda		F major	'y' with *idée fixe*

conclusion of the soprano monologue in F major balances the prevalence of that key in 'Pale amber sunlight', the setting for baritone of 'Exile' ('By the sad waters of separation'), which also concludes in F, reiterates the importance of C major from the opening partsong and love duet. In direct response to the soprano's entreaty to live for the moment, an imaginative tripartite structure of three distinctive thematic ideas ('x', 'y' and 'z') mirrors the baritone's sense of separation (verses one and two), the dim memory of his beloved (verse three) and desolation (verses four and five). Delius's recapitulation of verse one, which coincides with the textual variation of the opening line, also subtly incorporates the orchestral thematic material of verses four and five (see Table 9.1), while the melancholy coda combines the melodic fragment of verse three with the *idée fixe* in augmentation, memorably scored for the bass oboe.

Firmly cast in A minor, the third partsong of the cycle ('See how the trees and the osiers lie'), taken from 'In Spring' (*Decorations*), is a sophisticated example of stanzaic variation. Of the two seven-line stanzas, Delius set the first two lines to different music, but both are directed towards the *same music* for the next three lines. Each set of five lines has offered a vibrant vision of nature in springtime, so it would be typical of Dowson to accentuate, in the last two lines, the sense of regret at its passing, and in parallel, the transience of young love. This is highlighted by giving this text to the lovers, first to the baritone ('But the spring of the soul'), and then to the soprano ('But the flowers of the soul') whose music refers back to her former monologue ('Exceeding sorrow'). The soprano's gesture, in particular, seems to capture the seminal character of Dowson's inherent sorrowfulness, a sentiment exaggerated by the melancholy arabesques of the solo violin (arguably an autobiographical 'aside' from the composer), the affecting closing comment from the chorus ('bloom never again'), the simultaneous recurrences of 'y' (a reference to dim memory) and the *idée fixe*, which tie this music to the baritone's previous number.

The world-weariness of 'Spleen' (*Verses*) preoccupies the baritone's second song ('I was not sorrowful, I could not weep'), a lullaby troubled by memories that cannot be expunged. The first three couplets of Dowson's poem form the first section of the tripartite structure which moves from E major to its dominant. A mesmeric central paragraph, which neatly begins with the same words ('I was not sorrowful, but only tired'), gives vent to the baritone's tormented memories. These are, however, only partly assuaged by the return of the lullaby 'charm' and E major with its piercing major-seventh nuance.

Although Delius did not leave any clue as to a programme for his one and only song cycle, there are numerous indications within the choice and order of the songs to suggest a narrative. This is surely evident after the first (introductory) song where the lovers are presented. The soprano's monologue announces that they must part, a separation which vexes the baritone. Realising that their love, a passionate but fleeting one, can never return, the baritone is left with 'memories that could not sleep'. The role of the chorus, Greek-like, is essentially one of comment and reflection between the solo items. The narrative concludes with a finale in B flat major, in which Delius set what had already become Dowson's best-known poem 'Vitae summa brevis spem nos vetat incohare longam' ('They are not long, the weeping and the laughter').[23] The arrival of the finale, like a long-awaited cadence, is signalled by an orchestral transition through which Delius not only effortlessly provides a transition from E to B flat, but does so through the expressive lines of the cor anglais. It is with this optimistic revelation that the unison soloists, accompanied by the chorus, are reconciled in a stoical recognition of man's mortality, or as Heseltine put it, 'the *envoi* to life'.[24] At the beginning of the second verse, Dowson's famous line 'They are not long, the days of wine and roses', is given special emphasis in a rare functional perfect cadence into D minor, but it is after the final climax ('Our path emerges for a while'), and the reminiscences of 'Exceeding sorrow', that the emotional heart of the work is articulated. In a profoundly heart-rending coda, the

---

[23] Here Dowson quotes from Horace's *Odes*, Book 1.4 'The brief sum of life forbids us the hope of enduring long', echoing a similar sentiment in Psalm 90 (v. 10). An earlier version for solo voice and piano, in Jelka's hand, is dated 1906 (see *GB-Lbl* MS Mus 1745/2/6).

[24] *PH*, 122.

essence of Dowson's Shakespearean paraphrase, 'then closes within a dream' is eloquently captured in the languorous violin phrases (with their poignant ninth dissonances) and inner lines for horns, but most of all in the Lydian inflections accentuated by the lingering choral reiterations. With such a combination of gestures the final recurrence of the *idée fixe* is transcendentally charged with meaning. Heseltine maintained that, in the *Songs of Sunset*, Delius demonstrated a sense of 'unity and cohesion fully as satisfying as the most elaborate devices of formal structure by means which totally elude a formal theoretical analysis'.[25] Yet this comment, for all its implied 'anti-academicism', would be to deny Delius's subtle and sophisticated variegation of designs which he brought to both his solo and choral songs in the cycle; added to which one can also observe that the orbit of tonalities (C and F, A and E, and B flat) is far from arbitrary. Indeed it is the particular chemistry of Delius's language of orchestral gesture (those desolate, mournful calls of the cor anglais and bass oboe and the *cri de coeur* of the solo horn), sustained by harmonic moments of unbearable longing and searing flights of melody, that brings him so close to Dowson's inner realm of world-weariness and which places these settings apart from those by Scott, Quilter and Ireland.

After the completion of *Songs of Sunset* in 1907, Bantock (who shared a mutual interest in Dowson's poetry) thought of including the work in the Birmingham Orchestral Concerts that same year or in 1908,[26] but it was not actually performed until 16 June 1911 at Queen's Hall under Beecham and the Beecham Orchestra and the celebrated Edward Mason Choir, a choral society well known for its promotion of new British music. Critical reception was fair; there were no extremes in Delius's choral writing to excite consternation. Greatly moved by the work,[27] Haym gave a performance in Elberfeld on 7 March 1914, which acknowledged Delius's dedication to the Elberfelder Gesangverein. Yet, even though it was a piece of Damascene significance for the young and impressionable Philip Heseltine, the more intimate nature of the *Songs of Sunset* did not immediately encourage a flurry of performances. Although the work was published in 1911 (which facilitated the London performance), it did not capture the imagination in the same way as *Sea Drift* or *A Mass of Life*, and its next major performance was not until the Delius Festival of 1929.

---

[25] Ibid.

[26] Letter from Bantock to Delius, 13 October 1907, *DLL1*, 303.

[27] Carley, L., 'Hans Haym', 21.

DELIUS AND THE PARTSONG IDIOM

Although Delius had not attempted any *a cappella* choral composition since his days at Leipzig, there had been many instances of unaccompanied choral writing in the operas and in the choral works. Moreover, in these various instances, Delius's love of vocal part-singing (awakened by his experiences of hearing the negroes on the plantations in Florida and Virginia) allied itself closely with his particular bent for opulent harmony and rich sonority. Delius's interaction with choral music – with *Appalachia, Sea Drift, A Mass of Life* and *Songs of Sunset* between 1903 and 1907 – delineates an important period of his creative life when music for voices and orchestra became the focus of composition, one generated to a significant extent by the choral societies in Germany and in particular the enthusiasm of Hans Haym. A continuation of this focus can also be witnessed in the production of three partsongs composed between 1907 and 1908 which, in many ways, captures the quintessence of Delius's approach to choral writing. 'I have just managed to finish one part song "On Craig Ddu" Arthur Symons, which I send you', he wrote to Bantock. 'The other one I attempted does not yet please me, so I must live with it a bit longer. I find I can never do anything in a hurry, but will try to do some more of these things when the mood takes me'.[28] Delius's letter suggests that he had comprehended the advantage, in terms of royalties, of publishing partsongs for which there was a lucrative market. He had probably learned this from Bantock who was himself an active (and most original) composer in the genre. The 'other' partsong to which Delius referred was another setting of Symons, 'Wanderer's Song', for male chorus. A third partsong, 'Midsummer Song' (with a text probably by Delius) was composed in 1908; all three were published in 1910 by Harmonie. At least two of the partsongs affirmed the composer's new-found reputation with the English institution of the choral society (one just as vibrant, if not more so, than in Germany) and, of particular national significance, the competitive festival which, in the years prior to the First World War, was enjoying its apogee.

Delius took 'On Craig Ddu' from an early collection of Symons's symbolist poetry, *London Nights*. The title referred to a wooded upland on the southern side of the Vale of Llangollen close to where the poet lived, a still location disturbed only by the sounds of a local farm, flowing water and the wind. Though the partsong gives the impression of a seamless through-composed structure, Delius's form is remarkably subtle. The piece is in fact divided into

---

[28] Letter from Delius to Bantock, 15 December 1907, *DLL1*, 321.

two sections: the first consists of Symons's first verse (beginning in G major) and a 'refrain' in D minor; the second, longer in that it embraces the two remaining verses, is more tonally fluid, but also ends with the same refrain in D minor before cadencing in to G minor. Much of Delius's six-part texture relies on harmonic nuance and arresting 'sound moments' (particularly the dominant thirteenths) to give emphasis to the text, a fact emphasised by the lack of any real rhythmical interest. Yet it may be fairly argued that the paucity of rhythmical activity is deliberate in heightening the sense of stillness, an impression emphasised by the concluding tonic pedal, the evocative resolving added ninth and Delius's splendid quasi-orchestral scoring of the voices. After its publication, 'On Craig Ddu' was taken up as a test piece by the Blackpool Competitive Festival in 1910 where its difficulty and unfamiliarity of idiom was the source of some controversy. One may infer from the comments of William McNaught, one of the chief adjudicators, before the festival, that, among the various test pieces, Delius's partsong would prove especially challenging but that it was part of the festival's agenda to embrace new music and new choral techniques.[29] So it proved to be, and McNaught felt compelled to respond after the festival by acknowledging the '[peculiar] tonal idiom, the [indefinite] key, and [the] many discords difficult for singers to hold firmly'. 'A fine performance of this dreamy, moody piece', McNaught stressed with some equanimity, 'is very striking, but anything short of this is a misery to all concerned'.[30] The winner of the category was the Barrow Madrigal Society, a remarkable group of amateur singers, who performed the partsong as part of their London concert on 7 March 1912. Such enterprise left the critic of *The Musical Times* asking 'has any Metropolitan choir attempted this?'[31] Another of the award winners, the Blackpool Glee and Madrigal Society sang the partsong at the Schiller-Anstalt on 7 March 1911 and was much appreciated.[32]

Given the choice of Delius's second setting of Symons, 'Wanderer's Song' ('I have had enough of women'), it could only have been set for men's chorus; indeed, one wonders whether Delius had the German tradition of *Männerchor* in mind. One suspects that the poetical form – verses one and three begin with the same text – helped determine the ternary shape of the musical design.

[29] 'The Blackpool Festival', *The Musical Times*, Vol. 51 No. 804 (February 1910), Extra Supplement, 4.

[30] 'The Blackpool Festival', *The Musical Times*, Vol. 52 No. 816 (January 1911), Extra Supplement, 2.

[31] 'The Barrow Madrigal Society', *The Musical Times*, Vol. 53 No. 830 (April 1912), 256.

[32] *The Musical Times*, Vol. 52 No. 816 (February 1911), 121.

Although the outer verses exhibit some contrast in their opening declamation (in 4/4) and subsequent lyricism (in 6/4), and the last verse shows some inventive variation, especially at the close ('too deep to wake'), the incessant homophony of the central verse (hampered by the more restricted tessitura of the choral forces) provides insufficient contrast.

In 'Midsummer Song' Delius was perhaps in danger of allowing his preference for compound duple metre to become stereotypical. Hints of this over-reliance on compound metres were already present in *Sea Drift*, *A Mass of Life* and *Songs of Sunset* and we can also see it in 'Summer Landscape' and 'Wanderer's Song'. As Evans has suggested:

> To aggravate this monotony he [Delius] often chooses not the simplest yet most flexible of the common patterns 4/4, but the jog-trot 6/8, always a dangerous pattern for a composer not gifted in true rhythmic ingenuity (contrast Brahms). With its heavily marked stress, compound time is a snare also for a composer who relies on blocks of harmony rather than contrapuntally vitalized harmony. Really the two points are the same, since counterpoint is as much a matter of opposed rhythm as of opposed melody.[33]

The 'jog-trot 6/8' of 'Midsummer Song', no doubt intended by Delius to be a dance, is rescued by his imaginative 'instrumental' scoring of the eight-part texture which provides a degree of contrapuntal interest. The slower reprise of the opening paragraph is also effective as is his characteristic conclusion 'dying away to the end' with stoical 'heigh-ho'; and Delius succeeds in avoiding monotony in the central section's wordless 'la la' with some resourceful sustained countermelody which acts as a vital foil to the unchanging accompanimental rhythm. As Mitchell commented: 'This sort of gay, choral dance is a Delian speciality ... Even here, however, Delius is inclined to run his dancers out of rhythmic breath (cf. *A Mass of Life*), and 'Midsummer Song' might have been less exhausting for singers and audience had he a little curtailed his high spirits'.[34] 'Midsummer Song' was first sung by the Whitley Bay and District Choral Society under the indefatigable William Gillies Whittaker in December 1908. Whittaker had already introduced 'On Craig Ddu' to the same choir. In spite of vociferous opposition, he doggedly refused to drop the

---

[33] Evans, P., 'Delius', Evans Papers, *GB-DRu*.

[34] Mitchell, D., 'Delius: The Choral Music', *Tempo*, No. 26 (Winter 1952–1953), 12.

work,[35] which caused the choir to double their efforts. Whittaker (who came to admire Delius through his work for the Musical League) later gave the work with his famous Newcastle Bach Choir in May 1916. The Edward Mason Choir also performed 'Midsummer Song' in London on 27 February 1913 in a shared concert with the New Symphony Orchestra. Beecham was less fortunate however. 'On Craig Ddu' and 'Midsummer Song' were programmed for an all-Delius concert on 8 July 1914, but had to be omitted.

These three partsongs set a precedent for two later published works in the idiom which were performed by Charles Kennedy Scott, the celebrated conductor of the Oriana Madrigal Society. In a similar manner to Whittaker's promotion of Bach and contemporary British music, Kennedy Scott developed a reputation for the performance of Elizabethan music with his smaller choir of thirty-six voices, and to this was appended a fascination for new British works by Grainger, Holst, Balfour Gardiner, Benjamin Dale and Arnold Bax. 'On Craig Ddu' was given in one of their pioneering concerts at the Aeolian Hall on 11 April 1916. The two partsongs, *To be sung of a summer night on the water*, were completed in late spring 1917 and dedicated to Kennedy Scott and the Oriana Choir, though they were not performed until 28 June 1921 at the Aeolian Hall while Delius was in Norway. Romanticised agglomerations of Delius's more distant American memories, both wordless pieces expressed aspects of that former enchantment with a now imagined tropical landscape of the St Johns River. Both songs also make inventive use of a continuous variation technique and a through-composed structure. Comparable with the technique of 'Exceeding sorrow' in *Songs of Sunset*, the first song develops the opening four-bar phrase, or divisible sub-phrases, and dexterously moves individual bars of the melodic material between voices, thereby constantly inventing new countermelodies and new harmonisations in the other parts within the ever-changing texture of five or six voices. That Delius saw the song as a 'legato' continuum (further accentuating his instrumental concept of choral writing) is shown by his commas for breath.[36] Many of these are mid-phrase but are cleverly covered by other doubling voices, though most accomplished choirs would be accustomed to stagger the breathing to guarantee the sense of unbroken lines. The second song, for wordless choir and tenor solo (with vocalised syllables) is surely a conflation of the 'solo-basing and choir response' formula of the negro songs. The solo

---

[35] Whittaker, W. G., *Autobiography, 1903–1914*, 25.

[36] The instrumental nature of Delius's two wordless choruses is corroborated by Fenby's arrangement of them as *Two Aquarelles* for string orchestra, made with Delius's sanction in 1932.

tenor's synthetic folk material, presented over five bars, is a series of repeated fragments – A (one bar), A (one bar), B (half bar), B (half bar), C (half bar), C (half bar), C augmented (one bar) – which is subject to a variegational process of contraction and expansion in contrasting tonal areas. A reprise of the original melodic material in the tonic, D major, appears to signal the conclusion, although Delius's instinct for variation continues in the exquisite dying tones of the evocative coda.

Delius's final essay in the genre of partsong was a setting of Tennyson's 'The splendour falls on castle walls', completed in 1923. Some of this he was able to copy down himself, but it required the help of Jelka to produce the *Stichvorlag* for Oxford University Press which, as a young music publishing house, released it in 1924.[37] It was first given by Kennedy Scott in London on 17 June 1924, though it also appeared as a test piece for the enterprising Blackpool Festival in 1926. Of Tennyson's three verses, Delius set the first two. The structure might, in simple terms, be described as 'modified strophic' (AA') in that the second verse is a truncated version of the first. The idiom is very much the same chromatic one of 'On Craig Ddu', though the common time of the first four lines is complemented by 6/8 for the 'refrain' ('Blow bugles, blow'). In marked contrast, however, are the diatonic horn imitations of the separate choir of tenors and basses which provide an 'instrumental' dimension. This is particularly effective at the end of the shorter second verse where the distant horns are complemented by Delius's euphonious yet enigmatic half-cadences, their lack of resolution adding much to the evocation of the 'dying echoes'.

---

[37] See *GB-Lbl* MS Mus 1745/4/3.

CHAPTER 10

Symphonic Poems (I): *Brigg Fair, In a Summer Garden, Dance Rhapsody* No. 1 (1907–1912)

A RETURN TO THE ORCHESTRA

With the successes of *Appalachia, Sea Drift* and the revised Piano Concerto, and the accumulation of interest from British conductors such as Wood, Beecham and Bantock, the desire for Delius to return to the composition of orchestral music, where his true instincts lay, must have been almost irresistible. Orchestral programmes in London and the provinces, notably in Birmingham, Manchester, Liverpool and Glasgow, were alive more than ever due to the symphonic poem, and two of the Musical League's major forces, Elgar and Bantock, were prominent authors of this new, vibrant genre. Delius, of course, was himself the proud author of *Paris, Lebenstanz* and *Appalachia*, all of which had shown the assimilation of Strauss. These works had been very much a manifestation of his cosmopolitan existence and outlook, but with his next orchestral work, *Brigg Fair*, the public's perception of Delius as an Englishman seemed much more immediate (even though to Beecham the work had more to do with the classical phenomenon of pastoral and the eighth Eclogue of Virgil's 'Incipe Maenalios mecum, mea tibia, versus').[1] Beecham's comment was almost certainly levelled at the remarks of Heseltine, Gray, Hutchings and Fenby who all located *Brigg Fair* in the still, mist-ridden summer landscape of England.[2] A more likely reality is that we should not underestimate Delius's sense of opportunism; given the *Zeitgeist* of folksong collection and arrangement in England at the time (particularly with Vaughan

---

[1] *TB*, 166–7.

[2] See *PH*, 127; Gray, C., *A Survey of Contemporary Music* (Oxford: Oxford University Press, 1927), 73; *AH*, 83 (who quotes Gray); *EF*, 208, although Fenby counter-claimed that, such were his indelible experiences of Grez, he came to associate *Brigg Fair* with the surrounding countryside around the French village (*EF*, 209). Hutchings also supported his viewpoint by pointing out that *Brigg Fair* was Delius's most frequently performed work in England.

Williams, Holst, Sharp and Grainger himself), an orchestral piece based on a national tune was destined to win hearts and minds.

The spur to compose *Brigg Fair* is well known. Grainger had been actively collecting folksongs in rural Lincolnshire in 1905 where, by dint of its relative geographical isolation, it was still normal for local people to make their own entertainment. Moved by this social phenomenon, Grainger collected dozens of tunes, and took part in the Brigg Festival in 1906 as a conductor, directing choirs, soloists and the Brigg Brass Band in several of his folksong arrangements, including 'Brigg Fair', which was performed for the first time. The arrangement of 'Brigg Fair' (dedicated to Grieg), which had been recently published by Forsyth, turned out to be the highlight of the concert, thanks in no small part to Gervase Elwes as tenor soloist.[3] It is thought Delius first met the young Grainger in April 1907 at the house of John Singer Sargent. At a second meeting there was music at Grainger's London home including Delius's Piano Concerto, *Appalachia* and Grainger's own folksong arrangements. Apart from a good personal rapport and a degree of commonality in their musical values, Delius recognised a similar affinity for harmonisation which he recognised in the arrangements, especially of 'Brigg Fair'. 'But our harmonies are identical', Delius exclaimed,[4] clearly having observed Grainger's own innate grasp of that functional division between diatonic melody and chromatic harmony (for which a common link was Grieg) in the process of strophic variation. Grainger also claimed the same affinity after reading *Appalachia* for the first time: 'I was amazed to find that anything so like my own chordal style existed. It struck my mother the same way: "What piece of yours is that?" She called from the next room, taking for granted it was mine, yet not able to recognise it'.[5]

BRIGG FAIR: RHAPSODY AND VARIATION

Fenby maintained that Grainger had sent Delius his setting of 'Brigg Fair;[6] Heseltine stated that it was 'given to Delius' by Grainger,[7] and that the

---

[3] Bird, J., *Percy Grainger* (Oxford: Oxford University Press, 1999), 121. The tune was published in the *Journal of the Folk Song Society*, Vol. 2 No. 7 (1905), 80.

[4] Grainger, interview with John Amis, BBC, 14 June 1959, quoted in Bird, J., *Percy Grainger*, 126.

[5] Grainger, P., 'The Personality of Frederick Delius', in *DC*, 122.

[6] Fenby, E., *Delius* (London: Faber & Faber, 1971), 58.

[7] *PH*, 127.

Australian suggested that it might form the satisfactory basis of an orchestral work. Grainger also claimed that, after hearing his passacaglia *Green Bushes*, Delius composed both *Brigg Fair* and the *Dance Rhapsody* No. 1 'in somewhat similar passacaglia-like forms – as contrasted with the variation form he had used in "Appalachia"'.[8] This was an interesting if somewhat loose assertion. Delius might well have seen (and possibly heard) Grainger's *Green Bushes* which was completed between 1905 and 1906 during their first musical meeting in London, so there was the definite possibility that he was able to scrutinise Grainger's adaptation of passacaglia form (which also embraces sonata principles) and its seamless set of variations. The first phase of Delius's variations certainly reveals a seamless process in the same manner as Grainger's, though there is no evidence of any bass ostinato (as one finds in *Green Bushes*) which characterises the normative first phase of a passacaglia (cf. Bach or Couperin). Grainger is also only partly right in his point about *Appalachia*. Certainly, *Appalachia* was driven by the principle of 'character' variations, but Delius initially avoids this approach in the first part of his variation method; later, however, character variations do become a more prominent component of the structure.

Sketches of *Brigg Fair* occur on the same pieces of manuscript as *Songs of Sunset*,[9] and a notebook of 1905 to 1907 shows ideas for the middle section of the work.[10] There is also some evidence to suggest that Delius contemplated a chorus (just as he had done for *Appalachia*) in which the song might be sung at the conclusion, though, in the end, Delius abandoned this idea.[11]

Delius was, in fact, no stranger to folksong. His early notebooks reveal the collection of Norwegian tunes during his walking tours of the Jotunheim, and his harmonisation of them under the influence of Grieg. 'Brigg Fair' offered Delius the same potential as the tune for *Appalachia* – a diatonic melody which could be harmonised in many different ways – but where 'Brigg Fair' offered real potential was its unusual Dorian modality. In Grainger's harmonisation, its transposed Dorian G minor is spelled out from the beginning. In Delius's more ambiguous version, however, the dominant (D minor) tangentially accompanies the first three bars, before moving through its relative (F major)

---

[8] Grainger, P., 'The Personality of Frederick Delius', 128.

[9] See *GB-Lbl* MS Mus 1745/2/13/4. This shows the propinquity of ideas for 'Cynara' with those of *Brigg Fair*.

[10] A very early pencil sketch can be observed in *GB-Lbl* MS Mus 1745/2/13/5, ff. 117–19 and *GB-Lbl* MS Mus 1745/2/11/5, ff. 153–51 (notebook inverted) pertains to the middle section of the work.

[11] See *RT1*, 141.

to the unexpected tonal centre of G in b. 6. Here the major and minor modes are mixed (which includes a tantalising clash between the C sharp and C natural) before a *tierce de picardie* in b. 10 concludes the phrase. A passing modulation to G minor's relative, B flat, then occurs before a genuine perfect cadence is reserved for the last two bars (Example 10.1a) in the *minor* mode. Note also how Delius deftly phrases his accompaniment to cut *across* the phrasing of the folksong. This emphasis on D proved to be important for the opening of Delius's symphonic poem. It is precisely that pitch which begins the evocative 'Pan-like' flute cadenza of the introduction, and it is this same pitch which stands out as part of the added sixth of F minor harmony in b. 3 (a 'sound moment' Delius had surely learnt from the pastoral muse of section four of Part II in *A Mass of Life* – see b. 5), the fluctuation between the D major triads (replete with Lydian colour from the decorative filigree of the solo wind) and the augmented sixths for the rest of this idyllic passage, marked by Delius 'Lento Pastoral'.[12] The avoidance of G minor is therefore very much a characteristic, not only of the introduction and the melody but of the variations which follow. The profoundly pastoral atmosphere of the introduction to *Brigg Fair*, one which so many now associate with Delius as a 'pastoral' composer, is in fact an important structural conduit within the work. As we have observed in *Appalachia*, it was a device in variation form with which Delius was already familiar and one he also planned to use as a ritornello-like, unifying element to his successional design.

The tabular representation by Erwin Stein (a one-time student of Schoenberg) in the 1923 Universal edition of the miniature score provides a useful if basic overview of the sequence of variations, though nothing more in terms of their character and role. The first phase of the work, as Stein outlines, is the theme and a group of six variations. Delius sets about providing a series of increasingly esoteric and dense harmonisations of the modal theme, whose recurrences are easily identifiable by the incipit D–E–F of the theme's opening phrase and by the Delian thumbprint of the falling chromatic bass line. The spirit of the variations, especially from Variation 4 (which, in its reconstitution of the various rhythmical fragments of theme, acts as transition to variations 5 and 6), have an increasing dance character,

---

[12] It has always been a temptation to link this impressionistic opening with Debussy's *Prélude à l'après-midi d'un faune*, although Jelka Delius always maintained that her husband did not become acquainted with the work until 1909 when he was in London. Although Delius knew Debussy's music, notably *Pelléas et Mélisande*, it seems more likely that the opening music to *Brigg Fair* evolved as an aggregate of the picturesque passages of *Appalachia*, *Sea Drift* and *A Mass of Life*.

Example 10.1a. *Brigg Fair*, folksong melody and Delius's harmonisation.

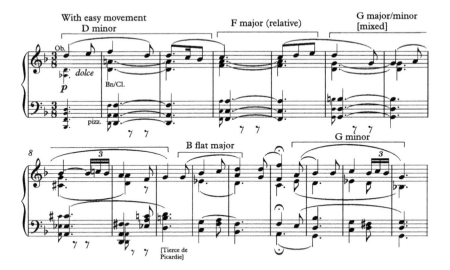

again suggesting Banfield's notion of 'Sellinger's round'.[13] Heseltine even went as far as to suggest that the semiquaver counterpoint, which continues to inhabit variations 5 and 6, where the melody returns intact in the horns and trumpet, was an unconscious reminiscence of the 'divisions' in which the 'old English composers of the time of Queen Elizabeth were in the habit of adumbrating the popular melodies of the day', another symptom, he argued, for the presence of the passacaglia style-form.[14]

Breaking the procession of variations, the slower tempo of the introduction is invoked with the reappearance of the flute cadenza underpinned by the same F minor and added-sixth sonority. Also having a precedent in *Appalachia*, this 'brief and lovely interlude', so-called by Heseltine,[15] has many interesting attributes. Voluptuously scored, its long, languorous melody embodies a marked contrast from the more lively dance rhythms, and one of its central melodic shapes (G–F–E–G–F) recalls similar phrases in *Lebenstanz* (second

[13] Banfield, S., 'La ronde se déroule: Delius and the Round Dance', *British Music Society Journal*, Vol. 6 (1984), 35.

[14] PH, 127–8. Perhaps influenced by Heseltine's impression, Fenby likened this part of Delius's variation process to William Byrd's *The Woods So Wild*; Fenby, E., *Delius*, 62.

[15] PH, 128.

subject) and *A Mass of Life* (Part I No. 2). Heseltine remarked that the melody was 'not derived from the main theme'; yet on examination the opening triplet (D–E–F) is surely the very same that begins 'Brigg Fair'. Delius's numerous repetitions surely also emphasise the link, and the descending triplet (G–F–E) relates to the theme's second bar. In addition, the descending chromatic inner lines, which on repetition of the melody translate to the bass, settle a connection with the descending bass lines of the previous variations. Hence it would be more accurate to claim the status of a variation for the interlude rather than as a separate entity (Example 10.1b). The order and nature of the variations in *Brigg Fair* are shown in Table 10.1.

After the interlude the 3/4 metre is reinstated and a second series of seamless variations, passacaglia-like in their repetitions, ensues, though it is not until the truncated Variation 9 that G minor is restored (Variation 8 is couched in D minor). At the conclusion of Variation 8, Delius also begins to introduce additional thematic and contrapuntal features. The first of these is a fluctuating bass figure (Example 10.1c) which is ambiguously suggestive of both D minor and F major (a sound highly reminiscent of the same ambiguous tonal relationship in the wedding procession of *A Village Romeo and Juliet*); this also recurs at the end of Variation 9 where F major is restored as the tonic. Variation 9 also introduces a new melodic counterpoint which frames the variation, and this spawns yet a further thematic countermelody in Variation 10 (Example 10.1d) with a waltz-like character. In addition, it is also worth noting that the initial three-note shape of the folk melody (D–E–F) is now goal-directed in that it defines F major rather than D minor. The momentum of Variation 10 is taken up by its close relation, Variation 11. Here Delius takes the opportunity to imbue the variation process with a new sense of fantasy

Example 10.1b. *Brigg Fair*, Variation 7, Interlude.

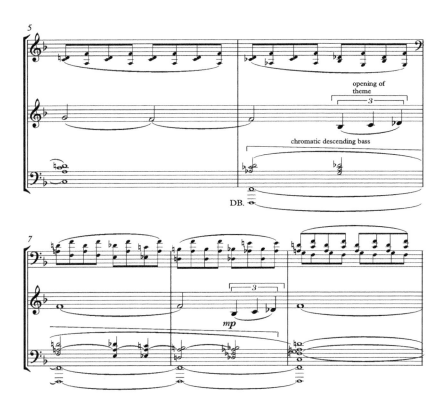

which is achieved by developing the waltz countermelody to the point of the work's first major climax, and a calming of its passions with a brief, hushed, but telling recurrence of the interlude at its close.

Casting the second group of variations in F major provided an effective tonal foil to the first group in G minor. It was also a measure of Delius's harmonic dexterity in that the pitches of the melody remained the same throughout. Having set a precedent of settled tonal areas for the previous two variation groups (analagous, one might argue, to the two opposing keys of a sonata structure), Delius used his third group of variations in a manner more analogous to a developmental phase. This is epitomised in Variation 12, cast in 4/4 metre, which begins in D minor (re-emphasising that tonality's association with the beginning of the original melody). There is, however, no conventional conclusion to this variation in G minor. Instead, Delius provides a modulatory transition in which a repetition of the theme, fully reconstituted, now appears as Variation 13 in the minor mode as G sharp minor. Grimley attributes this remote key area to the prevalence of A flat in the F minor

Table 10.1. *Brigg Fair*, order and nature of variations.

Section	Tempo/metre	Key	Comments
Introduction	Slow, 4/4	F major[6]	Flute cadenza/pastoral
Theme	Allegretto leggiero, 3/8	G minor	'Brigg Fair' tune
Variation 1	3/8	G minor	
Variation 2	3/8	G minor	
Variation 3	3/8	G minor	
Variation 4	3/8	G minor	Reconstitution of theme [transition]
Variation 5	3/8	G minor	
Variation 6	3/8	G minor	
Introduction	4/4	F major[6]	Recurrence of flute cadenza Long melody
Variation 7		F major	Interlude
Variation 8	Rather quicker, 3/4	D minor	Introduction of bells
Variation 9	3/4	F major	Truncated version of theme with new countermelody
Variation 10	3/4	F major	Introduction of 'waltz' countermelody
Variation 11	3/4	F major	'Fantasy' extension
Interlude	3/4	F major	Memory of previous interlude (molto tranquillo)
Variation 12	Slow. With solemnity, 4/4	D minor – V of B	Funeral march (I)
Variation 13	4/4	G♯ minor	Funeral march (II)
Introduction	4/4	F major	Cadenzas (more extended)
Variation 14		F major	Reminiscences of theme
Variation 15	3/8, Gaily	V of F major	Round dance
Variation 16	3/8	D minor	Round dance
Variation 17	3/8	F major	Round dance (full orchestra)
Variation 18	3/8	G minor	Round dance – restatement of original theme
Variation 19	Rather slower, 3/2	B♭ major	Finale – Paean
Variation 20	3/4	B♭ major	Coda

colour of the introduction (as the minor mode of F minor's relative, the tonal distance is not that considerable).[16] The ponderous, cortège-like character of variations 12 and 13 also suggests a break in the passacaglia process of the variation structure in that, as a marked transformation of the original

---

[16] *DG*, 198.

Example 10.1c. *Brigg Fair*, Variations 8 and 9, fluctuating bass figure.

Example 10.1d. *Brigg Fair*, Variation 10, waltz.

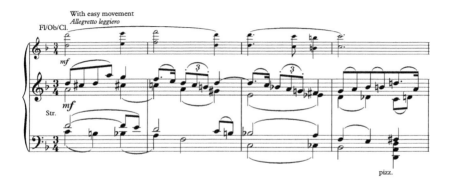

theme and accompaniment, they constitute 'character' variations much more similar to those of *Appalachia* (where, it should be noted, Delius included two such similar variations). As for the funeral character and rhythm of the two variations, Delius may well have followed the example of Grieg's string arrangement of 'Hjertesår' (a miniature set of variations) from his *Two Elegiac Melodies* Op. 34 where a similar rhythmic device is used.

From the funeral march, which represents the most distant (and most alien) tonal excursion from the theme's original orbit, Delius pulls the tonality rapidly back to the familiar territory of D minor with a recapitulation of the cadenzas from the introduction (using the same distinctive scoring for flute and clarinet). In this instance the introduction is more extended and sits on an A pedal (ambiguously balanced between V of D and I^6 of F. Besides the cadenza solos of the woodwind, evocations of mountain music (now familiar to us from *Paa Vidderne, A Village Romeo and Juliet* and *A Mass of Life*) are provided by the horns, together with a melancholy utterance from the cor anglais whose free line connects with a passing reminiscence of the funeral march and, with a closing reference to the entire theme in the clarinet, links this fantastical section more closely with the variation sequence.

These elements of 'fantasy', ones which give Delius's approach to form their individuality and special poetry, furnish an effective conduit to the last phase of the work, a final set of variations. Variations 15–17 more readily reveal the character of a country 'round dance' (very much in keeping with the type of maypole dancing Grainger would have witnessed in Brigg). The modal features of the melody evidently continued to fascinate Delius. Variations 15 sits on the dominant of C, while the melody, embarking from F, provides some attractive Lydian colour. Variation 16 (in the cellos and a singular instance of the melody as a bass voice) is based in D minor, while Variation 17 sits on the dominant of F. Finally, the original theme (Variation 18), scored for full orchestra, is restored in G minor before the theme is more spaciously reinterpreted as a paean of bells (recalling the same joyous music of Vreli and Sali's wedding in Scene 5 of *A Village Romeo and Juliet*). What is more, as we enter this clamorous coda, Delius deftly shifts the tonality to B flat. Besides the sense of drama this instils at the end of the work, Delius's true *coup de maître* is to reintroduce the folksong, its original pitches intact, while grounding the key, not in G minor, but in its relative; moreover, as the tempo and dynamic of the paean subsides, we are left with one last, reflective reference to the folk melody, gently imparted over a tonic pedal in which the inherent Lydian features of the tune (accentuated by B flat) add a poignant note of melancholy valediction.

Brigg Fair, one of Delius's orchestral masterpieces, reiterates the evident fondness the composer retained for variation form. In this latest work, however, we witness a rather tighter technique of organisation where, in addition to the variegation of the folk melody, we can observe Delius's more systematic and indeed more esoteric development of the melody's modal possibilities, together with his ingenious ability to assimilate this aspect within the increasingly broad range of his chromatic language. As an abstract work, bearing the title 'Rhapsody', it is highly satisfying as an inventive, free structure, but Delius's choice to publish the six verses (for which Jelka provided a German translation) of the folksong in the score published by Universal Edition may also suggest that he may have wanted to convey something of the sentiment of the lovers, their first encounter at Brigg Fair, their courting, the blithe bells of their wedding, and their vows to remain constant, but without relation to a programme. As *The Musical Times* related: '[It] is not, as might be imagined, descriptive of the hurly-burly of a country fair. The composer idealises love scenes, thoughts and moods, in music of tender and melancholy beauty'.[17] Yet it is surely the reflective sentiment of the last verse (which gives such piquancy to Grainger's vocal arrangement) which Delius hoped to convey in the oboe's wistful tone of the magical coda.

Brigg Fair was one of Delius's major successes in the concert hall. Having heard Beecham conduct *Paris* on 11 January 1908, Liverpool's music lovers heard Delius's new work under Bantock with the Liverpool Orchestral Society just a week later. The work received its first fully professional performance under Landon Ronald with the Hallé Orchestra in Birmingham Town Hall on 19 February, and it was just over a month later that Beecham first took up the work with the New Symphony Orchestra at Queen's Hall on 31 March. After the major exposure of *A Mass of Life* in 1909, the work enjoyed another flurry of performances, both abroad, in Zurich under Volkmar Andreae and in New York under Walter Damrosch in 1910. The international tirage of his music was increasing.

IN A SUMMER GARDEN: SYMPHONIC POEM *PAR EXCELLENCE*

It became a normal activity for Delius to revise his work after hearing its first performance. This was certainly the case with *Brigg Fair*. However, after the first performance of *In a Summer Garden*, which Delius himself conducted on 11 December 1908 at Queen's Hall for the Philharmonic Society, the composer withdrew the work while he made extensive revisions. It was not until 1912 when Max Fiedler conducted the revised version (the published version which Leuckart undertook in 1911) on 19 April with the Boston Symphony Orchestra that he was contented with the form and thematic material, after which the work received a good deal of national and international exposure and became more closely associated with Rossetti's lines from the *House of Life* ('All are my blooms; and all sweet blooms of love To thee I gave while Spring and Summer sang'). Fritz Stein, the German conductor, who worked with Nikisch and Sitt, directed its first European performance in Jena on 3 June 1913,[18]

---

[17] *The Musical Times*, Vol. 49 No. 780 (February 1908), 92.

[18] At this performance in Jena, the programme note featured a further unattributed quotation [Delius or Jelka?] which provides a description highly suggestive of the garden at Grez: 'Rosen, Lilien und tausend Blumen. Bunte Schmetterlinge flattern von Kelch zu Kelch und goldbraune Bienen summen in der warmen zitternden Sommerluft. Unter schattigen alten Bäumen ein stiller Fluss mit weissen Wasserrosen. Im Kahn, fast verborgen, zwei Menschen. Eine Drossel singt – ein Unkenton in der Ferne'. [Roses, lilies and a thousand flowers. Colourful butterflies

which was followed by Theodor Spiering, the Joachim pupil, concertmaster for Mahler while the latter directed the New York Philharmonic Orchestra, and guest conductor of the Berlin Philharmonic Orchestra, who gave it in Berlin on 4 November 1913. It was not until 18 December 1913 that Emil Młynarski, the Polish conductor, gave its first British hearing in Edinburgh, and the task of its first London hearing was given to the young Geoffrey Toye who also conducted the first performance of Vaughan Williams's *A London Symphony* in the same programme. Beecham, however, did not undertake a performance until 8 July 1914 when the work formed part of an all-Delius programme of *Brigg Fair* and the two small orchestral pieces, *On Hearing the First Cuckoo in Spring* and *Summer Night on the River*, music from *A Village Romeo and Juliet* and the *Dance Rhapsody* No. 1.

Like the fate of the Piano Concerto, *In a Summer Garden* was one of Delius's works to be heard in two quite different versions. Subject to more change and recomposition than any other of Delius's mature orchestral works, this most individual of his symphonic poems is not only testimony to his fastidious and self-critical acumen, but also to his intuitive sense of form and equilibrium. The *Stichvorlag* of the published version is now lost, but it is possible to study the surviving autograph of the first version over which he spent much time. A letter to Bantock, dated 30 June 1908, indicates that he was still making finishing touches to the score which, at that time, was called *Summer Rhapsody*.[19] Apart from the large numbers in blue pencil indicating the changing time signatures throughout the work in Delius's hand (which he put there to aid his direction of the first performance), one can observe the extensive pencil short-score reworkings at the foot of the pages and many crossings out.[20] A comparison of the two versions is also instructive in revealing a number of important choices

---

flutter from goblet to goblet and golden-brown bees hum in the warm, shivering summer air. Under shady old trees a quiet river with white water lilies. In the boat, almost hidden, two people. A thrush sings – a sound in the distance.] The quotation was also reproduced below the Rossetti quotation in the Universal edition of the score in 1921.

[19] Letter from Delius to Bantock, 30 June 1908, *DLL1*, 358.

[20] See *GB-Lbl* MS Mus 1745/1/23, ff. 1–24. An even earlier pencil draft can be observed in *GB-Lbl* MS Mus 1745/2/8. Here the title page provides interesting evidence of how Delius deliberated over his poetic titles. There are no less than ten different attempts before Delius arrived at his final choice (see also *RT2*, 173); it is also interesting to note that some of the titles were deployed elsewhere: *Summer Night / Rhapsody / Summer Sounds / Summer Rhapsody / A Song of Summer / A Summer Eve / A Summer Song / Summer / On a Summer Eve / In a Summer Garden.*

Table 10.2. *In a Summer Garden* (revised version), structural overview.

Thematic material	Key	Comments
First subject	G minor – V of G	'a', 'b', 'c'
Second subject	F major	'd', 'e'
Codetta	F major	Juxtaposition of unrelated triads
Central paragraph	E♭ major – D major	Extended lyrical theme
Tonal affirmation	D major	'b', 'd'
First subject and second subjects conflated	D major	'b', 'd', 'e'
First subject	G major	'a'
Coda	G major	Memory of 'd'

Delius made – since these involved matters of proportion, thematic material and tonal organisation, three factors which indicate that, in spite of those who believed the composer to be oblivious of such phenomena, formal and tonal considerations were clearly a priority in his mind.

The shape of *In a Summer Garden* is essentially ternary (ABA'). However, it is evident from the return of the A section (A') that the influence of sonata thinking is inherent in the highly modified nature of the material already used in the first section and of its strong directional momentum towards the tonic, G (see Table 10.2). More fascinating still, however, is the 'reversed' nature of Delius's reprise in A' where the first subject (notably the first thematic statement in G minor) returns obliquely before G major occupies the final bars. The manuscript of the original version also indicates that, like *Brigg Fair*, he initially wished to call it a 'rhapsody', though this subtitle did not figure in the published edition.

As is common in a good deal of Delius, the mixing of major and minor modes is a salient feature of his tonal organisation. *In a Summer Garden* begins in a modal G minor (Example 10.2a) with two statements of the same phrase ('a'). This is all we hear of this specific material until close to the conclusion of the work. Accompanying the second of these two phrases is what appears to be an elusive fragment ('b'), representative perhaps of a flitting butterfly or insect, and this composite thematic statement ends with a flourish from the flute ('c'). Delius's first paragraph is all about a constant variation of figure 'b' which takes in the first instance to a half close (three bars after Fig. 3). This figure, however, remains persistent, and embarking once again from G minor, Delius introduces two more short fragments 'd' and 'e' (Examples 10.2b and 10.2c) which also combine and develop as a form of second subject. This detailed process of developing small motives is something unique to this symphonic poem, an attribute to which Heseltine alluded when he poetically described the work as being 'built up of thematic *scrappets* that might well have been suggested by whispers of wind and the colloquy of birds'.[21] Payne has more incisively observed, however, that 'though not cast as a set of formal variations, it makes use of the technique'.[22] In fact it is through the agency of variation and his tessellated method of thematic ideas that Delius reaches his first climax and the secondary key of F major (a key anticipated in the flute phrase 'c'). This secondary material is the subject of further reworking and amalgamation of both first and second subjects blended with another somewhat new ingredient of Delius's style, the juxtaposition of unrelated triads (Example 10.2d). Delius's pointillistic orchestration, with its 'babble' of woodwind filigree, is also an

Example 10.2a. *In a Summer Garden*, opening idea
in G minor featuring fragments 'a', 'b' and 'c'.

---

[21] *PH*, 130.

[22] Payne, A., 'Delius's Stylistic Development', *Tempo*, No. 60 (Winter 1961–1962), 13.

indelible feature of the score and one that he learned from the pages of *Brigg Fair*. One other notable characteristic of the animated section between Figs 4 and 11 is how much Delius's secondary thematic material (especially 'd' and 'e') shares a similar angularity and rhythmic emphasis with Till Eulenspiegel's 'laughter' material in Strauss's tone poem, and how, in consequence, the playful, even jocular nature of this paragraph gradually becomes ever more suggestive of a scherzo.

Example 10.2b. *In a Summer Garden*, fragment 'd'.

Example 10.2c. *In a Summer Garden*, fragment 'e'.

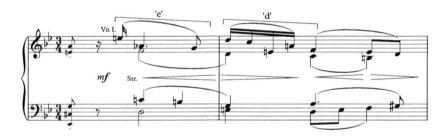

Example 10.2d. *In a Summer Garden*, unrelated triads.

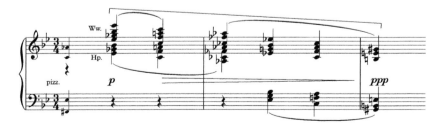

Delius's foil to this concatenation of individual melodic cells was a central paragraph of a long, self-developing theme for the violas (Example 10.2e). Although we have met such long, sustained melodies in Delian contexts such as *Lebenstanz* (second subject) and *Brigg Fair* (interlude), this particular example, with its quasi-operatic emphasis on melody, is a novel element of his mature orchestral style. Fenby suggested that it depicted the ebb and flow of the river at the foot of the house at Grez – but this is surely a 'love song' to Jelka whose dedication lies at the head of the score. Beginning in E flat major, the melody, in 6/4, is adorned by a pattern of accompanimental shapes in the upper woodwind which, ostinato-like, run the entire course of the opulent paragraph of string harmonies.

Concluding in D major, this splendidly sumptuous, self-contained, lyrical utterance yields to a resumption of the scherzo ideas, with particular reference to 'b' and 'd', though their interaction is curtailed by the work's second major climax in D major (see three bars before 17). It is as if Delius was determined to affirm this tonality as a central pillar to the tone poem before the process of working back to the tonic begins. Enchantingly, Delius lingers over this 'tipping point' of D major for some while – perhaps the most memorable moments of this celebration of D are the two 'pregnant' dominant elevenths (before Fig. 18). After Fig. 19, Delius's response to the reworking of the first and second subjects is to recapitulate them in conflated form in D major before the tonality swings back to G major at Fig. 25, an event which also marks the dissipation of the scherzo character. This restatement of the tonic occurs together with a restatement of 'a' (not heard since the opening bars), though this is adroitly veiled by the oblique dominant of E (after Fig. 23); Delius's delay of tonicisation is skilfully handled by way of a lyrical climax on the dominant of G (at Fig. 24) and the work concludes in characteristic fashion in total tranquillity, replete with the hallmarks of added-sixth, sonorous divided strings and the 'murmur' of woodwind. All in all, *In a Summer Garden* remains one of Delius's most sophisticated orchestral essays. In one sense the ever-shifting tempi of the work's thematic material, with its phraseological ebb and flow, convey an almost extemporary, prose-like fluency, and yet, on closer examination, the careful use of prelude and coda as a frame, and the assimilation of use of contrasting movement 'types' (scherzo, slow movement) within a larger ternary design reveal Delius's ability to think musically on several different abstract levels.

The original version of *In a Summer Garden*, a rather looser structure altogether, which Delius directed in 1908, shows a number of marked differences. The work commences with the same G minor theme 'a', but with the repetition of 'a', a plaintive phrase for oboe provides a counterpoint rather

Example 10.2e. *In a Summer Garden,* central viola theme.

than the familiar semiquaver motive, before 'c' (in a slightly different from) emerges on the flute. Delius's initial concept of his first subject was to be more languorous in terms of its harmonic content and the first point of repose is G major (rather than the D major of the revised version). What is evident is that Delius sensed that the first paragraph lacked enough rhythmical movement, so he resolved to introduce the semiquaver figure ('b'), present at a later stage of the work, to provide more forward motion as well as motivic tightness as a conduit to the more sprightly second subject. This material in the first version is recognisably similar in content to the revised one ('d' and 'e') as is the climactic modulation to F major and its prolongation, though the scoring is less cleanly executed. Indeed, after the first performance Delius opted to reorchestrate substantial sections of the work in tandem with his musical changes. Retaining the same orchestral forces including the glockenspiel, he nevertheless dispensed with the original idea of three tubular bells (used in the transition to the central melody and for the major climax of the reprise) and introduced a triangle.

The central melody in E flat is virtually identical in shape and progression to that of the later version, although Delius chose to double the viola with the cor anglais; moreover, the elaborate wind accompaniment of his revision replaced a much simpler matrix of wind figurations. With the commencement of the third section (A'), it is interesting to hear the semiquaver motive ('b') active in the developmental texture, and one suspects that it was this sound that persuaded Delius to utilise it to greater effect in the revised first subject and its transition to the second-subject material. Other things remained unchanged between the two versions – notably the full orchestral climax in D major together with the 'pregnant' dominant elevenths (though the tubular bells were excised). However, much of the last part of the first version Delius (rightly) elected to jettison. Lacking in vitality and motivic cohesion, the music sags conspicuously and Delius seemed uncertain of his tonal goal. Finally, a reprise of the first subject ('a') occurs in the horn in B flat minor which initiates the closing paragraph of the work, and a memory of the central melody (marked 'Very slow') inaugurates the short coda in F major, though perhaps wishing to link the conclusion with the first subject, the final progression is to B flat major, which seems entirely unsatisfactory and unbalanced. It is no wonder, therefore, that Delius felt moved to revise an extensive portion of this part of the structure.[23]

DANCE RHAPSODY NO. 1

Delius's *Dance Rhapsody* No. 1 was almost certainly the result of the reputation he had established as an orchestral composer with *Brigg Fair*; more significantly, the work shared a similar formal concept in its use of variation structure, introduction and interlude. Through its modification of the

---

[23]   The reception of the first version of *In a Summer Garden* was not helped by Delius's role as conductor (a skill for which he had little affinity or sufficient practical

Lincolnshire folksong, *Brigg Fair* had been strongly connected with Delius's love of the dance, in rather English terms; the *Dance Rhapsody* also reflected this tendency, albeit with an original tune, for popular melody. Moreover, the subdivision of its 2/4 metre into four groups of triplets alludes once again to Delius's predilection for the 'round dance'.

A pencilled draft score of the work is entitled *Harmonic Dances*,[24] an intriguing heading since it conceptually divulges Delius's preoccupation with harmony as an agency of variation and also suggests that the composer conceived of each variation as a dance in its own right. While the draft lacks the lively coda and some of the transitional passages between variations of the final version, it shows the same huge scoring (save for the heckelphone, which Delius replaced with a bass oboe) as *A Mass of Life*. Indeed, combined with the element of dance and popular melody, the colourful scoring of Delius's work suggests that it was almost designed to be a showpiece and that the attraction of its first performance with the London Symphony Orchestra in Hereford's Shire Hall would be enhanced by the composer's presence as conductor. Having been completed between February and April 1909,[25] the work was entirely well placed to satisfy the invitation by George Robertson Sinclair and the Hereford Three Choirs Festival for their 1909 programme, and it was performed there on 8 September.[26] Having failed to make an impression at the Philharmonic with *In a Summer Garden*,[27] and despite reassurances of private practice in front of a mirror, Delius's friends should have counselled him against a second appearance, but as Lloyd has asserted, premieres directed by their creators were a chemistry dear to those with one eye on the marketplace. Besides the precarious nature of Delius's conducting abilities, the performance at Hereford was hampered by the considerable difficulties occasioned by Delius's scoring of a bass oboe and sarrusophone. This had caused some difficulties in Beecham's performance of *A Mass of Life* in June of that year with the bass oboe, but at Hereford a heckelphone

experience) which, as the *Musical Standard* posited, only served to compound the work's negative criticism in the press.

[24]   See *GB-Lbl* MS Mus 1745/2/8.

[25]   See letters from Delius to Bantock, 17 February and 24 April 1909, *DTA*.

[26]   See Lloyd, S., 'Delius as Conductor', *DSJ* No. 46 (January 1975), 12.

[27]   Coates, E., *Suite in Four Movements* (London: Heinemann, 1953), 148. As a professional violist, Coates had rare first-hand experience of Delius's conducting at the Philharmonic of *In a Summer Garden*.

was used, though its inability to 'speak' marred what positive impression the press could gain.[28] As Beecham recalled in his experience with this work, Delius's choice of a bass oboe placed a serious obstacle in the work's road to acceptance:

> Now the bass oboe, like certain other members of the single- and double-reed families, is to be endured only if manipulated with supreme cunning and control; otherwise its presence in the orchestra is a strain upon the nervous system of conductor and players alike, a danger to the seemly rendering of the piece in hand, and a cause of astonishment and risibility in the audience. A perfect breath control is the essential requisite for keeping it well in order, and this alone can obviate the eruption of sounds that would arouse attention even in a circus.[29]

After Hereford, the work was given its first continental hearing in Berlin with the Blüthner Orchestra in the Blüthnerhalle under the direction of the Austrian composer and conductor Siegmund von Hausegger on 11 December 1911. Hermann Suter, its dedicatee, also conducted it in Basel. It was greatly admired by Grainger who made a two-piano / four-hands arrangement of the work in 1922 which Universal published in 1923.[30] Beecham also took up the work in an 'all-Delius' concert in London in 1911 when it was given in the same concert as *Songs of Sunset* (which also required a bass oboe) at Queen's Hall on 16 June; he also repeated it with the Hallé Orchestra in Manchester in the spring of 1912.

The scoring of the *Dance Rhapsody* – with its principal foci of oboe, cor anglais and bass oboe – was key to the work's personality as one can witness from the role of these double-reed instruments in the slow introduction. In the introductory bars of the draft score, Delius labelled the opening solo for cor anglais 'Caravanserai', connecting the aura of the music's exotic intervals with the caravans of the eastern trade routes. In the published version (the manuscript of which is now lost) by Leuckart of 1910, the dialogues between cor anglais and bass oboe, and clarinet with bass oboe, accentuate this romanticised relationship even further (as do the brief transitional passages), which have the effect of throwing into relief the Grainger-like 'walking'

---

[28]   Lloyd, S., 'Delius as Conductor', 13–14. See also 25n.

[29]   *MC*, 80.

[30]   See *GB-Lbl* Add MS 50886.

tune of the main variation series. Nevertheless, the 'reedy' timbre of the orchestration means that the element of exoticism is invariably present and is given additional perspective by the eastern 'dance interlude' (which is more suggestive of Rimsky-Korsakov's *Scheherazade*).

As mentioned above, Grainger claimed that his passacaglia *Green Bushes* had been influential in the conception of the *Dance Rhapsody*, in that, similar to *Brigg Fair*, the successional process of variations resembled that of a passacaglia paradigm. This was largely true, though another important element of the structure are the short transitions between each variation, a factor somewhat different from the seamless process of *Brigg Fair* in that, as a fundamental part of the structure, they are themselves subject to variation and the addition of 'exotic' phrases (mainly from the reed instruments). Scrutiny of the work's structure shows a further similarity to *Brigg Fair* in the use of an interlude; as mentioned above, the rather Russian flavour has a tangible link with the material of the introduction, though, as a contrast in style to the variations, its style and language seem reminiscent of earlier Delius.

The eleven variations themselves reveal an inventive set of features. Anticipated in the introduction, the theme, eight bars long, consists of two four-bar phrases which are musically similar in content, save for the first ending on a half-close, the second (for the most part) with a full cadence. In general this 4 + 4 phraseological pattern remains intact, and associated with one tonality, but, in the case of variations 3 (F sharp major to A major) and 9 (D major, F sharp minor and A major), these patterns are used as vehicles of modulation and are extended to twelve bars. In addition, a variant of the theme, which appears in the bass rather than as an upper line, is only six bars long (4 + 2). This occurs as Variation 2 in F sharp minor and recurs in a different orchestration between variations 7 and 8 in the same key. In terms of the work's proportions and tonal organisation, the variations are divided into two sets, the first four variations representing a microcosm of the seven variations which follow the interlude (see Table 10.3). Here A major encompasses two variations in (or which commence in) F sharp minor and F sharp major. This is also the pattern of the second group of variations except that F sharp minor encompasses two variations in (or which commence in) D major. One of the most inspired of the variations is, however, the penultimate tenth variation, scored for solo violin and 'con sordino' strings, which functions as a foil to the highly animated finale with its metrical conflict between duplets and triplets. Marked 'Molto Adagio', it is set apart from all the other variations for its pathos and intensity, as is the affecting melancholy of the preceding transition. As Heseltine wrote ecstatically:

Table 10.3. *Dance Rhapsody* No. 1, structural
overview of variations and transitions.

Section	Key	Comments
Introduction	Fluid	Fragments of theme and transition
Theme	A major	Oboe solo
Transition 1	A major	Flute solo
Variation 1	A major	Clarinet solo
Transition 2	A major	Cor anglais solo
Variation 2	F♯ minor	Strings (truncated) [variant of melody]
Transition 3	F♯ minor	Flutes/clarinets/timpani
Variation 3	F♯ major/ A major	Violin 1 (antecedent four bars); piccolo/flutes/oboes (full eight bars of theme)
Transition 4	A major	Flute/clarinet
Interlude	C♯ minor – F♯ minor	Full orchestra – through-composed; 'dance interlude'
Variation 4	A major	Flute/clarinet (Piú lento tranquillo)
Transition 5	A major	Omitted save cadence
Variation 5	A major	Full orchestra (with bass drone)
Transition 6	A major	Oboe/clarinet/bassoon
Variation 6	A major	Full orchestra (with drone)
Variation 3	F♯ minor	Full orchestra
Transition 7	F♯ minor	Trumpet/horn
Variation 7	D major	Flutes/clarinets
Transition 8	D major	[Extended] trumpets/strings/woodwind
Variation 8	D major – F♯ major – D major	Trumpet/oboe/cor anglais/flutes; 4 + 4 + 4 (12 bars)
Transition 9		Omitted
Variation 9	F♯ minor	Bass oboe [truncated variant – see Var. 3]
Transition 10	Fluid	Strings
Variation 10	A major	Violin solo + strings [con sordino] – Molto Adagio
Transition 11	A major	Reprise of introduction – clarinet/bass oboe
Variation 11	A major	Finale – full orchestra

The climax of the work is not dynamic, but comes at the music's ebb, a metamorphosis of the dance theme played by a solo violin against a background of divided strings [a Delian hallmark], an indescribable passage, "wonderful, causing tears", perhaps the most intense and *exalted* in all Delius's work. It has a wounding beauty which is all the more poignant for its evanescence – and which blinds one to the fact that the tumultuous coda, though completely satisfying in conception, does not and cannot ever quite come off in performance.[31]

In most instances the variations are followed by a transition (or what could also be described as a musical 'suffix' to the previous variation) which is usually four bars in length but is sometimes extended or even omitted altogether. As for the introduction, it does not play the same ritornello-like role of the corresponding material in *Brigg Fair*, except that Delius reserves a special place for its reprise, replete with a closing solo passage for bass oboe, between the eleventh and final variations.

By no means all commentators on Delius's music have found much to admire in the *Dance Rhapsody* No. 1. Payne considered it 'the least successful of all Delius's works for full orchestra. It is a set of formal variations, based on a very catchy tune, but the various episodes clank, and the sense of flow that keeps *Brigg Fair* moving is absent'.[32] Nevertheless, it is difficult not to admire Delius's harmonic resource with each successive variation as he puts into practice his well-established paradigm of a diatonic melody (albeit tinged with Lydian colour) supported by a falling chromatic bass line infused with complex harmonies. Although some of the variations are underpinned by pedal points (another of Delius's preferred methods) such as variations 6 and 7, this model figures as a constant feature, so much so that the final two variations embody an apotheosis of the technique. In addition, one cannot ignore the fact that, while the *Dance Rhapsody* shares a common approach to form with *Brigg Fair*, its scope, to show off the orchestra, is entirely different. Indeed, a scrutiny of the instrumentation of each variation and transition (Table 10.3) reveals a commitment to the art of orchestration, especially to the part played by the family of double-reed instruments, and the fact that Delius's intent in the *Dance Rhapsody* No. 1 was to write an orchestral work which differed in mood, form and technique from the challenging experiment of *In a Summer Garden*.

---

[31] *PH*, 129–30.

[32] Payne, A., 'Delius's Stylistic Development', 13.

CHAPTER 11

Homage to Jacobsen: *Fennimore and Gerda* and *An Arabesque* (1908–1913)

A NEW AUSTERITY

By the end of the first decade of the twentieth century, Delius was enjoying an acclaim about which he might only have dreamt ten years before. *A Mass of Life* had finally been heard in its entirety both in England and Germany, and the prospects of further performances seemed good. *Appalachia* had been performed in Hamburg; *A Village Romeo and Juliet* had been produced under Beecham's supervision at Covent Garden; Schuricht directed *Sea Drift* in Wiesbaden, *Brigg Fair* was given in Zürich and, as one of Delius's most popular works, was programmed in many major cities across Europe; there were also invitations from Bartók and Kodály, admirers of the *Mass*, to visit Budapest. In England his music was now a regular source of interest thanks to the support of his devotees such as Bantock, Beecham, Gardiner, O'Neill, Grainger and the youthful Philip Heseltine, still an Eton schoolboy. And in America, his ties with the plantation at Solana Grove were finally cut after it was sold to his old German friend and confidant, Hans Haym, whose son entertained aspirations to be a farmer.[1] Furthermore, in spite of difficulties with one of his principal publishers, Harmonie Verlag (which caused him to go to law), his music was now widely available in print which in itself helped to nourish its continued performance. Yet, a dark cloud hung over his life which now seemed set so fair, in that the syphilis contracted as a young man now began to manifest its tertiary symptoms as he reached the age of 50, a reality confirmed when he visited the sanatorium at the Swiss resort of Mammern for a cure.[2] Delius was unhappy at Mammern and hoped for something more positive when he entered another sanatorium in Dresden at the end of 1910. The prognosis was a major source of concern for Jelka and his friends though it is a testimony

---

[1] *DLL2*, 82.

[2] Ibid., 37.

to Delius's fortitude that he recovered sufficiently to return to composition. There was still much music in him, and he was anxious to spend his creative time in Grez and in Norway to make progress with new orchestral and choral works as well as a new opera.

Yet it was Beecham who noted that, with the composition of *The Song of the High Hills* (see Chapter 12), 'there was a certain austerity of manner that we have not encountered before'.[3] In truth, even before the composition of his largest tone poem, Delius had embarked on a more serious, introspective tributary of his art with his two sombre settings of Verlaine, 'La lune blanche' and 'Chanson d'automne' (which bear the imprint of *A Mass of Life* harmonically),[4] and even more so the denser and highly chromatic setting of W. E. Henley's 'The Nightingale', whose 'waltz' and emulation of birdsong provide a frame for the brief but passionate outburst at its centre ('For his song is all of the joy of life').[5]

FENNIMORE AND GERDA: A SECOND OPERATIC EXPERIMENT

Although relatively minor works in his output, the Verlaine settings and 'The Nightingale' were indicative of a more severe stylistic development in Delius's method and the principal object of this *modus operandi* was a new opera which occupied most of his creative time during 1909 and 1910. Since the completion of *A Village Romeo and Juliet* and *Margot la Rouge*, various subjects had appealed to him, but, for one reason or another, they all presented practical difficulties. Oscar Wilde's play *Salome* had been considered in 1903, which would have demanded the realist methods of *Margot la Rouge*. As it happened, Strauss got there first, much to the regret of Haym: 'What a pity that Strauss took the material away from you!', Haym opined. 'Couldn't you do it nonetheless, and especially now?'[6] Maeterlinck's *Pelléas* or another of the

---

[3] *TB*, 168.

[4] 'La lune blanche' dates from 1910 (*GB Lbl* MS Mus 17452/6/5) and was later published with Delius's earlier settings of Verlaine of 1896 in *Drei Lieder: Dichtungen von P. Verlaine* in that year. 'Chanson d'automne' dates from 1911 (see DTA OUP Acc. 229 for the autograph manuscript) but was not published until 1915 by Tischer & Jagenberg as one of *Fünf Gesänge*).

[5] This song (see DTA OUP Acc. 229) also dates from 1910 and appeared in Tischer & Jagenberg's *Fünf Gesänge* of 1915.

[6] See letter from Delius to Charles Russell & Co., 1 May 1903, *DLL1*, 215n.

Belgian playwright's dramas was also the subject of discussion at Grez, but Delius was unenthusiastic about Maeterlinck and the idea foundered.[7]

It was just before Christmas 1908 that Delius began work on his sixth operatic work, *Fennimore and Gerda*, based on two episodes from Jacobsen's celebrated novel *Niels Lyhne*. In fact, for much of the two years which Delius took to complete his new drama, his reference to it was always to the title (i.e. the main protagonist) of the novel.[8] In February 1909, in correspondence with Ethel Smyth, whose own opera *The Wreckers* he admired, he let it be known that he was 'hard at work on something new'.[9] It was, however, not until October 1910 that the first draft of the opera was completed.[10] Feeling revived after his illness he told Bantock: 'I am enjoying again excellent health – quite my old self again. I finished "Niels Lyhne" a few days ago'.[11] It was dedicated to Beecham who, delighted at the gesture, offered to do it in London. 'We will produce it here during this the coming season – de luxe – with the real cast of singers for the job'.[12] But Beecham, who now referred to the work as 'Fennimore', had not yet seen the score. In 1914, after the disappointment of Cologne's cancellation, Beecham still retained hopes of doing it in London. 'What about "Niels Lyhne"?' he asked; 'I should very much like to see it with a view to working it in to one of my Seasons'.[13] Beecham's intention to produce *Fennimore* clearly remained an imperative for Delius during the war, since, in 1919, he pressed Universal to send Beecham the vocal score. 'He is *very* interested in this work & it is expected that he will give it in the next spring season in London; thereafter he [intends] to go to the New York Metrop. Op. with his entire troupe & give it there as well'.[14] Yet, when Beecham did become acquainted with the work, he found himself entirely out of sympathy with its content, design and stylistic demeanour. So

[7] See letter from Jelka to Heseltine, 3 September 1929, *DLL2*, 354. After the completion of *Fennimore and Gerda* in 1914, both Heseltine (*PH*, 102n) and Clare Delius (*CD*, 196–7) made the claim that Delius was contemplating the further operatic subjects of *Wuthering Heights* and *Deirdre of the Sorrows*, though neither project was ever realised.

[8] See letter from Delius to Bantock, 17 December 1908, *DLL1*, 377.

[9] Letter from Delius to Ethel Smyth, 17 February 1909, *DLL2*, 9.

[10] The *Stichvorlag*, *GB-Lbl* Loan 54/2 is dated 1909/1910.

[11] Letter from Delius to Bantock, 26 October 1910, *DLL2*, 61.

[12] Letter from Beecham to Delius, 15 January 1911, *DLL2*, 66–7.

[13] Letter from Beecham to Delius, 1 October 1914, *DLL2*, 137.

[14] Letter from Delius to Universal, 14 August 1919, *MC*, 140.

much so, in fact, that he never conducted the work as a whole. Admiring the later section, entitled 'Gerda', which is very much shorter than its counterpart 'Fennimore', Beecham did perform this as well as Fenby's conflation of the orchestral interludes (now known as *Intermezzo from Fennimore and Gerda*) but the entire work he conspicuously avoided.

The choice of *Niels Lyhne* as a subject for Delius's opera almost certainly arose out of his love of Jacobsen's poetry. Somewhat more traditionally romantic than *Niels Lyhne*, the deep longing of such poems as 'Silkesko over gylden Læst', 'Løft de klingre Glaspokaler' or 'Det bødes der for' fulfilled a purpose for Delius in the mid-1890s with their suitable brevity for the *Danish Songs*; and the verse of Dowson in *Songs of Sunset* provided a fitting English equivalent in terms of sentiment and beauty of language. The ambience of *Songs of Sunset*, having been completed in 1908, may well have lingered in Delius's mind, but it must have also been the latency of *A Mass of Life*, with its rejection of Christianity that chimed with the attraction of Jacobsen's evangelical atheism. *Niels Lyhne*, finished in 1880, was very much a novel about self-examination. Unbelief – Christian unbelief – is central to its pages (the novel at one stage was to have been called *The Atheist*), but there are other aspects – human manners, art (and particularly artistic disillusionment), sex, love and man's place in nature – which figure prominently and express those turbulent and transitional times in which Jacobsen lived in the wake of the Darwinist revolution. The novel in its entirety focused, in particular, on Niels's unhappy and restive relationships with women in an era when women's position in society was rapidly changing. The lessons from Fru Boye and Fennimore, two of Niels's elusive lovers, were that women were no longer to be treated as objects of desire, fantasy and dreams, but as figures of equality. This proved to be a prism from which he attempted to shape his own life philosophy, coloured quintessentially by his hopes for an idealistic atheism embraced in his youth. Niels's *Weltanschauung* (which is proclaimed like the 'new Jerusalem' of the *Book of Revelation*) is best summarised in his conversation on Christmas Eve with Dr Hjerrild, a freethinker on religious matters:[15]

"But don't you see", exclaimed Niels, "that the day humanity can freely cry: there is no God, on that day a new heaven and a new earth will be created as if by magic. Only then will heaven become free, infinite space instead

---

[15] Jacobsen, J. P., *Niels Lyhne*, trans. Tiina Nunnally (London: Penguin Books, 1990), 106–7.

of a threatening, watchful eye. Only then will the earth belong to us and we to the earth, when the dim world of salvation and damnation out there has burst like a bubble. The earth will be our proper fatherland, the home of our heart where we do not dwell as foreign guests for a paltry time but for all our days. And what intensity it will give life when everything must be contained in life and nothing is placed outside of it. That enormous stream of love, which now rises up toward that God who is believed in, will bend back over the earth when heaven is empty, with loving steps toward all the beautiful human traits and talents with which we have empowered and adorned God in order to make God worthy of our love. Goodness, justice, wisdom, who can name them all? Don't you realize what nobility would spread over humanity if people could live their lives freely and meet their deaths without fear of hell or hope of heaven, but fearing themselves and with hope for themselves? How our conscience would grow, and what stability it would bring if passive remorse and humility could no longer atone for anything, and no forgiveness was possible except to use goodness to redeem the evil you so evilly committed".

It was a hard choice which confronted a deep personal loneliness. Suffering the death of no less than seven of his own kin, Niels is haunted by man's mortality throughout the novel. Indeed, at the very end, bereft of his dead wife (Gerda) and young child, he dies the stoical death of a soldier during the Dano-Prussian War of 1864, without the comfort of religious faith.

Much of this essential part of Niels's character and outlook (which is but a mirror image of Delius's Nietzschean rationale), is strangely omitted from the opera; indeed Niels, to whom there is a but a brief reference to his own artistic failures as a poet, is very much a diluted form of Jacobsen's much more psychologically tortured individual. Delius chose to concentrate his attention loosely on chapters 10 and 11 of Jacobsen's novel – those which focused on the episode in Niels's life of Fennimore, the daughter of Consul Claudi and the uncle of both Niels and his old school friend and painter, Erik Refstrup. At first, it would seem, judging by Delius's reference to the opera in correspondence, that Niels would be the centre of attention, but it is evident by the time of completion, and Beecham's letter to Delius in April 1910 (see above), that the weight of the drama had swung to Fennimore as the central character. She, after all, lies at the core of the 'love triangle' which forms the basis of Delius's narrative, and this undoubtedly persuaded him to dispense with the original title of *Niels Lyhne*.

It is significant that, at the beginning of the opera, on a summer evening, Niels, a man of the world who has travelled, listens to and watches Fennimore sewing. She is impatient to escape the confines of the house at Fordby, while Niels (who in the novel is recovering from the marriage of a former lover, Fru Boye, and the death of his beloved mother) is only too happy to enjoy the simple domestic joys of life in the country owing to his love for Fennimore. Niels's declaration is not what Fennimore wants to hear; she is more receptive to the energy and zest for life she sees in Erik, recently returned from Italy. And when Erik asks for a song, Fennimore sings a ballad of Svanhild ('Young Svanhild sat alone and sighed'), a legendary figure left to dream of a larger world which perfectly articulates her own sense of captivity. Fennimore and Erik declare their love; Niels is devastated, not only at losing Fennimore, but that her lover should be his only friend. Three years elapse in which time the marriage of Erik and Fennimore has not turned out well. Erik, now an embittered, sultry figure, who has turned to drink and undesirable company, can find no inspiration at their lovely home on the Mariagerfjord. To the relief of Fennimore, he writes to Niels to join him, in the hope that the stimulus to work might return and with it his former optimism. Niels arrives.

Fennimore, who admits that her marriage is unhappy, implores Niels to help her husband. So deep has Erik's despair become that, he tells his old friend, he has contemplated death. From his own experience (evident in the earlier chapters of the novel) Niels recommends travel, though Erik fails to see the benefit. Still unable to paint, Erik goes off with his drinking companions and dismisses the idea of help from his friend. Baffled by the behaviour of Erik, whom he once hero-worshipped in boyhood, Niels nevertheless tries to reassure a questioning Fennimore that his friend's muse might return. (As Niels observed: 'Sometimes a man of action feels a strange longing for something infinitely tender'. These words might easily have been Delius's own rather than Jacobsen's.) Yet, while expressing empathy for Fennimore's unhappiness, his promise to be her loyal friend has the effect of reviving his love for her. And when Erik returns to the house drunk, this only serves to propel Fennimore even more ardently towards an ever-receptive Niels. Fennimore resists, but declares that she cannot live without him. In this dilemma they embrace. From autumn, the scene passes to winter (as a projection of emotional desolation). Fennimore waits passionately for Niels to come. Instead a telegram arrives announcing Erik's death in an accident and that his body is to be returned to Mariagerfjord. In the shock of the event, Fennimore suffers a major crisis of conscience, blames Niels for her succumbing to him ('with all his poetry and beautiful speeches'), and spurns him. Her feelings turn to loathing as Niels is left bemused and abandoned. At this point Delius envisaged the end of the opera, to finish on a note of tragedy and irresolution, yet it remained the cause of indecision. Writing to

Emil Hertzka at Universal Edition in January 1913, he expressed a certain satisfaction with the German libretto, but otherwise retained reservations:

> In my opinion Fennimore as a libretto is dramatic and effective throughout with a slowly increasing dramatic interest ... The only thing in Fennimore which made me hesitate was the gloomy and unresolved ending & and it has been because of this that I have been occupying myself again in recent weeks with my Gerda music & have become convinced that the "Gerda" episode is necessary after all to round off the opera.[16]

To make this possible, Delius looked for requisite material in chapters 12 and 13 of the novel. In doing so, the emphasis swung back to the character of Niels, thereby shifting the emphasis of the whole opera to a narrative of his changing fortunes. In Jacobsen's text Niels 'wandered abroad' full of loneliness envying those with faith while he, without any, felt listless.[17] Another romantic liaison had presented itself, to a convalescing opera singer, but it came to nothing. At this point, Delius took up the narrative again. Finding solace in his father's estate at Lønborggaard, where he farmed; there he visited Councillor Skinnerup in Varde and became distracted by the councillor's four daughters. Niels falls for the oldest daughter, Gerda, who returns her affections. He introduces her to his estate and it concludes with the happy couple and of Niels having at last found contentment.[18] Thus, having based the opera on *one* episode of Jacobsen's novel, the definitive canvas of 1913 was based on two, a fact which Delius included in his published title: 'Zwei Episoden aus dem Leben NIELS LYHNES in elf Bildern nach dem Roman von J. P. Jacobsen'.

The organisation of Delius's plot followed the same experimental dramaturgical principles as *A Village Romeo and Juliet* – in other words voices, orchestra, plot and libretto combined to produce a succinct approach to drama in which old forms of operatic construction were jettisoned. During

---

[16] Letter from Delius to Hertzka, 24 January 1913, *DLL2*, 100–101.

[17] Jacobsen, J. P., *Niels Lyhne*, 165.

[18] This was not, of course, how the novel itself ended. During the course of the marriage Niels endeavoured to convince Gerda of the wisdom of his atheism as opposed to the tenets of her Lutheran faith. But, as Gerda fell ill, she fell back on the reassurances of her old beliefs before she died. To add to his torment, his young son also died soon afterwards, at which point, *in extremis*, he called upon God to help him. For Niels, on reflection, it was a 'fall from grace' the expiation for which was enlistment in the Danish army and a lonely death.

the course of his revisions for the end of *Fennimore and Gerda* he wrote to
Hertzka at Universal:

> Whatever is purposely not expressed in words, in order to avoid the
> notorious longueurs, is made complete by the music. The text is simply
> there as the basis & situation for the music and *must* in consequence
> absolutely not give the impression of being something complete in
> itself. The whole of modern literature has this defect: that is, theatrically
> effective libretti which in themselves are quite complete as stage plays &
> do not need any music at all. The *theatrical*-dramatic situation does not
> require any music at all & is diminished by it, while on the contrary the
> *musical*-dramatic situation comes into its own only through the music. I
> hope that you are enough of an artist to understand this, for herein lies
> the whole future of music drama. The same goes for A Village Romeo and
> Juliet though not yet quite so surely expressed as in Fennimore.[19]

Delius's final comments about the composition of *Fennimore* is highly
significant in that it indicates that the composer's approach to his latest opera
had been one of refining the techniques and methods he had exercised in his
fourth opera (see Chapter 6). In the process of composing *A Village Romeo
and Juliet*, he had realised that the traditional organisation of the operatic
canvas into individual acts and scenes no longer suited his concept of music
drama. However, we can also observe throughout the creation of this opera
the *change of concept* in that Delius had originally conceived the work in
acts but, after the first performances in Berlin in 1907, opted to change the
perception of the opera to one of six 'pictures' ('Bilder') or 'tableaux'. With
this significant transformation still fresh in his mind, he began *Fennimore*
with an even more radical vision. The opera would be even shorter than *A
Village Romeo and Juliet* and would consist of a series of terser 'Bilder' or
'pictures'. In fact, at around one hour and twenty minutes in performance, it
had more in common with the popularity of realist operas. Yet, even with this
succinctness of length, Delius typically made no compromise in his resources.
The orchestra required its usual augmented wind section, and in common
with those scores which were still fresh in his mind – *A Mass of Life, Songs of
Sunset* and *Dance Rhapsody* No. 1 – he required a bass oboe, a timbre he used
for moments of inner meditation.

---

[19] Letter from Delius to Hertzka, 24 January 1913, *DLL2*, 101.

Even more pervasive in *Fennimore*, however, is Delius's sense of dramatic and musical concentration. Each 'picture' is a distillation of the largely internalised 'action' of the drama in which the orchestra plays as significant a role (if not more so) as the characters. In much the same manner as *A Village Romeo and Juliet* and *Margot*, the music of *Fennimore* is essentially symphonic and Delius's innate sense of variation form (which we have witnessed time and time again in the symphonic poems) and continuous development constitutes the bedrock of the musical substance. For Delius this was a *vital* conceptual change in the way musical drama should be communicated. The libretto was no longer an agency to inspire the music; both elements occurred simultaneously as a creative impulse and both dimensions needed to embody the innermost meaning of the drama. In rejecting old operatic practices, Delius endeavoured somewhat polemically to enunciate this to his publisher:

> The successes enjoyed by certain modern operas have nothing whatever to do with their music & in consequence these compositions must soon disappear again. Their music *can* only be inferior, because a really sensitive artist could not possibly set such superficial libretti to music. It is only where text & music spring from the same source that a harmonic and living work can result.[20]

As Michel Fleury has remarked: 'In a symphonic poem or in an opera, and with a degree of precision increasing from the first genre to the second, the work of the imagination is partly assumed and channelled by the argument or the libretto'.[21] Indeed, so seminal was this dimension to Delius's understanding of opera that there were moments when meaning and emotion could be conveyed without words. It was this crucial step towards a more *instrumental* perception of music drama that Delius aspired to pursue in the condensed pages of *Fennimore*. As Fleury has commented appositely: 'Music allows thoughts and feelings to be expressed where words fail'.[22]

There are many familiar aspects of the first two 'pictures' of *Fennimore and Gerda* which recall earlier musical tropes and experimentations. The rich matrix of leitmotivs, which are here expressed with a new and more pithy

---

[20] Letter from Delius to Hertzka, 24 January 1913, *DLL2*, 101.

[21] Fleury, M., '*Fennimore and Gerda*: Une "expérience Délienne" aux multiples resonances', in Rossi, J. (ed.), *Frederick Delius et la France* (Paris: Delatour, 2014), 151.

[22] Ibid.

elegance, take their example from both *Romeo and Juliet* and *Margot*. Niels's probing, thoughtful upward-moving theme (Example 11.1a) is all-pervasive throughout the first 'picture' as, deeply enamoured, he observes Fennimore. She, by contrast, is more excitable, and her more rhythmically active leitmotiv (Example 11.1b) is drawn from *In a Summer Garden*, while her love for Erik derives from the familiar melodic figure from 'In the Seraglio Garden' and Part I No. 3 of *A Mass of Life* (Example 11.1c). In Fennimore's ballad, 'Jung Svanhild sass im Schloss allein', was Delius attempting to ape Jacobsen's own efforts as a balladist in 'Irmelin Rose' (from the *Danish Songs*) or 'Pagen højt paa Taarnet sad'? The trope of the 'Tenor voice on the water' in the second 'picture' is, of course, reminiscent of the bargemen in *A Village Romeo and Juliet*, and the nocturnal figurations at the beginning of this section have definite postludial affinities with *The Magic Fountain* and *Koanga*. In setting a precedent of short, epigrammatic episodes, the first two pictures reveal a sense of tighter tonal organisation than *Romeo and Juliet*. In the first picture, which leaps into the action without any orchestral 'Vorspiel', the tension between Niels's desire to find peace at home and Fennimore's desire to escape is palpable. This is immediately evident at the outset of the first 'picture' which begins on the dominant of F, and it is between this tonality (strongly associated with Niels) and C major that the first picture hovers. It continues to be discernible in other significant dramatic situations, such as when Niels expresses his frustration 'Oh, why did I not know you' where F is firmly accentuated; Fennimore then chaffs at her 'captivity' at which her longing to break out is resolutely underpinned by C, especially when she thinks of Niels's adventures in Copenhagen and Italy (see Fig. 5); yet F major returns when Niels is quick to remind her 'Oh, Fennimore, in the world one longs for one's homeland'. Erik's entrance is also supported by the dominant of F and this tonal centre persists until Fennimore breaks loose with her ballad. Even here, however, in the 'set piece' of the picture, Fennimore's frustration is made all the more vivid by the cadence into F minor at the end of her first verse ('for the joy of life I'm pining'). Only with the open-ended second verse is F finally discarded and with it twenty-eight bars of purely orchestral music in which Fennimore's hopes, through her love for Erik (see Example 11.1c), are allowed to develop.

The move from the first 'picture' to the second is played out without a break but the delineation is made clear by the change of key to C sharp minor and the introduction of the nocturnal material. Nevertheless, the delineation across the two 'pictures' is subtly smoothed by the sole presence of the orchestra and it is not until Fennimore's dreamy, love-enchanted entrance twenty-eight bars into the scene (a substantial proportion of the 'picture' as a whole) that text plays its attenuated part. In the slow-moving harmonic pace

Example 11.1a. *Fennimore and Gerda*, Niels's theme.

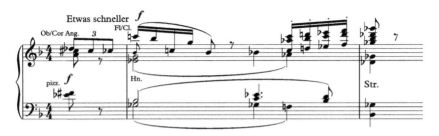

Example 11.1b. *Fennimore and Gerda*, Fennimore's theme.

Example 11.1c. *Fennimore and Gerda*, Fennimore's love for Erik.

of this nocturnal scene, C sharp minor (and numerous instances of Delius's favourite augmented sixth interjections) remains the predominant tonality, but as Erik and Fennimore declare their love for each other, C major, in a golden cloak of affecting melodic diatonicism comes to the fore. Much of this upsurging material, nuanced by the use of chromatic appoggiaturas, owes its character to those euphonious passages sung by Lili Béguin in Scene 2 of *Margot*. The display of ardour is also accompanied by a new thematic strand (Example 11.1d) which seems to consecrate this wonderful outpouring of 'white-note' melody. As these passionate bars subside, we are left with the added-sixth ruminations of *Songs of Sunset* as the lovers retire from the scene ('Yet 'tis no dream? Wondrous fulfilment'). The elation of C major, what is more, carries us through to the end of the 'picture' in spite of Niels's closing interjection of despair ('Fennimore, Fennimore, 'tis him you love') in F major before the end. At the conclusion of the first two 'pictures', Delius marked his

Example 11.1d. *Fennimore and Gerda*, the passion of Fennimore and Erik.

score with 'Ende des ersten Aktes. Pause 5 Minuten'.[23] There was undoubtedly a practical reason for this; time was required for a major change of scene. Nevertheless, Delius did not use the vehicle of different acts to define the remaining stages of his opera (i.e. there is no Act II or Act III) or group the remaining nine 'pictures'. Curiously Delius made no attempt to alter this which suggests that he wanted the first two 'pictures' to remain distinct and discrete from the rest of the opera – as if they were a prologue. An examination of the dramatic and tonal behaviour of later parts of the score suggests that this was precisely how he wanted the opening of his work to function.

Another reason for the marked distinction of the first two pictures from the rest of the opera is that the third 'picture' takes place three years later when Fennimore and Erik have moved to their new home on the Mariagerfjord; it is summertime. This third 'picture' and those that follow attempt to demonstrate Delius's intention to make the libretto and action as concise as possible in scenes which are minutes long in their contribution to the drama and which are organised by the larger umbrella of the passing seasons. Moreover, those seminal thematic fragments (see Examples 11.1a, 11.1b, 11.1c and 11.1d) form the basis of Delius's musical development as the narrative unfolds. At the outset of the third 'picture', C major persists, but its fervent edge has dissipated as can be heard in the more pervasive chromaticisms. Only with the prospect of Niels's visit does C major reassert itself in the form of Erik's revitalisation (see Fig. 26), and with Niels's entrance the tonality continues to provide a

---

[23] It is worth noting that Delius's insistence on short intervals was part of his operatic strategy.

sense of stability. Yet, underlying Niels's robust exterior we hear the sounds of Erik and Fennimore's love music from the second 'picture', now more fragile in manner, which signals a marked decline in their affections and optimism. The fourth 'picture', which depicts Erik and Niels together, is dominated by Erik's declamatory monologue. From C minor, which closes the third 'picture' and opens the fourth, the musical landscape becomes much more diffuse. References to Fennimore (before Fig. 36) and Niels serve as happy memories of the past, but a fragmentation of the love music brings into focus the decline in Erik's marriage, and his despair is expressed by the introduction of a new leitmotiv (Example 11.1e) which, featuring the downbeat triplet as a seminal rhythmic figure, is developed throughout the scene. The slightly longer fifth 'picture' begins with a lament as Erik loses heart at ever finding inspiration, a state of mind conveyed in Wagnerian terms (Example 11.1f); but the body of the 'picture' is focused on the degradation of Erik's character in the form of a demonic Scherzo ushered in by the tritone of the timpani. Although the Scherzo is effectively a through-composed, tonally fluid development in which fragments of the familiar leitmotivs come and go, there are significant passing moments such as the ironic toast to Erik by his 'boon companions' ('We'll drink a toast to the great painter') in C major, and when Fennimore begs Erik to consider his friendship with Niels (see Fig. 51 to Fig. 52), the material significantly turns to F major. At the centre of the Scherzo, as Erik recklessly leaves with his companions, it is the tragedy of Fennimore's despair which recalls the Wagnerian music at the beginning of the 'picture' (see six bars before Fig. 53). It is at this point, with the resumption of the Scherzo, that Niels steps in, in defence of Erik's talent, and by degrees, as Niels himself attempts to bring stability to his dialogue with Fennimore, the tonality returns robustly to C major. Of thematic significance in this process, however, is the appearance of the downbeat triplet (Example 11.1g – see Fig. 60) which signals a new liaison between Fennimore and Niels. 'You'll be my friend, Niels?', asks Fennimore, to which Niels eagerly replies: 'I've always been your friend'.

Little more than a transition, the sixth 'picture' retains the tempo of the Scherzo, but the mood turns to one of foreboding as the continued fragmentation of the love motive of Fennimore and Erik (Fig. 62) conveys a sense of hopelessness. As Erik arrives home drunk, Fennimore ignores him, and while Erik's motive attempts to turn the tonality back towards C (five bars before Fig. 67), the sense of revulsion gives way instead to A major, the key which concluded Erik's despondent dialogue with Niels at the end of the fourth 'picture'.

After a stipulated interval of three minutes (clearly required for the scene change), the season shifts from summer to autumn for the seventh 'picture'.

Example 11.1e. *Fennimore and Gerda*, Erik's despair.

Example 11.1f. *Fennimore and Gerda*, Erik's darkness.

The languorous preludial material, essentially in A minor (though towards the conclusion, Delius once again pulls the tonality back to C), owes much to the wistful lyricism of the first interlude of *Brigg Fair*. The first part of the 'picture', which opens in A minor, is an evocation of autumn emphasised by Delius's imagery of chromatically falling lines (one that looks forward to the opening movement of *North Country Sketches*). There is a solemn atmosphere as Fennimore and Niels exchange comments about nature's changing apparel, but, critically, a turn towards the symbolic stability of C major occurs when Niels grasps Fennimore's hand (two bars before Fig. 72) and, to use Delius's stage description, 'kisses her passionately'. Yet Fennimore is deeply confused: while wishing on the one hand to accept Niels's advances, she still feels a close bond and loyalty to her aberrant husband. References to the triplet leitmotiv hover in the background. Fennimore nevertheless realises that she cannot live without Niels and her new openness is harnessed to the reprise of the love music of the second 'picture'. C major, and the subdominant colouring of Niels's key of F major, spaciously support their embrace and the music reaches a new height of

Example 11.1g. *Fennimore and Gerda*, the love of Fennimore and Niels.

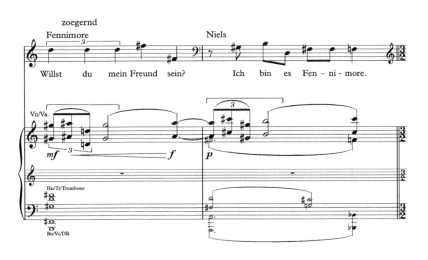

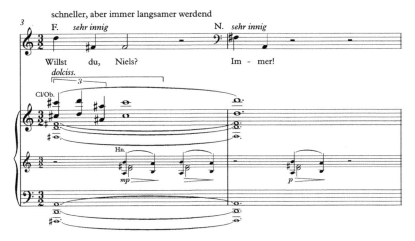

rapture (one to rival the high points of Vreli and Sali in *A Village Romeo and Juliet*). Yet the very climax of their dialogue is not to affirm C major as might have been expected. Instead, Delius very deliberately diverts the tonality away towards A major. This change of tonal direction cleverly gives the impression of inflaming their mutual passion and their adoring exchanges ('Beloved, Thine only, ever thine!'), but the cadence into A (as the curtain falls) signals a sense of pending tragedy as we are reminded in the figurations of the wind and harp of Fennimore's former love for Erik (three bars after Fig. 81).

After a further interval of three minutes, there is a change of scene to winter, and the bleaker eighth 'picture' opens with portentous sequential statements of Fennimore's leitmotiv, now considerably transformed to depict a highly conflicted woman. The 'picture' itself is a dramatic monologue for Fennimore. Initially, the scene is one of an expectant lover as she awaits the arrival of Niels (now freely acknowledged as her beloved). The inability of the music to settle tonally aptly reflects her restless demeanour, but it also provides apposite preparation for the terrible *anagnorisis* she is about to suffer as she receives the news of Erik's death in the telegram. This *peripeteia* unleashes a furious transformation in her behaviour as she becomes hysterical, haunted by her guilt, an emotion (Example 11.1h) which becomes increasingly and more violently persistent (see five bars before Fig. 95 and *passim*) as the scene runs its course. Indeed, by the end, the leitmotiv is subject to almost obsessive reiteration as Fennimore, in a state of profound agitation, not only renounces Niels but detests him for leading her on. Equally significant, too, is Delius's strategic use of A minor as the curtain falls at the end of the 'picture' (see Fig. 97), in which two citations of the leitmotiv initiate her meeting with Niels in the ninth 'picture'. The agitation of the eighth 'picture' continues in the ninth which proceeds without a break, but the musical preoccupation with the leitmotiv representing Fennimore and Niels's love is now combined with the persistent reference to Erik's despair (see Example 11.1e). As Niels attempts to reason with her, the guilt leitmotiv (by dint of its metrical augmentation) recurs with added venom. As Fennimore furiously orders him to leave ('Geh! Geh!' ['Go! Go!']), the dominant of C is announced (four bars before Fig. 104). This ominous moment makes way for a powerful orchestral postlude in C; it first depicts a forlorn Niels as he turns back towards the fjord before yielding to a funereal scene (in C minor) of the 'four dark figures ... bearing the body of Erik'. As Fennimore beholds this shocking scene, she

Example 11.1h. *Fennimore and Gerda*, Fennimore's guilt.

rushes up the steps of the verandah and collapses in the snow, accompanied by a final statement of the guilt leitmotiv for full orchestra in which a sense of malediction is powerfully stressed by the menacing C minor.

It was at this point that Delius originally envisaged the conclusion of the opera but was nonetheless concerned about the work's lack of resolution, not to mention its unrelenting reflection of Jacobsen's sense of fatalism. He therefore considered the addition of two more 'pictures' necessary not only to complete his dramaturgical adaptation but also to round off the *musical* argument.[24] The tenth and eleventh 'pictures' of the opera, bearing the title 'Gerda' (the only title he used for any of the pictures), provide a telling counterweight to the opening two scenes and Delius achieves this in several ways. The tenth 'picture', which takes up the narrative a further three years later, provides an image of the pastoral idyll. It is harvest time on Niels's estate and the evening brings a cessation of work. And this idyllic mindset reflects furthermore a healed man, full of memories and regrets, yet of an individual who, in spite of the trials and tribulations hurled at him, is not tainted by cynicism nor deterred by the possibility of finding love and contentment again. Delius's engagement with this psychological situation was profound. The opening transparent diatonicism of the orchestral prelude (among Delius's most searingly tender in its use of the solo oboe and divided strings) reinforces the pastoral representation (as does the distant sound of labourers in the fields with their 'la la' chorus), but its simplicity hides a phrase structure of some sophistication (ABACAA), one that also embodies yet another of Delius's variation series. This can be observed in the harmonic variety of each melodic repetition with its remarkable mixture of chromatic voice-leading and functional progressions. In addition, however, to the pastoral role of the prelude, the thematic material is imbued throughout by a diatonic transformation of Fennimore's leitmotiv in inversion (Example 11.1i), while the entire prelude is couched in F major, Niels's key, for whom the memory of Fennimore has now become a catharsis. This is indeed made clear in Niels's monologue, where, in acknowledging the sadness of his past life, he also recognises the joy of his homecoming, a desire craved at the beginning of the opera. Musical memories of Fennimore, as mentioned above, figure prominently, as does their former liaison, tinged with harmonic progressions of bitterness among the references to the triplet leitmotiv and to Erik's fecklessness. The recapitulation of these ideas, however, serves not

---

[24] Delius originally composed three additional 'pictures', but, as was his zeal for revision, the last two were elided (see *MC*, 107).

only as a useful means of musical reprise but also as a means of throwing into relief a climactic statement of the opening melody (in combination with the love music of Fennimore and Erik – see Example 11.1c), this time in C major; it also powerfully verifies that Niels himself has moved on emotionally ('I'm healed now'). Niels's new relationship with his old home is, moreover, confirmed by the response of the distant farm labourers whose wordless partsong adds a mystical dimension to the scene, though Delius's most poignant (and personal) touch is to provide one further variation (for strings only) of the opening melody as a nostalgic coda (a device he had used so effectively many years ago at the end of Act II of *Koanga*), back in F major.

The tenth 'picture' merges seamlessly into the eleventh, and from Niels's F major we shift to an unequivocal, serene C major. Slow moving in tempo, the idyllic prelude is no more than sixteen bars, but in that short period of extraordinary tranquillity, Delius is able to express, without words, Niels's innate sense of longing both in the memorable added major seventh sonority (a sound he must have gleaned from *On Hearing the First Cuckoo*) and in the plangent diatonic oboe solo. Here we are not only treated to an exquisite set of miniature harmonic variations (some of them subtly attenuated) but also to a microcosm of those two critical tonalities in the opera – C major and A minor.

The scene (as we learn from Delius's stage directions when the action begins) is spring – a (Nietzschean) time of renewal, and from a meditation of times past there is a regeneration of energy and movement in what is the longest 'picture' of the series. For this 'Epilogue', Delius chose a set piece, a sonata form, infused with exuberant dance (Table 11.1), a dramatic mechanism he had used before in the penultimate 'tableau' of *A Village Romeo and Juliet* (see Chapter 6). For the exposition of his sonata scheme, Delius uses the ensemble of Gerda and her sisters (who tease her about her feelings for Niels) and as C major yields to the dominant, G, they become more excited.

Example 11.1i. *Fennimore and Gerda,* transformation of Fennimore's theme.

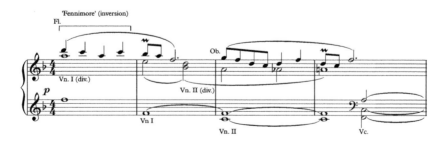

Table 11.1. *Fennimore and Gerda*, sonata structure of eleventh 'picture'.

Figure	Structural event	Key
	EXPOSITION	
118[+4]	First subject (Ingrid, Lila, Marit, Gerda); 'Humoresque' 4/4 and Waltz 3/4	C major
121[+5]	Second subject (they dance round Gerda)	G major
	DEVELOPMENT	
124[+1]	Slower. Niels and Gerda (love scene)	Fluid
	RECAPITULATION	
128[+4]	Reprise of prelude (love duet)	C major
131[+5]	Waltz (Gerda, Niels, Councillor, Ingrid, Lila, Marit)	C major
134[+4]	Postlude – reprise of preludial material	C major

In addition, the entire tissue of the music is imbued with a fluctuation of metres – 4/4 and 3/4 – as the dance shifts between the dotted rhythms of a 'Humoresque' and the invigorating lilt of the waltz. Just as in *A Village Romeo and Juliet*, Delius reserves the tender love encounter of Gerda and Niels for the fluid developmental phase of the movement. With a calming of the tempo, the leitmotiv of Niels's love for Fennimore recurs, but now marked 'dolce'. As their future together is resolved, a reprise of the preludial material (see Fig. 128[+4]) and their love duet mark a return to C major (see Fig. 130[-2]). This key, so central to the entire opera, is affirmed by the reoccurrence of the overjoyed female ensemble. As they return to the house, Niels and Gerda are left together on stage, their contentment underpinned by the wistful added-seventh sonorities from the opening of the 'picture' and by the fortifying C major chord which accentuates the opera's buoyant ending.

After completing the revision of his opera in 1913, Delius hoped that it would be performed in Cologne in 1914 with Gustav Brecher, the former celebrated Kappellmeister of the Hamburg Stadttheater (where he had conducted the premiere of Busoni's *Die Brautwahl*). Performances were planned for the autumn, and in July word came that a first performance was scheduled for 10 October. But, of course, the outbreak of war rendered this an impossibility and it was not until 21 October 1919, that the opera, revised in the meantime,[25] was finally performed under Brecher at the Frankfurt

---

[25] See *RT1*, 50.

Opernhaus.[26] Beecham, as mentioned above, conducted the 'Gerda' section at the Delius Festival in London on 24 October 1929, but never undertook the work in the opera house. After attending many of the rehearsals, Delius was present at the first night of the Frankfurt performances, but he never heard his last opera in England in its entirety. Indeed, only through the choral 'Intermezzo', sewn together by Fenby from the orchestral preludes to the tenth and eleventh 'pictures', has *Fennimore* remained an acknowledged work in Delius's output.

Performances of *Fennimore* have, it is true, proved a rarity. In *The Musical Times*, Heseltine wrote in praise of the work:

> "Fennimore and Gerda" ... is far more definite and compact in structure than "A Village Romeo and Juliet" ... Not only are the individual scenes more closely knit in the later opera, but there are greater firmness and coherence in the design of the whole work. Every "picture" is musical self-subsistent, generally built round an initial theme or rhythmic figure, and the logical development and flow of the music are never interrupted for the sake of thrusting the words into prominence.[27]

In truth, however, he was ambivalent about the work's success. He much admired the first nine scenes and wrote to the composer congratulating him 'on having made a big step forward towards the solution of the biggest problem connected with opera – that of fusing the demands of dramatic propriety and those of purely musical logic into a perfectly harmonious whole'.[28] Yet, three years later, in his book on Delius, he dismissed the last two 'pictures' of the work as a solecism:

> It is the disproportion and psychological falsity of the last section that jar. It is like a sugar-plum designed to take away the taste of the preceding tragedy, and one resents this, for the tragedy is convincingly complete in itself and, though it deals with but one episode, epitomizes the whole life of Niels Lyhne as Jacobsen conceived it. There is also a purely practical reason for the omission of the last two pictures. The Gerda episode occupies but one-fifth of the whole work; but that fifth is just long enough

---

[26] See letter from Delius to Hertzka, 5 May 1913, *MC*, 111.

[27] Heseltine, P., 'Delius's New Opera', *The Musical Times*, Vol. 61 No. 926 (April 1920), 238.

[28] Letter from Heseltine to Delius, 7 December 1919, *FDPW*, 302.

to make a programme containing *Fennimore and Gerda* as well as another opera too long, while *Fennimore and Gerda* alone does not constitute what the Germans call an *abendfüllendes Werk*. This fact alone has undoubtedly hindered the performance of the work at several German opera-houses which would otherwise have been glad to take it into their repertory.[29]

Heseltine undoubtedly raised the perennial problem with so much of Delius's operatic output (save perhaps *Koanga*) in that, with his artistic insistence on conciseness and shorter length, producers were always confronted with the problem of how to create a full evening's entertainment, not to mention the considerable orchestral resources the composer always required. Without 'Gerda', *Fennimore* would have been little more than a one-act opera of an hour's duration; with the addition of the last two 'pictures', the awkwardness of the work's duration became more acute. Moreover, we also know that Delius had very fixed and unwavering notions of the opera's production:

> All sets to be produced new according to drawings prepared in Denmark, which I shall provide myself. 8 different sets are required for the 11 scenes in the work, of which 2 represent rooms, the others landscape views which are, however, quite simple and dispense with large scale stage construction because for the most part, they consist of large painted views. I absolutely will not have my work produced with the usual horrendous and tasteless decoration which does not suit my music at all.[30]

The question of staging is a particularly fascinating aspect of Delius's operas as a whole. Throughout this analytical study much has been ascribed to the transcendent 'internalisation' of *Tristan*, *The Ring* and *Parsifal* and the way in which the agency of the orchestra has played a central part, especially in extended passages without the singers. A further contributory factor to the composer's vivid pictorial conceptulisation of his operatic works, however, might also have been his highly individual sensitivity to the phenomenon of staging, lighting techniques and the designs of the *mise-en-scènes*. Delius was, after all, married to an artist, and in the early days at Grez he had been surrounded by progressive painters and visual artists. Furthermore, during his Parisian years he had lived through a period of significant theatrical experiment with Adolphe Appia's innovative lighting and décor of Wagner's

---

[29] *PH*, 100.

[30] Letter from Delius to Hertzka, 5 May 1913, *MC*, 111.

operas (as articulated in *La mise en scéne du théâtre Wagnerien* of 1895 and *Musique et mise en scene* of 1897). A clue to the significance of this element in the creation of Delius's operatic 'musical vision' is in the elaborate stage directions which appear in his libretti and especially those which present serious practical challenges towards their visual and spatial realisation. The opening of the second 'picture' of *Fennimore* (not least after the relatively short expanse of the 'first' picture) presents such a challenge, as does the 'ninth' picture with the return of Erik's body, Fennimore's rejection of Niels and her collapse in the snow. The same could also be said for the realisation of Act II of *The Magic Fountain* where Watawa and Solano 'are for some time seen picking their way through the thick bush, then they disappear and night gradually falls over the scene'. And in *A Village Romeo and Juliet* the problem of how to stage the bargemen and the suicide of Sali and Vreli was one of the main reasons why Delius felt that his fourth opera had never received a sympathetic stage interpretation. Is it that in some way his imagination was anticipating the new art of montage and silent film? What is evident, however, is that by the middle of the First World War, Delius, aware of the difficulties of realising his operatic conceptions, showed himself to be well disposed to Heseltine's more abstract concept of staging *A Village Romeo and Juliet*. 'I propose to have no scenery', Heseltine stipulated, '– i.e. no set pieces: only plain curtains – possibly a suggestive back-cloth or two – nothing more – costumes of extreme simplicity. Perhaps, in the old Chinese fashion, one might have the stage-directions read out or thrown upon a screen before the commencement of each scene. In any case, the stage must be free from disturbing elements – the curtains or back-cloth beautiful but entirely free from any elaboration'.[31] To this Delius replied positively: 'I entirely agree that realism on the stage is nonsense & that all the scenery necessary is an "impressionistic" painted curtain at the back with the fewest accessories possible – Even furniture ought mostly to be painted – but one requires a real artist to have thoroughly understood the Drama & then to paint the scene after his own conception. In Germany this has been already tried with success'.[32] Beecham, who later saw this correspondence,[33] admitted his surprise at the highly reductive attitude that Delius had adopted:

> I can only remark that it is diametrically opposed to everything that [Delius] had ever said to me about the scenic side of his own operas. When

[31] *FDPW*, 225.

[32] *FDPW*, 230.

[33] *TB*, 177–8.

I revived *A Village Romeo and Juliet* in 1920, several letters passed between us touching the whole plan of production, and I received many sketches of scenery designed by Jelka herself. In the case of *Fennimore and Gerda* there are the most detailed directions throughout the score, indicating the kind of décor essential for each of the many scenes, some of which would suffer severely from the lack of appropriate or picturesque background.[34]

Besides offering these comments on the production and staging of *Fennimore and Gerda*, Beecham had numerous misgivings about another inherent difficulty of Delius's final opera – the attractiveness of the story and its unappealing *dramatis personae*. Unsympathetic characters, he believed, were hardly likely to draw enthusiastic audiences; nor was their introspective, psychologically driven dialogue. An experienced operatic conductor, accustomed to established conventions of memorable lyrical melody, well-drawn characters and clearly conceived libretti, Beecham considered the conflicted neurotic figure of Fennimore to require an actress of such accomplishment (which, he believed, was lacking in the operatic world of that time) in order to retain dramatic interest. Otherwise, he feared, the pessimistic effect of the opera, for all its grim Scandinavian realism, would quickly founder.[35] In contradistinction to Heseltine's viewpoint, Beecham found in 'Gerda' the only music of real dramatic significance, which is no doubt why it was programmed for the Delius Festival in 1929. Delius, on the other hand, believed his opera to be the most perfect fulfilment of his musico-dramatic adventures. As he told Hertzka: 'I consider this stage work the most complete that I have yet written and it should only appear under the most favourable conditions'.[36] In addition, he was convinced that the addition of the 'Gerda' episode had 'rendered it considerably more effective from a scenic standpoint',[37] and that had 'benefited greatly from this ending'.[38] To give Beecham credit, in spite of his lack of sympathy with *Fennimore*, he was much more willing than Heseltine to acknowledge the individuality of Delius's latest dramatic foray and 'that it might be unwise to assume that the last word has been said and that the time has come to write it off as an unskilful

---

[34] *TB*, 178.

[35] *TB*, 164–5.

[36] Letter from Delius to Hertzka, 9 February 1913, *MC*, 106.

[37] Ibid.

[38] Letter from Delius to Hertzka, 17 February 1913, *MC*, 107.

experiment'.[39] Yet, even though he suggested that a return to Jacobsen's original Danish text might provide a new insight, he remained circumspect in the light of Delius's austerity towards music and drama that such a method '[might] not have been carried a step too far'.[40] Jefferson similarly believed that the 'difficulties involved in staging and playing the opera [had] helped to consign it to near oblivion'.[41]

The subtitle of *Fennimore and Gerda*, 'Two Episodes from Jens Peter Jacobsen's Niels Lyhne', was, on Delius's part, a deliberate attempt to expunge the generic notion of opera. As he told Hertzka, 'I see from the choral parts that you entitle Fennimore 'opera'. The word 'opera' is inappropriate'.[42] This comment sheds significant light on Delius's own hopes for *Fennimore* as a new genre, aspirations which were essentially at odds with both Heseltine's and Beecham's understanding of the work. Though intended as individual 'scenes', Delius's 'pictures' were intended to be more than the traditional dramaturgical building blocks of conventional operatic fare. Governed by the larger scheme of changing seasons – an analogy of Niels Lyhne's own emotional cycle – the effect of each 'picture' was, as Boyle has suggested, to provide a miniature tone poem,[43] a realist commentary on each varying mood and human nuance. And the sum of these individual tone poems gave rise to a larger symphonic canvas, a musical *Gestalt* where orchestra, soloists and chorus participate as equal partners. It is, however, particularly on a *musical* level that *Fennimore* functions as, arguably, the most sophisticated of Delius's dramatic works. Since the composition of *Irmelin*, where it was evident that certain choices of keys played an important part in Delius's formal thinking, and important symbolic tonalities in Wagner's music dramas (such as D flat major and B major) were also appropriated for similar effect, it is evident that Delius was very much aware of the usefulness of individual keys to tighten the larger sense of dramatic structure. In *Fennimore* his use of tonality is more overt than in any of his other dramas. Indeed, it would be no exaggeration to describe the broader canvas as being *about* C, a tonal thread which underpins the central idea of the opera as a complex love story. It is C major that emerges in the love scene between Fennimore and Erik, and, after Erik's inspiration has withered, re-emerges with Niel's visit to the beleaguered couple. References

[39] *TB*, 165.

[40] Ibid.

[41] *AJ*, 64.

[42] Letter from Delius to Hertzka, 26 December 1913, *MC*, 125.

[43] *DN*, 236.

to C also figure prominently in the love between Fennimore and Niels, and it is to C *minor* that the Fennimore episode ends so darkly at the end of the ninth 'picture'. Yet the centrality of C also clearly spawned a second stratum of tonal symbolism, for Niels's own key of F major is also demonstrably present at important junctures of the drama (such as at the beginning, his later infatuation with Fennimore, and his healing in the tenth 'picture') and A major/minor features very much as a symbol of moral turpitude in the later scenes (as Fennimore is tortured by her faithlessness towards Erik). Given this perspective, Delius clearly decided that he required an affirmation of C major at the end of the opera which the somewhat precipitate (and rather melodramatic) C minor ending of the Fennimore episode could not conclusively provide. In so doing, Delius's creation of the two final 'pictures', strongly orientated around C, produced a telling symmetry with the two opening and well delineated scenes, both of which, dramatically speaking, share contrasting love scenes. One also senses, moreover, that in the last 'picture', Delius's 'set piece' in C major was intended to function very much as a 'finale', a rhetorical device which suggests that Delius had not quite, after all, abandoned those conventions of opera which he claimed to have rebuffed.

A RETURN TO JACOBSEN'S POETRY: *AN ARABESQUE*

While Delius was contemplating revisions of *Fennimore and Gerda*, his mind was also on the matter of setting Jacobsen's most admired poem, 'En Arabesk', in its German translation (made from the Danish by Jelka), choosing that language in part because of its German publisher but also because there was no market for the Danish language.[44] Although appreciating Delius's point, Beecham maintained, however, that, owing to the unsatisfactory nature of both the German and English translations, the work was best performed in Danish.[45] It was a view put into practice in 1955 when Beecham recorded it with Einar Nørby, the Danish bass-baritone. 'The effect', Beecham observed, '[was] surprising and beautiful'.[46] Although *An Arabesque* was completed in the autumn of 1911, Delius waited patiently for a first performance of the work in Vienna in November 1913. Having travelled to Austria to hear it,

---

[44] See letter from Delius to Ernest Newman, 19 August 1929, *DLL2*, 353. Heseltine provided an English translation.

[45] *TB*, 167.

[46] Ibid., 168n.

his hopes were subsequently dashed on account of poor, unusable orchestral materials.[47] In the end it became one of several works which had to await the end of the war before they were performed. After some revision during the war (Beecham recalled work on it when Delius was staying at his cottage in Watford),[48] it was finally first given in Newport Central Hall on 28 May 1920 where it was conducted by Arthur Sims with the Welsh Musical Festival Choral Society, the London Symphony Orchestra and the English operatic baritone Percy Heming. Delius was unable to be there and did not finally hear the work until it was performed under Beecham at the Delius Festival in London in 1929. It has remained one of his most neglected vocal works due in part to its relative brevity (about twelve minutes in duration) and the considerable orchestral resources it demands (besides the triple wind, it requires a bass clarinet, bass oboe, sarrusophone and celesta).

Jacobsen's poetry, with its powerful sense of psychological introspection, romantic symbolism and beguiling sensuality held Delius's attention much as the same sensual, symbolist verse of Verlaine had drawn him back to solo song. The theme of Jacobsen's poem has much in common with the 'Lorelei' legend made popular by Brentano and Heine in the early nineteenth century, and Keats's famous ballad 'La belle dame sans merci'. In 'Lorelei' an enchanted female bewitches unsuspecting men to their death; in Keats's verses a knight who, having been lured to the 'Elfin grot' by a temptress, only to see others 'death pale' who hold her in thrall, awoke to find himself on a cold hillside, alone and terrified. White has identified the connection of 'La belle dame' with Jacobsen's atmospheric poem.[49] 'Knowst thou Pan?', asks the disquieted individual at the beginning of the poem. Wandering in gloomy forests it is not, however, the traditional Pan he has encountered, but the 'Pan of Love', one beheld through a 'wondrous herb'. Drugged and spellbound (in the manner of Tennyson's 'Lotos-Eaters'), he has beheld his beloved. Yet this state of intoxication is a disturbing one (as it is in Keats's ballad), for this mesmerising maiden brings death in her dazzling chalice of poison from which men hasten to their doom. Fortunately for the knight in Keats's verse, he survives his ordeal. In Jacobsen's macabre psychological rumination, the fate of our protagonist is sealed in the sinister reiteration of the poem's ominous opening question.

---

[47] Letter from Delius to Jelka, 25 November 1913, *DLL2*, 114.

[48] *MC*, 142.

[49] White, J., 'Delius and La Belle Dame Sans Merci: The Hidden Meanings of *An Arabesque*', *DSJ* No. 120 (Spring 1997), 15–17.

The successful model of *Sea Drift*, with its solo baritone (as narrator and protagonist), 'commenting' chorus and orchestra, was also one ideally suited to *An Arabesque*. The recurrence of the sea as a powerful symbol in Whitman's poem also provided Delius with his formal rationale of a 'rondo', and many of the intervening choral episodes took the shape of partsongs, a genre for which, as we know, Delius felt great kinship. Jacobsen's poem, however, posed different problems. Much shorter, and without the reflective episodes ideally appropriate to chorus, a through-composed structure proved much more apposite for the constantly changing moods of each of Jacobsen's five stanzas. Mitchell has remarked, 'it is not … a true choral work but a lyric piece for baritone and orchestra with choral intrusions'.[50] Indeed, one might go further and describe the work as an operatic solo 'scena' with the unusual addition of a chorus.

Essential to the form of *An Arabesque* is the B major frame which is linked with the unique, lugubrious material for divided strings and which articulates both the seminal questioning at the beginning and end of the poem and the sense of uneasiness. The intricacy of Delius's thematic lines with their lower and upper chromatic appoggiaturas not only gives the music its sinister quality but also seems to negate any sense of tonal centre, an impression the composer evidently wished to convey in the light of Jacobsen's agitated text. The rest of the structure of *An Arabesque* is largely determined by the poetic form. The initial statement of B major presents two principal, contrasting thematic ideas – the first, a menacing, intimidating line low in the tessituras of the violas and cellos (Example 11.2a), the second, a more voluptuous outpouring in the richly divided strings (Example 11.2b), representative of

Example 11.2a. *An Arabesque*, opening gesture for lower strings.

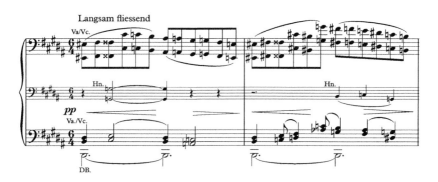

50 Mitchell, D., 'Delius: The Choral Music', *Tempo*, No. 26 (Winter 1952–1953), 12.

Example 11.2b. *An Arabesque*, divided strings and wind, Pan's theme.

Pan, the god of love. In making his first apprehensive entry ('Irrtest du je in dunkeln Wäldern, kennst du Pan?'), the solo baritone embarks from the dominant, F sharp minor (Fig. 1^{-3}), before closing out the first eight lines on the dominant of A. The second stanza, in which 'the beloved' is introduced for the first time, is adorned with some of Delius's most ornamental scoring. The extensive flute solo, embellished with harp, celesta and divided strings, affords a delicate, hypnotic image of Pan, one that Delius may well have drawn from his admiration for Debussy's *L'après-midi d'un faune*.[51] Throughout this paragraph, which is heavily adorned with decorative chromatic filigree, much of the sensuous luxuriance is associated with whole-tone parallelisms, shifting unrelated triads and climactic 'sound moments', though, amid the dense harmonic texture, A major remains in control of the tonal structure. The third stanza, the longest of the poem, is shared between the chorus and the soloist and commences with a fulsome statement of Pan's theme in the upper strings (see Example 11.2b), adorned by 'pipe' impressions in the wind. The chorus's physical description of the beloved retains a connection with the second stanza in its retention of A major which is more fully stated with the emergence of an important thematic fragment ('die kalten marmorweissen Hände ruhten in ihrem Schoss' – Example 11.2c). This material is then extended and developed towards the half close on the dominant of A ('Auf das taufeuchte Gras') which marks the end of the first important choral statement. The impression of this half cadence is one of gentle benevolence,

---

[51] See *AH*, 113.

but, as the second part of the stanza unfolds, which continues the process of development, the extreme cold of the beloved's gaze is portrayed in the greater dissonance of the choral gestures ('kalt und klar') and the high unison lines, while the orchestra punctuates the thematic reiterations with climactic triplets on the downbeat ('Jubel in ihrem Schmerz') as if to portray the sense of stabbing pain in her vanquishing glare. At the end of the stanza, Delius also leaves us in no doubt as to her capacity to spellbind all who look into her gaze with a beguiling lull in C major ('nur zwei wagten ihr zu trotzen ihre eigenen

Example 11.2c. *An Arabesque*, 'Die kalten marmorweissen Hände ruhten in ihrem Schoss'.

Example 11.2d. *An Arabesque*, Pan's spellbinding gaze.

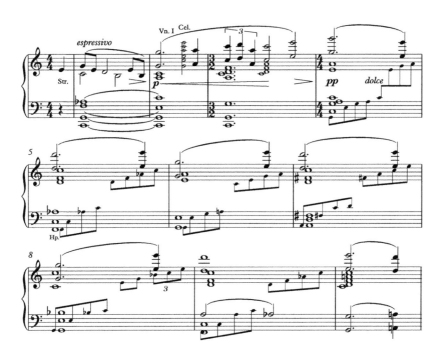

Augen') together with the composer's characteristic added-sixth melodic figurations (Example 11.2d).

The declamatory opening of the fourth stanza propels us towards the climax of the work in which our spellbound onlooker, hopelessly in thrall, observes the poisonous chalice and death which it brings to those irrevocably drugged by her allure ('und ihm der nun kniet zu ihren Füssen'), an event which summons a full-bodied recapitulation of Pan's theme (see Example 11.2b). As if to suggest that our onlooker, like other unfortunate victims, has passed the point of no return, Delius makes a significant final reference to A major, thereby reminding us of the intoxication associated with that key in the second and third stanzas; moreover, at the same time he skilfully connects the thematic material with that of the C major 'spell' at the close of the third stanza. This also coincides, adroitly, with the reiteration of text from the beginning of the third stanza ('Sie war wie Jasmins süssduftender Schnee') by the chorus. This confluence of thematic, textual and tonal components does not, however, mark the end of the fourth stanza, for, at this juncture, the closing lines of the baritone's declamation provide a conduit to the reassertion of B major. With this tonal recurrence, Delius took the first line of the last stanza, sung by the soloist and chorus ('Alles vorbei') to complete his musical paragraph, allying it subtly with a reprise of the 'spell' music. Such was the dramatic importance of this moment that Delius marked the final reiteration for alto and basses 'wie ein Hauch' ('with a sigh'), a complex gesture full of longing, regret and anguish at the hapless fate of those who gaze on Pan. The last stanza functions as a slow and contemplative coda in which the impressionist parallelisms of stanza two return, though now with a more dissonant piquancy in their evocation of the bleak heathland and the solitary thorn bush shedding its blood-reddened berries. This description is left to the baritone to complete the stark narrative in an eerie ambience of sustained string chords and arid pizzicato, while the prevailing sense of trepidation, also marked 'wie ein Hauch', is left to the baritone and chorus and to the restatement of the work's sinister opening theme (see Example 11.2a), its B major tonality now expressing an emotion quite at odds with its former Tristanesque associations.

PART III

FAME AND DECLINE

CHAPTER 12

Symphonic Poems (II):
Two Pieces for Small Orchestra, The Song of the High Hills, North Country Sketches (1911–1914)

TWO 'LYRIC PIECES' FOR SMALL ORCHESTRA: A TRIBUTE TO GRIEG

That Delius was still preoccupied with orchestral music and the symphonic poem is indicated by his return to the score *Lebenstanz,* or *Life's Dance* as he now preferred to call it.[1] After an airing under Enrico Fernandez Arbós in London in January 1908, Delius withheld the work. Still unpublished in 1912, it was revised with a new conclusion for publication by Tischer & Jagenberg of Cologne and first performed in this version (in the presence of the composer) by its dedicatee, Oskar Fried, in Berlin on 15 November 1912; the first English performance of the work was given by Balfour Gardiner at Queen's Hall on 25 February 1913. Delius always considered this symphonic poem to have been seminal to his development as a composer, and believed, as he explained to Tischer & Jagenberg, that it was among his finest orchestral essays, save for the frustration he had earlier felt for the conclusion: 'I consider the "Dance of Life" really to be my best orchestral work. I have had it in my file for some years now, as the ending did not quite satisfy me; but at last I have found what I was looking for & it is now a fully mature work'.[2] This and the revised version of *In a Summer Garden* rejuvenated his commitment to the genre of the symphonic poem and this was confirmed with the composition

---

[1] See *GB-Lbl* MS Mus 1745/1/17, ff. 1–44 in a copyist's hand which is signed and dated 1912 with English and Italian instrumentation rather than the French of the 1901 score (cf. *GB-Lbl* MS Mus 1745/1/16, ff. 1–28). On the title page (f. i) the German title 'Lebenstanz' is struck through in favour of 'Life's Dance'. Delius also used other titles such as *Dance of Life* and *Tanz des Lebens*.

[2] Letter from Delius to Tischer & Jagenberg, 20 March 1912, *DLL2*, 84.

of *Zwei Stücke für kleines Orchester*, written between 1911 and 1912 and also published by Tischer & Jagenberg in 1914. Until the composition of these two works for small orchestra, and since his accession to the Straussian paradigm of the 'high' romantic orchestral canvas, Delius had been unbending in his demands for the largest of instrumental forces and for the procurement of rare instruments such as the bass oboe and sarrusophone. No-one more aware of this was Grainger who, by 1912, was enjoying a good deal of success with the 'multi-scorings' of his folksong arrangements and other original pieces. 'I *do* wish', he wrote to Delius, 'you had in print some piece for not *too big* orchestra (4 horns, 2 trumpets, no strange woodwind, nor too many strings required) & not too wildly hard, that orchestras such as those at *Bournemouth Belfast*, etc could perform it, a piece that could be performed with an hours or ¾ hours rehearsal & then form part of general repetory [*sic*]. In all these towns they are conscious of your greatness & growing British fame & long to do something but are held back for want of instruments or fear of a difficultness beyond their powers'.[3] In his essay 'About Delius' for Hubert Foss's 'Additions, Annotations and Comments' in the revised edition of Heseltine's biography of Delius published in 1952, Grainger recollected that it had been around 1910 that Delius had complained that his orchestral works suffered from neglect in England. Grainger, a practical musician *par excellence*, had direct experience of good amateur orchestras all over England and recommended the remedy to 'write some short pieces for small orchestra … and English orchestras will devour them'.[4] Grainger also recalled that Delius's reply confirmed that he had already completed *On Hearing the First Cuckoo in Spring* [*Beim ersten Kuckucksruf im Frühling*] and a second piece, *Summer Night on the River* [*Sommernacht am Flusse*], was under way, though in fact the latter was finished in 1911, the former in 1912.[5] The *Zwei Stücke*, as *Stimmungsbilder* (symphonic poems, as advertised by the publishers) were therefore written very much as a response to the marketplace, a rare response for the composer in the domain of orchestral music, though one we have already witnessed in the area of solo song.

The pair was first heard at the Leipzig Gewandhaus on 23 October 1913 under Artur Nikisch. Having unsuccessfully courted Nikisch in Leipzig many

---

[3] Letter from Grainger to Delius, 5 March 1913, *DLL2*, 103.

[4] Heseltine, P. [Warlock, P.], *Frederick Delius*, reprinted with additions, annotations and comments by Hubert Foss (London: The Bodley Head, 1952), 172.

[5] The *Stichvorlag* of both pieces is now lost, although an undated draft of *On Hearing the First Cuckoo* survives (see *AU-Mgm* SM7, 72).

years earlier with his first major works, it must have been an experience of some satisfaction to Delius to hear his works in the location of his education. 'Nikisch played the 1st piece (Spring) much too slow – but very expressively the 2nd He played most beautifully – perfect – I asked him to play the 1st one faster at the Concert so I hope it will go off alright – Orchestra splendid'.[6] The first English performance took place under the aegis of the Philharmonic Society on 20 January 1914 and with the Dutch conductor, Willem Mengelberg.

Both pieces, profoundly connected with nature, are pastoral essays in compound time. *On Hearing the First Cuckoo*, in 6/4, is based on a similar pastoral miniature 'I Ola-Dalom, I Ola-Kjönn' ['In Ola valley, in Ola lake'] which Grieg published as No. 14 of his *19 Norwegischen Volkweisen* Op. 66. According to Grainger, it was he who played it to Delius when first they met in 1907,[7] although it is plausible that Delius had come across the piece much earlier during his friendship with Grieg during the mid 1890s. Paying no heed to the words and narrative of the original Norwegian, Grieg was more enamoured by the beauty of the folksong melody (as is evident from the 'Andante tranquillo' tempo marking), and Delius followed the example of his one-time mentor. Grieg's short essay in A major quotes the Norwegian melody three times, the first (in the top line) over a tonic–dominant drone, the second (in the tenor range) in F sharp minor, and the third (back in the top line) 'molto tranquillo' – in essence a diminutive, through-composed variation form. The melody itself had points of interest. Its diatonic simplicity had potential for harmonic variegation, and its phraseological organisation, 2 + 2 + 2 + 2 (Example 12.1a), also expounded an inbuilt structure of ABCB. And besides the bucolic drones, Grieg's use of syncopation, notably during the harmonisation of the melody in F sharp minor, was also a feature Delius harnessed in his own interpretation.

The Norwegian folksong was undoubtedly the principal focus of *On Hearing the First Cuckoo* (in keeping with Delius's subtitle in the printed score 'Introducing a Norwegian Folksong'), so it might be convincingly argued that the landscape Delius had in mind was Norwegian and one that was intended to be a tribute to Grieg. Yet, the choice of something so emblematic as the cuckoo, *the* symbol of the arrival of spring, also surely tapped into the marketplace for which he was writing. Delius's cuckoo is English and looked to those numerous native literary and poetic references understood and loved through every age from 'Sumer is icumen in', Shakespeare, the Silver Poets, Tennyson

---

[6] Letter from Delius to Jelka, 22 October 1913, *DLL2*, 112.

[7] Heseltine, P. [Warlock, P.], *Frederick Delius*, 172.

Example 12.1a. *On Hearing the First Cuckoo in Spring*, melodic structure.

and Christina Rossetti. In consequence Delius's approach was to *expand* Grieg's concept of variation with four repetitions of the folksong, and with each repetition to vary the order and number of appearances of each two-bar phrase, each harmonised differently. To the outer extremities of this variation structure Delius added self-developing preludial and postludial material ('x'), essentially cast in G major, and interspersed the folksong occurrences with ritornello-like passages derived from the falling first phrase of the folksong (see Table 12.1) which often interacted with the appearance of the familiar cuckoo motive and the assimilation of Grieg's accompanying syncopated drone figure.

The result of Delius's variation design is one of a seamless lyrical utterance where the sense of continuity is skilfully maintained, as Grimley has demonstrated, by a complex interrelationship of thematic cells.[8] This is executed by deftly avoiding the platitude of the cadence (which always seems tantalisingly out of reach), and by the inclusion of unexpected modulations, in particular the central, joyous move to E major which dominates Variation 2. The recovery from this third-related tonality is nimbly managed as is the diversification of tonalities which conclude each variation. Delius's final climax, which occurs in the last ritornello, is a subtle piece of legerdemain. A reprise of 'B', supported by a falling sequence of syncopated drones, leads to a final climax of tonal synchrony between E major and G major (4 bars after Fig. 10). This lack of tonal closure is then left to the truncated recapitulation of the introduction (cf. b. 3) to establish G major, though the pause on the dominant of E, four bars before the end, provides us with a memory of the work's climactic ambivalence. These delicate, understated 'structural happenings' are quintessential to an understanding of *On Hearing the First Cuckoo in Spring* and its elusive simplicity. Germane to the work's numinous signature, however, is its unresolved subdominant seventh which, judging by

8 DG, 24–7.

Table 12.1. *On Hearing the First Cuckoo in Spring*, structure of variations.

Section	Key	Comments
Introduction	G major	Preludial material 'x'
Folksong (Variation 1)	G major,	A (G major) + A (D major) +
	D major,	C (D major) + B (F♯ minor) +
	F♯ minor	B (F♯ minor)
Transition/ritornello	Fluid	Cuckoo
Folksong (Variation 2)	E major,	A (E major) + A (E major) +
	C♯ minor	C (E major) + B (C♯ minor)
Transition/ritornello	Fluid	Cuckoo
Folksong (Variation 3)	E major,	A (E major) + A (D major) +
	D major,	C (D major) + B (B minor)
	B minor	
Transition/ritornello	Fluid	Cuckoo
Folksong (Variation 4)	E minor,	A (E minor) + B (G major) +
	G major	C (E minor) + B (V of E?)
Transition/ritornello	Fluid	Cuckoo, climax with B (G major/V of E)
Coda	G major	Recapitulation of preludial material 'x'

the surviving manuscript materials, was originally more extensive in length.[9] Impeccably spaced for divided strings, this utterly memorable, perfumed sonority comes as a new and fresh enrichment to the composer's glossary of 'sound moments'. It is perhaps this deeply poetic gesture which gives meaning to Grainger's later remark when comparing Grieg's *Skizze* with Delius's amplification: 'while Grieg's is concentrated, pristine, miniature, and drastic, Delius' has the opulent richness of an almost over-ripe fruit and the luxurious long decline of a sunset'.[10]

Summer Night on the River, a nocturnal pastoral, might best be described as a binary 'Introduction and Song', a structural formula he would fall back on again for the later *Air and Dance* for string orchestra and *Caprice and Elegy* for cello and orchestra. Twenty-four bars of evocative music, somewhat redolent of the nature music in *In a Summer Garden*, constitute a preludial section, centred around A major, supported by extended pedal points. As Hutchings put it: 'harmony and texture are exquisitely nebulous, so that we are aware of the river

---

[9] See *GB-Lbl* MS Mus 1745/2/9, ff. 21–2. The process of reduction of this material can also be seen in the surviving sketch in *AU-Mgm*.

[10] Warlock, P. [Heseltine, P.], *Frederick Delius*, 173.

mist, "the unforgettable, unforgotten river smell", the rocking of a small craft, even the midges and scarcely audible noises of the warm night'.[11] It could be the river at the foot of Delius's garden at Grez, or, alternatively, a tropical, humid memory of the St Johns River in Florida. The parallel fourths of the opening 12/8, though more sensuous in their harmonic vocabulary, recall the same mechanisms of the entr'actes shared by *The Magic Fountain* and *Koanga* (both with strong American associations), though the highly chromatic 9/8 and 6/8 section which follows looks forward to the bleaker sounds of the first of *North Country Sketches* in its use of descending chromatic parallelisms. The 'Song' element of this exquisite miniature is taken up with variants of a rhapsodic melody (Example 12.1b) on solo strings, the timbres of which, in this section of the symphonic poem, seem more suggestive of an intimate chamber music. Delius also brings adroit control to the tonal design which evinces an arch scheme. After the 'introduction', based in A major, the 'song' begins in E major, before shifting climactically to C major (though the dynamic of the climax only once reaches a volume of 'f' in a piece essentially conceived around the hushed scale of 'p' to 'pppp') and this tonality carries us into the coda (in which Delius marked with some characteristic precision: 'The melody becoming softer and softer as if dying away in the distance') before A major is reasserted with one more curtailed version of the melody on a solo violin. At this juncture, the delicacy of Delius's scoring, with its divided string parts, solo trills, bowed and pizzicato textures, and the interjection of wind chords amounts to some of the most evocative sounds of nature he ever produced.

There can be little doubt that Delius's decision to produce the *Zwei Stücke* (which he dedicated to Gardiner) was a wise and practical one. With much reduced scoring for double wind, two horns and strings (*On Hearing the First Cuckoo* only uses a single oboe and flute), these pieces were immensely accessible to competent amateur orchestras, and Delius clearly gave considerable thought to the works' technical exigencies. Both are set at a leisurely tempo, neither requires excessive facility at the higher range of the instruments, and there is no rapid passagework or intricate fingerwork for either strings or wind. Of the two, *Summer Night on the River* makes more demands in terms of intonation and balance (largely because of its chamber music orchestration), and much of the solo work for wind and strings is exposed. Yet, at the same time, Delius was able to leave his hallmark in terms of the colourful scoring and the subtly unconventional structures he was always wont to create. In this sense there was still no concession and, to an

---

[11] *AH*, 86.

Example 12.1b. *Summer Night on the River*, rhapsodic melody.

audience, the simplicity in no way detracted from the quality of the musical experience. We can also see that Delius, himself a former string player, had thought sympathetically about his amateur players, for, especially in *On Hearing the First Cuckoo*, the idiomatic choice of key (G major – especially for strings), the restricted tessitura of string writing rarely straying beyond second position, and the ease of double stopping, much of it on open strings (*viz.* the opening for cellos and b. 5 for violas) were easily manageable. It was perhaps for this reason, and its more appealing melodic material, that *On Hearing the First Cuckoo* enjoyed a greater popularity than its nocturnal counterpart. Elgar, for one, much admired the piece and his admiration undoubtedly sprang from his own experiences as an amateur player during the 1880s and 1890s. He exhorted Delius to write more in this practical vein:

> I wish you would think out (I tremble in making any suggestion) some small composition suitable, as regards difficulty for small orchestras. Your "Cuckoo in Spring" is naturally very much loved and is within the capacity of some of the smaller organisations – we did it in Worcester which, apart from the festival, boasts of no great equipment. I want three movements – any poetic basis you like? Fontain[e]bleau – Grez – your own surroundings – you cannot help being a poet in sound and I say no more on this side of the matter. Something, or things, such as I have had the temerity to name, would bring your wonderful art among the devoted people who mean (and do) well in small things and cannot aspire to perform your large works: do not be angry![12]

Later, in 1930, when these miniatures had become an established part of the repertoire, it was no accident that Oxford University Press, a relatively new

---

[12] Letter from Elgar to Delius, *DLL2*, 424–5.

music publisher under the guiding hand of Hubert Foss, was keen to build up its 'democratic' strand in its 'Oxford Orchestral Series' where a large amount of repertoire of moderate difficulty, was arranged for amateur, school and college orchestras. By dint of the circumstances which brought Delius's *Zwei Stücke* to life, their place in the OUP catalogue therefore seemed entirely appropriate and ideal.

THE SONG OF THE HIGH HILLS: A RETURN TO THE EPIC

If we consider Grainger to have been an essential catalyst in the creation of the *Zwei Stücke*, the most diminutive of Delius's symphonic poems, then we should probably also credit the Australian with the largest of his orchestral works – almost half an hour in length – in a single movement. 'In a similar receptive (rather than originative) vein did Delius conceive his transcendental *The Song of the High Hills*, for all his 17 [*sic*] mountaineering trips to Norway it did not occur to him to write a work about the hills until he had heard my two *Hill-Songs*, the first written in 1901–1902, the second 1906–1907'.[13] As was the case with *Green Bushes*, Delius presumably saw these works when he and Grainger first met in 1907, and after the second *Hill-Song* had been completed. This latter work must have impressed Delius considerably since it is quoted in the concluding bars of *The Song of the High Hills*.[14] Grainger's two pieces are notable for other important features: the *Hill-Song No. 1*, at least in its original wind scoring, looks to the 'bagpipe' ethos of northern pipe music and its polyphonic, modernist harmony, while the *Hill-Song No. 2*, albeit drawn in part from its predecessor, trials a new concept of soloistic orchestration which anticipates the arrival of Schoenberg's *Chamber Symphony*. Grainger's austere essays (among his most challenging extended structures) might seem a world away from the vast opulence of Delius's orchestra which, in marked contradistinction to the *Zwei Stücke*, returns to the even larger, more sumptuous Strauss-inspired instrumentation of his earlier symphonic poems with its lavish string section, large woodwind, six horns, three trumpets, two harps, four timpani with three players (to enable harmonic interaction), celesta, glockenspiel, cymbals, bass drum and wordless chorus. Yet Delius's use of woodwind, especially the double reeds of oboe, cor anglais and

---

[13]   Warlock, P. [Heseltine, P.], *Frederick Delius*, 172–3.

[14]   This point is also mentioned in *DG*.

bassoons in the 'hill song' has a strong reminiscence of Grainger's wind sound (in works such as *Walking Tune* of 1905), and the modal elements (with which we are already familiar from *Brigg Fair*) have much in common with the both Grieg's and Grainger's delight in folksong and folksong arrangement. The notion of a 'Hill Song' remained uppermost in Delius's mind, since we can observe from the surviving manuscript sketches that his work revolved around the idea and mystical role of the wordless chorus as the principal focus.[15] This was Delius's 'Song' of the high hills and for its true realisation we return to the familiar *topos* of the 'unobtainable' distant choir symbolised by the composer's much-favoured eight-part song texture. Indeed, so prominent and significant is the role of the chorus in *The Song of the High Hills* that Delius consistently referred to it as a *choral* work.[16]

There are in fact numerous features which *The Song of the High Hills* shares with *Appalachia*. Both use the chorus as a focal and climactic part of the work, and both seek to incorporate the wordless choral element as an appendage of the orchestra. In the latter sense, however, *Appalachia* (experimental as it is) is less bold than the epic pages of his new elemental canvas. What is more, the chorus of *Appalachia* is deployed in a rather different, end-weighted manner where, as has already been mentioned, the work concludes with a dramatic 'scena'. In *The Song of the High Hills*, the chorus, as a much more intrinsic part of the *instrumental* conception of the work, plays a more integrated role in Delius's modified ternary thinking.

Hopes to perform *The Song of the High Hills* before the war came to nothing, as did others under Grainger in America during the war years. Ultimately it had to wait almost a decade until Albert Coates conducted it at Queen's Hall for the Royal Philharmonic Society on 26 February 1920. Of Coates's interpretations, Delius was never entirely confident. As he remarked to C. W. Orr, 'Coates evidently did not quite know what to do with my music – It was unfamiliar to him & I am afraid he had not occupied himself sufficiently with the score'.[17] He was, however, much happier with the performance in which the choral part was sung by Charles Kennedy Scott's

---

[15] See *GB-Lbl* MS Mus 1745/2/13/5 for sketches and drafts in which the choral part of the figures conspicuously. This is also the case with the one page of a draft sketch in *AU-Mgm* MG/DELI-27-2.

[16] See letter from Delius to Heseltine, 4 December 1911, *DLL2*, 66, and Heseltine's response of 28 February 1912, *DLL2*, 81. Also letter from Delius to Bantock, 24 April 1912, *DLL2*, 82.

[17] Letter from Delius to C. W. Orr, 16 May 1920, *DLL2*, 231.

Oriana Choir. 'Why not give the Song of the High Hills again with that lovely Kennedy Scott chorus?', he wrote to Norman O'Neill, by then a Director of the Royal Philharmonic Society.[18] Not only was Kennedy Scott's famous choir well known for its interpretations of Delius's partsongs, but they also became closely associated with equally sympathetic performances of *Sea Drift* and *A Mass of Life*.

Typically diffident about the detail of the work, Delius insisted on an 'anti-intellectual' description of *The Song of the High Hills* for the programme notes of the first performance: 'I want the note on 'The Song of the h. hills to be as short & simple as possible – I have tried to express the joy & exhilaration [*sic*] one feels in the Mountains & also the loneliness & melancholy [*sic*] of the high Solitudes & the grandeur of the wide far distances. The human voices represent man in nature; an episode, which becomes fainter & then disappears altogether'.[19] Original sketches reveal that Delius had various perspectives that he wished to explore (much like when he took time to settle on a title for *Songs of Sunset* and *In a Summer Garden*). Early ideas varied from 'Symphonie. Mountain Sounds / (Poem of the Mountains) / The Song of the Mountains / Mountain Song', while another pencil sketch is much more general in its description 'Songs of Nature'.[20] There is some suggestion here that Delius more clearly saw his work as a large-scale symphonic poem, perhaps on a comparable scale with the multi-movement design of *Ein Heldenleben*. Certainly the German translation of Delius's work, *Das Lied von den hohen Bergen*, falls within a similar plane of repertoire as Mahler's earlier *Das Lied von der Erde*, and its subject matter also has much in common, as Grimley has suggested, with von Hausegger's contemporaneous *Natursymphonie* (1911), Strauss's *Alpensinfonie* (1915) and Zemlinsky's *Lyric Symphony* (1922–1923).[21] Of course Delius had visited this territory of 'mystical nature' before in his two early Ibsen-inspired interpretations of *Paa Vidderne* as well as *Over the Hills and Far Away*, but, in truth, it is more likely that Delius was looking to return to the epic expression of *A Mass of Life* (and more specifically the opening of Part II) but now in the form of a hybrid orchestral work with chorus.

The Song of the High Hills has attracted a wide variety of structural interpretations over its hundred years of existence. Heseltine began by virtually ascribing a poetic programme to the work:

[18] Letter from Delius to Norman O'Neill, 20 August 1922, *DLL2*, 258.

[19] Letter from Delius to Norman O'Neill, 10 February 1920, *DLL2*, 228.

[20] See *BG-Lbl* MS Mus 1745/2/13/5, ff. 51–2.

[21] *DG*, 231.

The structure of *The Song of the High Hills* is like the rugged outline of a great range of mountains whose heights are hidden from the eyes in cloud. The music is full of a sense of spacious solitudes and far horizons. The elation of the ascent is succeeded by a mood of ecstatic contemplation, and the soul rises through the pure still air to the very heights of rapture, losing all consciousness of itself as the mountain-tops are lost from the ken of man, among the wandering mists and the eternal snows.[22]

Beecham, by contrast, hit on the differentiation of material between the 'frame' of the symphonic poem and its central portion:

It is built on an heroic scale and the inspiration is on an exalted level throughout. It has also a certain austerity of manner that we have not encountered before, and which appears to be associated in the composer's mind with the emotions roused by the contemplation of great heights. The ascent and descent from the High Hills is cunningly depicted in music of a totally different character from that which greets us when the summit has been attained, where we have a magical sequence of sounds and echoes, both vocal and instrumental, all culminating in a great outburst of tone that seems to flood the entire landscape. The first entrance of the full choir singing as softly as is possible is surely a stroke of genius, and of its kind without equal, either in him or any other composer.[23]

Fenby's and Mitchell's understanding of the work's architecture generally conformed with both Heseltine's and Beecham's analogy of landscape and self-communion, and of the physical challenge faced by the ascent, ultimately alleviated by reaching the summit and the relief of the descent.[24] This image has been enshrined in the brilliant if fictitious sequence of Russell's documentary film *A Song of Summer*. Boyle took pains to correct the myth, reinforced by former biographers and by Russell's 1968 film, that a gruelling seven-hour ascent and the purpose of carrying Delius up the mountain from their 'hut' at Leskaskog in 1923 on a chair with poles had been to witness the sunset across the Tafjord mountains. This was not true (the party was home before any sunset took place), nor was the seven-hour ordeal to the summit

---

[22] *PH*, 126.

[23] *TB*, 168.

[24] Mitchell, D., 'Delius: The Choral Music', *Tempo*, No. 26 (Winter 1952–1953), 15.

of Liahovdane as portrayed so movingly in the film.[25] Nonetheless, the
courage shown by Grainger, Jelka and Senta Mössmer (their young Tyrolean
maidservant and cook) to convey him there under difficult conditions, in
the knowledge that it was probably the last time he would see the distant
mountainscape that he adored, has a genuine, affecting profundity. Grainger
made his arrangement of *The Song of the High Hills* in America in November
and December of 1923, presumably after he had performed this selfless act for
his friend.[26] This connection, moreover, was poignantly reinforced in Russell's
film where the 'hill song' section of Delius's work, in Grainger's arrangement,
is played by Grainger and Fenby while the then blind Delius listens attentively
from his bedroom.

As a comprehensive rationalisation of his study of Delius and Norway,
Boyle inevitably sees *The Song of the High Hills* as the culmination of his
'mountain music' metaphor in which his use of 'peaks' and 'plateaus'
provides an interesting (if not entirely convincing) allegory and of how this
relationship with nature helped to generate his attitude to form.[27] Both he
and Guinery perceive the work as a tripartite structure, in which the three
sections are composite in construction. Guinery's assessment suggests an
Exposition–Recapitulation model in which the 'Great Solitude' (as described
by Delius), embodied by the central 'Hill Song', undergoes a process of
development before being restated.[28] To Matthew-Walker the grandiloquent
scale of *The Song of the High Hills* constitutes a wordless symphony (a term
we know Delius used in his sketches to describe the work) in four continuous
sections, and to this structural understanding is adjoined an additional level
of 'two orchestras', the one more immediate, the other distant and removed.[29]
Holten cleaves to the notion of 'four big climaxes'(Figs 7–8, 16–17, 33–34
and 44–45), each preceded by substantial accumulations of thematic working
out, and with each climax a rapid falling away of tension; but, like Heseltine
and Beecham decided, the achievement of the summit allows the composer

[25] See *DN*, 293–4.

[26] See *GB-Lbl* MS Mus 1745/1/22, ff. 16–30. The second piano part has markings by
      Delius. See also *RL*, 83. For a facsimile of a page from the first part of Delius's work
      in Grainger's arrangement, see Fenby, E., *Delius* (London: Faber & Faber, 1971), 71.

[27] See *DN*, 250–60.

[28] Guinery, P., '*The Song of the High Hills*: A Musical Analysis', *DSJ* No. 138 (Autumn
      2005), 67.

[29] Matthew-Walker, R., 'Aspects of *The Song of the High Hills*: A "Symphony for Two
      Orchestras (In Tribute to Edvard Grieg)"', *DSJ* No. 138 (Autumn 2005), 72–3.

to bask in the magnificence of the mountainous landscape.[30] Palmer perceives *The Song of the High Hills* as an 'epic nature-drama' in no less than nine distinct, yet interrelated sections, but key to his reading is the central section, the antecedent of which he understood to be the 'tiny crystalline impressions of the Norwegian countryside which formed part of the legacy of Grieg'.[31] Grimley, informed by his 'sense of place', also sees Delius's scheme as one of ten contrasting sections,[32] characterised by the composer's favoured modes of expression – 'introduction', 'idyll', 'rhapsody' and 'hill song' – all of which contribute to a hybrid tessellation of styles imbued by Norwegian hill sounds such as the kulokk,[33] and (as Matthew-Walker has also alluded) by quasi-Norwegian folksong explored by Grieg in his *Lyric Pieces*, particularly those permeated with Lydian inflections (a notable Norwegian characteristic).

The Song of the High Hills also offers other formal perspectives. One, close to that of Guinery and Matthew-Walker, is that it is made up of *two* ternary structures, one embracing the other (Table 12.2).

This reading of the work emphasises the *composite* nature of the first section which is rich in thematic material. The introduction (Example 12.2a) establishes that Ibsen-inspired melancholy engendered by seclusion in a vast landscape. The sense of struggle (which clearly provoked Beecham and Heseltine to associate this music with physical exertion) is well differentiated by its character of invertible two-part counterpoint (Example 12.2b), though this aspect is arguably overworked by the composer. A variant of this material, combined with the same chromatic counterpoint of quavers, continues in E major and reaches a climax marked by a transitional passage featuring Delius's familiar 'nature' music (as we have met so many times in *A Village Romeo and Juliet*, *A Mass of Life* and *Brigg Fair*), though here coloured by the sounds of Norwegian Lydian folk song. A new episode in C major (a conspicuous contrast in its use of diatonicism), distinctive in its use of harmonic parallelisms, provides a welcome relief before the contrapuntal material returns almost irresistibly. Arrival in D major and a second major climax marks the end of the first section, whereby the metre changes from Delius's much-favoured 6/4 to 4/4 to accommodate a new

[30] Holton, B., 'On Conducting the Song of the High Hills', *DSJ* No. 138 (Autumn 2005), 75.

[31] Palmer, C., *Delius: Portrait of a Cosmopolitan* (London: Duckworth, 1976), 53.

[32] *DG*, 233.

[33] Ibid., 236; see also *DN*, 52.

Table 12.2. *The Song of the High Hills*, overview of ternary structure.

Score ref.	Section	Key/mode	Comments
	EXPOSITION		
b. 1	A^1, Introduction	G minor	Inner melancholy (Ibsen)
Fig. 2	A^2	C minor	Two-part counterpoint
Fig. 4	A^3	E major	Two-part counterpoint
Fig. 8	Transition	E Lydian	Impressionistic
Fig. 11	A^4	C major	Intermezzo
Fig. 14^{+4}	A^2	Fluid	Resumption of two-part counterpoint
Fig. 18^{+5}	B (A)	D Dorian	'Hill Song' with variations
Fig. 21^{+4}	(B)	D major	'Mountain impression'
Fig. 25	(A)	E♭ minor	'Hill Song' development
Fig. 30	(A)	E Dorian	'Hill Song' reprise
	RECAPITULATION		
Fig. 35	A^1	E minor	Introduction
Fig. 38	A^3	F major	Without counterpoint
Fig. 41	A^2	F major	Two-part counterpoint
Fig. 46^{-4}	Transition	A Lydian	Impressionistic
Fig. 48	A^1	A Lydian	Introduction
Fig. 49	(B)	G♯ Dorian	Memory of 'mountain impression'

Example 12.2a. *The Song of the High Hills*, opening idea.

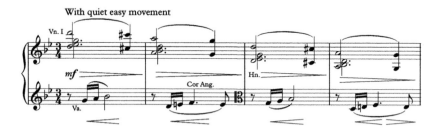

thematic departure within his 'great solitude'. A quasi-Norwegian folksong
(Example 12.2c) in the Dorian mode, the 'Hill Song', forms the central focus
of this 'inner' ternary structure, though Grimley's insightful analysis points
to Delius's overarching process of a variation scheme, which we have met so
many times, as a generative method in his symphonic music. After twelve bars
of hushed transition, bars which Beecham pronounced as 'visionary' with the

Example 12.2b. *The Song of the High Hills*, two-part invertible counterpoint.

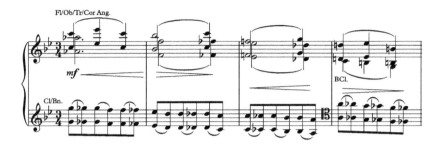

Example 12.2c. *The Song of the High Hills*,
synthetic Norwegian folksong, 'Hill song'.

appendage of mystical, wordless voices 'in the far distance', the 'theme and variations' commences with the 'wind band' replete with a countermelody in the upper strings, and momentarily ceases with a variation initiated by the solo trumpet (an orchestrational hallmark from as far back as the second subject of *Paris*). As an interlude to the first phase of variations, another impressionistic episode ensues, inaugurated by distant tenors (Example 12.2d). With the high tessitura of the upper strings, harp, celesta, flute and piccolo this is surely the rarified air of the high peaks. To this shimmering agglomeration Delius adds fragments of the 'kulokk' (Example 12.2e) mountain cry and sounds imitating a low horn (Example 12.2f) together with an original 'harmony' of timpani. After this luminous evocation has ceased, the 'Hill Song' returns in a new variation sung a by a solo tenor whose loneliness is enhanced by the remoteness of E flat minor (entirely distant from the D Dorian of past variations). This is a moment of extraordinary intensity before Delius's tonal 'correction' to E minor and the entry of the eight-part wordless chorus in that key. This resumption of the 'Hill Song' forms the emotional heart of the work. In part, since the brief earlier interjection of the voices, there has been a lingering sense of expectation of the chorus's 'need' to express itself through the folksong medium, but the eight-part texture of the chorus signals a special form of 'homecoming' for Delius and his love of the dense, harmonic sonority of the unaccompanied partsong. A manifestation of that unattainable moment of ecstasy in the Floridian tropics is here most powerfully realised and expressed, made more intoxicating by the addition of the soprano and tenor soli – a spiritual embodiment of the two lovers. The recommencement of the 'Hill Song' also continues the process of variation and carries it to a new height of elation (reminding us of the demanding choral material of *A Mass of Life*) before the pangs of melancholy return in the reprise of the introductory music (A^1). This, and a curtailed version of A^3 (in which the contrapuntal element is only latterly re-established in F), constitute a powerful sense of sonata recapitulation. After the final climax, and another Lydian transition of nature music, it is a memory of 'eternal nature' (from the impressionistic epicentre of the work) that forms the introspective coda.

A 'SYMPHONY' OF SYMPHONIC
POEMS: *NORTH COUNTRY SKETCHES*

It is an indication of the epic nature of *The Song of the High Hills* that its length exceeds that of all four symphonic poems which constituted the *North Country Sketches*, composed between 1913 and 1914 and dedicated to Albert

Example 12.2d. *The Song of the High Hills*, episode introduced by tenors.

Example 12.2e. *The Song of the High Hills*, 'kulokk' fragment.

Example 12.2f. *The Song of the High Hills*, low mountain horn.

Coates.[34] It is also significant that, having experimented with impressionistic techniques in the central paragraph of *The Song of the High Hills*, Delius should have chosen to extend this spirit of exploration in what proved to be his most adventurous, modernist orchestral work. In what he described to Heseltine as 'shortish Orchestral pieces',[35] his final use of the term 'sketch' insinuated a structure more diminutive in length; but there is also the suggestion of a more abstract, free approach to form and content. At the time of writing to Heseltine, Delius had written three movements, most likely the first, second and final movements (which, incidentally, already bore the title *North Country Sketches*),[36] since by the time he was corresponding with Beecham, the latter referred to a 'new Orchestral Dance',[37] which, one assumes, was what became the third movement, 'Dance'. Although Delius characteristically had

[34] The autograph title page of *North Country Sketches* is dated 1914 – see *GB-Lbl* MS Mus 1745/1/24, f. 1; however, the individual movements indicate that the first two movements (ff. 2 and 12) were completed in 1913, the second two in 1914 (ff. 16 and 31).

[35] Letter from Delius to Heseltine, 11 March 1914, *DLL2*, 123.

[36] Letter from Beecham to Delius, 25 October 1914, *DLL2*, 139.

[37] Ibid.

no detailed or stipulated programme in mind for the individual movements, there was undoubtedly an overlying scheme to the first, second and fourth movements in terms of the seasons and their sense of renewal (which may well have lingered in his mind from *A Mass of Life* and the plot of *Fennimore and Gerda*). As Heseltine described:

> We have mood pictures of autumn, when the "wind soughs in the trees",[38] a *Winter Landscape*, and – significantly placed *after* the melancholy of autumn and the gloom of winter – *the March of Spring* over woodlands, meadows and silent moors,[39] portraying the gradual awakening of Nature from its winter sleep,[40] the rising of the sap in the trees, the opening of the green leaves, and the blossoming of the flowers until all Nature bursts into a paean of delight and joy. Linked with these Nature impressions is a *Dance*, with no specific programme, though its uncertain, tentative beginning and abrupt conclusion lead one to picture it as a spell of fireside musing over the past, a tale within a dream – and one of the loveliest short pieces Delius has ever written.[41]

Having originally thought of the fourth movement as a dance, Delius clearly felt its dance character was not pronounced enough, and that there was a need for a faster, more vigorous movement, given the otherwise predominant slower tempi of the work. In placing the dance movement third, it was as if Delius was aping the position of the traditional dance movement of a symphony; indeed, one may conjecture that the four movements of the *North Country Sketches* came as close as Delius ever ventured to a more conventional four-movement symphony. That it was also evocative of an English landscape, and with the mention of the 'silent moors', the rugged Yorkshire country outside Bradford where Delius had grown up, was probably reinforced by the straitened European circumstances in which he and Jelka found themselves in

---

[38] The original title was 'The wind sounds in the trees' – see *GB-Lbl* MS Mus 1745/1/24, f. 1 (cf. f. 2). An even earlier title, 'Autumn: The wind sounds in the forest' can be observed in *GB-Lbl* MS Mus 1745/2/8/4 (also dated 1913), though 'The wind soughs in the trees' is written above in typescript.

[39] Delius also appears to have conceived this movement as a dance – see *GB-Lbl* MS Mus 1745/2/8.

[40] It is significant that Heseltine uses the term 'awakening' here, since it is evident from *GB-Lbl* MS Mus 1745/1/24, f. 1 that the fourth movement was originally entitled 'Spring's awakening' (the erasure of which is evident on the title page).

[41] *PH*, 119.

1914 and the succour they sought in Britain with Beecham in the first stages of the war (fortunately Delius astutely always kept his British passport). Although music-making in London was more restricted during the war years, Beecham was still able to mount a performance at Queen's Hall on 10 May 1915 with the London Symphony Orchestra (probably also made practical by the more standard orchestration). Publication of the work was, however, severely delayed until 1923 when it was taken on by Augener, the same year it received its German premiere in Frankfurt.

Delius's *North Country Sketches* represent the apogee of the composer's attraction to modernism, but at the same time they also demonstrate his awareness of new European developments and of his ability and readiness to marshal his material in novel ways. Although seemingly isolated at Grez for months at a time, he was far from ignorant of new musical trends and much of his travel to Germany and London, as well as Paris, invariably gave him a flavour of the contemporary generation. His contact with the Musical League had, of course, given him access to the current English scene, among them Bantock, Elgar and Grainger, but also others such as Cyril Scott. To Elgar's music he remained equivocal. For the culture of oratorio and the Bible (for which he outrightly condemned Parry), he had little time, but he admired Elgar's forays into the genre of the symphonic poem, notably *Falstaff*. Yet he lacked patience with Elgar as a symphonist, having attended the first London performance of the composer's First Symphony under Richter at Queen's Hall on 7 December. Impervious to the adulation it received, he complained to Bantock that 'it [was] a work *dead born*'.[42] Years later he received a copy of the work from C. W. Orr but found the invention 'weak'. 'Whenever he gets a good theme or nice harmonies', Delius retorted, 'they remind me of Parsifal or Brahms – He never seems to have outlived his admiration for the "Good Friday magic music"'.[43] Yet he had grown to admire the early symphonies of Mahler, especially the 'Resurrection', and Mahler's reputation as a conductor had incited Delius to suggest him as the conductor of the Musical League's festival in 1909.[44] Correspondence with Bartók brought him into critical contact with

---

[42] Letter from Delius to Bantock, 17 December 1908, *DLL1*, 377.

[43] Letter from Delius to C. W. Orr, [June/July 1918], *DLL2*, 189.

[44] Letter from Delius to Bantock, 7 January 1909, *DLL2*, 3. Delius had also intended to hear Mahler's Eighth Symphony at the Lower Rhine Festival in Cologne on 8 June 1913, but being weary of other German works which did not impress him, he forewent the experience (*DLL2*, 108n). This impression of Mahler prevailed into the early 1920s (*DLL2*, 242), but by the end of the decade he somewhat egocentrically condemned as banal the genre of the symphony with all its 'long

the Hungarian's Suite No. 2,[45] and he was thoroughly receptive to Stravinsky whose *Le Sacre du Printemps* he certainly attended on that fateful night in Paris on 29 May 1913.[46] We know he also attended *L'oiseau de feu* on 23 May, and had been given free entry by the impresario Astruc to any new work that appealed to him.[47] At that time he was greatly attracted to what Stravinsky was doing – 'your music interests me enormously', he told Stravinsky, 'something I cannot say for most of the music I have heard for a very long time'.[48] Yet by 1921, Stravinsky had lost its appeal and *Le Sacre*, which he heard in London, had become nothing more than 'an Anti-musical pretentious row'.[49] He was curious about Schoenberg, largely because Heseltine's first article, 'Arnold Schoenberg', had been published in the *Musical Standard* in September 1912. His response to Schoenberg's *Harmonielehre* was positive – 'it is by far the most intelligent Harmony I ever read', he wrote back to Heseltine[50] – yet he was characteristically reticent of the Austrian's theoretical approach to composition. 'He seems to be very *Academic* à rebours', he complained.[51] But Delius's resistance tended always to be predicated on a fear of too much cerebral calculation. Composition, as he understood it, was a process of emotion which precluded intellectualism. This was his reaction after hearing Schoenberg's *Chamber Symphony* in Cologne: 'It is very dry & unpoetical & and entirely intellectual – but did not sound bad at all – At times quite like Strauss in Heldenleben – & sometimes quite interesting – But what sometimes sounds very bad on the piano – sounds quite tame on the Orchestra – I agree with every effort of the young school to do something new – but I disagree with music becoming a merely mathematical, & intellectual art'.[52] This was an argument, curiously, that he also levelled at Sibelius who, as a mutual friend of Busoni's, he had known and admired during the late 1890s. 'I like Sibelius', he told Fenby, 'he's a splendid fellow. I often met him at Busoni's house. Elgar brought me an album of his records – the Fifth Symphony, *Tapiola*,

---

drawn out movements padded with dull development'; see Lloyd, S. (ed.) *Fenby on Delius* (London: Thames Publishing, 1996), 35.

[45] Letter from Delius to Bartók, [September 1910], *DLL2*, 58.

[46] Letter from Delius to Stravinsky, 27 May 1913, *DLL2*, 107.

[47] Letter from Delius to Jelka, [23 May 1913], *DLL2*, 106.

[48] Letter from Delius to Stravinsky, 27 May 1913, *DLL2*, 107.

[49] *DLL2*, 238.

[50] *DLL2*, 92n.

[51] Ibid.

[52] Letter from Delius to Heseltine, 11 March 1914, *DLL2*, 123.

and *Pohjola's Daughter* – very good in their way, but he always uses the same procedure to get the music going and that irritates me. A Lot of his work is too complicated and thought out'.[53]

We also know that Delius was also receptive to the music of Debussy after attending two of the early performances of *Pelléas et Mélisande* and that he had felt some affinity for the Frenchman's harmony. *L'Après-midi d'un faune*, according to Jelka, he heard much later in 1909.[54] It seems likely, however, that Delius was familiar with a good deal more of Debussy's music after hearing *Pelléas* in 1902 than he committed to correspondence. It also seems to have been the perception of Constant Lambert.[55] As Delius told C. W. Orr in 1917, 'Debussy wrote his best things before 30 & got gradually more superficial & uninteresting – The same with Ravel who is even cleverer than Debussy but even more flimsy and superficial – But their chief idea is to startle & be brilliant'.[56] Of Florent Schmitt, he was surprisingly dismissive. 'The intelligence of Florent Schmitt is rather simple', he pronounced to C. W. Orr in 1919; 'I don't quite understand why anyone attaches any importance to what the French clique in Paris think or say about English music & composers – They are so narrow that they only like what resembles their own Lollipops'.[57] As for incipient Neo-Classicism, he had little time. 'Look with what ease hundreds of young composers are quietly expressing themselves in the so called "new idiom". Otherwise the wrong note system'.[58] As for Italian Neo-Classicists such as Casella: 'now he imitates the Paris clique'.[59]

Having shown a predisposition towards impressionistic methods in the central section of *A Song of a High Hills*, Delius continued to pursue the potential of colouristic techniques of French music in the first two of his *North Country Sketches*. After establishing a sound-world of fourths and fifths in the opening eight bars of 'Autumn: The Wind Soughs through the Trees', this harmonic template is translated into an accompanying counterpoint of superimposed consecutive fourths (as a symbol of the moaning wind) whose austere sounds later form a richer sonority of dominant thirteenths

---

[53] *EF*, 123.

[54] Letter from Jelka to Heseltine, 3 September 1929, *DLL2*, 354.

[55] Lambert, C., *Music-Ho! A Study of Music in Decline* (London: Harmondsworth, 1934), 25.

[56] Letter from Delius to C. W. Orr, 10 April 1917, *DLL2*, 178.

[57] Letter from Delius to C. W. Orr, [July 1919], *DLL2*, 217.

[58] Letter from Delius to Heseltine, 27 May 1917, *DLL2*, 179n.

[59] Letter from Delius to C. W. Orr, [July 1919], *DLL2*, 217.

(Example 12.3a – 'x'). This particular component of the movement forms part
of a matrix of contrasting, differentiated musical ideas closely associated with
orchestral tone colours and timbres, which has much in common with those
techniques developed by Debussy – as one sees, for example, in the *Nocturnes*
(1901), the beginning of Act I of *Pelléas* (1902), the two books of *Images*
(1901–1907), *La Mer* (1903–1905) and the *Images pour Orchestre* (1905–
1912). Delius's consecutive triads in second inversion Payne also attributed
to Debussy (Example 12.3b – 'y') noting that, while long strings of identical
chords are common in the latter, they are rare in Delius's music,[60] and these
are contrasted with strings of minor and augmented triads. Differentiation
also extends to a diatonic fragment (Example 12.3a – 'z') which also combines
with the consecutive fourths in a chromatically falling sequence of phrases,
and Delius's canvas is, like that of *Summer Night on the River*, set against a
backdrop of dynamics ranging from 'mf' to 'pppp'. The initial interaction of the
individual thematic components is based around G and its dominant, but this
soon moves on to quasi-improvisatory episodes on C (three bars after Fig. 5)
and on B (two bars before Fig. 7). A point of return is marked by the reprise
of 'y' and the 6/4 parallelisms before this section of the 'fantasy' structure is
curtailed. At Fig. 11 a transition, marked 'Slow and more deliberate', anticipates

Example 12.3a. *North Country Sketches*, 'The Wind Soughs
through the Trees', sonority of dominant thirteenths, 'x'.

60   Payne, A., 'Delius's Stylistic Development', *Tempo*, No. 60 (Winter 1961–1962), 15.

the augmented note values of the coda, a microcosm of the main movement in that 'x', 'y' and 'z' appear simultaneously, the full melodic statement of 'z' appears in augmentation (its two phrases in reverse order) as an upper voice, and two statements of 'z' (to C and F), a fourth apart, ape those of G and C earlier in the movement. Ultimately it is to C major that the work finally gravitates, still haunted by the bleakness of 'y'.

Winter Landscape, even more of a 'sound picture' than its antecedent, is no less unusual in its process of structural cohesion, but this time the movement relies almost entirely on the unifying thread of an ostinato (Example 12.3c) which, save for a total of fifteen bars, runs throughout the entire movement. To this Delius adds two cycles of variations, ones that are heard contiguously on a short falling phrase. The climax of each cycle is a variation fully harmonised with a short thematic suffix (which Delius marks 'Very sustained'), the first on the dominant of A, the second on the dominant of E, though neither dominant successfully tonicises in spite of each cycle's tendency to move increasingly to a richer harmonic palette. While there is no sense of finality to this portrayal

Example 12.3b. *North Country Sketches*, 'The Wind Soughs through the Trees', consecutive triads in second inversion, 'y'.

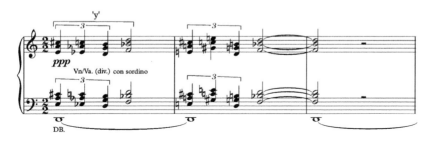

Example 12.3c. *North Country Sketches*, 'Winter Landscape', ostinato.

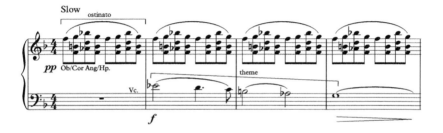

of nature's 'icy blast' in the D flat drone which underpins the last variation (and characteristically dies away to 'pppp'), Delius subtly lends this shorter 'sound-world' a sense of reprise with the ostinato whose same pitches began the movement and the upper strings' same 'whistling' synthetic harmonics.

As if to confirm its 'symphonic' status within the four-movement scheme, the 'Dance' is a ternary structure, featuring a lively mazurka and a trio in 4/4. Like so many of Delius's internal structures, it features a series of thematic repetitions in which variety is gained by the variation of instrumentation, tonality and subtle modal change. At first Delius's Nietzschean mazurka fluctuates between F sharp minor and A major but shifts to F major as the dance gathers momentum, and Delius's ever-present harmonic resource gives us a variation in A minor and a conclusion on the dominant of C. A particularly interesting feature of the dance melody is its folk-like 'Scotch snap' which it gains along the way. Delius most likely appropriated this rhythmical trait from his setting of Fiona McLeod's 'I-Brasîl', which he composed in January 1913 (and published with Tischer & Jagenberg in 1915),[61] where the folk-like vocal melody is heavily imbued with the same feature.[62]

The 'Trio' more unconventionally fluctuates between a new theme in 4/4 and intrusions of the mazurka (as if was being reworked). Ultimately the dotted rhythms of the mazurka usurp the more tranquil demeanour of the 'Trio' idea, and this provides a happy transition to the mazurka's reprise in F sharp minor. The return of the 'Dance', consistent with its Nietzschean spirit, instigates an increase of tempo and a sense of Dionysiac abandon as the original variations are forsaken. Delius heightens this perception momentarily with a reflective pause in which the mazurka, now stripped of its dotted rhythms, is wistfully heard on a solo violin, but the momentum of the dance is irresistible and the Bacchanale resumes with even greater vigour with a recapitulation of the original dance theme, though now in the guise of a giddy waltz. The recapitulation, what is more, is marked by a return of the original key, F sharp minor, though, with the waltz's new-found energy, it is D major that asserts itself, only to be contradicted by F sharp minor in the final two bars.

---

[61]　See letter from Delius to Heseltine, 11 January 1913, *RT2*, 118.

[62]　It is, perhaps, ironic that this rhythmical feature, associated with Scottish folksong, should have emerged in conjunction with an Irish text. 'I-Brasîl' was the name given to the old country of legend in the Atlantic. Threlfall also suggests that this song formed part of a pair of Irish songs, a conjecture predicated on the incomplete sketches of a setting of W. B. Yeats's 'The Lake Isle of Innisfree' (which can be found in *AU-Mgm* SM7 74).

The final symphonic poem of *North Country Sketches*, 'The March of Spring: Woodlands, Meadows and Silent Moors', bears the imprint of Delius's youthful memories of his Yorkshire home; moreover, the movement functions as a buoyant finale to the larger cycle of four movements with its opulent instrumentation. Indeed, much of this finale is predicated on the rationale of orchestral pigments, striking 'sound moments' (within a context of almost complete chromatic saturation), whole-tone scales and progressions (in which the Lydian mode is a prominent component), the juxtaposition of unrelated triads and the composer's subtle spacing of individual harmonies. In this respect alone Delius's score, a *tour de force* of orchestration, rivals those contemporaneous scores of Schmitt's *Rêves*, Debussy's *Rondes de Printemps* and *Jeux* and Ravel's *Ma mère l'Oye* and the two *Daphnis et Chloé* Suites, particularly for its balletic syntax. The description of the movement is significant in two senses. The actual 'march' of the symphonic poem takes place at a very late stage in the structure, in the key of A minor, and the march melody, another example of Delius's synthetic folk melodies, replete with Scotch snap, looks back to the 'Dance' but also forward to *Poem of Life and Love* (and its revised counterpart *A Song of Summer*). In another sense, however, the title also refers to a more inexorable forward motion towards the dramatic entrance of the march (this was presumably behind Delius's initial title of 'Spring's awakening'). The opening statement in C major, for cello, viola and violin solos, is a caprice in which the sumptuous wind filigree reminds us of the rich motivic canvas of *In a Summer Garden*. The goal of a second, contrasting section (which commences with a lyrical oboe solo in F major) is an ebullient D major (five bars after Fig. 44) in which Delius's impressionistic credentials are made plain in the triadic juxtapositions of the harps, the Lydian woodwind scales, string figurations (after Fig. 45), harmony and timbres which anticipate the extraordinary conclusion of the *Requiem* written during the war. At this point Delius develops his 'caprice' idea until, in a mood of more tranquil elation, it returns to C major as a point of reprise (Fig. 48), and this is matched by a climactic recapitulation of the secondary material, again based on a more extended D major (see Figs 50–53). Having completed this part of the movement with its sonata-like contrasting thematic elements (though refusing to conform to the form's more conventional tonal behaviour), the last twenty-six bars are taken up with a completely new and unexpected march theme which functions as a triumphant codicil. This begins in A minor, but, as we know from Delius's treatment of modal melody, his final tonic can vary, as it does here to D minor, though with great subtlety, for D becomes part of an added sixth of the closing F major harmony whose own crystallisation is momentarily clouded by the lower G sharp appoggiatura of the violas and second violins.

Though it constitutes a less well-known domain of Delius's orchestral output – it has never enjoyed the same adulation as *In a Summer Garden* or the *On Hearing the First Cuckoo* as concert pieces or as the subject of recording – the *North Country Sketches* undoubtedly represents a high-water mark in his composition of the symphonic poem as a genre. 'All musicians think it is one of Fred's finest works', Jelka claimed,[63] and as Payne remarked, 'the work as a whole is one of the composer's most highly organized scores, a mine of information on his orchestral methods, and some of the loveliest music he ever wrote'.[64] To this one might add an intuitive flair for free forms and an inclination to pursue new and individual ideas of cohesion alien to our normal experience. In this sense Delius brought a new perspective to the symphonic poem which, in the years directly before the First World War, was still experiencing a time of fecund activity. In England this was true of Bantock, but especially so of Holbrooke, Bridge and Bax whose programmatic elements contributed significantly to the formal part of their compositions in the idiom. Delius was, as we have seen, largely averse to the affixation of programmes, nor was he inclined, like Strauss, Bantock, Elgar and others, to use a programme as a potentially inexhaustible means of varying the sonata paradigm. As Peter Evans has incisively commented:

> Delius did not use complex programmes in his tone-poems, as did Strauss, and good proportions when he did achieve them, are the result of instinct. This does not mean that Delius patched together passages as they occurred to him, one by one. Though this is almost true of some of the early and of the late dictated works, the mature works show an architectural intent which must have preceded the actual composition – "A Song of the High Hills" for example (strictly a choral and orchestral work but without words) shows a very purposeful sweep up to a climax and a recession. But this, and all his formal successes, are not achieved by the classical gambits of restatement and [figure] development. Restatement, if it does occur is in the nature of an affectionate reminiscence rather than a stroke of rhetoric. Uniformity is more likely to come from the persistent use of some decorative arabesque (in the w.w. [woodwind]) than from definitive melodic outlines. We cannot criticise these methods if their success is evident, as we find it to be in the greatest of the orchestral works – "In a summer garden", a masterpiece

---

[63] Letter from Jelka to Adine O'Neill, 30 March 1923, *DLL2*, 270.

[64] Payne, A., 'Delius's Stylistic Development', 15.

of instinctive design, "Paris", The North Country Sketches and the well-known pieces for small orchestra.[65]

In consequence, Delius's entirely individual approach to the symphonic poem as a genre had the capability of reaching new heights by dint of his untrammelled perception of form, lyricism, rhapsody and orchestral elegance. As Evans, once again, has astutely observed: 'By rejecting the classical concept of development, Delius denied himself perhaps the only fully proven method of securing convincing *absolute* structures, yet in his free tone-poems he may be claimed to have produced more truly "Romantic" forms by sheer instinct than did the 19th-century composers with their dependence either on existing moulds or the equally Procrustean demands of a programme'.[66]

---

[65] Evans, P., 'Delius', Evans Papers, *GB-DRu*.

[66] Ibid.

CHAPTER 13

Music of the War Years and After (I):
Dance Rhapsody No. 2, *Requiem,*
Eventyr, A Song Before Sunrise, Poem
of Life and Love, Hassan (1914–1923)

CREATIVE APOGEE AND DECLINE

In many ways the outbreak of war in August 1914 could not have occurred at a worse time for Delius. Performances of his music in England and Germany were at an all-time high. As Carley has noted, he bathed in London's musical scene, enjoyed concerts and operas, and was wined and dined in the capital's most elevated social circles,[1] even at 10 Downing Street where he lunched with Prime Minister Asquith.[2] Beecham, Wood and others were keen to take on any new works he produced and many of the younger generation, such as Norman O'Neill, Heseltine and Grainger – devoted disciples of Delius's art – continued to help with the promotion of his music. But in the light of the alarming European political events and the extraordinary speed with which nations were being catapulted towards disaster, Delius must have sensed that it was almost inevitable that major military disruption would come. Writing to Heseltine on 30 July, only days before the outbreak of hostilities, he remarked: 'I do hope War will not break out & knock all Art and Music on the head for years'.[3] The war did indeed bring disorder to Delius's life at Grez. As the Germans made what seemed like their unstoppable advance towards Paris, Grainger's exhortation that he should leave for England and then cross to the United States appeared rational. Although he was forced to leave Grez with Jelka in September, the couple returned home after news of the allied

---

[1] *DLL2*, 116–17.

[2] Ibid.

[3] Letter from Delius to Heseltine, 30 July [1914], *DLL2*, 136.

counterattack which gave reason for optimism. Beecham, however, advised that they set up home for the time being in his house in Watford. Here they could observe the war from a safe distance and Delius could enjoy in London, Manchester (where Beecham had conducting commitments with the Hallé Orchestra) and elsewhere England's musical life, albeit changed radically by the exigencies of war. This beneficial experience included performances of his own music, including the Piano Concerto and *Sea Drift* and a number of his new concertos and chamber works. Such performances provided a modicum of income when royalties from Germany and Austria had evaporated.

Immersing himself in what London and Manchester could provide seemed conducive to creativity, but, perhaps inevitably, for all his physical strength and activity, his dormant affliction of syphilis was bound to return, and did so with more regular and worrying recurrence. Signs of paralysis began to manifest themselves in 1915, and after treatment in London, Delius and Jelka spent about five months in the mountainous country of Norway on the Nordfjord. Here he recovered sufficiently to return to Grez in November and here they passed the rest of the year and 1916 in solitude (with occasional visits to Paris to see their American friends, the Clews). But symptoms returned in June 1917 which necessitated a stay at a Normandy spa and then a holiday in Brittany. This pattern of recurrences and bouts of good health became more regular as the years went on. In January 1918 he was in a Paris sanatorium before taking time away in the summer in Biarritz with Jelka. After returning to their Grez home, which had been vandalised by occupants, a decision was made to spend some time in London. Money was short, and Beecham's own straitened financial circumstances meant that their own impecunious difficulties were exacerbated. Thanks to the intervention of Henry Wood, they briefly rented a house from him in St John's Wood before taking an apartment in Belsize Park.

Even though Delius had to contend with the lingering uncertainty of the war years, the increasing evidence of his uncurable illness and the changing circumstances of his residence in France, England, Norway and (after the war was over) Germany, it remains a remarkable fact that his creative energies remained undimmed. Ironically, it allowed for extended periods of isolation without disturbance which permitted him to focus his mind. In this way he completed three significant orchestral works, *Dance Rhapsody* No. 2 (1916), *Eventyr* (1917) and *Poem of Life and Love* as well as the shorter *A Song before Sunrise*, the last two in Biarritz in 1918. He was also able to finish composing his *Requiem* in 1914, though further work continued until at least 1916 with the composition of the last movement. Moreover, as will be discussed in Chapter 14, the more austere style of *Fennimore*, *The Song of the High Hills* and

North Country Sketches also appears to have encouraged Delius to explore the even more formalist musical idioms of chamber music and the concerto.

Ironically, as war ended, more turmoil came to the Delius household. Before he could return to Grez in October 1919, and in spite of his more fragile physical condition, he and Jelka lived a somewhat itinerant existence. After giving up their apartment in Belsize Park, they spent short periods in Sussex, a Kensington hotel and Cornwall. After this they made for the familiar region of Valdres in Norway until September, when a return journey to Grez included a stay first in Christiania and then in Frankfurt where *Fennimore and Gerda* was performed under Brecher in October. It was not until 1920, back in Grez, that Delius could resume a familiar routine of composition that he had enjoyed before the war. Work began on another Whitman choral work which would later materialise as the *Songs of Farewell,* but the most revitalising opportunity came with the composition of incidental music for James Elroy Flecker's play, *Hassan,* completed in 1921 along with a Cello Concerto for Beatrice Harrison.

Nevertheless, Delius's *Wanderlust* continued with visits to Frankfurt during the winter of 1920 and 1921, to London (which included performances of the numerous unheard works completed before and during the war), and to Norway where, during a holiday of 1921, they resolved to construct a modest chalet above the village of Lesjaskog. This proved to be a bolthole for them for the next two years, but as Delius grew weaker and his illness more acute, travelling became increasingly problematic. In January 1922 the symptoms came on again but with greater intensity, persistence and discomfort. Some alleviation resulted from time at a Wiesbaden spa, but all else was curtailed. Time spent at Lesjaskog in the summer and a stay in Frankfurt during the winter of 1922 and 1923 enlivened him, but the decline in his health – paralysis and signs of blindness – was inexorable, one which ten weeks at another spa at Bad Oeynhausen did little to alter. By January 1923, as Jelka witnessed in dismay to her friends Henry and Marie Clews: 'I have been silent so long. We have had such terrible times and I was too depressed to write about it: Fred has been seriously ill the whole dreadful year of 1922'.[4] Moreover, she attributed the steepness of her husband's deterioration to the war: 'I believe', she told the Clewses, 'in my mind there is no doubt that all the harassing cares of the war and the endless after war period (our sequestered money is not all paid back yet!) contributed very much to this breakdown of his'.[5] Closer to the truth,

---

[4] Letter from Jelka Delius to Henry and Marie Clews, 23 January 1923, *DLL2*, 263.

[5] Ibid.

however, was a denial of the real causes of Delius's malady – that a cure was impossible. Even in 1924, when the symptoms were incontrovertible, the hope for a cure continued.[6] As Beecham observed, 'the blind belief in homeopathy prevailed and nothing came of it. The disease took precisely the course my expert had predicted, and Delius, although surviving another eight years, spent the last six of them in total blindness and paralysis'.[7] The isolation of Grez also concerned them as Delius's affliction worsened. They thought of selling the house, but commercial conditions and property law in France at that time militated against such action.[8] Fortunately, Balfour Gardiner stepped in and bought the house from them, providing much-needed capital for the cash-strapped couple, and the hope that, by relieving Delius of financial worry, a return to creativity would be more amenable. Though he retained the will to compose, necessary for the completion of the final version of the *Hassan* music for London (in which Grainger assisted), the Violin Sonata No. 2 and the partsong 'The splendour falls', Delius nevertheless required the stalwart help of Jelka who painstakingly acted as amanuensis.[9] And though other works were sketched during the course of 1924 – *Poem of Life and Love*, the *Fantastic Dance*, movements of a Third Violin Sonata and a setting of Henley's *A Late Lark* – there was no immediate prospect of sustained composition.

A DANCE INTERLUDE: *DANCE RHAPSODY NO. 2*

It was evident from the 'Dance' movement which he appended to *North Country Sketches* in 1914, and the short *Air and Dance* for string orchestra composed in 1915, that the spirit of the dance remained a potent stimulus for Delius's orchestral music. Interest in his *Dance Rhapsody No. 1* had been heightened by the prospect of it being turned into a ballet for Nijinsky to

---

[6] See letter from Delius to Heseltine, 23 March 1924, *DLL2*, 289.

[7] *MC*, 188.

[8] Letter from Jelka Delius to Henry and Marie Clews, 23 January 1923, *DLL2*, 264.

[9] The increasing participation of Jelka can be observed in the surviving manuscripts. The Violin Sonata No. 2 (*GB-Lbl* MS Mus 1745/2/5) shows Delius's pencil sketch (ff. 83–7) and a further ink and pencil sketch by Delius (ff. 88–99). Another incomplete version is, however, entirely in Jelka's hand (ff. 99–102). Sketches of the Violin Sonata No. 3 (*GB-Lbl* MS Mus 1745/2/5) also shows Jelka's participation (along with Fenby's later interventions) in the heading of the work (f. 105), some pencil sketches of the beginning of the second movement (dated 11 November

dance in 1914,[10] and it received its first American performance in Minnesota on 5 November that year. These two events may well have provided the stimulus for the production of the *Dance Rhapsody* No. 2, completed at Grez (according to the manuscript) in the spring of 1916.[11] '[I] am now writing a "dance"', he told Heseltine, 'which I think is going to be good'.[12] Delius entertained high hopes, with the assistance of Grainger, of having it performed and published in the United States, but this did not materialise. It was not until 1923, when Augener published the full score, that Henry Wood conducted it at Queen's Hall at the last night of the Proms on 20 October, though the composer remained unhappy with Wood's choice of tempi.[13]

Perhaps most interesting about the *Dance Rhapsody* No. 2 is that, like its earlier counterpart, it is based on the variation principle. However, in this instance, within the larger ternary structure of the work, the variation method is applied freely, flexibly and notionally as part of an imaginative symphonic conception. Like the 'Dance' from *North Country Sketches*, the central theme of the work (Example 13.1a) is strongly preoccupied with the mazurka's rhythmic feature of the emphatic second beat in bars 1 and 2 ('a'), but there are at least three other salient features – the triplet and quaver motion of b. 3 ('b') which is repeated in bars 6 and 9, the upward motion of the cell in b. 4 ('c'), repeated in bars 10 and 12, and a second mazurka rhythm in b. 7 ('d') which is invariably linked with the rising quaver movement in the following bar. Couched in A minor, this thirteen-bar unit is curtailed by the faster interjection of a waltz ('e'), characterised by false relations and parallelisms from the full orchestra, an idea which punctuates Delius's variations and which is also subject to its own process of modification (Example 13.1b). The first notional variation (bb. 22–63) is considerably longer than the theme itself and consists of three subsections, the first of which develops 'c' and 'd', the second 'b', and the third constitutes a variegated reprise of the first eight bars

1924 – f. 115) and a substantial portion of the last movement (various sketched passages are dated between 19 September and 16 October 1924 – ff. 120–32). Further evidence of Jelka's hand can be seen in other surviving sketches of the Violin Sonata No. 3 (*GB-Lbl* MS Mus 1745/4/5), the String Quartet (*GB-Lbl* MS Mus 1745/2/5, ff. 176–91), 'The splendour falls' (*GB-Lbl* MS Mus 1745/2/5, ff. 33–9) and the *Stichvorlag* (*GB-Lbl* MS Mus 1754/4/3, ff. 4–7) and part of *Poem of Life and Love* (*GB-Lbl* MS Mus 1745/1/32, ff. 24–33).

10 See letter from Delius to Jelka, [23 June 1914], *DLL2*, 129.

11 See *GB-Lbl* MS Mus 1745/1/28, ff. 1–26.

12 Letter from Delius to Heseltine, 11 June 1916, *DLL2*, 167.

13 See *DLL2*, 384.

of the original theme. A second waltz interjection, of only four bars, gives way to a similarly brief third variation of only eleven bars, and this is succeeded by a third waltz utterance of six bars in length. As if to accentuate the brevity of these statements, and to act as a balance to the first variation of forty-one bars, Delius's fourth variation (bb. 87–120), is considerably longer at thirty-three bars. There is also, in its latter stages, a suggestion that the 'dance' element of the mazurka is about to break loose. This is, however, attenuated by a further eight-bar interjection of the waltz, which not only acts to temper the mazurka's latent energy, but also functions as a conduit to a reprise of the original theme (b. 134). The 'trio' of the *Rhapsody*'s ternary form is notable for its extended melody of twenty-eight bars (a character it shares with the central section of *In a Summer Garden*) which functions as a major contrast to the free variation structure of the first part. Yet it too is ultimately a set of six miniature variations based on the first cell of four bars (bb. 147–50). More crucially, Delius allows his composite theme to modulate until it reaches an augmented sixth on B flat. This permits a final interjection of the waltz theme on the dominant of D before Delius effects a reprise of the first section in what constitutes a final variation. This 'finale' has several important features. First of all Delius does not return to A minor, the key of the first section. He also tantalisingly delays tonicisation in a more extended developmental paragraph in which the 'dance', a conflation of the mazurka (especially figure 'd') and waltz material, becomes increasingly animated. The tonal objective, moreover, is F (stated in both its minor and major modes), latently present in the earlier variations (e.g. bb. 36–8 and 78–81) but never unequivocally expressed, and it is this key centre which underpins the flute cadenzas and the cor anglais' thematic memory (decorated by the added-sixth motive familiar from *Songs of Sunset*) of the coda. The 'ternary' form of *Dance Rhapsody* No. 2 therefore requires revisiting in that, although it outwardly presents an ABA form, it is, in reality, a flexible variation structure with an 'interlude'.

A 'PAGAN' REQUIEM: SEQUEL TO *A MASS OF LIFE*

We have evidence that Delius contemplated writing some form of Requiem as far back as the summer of 1902 when such a work was discussed with the French writer and critic Robert d'Humières.[14] Nothing came of this project, and we know nothing of what form or scale Delius had conceived for it, but in

---

[14] See letter from Delius to Jelka, [May/June 1902], *DLL1*, 201–2.

Example 13.1a. *Dance Rhapsody* No. 2, central mazurka theme.

Example 13.1b. *Dance Rhapsody* No. 2, waltz idea.

September 1913 he began work in earnest on a Requiem for soloists, double choir and orchestra. This may have been motivated by the performances of his Nietzsche-inspired revision of *Lebenstanz* which received hearings in Berlin and London, but it was just as likely that he was buoyed up by the continued public acclaim for *A Mass of Life* which Beecham performed at Covent Garden on 20 January 1913. Throughout the summer of 1914 he devoted his energies to the work, and manuscript evidence shows that it was drafted at least twice before it was pronounced 'ready' to Heseltine in October of that year.[15] Clearly, however, the work was not finished to Delius's satisfaction, for we know that he was still engaged with the score in 1915 when he was living in Watford.[16] Indeed, it was not until January 1916, back at Grez-sur-Loing, that he informed Heseltine that he was 'hard at work on the end of my "Requiem"'.[17] Both Wood and Beecham expressed interest in the new work,[18] and Delius entertained the unlikely prospect of directing a performance in America;[19] but, in reality, there was little chance of any performance until after the war, by which time, *post hoc*, he was able to dedicate the published score by Harmonie 'To the memory of all young Artists fallen in the war'.[20]

Delius entertained major ambitions for this new choral work, perhaps as a possible sequel to the *Mass* in that, like its earlier counterpart, it was conceived in *German* and was almost certainly intended for the same public (such as Elberfeld) which had acclaimed the *Mass* a decade earlier. Indeed, at half an hour's length, it practically provided a symmetrical counterpart to the first part of the *Mass*, placing the latter's second part, of an hour's duration, at the centre. Proclaiming the work a 'Pagan Requiem' to Ernest Newman and to Grainger,[21] he confided to Hertzka at Harmonie that it was a work 'which will achieve the greatest significance in Germany'.[22] By this Delius surely implied that the audience which had readily imbibed the Nietzschean message of the *Mass* would also enthusiastically accept the pantheistic meaning of his new work which '[insisted] on the Reality of Life'.[23] That Delius held fast to this

---

[15] Letter from Delius to Heseltine, [26 October 1914], 141. This concurs with the date on the autograph manuscript (*GB-Lbl* Loan 54/4) and the published score. Two incomplete pencil drafts also exist in full score – see *GB-Lbl* MS Mus 1745/2/13/5, ff. 86–101 and ff. 102–16.

[16] *DLL2*, 145.

[17] Letter from Delius to Heseltine, 22 January 1916, *DLL2*, 163.

[18] See letter from Delius to Jelka, [3 July 1914], *DLL2*, 135 and letter from Beecham to Delius, 1 October 1914, *DLL2*, 137.

[19] See letter from Delius to Heseltine, [26 October 1914], *DLL2*, 141.

[20] See letter from Delius to Grainger, 16 January 1919, *DLL2*, 211.

[21] See letters from Delius to Newman, 31 January 1919, and to Grainger, 17 December 1919, *DLL2*, 213 and 224.

[22] *DLL2*, 225n.

[23] 'London Concerts', *The Musical Times*, Vol. 63 No. 951 (May 1922), 342.

view is evident from a letter to Universal in 1919: 'there are so many more opportunities for performances of it in Germany & Austria. With the choir situation here it is far too difficult'.[24]

Much of the text's sentiment was derived and paraphrased from Nietzsche and Schopenhauer. To what extent, however, is difficult to determine. Carley has suggested that Mahler's *Das Lied von der Erde* of 1911 might well have been a more direct influence, but can only speculate as to whether Delius ever saw a score of this work.[25] Numerous texts from the Old Testament (such as the Psalms, Ecclesiastes, Proverbs and the Song of Solomon), Shakespeare and Tennyson also appear to have played their part. How and when the libretto was constructed remains unclear. Delius may have had an original hand in it; yet the task of constructing a German libretto, perhaps with Delius's initial advice as to content, was entrusted to Heinrich Simon, the owner and editor of the *Frankfurter Zeitung*, with whom Delius had become acquainted as an adept translator of English during his visits to the German city;[26] Simon, an occasional visitor to Grez, also prepared a small biography of Delius for Verlag Piper in Munich which was intended to mark Delius's sixtieth birthday.[27] Apparently this never made it into print. Although the score made no acknowledgement of Simon's participation, the accompanying programme note for the London performance confirmed that the text had been prepared 'by an anonymous German', and this has been confirmed more recently by the evidence of Simon's request for a royalty.[28] For the English translation, Delius originally approached Ernest Newman. 'It is written in the style of the old Testament & it is short', he explained. In the end, however, after Newman turned down the invitation, it fell to Heseltine who, after various deliberations with Delius, elected to retain the old language of the King James Bible.[29] It is not one of Heseltine's best efforts even though it was

---

[24] Letter from Delius to Universal, 18 November 1919, *MC*, 140–41.

[25] Carley, L., 'Delius's Song of the Earth', *Fanfare from the Royal Philharmonic Society*, No. 3 (Spring 1994), 3–4.

[26] *MC*, 166.

[27] Ibid., 178. There is much evidence of Simon's continued interest in Delius's music after his death in 1934. As a Jew he was forced out of Germany in 1934, and after periods in Switzerland, Palestine and England, arrived in Washington, DC in 1940. There he was murdered in 1941. Two years later, his liberal-leaning newspaper was suppressed; see Carley, L., 'Benno Carl Reifenberg (1892–1970)', *DSJ* No. 165 (Spring 2019), 10–12.

[28] 'London Concerts', *The Musical Times*, Vol. 63 No. 951 (May 1922), 342.

[29] See letter from Delius to Heseltine, 3 October 1920, *FDPW*, 302.

sanctioned by the composer – he was never sympathetic to the task (though he never told Delius of his lack of interest) – and it might now be superseded by a more discerning translation.

That Delius wished to reconnect with the kind of epic expression of *A Mass of Life* is evident not only from the vast orchestral resources (including bass oboe, six horns, three trumpets, sarrusophone, and a large contingent of percussion, harp and celesta) – again Delius was not about to compromise his resources for half an hour's music – but from the call for double choir, a vocal feature particular to the *Mass*. Throughout the *Requiem* one is continually conscious of the increased sonority of the choral sound, especially in Delius's use of amplified vocal tessitura. These attributes, what is more, are symptomatic of a much-enhanced choral role in the work. A subject of much controversy, the content of the *Requiem* was essentially driven by Delius's zeal for atheism, one that, in connection with the subject of death, evidently exercised his sense of antagonistic evangelism. As the programme note didactically avowed: 'It [preached] that human life is like a day in the existence of the world, subject to the great laws of being'.[30]

The first two sections, musically linked, are complementary. The former, a solemn funeral march marked 'feierlich' (a term one more usually encounters in Bruckner), largely drawn from Ecclesiastes and Shakespeare's *The Tempest*, conveys man's insignificant existence within the universe, and that, with the inevitability of ageing and death, man confronts the fundamental truths that 'all is vanity', that religion offers only empty promises and that, at the end, eternal sleep awaits. The latter, probably based on a range of Nietzsche's writings – *Zarathustra*, *Ecce Homo* and *The Gay Science* – is one more of consolation, for with the knowledge of annihilation, man should enjoy life to the full (a sentiment echoed in Ecclesiastes 8:15 and Paul's citation in Corinthians 15:32). Both these movements are shared between baritone soloist and chorus. The third part, by contrast, is, save for a short reflective comment from the chorus, a monologue for baritone. Entitled 'à la grande Amoureuse' in the manuscript, it might well have drawn its text from the Song of Solomon, given its praise of love and the beloved ('Die Geliebte meines Herzens war eine Blume'). As Delius attempted to articulate: 'Often a man is judged worthless to the world and its laws, who should be exalted by praise for his human goodness, and the love of which he freely gives'.[31] A counterpart is provided by the more Nietzsche-inspired soprano monologue in the fourth

---

[30] 'London Concerts', *The Musical Times*, Vol. 63 No. 951 (May 1922), 342.

[31] Programme note for 23 March 1922. This is also quoted in full in *CD*, 195.

section ('Ich preise den Mann, der die Welt liebt und sie dennoch lassen kann') which honours a man who, after a fulfilling life, can look death in the face without fear. 'Thus', Delius affirmed, 'independence and self-reliance are the marks of a man who is great and free. He will look forward to his death with high courage in his soul, in proud solitude, in harmony with nature and the ever-recurrent, sonorous rhythm of birth and death'.[32] It is this 'harmony with nature' that forms the fifth part, focusing on the Nietzschean concept of 'eternal recurrence' ('Unendlicher Kreislauf, aller Dinge ewige Wiederkehr') in its celebration of springtime in much the same way as the conclusion of the *Mass* with its combination of solemnity, paean and nature mysticism.

The funereal opening movement, an arch form, is very much dominated by a partsong in eight parts ('Es gleicht ein Tag dem andern, denn jeder is vollendet in der Nacht'). Somewhat subtly, Delius allows the tonality to hang equivocally between the E minor of the sombre orchestral statement and C major which marks the beginning of the partsong. C major also underpins the next section of dialogue between the baritone and chorus ('Wir sind nur wie ein Tag'), a passage especially effective in its richly modified choral version. A return of the funereal material in G minor ignites a new, more tonally fluid phase, central to which is the didactic pronouncement 'Du bist verganglich und du musst vergehn'. The choral response – a repetition of the baritone's text – is one of great beauty not only in its harmonic nuance but also its melodic sweep through the soprano's high B flat and A. This climax in a passing D minor facilitates the recapitulation of the partsong which, after subsiding from an impassioned climax, subsequently cadences in C minor. A postludial transition, in which the funereal theme plays a conspicuous part, yields to a satirical choral outburst of both Christian and Islamic exclamations. Rhythmically banal and thematically repetitive, it is regrettable that Delius needed to include this bombastic gesture, presumably intended as a sardonic representation of the world's two largest religions. That Delius was considering how best to characterise religious ceremony among the world's religions is evident from a letter written to Newman in October 1913: 'If you had to characterise the 4 principal religions in music – which religious melodies used in the several religious ceremonies would you choose? – In other words – what themes do you consider would characterise the best the Christian – Mohamedan – Jewish & Boodhist religions?'[33] This notion was clearly abandoned, however, and no doubt wisely. Satire and parody are, at the best of times, difficult enough to

---

[32] Ibid.

[33] Letter from Delius to Newman, 10 [October] 1913, *DLL2*, 111.

express in musical terms (as we know from Mahler), and this was not an area of rhetoric familiar or well suited to the aesthetic of Delius's style. But if one chooses to ignore this solecism, the second movement is itself a rather affecting 'introduction and air', the latter (surely based on Nietzsche) a gentle melody or 'song' (Example 13.2a) sung by the baritone and amplified magnificently by the chorus ('Die lebenden wissen, dass sie sterben müssen'). In a harmonic world more reminiscent of *North Country Sketches* and *The Song of the High*

Example 13.2a. *Requiem*, 'Die lebenden
wissen, dass sie sterben müssen', baritone.

Hills, the baritone's invitation 'eat, drink and be merry' (an imperative from Ecclesiastes) is lucidly articulated and provides an apt conduit for the reprise of the 'air' in a more remote context for sopranos and altos.

The largely through-composed monologue for baritone (based, like the first movement, in C), with its more symphonic demeanour, has a good deal more in common with those solo movements of *A Mass of Life* and *Songs of Sunset*, particularly in its constant reworking of the movement's seminal thematic 'love' figure (Example 13.2b), an idea Delius lifted from *Margot la Rouge*. Introduced in b. 7, this figure is germane to the voluptuous choral amplification which embarks from the dominant ('In Ihren Blütenblättern wohnt die Liebe') and to the baritone's subsequent adulation of his beloved ('so würden alle meine Geliebte mit mir preisen'). A diatonic transformation of the opening motive in b. 1, with its distinctive Wagnerian lower chromatic appoggiatura moving to the added sixth, the sensual properties of the idea suggest that *Tristan und Isolde* still informed Delius's harmonic and gestural vocabulary, a fact confirmed by the intrusion of the 'Tristan' chord in the coda.

After the more declamatory prelude to the fourth part ('Ich preise den Mann'), the second part consists of two subsections, the first 'an ascension to the mountain tops' appropriately scored for high strings and horns (the allusion to Norway is plain enough), while the more protracted second is a nocturne ('und der Abend breitet seine Hände segnend aus') where encroaching darkness is evoked by a series of variations on a two-bar cell of falling thirds (Example 13.2c). It is this idea we hear more baldly at the movement's conclusion on a solo bassoon. The mountainous landscape ('Noch liegt Schnee auf den Häuptern der Berge') at the opening of the fifth part of the *Requiem*, with its crystalline scoring for upper strings and celesta, again owes much to the impressionism of *The Song of the High Hills*. Indeed, the entire picture of 'eternal renewal' (conceived as one panoramic through-composed canvas) surely rivals, if not supersedes, the paean of *A Mass of Life* in its pictorial immediacy. Besides the infectious sense of procession (which vividly recalls the end of the *Mass*), the combination of the arresting

Example 13.2b. *Requiem*, 'love' figure.

progressions of Delius's 'hymn' ('Aller Dinge ewige Widerkehr') and the enhanced choral sonority provide an imposing preface to the portrayal of spring. With springtime invoked, Delius's inclusion of the cuckoo (which he instructed in the score 'to be heard') and a pastoral oboe counterpoint in 6/4 (Lydian in character) in E major was surely intended to make allusion to *On Hearing the First Cuckoo*, an insinuation reinforced by its repetition in G flat. The Lydian melody is, however, given its greatest accentuation as a counterpoint to the chorus's final exclamation ('Frühling!') in D major, and it is in this key that the Requiem concludes in a visionary manner quite unique in the composer's output. As an aftermath to the brass fanfares (after Fig. 45), Delius's increasingly elliptical cadential progressions marked 'p' are answered by the melancholy 'cris de coeur' of the strings marked 'f' (such augmented harmonies ring true as quintessential of the composer). A response to this dramatic rhetoric are twenty preternatural bars of D major in support of a magical texture of mantra-like Lydian thematic cells in the wind, a tolling bell effect, offstage horns (which he requests be 'in the far distance'), further allusions to the Lydian pastoral self-quotation in the first violins and decorative embellishments from the harp and celesta. In this music Delius seems almost to take a step beyond the experimental aura of the *North Country Sketches*.

It was not until 23 March 1922 that the *Requiem* was given its first hearing at the Royal Philharmonic Society, in Heseltine's English translation and under the direction of Albert Coates; the choir was trained by Kennedy Scott. Delius, unwell and taking the waters in Germany, was unable to be present, but he was able to attend the first German performance in Frankfurt under Oskar von Pander on 1 May. German reception was cordial but in England, still coming to terms with its losses after the war, it was an inauspicious time for the proselytisation of such a stark Nietzschean message. As the columnist of *The Times* remarked: 'Its words are little more than a dry rationalistic tract, and are about as amenable to musical treatment as the Church Catechism would be'.[34] Colles, writing in *The Musical Times*, was no less accommodating:

Example 13.2c. *Requiem*, cell of descending thirds.

---

[34] *The Times*, 24 March 1923.

'It preached, and that was a good deal of the offence. The sacrifice in the war of the lives of young artists (and of young butcher-boys too, for that matter) seemed a theme for more humility. Who are we, their survivors and their beneficiaries, to "preach" so dogmatically about the motives and the end of their being?'[35] Clare Delius, 'chilled by [Delius's] philosophic detachment', expressed her consternation at her brother's attitude to the war when they met during the war years in London: 'In our talk in Pembridge Gardens I quickly abandoned the subject of the War. Fred seemed to me to be in a fever of thwarted creative longing. He wanted to "carry on" with his work as he had always carried on with it, and the war figured to him as an outrageous interruption'.[36] Beecham, however, could not hide his unbridled excoriation. Not only was the work ill-timed and lacking the 'invention equal to that of any preceding work of similar dimensions' (which, he maintained, was the key to its subsequent neglect),[37] but, 'through the state of self-delusion into which most composers and authors fall over the value of their own works', it was 'an unattractive manifestation of growing egoism' fuelled by his sequestered existence at Grez.[38] As with *Fennimore and Gerda*, Beecham never performed or recorded the work. Heseltine was no less polemic and declared it the 'weakest of all Delius's mature works', blighted by a lack of 'coherence and organic unity as well as the text',[39] while Hutchings advocated the more reconciling message of *Songs of Sunset* which '[dealt] with the same theme as the "Requiem" – the beauty of life and its transience – but without the didactic queasiness'.[40] In 1936 Fenby also condemned it as 'the most depressing choral work I know' (though later changed his mind).[41] The inappropriate time of the *Requiem*'s premiere almost certainly contributed to its silence, and the tragedy of the Second World War only served to hinder its exhumation. After a performance on 6 November 1950 in Carnegie Hall, New York, under William Johnson, it would be another fifteen years until Charles Groves performed it in Liverpool on 9 November 1965. Since then it has received several commercial recordings and has been issued on at least two occasions alongside *A Mass of Life*. Such an apposite coupling would be

---

[35] 'London Concerts', *The Musical Times*, Vol. 63 No. 951 (May 1922), 342.

[36] *CD*, 196.

[37] *TB*, 172.

[38] Ibid., 173.

[39] *PH*, 116–17.

[40] *AH*, 110.

[41] *EF*, 102.

enhanced further if the *Requiem* were to be sung in German. Nonetheless, the availability of recordings has eventuated a re-evaluation. Aside from the unpalatable text, and the unequal level of inspiration, there is much in the score of merit, not least the first and second movements for all their harmonic astringency. And it is hard to ignore the singular modernist vision and experiment of the last movement, a fact which was surely instrumental in Fenby's *volte-face*.[42]

EVENTYR: NORWEGIAN TRIBUTE
AND ORCHESTRAL SHOWPIECE

Eventyr is unique in Delius's output as a work inspired by folklore. Composition on it had begun in the first few months of 1915, in Watford. Delius and Jelka spent the winter months at Grez acquainting themselves with the writings of Peter Christen Asbjørnsen and his colleague, Jørgen Engebretsen Moe as a distraction from the constant concerns of the war situation. Delius's attraction to Norwegian folklore must also have articulated a longing for the isolation and tranquillity which Norway afforded during the European conflagration. In the summer of 1913, as Boyle has chronicled, Delius spent an idyllic holiday on the Gol and Hardangervidda plateaus (the very location of his early discoveries of the Norwegian landscape) before meeting up with Jelka at the Grieg home in Bergen where they were welcomed by Nina Grieg.[43] After the disruptions of 1914, their trip to the Nordfjord in the summer of 1915 must have seemed cathartic, not least because a conclusion to the war appeared elusive. 'Since I left England my spirits have been gradually rising & in the highlands of Norway, away from all humans I really got my old self back again', he told Heseltine.[44] But, after 1915, sailing restrictions prohibited travel to Norway which effectively attenuated one vital form of therapy as his illness worsened. *Eventyr*, and its completion in 1917, surely expressed something of the composer's longing for a world, albeit temporarily, beyond his grasp. Equally important, moreover, *Eventyr*, an orchestral showpiece, marked a return of a more overt expression of his

---

[42] See Fenby, E., sleeve note to EMI recording *ASD 2397* (1968), reprinted in Lloyd, S. (ed.) *Fenby on Delius* (London: Thames Publishing, 1996), 186–7.

[43] *DN*, 264.

[44] Letter from Delius to Heseltine, 12 October 1915, *FDPW*, 185.

affinity for Norwegian culture which had remained understated (such as in *The Song of the High Hills*) after the debacle of *Folkeraadet*.

Beecham tells us that, in the first phase of sketches, *Eventyr* was conceived 'in a somewhat casual way during his residence at Watford in 1915, but the revised score is on a considerably larger scale than originally planned'.[45] Although it requires the same large contingent of woodwind, there is no need of a bass oboe or additional horns. Nevertheless, Delius still requires his two harps, three trumpets and a battery of percussion including a gong, xylophone, bells, celesta and, most unusually, an offstage group of twenty men's voices. A significant feature of *Eventyr* (which, in this context, means 'fairy tale' or 'folk tale' in Norwegian) is its title. It is clear from the autograph manuscript, and from concert advertisements, that he vacillated between the Norwegian title and a more decorous English one, 'Once upon a time' (not, it should be emphasised, a translation of the Norwegian) and an additional attribution 'after Asbjørnsen's Folklore' ('fairytales' is crossed out).[46] Furthermore, the subtitle, 'A Ballad for Orchestra', also suggests that the work embraced some element of narrative or story, a factor which added to the debate as to whether Delius's tone poem contained programmatic features.[47] It was generally Delius's wont, as we have seen in such earlier orchestral essays as *Paris*, *Lebenstanz* and *In a Summer Garden*, to avoid the idea of a prescribed programme. This represented one end of the discourse which had exercised two of the most central protagonists and authors of symphonic poems in Britain, Bantock and Wallace, in the first decade of the twentieth century. Bantock's prescription (which mirrored that of Strauss) advocated a programme which, as a fertile 'well spring', could give rise to an almost limitless font of new symphonic structures At the opposite end lay the notion of a *Stimmungsbild* or 'general impression', a notion promoted by Wallace and one, from what evidence we have, Delius endorsed. Nevertheless, these polarised prescriptions left ample room for a conflation of both (as *Paris* suggests), and, in *Eventyr*, Delius's vivid characterisations and impressions merged with more vivid portrayals of particular stories, or, more precisely, *parts* of particular tales. As Rosa Newmarch – the author of the programme note for the first performance on 11 January 1919 and one which was almost certainly sanctioned by the composer – wrote: 'The music

---

[45] *TB*, 181.

[46] See *GB-Lbl* MS Mus 1745/1/29. See also Iliffe, B., '*Eventyr* and the Fairy Tales in Delius', in *FDML*, 276–7.

[47] See *DN*, 275–6 and Iliffe, B., '*Eventyr* and the Fairy Tales', 278ff.

of 'Once upon a time' reflects the general atmosphere of these traditions, but does not set out to illustrate a specific tale. It has no concrete literary programme, but it presents a series of pictures, simple yet subtle, that bring back to us many half-forgotten memories of days when romance and fantastic adventure was as real to us as the commonplaces of everyday life'.[48] On the authority of the composer, Fenby identified two groups of thematic ideas, the first representative of the 'warmhearted superstitious peasantry', the other, 'the eerie intervention in their lives of the fantastic creatures of Norwegian legend',[49] and the delineation of these two groups of ideas was strengthened by the amiable, sonorous scoring for strings of the former, and the more menacing timbres of the woodwind, brass and xylophone for the latter. These thematic ideas do in fact help to shape a sonata scheme in D minor which is very much a focus of the larger structure (see Table 13.1). The opening idea (Theme 'a'), which outlines a half-close in D minor, almost seems to enunciate the syllables of 'Once upon a time' (as in Norwegian 'Det var en gang'), though it is the second theme ('Theme 'b'), in the tonic major, that establishes the key. Two more thematic strands (Themes 'c' and 'd') introduce the 'Underjordiske', the 'unearthly ones' – trolls, hobgoblins, pixies, giants – though it is the more threatening sounds (Theme 'e') of what are surely malign trolls and hobgoblins (accentuated by the xylophone) which Delius uses as a transition to a group of second subjects in the dominant, A. These also reiterate the contrast of the good-natured peasantry (Theme 'f'), trolls and their best deterrents, church bells (Theme 'g'). Such contrasts might happily illuminate many of Asbjørnsen's collected folk tales – one thinks of classics such as 'Askeladden som stjal sølvendene til trollet' ['Boots and the troll'] or 'Askeladden som kappåt med trollet' ['Askeladden who had an eating match with the troll'], 'Herreper' ['Lord Peter'] or 'Risen som ikke hadde noe hjerte på seg' ['The giant who had no heart']. However, Iliffe has suggested the depiction of a particular tale on account of Jelka's description in letters to Heseltine and Fenby.[50] It concerns more specifically an extended passage in the development, framed by two statements of D minor, which reiterate the trolls and hobgoblins and one of those frightening episodes in 'Enkesønnen' ['The widow's son'] where the son of a poor widow, apprenticed to a brutal troll, escapes on a magic horse, only to be chased relentlessly through the forest by the troll and his gang. Initiated by statements of Theme 'a' and the

---

[48] Quoted in Iliffe, B., 'Eventyr and the Fairy Tales', 278.

[49] Fenby, E., Delius (London: Faber & Faber, 1971), 74.

[50] Iliffe, B., 'Eventyr and the Fairy Tales', 281–2.

Table 13.1. *Eventyr*, structural overview.

Bars	Theme	Key	Comments
	EXPOSITION		
	(First-subject group)		
1–20	Theme 'a'	D minor	'Once upon a time'
21–32	Theme 'b'	D major	'Peasants'
33–40	Theme 'c'	V of E (minor)	'Underjordiske' and other fantastic creatures
41–44	Theme 'd'	D minor	'Underjordiske' and other fantastic creatures
45–48	Theme 'e'	Transition	'Trolls and hobgoblins'
	(Second-subject group)		
49–56	Theme 'f'	A major	'Peasants'
57–78	Theme 'e'	A minor	'Trolls and hobgoblins'
79–86	Theme 'g'	A minor	Codetta – tolling bell
	DEVELOPMENT		
87–107	Theme 'f'	A minor (fluid)	
108–118	Theme 'e'	D minor	'Trolls and hobgoblins'
119–169	Theme 'a'	G minor / D minor / E minor	Episode from 'Enkesønnen'
170–187	Theme 'e'	D minor	'Trolls and hobgoblins'
188–215		(V of D)	Pealing bells
	RECAPITULATION		
216–229	Theme 'b'	D major	'Peasants'
230–end	Theme 'f'	F major	'Peasants'

'underjordiske' (Theme 'c'), the awful chase is illustrated by the rising pitch of galloping figurations in the orchestra and the 'wild shouts' (to use Delius's description in the score) of twenty mens' voices.[51] Only with the deterrent of pealing (and tolling) bells (from b. 188) is the troll and his gang thrown back and peace is restored by the recurrence of D major (b. 216), marked by the recapitulation of the first 'peasant' theme (Theme 'b'), while the second subject ('Theme 'f') brings the work to a conclusion in F major, a consequence of the first subject's quizzical half-closure in that key.

Eventyr demonstrates a fascinating conciliation between the programmatic and the more formal *Stimmungsbild* in that it shows Delius working within

---

[51] Ibid., 284–5.

the well-established scheme of sonata principles where, with a rich tapestry of thematic ideas, he provides picturesque and vivacious impressions of Asbjørnsen's folk tales. However, within the context of the developmental section of the piece (a much-favoured and apposite juncture for turbulence and dramatic climax within the programmatic domain), he provides a much more illustrative account of one of the folk tales (or at least one of its seminal scenes). In particular, this makes sense of the two 'shouts' for male voices which have always remained a somewhat enigmatic feature of the work and Delius's idiomatic identification of it as a ballad.

TWO TONE POEMS OF 1918: *A SONG BEFORE SUNRISE* AND *POEM OF LIFE AND LOVE*

It is an indication of Delius's physical resilience that, even after the completion of *Eventyr* in 1917, his creative vitality was not impaired, nor had his first love, the orchestra, declined in its appeal. With the lack of incoming royalties from Harmonie and Universal, Delius needed money, and after the war, rampant inflation in Germany meant that what was payable proved worthless. But, it should be added, much of what he had produced orchestrally during the war years required his usual large forces, so it is probable that the motivation behind the production of *A Song before Sunrise*, an orchestral miniature of moderate technical difficulty, of around six minutes in length, with a reduced contingent of woodwind and two horns (forces comparable with those of the *Zwei Stücke*), was to attract the increasing number of amateur orchestras in Britain. Cast in Delius's favoured 6/8, and the uncomplicated key of F major, it is a gentle pastoral, evoking the composer's predilection for the 'round dance'. The smaller forces, like those of the *Zwei Stücke*, by no means attenuate the imaginative colour of the orchestra. The wind, in particular, provide numerous nocturnal sounds – birds, insects; and Delius, according to Fenby, even alluded to 'cock-a-doodle-doo' at the end.[52] The body of the work, however, is contained, typically, in the rich texture of the nine-part string orchestra which exactly mimics the divisions of *On Hearing the First Cuckoo*. Although the two pieces provide ample evidence for Delius's lyrical music, they differ markedly in structure. Whereas *On Hearing the First Cuckoo* divulged the composer's love of variation form, *A Song before Sunrise* is a subtle sonata structure (Table 13.2). The first subject, rather more substantial

[52] Fenby, E., sleeve note to EMI Classics recording *CDZ 5 75293 2* (1968).

Table 13.2. *A Song before Sunrise*, structural overview.

Bars	Structure	Key	Comments
	EXPOSITION		
1–12	Theme 1a	F major	First subject (part 1)
13–22	Theme 1b	F major	First subject (part 2)
23–26	Transition	Dominant preparation	
27–36	Theme 2	C major	Second subject (two variations)
37–41	Theme 2	Bb major	Second subject (third variation)
	DEVELOPMENT		
42–76	New thematic episode	Fluid	
	RECAPITULATION		
77–88	Theme 1a	F major	First subject (part 1)
89–98	Theme 1b	F major	First subject (part 2)
99–106	Transition	Dominant preparation	
107–119	Theme 2	C major	Second subject (two variations – more extended)
120–124	Theme 2	Eb major	Second subject (third variation)
125–end	Coda	C major	

than the second in terms of length and self-development, is based in F and consists of two distinctive thematic departures. After a short transition, a second subject in the dominant, presented in three variations, concludes with a diversion to B flat major. The development, perhaps an evocation of the dawn chorus with its bubbling woodwind passages, provides a new episodic diversion. Dominant preparation for the recapitulation provides further nocturnal utterances (and what is surely a cock crowing – bb. 74–5) before a restatement, much of which is a literal repetition of the exposition, save for the extended second subject of which the third variation appears in E flat major (down a fifth – a common recapitulatory practice). And, like numerous codas, Delius quizzically concludes away from the tonic, in C major.

Owing to Delius's illness, the lot of seeing *A Song before Sunrise* into print with Augener in 1922 fell to Heseltine, the work's dedicatee.[53] Heseltine repaid the compliment in a work of comparable design, character and metre (indeed,

---

[53] See *FDPW*, 388–9.

it might even have been a tribute to the gift of Delius's piece), his *Serenade* for Delius's sixtieth birthday of 1923 [*sic*], the same year as the first performance was given by Henry Wood at Queen's Hall on 19 September 1923.

At much the same time as *A Song before Sunrise* was being completed in Biarritz, Delius was also working on another large-scale orchestral canvas, *Poem of Life and Love*, a work to which, like *Appalachia*, he referred to as 'symphony',[54] though this was clearly interchangeable with his concept of the tone poem. It was to Grainger that he announced he had completed the piece in July 1918,[55] and Jelka, undoubtedly delighted that, in spite of his increasing spells of illness, he was composing, remarked to Edvard Munch: 'Fred has been working splendidly and has quite finished his Symphony. He calls it "A poem of Life and Love", and it really is that, so emotional and warm and flowering forth so wonderfully!'[56] Delius then laid aside the score while *Fennimore and Gerda* received its first hearing in Frankfurt; and other works, notably the *Songs of Farewell* (see Chapter 15) and the Cello Concerto (see Chapter 14), as well as the commission to write the incidental music for *Hassan*, were significant enough distractions to prevent him from revisiting the score until the end of 1921. At this stage, having either lost or mislaid half the work, he had doubts about whether he could ever finish it.[57] By 1923 his ability to see and to write had seriously deteriorated and Jelka had begun to assume the role of amanuensis, assisting him with copying out parts of the score. What is more, progress was interrupted by the need for new music for *Hassan* (see below) and the attendance of its rehearsals and performances in London. Writing to Grainger in January 1924, Jelka commented: 'With what difficulty he is dictating me an orchestral score, his mind so active and bright, and he so hampered by his invalid limbs'.[58] Yet, in March 1924, while they were staying in La Napoule (where the Clews owned the 'fortress Chateau de la Napoule'), Delius was still determined to make progress with the work. 'We are to get a piano from Cannes today', she wrote to the novelist Sydney Schiff (known under the pseudonym Stephen Hudson), 'and then we shall go on with the new orchestral work that Fred has so at heart!'[59] The tone poem

---

[54] See letter from Delius to Henry Clews, 20 June 1918, *DLL2*, 188.

[55] Letter from Delius to Grainger, 20 July 1918, *AU-Mgm*.

[56] Letter from Jelka to Edvard Munch, 30 July 1918, *DLL2*, 193n.

[57] Letter from Delius to Heseltine, 14 October 1921, *FDPW*, 369.

[58] Letter from Jelka to Grainger, [24 February 1924], *DLL2*, 288.

[59] Letter from Jelka to Sydney Schiff, 25 March 1924, *DLL2*, 290n.

was left still unfinished in 1928 when Balfour Gardiner made a version for two pianos from the revised material left with Jelka's support, though it was finally completed by Fenby after his arrival at Grez in 1928. It was in this version that Gardiner and Fenby played the work to Delius on several occasions, hearings which persuaded him to think decisively about its future.

Delius's reluctance to release *Poem of Life and Love* was prudent. An examination of the score as left completed by Fenby reveals an unconventional sonata scheme (see Table 13.3). Although we have no programme note or surviving description or impression of what Delius intended for his tone poem – and we can only guess the various moods and dispositions from the thematic rhetoric – it seems evident from the abundance of thematic material that he had some, albeit very broad, narrative in mind to express the idea of 'life and love' in a series of symphonic episodes. Furthermore, these episodes would feature a process of thematic interaction and transformations in which, one suspects, in much the same manner as *Eventyr*, a compromise between 'impression' and definitive programme underpinned the form. The systemic problem with *Poem of Life and Love* is the highly variable quality of its thematic material. Profoundly disappointed by its quality, Fenby even described it as being 'the work … by a student in Delius's manner'.[60] An inauspicious, tonally oblique introduction, dominated by a melodic fragment for cellos, Theme 1a (Example 13.3a), gives way to a more animated paragraph in G minor whose melody, Theme 1b (Example 13.3b), is derived from the introduction. Strangely regressive in its rhythmical blandness, this material is uncharacteristically melodramatic and, to make matters worse, the transition to a second thematic departure, Theme 2, in the tonic major at b. 58, is also eccentrically inept (Example 13.3c). Much more representative of Delius's style and lyricism is the second subject in D major, Theme 3 (Example 13.3d), with its pungent Lydian and flattened seventh inflections, and the synthetic 'folksong' in D minor, Theme 4 (Example 13.3e), replete with 'Scotch snap' (a trait adopted from the 'Dance' in *North Country Sketches*). Problems of continuity return with the over-protracted development saved only by the new, slow episode at b. 207 (Theme 6), where the invention is of a higher quality. The recapitulation, with its new countertheme (Theme 7), is awkwardly pedestrian and banal, but, like the exposition, is rescued by the second subject. Initially presented in B flat major, its move to D major (which mimics the shift to F sharp major in the exposition) yields to the

---

[60] *EF*, 17.

Table 13.3. *Poem of Life and Love*, structural overview.

	Bars	Theme	Key	Tempo/metre/dynamics	Comments
INTRODUCTION	1–18	1a, 2	Fluid	Very slow, 3/2	Fragment in cellos/woodwind
	19–57	1b [hiatus at b. 58]	G minor	Animated, 4/4	First-subject group, derived from Theme 1a
	58–73	2, 1a	G major		
	74–95	3, 2	D major	Slow and very quietly, 3/2	Second-subject group, Lydian character
	96–117	4	D minor		'Folk' tune, concludes on V of D
DEVELOPMENT	118–177	1b, 2	Fluid	Commodo, 4/4	Introduction of new thematic fragment in b. 163 (Theme 7)
	178–191	5	Fluid	Rather quicker	
	192–206	1b, 3, elements of 2	Fluid	More quietly, 4/4	Concludes in F minor
	207–246	6, 3, 1b, 4	F major	Very slow, 4/4	Concludes with V–I to G minor
RECAPITULATION	247–284	1b, 7	G minor	Animated, 4/4	Theme 7 forms a countermelody to Theme 1b
	285–296	2	G major		
	297–320	3, 2	Bb major	Slow and very quiet, 3/2	Concludes on V of D
	321–344	4	D major	A tempo, quicker, 2/2	Climactic section
	345	4	D major	Rather slower	Coda

work's substantial and distinctive climax before the work concludes typically in a hushed manner.

The incoherent nature of *Poem of Life and Love* may have been symptomatic of Delius's circumstances. The conditions for revising the work with Jelka, who, for all her devotion, was no professional musician, were fraught with difficulty, and, as we know from the nature of Delius's illness, concentrated periods of work were a rare commodity. However, his attachment to the work meant that it remained at the forefront of his mind, should an opportunity present itself for a thorough revision, and this, as we know, materialised with the arrival of Eric Fenby in October 1928.

Example 13.3a. *Poem of Life and Love*, Introduction, opening fragment.

Example 13.3b. *Poem of Life and Love*, animated theme in G minor.

Example 13.3c. *Poem of Life and Love,* transitional material.

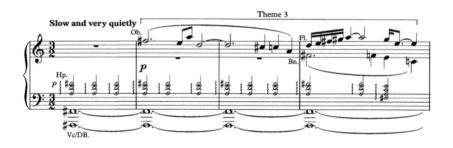

Example 13.3d. *Poem of Life and Love,* second subject.

HASSAN: A RETURN TO THE THEATRE

There is something perhaps poetic in the fact that Delius's last (largely) unaided score should have been incidental music for the stage, the very idiom which had whetted his appetite as a fledgling composer fresh out of Leipzig in 1888, initially with Bulwer Lytton's *Zanoni* and later with Ibsen's *Emperor and Galilean* and *The Feast at Solhaug.* Moreover, his music for Heiberg's *Folkeraadet* of 1897, notwithstanding its political controversy, had proved an important catalyst in the development of his style at the turn of the century, particularly with works such as *Paris, Lebenstanz, A Village Romeo and Juliet* and *Appalachia.* It is not without interest, too, that Delius should have found himself associated with the work of James Elroy Flecker, another *fin-de-*

Example 13.3e. *Poem of Life and Love*, synthetic folksong.

siècle author, like Ernest Dowson, to have died young. In both instances, it is difficult not to feel in Delius's music a sense of poignancy.

In the case of James Elroy Flecker, his 'poetic prose play' *Hassan* was completed in August 1913, by which time the author was seriously ill with tuberculosis but still buoyed up by the prospect of his play being produced in London. Indeed, Flecker, who earned a living in the Consular Service as an oriental linguist in the Levant, placed his hopes on the success of *Hassan*. Recognised by Edward Marsh, the editor of *Georgian Poetry*, as a poet of real potential, Flecker appeared in the first two volumes of that publication between 1911 and 1915 and his work received positive reviews. *Hassan*, however, was considered his masterpiece, and Flecker placed his hopes in Marsh to have it staged. At first, the response was mixed, but Marsh stood by the play and considered it a commercial proposition.[61] Until about a year before his death, Flecker worked on the play and it grew into five acts under the watchful eye of Marsh who oversaw its publication by Heinemann in 1922. Perhaps the saddest aspect from Flecker's point of view was that, with the outbreak of war, he knew that any immediate prospect of *Hassan* being produced had been negated and that he would not live to see his play on the stage. 'It is a masterpiece', Flecker told his mother in the autumn of 1913, 'but I shall never live to see it come into its own'.[62]

After receiving the typescript of *Hassan* in 1913,[63] Basil Dean, actor and theatrical producer, longed for the opportunity to stage the play in London. Originally Marsh had thought that Beerbohm Tree might produce it. Tree thought it too long, which prompted Tree's daughter, Viola, herself an actress,

---

[61] Redwood, D., *Flecker and Delius: The Making of 'Hassan'* (London: Thames Publishing, 1977), 18.

[62] Ibid., 11.

[63] Ibid., 6.

to pass the play on to Dean who, at that time, was assistant producer to Tree at Her Majesty's Theatre. Dean was well known as an innovator, a reputation he had established with the Liverpool Repertory Company where he had experimented with new, imaginative sets, costumes, and lighting effects. After moving to London to work with Tree, he was urged by Viola to give her father new ideas, and one of these was the possibility of *Hassan* which Dean considered ripe as an agency for 'total theatre'.[64] The war intervened, and Dean joined the Cheshire Regiment where his skills enabled him to manage the 'Navy and Army Canteen Board', a body which looked after theatres, cinemas and touring companies. After the war, Dean returned to the theatre and founded RandeaN, a company which lasted for ten years and stood at the forefront of British theatre during the 1920s. *Hassan* had not lost any of its appeal to him, and it was one of the priorities of that important decade, with a solemn undertaking to Flecker's wife Hellé (which gave rise to a substantial and, at times, emotionally charged correspondence), that the play be produced.[65]

The part played by music in *Hassan* was considerable and was part of the *Gesamtkunstwerk* of Dean's scheme to involve music at a substantial level. This was also the desire of Flecker and his widow who rather unreasonably expected the play to be staged in 1919. After 1919 gave way to 1920, Hellé Flecker threatened to take the play elsewhere.[66] In May of 1920, Dean and Hellé began to discuss the music of *Hassan* and their first choice was Ravel. He expressed interest in the project but was unsure of the time frame. While Ravel procrastinated, other names were considered including Jean Roger-Ducasse, the star pupil of Fauré, Harold Samuel, a composer of sorts though better known as a Bach pianist, Arnold Bax, Herbert Howells, Edward Dent and Rutland Boughton. Ravel's response was negative; he was too occupied with his one-act opera, *L'enfant et les sortilèges*. Having made little progress by June, Dean then suggested Delius whose music he knew, but his choice was confirmed after hearing Beecham's revival of *A Village Romeo and Juliet* at Covent Garden. After making contact with Delius, Dean travelled to Grez on 15 July where he read the whole drama to an increasingly interested

---

64 Ibid., 6–7. Dean's passion for 'total theatre' eventually evolved into a passion for talking films (of which he became an early pioneer). His later associations with the British film industry are well known.

65 See *GB-Mr* GB 133 DEA, Basil Dean archive.

66 Redwood, D., *Flecker and Delius*, 25.

composer.[67] A week or so later, Hellé Flecker also visited Grez to discuss her own understanding of the music involved. Both noted Delius's deteriorating health, though evidently neither was too concerned that the task would be physically beyond him. In fact, Delius felt that, with the assistance of Jelka and Heseltine (who consented to write out the full score from Delius's pencil drafts), he would be able to complete this rare commission. Only one hurdle remained. After twenty years of working almost exclusively with large orchestral forces, Delius was preoccupied with the challenge of writing for only twenty-one players, and wanted a larger ensemble. Dean was concerned too, and briefly considered approaching Boughton if Delius could not be placated; in the end, however, they reached a compromise of twenty-six players, and though Delius continued to lobby for a larger orchestra,[68] he got to work immediately in the knowledge that the music would be required for the rehearsals in August 1921 and the first night in September.

National political circumstances in 1921 – a credit 'squeeze' to curb individual spending – caused the postponement of *Hassan*; moreover, Dean was also preoccupied with finding a theatre larger than St Martin's Theatre which normally housed RandeaN's productions. A breakthrough came when Dean was asked to direct Arthur Pinero's *The Gay Lord Quex* at His Majesty's Theatre in 1923; Dean agreed on the proviso that *Hassan* could be staged there immediately afterwards. Another event which intervened was the German production of the play. As far back as 1914, Ernst Freissler had made a translation of Flecker's play and plans were being made for a production when the war began. After the war, the performance of plays by contemporary English authors met with hesitation in German theatres, and just as with Dean's circumstances, Freissler required a theatre large enough for the production. This was eventually discovered at Darmstadt, and its impresario, Hartung, hoped to open the production in January 1922. It was not, however, until 1 June 1923 that *Hassan* opened; Delius was unable to attend. Dean and Hellé were, however, able to see the Darmstadt production. Dean was greatly disappointed and felt the music had been treated rather indifferently. 'It did not seem to me that the audience were made sufficiently aware of the music', he told Delius, 'nor did it appear that the music had been so handled as to aid the atmosphere. Neither the poet's nor the musician's point of view

---

[67] See *DLL2*, 232n.

[68] See Redwood, D., *Flecker and Delius*, 60.

was realised, and as to a union between the two elements, that had not been thought of'.[69]

After witnessing the Darmstadt production, Dean was convinced that his original musical conception was inadequate. Having initially believed that individual preludes to the acts and between the scenes would be sufficient, he now knew that he would have to request several additional pieces from Delius who was about to leave for Norway. Not surprisingly, he met with protests from the composer, not only because music had to be composed quickly before the production in September, but because Delius's illness had progressed significantly since 1920 and he was more reliant than ever on the help of Jelka and his friends. A good deal of the additional music was written at Leskaskog, and a visit of Grainger occasioned his composition of the 'General Dance' for Delius to orchestrate.[70]

An account of the additional music for the 1923 London production was provided by an article in the *Daily Telegraph* by Heseltine,[71] and a full tabular representation of the music as it took place in the production was listed by Christopher Redwood.[72] This gives a comprehensive idea of the extent of the music, how it contributed to Dean's paradigm of 'total theatre' and the elaborate concept that Dean wanted to achieve.[73] As the *Daily Mail* anticipated, the presence of Delius's score '[promised] to be far more serious than the usual interludes'.[74] Delius also latterly recognised that Dean's instincts had been right. 'I understand now', he explained to Grainger, 'that there really was too little music before I had written the additions, especially for the last 2 scenes, where music goes on almost all the time ... *Our* ballet piece was a *great success* and brought just a vigorous contrast to the rest'.[75] *Hassan* opened on 20 September 1923 under the direction of Eugene Goossens; it played triumphantly to packed houses and had a run of 281 performances (directed by Percy Fletcher) which also extended to the provinces. 'The applause was deafening', Dean recollected. 'I fled back to the shelter of the office, where I was eventually found by the theatre manager, unsympathetic to my trembling

---

[69] Letter from Dean to Delius, 19 June 1923 in Redwood, D., *Flecker and Delius*, 44.

[70] Bird, J., *Percy Grainger* (Oxford: Oxford University Press, 1999), 214.

[71] Heseltine, P., *Daily Telegraph*, 23 September 1923.

[72] Redwood, C., 'A Note on the Music', in Redwood, D., *Flecker and Delius*, 76–7.

[73] Dean, B., *Seven Ages: An Autobiography, 1888–1927* (London: Hutchinson, 1970), 182.

[74] Redwood, D., *Flecker and Delius*, 69.

[75] Letter from Delius to Grainger, 29 September 1923, *DLL2*, 280–81.

and my tears ... I remember little of my curtain speech, save that I had the wit to say how glad I was that after nearly ten years of struggle, I had been able to keep my promise to the poet'.[76] To Dean's astonishment, however, it was a complete failure in New York's Broadway and had to be withdrawn after two calamitous weeks at the Knickerbocker Theatre with the loss of £100,000. For Delius, on the other hand, the commercial success in London was extremely welcome. This and Gardiner's generous purchase of the house at Grez placed him and Jelka in a more comfortable pecuniary position for the rest of their lives.

The *Hassan* commission furnished Delius with the rare opportunity to revisit musical essays of more reduced scale which, for the most part, he had not composed since the 1890s. Delius was also no stranger to exoticism. The sound of the harmonic minor scale with its characteristic augmented second was something which coloured the introduction of the *Dance Rhapsody* No. 1; and the 'interlude' to that variation structure, somewhat Caucasian in atmosphere, revealed Delius's interest in the music of 'The Five'. The music of Rimsky-Korsakov, Borodin and Balakirev had begun to establish itself in the western repertoire during the first years of the twentieth century, and Beecham, in particular, had done much to promote Rimsky-Korsakov's operas, Borodin's *Prince Igor* (which we know Delius admired) and Stravinsky's *The Firebird* in London in the years before the war. In addition, the ballet music which Dean required was directed by no less than the great Russian dancer and choreographer, Michel Fokine, whom Dean had brought over specially from America. It is also worth noting that the idiom of incidental music was experiencing its heyday in the European theatre before the advent of film and sound in the mid-1920s, when one of Delius's closest friends, Norman O'Neill, stood at the head of those professional composers and conductors who made their names in the theatre. O'Neill, specifically, had been recognised for his music to Maeterlinck's *The Blue Bird* (1909), Lord Dunsany's *The Golden Doom* (1912) and J. M. Barrie's *Mary Rose* (1920) at the Haymarket Theatre, as had Roger Quilter for the Christmas play *Where the Rainbow Ends* (1911), which enjoyed an extended popularity.

One of the major attributes of Flecker's play was that it offered Delius a broad range of emotional subject material. This he had responded to immediately during Dean's first visit to Grez when the play had been read to him.[77] Apart from the elements of spectacle, a combination of seduction,

---

[76] Dean, B., *Seven Ages*, 188.

[77] See *DLL2*, 232n.

revenge, love, horror and disillusionment pervaded the pages of the play (though the Lord Chamberlain, Lord Cromer, required reassurance that there would be no realistic representation of torture on the stage).[78] But *Hassan* also presented Delius with other more esoteric opportunities. Complex in its range of scenes and character roles, *Hassan* has been compared with *The Tempest* in its mixing of magic and realism.[79] As one critic of *The Times* perceived, it was 'a play of Persia, a love story almost approximating to Greek tragedy'.[80] And for this reason alone, some commentators rightly remarked that the play was much more than the major spectacle and pageant afforded by the lavish production.[81] After Hassan is condemned by the Caliph to witness the appalling, sadistic death of Rafi and Pervaneh (a couple who choose a day of love followed by unimaginable torture, rather than banishment for Rafi, and a life for Pervaneh in the Caliph's harem), 'an inspissated gloom' hangs over the play from which one seeks moral escape.[82] As Ishak, Hassan's friend, put it in Act V Scene 1: 'I am leaving this city of slaves, this Baghdad of fornication. I have broken my lute and will write no more qasidahs in praise of the generosity of kings. I will try the barren road, and listen for the voice of the emptiness of earth. And you shall walk beside me'. Samarkand thus becomes not only a destination of physical flight but one of philosophical and utopian refuge.

Many aspects of *Hassan* read in a similar manner to incidental scores of the past and present. Short passages of introductory fanfares (as at the beginning of Act II), brief thematic interludes of no more than a few bars are among the many aphoristic comments that Dean felt were necessary for the play's coherence. There was, however, opportunity in the Preludes and Entr'actes for Delius to expand his musical thought into a series of highly attractive miniatures. This is certainly true of the Prelude to Act I where Hassan's exotic melody (in B minor), associated with the reedy hues of the cor anglais and oboe, frame a longer, developed melody which reaches the dominant of D at its climax. The hushed 'pppp' conclusion is also redolent of so many other Delius orchestral works, as is the final gesture on the cor anglais which is yet another borrowing of that dream-like figure from 'In the Seraglio Garden' and *A Mass of Life*. The Interlude between Act I Scenes 1 and 2 was an exercise in woodwind arabesques and cadenzas based on Delius's familiar 'added notes'

---

[78] Dean, B., *Seven Ages*, 183.

[79] *MLPG*, 401.

[80] *Daily Mail*, 14 September 1923.

[81] *Daily Mail*, 21 September 1923.

[82] *The Times*, 21 September 1923.

of a sixth, seventh and ninth, and the 'Serenade', from Act I Scene 2 (and the most enduring number of Delius's score), provides an archetypal example of the composer's 'bifurcated' model of diatonic melody and chromatic accompaniment. It was as if Delius looked back, nostalgically, to the pages of *Koanga*. Clearly intended as a 'feature' of the play, it recurred later in Act I and was repeated (as a vocalise for tenor solo), more fully scored in Act III, as an interlude between Scenes 1 and 2. There was also a place for Delius's paradigm of the distant wordless chorus, notably the seamless twenty-one bars used in Act I (an example which might easily have figured as a third song to those for *To be sung of a summer night on the water*). Wordless chorus is most effectively deployed at the end of the Preludes to Act III and Act V, but there is also room for homophonic partsong as with the 'Chorus of Beggars and Dancing Girls' in Act II. The male chorus of beggars in Act II seems, by comparison, to be more stilted, but Delius's former experience of ballet music with female chorus (as one finds in *The Magic Fountain* and *A Mass of Life*) is put to good use in the sensuous 'Chorus of Women'. Indeed, the ballet music in *Hassan* was an ornate affair which prompted some of Delius's best music (e.g. the 'Divertissement'), with Grainger's 'General Dance' (perhaps somewhat more rhythmically dynamic than we find in Delius's style) offering a fascinating intersection of the two composers; while the Beggars' Dance was clearly influenced figuratively and modally by the second subject of *Poem of Life and Love* and its Griegian similarity to *Florida*. As Grainger later remarked: 'It was not *the scoring* of Hassan I helped him with. He wanted 3 minutes (about) more music for a ballet section, and this I composed and scored (I forget whether I used any of his themistic material or not)'.[83] Three other miniature movements are worthy of note. 'The Procession of Protracted Death' from Act V is a strangely austere march (replete with xylophone interjections), appropriate to the horrific execution scene which Hassan is forced to witness. This contrasts markedly with the languid, gossamer Prelude to the last scene, elaborately scored for strings, harp and wind, which is a unique piece of impressionism in the composer's output. Moving on without a break, the mesmeric closing scene, another procession in which Hassan and Ishak join the merchants and pilgrims on the 'Golden Road to Samarkand', reveals Delius's own instinct for the theatre. Full of his 'added chords', whose inner parts continue to shift kaleidoscopically, the movement recalls the opening material of Act I, while holding our attention with its ostinato string and harp figures and evocative isolated phrases for wind. The chorus's line 'We take the

---

[83]   Letter from Grainger to Fenby, 1936, quoted in Redwood, D., *Flecker and Delius*, 78.

golden road to Samarkand' becomes another adjunct to the ostinato, and its rich, harmonised form (which gravitates to E flat rather than C) provides not only an additional sense of colour but also a hauntingly quizzical note to the end of the play as the 'caravan' eventually moves out of sight, still suspended on its unresolved pedal of G.

Beecham claimed that the final spell of Delius's creative activity, 1915–1923, was 'one of progressive decline',[84] but that in *Hassan* 'the ancient fire [burned] brightly for a few rare moments'. Certainly, *Hassan* seemed to appeal to an earlier stylistic fertility which can be traced back to the unpretentiousness of *Florida* and the *Drei Symphonische Dichtungen* of the composer's first creative years. In his concert performances of extracts from the score, Beecham used the original orchestration, but, at the behest of Balfour Gardiner, who believed that, as a choral suite,[85] it would 'be a useful addition to the répertoire of small choral societies',[86] and, thereby, the source of some useful income, Delius took the opportunity with Fenby's assistance to reorchestrate a number of the movements (Prelude to Act I, Prelude to Act II and ballet, Serenade, 'The Procession of Protracted Death' and the final Desert Scene) for full orchestra. Later the preludes to Acts I and II were excised to produce a shorter suite which was first broadcast by the BBC (with the pieces in reverse order) under the direction of Victor Hely-Hutchinson on 1 August 1933.

[84] *TB*, 221.

[85] Although the addition of chorus further complicated the question of resources for *Hassan*, Delius disliked the purely instrumental arrangements of the vocal numbers. As he remarked to Beecham (letter from Delius to Beecham, 23 March 1934, *DLL2*, 446): 'I have never been quite pleased with Hassan arranged without the voices. Or is it that this music belongs so entirely to the theatre?'

[86] Letter from Gardiner to Delius, 21 March 1929, *DLL2*, 348.

CHAPTER 14

Music of the War Years and After (II): Violin Sonata No. 1, Double Concerto, Cello Sonata, String Quartet, Violin Concerto, Cello Concerto, Violin Sonata No. 2 (1914–1923)

It is one of the most puzzling aspects of Delius's creative path that, between 1914 and 1923, while also occupying himself more amenably with the composition of that most romantic of idioms, the symphonic poem, he became consumed with the need to write a series of instrumental works entirely dependent on the classical imperatives of sonata and concerto. Beecham was baffled; he considered the enterprise a failure, save for the Violin Concerto,[1] and expressed a relief in the restoration of the composer's natural gifts in the freer forms of *Eventyr*, *A Song Before Sunrise* and, even more so, in *Hassan*.[2] Heseltine was similarly hesitant: 'Delius is not seen at his best in those works whose form is dependent upon the development of contrasted themes in a certain relation preordained by tradition'.[3] While Evans, perhaps the most eloquent of all, remarked: 'Where we may find them [Delius's compositional methods] to fail is in those works which by their medium invite comparison with the classics on which our musical experience is based. Even by their titles alone, the Delius concertos and sonatas compel us to apply terms of evaluation foreign to the composer's nature'.[4]

---

[1] *TB*, 217.

[2] Ibid.

[3] *PH*, 136.

[4] Evans, P., 'Delius', Evans Papers, *GB-DRu*.

Delius never gave his reasons for wishing to revisit more classical idioms that he had only briefly explored in the past. The Violin Sonata in B major of 1892, a perhaps overblown work, had been long since shelved, as had his Suite for Violin and Orchestra; and, for all its popularity and number of performances, his Piano Concerto never met with his greatest satisfaction. Nevertheless, Delius evidently believed that the possibilities of rhapsodic lyricism and thematic variation, seminal to his style and *modus operandi*, might be a productive source of new forms, and, given his zeal to explore new structural ideas in his symphonic poems, the traditional sonata and concerto seemed a ripe field for his attention and one to which he evidently felt he could make a novel and creative contribution. In consequence, this gave rise to a new and heightened awareness of the role of thematic material and the integral role of key in his style. With regard to the latter, in particular, we find that Delius seemed to discover a new simplicity in his favoured one-movement forms, expressed by a new contrapuntal fluency, the choice of uncomplicated tonalities (e.g. C major, A minor, D minor and F) and the process of 'dual functionality' in his structural thinking.

VIOLIN SONATA NO. 1

Ideas for the first two movements of the Violin Sonata No. 1 had been sketched as far back as 1905,[5] when he had showed the work to the violinist Achille Rivarde.[6] Rivarde was, by then, an established violin teacher at the Royal College of Music and is reputed to have performed the work privately.[7] But it was not until 1914 that Delius decided to revisit the work in order to add a final movement. The addition of this movement was clearly to provide balance and resolution to an otherwise incomplete structure which, given the absence of movement designations (i.e. I, II, III), the composer wished to convey as one extended movement. Such thinking was very much in keeping with Delius's approach to multi-movement structures. It is evident from the earlier Piano Concerto – in the initial *Fantasy* for Piano and Orchestra and the revised version of the Concerto in one movement – but there are numerous instances

---

[5] See *GB-Lbl* MS Mus 1745/1/34, ff. 1–12.

[6] Harrison, M., 'The Music of Delius', *Proceedings of the Royal Musical Association*, Vol. 71 (1944), 47.

[7] Ibid.

in works such as *The Song of the High Hills* and *North Country Sketches* where a Gestalt theory appears to be in operation.

The first movement of the Sonata begins with a thematic idea in the violin (Example 14.1a) featuring an extended dominant pitch (A) and a series of descending fourths (a feature also present in the right-hand accompaniment in b. 1). Delius uses this melodic idea as a departure no less than three times in the next fourteen bars and on each occasion the idea undergoes fresh development. Such a process we have met many times in the way Delius generates his musical paragraphs. Here, however, in this balder, more naked 'absolute musical' idiom for violin and piano, it is arrestingly evident how significant these melodic repetitions are, shorn of their orchestral timbre, to the broader method of fragmentation, and how Delius invariably used them to introduce additional counterpoints (such as the one in b. 8) as part of his variation technique. At the same it also revealed a density of harmonic rhythm in the piano part which, at times, leads Delius into a minefield of textural banality and stereotype when his goals do not appear to be well defined (e.g. bars 12–16). At b. 17 Delius presents a counterstatement (Example 14.1b), a new thematic cell of two bars which is subject to the same form of treatment as the first subject, but is strongly differentiated by its rhythmical character,

Example 14.1a. Violin Sonata No. 1, first movement, opening theme.

differing accompanimental figuration and the prevalence of sensual dominant-thirteenth harmony at the beginning of each phrase. More fluid tonally, this idea also contrasts markedly with a third thematic statement in G minor at b. 32 which briefly intervenes for four bars. Of particular interest here is Delius's use of the two invertible contrapuntal lines between the violin and the right hand of the piano (Example 14.1c). From a dynamic of 'p', this idea swells rapidly to 'ff' as the movement breaks out into a more passionate series of variations of the counterstatement, one encapsulated by the climactic solo piano in bars 43–6. Clearly constituting a form of developmental paragraph, this turbulence is, however, undermined by the return of the third thematic idea. In emulating the same dynamic properties as its expositional appearance, the two further statements of this lyrical material hasten towards an 'ff' climax by making fertile use of the contrapuntal invertibility (cf. bb. 47–52 and bb. 53–8). After a short transition, the quicker cadenza-like passage (bb. 61–71) pulls us back towards D, strongly confirmed by the dominant harmony of b. 71, though before the restatement of the first subject in b. 77, Delius cannot resist a sense of 'false' recapitulation in bars 72–5.

Example 14.1b. Violin Sonata No. 1, first movement, counterstatement.

Example 14.1c. Violin Sonata No. 1, first movement,
third thematic statement, invertible counterpoint.

The recapitulation appears to begin conventionally enough in D minor but as Delius binds both the first subject and the counterstatement more closely to the tonic, the process of variegation is inevitably changed. Delius also makes no reference to his third subject. In consequence the much-truncated recapitulation, which concludes with a final fragment of the counterstatement leaves us with the inescapable impression that a new departure is about to happen. Moreover, the augmented sixth (bb. 119–20) on B flat, which might have resolved on V of D, resolves plagally onto F^7 as we head into a new movement, marked 'molto moderato'. Effectively a slow movement, or at least an extended 'intermezzo', this reverie, dominated by the violin, is paradigmatical of Delius's instinct for monothematic development. The die is cast in the first two antecedent bars (bb. 121–2) and the three consequent bars (123–5) which carry the tonality to a 6/4 of C major (Example 14.1d), though resolution of this key is characteristically delayed until bb. 180–81 (with significant passing references in bb. 141, 147 and 155). An augmented version is added to the mix in b. 133 which, by degrees, begins to adopt the identity of parallel seventh harmonies in last inversion (see bb. 182–4) as we move towards the coda.

Example 14.1d. Violin Sonata No. 1, slow movement, first theme.

After concluding on the dominant of C, Delius furiously embarks on his finale in the unexpected key of B minor (Example 14.1e). The movement is constructed in three clear parts. The outer sections unambiguously constitute the bones of a sonata design (see Table 14.1a) in which there are two contrasting thematic subjects. In the exposition, Delius makes use at first of a conventional classical relationship of B minor and its relative major, D, though the extension of the second subject (which is conspicuously developmental in scope) restates the first subject in the submediant minor, G minor, before D minor returns in the closing bars. The recapitulation follows a similar if modified thematic pattern, though it is E major that Delius chooses for his second subject and (more conventionally) E minor for the restatement of his first subject. More exceptional, however, are the twenty-three bars, marked 'slow and mysteriously' (bb. 78–101) which replace the conventional development. Here Delius presents us with a second self-developing slow movement.

Though the long melody in the violin is tonally fluid (analogous to the standard behaviour of a developmental paragraph), it is ultimately goal-directed towards D major (b. 93) before B minor is once more established. Its lyrical contrast, moreover, with the turbulence of the rest of the finale is vivid. Furthermore its position has a larger syntactical effect on the perception of the sonata's larger structure, for besides understanding the work as a three-movement design, it is also possible to observe it as a scheme in five movements, in which the two slow movements provide interludes (Table 14.1b).

The tonal insistence on D major in the coda of the last movement, together with the (albeit somewhat artificial) cyclic reference to the first subject of the first movement, also warrants us to consider the broader consequences of the whole work.

Example 14.1e. Violin Sonata No. 1, Finale, opening theme.

Table 14.1a. Violin Sonata No. 1, Finale, structural overview.

	Bars	Theme	Key	Tempo/metre/dynamics	Comments
EXPOSITION	1–27	First subject	B minor	With vigour and animation	
	28–38	Second subject	D major	Più tranquillo	Rhythmically related to first subject
	39–72	First subject	G minor	Tempo I	Fluid and lyrical/developmental
	73–76	First subject	D minor (V)	Becoming softer and slower	
	77–78	Transition			
[DEVELOPMENT]	79–93	New thematic idea	D major?	Slow and mysteriously	Second slow movement? Goal-directed towards D?
	95–102	Transition	V of B	Molto tranquillo	
RECAPITULATION	103–129	First subject	B minor	Tempo I	
	130–139	Second subject	E major	Più tranquillo	
	140–155	First subject	E minor	Tempo I	
	156–161	Transition	D major		
	162–172	First subject of first movement	D major	Very quick	Cyclic reference
	173–176	First subject	B minor/major	Tempo I	

Table 14.1b. Violin Sonata No. 1, scheme of the entire work.

Movement	Key
First movement (moderato)	D minor
Slow movement 1	C major
Finale (exposition)	B minor
Slow movement 2	D major
Finale (recapitulation)	B minor – D major – B minor

The first hearing of the Violin Sonata No. 1 was in the Houldsworth Hall, Manchester, on 24 February 1915. Taking advantage of Beecham's connections with the city and the Hallé Orchestra, Delius secured a performance by the Hallé's leader, Arthur Catterall, accompanied by Robert Jaffrey Forbes, a distinguished Manchester concert pianist. Catterall and Forbes also performed the Sonata in London on 29 and 30 April attended by the composer. Soon after it was also played by the young May Harrison accompanied by Harty on 16 June. According to Harrison, Harty painstakingly corrected Delius's manuscript, and, after the performance, took the corrected version to Forsyth. 'But by some extraordinary chance, the wrong part got published, and, as far as I know, Harty's wonderful work was irretrievably lost'.[8] The piano part of Forsyth's edition was in fact carried out by Forbes who no doubt insisted, as the work's first executant, that the publisher accept his editorial standpoint and revisions. The truth is, Delius's manuscript required extensive revision, a fact pointed out by Threlfall who also drew attention to the considerable amount of surviving sources, including Delius's autograph manuscript.[9] In 1928, Bax, who remained a keen proponent of the work, broadcast it with May Harrison.

DOUBLE CONCERTO: CONCERTO AS LYRIC FORM

In her paper for the Royal Musical Association of 22 March 1945, May Harrison recalled how she and her sister, Beatrice, the celebrated cellist, first encountered Delius in Manchester on 3 December 1914 when they both

[8] Harrison, M., 'Delius', in DC, 102, quoted in Dibble, J. C., *Hamilton Harty: Musical Polymath* (Woodbridge: Boydell & Brewer, 2013), 119.

[9] See RT2, 102–3 and Threlfall, R., 'Delius's Violin Sonata (No. 1)', *DSJ* No. 74 (January 1982), 5–12.

participated in a Hallé Concert at the Free Trade Hall. The main reason for Delius's attendance at the concert – it was his first visit to Manchester, which he disliked intensely[10] – was that Beecham planned to direct two pieces from *A Village Romeo and Juliet* (Scene 5 and *The Walk to the Paradise Garden*), but the programme also included Balakirev's *Thamar* and Brahms's Double Concerto featuring the Harrison sisters as soloists.[11] '[Delius] came into the artists' room with Mr Langford, the well-known critic, at the rehearsal', Harrison recalled. 'At that time Delius was well and vigorous. He told us that he usually had not much liking for Brahms, but that the Double Concerto had greatly impressed him, and had given him the idea possibly of writing a double concerto also for violin, cello and orchestra'.[12] As Harrison insinuated, it was Samuel Langford, the Leipzig-educated Manchester critic, who facilitated the introduction, as much, one senses, from his admiration for the Harrisons' brilliant playing as from his veneration of Delius's music. '[He] is the most rare spirit in English music and the most delicate and subtle of our English harmonists. No movement in music would be more welcomed by the musicians amongst us than the fuller exploration of his works'.[13]

Delius began work on his Double Concerto by the end of April 1915 and completion of the score must have occurred sometime towards the end of November, for we know that, by Christmas, Heseltine had produced a pianoforte score which the Harrison sisters required for rehearsal.[14] During the course of 1915 and 1916, Delius saw a good deal of them when he visited either London or the Harrison home on Ditton Hill in order to go through the score.[15] According to Beatrice, the finished score posed some serious problems for her instrument:

> The strange thing was that it was written in unison and technically was almost impossible to play but with Delius himself and Peter [*sic*] Heseltine at the piano, we rewrote the cello part and made it playable. Delius sat for hours with a large cushion and the score on his knees, surrounded by four of our Scottie dogs, who took a great interest in the proceedings and

[10] See *DLL2*, 142n.

[11] Kennedy, M., *The Hallé Tradition: A Century of Music* (Manchester: Manchester University Press, 1960), 190.

[12] Harrison, M., 'The Music of Delius', 43.

[13] Kennedy, M., *The Hallé Tradition*, 190.

[14] Letter from Delius to Heseltine, 21 December 1915, *DLL2*, 158.

[15] Harrison, M., 'The Music of Delius', 44.

periodically licked his fingers which made him jump, throw everything in the air and have to begin again. Heseltine banged out the orchestral part, while I, hot and anxious, played each passage over and over again until Delius was satisfied that it corresponded perfectly with the violin. All this took weeks but at last it was finished.[16]

As with his orchestral tone poems, Delius had high hopes that the Double Concerto might be given during the winter season of 1916, though this did not materialise,[17] and the hope lingered that the Concerto might be performed in the USA, but, as we know, illness, the war and lack of money made the notion of travel impossible. The Harrison sisters were also in America for a tour at the end of 1916 and there was much enthusiasm about the Double Concerto amongst the New York 'Friends of Music'. As Beatrice explained:

> Every one over here is most excited about your beautiful Double Concerto & Mrs Lanier [a prominent New York patron and manager of the "Friends"] told me to ask you to send over the Score of the Double Concerto at once, & the Conductors want to see & study it, & she does want it by the spring, & she does hope she can fix it up for us to play it next year at the "Friends of Music". The Boston Symphony Orchestra is most anxious to have it I hear, also the New York Philharmonic, every one is thrilled about it. I do hope you will be able to come over to England this summer, & May and I will work & study it, & get it as one instrument, as I think we really do understand your exquisite music a little bit, & I think you know how we love it.[18]

The Concerto was rehearsed with Orr at the piano in or around July 1920 while Delius and Jelka were in Cornwall. By then the work was destined to have its London premiere in the next London season when Wood conducted it at Queen's Hall with the Harrison sisters on 21 February 1920. 'The Concerto went wonderfully well', Delius recalled to Jelka, 'The girls played superbly & Wood surpassed himself – It was enthusiastically received – The house was crowded – the best of the season'.[19]

---

[16] Harrison, B., *The Cello and the Nightingales: The Autobiography of Beatrice Harrison*, ed. Cleveland-Peck, P. (London: John Murray, 1985). 104.

[17] See letter from Delius to C. W. Orr, 26 May 1916, *DLL2*, 166.

[18] Letter from Beatrice Harrison to Delius, 11 January 1917, *DLL2*, 177.

[19] Letter from Delius to Jelka, [22? February 1920], *DLL2*, 227.

Brahms's Double Concerto (for which the Harrison sisters were famous) may have been the stimulus to re-enter the world of the concerto, but he was in no frame of mind to revive the kind of large-scale Romantic model which had been suggested by Szántó's 'transformation' of his piano concerto, nor of the post-Brahmsian classical paradigms such as that of Elgar (which he found 'very long and dull').[20] As Evans has commented, 'concerto is a far more complex structure even than symphony and requires most delicate organisation not only of the material but of the interrelations of the two opposed forces. Delius ignores the latter requirement in favour of sustained rhapsody by the soloist; even when the thematic interest passes to the orchestra it is hidden by the wealth of decoration in the solo part. This treatment might be acceptable were it moulded into a succinct formal design, but he rarely makes any attempt to curb the endless lyricism'.[21]

This is entirely true of the construction and *modus operandi* of the Double Concerto, which relies strongly on variation processes which we have already met in so many of Delius's own brand of symphonic structures. Moreover, the Double Concerto confirms the composer's preoccupation with one-movement forms with a conciseness of structure (at a length of roughly twenty minutes by comparison with traditional three-movement schemes of thirty to thirty-five minutes). Also a general rejection of lengthy developmental paragraphs is enshrined by a strong allusion (like that of his Piano Concerto in its one-movement form) to exposition and recapitulation as 'first' and 'last' movements which embraces even lyrical effusion in a 'slow' movement. In her analytical notes for the first performance in 1920, Newmarch noted: 'The old three movements are still faintly discernible, the middle section being clearly a survival of the usual slow movement, while the first and last parts not only retain roughly the sonata-form with its first and second subjects, but moreover, at the same time, the function of exposition and recapitulation. The composer has merely rendered the rigorous old formulae more pliable in order to adapt them to his poetical ideas, which he is unwilling to sacrifice to any exigencies of strict form'.[22]

Newmarch's thoughtful and perceptive assessment of Delius's structure captures a modicum of the complexity of Delius's lyrically driven form, though there are also other noteworthy aspects (the climactic, closing role of the 'slow' movement and the interaction of sonata methods with variation processes,

[20] See letter from Delius to C. W. Orr, [June/July 1918], *DLL2*, 189.

[21] Evans, P., 'Delius', Evans Papers, *GB-DRu*.

[22] Newmarch, R., Analytical notes for the programme on 21 February 1920.

and Delius's residual use of 'ritornello' as a structural device) which are not mentioned but which compensate for those normative cohesive elements, and which commonly lend concerto form its traditional coherence and syntax. The opening of the Double Concerto begins with a short orchestral statement in C minor of eight bars (Example 14.2a) followed by a cadenza of seven bars on IV of C minor for the two soloists. This unassuming introduction, whose simple function is to bed down a sense of the tonic key, establishes an opening formula which Delius employed in his Violin Concerto. Having stated his introduction, Delius launches into his exposition without ceremony. His first theme, outlining a strong, almost Neo-Baroque two-part counterpoint for the soloists (Theme 1), sets out from C minor in what is a fascinating matrix of variations cast on two levels. Delius's theme (essentially in the solo violin) is made up of a series of four-bar phrases, with each succeeding phrase based on the rhythmical formula of the first. The result is a cumulative, *composite* theme of sub-variations, embellished by counterthematic strands from the solo cellist (Example 14.2b). The first thematic utterance, the theme plus four additional variations, moves from C minor to V of F sharp before a short transition in B minor provides a conduit to a first composite variation and sub-variations at b. 44. This new variegation is initiated by the cello in E minor, though the five sub-variations are increasingly shared by the two soloists. A second phase of variations at b. 68 occupies the tonal area of A flat major and G sharp minor and interacts subtly with a new thematic departure from the orchestra (as second subject – Theme 2) and this occurs again in a third phase from E flat minor in b. 97, shrewdly enhanced by a new thematic filigree introduced in b. 95, lending the variations a more tranquil character and mood. The presence of this second theme, in a contrasting tonal area, brings an additional layer of complexity in that the variations design conflates

Example 14.2a. Double Concerto, opening orchestral statement.

Example 14.2b. Double Concerto, thematic statement for violin and cello.

with the aura of a larger sonata expositional scheme. This is appropriately complemented by the final (fourth) set of variations initiated at b. 118, which, more fragmentary in its thematic treatment, and more tonally fluid, is more analogous to a sonata development.

Concluding obliquely, on the dominant of B, this first chapter of Delius's concerto structure, with its 'variation mindset', is replaced by a slow movement of quite different character, and a suggested modulation to B is deflected by a shift to G major and the presentation of a more extended diatonic melody (Theme 3 – see Example 14.2c) which might easily have come from Delius's pen in the 1890s. The arrival of the dominant key, conspicuously absent in the opening movement, lends an aura of brightness and optimism to the score as does the embedding of the tonality between bars 140 and 173. Yet more vivid, however, is G's own dominant, D major, which Delius deploys to underpin a counterstatement to Theme 3. This musical event, which introduces yet another important and substantial thematic element – Theme 4 (Example 14.2d) – was evidently considered emotionally central to the concerto scheme. This is made plain, firstly by the introduction of the 'ritornello' in b. 174 and its placing on one of Delius's typically strategic augmented-sixth harmonies (on B flat). Positioned above one of Delius's classic dominant pedal points, the intensely nostalgic Theme 4 is characterised by its repetitive melodic figure and its climactic secondary seventh (b. 186). Having modulated to D major, Delius sets about the process of resolution, but *not* with a restatement of G. Instead his sights are on the larger bones of the structure and the return of the first movement.

Example 14.2c. Double Concerto, slow movement, opening theme.

Example 14.2d. Double Concerto, slow movement, secondary theme.

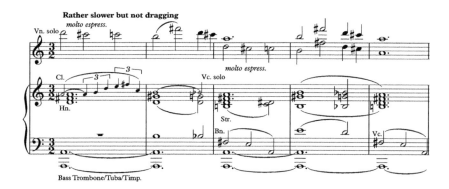

This is adroitly anticipated first by the recapitulation of Theme 3 in C major in b. 199 and by thirty bars of cadenza accompanied by the orchestra (had Delius gleaned this technique from his hearing of Elgar's Violin Concerto?) in bars 211–41 in which elements of Theme 4 and the ritornello combine developmentally.

The extended dominant pedal which underpins the cadenza yields to a recapitulation in C minor of Theme 1 in b. 242. At this point the dual-functional exposition of variation and sonata proceed as before, though the groups of sub-variations are reduced in length; in addition, Delius's second subject embarks from A major (in b. 289), and from A minor (b. 309) the tonality is steered back to C (b. 317), provoking the recapitulation of Theme 3 (b. 327), not only in a new rhythmical guise but also in a transformed role that now more auspiciously anticipates the restatement of Theme 4. In typically Delian fashion, the reprise of Theme 4 (b. 335) is an understated affair in terms of its dynamic level (marked 'Very quietly'), but its impact is one of considerable lyric intensity enhanced by Delius's remarkably original scoring for tremolando woodwind, by the affecting diatonic climax and the swell of the orchestral comment which follows. As Grimley has informed us, Delius's incorporation of the 'ritornello' in the closing bars was not thought of until late in the compositional process,[23] but its tonic minor inflections provide an entirely apposite rumination before the work ends in a silken glaze of C major. Moreover, in these last few bars, where the ritornello and Theme 4 gently intertwine, Delius brings his seemingly boundless harmonic palette to bear in one more harmonic variation (b. 363).

An often neglected work, Delius's Double Concerto is in fact a highly sophisticated structure. Recycling and revising the model of his one-movement plan in the Piano Concerto, he was able to bring to this unusual soloistic combination an entirely fresh and intricate set of schematic perspectives (see Table 14.2). In a most original fashion Delius was able to create a symphonic dimension in his first movement through a skilful conflation of both sonata and variation principles which, through the composer's ample font of lyricism, allowed the music to move forward in ever-changing thematic guises. The Concerto is also a fine example of how two contrasting movements also combine to form an overarching, dual-functioning sonata dialectic, which permits the recapitulation of the slow movement (and Theme 4) to behave as a convincing apotheosis to the entire work. It was this mode of thinking which would inspire his later concertos and indeed the configuration of his Cello Sonata and Violin Sonata No. 2.

STRING QUARTET: AN UNSYMPATHETIC IDIOM

The early years in Paris had witnessed the production of a Quartet in C minor, a work largely inspired by Grieg's Op. 27. The work was mentioned in correspondence between the two men in 1888,[24] and it was also scrutinised by Sinding in the hope that the Brodsky Quartet might take it up in Leipzig. Further attempts at quartets in 1889 and 1893 came to nothing,[25] so it was well over twenty years before he considered the idiom again, and it may well be that, like the production of the Double Concerto, his String Quartet of 1916 was the result of hearing the London String Quartet in Manchester at the end of 1915 which Albert Sammons led. The London String Quartet was well known for its enterprising concerts of new British music, which included works by

---

[23] *DG*, 282–6.

[24] See letter from Delius to Grieg, [mid-December 1888] and from Grieg to Delius, 30 December 1888, *GD*, 68 and 70.

[25] See *RT1*, 175.

Table 14.2. Double Concerto, structural overview.

Mvt	Sonata function	Overarching function	Bars	Structural event	Theme	Key	Tempo/metre/dynamics
I	E ⎡ S1	E ⎡ S1	1–14	Ritornello	Introduction	C minor	4/4, Quietly
			15–36		Theme 1 + sub-var.	C minor	With moderate speed
			37–43		Transition	B minor – V of E	Rather quicker
			44–67		Var. 1	E minor	Rather quieter
	⎣ S2	S2	68–94		Var. 2/Theme 2	A♭ major/G♯ minor	A tempo, quicker
			95–117		Var. 3	E♭ major/minor	Rather slower, molto tranquillo
			118–139		Var. 4 + coda	Tonally fluid	
II	S2		140–173		Theme 3	G major	A tempo, slow
			174–178	Ritornello	Introduction	Aug. 6th	Rather quicker, molto tranquillo
			178–198		Theme 4	D major	Rather slower but not dragging
			199–210		Theme 3	C major	Slow
		⎦	211–241	Ritornello [cadenza]	Introduction	V of C	Quicker
I	R ⎡ S1	R ⎡ S1	242–263		Theme 1	C minor	Tempo I
			264–270		Transition	B minor – V of E	Rather quicker, tranquillo
			271–288		Var. 1	E minor	
	⎣ S2		289–312		Var. 2	A major	Quicker, a tempo
			313–334		Var. 4/Theme 3	V of C	
II	S2		335–351		Theme 4	C major	Very quietly
		⎦	352–368	Ritornello	Introduction	C minor/major	Tempo I, molto tranquillo

I: First movement II: Second movement E: Exposition S1: First subject S2: Second Subject

Smyth, Bridge, Vaughan Williams, Holbrooke and McEwen, and it showed the same eagerness to perform Delius's quartet on 17 November 1916 at the Aeolian Hall. This first hearing featured the piece in its initial conception, as a three-movement work which had been completed during the months of April, May and June that same year. Flanked by two quicker movements, the first in G (though it ends quizzically in E minor), the last in D, an 'inner' emotional core in the form of a much longer slow movement was named 'Late Swallows'. The two outer movements are based loosely on the abridged sonata principle in that they both essay exposition and recapitulation of material but omit the developmental process. The first movement, more pastoral in mood, has moments of melancholy rumination, occasionally redolent of Ravel's Quartet, a work Delius knew well. The finale, which enjoys a greater sense of thematic differentiation, encapsulates the relationship between B flat and D in its 26-bar introduction. The first subject, in B flat major (Example 14.3a), has a strikingly American pentatonic character (though its later presentation in octaves with the first violin is also distinctly Griegian, and distinctly reminiscent of Delius's song 'Black Roses'). Delius also employed this idea for his second subject in D major though in association with other contrasting material including the rustic 'pesante' dance which emerges shortly before the exposition's closure. This process is repeated in curtailed form for the reprise where D major becomes the unambiguous goal. As Grimley has demonstrated, the central slow movement (which is considerably longer than its outer counterparts), was reworked extensively before Delius settled on a form which began and concluded in C, while the slow dance is simpler in texture and begins with a striking image of flight in the first violin's opening phrase.[26]

Dissatisfied with the work in this form, Delius added a Scherzo in May 1917 and took the opportunity to revise the work which the London Quartet, this time with James Levey as the quartet's leader, performed it at the Aeolian Hall on 1 February 1919, though Jelka always maintained that the Quartet never understood it.[27] The addition of the gossamer Scherzo, of little more than three minutes' music, provided an appealing 'intermezzo' (Example 14.3b) between the first movement and 'Late Swallows', while the adroit yet elusive tonal behaviour of its beautifully crafted sonata scheme, which gravitates between G minor (at the opening) and E minor (at the close), secures a more tangible link with the tonal properties of the first movement. By the same token, all the

[26] Grimley, D., 'Chasing Late Swallows', *DSJ* No. 160 (Autumn 160), 43–6.

[27] Letter from Jelka to Heseltine, 8 September 1926, *DLL2*, 316n. The work received a rather more sympathetic performance by the Virtuosi Quartet at the Delius Festival on 23 October 1929.

Example 14.3a. String Quartet, Finale, principal theme.

sections of 'Late Swallows' (including the outer sections in 4/4) were recast around D major, which helped tie the movement more closely with the end-weighted tonality of the finale, thus creating a cohesion of two halves.

Another fascinating aspect of 'Late Swallows', as Threlfall and Grimley have cited, is the extent of its thematic borrowing from Delius's American works (namely *Florida*, *The Magic Fountain* and *Koanga*),[28] a capacity consistent with the 'banjo'-like first subject of the finale, in particular the dramatic crux where Solano and Watawa kiss before their deaths in the 'Fountain of Youth'. Likewise, Buckley has made a connection with *Frühlingsmorgen*.[29] Given Delius's increased physical incapacity (and there is ample evidence of Jelka's help as a copyist in the work), it is not perhaps surprising that he should have sought some inspirational assistance from earlier sketches.

For all its corners of lyrical beauty and eloquence, Delius's String Quartet nevertheless presents us with various problems. Although the composer no doubt thought it possible to transform the idiom from one that was traditionally contrapuntal in discipline into one that suited his own stylistic imperatives, his desire for *sonority* (engendered by his desire for a rich harmonic environment) gave rise to an incessant, unvarying texture. With the exception of some passages in the Scherzo, all four instruments play without a break, presenting a major challenge of the performers to avoid monotony. Heseltine ultimately

---

[28] See *RT1*, 180, Grimley, D., 'Chasing Late Swallows', 48.

[29] Buckley, R., 'Recording Reviews', *DSJ* No. 135 (Spring 2004), 62.

Example 14.3b. String Quartet, Scherzo, opening.

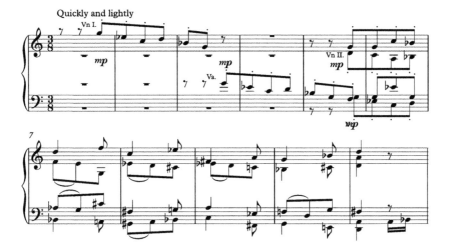

considered that Delius's understanding of the quartet idiom was flawed.[30] Symptomatic of this failure was the tendency to treat the quartet as if it were an orchestra-*manqué*; this is true not only of the first movement and finale, but also of the work's centrepiece, the slow movement. Hutchings remarked that "'Late Swallows", though pure chamber music, has the effect of a tone poem. Between a prelude steeped in autumnal atmosphere, which returns at the conclusion of the piece, is a masterly stretch of visual and aural suggestion, comparable with *Summer Night on the River*.[31] This is an interesting comparison, though surely a more obvious precedent for Delius's extended melody and repetitive accompanimental figurations must be the central paragraph of *In a Summer Garden*. Such orchestral affinity must have struck Eric Fenby when he produced his arrangement for string orchestra in 1963.

VIOLIN CONCERTO

If the Harrison sisters (and Brahms) were the vital catalysts behind the conception of the Double Concerto, then it is likely that Albert Sammons played a similar role in the creation of Delius's Violin Concerto. Sammons

---

[30] See *EF*, 65.

[31] *AH*, 152.

swept to fame as a virtuoso violinist in November 1914, having replaced Kreisler (who had joined the Austrian army) in a performance in London of Elgar's Violin Concerto under Vasily Safonov. Sammons repeated his success on 13 May 1915 under Elgar's direction in the second concert of a festival of British music. Among the ecstatic critics was Heseltine who commented in the *Daily Mail* that 'the mingled strength and tenderness of his tone, coupled with brilliance and execution and flawless intonation, made of his performance a miracle of beauty'.[32] Also in the same programme was Delius's Piano Concerto and among the audience was its composer. Wetherall has conjectured that a chance meeting took place between Sammons and Delius at this concert or at a time in close propinquity, since the following year Delius composed his Violin Concerto which bore the dedication 'For Albert Sammons'.[33] Much of the work was composed in the last months of 1916 though it was not performed until 30 January 1919, when Sammons performed it with the young Adrian Boult, then making his debut at the Royal Philharmonic Society. At this time Sammons was still in uniform (as a member of the Grenadier Guards band) and was refused leave of absence the night before the morning rehearsal and concert. Only after two members of the Royal Philharmonic intervened was Colonel Sir Henry Streatfeild able to grant the necessary leave to save the situation. Sammons, who had met several times with Delius at his London flat in Belsize Park, well remembered the composer's apoplexy when he broke the news of his bandmaster's intransigence.[34] The reception of Delius's concerto was tumultuous and it was equally greeted with enthusiasm when Sammons performed it with Harty in December 1919 and with Boult again in January 1920.[35] In later years it was also to attract violinists of the calibre of May Harrison, Orrea Pernel, Bronislaw Hubermann and Jean Pougnet, though it remained a work closely associated with Sammons who also performed it with Beecham at the Delius Festival in 1929.

A tightly constructed canvas lasting around 24–25 minutes, the Violin Concerto is perhaps simpler in design than the Double Concerto, but it is considerably more complex in terms of its thematic activity and detail. The seemingly inauspicious two bars of the opening are in fact a deft microcosm of

---

[32] Wetherall, E., *Albert Sammons, Violinist: The Life of 'Our Albert'* (London: Thames Publishing, 1998), 34.

[33] A letter from Delius to Grainger, dated 5 October 1916, also insinuates that, had the Violin Concerto gone to America for performance, Delius had Kreisler (who was by then in New York) firmly in mind to play it (see *DLL2*, 170).

[34] Wetherall, E., *Albert Sammons*, 45.

[35] Kennedy, M., *Adrian Boult* (London: Hamish Hamilton, 1987), 67 and 73.

the work's tonal argument between D minor and F major (as well as their major and minor equivalents) as is the D minor seventh chord of b. 3. Moreover, as Deryck Cooke has demonstrated, the opening melodic 'shape' of bb. 1–2 is also generative of several important thematic fragments. In fact Cooke, in a crusade to vindicate his belief in *form* in Delius's music, went so far as to suggest that three fundamental 'shapes' provided a seed bed for the creation and inter-relation of as many as nine thematic ideas across the entire canvas.[36] Cooke may be criticised for his over-reliance on the methods of Rudolf Réti and Hans Keller, but his article is nevertheless indicative of the concentration of Delius's melodic thought and lyrical flight throughout the work. In the same manner as the Double Concerto, Delius also brings the same process of 'dual functionality' to his structure, though with interesting differences, and his manipulation of tonality is particularly adroit (a dimension to which Cooke gives less attention).

After the first two bars, Delius's soloist promptly appears with the first important thematic idea (Example 14.4a) in 4/4, and as adjuncts to this are three significant melodic fragments (two of them notably contrasted by their 12/8 metre in bars 9 and 14 – see Examples 14.4b and 14.4c, while 14.4d conflates 4/4 and 12/8). The constant interaction of these ideas, delineated by their metrical properties, provides one dimension of Delius's lyrical development and elasticity. Another is the series of strong 'departures' of Theme 1a in F minor which lends an impression of variation technique;

Example 14.4a. Violin Concerto, opening theme for violin (Theme 1a).

---

[36] See Cooke, D., 'Delius and Form: A Vindication', in *DC*, 249–62. Originally published as Cooke, D., 'Delius and Form: A Vindication', *The Musical Times*, Vol. 103 No. 1432 (June 1962), 392–3 and No. 1433 (July 1962), 460–65, and reprinted later in Cooke, D., *Vindications: Essays on Romantic Music* (Cambridge: Cambridge University Press, 1982), 123–42.

Example 14.4b. Violin Concerto, additional thematic strand (Theme 1b).

Example 14.4c. Violin Concerto, additional thematic strand (Theme 1c).

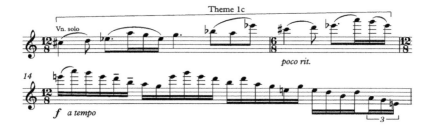

Example 14.4d. Violin Concerto, additional thematic strand (Theme 1d).

moreover, at strategic points in the structure, Delius interrupts the continuity with an augmented sixth on B flat. In the first two instances this 'resolves' to F minor (b. 24) and V⁷c of G (b. 62) respectively. On the third occasion, the resolution is more conventional in its progression to V of D (b. 78) and in the introduction of the fanfares, though, as is evident from the cadence (bb. 91–3), neither D minor or F major is unequivocally stated (see Table 14.3a).

Delius's slow movement, an ABAB scheme (see Table 14.3b), begins unequivocally in F major with what must be one of the composer's most rhapsodic inventions (Theme 2 – see Example 14.4e). Much of the space given to its expansion, however, is in D minor and D major (bb. 104–17), and this treatment is allied with the introduction of a secondary 'folksong' idea (Theme 3 – Example 14.4f) with characteristic Scotch snap (bb. 109–11) which is also used to close the B section (bb. 128–31). The recapitulation of Theme 2 in F major (b. 132), even more ravishing in its higher tessitura, is similarly ephemeral before D major takes over for a second time (b. 136).

Table 14.3a. Violin Concerto, first movement, structural overview.

Bars	Theme	Key	Tempo / Metre
1–2	Introduction	D minor/F major	With moderate tempo
3–8	Theme 1a	D minor	4/4
9–13	Theme 1b	C minor	12/8
14–16	Theme 1c		12/8
17–21	Continuation	V of D	12/8
22–23	Interruptive augmented 6th based on Theme 1a		4/4
24–28	Theme 1a (Var. 1)	F minor	4/4
29–30	Theme 1d	C major	4/4
31–39	Theme 1a	Fluid	4/4
40–48	Themes 1b and 1d	Fluid	12/8
49–56	Theme 1a (Var. 2)	F minor	4/4
57–59	Theme 1b		12/8
60–61	Interruptive augmented 6th based on Theme 1a		4/4
62–75	Theme 1d	Fluid	12/8
76–77	Interruptive augmented 6th based on Theme 1a		4/4
78–88	Fanfares + Theme 1b	V of D	4/4 + 12/8
89–93	Theme 1a	D minor – F major?	4/4

The principal difference about Delius's restatement is, however, its more protracted closure in which use of the 'folksong' figure is considerably expanded (bb. 145–66).

At this point Delius embarks on an accompanied cadenza of thirty bars – a device he had already used in the Double Concerto – and, as Cooke has alluded, the increasingly decorative filigree of the violin part is a set of miniature variations based on the first two bars (bb. 168–69), itself derived from a synthesis of Themes 1a and 1c.[37] The variations are also organised into two groups which conclude on V of D, the first, of only three variations, in b. 174, the second of nine variations, in b. 195 which provides dominant preparation for the restatement of the first movement. It might also be argued that the cumulative effect of the variations, the fluid nature of the tonal behaviour and the concluding dominant preparation provide an analogous parallel of a sonata

[37] Cooke, D., 'Delius and Form', in DC, 260.

Example 14.4e. Violin Concerto, slow movement, main theme (Theme 2).

Example 14.4f. Violin Concerto, slow movement, 'folksong' theme (Theme 3).

Table 14.3b. Violin Concerto, second movement, structural overview.

Bars	Section	Theme	Key
	EXPOSITION		
94–103	A	2	F major (to B major)
104–117	B	2, 3	D minor/major
118–127	Development	2	Fluid
128–131	Closing material	3	Fluid
	RECAPITULATION		
132–135	A	2	F major
136–144	B	2	D major
145–166	Closing material	3	D minor

Table 14.3c. Violin Concerto, structural overview.

Bar	Sonata function	Movement	Theme	Key
	EXPOSITION			
1–93	First subject	1	1a, 1b, 1c, 1d	D minor/F major
94–166	Second subject	2	2, 3	F major/D minor
167–196	DEVELOPMENT	Cadenza	1a, 1c	V of D
	RECAPITULATION			
197–258	First subject	1	1a, 1b, 1c, 1d	D minor/major, V of F
259–266	Second Subject	3 (Scherzo)	1b	Fluid
267–288		(Trio)	2 (transformation)	D major, V of F
289–313		(Scherzo)	1b	Fluid
314–341	Coda	Epilogue	1a	F major

development which is especially pertinent to an understanding of Delius's dual-functional scheme (see Table 14.3c).

The recapitulation of the first movement commences with the same ambiguous statement of D minor, though it is evident from two prominent statements of Theme 1b in D major (see bb. 215 and 236) that Delius is keen to emphasise the importance of this alteration of modality. Significantly truncated in length, the order of thematic ideas is conspicuously modified. The one appearance of the dramatic augmented sixth (b. 217) gives rise to a departure of Theme 1a in B flat minor (b. 219) rather than F minor of the exposition (Var. 1). The second appearance of Theme 1a (as Var. 2) does, however, make its appearance in F minor (b. 245) in anticipation of the return of the fanfares on the dominant of F (b. 248).

Confounding our expectation of the recapitulation of the slow movement, Delius gives us a 'dance Scherzo' in 12/8 in which we are once again in the familiar territory of 'Sellinger's Round' and the folksong variations of *Brigg Fair* (not to mention *A Song Before Sunrise* yet to be composed). Indeterminate in terms of its tonality, the Scherzo (based on Theme 1b) yields to a counterstatement – effectively the 'trio' – in the violin in 4/4, a further indication of Delius's continuation of the 4/4–12/8 metrical dialectic of Theme 1d. This is also clearly a transformation of the principal theme of the slow movement (Theme 2). Again, the tonality is ambiguous: at first Delius seems set on accentuating D major (see bb. 274–9), but at the conclusion of this section it is to a half-close in F that the violin, in its rich lowest register, settles (b. 288). Resolution into F is, however, denied by a restatement of the Scherzo whose longer duration and tonal uncertainty is this time adeptly deployed, by gradual steps, to cadence into F (b. 314), thereby facilitating an epilogue of searing lyrical beauty in which the metrical (4/4), thematic (Theme 1a) and tonal (F major) components of the concerto achieve an ultimate fusion. What is more, it provides a successful alternative 'solution' to Delius's dual-functional structure in what Payne aptly described as 'very like a tone poem with a solo violin as the protagonist'.[38] This idea of the 'protagonist' is a powerful image in Delius's Violin Concerto, for, not only was it the composer's own instrument, but its presence in so many of his scores – *Paris, Lebenstanz, A Village Romeo and Juliet, Sea Drift, Songs of Sunset* – seems to express an intimacy of the most personal kind. Indeed, one might even suggest that the intimacy is autobiographical in sentiment. It is, therefore, almost unavoidable not to perceive, through the endless, yearning strains of the Concerto, a sense of emotional culmination in these many intimate 'commentaries', leaving the indelible impression that the work is one of the composer's most singularly private utterances.

BEATRICE HARRISON AND
TWO WORKS FOR SOLO CELLO

Just as Delius's Violin Concerto (and its reception) had reflected the meteoric rise to fame of Albert Sammons, Delius's two major works for solo cello expressed his admiration for Beatrice Harrison. His acquaintance had of course been cemented during their collaboration on the Double Concerto, but it is in the Cello Sonata of 1916, published by Winthrop Rogers in 1919, that the composer made his first gesture of approbation and dedication. As Payne has aptly remarked, 'lack of an orchestral palette to bring his harmony to life places the top line in ascendancy'.[39] This is particularly true of the Cello Sonata where Delius gives his soloist very little rest. In one sense, of course, the score is yet another confirmation of how important Delius's melodic aptitude remained as a central point of cohesion, but, like the String Quartet, another over-dense work, its somewhat relentless pianistic homophony and textural differentiation (especially between first and second subjects) present major challenges for the two performers.

Formally the Cello Sonata is rather simpler in its manifestation of Delius's predilection for one-movement schemes and is also much shorter at around

---

[38]   Payne, A., 'Delius's Stylistic Development', *Tempo* No. 60 (Winter 1961–1962), 16.
[39]   Ibid.

thirteen minutes. In fact, Delius's preferred dialectical scheme, as witnessed in the Double Concerto and Violin Concerto, is jettisoned here in favour of a less complex sonata-rondo (see Table 14.4) where Theme 1a acts as the all-important 'rondo' in its three appearances in the tonic, D major. By contrast, the slow movement, consisting of two distinct thematic ideas in D minor and D major, makes but one appearance as a replacement for the development. Although Themes 1a and 2a have a distinctly Griegian flavour in the manner of the piano's octave configuration (note the octave doubling between the upper and lower voices) – and one wonders whether Delius might even have been paying tribute to his old friend's Sonata Op. 36 of 1883 – the most interesting feature is the sharing of similar material with the Violin Concerto. This can be heard in the closing bars of the first subject (Theme 1d – bb. 43–4 and bb. 220–21) which resemble the 'fanfares' in the first movement, and, even more luxuriantly, the quaver figure of bb. 144 which appears on four more occasions. Harrison first performed the Sonata with Hamilton Harty at the Wigmore Hall on 31 October 1918 and she gave a rare hearing of it in Paris with the Russian pianist, M. Yovanovitch on 6 June 1919 at the Salle Gaveau. Besides Harty, Harrison also performed it with other noted pianists such as Harold Craxton, and also her sister Margaret Harrison. But the sonata was also

Table 14.4. Cello Sonata, structural overview.

	Bars	Theme	Section	Key
FIRST MOVEMENT	1–21	1a	A	D major
(EXPOSITION)	22–29	1b		D minor
	30–42	1c		Fluid
	43–46	1d		V of D
	47–83	2a	B	F major/V of D
	84–114	2b		D♭/fluid
	115–127	1a	A	D major
SLOW MOVEMENT	128–142	3	C	D minor
(DEVELOPMENT)	143–170	4		D major
FIRST MOVEMENT	171–191	1a	A	D major
(RECAPITULATION)	192–207	1b		D minor
	208–219	1c		Fluid
	220–223	1d		V of D
	224–246	2a	B	D major
	247–265	2b		D major

championed by the Russian cellist Alexandre Barjansky, who toured the work in Germany. Barjansky's performance of the sonata in the composer's music room at Grez is picturesequely documented in *Delius As I Knew Him*.[40]

Having participated closely with Delius and her sister, May, on revisions for the Double Concerto in 1916, Beatrice travelled to the United States armed with the promise that Delius would write a Cello Concerto for her.[41] In fact it was not until after the Harrison sisters gave their performance of the Double Concerto in London, in February 1920, that Delius began to sketch the work at Grez at the request of Beatrice.[42] His real commitment to the work did not begin, however, until March 1921 when he and Jelka had an apartment in Swiss Cottage. Using all his dissipating strength, he completed the Cello Concerto by May, work which was punctuated by visits to see Beatrice at their farmhouse near Thames Ditton in Surrey. With the help of the Gloucestershire composer Charles Wilfred Orr, a copy of Delius's score was made, and the score was published by Universal in 1922, Heseltine having assisted with the proofs.[43] It would be the last of Delius's major works which he was able to compose unaided.

While staying in their small cottage in Lesjaskog in August 1922, Delius asked O'Neill if the Royal Philharmonic Society would like the first performance of the Cello Concerto with Beatrice Harrison, and suggested that it might form the centrepiece of an all-Delius concert.[44] O'Neill, as an influential voice at the Society, engineered the event, but it did not take place until 3 July 1923 under Eugene Goossens's direction – when it was taken far too slowly.[45] Before this date, however, Delius had been invited to Frankfurt for a number of concerts to celebrate his sixtieth birthday (even though it would soon be discovered that his birth took place in 1862!). On 1 March, in a programme which included *The Song of the High Hills* and *North Country Sketches*, Barjansky performed the Concerto under the direction of the Danish-born composer and conductor Paul von Klenau, having first given it in Vienna to some acclaim on 31 January under Ferdinand Löwe. As a champion of the Cello Sonata, Barjansky also promoted the Cello Concerto

40   *EF*, 26.

41   Harrison, B., *The Cello and the Nightingales*, 104.

42   *TB*, 188.

43   Orr's copy of Delius's pencil original (*GB-Lbl* MS Mus 1745/2/3) survives in the British Library, *GB-Lbl* Loan 54/5, dated 1921.

44   Letter from Delius to O'Neill, 20 August 1922, *DLL2*, 258.

45   Letter from Jelka to Adine O'Neill, 20 January 1926, *DLL2*, 312.

in Germany, but it was Harrison who made the work her own. Delius came to admit that Barjansky, 'who played so awfully well, has a tendency to play too fast', while he maintained that Harrison had a better understanding of his tempi.[46] In January 1927, in the company of her mother Annie, sister Margaret and the accompanist Gerald Moore, Beatrice played both the Cello Sonata and Concerto to Delius at Grez,[47] and that same year was moved to write down her thoughts on the work in August 1927.[48] It is something of a shame, nevertheless, that, having recorded the Sonata with Harold Craxton, she did not record the Concerto.

More akin to the length of the Double Concerto (and somewhat shorter than the Violin Concerto), the Cello Concerto continues to explore Delius's concise one-movement paradigm. However, with the exigencies imposed by writing for the solo cello and a full-size orchestra (which Delius had clearly understood, like Elgar before him), the work has a fragility and lyricism distinct from the two other concertos. This can be felt not only in the lightness of the orchestral scoring, where Delius's familiar matrix of wind counterthemes and rich divided string textures are given room to breathe, but also in the more delicately proportioned structure of the work where Delius's series of sonata schemes are uniquely executed 'in miniature'.

The Cello Concerto's longer introduction (bb. 1–23), partly conforms with the freer rhetoric of a cadenza (not unlike the beginning of Elgar's concerto). Dominant preparation also underpins the first fifteen bars, before the orchestra provide a serene transition to the beginning of the first movement. Delius's first subject (b. 16) somewhat unusually begins obliquely on the Neapolitan of A minor (Example 14.5a) and studiously avoids the tonic until bb. 31–5 at which point he rapidly moves to the relative major (b. 36) in order to present the brighter second subject in C major (Example 14.5b), somewhat understated in the first violins given the soloist's more assertive countertheme. Indeed, it is only with the soloist's uptake of the second subject, repeated in A major (b. 43), that the second subject becomes more melodically conspicuous. A return to the first subject in D major (b. 49) heralds a period of greater tonal instability and from here Delius embarks on the development of his two subjects with the same miniaturist precision that he deployed in his exposition. Passing through B major, a more climactic D flat and A major, the second subject presses on to the subdominant, D major,

[46] Harrison, B., *The Cello and the Nightingales*, 118.

[47] See Moore, G., *Am I Too Loud?* (London: Hamish Hamilton, 1962), 71–2.

[48] Harrison, B., *The Cello and the Nightingales*, 118–20.

Example 14.5a. Cello Concerto, first movement, first subject.

Example 14.5b. Cello Concerto, first movement, second subject.

at which point the first movement breaks off in characteristic fashion to make way for the slow movement.

Reminiscent of Delius's pastoralism in *Summer Night on the River*, the opening idea of the slow movement, with its lilting parallelisms is another of the composer's gentle round dances (b. 94). Shifting, with some legerdemain, to D flat, in a new variation for the subtle hues of the muted horns and solo violin (Example 14.5c), the soloist embarks on a euphonious second subject, also in D flat (Example 14.5d) and also diminutive in duration (bb. 114–23). Central to the slow movement, however, is the development of the first subject (Theme 3) which takes the form of a series of variations in the orchestra, replete with countermelody, duly embellished by the soloist. Given the predominance

Example 14.5c. Cello Concerto, slow movement, opening idea.

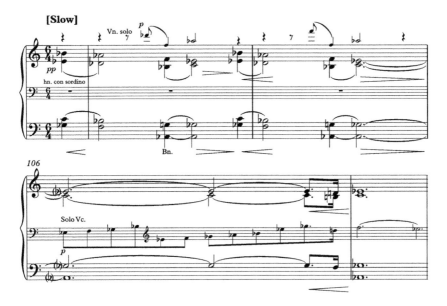

Example 14.5d. Cello Concerto, slow movement, second subject.

of this thematic material, Delius deftly dispensed with the reprise of the first subject in the tonic, leaving this role to the second subject (Theme 4), whose unworldly restatement is translucently supported by divided upper strings and wind (b. 185).

Closure of the slow movement yields to the recapitulation of the first movement and to first subject (b. 205) and second subject (b. 216) in A minor and major respectively. A second statement of the second subject

shifts to the subdominant (D major) which invokes dominant preparation
for that key in the remaining bars of this much truncated section, replete with
a cyclic memory of Theme 3. Avoiding the platitude of a perfect cadence
into D, Delius embarks on a new movement by introducing a new theme
(Theme 5) through the agency of the soloist. Marked 'with animation' and
'Allegramente' (meaning 'cheerfully' in Italian), it is one the composer's most
characteristic examples of a transparently *diatonic* melody subtly coloured by
the hues of Delius's chromatic palette (Example 14.5e). A transition full of
Debussyan whole-tone harmony seems to anticipate a counterstatement in E
(given the dominant preparation in bb. 285–9), but this is shrewdly obviated
by a move to G major (b. 290) and a new lyrical outpouring loosely derived
from Theme 4 (and a strong rhythmical resemblance to the opening theme
of the Violin Concerto). In truth, G major forms little more than the point of
embarkation for this thematic idea. In keeping with the 'miniaturist' mindset
of this concerto, Delius's short thematic gesture expands into a developmental
space used to anticipate the recapitulation of Theme 5 (b. 318). The arrival
of the dominant of D in b. 315, with its delicate added-sixth sonority, hushed
wisps of woodwind counterpoint and the lone sound of the cello, must surely
represent the quintessence of Delius's art. The restatement of Theme 5
(b. 318), enhanced by its appearance in the orchestra, also disguise a conflation
with Theme 6 which emerges as a counterpoint in the solo cello. But perhaps
Delius's most telling gesture in the entire concerto is the unexpected return to
G major for the magical coda, a captivating closing episode of nineteen bars
in which Themes 5 and 6 articulate a world of Arcadian paradise. Rivalling

Example 14.5e. Cello Concerto, Finale, principal theme.

Table 14.5. Cello Concerto, structural overview.

	Bars	Section	Theme	Key	Tempo/metre/dynamics
	1–23	Introduction	Cadenza	A minor	Slow
FIRST MOVEMENT	24–35	Exposition (1st sub.)	1	A minor	Meno mosso
	36–40	(2nd sub.)	2	C major	
	41–48		2	A major	
	49–55	Development	1	D major	
	56–61		1	B major	
	62–72		2	Db major / Bb major	
	73–79		2	A major – V of D	
	80–86		1	D major	
	87–93		2	D major	Becoming slower
SLOW MOVEMENT	94–113	Exposition (1st sub.)	3	D major / Db major	Slow
	114–123	(2nd sub.)	4	Db major	
	124–184		3	Fluid (development) – V of D	
	185–204	Recapitulation	4	D major	Very quietly
FIRST MOVEMENT	205–215		1	A minor	Con moto tranquillo
(REPRISE)	216–230		2	A major	
FINALE	231–289		5	D major	With animation
	290–317		6 (derived from Theme 4)	G major	Rather slowly, very quietly
	318–339		5, 6	D major	Tempo I
	340–358		5, 6 (coda)	G major	Quietly

the pathos of the epilogue of the Violin Concerto, this exceptional conclusion highlights yet a further variant of Delius's one-movement essays (see Table 14.5) in which the final movement harnesses a quite different rhetorical world, shaped by the diminutive component parts of its structure. This is not a concerto with symphonic aspirations as is the Violin Concerto with its grand gestures and probing pathos; rather, Delius's concept of the Cello Concerto seems to have been one of chamber music, in which his genius for 'cut glass crystal' orchestration is the seminal ingredient, and it is no more germanely exemplified than in the work's unique finale which seems to transform the very concept of concerto into one informed by the modernism of Neo-Classicism and the preference for slighter, anti-symphonic proportions.

VIOLIN SONATA NO. 2:
A DUAL-FUNCTIONAL CULMINATION

It demanded a considerable effort from Delius to complete the Cello Concerto, and progress would undoubtedly have been slower without Orr's help as a copyist, Heseltine's assistance with the proofs and Jelka's constant presence for any necessary dictation. His last stay in 1923 at Lesjaskog in Norway did not bring the improvement in health that he had hoped for. Yet, such was Delius's compulsion as a composer that he was undeterred by the effort necessary to have his music copied down. Jelka, who had the ability to write musical notation (and, where necessary, to play the material over on the piano), was able to copy from her husband's manuscript as well as take dictation for another violin sonata and the Tennyson partsong 'The splendour falls', and in her hand the manuscript materials were sent to London where, under the aegis of Hawkes & Sons, the new Sonata was edited by Sammons and Howard-Jones.[49] As seasoned performers of Delius's music, both men gave the first performance of the Sonata at the Westminster Music Society on 7 October 1924 and later recorded it with Columbia in 1925. Sales of the work in 1924 were, according to Heseltine, a great success,[50] an outcome which no doubt ultimately persuaded the celebrated violist Lionel Tertis, then at the zenith of his career, to publish his adaptation for viola in 1932.

---

[49] Delius's various drafts of the Violin Sonata No. 2 in addition to a complete draft can be examined in *GB-Lbl* MS Mus 1745/2/5, ff. 83–102. Jelka's *Stichvorlag* for the publisher can be seen in the Boosey & Hawkes Accession at *GB-Lbl* MS Mus 1745/3/17.

[50] *FDPW*, 474.

The last of Delius's instrumental works to experiment with one-movement form, the Violin Sonata No. 2 was a notable achievement not only because of the challenging circumstances of composition and preparing the materials for publication, but because it attempted to move the dual-functional form up to a new level of intellectual thinking, even beyond the formal concentration of the Cello Sonata whose shorter length it shares. Like its predecessors, the work is dominated by the sustained lyrical invention of the solo violin, but the piano has a much greater interactive role to play (which renders the work a much more successful representative of the medium), and the interplay of the two protagonists often gives rise to a wider variety of thematic ideas. Couched in C major (another of Delius's 'uncomplicated' keys), the opening melody for the violin is a luxuriant entity of twenty-two bars (Example 14.6a), essentially borrowed from the discarded melody from *Poem of Life and Love* (from b. 19). Its climax is marked by a rich descending sequence (bb. 14–16) as it emerges in the dominant (bb. 19–22). A more lively transitional section (bb. 23–44), which adroitly hangs between E minor and G major, derives its falling phrases from bars 3–4 and 6–7 (Example 14.6b). Combined with a third melodic fragment (bb. 45–74), more tranquil in character

Example 14.6a. Violin Sonata No. 2, first movement, opening theme.

Example 14.6b. Violin Sonata No. 2, first movement, transitional idea (1).

Example 14.6c. Violin Sonata No. 2, first movement, transitional idea (2).

Example 14.6d. Violin Sonata No. 2, first movement, second subject.

Example 14.6e. Violin Sonata No. 2,
transition between first and second movements.

Example 14.6f. Violin Sonata No. 2, slow movement, principal rhapsodic theme.

(Example 14.6c), this provides a link to the second subject, a composite idea featuring an upsurging Griegian idea for the piano and a falling dotted rhythm (Example 14.6d) formed around G. Following the pattern of other Delius sonatas (and concertos), the first-movement sonata structure breaks off here through the agency of a short transition (Theme 5 – Example 14.6e)

Table 14.6. Violin Sonata No. 2, structural overview.

	Bars	Section	Theme	Key	Tempo
FIRST MOVEMENT	1–22	First subject	1	C major	Con moto
	23–44	Transition (scherzo)	2	E minor/G major	Poco più mosso
	45–74		3	Fluid	Poco più tranquillo
	75–102	Second subject	4 (composite)	G major	Poco meno mosso
	103–106	Transition	5	Fluid	Più tranquillo
SLOW MOVEMENT	107–134		6	F major	Lento
	135–155	Development (scherzo)	2	Fluid	Vivace
	156–164	Transition	5	Fluid	Poco più lento – Lento
	165–192		6	F major	Lento
FINALE	193–217	(March)	7	C major	Molto vivace
(RECAPITULATION)	218–228	Transition		Fluid	Meno mosso
	229–232	Second subject	4	V of G	
	233–241	First subject	1	G major	
	242–246		5	C major	Più lento
	247–255	First subject	1	C major	[Come prima]
	256–259	Second subject	4	C major	
	260–269	Second subject	4, 7	C major	Poco più vivo
	270–280	(March)	7	C major	Molto vivace

to enter a slow movement in F major (b. 107), another of Delius's prolonged rhapsodic utterances (Example 14.6f) apportioned between violin and piano. The design of Delius's slow movement is, however, quite different from past essays in that its ternary scheme embraces a central paragraph (the 'trio') in which the transitional material of the first movement is recalled (Theme 2), its tonally fluid behaviour fulfilling the role of a development (bb. 135–55). At the tail end of this developmental phase, Delius somewhat poetically appends his transitional material (Theme 5) in a more protracted, cadenza-like flight of fancy (bb. 156–64), partly accompanied by the piano before the slow movement enchantingly recurs (in muted form as suggested by both Sammons and Tertis). Alighting on V of C (b. 192), the slow movement yields, not to a recapitulation of the first movement, but to a terse finale which begins with an entirely new march-like idea. Performing the rhetorical role of an introduction, Delius's new theme in C major paves the way for the recapitulation of both first and second subjects (bb. 229–41) in reverse order (in the dominant) before a brief, restrained reference to Theme 5 provides a transition to a full, ebullient reprise of both ideas in the tonic, C major, leaving the march to close off the work in buoyant and determined fashion.

Although we have met certain structural processes of Delius's concertos and chamber works before in the Violin Sonata No. 2, particularly the composer's favoured dialectical opposition of first-movement and slow-movement styles, it is clear from other factors that he intended to extend the concept of his dual function to incorporate other features of the traditional sonata scheme (see Table 14.6). It is notable, for example, that the element of 'Scherzo' (which had featured in the finale of the Violin Concerto) here has two roles, first as a significant thematic transition (Theme 2) in the first movement, and later as both a 'trio' and 'development' between the two main thematic pillars of the slow movement (itself unusual as a ternary form). While one of the structural roles of the finale is to provide a thematic and tonal recapitulation of the first movement, it is enacted here with important differences. The creation of the new, 'march' theme gives the last movement a strong character, lending it a distinct individuality of its own. Given the dominant role of the 'march', Delius's manner of reaffirming the first and second subjects from the first movement (and Theme 5) is both to *combine* them with the 'march' and to *integrate* them within the finale's own concentrated abridged sonata scheme. The effect of this highly sophisticated treatment can be felt with particular force in the last thirty-nine bars where all three principal themes coalesce in a broad and compelling statement of C major, rounding off not only the last movement but the entire sonata to boot.

CHAPTER 15

The Last Years of Creativity: *A Song of Summer, A Late Lark, Cynara,* Violin Sonata No. 3, *Songs of Farewell, Irmelin Prelude, Fantastic Dance, Idyll* (1923–1934)

After the completion of the Violin Sonata No. 2 in 1923 Delius enjoyed some alleviation in his financial circumstances. This was, in part, helped (as has been mentioned above) by Balfour Gardiner's generous intervention to buy the house at Grez so that Delius and Jelka could enjoy old age. And more to the point, much of Delius's income from royalties, shares and family went fruitlessly on cures which brought little relief from his encroaching illnesss. 1923 also marked his last sojourn to Lesjaskog, and a trip to Rapallo during the winter months was the last journey he was able to make, save for the curative baths at Cassel, before it became impractical to leave Grez; and, by 1925, even these came to an end as Delius lost faith in his German doctors. At this juncture, the legacy of tertiary syphilis had left him completely blind and without the use of his arms or legs, making it imperative to seek the help of live-in male nurses (the so-called Brüder) who could not only feed and dress him, but carry him everywhere around the house. Thus life at Grez became monotonous, punctuated only by occasional excursions in the car they purchased (but which always required a chauffeur), news of performances of his music in Germany (where, through the offices of Schuricht, enthusiasm for his music had clearly not been impaired by the war), Austria, England, and through the efforts of Grainger, in America. And, in the knowledge that he was housebound, many of his musician friends – Grainger, Gardiner, Bax, the young Patrick Hadley, Cassirer, Fried, Edward Dent, Roger Quilter, O'Neill, Frederic Austin, E. J. Moeran, Kennedy Scott, Heseltine, Cecil Gray, the Barjanskys, the Harrison sisters and Gerald Moore, Heinrich Simon, the Howard-Joneses, Nadia Boulanger and Florent Schmitt – loyally paid their social visits. Live performances, especially of his own music, from those such as Grainger, Barjanksy, the Howard-Joneses and the Harrisons, revived him, and, thanks to the technological advent of the gramophone, the radio, the

BBC (as well as other European broadcasting corporations) as well as the installation of electricity at Grez, he was able to listen to the few recordings of his music that were available (such as the *Dance Rhapsody* No. 1, *Brigg Fair, On Hearing the First Cuckoo in Spring* and excerpts from *Hassan*) as well as broadcasts of concerts from London and elsewhere.

A physical invalid Delius may have become, but his mental powers were unaffected, and the Nietzschean thirst for work was no less vibrant. His isolation at Grez may have helped to fuel his largely uncurbable egotism and his sense of his own musical importance – manifested by the conspicuously inflated preference of his own music over that of others – but the compulsion to create remained a deep source of frustration. With the *Five Piano Pieces* of 1923, Jelka 'made her debut as amanuensis' and explained to Adine O'Neill that Delius could not write 'and has to dictate it all to me and I find it pretty difficult'.[1] In this way the Violin Sonata No. 2 and the parstong 'The splendour falls' were completed. What is more, Delius was not cowed by his physical circumstances to attempt the more challenging task of orchestral music. 'With what difficulty he is dictating me an orchestral score', she wrote to Grainger, 'his mind so active and bright, and he so hampered by his invalid limbs'.[2] At intervals throughout 1924 the dictation continued. 'He is composing all the time, dictating it to me, which is a rather difficult task', Jelka reiterated, 'but he has got quite accustomed to it'.[3] In this way, *A Late Lark* was begun and other works, notably *Fantastic Dance* and the Violin Sonata No. 3 were sketched. Confiding to Grainger, she admitted 'I do feel so lonely in my dreadful responsibility about Fred – and I feel so tired sometimes that my resources in keeping up his spirits are so minimized'.[4] As time went on, dictation became more toilsome. 'The difficulties are so great', she told Heseltine, 'as he cannot see what he has written, I mean: dictated. But I can play it to him. *It could be done* and it would be so good, and he would think about music again'.[5]

In reality, in spite of her valiant efforts, Jelka was an amateur, and the dictation of Delius's music required a professional which was beyond

---

[1] Letter from Jelka to Adine O'Neill, 30 March 1923, *DLL2*, 269.

[2] Letter from Jelka to Grainger, [24 February 1924], *DLL2*, 288. The orchestral work is not specified but it may still have been *Poem of Life and Love*, left in an unsatisfactory state after its initial completion in 1918.

[3] Letter from Jelka to Adine O'Neill, 17 October 1924, *DLL2*, 294.

[4] Letter from Jelka to Grainger, 28 March 1925, *DLL2*, 300.

[5] Letter from Jelka to Heseltine, [July 1926], *DLL2*, 316.

their practical and financial circumstances. Beecham, preoccupied with major family financial problems, was in no position to assist. Gardiner had committed himself to the development of his Dorset estate; Grainger and Heseltine – two figures most sympathetic to aid Delius – had to make their own livings. Indeed, Heseltine was in such dire financial straits that he was forced to give up the cottage where he resided with E. J. Moeran at Eynsford, Kent, and reluctantly return to the family at Cefn Bryntalch in North Wales. Besides, his friendship with, and devotion to, Delius cooled after 1925 as is evident from the dearth of correspondence until 1929,[6] and his youthful rapture for Delius's music had been replaced by a more critical, disparaging attitude (not unlike Nietzsche's rejection of Wagner).[7] It must, therefore, have seemed like manna from heaven when the young Eric Fenby's letter arrived. Brought about by his reading of the composer's physical plight in the press,[8] his selfless offer, which came with little more than the obligation to feed and house him, and to cover his travel, could not have suited Delius's parlous predicament more appropriately.

At the same time, Delius knew nothing of Fenby beyond the few details of his letters, and though he shared the happy common denominator of being a fellow Yorkshireman, the man from Scarborough was an unknown quantity. Only twenty-two and barely out of his youth, Fenby seemed precariously young, but he was not without experience. An organist, with those particular skills common to organists (as had been the case with Thomas Ward) – namely an affinity for harmony and counterpoint, score reading, transposition and an inclination towards versatility in other areas of music such as conducting, choir training and accompanying – Fenby had cut his teeth in Scarborough's musical world as an articled pupil of Claude Keeton, organist of St Martin-on-the-Hill (well known for its Pre-Raphaelite windows). He was a cinema organist (for which he developed an ability for improvisation and extemporisation), as portrayed at the beginning of Ken Russell's film, and this skill fuelled his appetite for composition.[9] He was also a capable pianist and repetiteur, all of which placed him in demand among the local choral

---

[6] See *FDPW*, 422 *passim*.

[7] *TB*, 200.

[8] *EF*, 8.

[9] Immensely self-critical, Fenby destroyed much of his work. Though the clever light overture, *Rossini on Ilkla Moor*, is often cited, a better indication of Fenby's creative powers can be heard in his film score for Hitchcock's *Jamaica Inn* of 1939.

societies; and there was also the attraction of the Scarborough Spa Orchestra (which still exists), founded in 1912 by its director, Alick Maclean, which was a source of local pride.

A SONG OF SUMMER

Fenby arrived at Grez in October 1928. His services were put into action immediately as an accompanist for Barjansky. But very soon he was also involved in Delius's principal agenda of completing unfinished works. At the top of this agenda was *Poem of Life and Love* which Gardiner had already begun to transcribe into short score in anticipation of Fenby's arrival and for his first dictation with Delius.[10] Fenby was to finish it in order to assess its worth. This task brought to the fore a critical attribute which Jelka had lacked. Fenby's musicianship was possessed of an incisive self-criticism which quickly perceived how flawed the work was.[11] With Gardiner's arrival, the symphonic poem, now completed in piano score, was played to him several times. There was no reaction from the composer, and to Fenby the work in its present state required an amount of surgery that might have seemed anathema to Delius. The challenge, moreover, brought into question, as far as Gardiner was concerned, the realistic possibility of Delius ever being able to compose again given his physical condition.[12] Jelka, on the other hand, would brook no denial. Intimidated by Delius's thorny temperament, Fenby was at first reluctant to announce his verdict about the symphonic poem, and matters were not improved by notoriously unhappy first attempts at dictation (for what proved to be the 'trio' of the Violin Sonata No. 3), in which Delius demonstrated an almost heroic inability to understand the basic practicalities of musical communication. Had it not been for Jelka's unwavering belief, Fenby's generosity might have been exhausted there and then. But, forgetting his youth, he vehemently stood up to Delius, at first unaccustomed to blunt criticism, with the intention that a level of mutual respect between them would be established. Such respect was ultimately cemented by Delius's

---

[10] See inscription of *Poem of Life and Love*, GB-Lbl MS Mus 1745/1/32, f. 14. The first copy of the two-piano score is in Gardiner's hand (ff. 1–13v); the second is in Gardiner's hand until f. 23v when it is taken over by Fenby's (ff. 24–5).

[11] *EF*, 17.

[12] *EF*, 27–8.

request that Fenby would work at the symphonic poem; 'select all the good material, develop it, and make a piece out of it yourself. Now take your time; never hurry your work, whatever you do!'[13]

Besides probing Fenby's creative instincts, Delius's encouragement was also surely designed to test the young Yorkshireman's musical capabilities – the extent of his musical vocabulary, his critical acumen and his potential to deal with, and comprehend, the syntax of Delius's style. Fenby responded positively to the task; Delius was impressed by his sense of stylistic empathy, and, convinced that they could work together, was energised into his own revision of the work.[14] Although the process of dictation was laborious and exhausting for Delius – he was often not capable of dictating for long periods because of frequent bouts of pain – there was a genuine meeting of minds. Hurdles such as those of national musical nomenclatures – Delius used the German, Fenby the English – were overcome. In fact, as the two began to work together, it became evident that, after some brusque expressions of opinion (Delius still hoped to retain some of the rejected ideas),[15] much of the material for *Poem of Life and Love* should be rejected, and the piece turned into a new orchestral work, a fact confirmed by Fenby.[16] Indeed, with the exception of a few short passages, the only music to be retained was the beautiful Lydian music of the second subject (see Chapter 13). Whether Fenby's own creative solution to the score played a major part in this assessment, we cannot be certain, but it was a critical decision well made.[17] Progress on *A Song of Summer* was painfully slow and went on from 1928 into the spring of 1929. Writing to Grainger in August 1929, Jelka remarked to Grainger: 'Since your departure Fred has written quite a new opening to the Orchestral piece and Fenby did remarkably well in helping him'.[18] Clearly the work had been a major artistic burden to both her and Delius, for in another letter to Grainger she declared: 'It is a lovely short piece now. After the terrible vicissitudes thro' which it went since years, I could never have believed that it would sound so natural'.[19]

---

[13] Ibid., 35.

[14] *EF*, 37.

[15] Ibid., 50.

[16] See *GB-Lbl* MS Mus 17545/1/32, f. 14. 'Most of this work was rejected and the material used for A Song of Summer. Eric Fenby'.

[17] *EF*, 49–50.

[18] Letter from Jelka to Grainger, 27 August 1929, *DLL2*, 348n.

[19] Letter from Jelka to Grainger, 4 November 1930, *DLL2*, 368.

Example 15.1a. *A Song of Summer*, Theme 2.

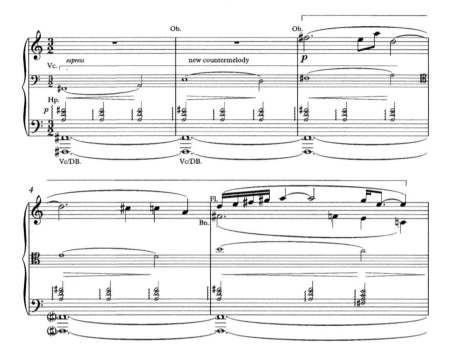

The result was a considerably truncated sonata structure of 155 bars in D major (as opposed to the 359 bars of the original symphonic poem) where the second-subject group of *Poem of Life and Love* (see Examples 15.1a, 15.1b and 15.1c) now formed the first (Themes 2 and 3) *and* second subjects (Themes 3 and 4) of a tighter, new design (see Table 15.1).[20] Around this material was constructed a new introduction (Example 15.1d – Theme 1), thematically interconnected with the cello countermelody and the upward flight of the flute motive of Theme 2, the opening figure of Theme 3 (in the high violins) and a horn 'call' deployed at the beginning of the development.[21] A short developmental episode is used to approach the work's dynamic climax at b. 72 (essentially a reworking of Theme 1), and the postlude was originally

---

[20] Table 15.1 owes much to Robert Threlfall's concordance in *RT2*, 155.

[21] The dictated introduction is famously recounted in *EF*, 132–47 as an indication of how Delius worked.

conceived in a first draft of the revised work as the opening. In this much abridged version, *A Song of Summer* was published by Boosey & Hawkes in 1931 and the *Stichvorlag* eventually presented to the University of Jacksonville. It was first heard at Queen's Hall on 17 September 1931 under the direction of Henry Wood (among a plethora of orchestral works and songs by the composer) and later became famous as the borrowed title of Russell's 1968 film for the BBC's *Omnibus* series.

Example 15.1b. *A Song of Summer,* Theme 3.

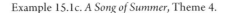

Example 15.1c. *A Song of Summer,* Theme 4.

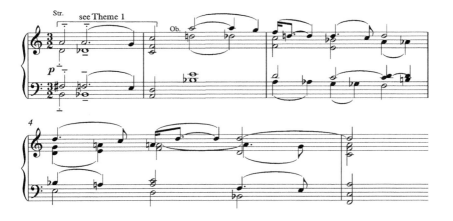

Table 15.1. A Song of Summer, structural overview.*

	Bars	Section	Theme	Key	Comments
EXPOSITION	1–15	Introduction	1 (with connections to 2 and 3)	D major	Dictated to Fenby
	16–37	First subject	2, 3	D major	Corresponds with bb. 74–94 in PLL
	38–55	Second subject	3, 4	F major / A major	Corresponds with bb. 95–112 in PLL
DEVELOPMENT	56–63			Fluid	Dictated to Fenby
	64–67			Fluid	Corresponds with bb. 161–164 in PLL
	68–71		Derived mainly from 1	Fluid	Corresponds loosely with bb. 64–67 in PLL
	72–76			Fluid	Corresponds with bb. 137–141 in PLL
	77–89			Fluid	Dictated to Fenby, although bb. 86–89 closely correspond with bb. 115–117 in PLL.
RECAPITULATION	90–109		2, 3	Bb major / D major	Corresponds with bb. 297–314 PLL
	110–146		3, 4	D major	Corresponds with bb. 315–351 PLL
	147–155	Postlude	4, 1	D major	This was originally dictated as an opening to the work.

* Compare with the structural overview of A Poem of Life and Love in Table 13.3.

Example 15.1d. *A Song of Summer*, Theme 1 (introduction).

CYNARA AND A LATE LARK: DELIUS AND THE SOLO 'SCENA'

At the beginning of 1929 Fenby was not only preoccupied with *A Song of Summer* but also the preparation of a 'choral suite' of pieces from *Hassan* at the behest of Gardiner.[22] The latter was completed in May. Fenby, whom Delius referred to as his 'musical secretary',[23] had arrived at Grez at an auspicious time, since Beecham had announced that there would be a festival of six concerts of Delius's music in London throughout October and one at the beginning of November 1929. Not only would Fenby's services be required with the logistics of the festival,[24] but the various concerts opened up opportunities for the performance of unfinished works. At the same time as he was working on *Hassan*, Fenby also made copies of three of the *Danish*

---

[22] See letter from Gardiner to Delius, 21 March 1929, *DLL2*, 348–9. See also *EF*, 50.

[23] Letter from Delius to Beecham, 10 March 1929, *DLL2*, 347.

[24] *EF*, 88.

Songs – 'Summer Nights', 'Wine Roses' and 'Red Roses' – as preliminary work for the festival (though they were not actually performed). Fenby's acquaintance with 'Summer Nights' (one of the most original of this fine collection of songs) must surely also have reminded him of its affinity with *A Late Lark* which Delius had managed to sketch in brief in 1924, and dictate to Jelka during 1925 before his sight had finally failed.[25] After it was exhumed by Fenby, several parts of the vocal line needed to be added by dictation along with some minor alterations elsewhere, before a fair copy could be made. It was then included in the first concert of the Delius Festival on 12 October 1929 when it was sung by Heddle Nash under Beecham's direction.

Much like Delius's impressionistic setting of Drachmann in 1897, *A Late Lark* has a similar, tranquil demeanour of declamation (though gently lyrical in delivery), and its slow harmonic change in the accompaniment, punctuated with and propelled by short comments from the wind and solo violin, has more in common with the idiom of 'scena' than orchestral song. Given the time of its composition, when there seemed no further prospect of creativity in his life, one wonders whether Delius's interpretation of W. E. Henley's contemplative acceptance of death ('Margaritae Sorori' from *Life and Death (Echoes)*) was one of personal valediction. Consisting of no less than seventy-one bars, the form of the 'scena' is largely determined by Henley's three verses. Beginning on a dominant eleventh of F, the first verse is deeply pregnant with nostalgia. The nocturnal impression of the 'late lark' (Example 15.2a) in the solo oboe is a compelling one, but there is something even more enthralling in the shift to D major (b. 13) and B major (b. 18) where the announcement of the work's central theme (b. 13) seems reminiscent of earlier Delius, and in particular thematic elements of *Koanga*, *Paris* and *Appalachia* (Example 15.2b). This thematic strain, which helps to define the A major framework of the second verse, enunciates the sense of transformation ('The spires shine and are changed') and the coming of night ('and the darkening air thrills with a sense of triumphing night'). With the arrival of the third verse ('So be my passing!') the tonal spell of A major is broken, but the spirit of the 'late lark' is deftly recalled by a 6/4 chord of D major and a reiteration of the 'lark' fragment. At this juncture Delius unexpectedly steers the music onto a 6/4 of E flat ('let me be gathered to the quiet west'), a modulation articulated by a final statement of the core theme, but this movement flatwards is serenely contradicted by F major which provides both a radiant conclusion and a resolution to the open-ended first verse.

---

[25] See *GB-Lbl* MS Mus 1745/2/6. See *EF*, 70–71.

Example 15.2a. *A Late Lark*, the 'late lark' (opening).

Example 15.2b. *A Late Lark*, 'transformation' theme.

In addition to *A Late Lark*, Delius was also keen to exhume a setting of much earlier work which had originally been intended for *Songs of Sunset*. Revisiting Dowson's 'Non sum qualis eram bonae sub regno Cynarae' revealed in Delius the fact that some musical enterprises in his past had remained unfulfilled, or that some of his musical invention had been put aside without realising its full potential. It was during the summer of 1929, when Heseltine was visiting Delius at Grez, that he came across the 'almost completed full score' of *Cynara*, planned on very big lines, and containing some excellent music. 'I knew he had once attempted this poem, but I had no idea he had got so far with it. He had completely forgotten it – it is more than twenty years old – but it was copied out and played to him, and he managed to dictate the last few bars of the music'.[26] As Heseltine deftly remarked some six years earlier in his book on Delius, 'The setting of "Cynara", Dowson's most perfect poem, which was to have formed the climax of the work [*Songs of Sunset*],

---

[26] Letter from Heseltine to Colin Taylor (Eton), 6 August 1929, *FDPW*, 464n.

was wisely omitted, as tending to disturb the proportions and interrupt the mood-sequence of the whole'.[27] Inspired by Horace's *Odes*, Book 4.1, 'Non sum qualis', Dowson's use of the Alexandrine lines of twelve syllables, with its dream-like flow and archaic language, conjured up a 'Pre-Raphaelite' image with its 'pale, lost lilies', though the 'bought red mouth' was more redolent of the prostitute.[28] Germane, however, to the poem was the overwhelming fixation with lost love, the reigniting of an old, tender flame, and a deep sense of remorse engendered by debauchery and indulgence; all these were embodied in the subtly modified recurrences of the refrain 'But I was desolate and sick of an old passion … I have been faithful to thee, Cynara! In my fashion'. In setting all four verses of Dowson's poem, Delius's inspiration extended to the best part of ten minutes of music, far longer than the average length of four minutes for each item in the cycle.[29] Indeed, the scale of *Cynara* had more in common with the epic nature of *A Mass of Life*, amounting to a quasi-operatic structure in its mixture of declamation and lyrical arioso.

Though the 'scena' begins elegiacally in an oblique G sharp minor, the entry of the solo violin establishes E major, a tonality Delius probably chose because of its connection with the penultimate song, 'I was not sorrowful', in the cycle's course of chosen tonalities. It was in this key that the draft manuscript concluded with the phrase 'Then falls thy shadow, Cynara!' (see b. 163). This left Delius with several additional lines to dictate to Fenby, a task completed 'after some painful and frustrating hours of work'.[30] For the first performance at the Delius Festival on 18 October 1929 with John Goss and the BBC Symphony Orchestra under Beecham, the work ended on a simple chord of E major. Delius considered this unsatisfactory so, after its London hearing, it was further revised to include a coda of eight bars, reiterating the thematic material in E major from the prelude (bb. 7–10) and a further reinforcement of the tonality, replete with added sixth, in the closing four bars. As Fenby recollected: 'It is not one of Delius's happiest inspirations, but there

---

[27] *PH*, 123n.

[28] Reumens, C., 'Poem of the week: Non sum qualis eram bonae sub regno Cynarae by Ernest Dowson', *The Guardian*, 14 March 2011.

[29] There is also some suggestion from the drafts and sketches (see *GB-Lbl* MS Mus 1745/2/13/4) that Delius originally intended to incorporate a chorus (which would echo the end of the refrain), though this was eventually jettisoned in favour a solo number.

[30] *RT1*, 81. See also Fenby, E., *Delius* (London: Faber & Faber, 1971), 82. Fenby also recalled that Delius revised the accentuation of 'Cynara' so that the emphasis was placed on the first syllable (i.e. '*Cyn*-a-ra').

was a moment in the green-room at Queen's Hall when, suddenly coming in from the noise of the street, I heard the distant sounds of its quietly ascending introduction for divided strings as it was being rehearsed, and there seemed to be no fairer music in the world than this. But, then, I was starved. I had not heard the sound of the orchestra in the concert-room for over a year'.[31]

Although there is a considerable degree of chromatic fluidity throughout the structure of *Cynara*, Delius nevertheless maintains a subtle but firm control in his adherence to E towards the end of each verse. At the conclusion to verse one this can be felt in the dominant harmony of bb. 53–5, in the shift to B major at the end of verse two (bb. 91–3) and the cadence into E major at the end of verse three (bb. 133–8), while the last four lines of verse four are pungently imbued with E major as we arrive at one of Dowson's most moving lines – 'Then falls thy shadow, Cynara! The night is thine' (which textually reiterates line two of verse one). Verses one and three, with their preponderance of D major and minor, are linked by their Bacchanalian theme of wine and the dance, especially verse three where the waltz is a prominent feature ('Dancing, to put thy pale, lost lilies out of mind'), and at the beginning of verse four where the first line of text acts as an important conduit to the reprise of E major ('I cry for madder music and for more wine!'). Here the connection with the 'Tanzlied' of *A Mass of Life* seems especially palpable. Equally important, however, as a Wagnerian motivic 'cement' is the continuous recurrence of the *idée fixe* (see Chapter 9) which is of a symphonic intensity comparable with the second song ('Cease smiling, dear'). This not only imbues much of the orchestra's thematic undercurrent, but it also occurs at significant structural moments such as the end of each refrain.

Perhaps the saddest legacy of *Cynara*, a ruefully introspective work, is that it was prepared for publication by Heseltine in 1930 (both vocal and full scores appeared with Boosey & Hawkes in 1931). Although his attachment to Delius's music had cooled markedly in the 1920s, the part he played in the organisation of the Delius Festival and his attendance at the concerts had revived his enthusiasm for there was no-one to rival his knowledge of the composer's music. Thus, as Jelka remarked, 'next to Beecham, [he was] the *soul* of the thing'.[32] After the news of Heseltine's death in his London apartment reached Grez, Delius, crushed by the catastrophe, dedicated *Cynara* to his memory.[33]

---

[31] *EF*, 70.

[32] Letter from Jelka to Edith Buckley Jones, January 1931, *FDPW*, 514.

[33] Letter from Jelka to Sydney Schiff, [January 1931], *FDPW*, 509.

VIOLIN SONATA NO. 3: A CLASSICAL REJUVENATION

After the dictation of those necessary parts of *Cynara* and *A Late Lark*, and hearing the works in the concert hall during the Delius Festival, Fenby recalled that the experience brought a renewed confidence in himself as well as Delius.[34] So much so in fact that Delius much looked forward to resuming work in 1930 after Fenby returned from Scarborough. The Violin Sonata No. 3 took shape between February and May 1930. Some sketches of the first movement had been made by Delius in 1916,[35] no more than a few bars of a second movement are dated 11 October 1924, and draft material for the last movement, dictated to Jelka, is dated between 9 September and 20 October 1924.[36] As Fenby recalled: 'The few odds and ends of sketches – the opening bars, a subsidiary theme, and the germ for the second subject of the first movement, a few bars of the second movement, and the themes for the last movement – dated from the war years'.[37] Though there was relatively little material, the work was dictated with rapidity, though the manner was never, to use Fenby's words, 'calm and leisurely'.[38] In May, May Harrison, to whom the Sonata was dedicated, came over to Grez to play the work over for the composer. It was first given by Harrison accompanied by Bax (who took a particular interest in Delius's chamber music) at the Wigmore Hall on 6 November 1930.

As had already been fortunately determined with *Poem of Life and Love*, Delius felt an affinity for Fenby's own creative musicianship and as the two worked, the process of dictation must have assumed a forward propulsion through Fenby's own instincts to anticipate the next harmony, or the next gesture. 'When I was not writing during his dictation', he remarked, 'I was feeling my way at the keyboard, striking every note immediately after he had named it, and anticipating wherever possible what I thought would be the next chord as well as my musical instincts and his verbal directions would allow me'.[39] From time to time, he would stumble on the right progression,[40] but more often than not, Fenby's understanding of Delius's thought processes and style permitted him to enter the spirit of the work along with the composer. In

---

[34] Fenby, E., *Delius*, 83.

[35] See *GB-Lbl* MS Mus 1745/2/5, ff. 105–6.

[36] Ibid., ff. 115–16 and ff. 120–32.

[37] *EF*, 91.

[38] Ibid., 147.

[39] Ibid., 149.

[40] Ibid., 149.

fact, Delius commented that Fenby could 'finish his sentences for him'. To this Fenby added that 'it was no use remaining passive and merely taking down the notes (even if one could have done at the speed at which he dictated), particularly with a man like Delius, who never repeated himself unless he could help it'.[41] For Jelka, who could not offer these musical attributes, Fenby's assistance was nothing short of extraordinary, as she described to Grainger: 'Fenby returned to Grez in Febr. and they at once set to to compose Fred's 3ᵈ Violin-Sonata, of which Fred had dictated sketches and snatches and a few opening pages to me in 1923–1924. But he was wonderfully alert, dictating to Eric, correcting, changing, making quite new suggestions. The result (as it seems to me), is a very flowing, melodious Sonata – serene and less wistful than No. 2'.[42]

Delius's Third Sonata was indeed very different from his other sonatas for violin and for cello in that he opted for a much more traditional, more classical three-movement scheme (a fact evident from the earliest sketches in 1916 and 1924) rather than the more esoteric dual-functional, one-movement schemes such as that of the Cello Sonata and Violin Sonata No. 2. It was probably for this reason that Fenby suggested it was 'the best of the three [violin] sonatas to introduce young players to Delius',[43] in that its three short movements (markedly shorter than those of the Sonata No. 1) were more approachable in scope and structure. The simplest of the three movements is without doubt the central Scherzo which follows an uncomplicated ternary design, the outer sections being firmly rooted in D minor, the 'trio' (the subject of Fenby's first uncomfortable dictation) another of Delius's quasi-folk songs in G minor. The first movement, an extensively modified sonata scheme, follows a more unconventional path. Though more clearly delineated in terms of its thematic events (an indication, perhaps, of its compositional process), the movement sets up an interesting interaction of tonalities which will prove important for the rest of the work. Setting out in G minor the first subject (A) yields to a more sequential transitional phase (B) which modulates to the more stable key of the dominant, D major (C). This stability, moreover, is accentuated by the simple diatonicism of Delius's melody, harmonised in the composer's typically bifurcated manner with its chromatically descending bass line. The restatement of material is altogether more complex. The first subject, which embarks from the dominant of G, behaves more like a development

---

[41] Ibid., 99.

[42] Letter from Jelka to Grainger, 4 November 1930, *DLL2*, 368.

[43] Fenby, E., *Delius*, 84.

Table 15.2. Violin Sonata No. 3, first movement, tonal and thematic overview.

Bars	Thematic material	Section	Key
1–13	First subject	A	G minor
14–30	Transitional material	B	Fluid
31–42	Second subject	C	D major
43–64	First subject (development)	A	Fluid (V of G)
65–75	Transitional material	B	Fluid
76–95	Second subject	C	E major

with its unstable tonal demeanour, as does the transitional material which follows. Stability occurs once more with the second subject which returns in E major and it is in this key that the movement concludes (see Table 15.2). The Scherzo, as mentioned above, is a simple tripartite structure in D minor, though it is worth noting that G minor (prominent at the beginning of the first movement) is employed for the 'trio' (rather than the A minor Delius originally envisaged).[44] Moreover, it is interesting to note that the reprise of the Scherzo begins in G minor, necessitating some modification of the material to restore D minor at the end. By comparison, the finale is more eccentric. What seems rhetorically like an introduction, balanced between a modal E minor (reminiscent of Grieg) and G major (bb. 1–18) is in fact part of a musical frame, since Delius reserves the return of this material until the very end (bb. 108–18) where it cadences in D minor. The main body of the movement, marked 'Con moto', is a more sophisticated sonata structure. The first subject, made up of several thematic strands, refuses to settle tonally. Suggestive of E minor in its opening bars (bb. 18–22), its climactic arc (b. 29) hints strongly at D major, while a third component (b. 44) strongly insinuates G major. However, it is only when we reach b. 53 that G major becomes more definite with the establishment of the second subject which is shared between the piano and violin (bb. 53–62). A restatement of the second subject in D major (bb. 72–9) marks the beginning of the recapitulation immediately after which recurs the last of the three fragments of the first subject (bb. 80–85), also essentially defined by that key. At this juncture, Delius incorporates a cyclic reference to the 'trio' of the second movement (bb. 85–9), before reaching the climactic recurrence of the movement with the second subject

[44] See *EF*, 32.

('con passione') in B flat major. This deft tonal divergence smooths the way for a final statement of the first subject in G minor (a final reference to a key which has figured conspicuously throughout the entire sonata) before the 'frame' brings the movement to a close in a tranquil D minor.

SONGS OF FAREWELL: A WHITMAN HOMECOMING

After completion of the Violin Sonata No. 3, and its scrutiny by May Harrrison, Delius composed the *Caprice and Elegy* for her sister's American tour. These two works were, however, only a preparation for a much more ambitious task, the realisation of which Delius must have been hoping to undertake since ideas were sketched in 1920 while he was also working on the music for *Hassan*. This is confirmed in a letter he wrote to Orr where he mentioned in passing: 'I am working on another choral work'.[45] This he had also indicated to Universal the day before.[46] Work, however, had to be postponed because of the pressures of getting *Hassan* completed. An indication of preliminary work survives, including a detailed pencil draft of the first movement of the full score,[47] and there is evidence of Delius's first sketches for the entire work in short score,[48] which corroborates Jelka's assertion to Newman that 'the work was entirely sketched out in 1921 or 1920, when he put it aside to do the Hassan music'.[49] Fenby also mentioned that the orchestral introduction was sketched in full score so this also provided tangible material for future dictation.

One may only conjecture as to why Delius wished to return to the tried-and-tested *topos* of the choral work for double choir and orchestra, but he may well have still required some form of creative catharsis to express the idea of valediction in the same epic mould as *A Mass of Life* and the *Requiem* (both of which required the denser choral sonorities and more expansive vocal tessituras of Delius's characteristic scoring for double choir). This must have struck the young Fenby when Delius urged him to reach for the thirty-two-stave manuscript paper. The orchestra was to be typically large once again (though not quite on the same scale as *A Mass of Life* or the *Requiem*

---

45 Letter from Delius to Orr, 16 May 1920, *DLL2*, 231.

46 Letter from Delius to Universal, 15 May 1920, *DTA* (see also *DLL2*, 226).

47 *GB-Lbl* MS Mus 1745/2/13/5, ff. 128–32 (see also *RT2*, 41).

48 *GB-Lbl* MS Mus 1745/2/9, ff. 15–25.

49 Letter from Jelka to Newman, 28 October 1930, *DTA*.

in terms of brass and wind) and the strings would be subject to their habitual divisions. Jelka had been responsible for the choice of words from Whitman's *Leaves of Grass* which also no doubt awoke Delius's rather earlier affinity for Whitman's verse in *Sea Drift*. There the rondo form and interpolation of partsongs between the passages of solo declamation and arioso had been a vibrant stimulus towards a final, highly cohesive, symphonic choral form. Perhaps aware that large-scale, extended choral canvases were physically beyond him by 1920, Delius sought the opportunity to explore the idiom of orchestral partsong which he had worked so fruitfully into a similar, coherent cycle in *Songs of Sunset*.[50] The sentiments of leave-taking, similarly expressed in *A Late Lark*, had also become a preoccupation of the composer. Indeed, the notion of the 'last farewell' and death were evident in his first thoughts of the title, *The Last Voyage*.[51] As Jelka attempted to enunciate to Grainger, the cycle consisted of '5 poems, or fragments, all about the Sea and embarking on the last great voyage. It is for Double Chorus and Orchestra (no Solists [*sic*]) and really it seems quite up to the finest of his works'.[52] Fenby's description of the 'programme' of the five partsongs is particularly adroit:

> in the first three movements, the composer gives voice to the "silent backward tracings", the "meditations of old times resumed – their loves, joys, persons, voyages", that delight the heart of man in the twilight of his days. The great forces of Nature are saluted in turn, and in the fourth and fifth movements, with a joyous leave-taking, the old sailor, bidding farewell to "land and life", speeds from the shore upon the endless chartless voyage of Death to the sound of the hushed voices of his friends in the final *pianissimo* chord, "Depart!"[53]

While it is true that Delius makes full use of Whitman's maritime analogies in the cycle, in the first of the partsongs the nostalgic sense of 'backward tracing' is to rural nature, to the very heart of Delius's sense of pastoral landscape and the dream-soaked idyll. A conflation of lines from two poems, 'Memories'

[50]   See Mitchell, D., 'Delius: The Choral Music', *Tempo*, No. 26 (Winter 1952–1953), 17.

[51]   Letter from Jelka to Grainger, 1 November 1930, *DLL2*, 368. Within a few weeks Jelka informed Fenby that Delius had changed the title to *Songs of Farewell* (see letter from Jelka to Fenby, 21 November 1930, *DLL2*, 371).

[52]   Ibid.

[53]   *EF*, 102.

and 'Out of May's Shows Selected' in *Sands at Seventy*, Whitman's poetic evocation chimed perfectly with the ethos of Delius's 'summer music' *par excellence*, pungent with scent, the intensity of afternoon sunshine and vivid colours. This is conveyed with so many of the composer's thumbprints – the added sixth of the first orchestral sonority, the downbeat triplets of bars 4 and 5, and their familiar melodic shapes, the *topos* of the falling chromatic bass line, the shifting kaleidoscope of Delius's choral homophony, and the elliptical final cadence. Delius defines the first line and a half in D major, and it is this key, replete with pastoral drone, that characterises the short orchestral interludes of bb. 12–17 and 27–32. This music is very much part of Delius's own 'backward tracing', for, with the prominence of the horn calls, this is mountain music from Norway. After a short choral statement which carries us from D minor to F sharp major (in illustration of human loves and joys), D major is restored by the second interlude. A second deviation from D (b. 33) builds a new tension with its powerful voice-leading in the bass, the goal being the dominant in b. 43 where the marking of 'largamente' fortifies the sequential writing ('The yellow, golden, transparent haze') which follows. The sequential phase from the dominant, and from the tonic in b. 50, moreover, borrows the same melodic and harmonic model the composer had deployed (albeit on a considerably larger scale) in *The Song of the High Hills* (see Fig. 82[+4]) in much the same ecstatic context. An unconscious reference, perhaps, but a thoroughly apt one nevertheless.

'From Montauk Point' (also from *Sands at Seventy*) formed the basis for a spacious seascape in the second song. Cast in C major, its frame consists of an undulating theme for cellos. A secondary idea, an ostinato (Example 15.3), underpins the entire choral statement, culminating in a more turbulent conclusion ('the snowy, curling caps, that inbound urge and urge of waves') strongly reminiscent of *Sea Drift*. The cello theme also figures prominently in the third song (lines 9, and 11–20 from *Passage to India*) which, as

Example 15.3. *Songs of Farewell*, 'I stand as on some mighty eagle's beak', ostinato.

Mitchell has suggested, links the second and third songs together as a slow movement.[54] The third song, in particular, has much of the intensity of *A Mass of Life*, not only in its persistent development of the material after b. 128 (strongly reminiscent rhythmically of the *Dance Rhapsody* No. 2) but also in its demanding vocal range for the chorus, epitomised by the climactic top C for soprano (b. 157) as the soul breaks its bonds ('Away O soul!'). In response to the reflective postlude of the third song, 'Joy, shipmate, joy!' (from *Songs of Parting*) is a sturdy march whose two melodic elements are supported respectively by a robust cycle of fifths and a descending chromatic bass (two immediately recognisable Delian hallmarks). It is the second of these that is developed initially by the succeeding choral statement, allowing the fifths material to have its impact in the orchestral reprise (b. 199). For the last song, 'Now finale to the shore' (also from *Songs of Parting*) which Mitchell aptly describes as an 'Epilogue', the choral style fluctuates between declamation and lyricism. Again deploying some powerful voice-leading, the soprano builds registrally by degrees to the final apogee ('Depart upon thy endless cruise old Sailor'), marked by the climactic 6/4 (b. 234) which presages the final establishment of D major from b. 242. What is more, this authoritative peroration is enriched by memories of the first song (its own climax) and the mesmeric cello theme of the second and third songs, while the final choral sonority, with its prominent added sixth in the soprano, seems like an echo of the same chord which began the cycle in bb. 1–2.

Delius had hoped that Beecham would take on the first performance of the *Songs of Farewell*,[55] but in the end news of Delius's work excited the attentions of Elizabeth Courtauld, wife of the industrialist, philanthropist and art collector Samuel Courtauld, who had agreed to sponsor a series of popular subscription concerts in London. A visit to Grez by Elizabeth Courtauld secured the premiere with Bruno Walter, though this responsibility eventually fell to Malcolm Sargent, the series' chief conductor, on 21 March 1932 at Queen's Hall with the London Symphony Orchestra and Philharmonic Choir. The first time Delius was able to hear the work was in a broadcast of 5 February 1933. The partsongs were a heroic achievement against the odds, or, as Fenby described them, 'a monument of what can be done when, the body broke, there still remains in a man the will to create'.[56]

[54] Mitchell, D., 'Delius: The Choral Music', 17.

[55] *EF*, 114.

[56] Ibid., 101.

OPERATIC EXHUMATION: *IRMELIN* AND *IDYLL*

The exertions of dictating left Delius exhausted; for Fenby, however, the strain was clearly much greater. As he left Grez in early October of 1930, feeling 'like a worn-out old man', he found it necessary to remain in England for much of 1931 rather than return to France as had been formerly arranged.[57] After the premiere of *A Song of Summer* on 17 September which Fenby was able to hear in London, he arrived back at Grez in October when he was able to oversee the completion of the *Hassan* Suite and take dictation of the *Fantastic Dance*, a work sketched in or around 1924. The first twenty bars of the work already existed in a draft pencil full score,[58] while some material for the middle section survive in the form of pencil sketches.[59] The task was to 'compose out' this material into a simple ternary form. Although the 'whole tone' element is a striking feature of the work, much of this piece (arguably Delius's final Nietzschean allusion towards the 'dance') owes its waltz *topos* and many of the orchestral gestures to *Paris* and *Lebenstanz*, though its more austere thematic and harmonic countenance has more in common with the later *Dance Rhapsody* No. 2.

The focus of Fenby's task until the final months of 1931 had been essentially to *finish* those works uppermost in Delius's mind which had been left frustratingly incomplete by the degeneration of his physical powers. At the end of 1931, however, Delius appears to have been motivated by regret, or at least disappointment, that some of his completed work had never reached the public ear. One of these was his earliest opera, *Irmelin*, for which he evidently retained an affection. With Fenby's assistance, a miniature ternary structure was completed in F sharp major using material from the Prelude and conclusion to Act I and the transposition of material from Act III (see Table 15.3).[60] Sadly, Delius did not live long enough to hear it performed. Beecham, who later expressed his own admiration for the opera (and later constituted a Concert Suite from Act II), included it as an interlude in Act III of the revival of *Koanga* at Covent Garden in September 1935. Its first concert performance had to wait until 1 April 1937 when Beecham conducted it at Queen's Hall.

More substantial than *Irmelin*, however, was the disinterment of his one-act opera *Margot la Rouge* which, in spite of its publication in vocal score in 1905

[57] *EF*, 114.

[58] See *GB-Lbl* MS Mus 1745/2/9, ff. 26–9.

[59] Ibid., ff. 30–31.

[60] Much of this concordance is available in *RT2*, 158.

Table 15.3. *Irmelin* Prelude, derivation of material from the opera.

Irmelin Prelude (1931)			
Bars	Section	Key	Correspondence with *Irmelin* opera (1890–1892)
1–24	A	G♯ minor – F♯ major	Condensed from bb. 1–46 Prelude to Act I
24–27		F♯ major	Irmelin's leitmotiv (see bb. 39–41) Act III
27–32	B	F♯ minor	cf. (in E♭ minor) bb. 42–7 Act III
32–33		A major	bb. 47–8 (in D♯ minor) Act III
34–42		F♯ minor	Repeat of material in bb. 42–8 in Act III and developed
42–52		F♯ major	bb. 49–58 (in E♭ major) Act III
53–61	A	F♯ major	bb. 17–25 Act I
62–64		F♯ major	bb. 690–92 (in G major) Act I

in Paris, had never seen the light of day. Fenby had returned to Scarborough for Christmas in 1931 where the strain of the work and his isolated life at Grez finally caught up with him in the form of a nervous breakdown.[61] He did not return to France until August 1932 at which time, sanctioned by Delius, he arranged the two wordless partsongs, *To be sung of a summer night on the water*, for string orchestra. As for *Margot*, the decision was made to jettison the old libretto and to see whether, *post hoc*, Robert Nichols, the English writer, poet and playwright, might be able to adapt the music to new words. According to Fenby, Nichols (who had been undoubtedly aware of the former love story by Rosenval) adapted a new story from a further compilation of words from Whitman's *Leaves of Grass* which would involve two soloists, a baritone and soprano.

Nichols, who had a considerable empathy for music, had heard the *Songs of Farewell* on 21 March 1932 and was greatly enthused by the work.[62] He, too, had visited Delius at Grez, and imbibed something of the composer's love of Nietzschean stoicism. More importantly, Nichols understood the artistic task before him: 'Delius, by virtue of his capacity to communicate the substance of life's stillest hours, is an exalted and tragic idyllist, the tone-poet of an extreme felicity, on whom "the burden of mystery" hangs heavy because it is never shirked'.[63]

---

[61] *EF*, 114.

[62] See letter from Jelka to Grainger, 23 March 1932, *DLL2*, 405.

[63] Nichols, R., 'Delius As I Knew Him', in *DC*, 115.

The choice to base his words on Whitman's poetry – freely taken and arranged from *Children of Adam, Calamus, The Sleepers* and *Songs of Parting* – was therefore an altogether sensitive and sympathetic one given Delius's affinity for the American's verse. Jelka considered it a process of emancipation: 'all that lovely music is freed from the beastly subject for which it was always much too good and refined. All the knife and murder bits are eliminated and the music really miraculously adapted to the new words, an exhalted [*sic*] Love-poem'.[64] Jelka's description was precise. All the 'naturalist' element of the opera was discarded, which included the storm music and rapid dialogue that dominated Scene 3 and the violence of Scene 7. In terms of constructing the new, shorter work, the task of reconstituting the musical structure was not especially problematical. As is evident from Table 15.4, the *Idyll* retained the chronological order of material from the opera (as one can see in Scenes 1, 2, 4, 5 and 6). Only at the very end, where it was clearly decided to restore E major, the key of the Prelude and the baritone's reappearance at 'Behold me when I pass', did Delius resolve to employ the lyrical material from the end of Scene 4 (where the key is a radiant E major) as a 'tranquil' finale ('Sweet are the blooming cheeks of the living'). In the original version first performed at Queen's Hall with Dora Labbette, Roy Henderson, Henry Wood and the BBC Symphony Orchestra on 3 October 1933, the work began with the beginning of Scene 1, but after this performance Delius thought to make the work more convincing with the Prelude to the opera by beginning with its opulent establishment of E major at its conclusion – at which point the first

Table 15.4. *Idyll*, reconstitution of material (from the opera) and key structure.

Text	Voice	Key	Scene in *Margot la Rouge*
Prelude (revised version)		E major	(Same as opera)
'Once I passed through a populous city' (first version)	Baritone	E minor	Scene 1
'Again we wander'	Baritone	C minor	Scene 2
'Day by day and night'	Soprano	F major	Scene 2
'Behold me when I pass'	Baritone	E major	Scene 4
'I am she who adorned herself'	Soprano	E♭ major	Scene 5
'This is thy hour O soul'	Baritone	D major	Scene 6
'Sweet are the blooming cheeks of the living'	Baritone	E major	Scene 4

[64] Letter from Jelka to Beecham, 16 October 1932, *DLL2*, 410.

twelve bars of Scene 1 were discarded.[65] Delius's principal undertaking was to readapt the original French style of syllabic delivery to a much more lyrical combination of declamation and sustained melodic lines better suited to the scansion, assonance and accentuation of English. In some instances, this meant preserving the original melodic lines (though often with rhythmical modifications); in others, it frequently involved quite new vocal invention which Delius had to dictate to Fenby. This took place, according to the preface of the published vocal score by Boosey & Hawkes, in September and October of 1932. The result was a transformation of the composer's original operatic concept in which Delius's natural gift for lyricism gained a new coherence without the distraction of *verismo*, a dramatic temperament for which he had limited affinity. Furthermore, the new form, cohesively cemented by the glue of E major, worked without detriment to Delius's rich matrix of thematic material which, allied to its new English words, still retained its fervour and immediacy.

Beecham described the collaboration of Delius and Fenby as 'heroic', but he chose to be more candid about what he considered the true value of those pieces produced between 1929 and 1933: 'It would be idle if in our admiration for the remarkable qualities of the two participants we ignored the plain fact that it gives us little of Delius that we did not know before; and even that little does not ring with the sound of unadulterated inspiration. Let us honour it as a noble experiment and leave it at that'.[66] Beecham's comments have a refreshing frankness. In truth, the works dictated to Fenby were always likely to be circumscribed by their challenging circumstances. There was no prospect of the production of anything of a very large scale; indeed, an examination of the list of works added to Delius's catalogue reveals a series of miniatures or, in the case of *A Song of Summer*, the *Songs of Farewell* and the *Idyll*, a tendency towards truncation. Nevertheless, these works provide a unique insight into the composer's creative powers and into those artistic values and aesthetic ethos which remained potent in a Neo-Classical age where the Romantic individualism of Delius's music had been superseded by a new, starker modernism. As Gray pronounced: 'The music of Delius belongs essentially to the same phase of romanticism as the art of Flaubert, Gaugin, Verlaine, and Baudelaire. They are alike possessed by the nostalgia of the infinite and the unappeasable longing for an impossible bliss'.[67]

---

[65] *RT1*, 72.

[66] *TB*, 218.

[67] Gray, C., *A Survey of Contemporary Music* (Oxford: Oxford University Press, 1927), 76.

Frederick Delius died at Grez in the small hours of Sunday, 10 June 1934. Jelka, suffering following an operation for cancer in hospital, was brought back in time to be with him at the end, even though the wounds from her surgery had not yet healed. She was ever-thankful to her doctor for making this possible. 'I owe it to him that I had a few days with Fred and to have seen his happiness about it … I am getting better, but shall never be my old self again – But what does it matter now?'[68] After temporary burial in the graveyard at Grez, Delius's coffin was removed to England and reinterred at St Peter's Church, Limpsfield, Surrey, on 26 May 1935. Jelka, who developed pneumonia on her way to England, died in a Kensington nursing home on 28 May. She was buried just a few days later next to her husband at Limpsfield.

[68] Letter from Jelka to Marie Clews, 22 June 1934, *DLL2*, 454.

Epilogue

The central issue of this study of Delius's music has been to examine the composer's musical style and ethos with a particular emphasis on its formal coherence and cohesion, since the latter has always remained an issue of controversy and disagreement among Delius's critics and, most of all, his detractors. To some extent Delius himself did not assist the reception of his own music in denouncing the benefits of musical education, and more specifically his own at the Leipzig Conservatoire. His comments, according to Fenby, about Leipzig, made in an era when (a) technical mastery was increasingly considered a trammel to genuine creativity, (b) academicism a synonym for pedestrianism, and (c) autodidacticism a virtue, have, nevertheless, to be accepted 'with a pinch of salt'. Delius may have learned the rudiments of music from Thomas Ward, but his musical technique almost certainly widened exponentially during his two years at Leipzig – *Florida* and *Hiawatha* both demonstrate how far he had come – and, even then, he had mastered sufficient technique to allow some of his original imagination to reveal itself. Judging from the counterpoint he had learned with Jadassohn, a third year at Leipzig might have proved additionally beneficial had he possessed the patience to stay on, not least because it might have enhanced his appreciation of counterpoint as an emancipating compositional force. But Delius was eager to get on and he chose the more empirical path of self-communion to develop his style, by private study of Grieg and by copying parts of Wagner's operas, besides frequenting the concert hall and opera theatres as much as was physically possible during the 1890s. In many ways these years more fully constituted his 'university' education, though the life and values Delius chose to pursue made the process of development as a composer that much more complex, protracted and hard-won.

Delius is well known to have shunned the idea of 'formal' structure, and over the years this has not been helped by observations such as 'the intellectual content of Delius's music is perilously thin', or that form in Delius 'was unimportant'. For many, of course, this chimed with the notion that his music was 'self-governing and self-reliant' rather than conforming to some preconceived impediments imposed by academic exigency.[1] Nonetheless, a detailed study of his music shows without a scintilla of doubt, that he perfectly understood the demands and possibilities of form and tonality which had largely been instilled in him at Leipzig and in his conversations with Grieg, Sinding, Busoni, Schmitt and others, that he was no stranger to the classical concepts of sonata form and organicism, and that he learned to apply the potential structural benefits of variation form as an integral part of the expansion of his harmonic language.

Delius's interest in opera was probably formed while he was still a young man in Bradford. His attraction to Wagner's music was almost certainly established when he was a Bradford schoolboy (with *Lohengrin*), and in London as a student at Isleworth, but it was reinforced indelibly while he was a student in Leipzig. The 1890s as a decade is very much about the development of Delius's Wagnerian techniques – through the melodrama *Paa Vidderne*, the 'scena' *Sakuntala*, and the four operas *Irmelin*, *The Magic Fountain*, *Koanga* and *A Village Romeo and Juliet*, a cycle of works which reveals an astonishing mastery of declamation, leitmotivic technique and symphonic process as well as the crystallisation of Delius's *own personal* awareness and grasp of opera as an idiom and where, in his view, it was destined. In these works we not only observe Delius's increasing mastery of the orchestra (a skill for which he is unjustifiably neglected as a great innovator and an original), but, perhaps even more significantly, the employment of the orchestra in the furtherance of opera as a new, symphonic genre. In the little-known *Irmelin* it is possible to perceive the exceptional progress Delius had made in the period of four years since leaving Leipzig and how he was already learning to assimilate and develop the 'Liebestod' concept of *Tristan und Isolde*; moreover, he had already understood the concept of the orchestra as the symphonic 'spearhead' in opera and how opera itself, as a German progressive idiom, was an *instrumental* art rather than a vocal one. *Tristan*, above all, appears to have been both a musical and dramatic benchmark by which to measure and evaluate his operatic enterprises. This is certainly true of *The Magic Fountain*, especially the love music of Act III, and even more so in the lengthy passage of purely orchestral music which concludes Act III of *Koanga*. By the time we reach Delius's fourth music drama, *A Village Romeo and Juliet*, written between 1898 and 1901, we witness a composer in full control of his resources and technique. Arguably one of his finest and most powerful works,

---

[1] See Collins, S., 'Anti-Intellectualism and the Rhetoric of "National Character"', in Dibble, J. and Horton, J. (eds), *British Musical Criticism and Intellectual Thought 1850–1950* (Woodbridge: Boydell & Brewer, 2018), 218–19.

and notwithstanding the problems it poses for impresarios, *A Village Romeo and Juliet* reveals an astonishing fecundity of thematic material developed with a new-found confidence and vision in which the role of orchestral music is as vital as that delivered by the singers and chorus. Rich in 'partsong' (which he had inherited from his previous three music dramas) and more extended orchestral 'tone poems', the Fair scene is a brilliant example of an orchestral and choral sonata form which, in the 1907 version of the opera, was followed by the most symphonic of all Delius's interludes, *The Walk to the Paradise Garden*, a superbly constructed microcosm of the entire opera. Delius's music drama also concludes with his most overt acknowledgement of *Tristan* in the love duet, couched in that most Tristanesque of keys, B major, and the valedictory gestures of the bargemen. The later conceptual development of casting *A Village Romeo and Juliet* in the form of six 'scenes' or tableaux was symptomatic of Delius's desire to steer opera in the direction of a more *concise* experience. A flirtation with one-act opera in *Margot la Rouge*, a work by no means lacking in inspired material, was unsuccessful; however, the culmination of Delius's aspiration for dramatic terseness was the composition of *Fennimore and Gerda*, described as 'Two episodes from the life of Niels Lyhne' but formally the organisation of selected texts from Jacobsen's novel into eleven 'pictures', a formal structure which, besides its wealth and careful control of leitmotivic material, appears to have encouraged Delius to think in a more strategic manner of tonal hierarchies with C major at its centre.

Opera may have been one of Delius's major artistic preoccupations, but there were other genres that contributed extensively to the development of his style and ethos. One was undoubtedly the solo song, an idiom for which he is not widely celebrated, and yet his output of songs, certainly until 1910, provides a rich catalogue of the composer's handling of miniature vocal structures. From Griegian beginnings in the two sets 'aus dem Norwegischen', a deferential nod to German lieder in the Heine songs, the English song market in settings of Shelley, and the French symbolist 'mélodie' in the poems of Verlaine, there is a perceptible line of stylistic evolution in terms of form, tonal treatment and, above all, *harmonic language* in which one can identify the song as the object of experiment. In fact, many of Delius's songs can be understood as 'studies' in preparation for larger works. This is particularly true of his first setting of 'Lyse Nætter' (Drachmann) which is essentially an exercise in Tristanesque harmony comparable with Wagner's 'Träume – Studie zu Tristan und Isolde' from the *Wesendonck Lieder*, and the *Seven Danish Songs* where, through a range of fertile song forms – ballad, stanzaic and through-composed – a confluence of Delius's mastery of more advanced Griegian harmony and Wagnerian chromaticism provides a catalyst to a perceptibly new voice in a second version of Drachmann's poem ('Summer Nights') and the striking selection of Jacobsen's poems (notably 'Silken Shoes' and 'Let springtime come'). The same zeal for experiment can be witnessed in *Lieder nach Gedichten von Friedrich Nietzsche* which, if anything, demarcate the most advanced limits of Delius's harmonic practice, though later songs such as 'Schwarze Rosen' and 'Summer Landscape' continue to anticipate linguistic advances in the composer's larger choral works.

Delius's affinity for the large-scale choral work did not spring, as it did for so many English composers, from the English choral tradition, but from the institution of the *Chorgesangverein* in Germany, though, of course, as Delius's music became better known in England, the country's tradition was well placed to perform, appreciate and assimilate it. The choral work as genre suited Delius's artistic outlook principally as a synthesis of those agencies which expressed his romantic ideals. One, already mentioned, was opera and theatre, though in the case of his choral works, these canvases allowed him to *internalise* his personal convictions, notably in respect of Whitman, Nietzsche, Jacobsen, and the subject of atheism, which, in the context of opera, would have encumbered the dramatic momentum. There were other reasons too: another of Delius's predilections was the genre of the partsong – one which chimed with his affinity for harmony and the elation of singing in multiple parts (necessary for the complex chords), derived, it is so often claimed, from his days in Florida listening to the improvised choral harmony of his neighbouring black workers. It is, in fact, possible to witness this inventive partiality in his first four operas where the chorus is treated as a fertile component of the *dramatis personae*, but it is with the creation of his extended choral essays that we witness the effect and presence of the chorus on his choice of forms. In *Appalachia*, the eight-part *a cappella* chorus (as a memory of the negro choir) provides the apex of his variation structure. In *Sea Drift* the choral partsong provides a series of interlude-reflections as episodes within the composer's deft rondo form, as well as the vehicle for the work's major Tristanesque climax. In *A Mass of Life*, his grandest synthesis of opera and vocal forces (in which he expressly composed for double choir) and his most substantial homage to Nietzsche and *Also Sprach Zarathustra*, the use of sonata, chorale forms, partsong, ritornello, variation and fugue (or more specifically a 'dance-fugue') bears witness to the range and fertility of his choral structures. Moreover, the presence of the dance as a recurrent *topos* in the *Mass* represents a culmination of his obsession with the 'waltz' (as found in *Paris* and *La Ronde se déroule*) and its consecration in Nietzsche's writings and beliefs. Although *A Mass of Life* may be his most epic choral utterance (which he tried to recapture with less success in the *Requiem*), the quintessence of

Delius's most personal choral forms may be found in *Songs of Sunset*, where the solo song and partsong intermingle within the larger frame of the romantic idiom of the song cycle. As a vehicle of reflective commentary, the chorus is also incisively used in *An Arabesque*, Delius's choral tribute to Jacobsen and an unusual example of an operatic 'scena' with chorus. The *a cappella* partsong, though not especially numerous in Delius's output, is nevertheless a significant facet of his choral output, whether in the form of the nature impression 'On Craig Ddu' (which so enthused the young Philip Heseltine), the choral dance 'Midsummer Song' or the negro-inspired wordless partsongs *To be sung of a summer night on the water*. The wordless chorus in eight parts was, however, to be more fully exploited in *The Song of the High Hills*, a symphonic poem no less fecund in structure than *Appalachia*. And from his last creative phase, the series of Whitman choral 'fragments', the *Songs of Farewell*, also calls for eight-part chorus as part of a cycle of valedictory orchestral partsongs.

Central to Delius's exploration of form and the evolution of his distinctive harmonic voice was *instrumental music*, essentially through the agency of the orchestra, a germane stimulus to his creative juices. The simple Griegian forms of *Florida* have already been cited, as well as those throughout the 1890s when he experimented with a range of formal types. The early efforts of his Parisian years suggest the influence of Bizet, Delibes and Massenet where orchestral technique, colour, timbre and nuance formed part of a French composer's armoury, especially in the guise of the orchestral suite. Essays such as *Summer Evening* and the orchestral *Paa Vidderne*, still largely reminiscent of Grieg, begin to a show a more imaginative approach to sonata form, but it is not until we reach the Fantasy Overture *Over the Hills and Far Away* and the *American Rhapsody* that we begin to witness more formal experiment. In the *American Rhapsody*, in particular, Delius's use of variation form (for which he had shown an early interest in the Leipzig *Rhapsodische Variationen*) marked a significant new departure which coincided with the consolidation of a major stylistic feature – the bifurcation of (diatonic) melody and (chromatic) accompaniment – one which Delius may well have gleaned from the example of Grieg's harmonic experiments of the late 1890s. Although a glimpse of Delius's harmonic resourcefulness in conjunction with variation form can be observed in the *American Rhapsody*, and the discovery of its greater potential can also be discerned in other, richer contexts such the harmonisation of negro tunes in *Koanga*, the second subject of *Paris* and the choral conclusion of *Appalachia*.

Delius was one of many to be affected by the popularity of Richard Strauss's symphonic poems in the concert halls of Europe and he clearly learned much from *Till Eulenspiegel*, *Tod und Verklärung* and *Ein Heldenleben*. The fecundity of Strauss's programmatic forms and the wide variety of sonata schemes spawned by these programmes, animated by a new standard of opulent orchestral technique, undoubtedly encouraged Delius to explore new and unconventional interpretations of sonata dialectics and formal hybridisation in his own works. This is evident in his incidental music to *Folkeraadet* and the symphonic poems *La Ronde se déroule* (later *Lebenstanz*), *Paris* and *Appalachia*. Exhibiting the greatest hybridity is *Appalachia* which reaffirms Delius's fascination for variation form. Based on an American negro song, the 'characteristic' variations not only articulate some form of programme (though this is unspecified) but the culmination of the variation set, an eight-part *a cappella* chromatic harmonisation of the theme with text, motivated by the composer's love of multi-voiced part writing, giving rise to a dramatic 'scena', deeply moving in its solemn evocation of slaves forced to leave their homes in the early morning. Even more adroitly, Delius then conflates this episode with the finale in which the introduction and negro theme are conflated.

Delius clearly valued the creative and formal potential of variation form as is evidenced by *Brigg Fair* and the *Dance Rhapsody* No. 1, but there is also much to be said for the variation as 'symphonic process' in most of Delius's orchestral works in his later music, whether in (arguably his masterpiece) *In a Summer Garden*, the four *North Country Sketches* (the nearest Delius came to the composition of a four-movement symphony), the miniature symphonic poems of *On Hearing the First Cuckoo in Spring* and *Summer Night on the River* (both of whose elaborate phrase structures are derived from self-developing variation methods) or the substantial impressionistic edifice of *The Song of the High Hills* (where the wordless chorus is itself a series of variations), the *Dance Rhapsody* No. 2, *A Song before Sunrise* and even parts of *Hassan*. More fascinating still is the interaction of this variation process with Delius's imaginative manipulation of sonata principles which, notwithstanding the accusations of formlessness from his detractors, he never abandoned.

That Delius possessed a sound understanding of form in the context of 'absolute music' is evident from the period between 1914 and 1921 when, whether by circumstance or desire, he devoted a substantial amount of time to the composition of solo sonatas and concertos. Counter-intuitive as these classical forms may have seemed to a composer supposedly dedicated to the notion of musical 'instinct' and anti-intellectualism and to an art driven above all by lyricism, the works of this seven-year period reveal a formal astringency and variety which suggests that the composer, in his maturity, was willing to bring a new, more cerebral attitude to his structural organisation and also one of greater formal concentration. One also suspects that Delius had learned much from the chequered experience of his early Piano Concerto (a work which, nevertheless, remained enormously popular and frequently performed during his lifetime). Most interesting about the lesson of this work was that its original one-movement, dual-functional sonata conception (as the *Fantasy for Piano Orchestra* and later as the revised version of the Piano Concerto), with its inclusion of a central slow movement, was precisely the model Delius chose to pursue in his later concertos and much of his chamber music. This was certainly true of the Double Concerto (with its own additional level of variation form), the highly original Violin Concerto (with its unusual accompanied cadenza of variations and closing Scherzo) and the concentrated, more diminutive scheme of the Cello Concerto's multi-movement structure. Further reworkings of this paradigm can be observed in the Cello Sonata and the structurally resourceful Violin Sonata No. 2.

The sonatas and concertos brought Delius's structural thought into sharper relief and this, with the help, sympathy and critical acumen of Eric Fenby, appears to have acted positively on the last works which came from his pen, the material of which underwent a reductive process of truncation, notably in *A Song of Summer*, *Cynara*, the *Idyll* and the most classical of his solo sonatas, the Violin Sonata No. 3, while the epigrammatic *Songs of Farewell* were essentially choral aphorisms bound together as a cycle. A closer study of Delius's sonatas and concertos also serves to demonstrate how deft he could be in his formal thinking and that he was by no means adverse to the perception of his music at macro-architectonic level. Indeed, extending this insight to the works of his maturity reveals a composer of considerable subtlety whose rebuttals about 'form' were merely a fashionable, anti-intellectual defence mechanism, yet one that has, arguably, deterred us from extending a clinical and analytical eye to the subtleties of his highly individual creative powers, perhaps believing that his art would be impervious or resistant to such examination. Delius's own verdict of form as the 'imparting of spiritual unity to one's thought' may seem poetically evasive,[2] but it articulates more precisely something closer to the Teutonic metaphysical ideals of form and style which Wagner had embraced in his own writings. Complex, unconventional and problematic Delius's musical style may be, but an interrogation of his scores has the potential to yield a rich harvest of subtleties (and weaknesses) of which the composer was as capable as any of his continental or British contemporaries. There may have been some truth in Elgar's comment 'my music will not interest you, Delius: you are too much of a poet for a workman like me!';[3] but this should not blind us to the

---

[2] Cooke, D., 'Delius and Form: A Vindication', reprinted in *DC*, 252.

[3] *EH*, 124.

reality of Delius's careful formal methods (and the surviving sketch materials demonstrate just how self-critical he was in reaching the definitive versions of his published works). Hutchings' remark, that 'the principles of classical structure are utterly foreign to Delius's nature',[4] also a popular *topos*, has also distracted us from the self-evident truth that Delius not only understood 'classical' forms such as sonata, rondo, sonata-rondo and (especially) variation, but used them and thought within their parameters, however eccentrically, on a habitual basis. If anything, it might be argued, his awareness of the strictures of formal architecture became keener and more finely tuned in the years immediately before and during the First World War. Nevertheless, it is during that extraordinary period of inventive – one might say instinctive – fecundity between 1899 and 1908, the period which produced *Paris, A Village Romeo and Juliet, Appalachia, Sea Drift, A Mass of Life, Songs of Sunset, Brigg Fair* and *In a Summer Garden,* that we require a true appreciation of Delius's exceptional and imaginative formal powers, for it is by comprehending the architectural precision of these works, over and above those accepted originalities of lyricism, orchestration and a unique harmonic language, that we do the composer ultimate justice.

---

[4] *AH,* 92.

Bibliography

Abraham, G. E. A., 'Delius and His Literary Sources', *Music & Letters*, Vol. 10 No. 2 (April 1929), 182–8.

Allen, W. F., Ware, C. P. and Garrison, L. M. (eds), *Slave Songs of the United States* (New York: A. Simpson & Co., 1867).

Anderson, H., 'Vilhelmine: The Muse of Sakuntala', *Delius Society Journal*, No. 127 (Spring 2000), 11–15.

Baker, H. A., 'A Decadent's Nature: The Poetry of Ernest Dowson', *Victorian Poetry*, Vol. 6 No. 1 (1968), 21–8.

Banfield, S. (ed.), *The Fourth Delius Festival*, 8–14 March 1982, University of Keele, 1982.

Banfield, S., 'La ronde se déroule: Delius and the Round Dance', *British Music Society Journal*, Vol. 6 (1984), 26–37.

Banfield, S., *Sensibility and English Song* (Cambridge: Cambridge University Press, 1985).

Bartók, B., 'A Delius Premiere in Vienna', in Suchoff, B. (ed.), *Béla Bartók Essays* (London: Faber & Faber, 1976), 449–50.

Beecham, T., *A Mingled Chime* (London: Hutchinson & Co., 1944).

Beecham, T., 'An Unknown Opera of Delius's Youth', *Daily Telegraph* and *Morning Post*, 21 March 1953.

Beecham, T., *Frederick Delius* (London: Hutchinson, 1959).

Beecham, T., 'Beecham on Delius', in Redwood, C. (ed.), *A Delius Companion* (London: John Calder, 1976), 65–73.

Bergsagel, J., 'Delius and Danish Literature', in Carley, L. (ed.), *Frederick Delius: Music, Art and Literature* (Aldershot: Ashgate, 1998), 290–310.

Bird, J., *Percy Grainger* (Oxford: Oxford University Press, 1999).

Böhm, C. (ed.), *Mahler in Leipzig* (Leipzig: Kamprad, 2011).

Boyle, A., *Delius and Norway* (Woodbridge: The Boydell Press, 2017).

Buckley, R., 'Recording Reviews', *Delius Society Journal*, No. 135 (Spring 2004), 61–3.

Butcher, A. V., 'Walt Whitman and the English Composer', *Music & Letters*, Vol. 28 No. 2 (April 1947), 154–67.

Carley, L., 'Hans Haym: Delius's Prophet and Pioneer', *Music & Letters*, Vol. 54 No. 1 (January 1973), 1–24.

Carley, L., *Delius: The Paris Years* (London: Triad Press, 1975).

Carley, L., *Delius: A Life in Letters, Vol. 1: 1862–1908* (Aldershot: Scolar Press, 1983).

Carley, L., *Delius: A Life in Letters, Vol. 2: 1909–1934* (Aldershot: Scolar Press, 1988).

Carley, L., *Grieg and Delius: A Chronicle of their Friendship in Letters* (London and New York: Marion Boyars Ltd, 1993).

Carley, L., 'Delius's Song of the Earth', *Fanfare from the Royal Philharmonic Society*, No. 3 (Spring 1994), 3–4.

Carley, L., '*Folkeraadet*: Performance and History', in Carley, L. (ed.), *Frederick Delius: Music, Art and Literature* (Aldershot: Ashgate, 1998), 211–59.

Carley, L., *Edvard Grieg in England* (Woodbridge: The Boydell Press, 2006).

Carley, L., 'Benno Carl Reifenberg (1892–1970)', *Delius Society Journal*, No. 165 (Spring 2019), 8–13.

Carley, L. and Threlfall, R., *Delius: A Life in Pictures* (Oxford: Oxford University Press, 1977).

Chamier, J. D., *Percy Pitt of Covent Garden and the BBC* (London: Edward Arnold, 1938).

Chatterton, J., 'The Morning and Afternoon of Delius', *The Sackbut* (October 1929), 77–8.

Chop, M., *Frederick Delius* (Berlin: Harmonie Verlag, 1907).

Chop, M., 'Frederick Delius: Eine biographische Studie mit Bildbeilage', *Musikalisches Wochenblatt*, Nos. 35–37 (1907).

Chop, M., *Der Fall Delius in Berlin ('Romeo und Julia auf dem Dorfe')*, Kritik der Kritik, Part 10 (Berlin: Schlesische Verlagsanstalt, 1907).

Chop, M., 'Frederick Delius: Biographie', in *Monographien moderner Musiker*, Vol. 2 (Leipzig: C. F. Kahnt Nachfolger, 1907), 84–97.

Chop, M., '"Frederick Delius: Romeo und Julia auf dem Dorfe": Uraufführung an der Berliner Komischen Oper (21 February 1907)', *Deutsche Musikdir.-Zeitung*, Nos. 10–13 (Hanover: Verlag Lehne & Komp., 1907).

Chop, M., 'Tonsetzer der Gegenwart: Frederick Delius, Sein Leben und Schaffen', *Neue Musik-Zeitung*, Vol. 31 (1910), 310–14.

Coates, E., *Suite in Four Movements* (London: Heinemann, 1953).

Collins, S., 'Anti-Intellectualism and the Rhetoric of "National Character"', in Dibble, J. and Horton, J. (eds), *British Musical Criticism and Intellectual Thought 1850–1950* (Woodbridge: Boydell & Brewer, 2018), 199–234.

Cooke, D., 'Delius and Form: A Vindication', in Redwood, C., *A Delius Companion* (London: John Calder, 1976), 249–62.

Cooke, D., 'Delius the Unknown', *Proceedings of the Royal Musical Association*, Vol. 89 (1962), 17–29.

Cooke, D., *Vindications: Essays on Romantic Music* (Cambridge: Cambridge University Press, 1982).

Creuzburg, E., *Die Gewandhaus-Konzerte 1781–1931* (Leipzig: Breitkopf & Härtel, 1931).

Dahlhaus, C., *Nineteenth-Century Music*, trans. J. Bradford Robinson (Berkeley, CA: University of California Press, 1989).

Dean, B., *Seven Ages: An Autobiography, 1888–1927* (London: Hutchinson, 1970).

Debussy, C., *Monsieur Croche et autres écrits* (Paris: Gallimard, 1971).

De Lara, I., *Many Tales of Many Cities* (London: Hutchinson & Co., 1928).

Delius, C., *Frederick Delius: Memories of My Brother* (London: Ivor Nicholson & Watson Ltd, 1935).

Delius, F., 'At the Cross-roads', *The Sackbut* (September 1920), 205–8.

Delius, F., 'Recollections of Strindberg', *The Sackbut* (December 1920), 353–4.

Dent, E., *Ferruccio Busoni* (London: Eulenberg, 1974).

Dent, E., 'English Opera in Berlin', in Redwood, C. (ed.), *A Delius Companion* (London: John Calder, 1976), 25–30.

Dibble, J., *C. Hubert H. Parry: His Life and Music* (Oxford: Oxford University Press, 1992; rev. 1998).

Dibble, J. C., 'Fantasy and Hybridisation in the British Variation Tradition', in Dibble, J. and Zon, B. (eds), *Nineteenth-Century British Music Studies*, Vol. 2 (Aldershot: Ashgate, 2002), 235–45.

Dibble, J. C., *Charles Villiers Stanford: Man and Musician* (Oxford: Oxford University Press 2002).

Dibble, J. C., *Hamilton Harty: Musical Polymath* (Woodbridge: Boydell & Brewer, 2013).

Dibble, J. C., 'The Partsong as *Topos* in the Music of Frederick Delius', keynote lecture for the one-day conference on Delius at the British Library, 15 July 2016.

Dibble, J. C. and Horton, J. (eds), *British Musical Criticism and Intellectual Thought 1850–1950* (Woodbridge: Boydell & Brewer, 2018), 218–19.

Dowson, E. C. and Symons, A., *The Poems and Prose of Ernest Dowson, with a Memoir by Arthur Symons* (London: J. Lane, 1905).

Eccott, D., '*Margot la Rouge*' Parts 1 and 2, *Delius Society Journal*, No. 69 (1980), 9–14 and No. 70 (1981), 8–15.

Elkin, R., *Royal Philharmonic: The Annals of the Royal Philharmonic Society* (London: Rider & Co., 1946).

Evans, E., 'Delius: A Personal Reaction in the Form of a Letter', *The Sackbut* (December 1929), 118–23.

Fauser, A., and Everest, M. (eds), *Music, Theater and Cultural Transfer 1830–1914* (Chicago: Chicago Press, 2009).

Fenby, E., *Delius* (London: Faber & Faber, 1971).

Fenby, E., *Delius As I Knew Him* (London: G. Bell & Sons Ltd, 1981 [1936]).

[Fenby, E.] 'Eric Fenby in Interview with Robert Layton', *Delius Society Journal*, No. 106 (Winter/Spring 1991), 3–11.

Fifield, C., *True Artist and True Friend: A Biography of Hans Richter* (Oxford: Oxford University Press, 1993).

Fleury, M., 'Fennimore and Gerda: Une "expérience Délienne" aux multiples resonances', in Rossi, J. (ed.), *Frederick Delius et la France* (Paris: Delatour, 2014), 147–75.

Foreman, L., 'Oskar Fried: Delius and the Late Romantic School', *Delius Society Journal*, No. 86 (April 1983), 4–21.

Franklin, P., *Reclaiming Late-Romantic Music: Singing Devils and Distant Sounds* (London and Berkeley, CA: University of California Press, 2014).

Gillespie, D., *The Search for Thomas F. Ward: Teacher of Frederick Delius* (Gainesville, FL: University Press of Florida, 1996).

Goldbach, K. T., 'Remarks on Delius's Violin Teacher, Carl Deichmann', *Delius Society Journal*, No. 154 (Autumn 2013), 74–88.

Grainger, P., 'The Personality of Frederick Delius', in Redwood, C. (ed.), *A Delius Companion* (London: John Calder, 1976), 117–29.

Grainger, P., 'About Delius', in Gillies, M. and Clunies Ross, B. (eds), *Grainger on Music* (Oxford: Oxford University Press, 1999), 361–8.

Gray, C., *A Survey of Contemporary Music* (Oxford: Oxford University Press, 1927).

Gray, C., *Predicaments or Music and the Future* (Oxford: Oxford University Press, 1936).

Gray, C., *Musical Chairs or Between Two Stools* (London: Home & Van Thal, 1948).

Gray, C., 'Memories of Delius', in Redwood, C. (ed.), *A Delius Companion* (London: John Calder, 1976), 135–45.

Grayson, D., 'Finding a Stage for French Opera', in Fauser, A. and Everest, M. (eds), *Music, Theater and Cultural Transfer: Paris, 1830–1914* (Chicago: University of Chicago Press, 2009), 127–56.

Grew, S., 'Frederick Delius', *The Sackbut* (October 1922), 67–71.

Grimley, D. M., *Grieg: Music, Landscape, and Norwegian Identity* (Woodbridge: Boydell & Brewer, 2006).

Grimley, D. M., 'Chasing Late Swallows', *Delius Society Journal*, No. 160 (Autumn 2016), 37–51.

Grimley, D. M., *Delius and the Sound of Place* (Cambridge: Cambridge University Press, 2018).

Guillot, P., *Déodat de Sévérac: La musique et les lettres* (Paris: L'Harmattan, 2000).

Guinery, P., '*The Song of the High Hills*: A Musical Analysis', *Delius Society Journal*, No. 138 (Autumn 2005), 56–67.

Guinery, P., '*Appalachia*: A Musical Analysis', *Delius Society Journal*, No. 141 (Spring 2007), 36–51.

Haddon Squire, W. H., 'Delius and Nietzsche', *Tempo*, No. 7 (Spring 1948), 27–30.

Harrison, B., *The Cello and the Nightingales: The Autobiography of Beatrice Harrison*, ed. Cleveland-Peck, P. (London: John Murray, 1985).

Harrison, M., 'The Music of Delius', *Proceedings of the Royal Musical Association*, Vol. 71 (1944), 43–8.

Harrison, M., 'Delius', in Redwood, C., *A Delius Companion* (London: John Calder, 1976), 101–6.

Haym, H., 'Frederick Delius: *A Mass of Life* – Introduction to the Words and Music', trans. B. Gardiner (Vienna: Universal Edition, 1925), originally published in German (Vienna: Universal Edition,1914).

Heldt, G., 'Delius' *Song of the High Hills* und die Idee einer Volkmusik ohne Worte', in Tadday, U. (ed.), *Musik Konzepte, Neue Folge: Frederick Delius*, No. 141/142 (July 2008), 53–81.

Heseltine, P., 'Some Notes on Delius and His Music', *The Musical Times*, Vol. 56 No. 865 (March 1915), 137–42.

Heseltine, P., 'Delius's New Opera', *The Musical Times*, Vol. 61 No. 926 (April 1920), 237–40.

Heseltine, P., *Frederick Delius* (London: The Bodley Head, 1923).

Heseltine, P., 'Frederick Delius', in Eaglefield-Hull, A. (ed.), *A Dictionary of Modern Music and Musicians* (London: J. M. Dent, 1924), 116–17.

Heseltine, P., 'The Works of Delius', *The Musical Times*, Vol. 68 No. 1013 (July 1927), 643.

Heseltine, P. [Warlock, P.], *Frederick Delius*, reprinted with additions, annotations and comments by Hubert Foss (London: The Bodley Head, 1952).

Hold, T., 'Grieg, Delius, Grainger and a Norwegian Cuckoo', *Tempo*, New Series, No. 203 (January 1998), 11–19.

Holland, A. K., *The Songs of Delius* (Oxford: Oxford University Press, 1951).

Holten, B., 'On Conducting the Song of the High Hills', *Delius Society Journal*, No. 138 (Autumn 2005), 75–84.

Huismann, M. C., *Frederick Delius: A Research and Information Guide*, 2nd edn (London: Routledge, 2009).

Hull, R. H., 'The Quintessence of Delius', *The Musical Times*, Vol. 68 No. 1012 (June 1927), 497–500.

Hutchings, A., 'Nietzsche, Wagner and Delius', *Music & Letters*, Vol. 22 No. 3 (July 1941), 235–47.

Hutchings, A., *Delius* (London: Macmillan, 1949).

Hutchings, A., 'Delius's Operas', *Tempo*, No. 26 (Winter 1952–1953), 22–9.

Iliffe, B., '*Eventyr* and the Fairy Tales in Delius', in Carley, L. (ed.), *Frederick Delius: Music, Art and Literature* (Aldershot: Ashgate, 1998), 273–89.

Jacobsen, J. P., *Niels Lyhne*, trans. Tiina Nunnally (London: Penguin Books, 1990).

Jefferson, A., *Delius* (London: J. M. Dent & Sons Ltd, 1972).

Jenkins, L., *While Spring and Summer Sang: Thomas Beecham and the Music of Frederick Delius* (Aldershot: Ashgate, 2005).

Jones, P., 'Delius and America: A New Perspective', *The Musical Times*, Vol. 125 No. 1702 (December 1984), 701–2.

Jones, P., 'Delius's Leipzig Connections 1886–1888', *Delius Society Journal*, No. 102 (Autumn 1989), 3–14.

Jones, P., 'A Reluctant Apprentice: Delius and Chemnitz', *Delius Society Journal*, No. 118 (Winter/Spring 1996), 17–29.

Jones, P. (ed.), *The Collected Writings of the German Musicologist Max Chop on the Composer Frederick Delius* (Lewiston, NY, Queenston, ON and Lampeter: Edwin Mellen Press, 2002).

Keary, C. F., *Norway and the Norwegians* (London: Percival & Co., 1892).

Keary, C. F., *The Brothers: A Masque* (London: Longmans, Green & Co., 1902).

Keller, G., *Romeo und Julia auf dem Dorfe*, trans. Von Schierbrand, W. (Berliner Bilinguale Ausgabe, 2015).

Kemble, F., *Journal of a Residence on a Georgian Plantation in 1838–1839* (London, 1863).

Kennedy, M., *The Hallé Tradition: A Century of Music* (Manchester: Manchester University Press, 1960).

Kennedy, M., *Adrian Boult* (London: Hamish Hamilton, 1987).

Kirby, C. S., "*The Art-Twins of Our Time-Stretch*": Percy Grainger, Frederick Delius and the 1914–1934 American "Delius Campaign", MA Thesis, Melbourne University 2015.

Lambert, C., 'The Art of Frederick Delius', *Apollo* (November 1929), 315–16.

Lambert, C., *Music-Ho! A Study of Music in Decline* (London: Harmondsworth, 1934).

Lee-Browne, M. and Guinery, P., *Delius and his Music* (Woodbridge: The Boydell Press, 2014).

Lindskog, A., 'Composing Landscapes: Musical Memories from Nineteenth-Century Norwegian Mountain-Scapes', *Landscape History*, Vol. 34 No. 2 (2013), 43–60.

Lindskog, A., 'Narrating Place and Perspective: Frederick Delius and Ibsen's Paa Vidderne', *Scandinavica*, Vol. 52 No. 1 (2013), 71–98.

Little, T., 'Delius's Violin Concerto: A Performer's View', *Delius Society Journal*, No. 91 (Autumn 1986), 3–19.

Lloyd, S., 'Delius as Conductor', *Delius Society Journal*, No. 46 (January 1975), 4–20.

Lloyd, S., 'The Rumble of a Distant Drum [Granville Bantock]', *Delius Society Journal*, No. 80 (October 1983), 5–28.

Lloyd, S., *H. Balfour Gardiner* (Cambridge: Cambridge University Press, 1984).

Lloyd, S., *Sir Dan Godfrey: Champion of British Composers* (London: Thames Publishing, 1995).

Lloyd, S. (ed.) *Fenby on Delius* (London: Thames Publishing, 1996).

Lobedanz, E., *Ausgewählte Gedichte von B. Björnson und anderen neueren nordischen Dichtern* (Leipzig: Wilhelm Friedrich Verlag, 1881).

Lowe, R., 'Delius's First Performance', *The Musical Times*, Vol. 106 No. 1465 (March 1965), 190–92.

Lowe, R., 'Frederick Delius and Norway', *Studies in Music*, Vol. 6 (Perth: University of Western Australia, 1972), 27–41.

Lowe, R., *Frederick Delius 1862–1934: A Catalogue of the Music Archive of the Delius Trust, London* (London: Delius Trust, 1974).

Lyle, R., 'Delius and the Philosophy of Romanticism', *Music & Letters*, Vol. 29 No. 2 (April 1948), 158–64.

Matthew-Walker, R., 'Delius' *Brigg Fair* in Words and Music', *Delius Society Journal*, No. 129 (Spring 2001), 7–29.

Matthew-Walker, R., 'Aspects of *The Song of the High Hills*: A "Symphony for Two Orchestras (In Tribute to Edvard Grieg)"', *Delius Society Journal*, No. 138 (Autumn 2005), 68–74.

Matthew-Walker, R., 'Aspects of Delius's *A Mass of Life*', *Delius Society Journal*, No. 144 (Autumn 2008), 38–44.

Mitchell, D., 'Delius: The Choral Music', *Tempo*, No. 26 (Winter 1952–1953), 8–17.

Montgomery, R. and Threlfall, R., *Music and Copyright: The Case of Delius and his Publishers* (Aldershot: Ashgate, 2007).

Moore, G., *Am I Too Loud?* (London: Hamish Hamilton, 1962).

Moortele, S. V., *The Romantic Overture and Musical Form from Rossini to Wagner* (Cambridge: Cambridge University Press, 2017).

Nichols, R., 'Delius As I Knew Him', in Redwood, C., *A Delius Companion* (London: John Calder, 1976), 113–15.

Nietzsche, F., *The Birth of Tragedy: or, Hellenism and Pessimism*, 3rd edn, ed.
Levy, H. (London: George Allen & Unwin, 1923).

Nietzsche, F., *Thus Spoke Zarathustra*, with an introduction by R. J. Hollingdale
(London: Penguin Books, 1960).

Orr, C. W., 'A Mass of Life', *Delius Society Journal*, No. 104 (Spring/Summer
1990), 15–16.

Palache, J., 'Debussy as Critic', *The Musical Quarterly*, Vol. 10 No. 3 (July
1924), 361–8.

Palmer, C., 'Delius and Percy Grainger', *Music & Letters*, Vol. 52 No. 4 (October
1971), 418–25.

Palmer, C., *Delius: Portrait of a Cosmopolitan* (London: Duckworth, 1976).

Payne, A., 'Delius's Stylistic Development', *Tempo*, No. 60 (Winter 1961–
1962), 6–16 and 23–5.

Payne, A., 'Delius, Frederick', in Sadie, S. (ed.), *The New Grove Dictionary
of Music and Musicians*, 2nd edn (London: Macmillan, 2001), Vol. 5,
338–43.

Plesner, A. and Rugeley-Powers (eds), *Arne: A Sketch of Norwegian Country
Life* (Cambridge and Boston, MA: Sever, Francis & Co., 1869).

Puffett, D., 'A Nietzschean Libretto: Delius and the Text for "A Mass of Life"',
Music & Letters, Vol. 79 No. 2 (May 1998), 244–67.

Randel, W., '*Koanga* and its Libretto', *Music & Letters*, Vol. 52 No. 2 (April
1971), 141–56.

Randel, W., 'Delius in America', in Redwood, C. (ed.), *A Delius Companion*,
revised reprint (London: John Calder, 1980 [1976]), 147–67.

Randel, W., 'More on that Long-lost Mistress', *Delius Society Journal*, No. 96
(Spring 1988), 8–13.

Redwood, C. (ed.), *A Delius Companion* (London: John Calder, 1976).

Redwood, C., 'A Note on the Music', in Redwood, D., *Flecker and Delius: The
Making of 'Hassan'* (London: Thames Publishing, 1977), 74–82.

Redwood, D., *Flecker and Delius: The Making of 'Hassan'* (London: Thames
Publishing, 1977).

Ridderbusch, M. R., 'The "Delius in Danville" Festival', *Delius Society Journal*,
No. 122 (Winter 1997), 35–49.

Riedel, S., 'Mahler in Leipzig: His First Season', in Böhm, C. (ed.), *Mahler in
Leipzig* (Leipzig: Kamprad, 2011), 39–88.

Rippin, J. W., 'Delius Requiem', *Musical Opinion* (May 1966), 465–7.

Rippin, J. W., 'The Choral Music of Delius' (unpublished).

Rossi, J. (ed.), *Frederick Delius et la France* (Paris: Delatour, 2014).

Runciman, J. F., 'Fritz Delius, Composer', in Redwood, C. (ed.), *A Delius
Companion* (London: John Calder, 1976), 13–18.

Russell, D., *Popular Music in England, 1840–1914: A Social History*, 2nd edn (Manchester: Manchester University Press, 1997).

Saylor, E., 'Zwei Zusammen: Delius und die Texte Walt Whitman', in Tadday, U. (ed.), *Musik Konzepte, Neue Folge: Frederick Delius*, No. 141/142 (July 2008), 159–78.

Seeley, P., 'Fritz Delius: The Bradford Years', *Delius Society Journal*, No. 58 (December 1977), 5–11.

Smith, J. Boulton, *Frederick Delius and Peter Warlock: A Friendship Revealed* (Oxford: Oxford University Press, 2000).

Stang, R., '*Paa Vidderne* in Historical Perspective', *Delius Society Journal*, No. 108 (Winter/Spring 1992), 3–8.

Stevenson, R., 'Delius's Sources', *Tempo*, No. 151 (December 1984), 24–7.

Streatfeild, R. A., 'Delius, Frederick', in Fuller Maitland, J. A. (ed.), *Grove's Dictionary of Music and Musicians*, 2nd edn (New York: Macmillan, 1911), Vol. 5, 629–31.

Tadday, U. (ed.), *Musik Konzepte, Neue Folge: Frederick Delius*, No. 141/142 (July 2008).

Threlfall, R., 'The Early History of *Koanga*', *Tempo*, No. 110 (September 1974), 8–11.

Threlfall, R., 'Delius's Unknown Opera: *The Magic Fountain*', *Studies in Music*, Vol. 11 (Perth: University of Western Australia, 1977), 60–73.

Threlfall, R., *A Catalogue of the Compositions of Frederick Delius: Sources and References* (London: Delius Trust, 1977).

Threlfall, R., 'Delius's Violin Sonata (No. 1)', *Delius Society Journal*, No. 74 (January 1982), 5–12.

Threlfall, R., 'Delius: A Fresh Glance at Two Famous Scores', *The Musical Times*, Vol. 125 No. 1696 (June 1984), 315, 317–19.

Threlfall, R., *Frederick Delius: A Supplementary Catalogue* (London: Delius Trust, 1986).

Threlfall, R., 'Delius's Student Exercises: A Fresh Look at the Chronology', *Delius Society Journal*, No. 104 (Spring/Summer 1990), 3–5.

Threlfall, R., *Delius' Musical Apprenticeship* (London: Delius Trust, 1994).

Threlfall, R., 'A Note on Watawa – Last of Her Race', *Delius Society Journal*, No. 118 (Winter/Spring 1996), 34–5.

Threlfall, R., 'An Early Manuscript Reappears', *Delius Society Journal*, No. 130 (Autumn 2001), 19–21.

Turner, W. J., *Music and Life* (London: Methuen, 1921).

Wetherall, E., *Albert Sammons, Violinist: The Life of 'Our Albert'* (London: Thames Publishing, 1998).

White, E. W., *A History of English Opera* (London: Faber & Faber, 1983).

White, J., 'Delius and La Belle Dame Sans Merci: The Hidden Meanings of *An Arabesque*', *Delius Society Journal*, No. 120 (Spring 1997), 11–17.

White, J., 'Words without Music: The Literary Sources of the Delius Operas', *Delius Society Journal*, No. 135 (Spring 2004), 7–31.

Whitman, W., *The Complete Poems*, ed. Murphy, F. (London: Penguin Books, 1975).

Wood, H., *My Life of Music* (London: Victor Gollancz, 1938).

Index of Works

Index